SA-Führer

THE SENIOR LEADERSHIP OF HITLER'S STORM TROOPS
1920-1945

SA-Führer

THE SENIOR LEADERSHIP OF HITLER'S STORM TROOPS
1920-1945

VOLUME 1
OBERSTER SA-FÜHRER & SA-STABSCHEF

Michael D. Miller and Andreas Schulz

To my friend Gary Costello, who volunteered—selflessly and without hesitation—

his exemplary research and translation skills to this project.

First published in Great Britain and the United States in 2025 by Fonthill
An imprint of
Pen & Sword Books Ltd
Yorkshire – Philadelphia
www.fonthill.media

Copyright © Michael D. Miller & Andreas Schulz 2025

ISBN 978-1-78155-922-2

The right of Michael D. Miller & Andreas Schulz to be identified as
Authors of this work has been asserted by them in accordance
with the Copyright, Designs and Patents Act 1988.

A CIP catalogue record for this book
is available from the British Library.

All rights reserved. No part of this book may be reproduced or transmitted in any form
or by any means, electronic or mechanical including photocopying, recording or by any
information storage and retrieval system, without permission from the Publisher in writing.
NO AI TRAINING: Without in any way limiting the Author's and Publisher's exclusive rights
under copyright, any use of this publication to 'train' generative artificial intelligence (AI)
technologies to generate text is expressly prohibited. The Author and Publisher reserve all
rights to license uses of this work for generative AI training and development of machine
learning language models.

The Publisher's authorised representative in the EU for product safety is
Authorised Rep Compliance Ltd., Ground Floor,
71 Lower Baggot Street, Dublin D02 P593, Ireland.
www.arccompliance.com

For a complete list of Pen & Sword titles please contact
PEN & SWORD BOOKS LIMITED
47 Church Street, Barnsley, South Yorkshire, S70 2AS, England
E-mail: enquiries@pen-and-sword.co.uk
Website: www.pen-and-sword.co.uk
Or
PEN AND SWORD BOOKS
1950 Lawrence Rd, Havertown, PA 19083, USA
E-mail: Uspen-and-sword@casematepublishers.com
Website: www.penandswordbooks.com

Foreword

The reference works by Michael Miller and Andreas Schulz, painstakingly compiled on the basis of meticulous research, are a great help to historians of the Third Reich and to anyone wishing to learn precise biographical and career details of the Nazi leadership. This latest volume, providing a plethora of personal data on the SA leadership, is no exception. I know of no comparable compilation. It would have saved me much endeavour had it been available when I was writing my biography of Hitler. I am sure it will now be warmly welcomed, as it deserves to be, by scholars and students of Nazi Germany, and I'm very happy to record my own pleasure at its publication.

Sir Ian Kershaw

SA-Stabschef Ernst Röhm poses with the senior leaders of the *Sturmabteilung* in 1932. (Heinrich Hoffmann, *Das Braune Heer. 100 Bilddokumente: Leben, Kampf und Sieg der SA und SS* [1932])

SA-Führungstagung (leadership conference) in Friedrichsroda, 21.01.1934: Hitler meets with the senior leadership of his *Sturmabteilung*. From right to left: *SA-Sanitäts-Obergruppenführer* Dr. Paul Hocheisen, *SA-Gruppenführer* Elhard von Morozowicz-Wuhden (died 31.01.1934 of injuries sustained in an automobile accident), *SA-Gruppenführer* Georg von Detten (murdered, 01.07.1934, during the SA purge), *SA-Obergruppenführer* Adolf Hühnlein, *SA-Obergruppenführer* Hans Georg Hofmann, *SA-Obergruppenführer* Georg Oberdieck, *SA-Obergruppenführer* Curt von Ulrich, *SA-Stabschef* Ernst Röhm, and *SA-Obergruppenführer* Franz Ritter von Epp, and *Oberster SA-Führer* Hitler. (NARA, Heinrich Hoffmann Collection)

Acknowledgments

The following individuals provided invaluable assistance in the creation of this and future volumes.

Helly Angel
Ignacio Arrondo Perals
Robert Bailey
Stefan Barber
Roger James Bender (†)
Erich Benndorff
Dr. Philip W. Blood
Patrick Butcher
Prof. Randall Bytwerk
Prof. Bruce Campbell
Jeff Clark
Mark Costa
Gary Costello
Howard Davies
Ann Farr
Frederick Froberg
Derek Gloster
Joshua Greenland (Fonthill Media)
Victor Gross Militärische Antiquitäten
Todd Gylsen
Jasper Hadman (Fonthill Media)
Jamie Hardwick (Fonthill Media)
Richard Hargreaves
Laurens Hessels
Ben Humphrey (†)
Simon James
Georges Jerome
Glenn Jewison
Igor Karpov
Sir Ian Kershaw
Katrina Kidwell-James
Jerry Luisi
Sten Lundø
Rick Lundström (†)
Ken McCanliss
Dr. Geoffrey P. Megargee (†)
Christian Merker (Helmut Weitze Militärische Antiquitäten KG, Hamburg)
Gary Merlie
Peter Mertlseder
Mari Miller (†)
Hugo Morsink
Yves Müller
Phil Nix (†)
Dave Overcash
Bill Panagopulos (Alexander Historical Auctions LLC)
Greg Pearce
Duncan Rogers
Marc Romanych (Digital History Archive)
Ian Sayer
Michal Sika
Albert Smetanin
Claus Strobl
Alan Sutton (Fonthill Media)
Jamie Sutton (Fonthill Media)
Piotr Szarafinski
Blaine Taylor (†)
Steven Tyas
James Webb
Dr. Andrew Wackerfuss
Marcus Wendel
Max Williams
Christopher Yahnke (†)
Mark C. Yerger (†)
Dr. med. Dieter Zinke (†)
Andrey Zubkov

Weimar, 12.12.1934. The funeral of *SA-Gruppenführer* Dr. Gustav Zunkel, who died of injuries sustained in an auto accident on 08.12.1934. From left to right: Dietrich von Jagow, Arthur Böckenhauer, Adolf Kob, Dr. Emil Ketterer, Otto Schramme, Dr. Heinrich Bennecke, Siegfried Kasche, Joachim Meyer-Quade, Johann Heinrich Böhmcker, Kurt Lasch, Otto Herzog, Herbert Fust, and Arthur Rakobrandt. (NARA, Heinrich Hoffmann Collection)

SA-Stabschef Schepmann presides over an *SA* leadership conference in 1943. From left to right: *SA-Obergruppenführer* Max Jüttner, Schepmann, *SA-Gruppenführer* Hans Petersen, *SA-Gruppenführer* Leonhard Gontermann, *SA-Gruppenführer (V)* Ernst Beißner, *SA-Obergruppenführer* Heinrich Böhmcker, *SA-Obergruppenführer* Herbert Fust. In the foreground, left to right: *SA-Gruppenführer* Erich Hasse and *SA-Gruppenführer* Robert Schormann. In profile at right: *SA-Brigadeführer (S)* Dr. Rudolf Holtgrave. (Igor Karpov)

Contents

Foreword by Sir Ian Kershaw   5
Acknowledgments   7
Commonly Used Abbreviations   11
Introduction   13

The Biographies

Adolf Hitler   17
Emil Jules Wilhelm ("Moritzl") Maurice   69
Julius Johann ("Hans") Ulrich Klintzsch   89
Hermann Wilhelm Göring   112
Hans Walter Buch   418
Alfred Max Ludwig Hoffmann   460
Wilhelm Pleickart Ludwig Adolf Arthur Freiherr Marschall von Bieberstein   464
Franz Ferdinand Felix von Pfeffer   469
Dr. phil. h. c. Otto William (Wilhelm) Heinrich Wagener   501
Ernst Julius Günther Röhm   511
Viktor Heinrich Lutze   599
Max Paul Wilhelm Werner Jüttner   679
Friedrich Wilhelm ("Willi") Schepmann   706

Appendix I: Comparative Table of Ranks   758
Appendix II: Glossary of German Military & Political Terms   759
Appendix III: Glossary of German Military, Political,
    and Civil Decorations & Awards   776
About the Authors   783

Berlin, 19.11.1943: *SA-Stabschef* Schepmann addresses a conference of active and honorary SA leaders. (NARA, Hermann Hoffmann Collection)

Bevergern/Westfalen, 04.05.1944: Memorial service marking the first anniversary of Viktor Lutze's death. From right to left: Deputy *Gauleiter* (Westfalen-Nord) and *SA-Gruppenführer* Peter Stangier, *SA-Obergruppenführer* Max Jüttner, *SA-Gruppenführer* Wilhelm Heitmüller, *SA-Gruppenführer* Hans Petersen, *SA-Stabschef* Wilhelm Schepmann, *SA-Obergruppenführer* Heinrich Böhmcker, Frau Paula Lutze, *SA-Gruppenführer* Paul Faßbach, *General der Flakartillerie* August Schmidt (Commander of *Luftgau VI*, Münster), August Lutze (Viktor's father), and *SA-Gruppenführer (S)* Dr. Kurt Blome. (NARA, Heinrich Hoffmann Collection)

Commonly Used Abbreviations

Abbreviation	German Meaning	English Meaning
a. D.	*ausser Dienst*	Retired; on the inactive list [term following *Wehrmacht* or *Waffen-SS* rank, e.g., *Oberst a. D.*]
d. R.	*der Reserve*	Of the reserves [term following *Wehrmacht* or *Waffen-SS* rank, e.g., "*Oberst d. R.*"]
Dr. h. c.	*doctor honoris causa*	Honorary doctor's degree
Dr. Ing.	*Doktor Ingenieur*	Doctor of Engineering
Dr. jur.	*doctor juris*	Doctor of Jurisprudence/Law
Dr. med.	*doctor medicinae*	Doctor of Medicine
Dr. phil.	*doctor philosophiae*	Doctotr of Philosophy
Dr. rer. Pol.	*doctor rerum politicarum*	Doctor of Political Science
e. h.	*Ehrenhalber*	Honorary
e. V.	*eingetragener Verein*	A registered society (e.g., "*Lebensborn e.V.*")
Gestapo	*Geheime Staatspolizei*	Secret State Police
HSSPF	*Höhere SS-und Polizeiführer*	Higher and Police Leader
i. G.	*im Generalstab*	In the General Staff [term following *Wehrmacht* rank, e.g., "*Oberstleutnant i. G.*"]
Kripo	*Kriminalpolizei*	Criminal Police
k.u.k.	*kaiserlich und königlich*	Of or pertaining to the Imperial and Royal armed forces of the Austro-Hungarian Empire
m.d.F.b.	*mit der Führung beauftragt*	Temporarily charged with leadership or command
m.d.F.d.G.b.	*mit der Führung der Geschäfte beauftragt*	Temporarily charged with the leadership of affairs
m.d.k.F.b.	*mit der kommissarischer Führung beauftragt*	Temporarily charged with acting leadership
m.d.W.d.G.b.	*mit der Wahrnehmung der Geschäfte beauftragt*	Temporarily charged with the conduct of affairs

NSDAP	*Nationalsozialistische Deutsche Arbeiter Partei*	National-Socialist German Workers Party
NSKK	*Nationalsozialistische-Kraftfahrkorps*	National-Socialist Motor Corps
NSV	*Nationalsozialistische Volkswohlfahrt*	National-Socialist People's Welfare Organization
SA	*Sturmabteilungen*	Storm Troops
SD	*Sicherheitsdienst*	Security Service
Sipo	*Sicherheitspolizei*	Security Police
SS (ᛋᛋ)	*Schutzstaffel*	lit. Protection or Guard Detachment
ß	*Eszett (ss)*	Not an abbreviation per se, but a character which represents the *"scharfes S"* (sharp S) in certain German words, such as *"preußisch"* (Prussian) and *"Stoßtrupp"* (shock troop)
z.b.V.	*zur besonderer Verwendung*	For special employment

Introduction

How did Adolf Hitler, who had never risen higher in military service than the rank of lance-corporal, attain mastery over Germany and most of Europe? Many factors contributed to the emergence of the Third Reich; prominent among these were the actions of Hitler's earliest paramilitary army, the *Sturmabteilungen* (SA, Storm Troops), and the men chosen by the *Führer* to lead it. An unswervingly loyal, highly disciplined militant force is as essential to the establishment and maintenance of a dictatorship as the dictator himself. Although Hitler ultimately culled the SA of its most revolutionary elements, there remained in it and the other Party-affiliated organizations a spirit of fanatical, sometimes mindless worship of its supreme leader. *Gauleiter* Josef Bürckel, one of Hitler's most tireless and devoted subordinates (and an honorary *SA-Obergruppenführer*) spoke for millions of his countrymen when he closed a 1935 speech with the words, "Our eternal prayer, however, is always and forever: God preserve the *Führer!*"

This series analyzes the lives and careers of the senior SA leadership. Many of them were, like their leader, veterans of World War I who had found themselves stunned, bitterly disillusioned, and in many cases unemployed and destitute in the aftermath of that four-year struggle. They eagerly sought the opportunity to return to uniform, battled the enemies of the Nazi Party in the streets of interwar Germany, and saw their efforts rewarded by their own leader's betrayal, as he essentially decapitated his SA in favor of its own subordinate formation, Heinrich Himmler's SS, in the so-called "Night of the Long Knives" (30 June to 1 July 1934). The SA did not end with that devastating blow, however, and despite its loss of prestige and power, it was to play an important role in military training and internal security within and outside the borders of the Reich. During World War II, many of its leaders were tasked with administering occupied territories and representing Germany's interests as ambassadors to other Axis nations. Still others, men of all SA ranks, served individually as members of the German *Wehrmacht*, tens of thousands of them losing their lives on all fronts and many of them receiving the highest awards for bravery and leadership.

This first volume, relying largely on official personnel files and other contemporary documentation, analyzes the lives and careers of the thirteen highest-ranking SA leaders—men who held the ranks of *Oberster SA-Führer* and *SA-Stabschef*. As with my previous books on leaders of the SS and NSDAP, it is my hope that it will provide the most comprehensive picture yet published of the *hauptamtlicher* (full-time, actively serving) and *ehrenamtlicher* (honorary) *SA-Führer*.

Michael Miller, 2025

Viktor Lutze and the top leadership of the SA, photographed at the Reich Propaganda Ministry in Berlin, 01.11.1934.
　First row, left to right: Dr. Otto Marxer, Lutze, and Karl-Siegmund Litzmann.
　Second row: Max Luyken, Wilhelm Schepmann, Siegfried Kasche, and Hermann Reschny.
　Third row: Otto Schramme, Dietrich von Jagow, Adolf-Heinz Beckerle, Arthur Böckenhauer, and Gustav Zunkel.
　Fourth row: Hans Friedrich, Herbert Fust, Hans-Günther von Obernitz, Heinrich August Knickmann, Otto Herzog, and Arno Manthey.
　Fifth row: Johann Heinrich Böhmcker, Joachim Meyer-Quade, Wilhelm Helfer, Heinrich Schoene, Dr. Emil Ketterer, Max Jüttner, and Emil Steinhoff.
　Sixth row: Arthur Rakobrandt and an unidentified *SA-Obersturmführer*; and behind Rakobrandt, Hans Elard Ludin. (Michal Sika)

The Biographies

Volume 1
Oberster SA-Führer
and
Stabschef der SA

Hitler in June 1923, photographed by Heinrich Hoffmann. (NARA, Heinrich Hoffmann Collection)

Adolf Hitler
Oberster SA-Führer
(30.08.1930–30.04.1945)

*	20.04.1889 in Braunau am Inn/Oberösterreich/Österreich-Ungarn.
†	30.04.1945 in the *Führerbunker* of the *Reichskanzlei*, Berlin, together with his wife, Eva Braun-Hitler. According to the accounts of his personal adjutant, *SS-Sturmbannführer* Otto Günsche, and valet, *SS-Sturmbannführer* Heinz Linge, he shot himself in the right temple with a 7.65-mm Walther Model PPK pistol (at 15:30 hours, according to Günsche, or 15:50 per Linge's account).
NSDAP-Nr.:	1 (Enrolled in the *Deutschen Arbeiterpartei* [DAP] with Nr. 555, 18.09.1919. Left the NSDAP, 11.07.1921; re-enrolled with NSDAP-Nr. 3.680, 26.07.1921; re-established the NSDAP and assumed NSDAP-Nr. 1 on 27.02.1925)

Promotions:

00.08.1914	*kriegsfreiwilliger Rekrut*
03.11.1914	*Gefreiter d. R.* (*mit Wirkung vom* 01.11.1914)
29.07.1921	*Erster Vorsitzender der NSDAP*
27.02.1925–30.04.1945	*Führer der NSDAP*
30.08.1930–30.04.1945	*Oberster SA-Führer*
30.01.1933–30.04.1945	*Reichskanzler*
00.08.1934–30.04.1945	*Führer und Reichskanzler*. Title created when Hitler united the office of *Staatsoberhaupt* (*Reichspräsident*) with that of *Reichskanzler*.
02.08.1934–30.04.1945	*Oberster Befehlshaber der Reichswehr* (redesignated *Wehrmacht*, 21.05.1935)
19.12.1941–30.04.1945	*Oberbefehlshaber des Heeres*

Career:

02.05.1895–00.00.1896	*Volksschule* in Fischlham bei Lambach.
00.00.1896–00.00.1898	*Klosterschule* (*Volksschule*) of the Stift Lambach.
00.00.1898–00.00.1900	*Volksschule* in Leonding bei Linz.
00.00.1900–00.00.1904	*Staatsrealschule* in Linz.
00.00.1904–00.00.1905	*Staatsoberrealschule* in Steyr.
Fall 1905	Absent from school due to illness (pulmonary apicitis), then lived a shiftless existence and sought to become a painter or architect.
00.09.1907	Unsuccessfully applied to the *Kunstakademie* (Academy of Fine Arts) in Wien, having settled in that city following the death of his mother. He supported himself through work as an assistant construction worker and sales of his own paintings.
00.00.1909–00.00.1910	Resident of a shelter for the homeless.
00.00.1910–00.05.1913	Lived in a *Männerheim* (men's home).
24.05.1913	Moved to München to avoid conscription into the k.u.k. (Austro-Hungarian) army (according to his own account, this move occurred on 24.12.1912). Hitler should have reported for duty in 1909. In 1913, the Linz magistrate tried to find the fugitive. After lengthy research, his whereabouts in München were traced in

	January 1914. The Linz magistrate then had the Austrian consulate general in München serve Hitler with a summons to appear. In it, Hitler was threatened with arrest and a fine if he did not comply with the obligation to report to Linz. The Consulate General in Munich was asked to arrange with the Bavarian authorities for Hitler's extradition to the nearest Austrian border authority, if necessary. The consulate general then reported to Linz that Hitler was "afflicted with a condition that makes him unfit for military service." At Hitler's request, he was finally allowed to report for conscription in Salzburg on 05.02.1914. The Salzburg *Stellungskommission* (draft board) found Hitler, who gave his occupation as "artist and writer," "too weak" and declared him unfit for military service.
00.08.1914	Reported for duty as a *Kriegsfreiwilliger* in the Royal Bavarian Army.
16.08.1914–01.09.1914	Assigned to *6. Rekruten-Ersatz-Bataillon/2. Kgl. Bayerisches Infanterie-Regiment Nr. 16* (Regiment List).
01.09.1914–09.11.1914	Assigned to *1. Kompanie/Kgl. Bayerisches Reserve-Infanterie-Regiment Nr. 16*, assigned as a *Meldegänger* (dispatch runner) on the Western Front. He first entered combat on the Yser on 29.10.1914. The following is a listing of combat engagements in which he participated from 1914 to 1918:

30.10.1914–24.11.1914	In combat at Ypres
25.11.1914–13.12.1914	Trench warfare in Flanders
14.12.1914–24.12.1914	December Battle of Flanders
25.12.1914–09.03.1915	Trench warfare in Flanders
10.03.1915–14.03.1915	Combat at Neuve Chapelle
15.03.1915–08.05.1915	Trench warfare in Flanders
09.06.1915–23.07.1915	Combat at La Bassé and Arras
24.07.1915–24.09.1915	Trench warfare in Flanders
25.09.1915–13.10.1915	Combat at La Bassée and Arras
14.10.1915–29.02.1916	Trench warfare in Flanders
01.03.1916–23.06.1916	Trench warfare in Flanders (Artois)
24.06.1916–07.07.1916	Feint attacks and reconnaissance in preparation for the Battle of the Somme
08.07.1916–18.07.1916	Trench warfare in Flanders
19.07.1916–20.07.1916	Combat at Fromelles
21.07.1916–25.09.1916	Trench warfare in Flanders
26.09.1916–05.10.1916	Combat on the Somme
06.03.1917–26.04.1917	Trench warfare in Flanders
27.04.1917–20.05.1917	Combat at Arras
21.05.1917–24.06.1917	Trench warfare in Flanders (Artois)
24.06.1917–21.07.1917	First phase of operations in Flanders
22.07.1917–03.08.1917	Second phase of operations in Flanders
04.08.1917–10.09.1917	Trench Warfare in Oberelsaß
18.10.1917–02.11.1917	Rearguard actions south of the Ailette
03.11.1917–25.03.1918	Trench warfare north of the Ailette
27.05.1918–30.06.1918	Combat at Soissons and Reims
14.06.1918–30.06.1918	Trench warfare between the Oise and the Marne
05.07.1918–14.07.1918	Trench warfare between the Aisne and the Marne

15.07.1918–17.07.1918	Offensive operations on the Marne and in Champagne
18.07.1918–25.07.1918	Defensive operations between Soissons and Reims
26.07.1918–29.07.1918	Mobile defensive operations on the Marne
21.08.1918–23.08.1918	Combat near Monchy-Bapaume
28.09.1918–15.10.1918	Defensive operations in Flanders

09.11.1914–07.10.1915	Assigned to the *Regimentsstab/Kgl. Bayerisches Reserve-Infanterie-Regiment Nr. 16*.
00.10.1916	Lightly wounded in the face by a shell fragment.
05.10.1916	Wounded in action (left thigh) near Le Bargur.
07.10.1915–07.10.1916	Assigned to *3. Kompanie/Reserve-Infanterie-Regiment Nr. 16*.
09.10.1916–01.12.1916	Hospitalized in the *Militärlazarett Beelitz*.
03.12.1916–05.03.1917	Assigned to *4. Kompanie/I. Ersatz-Bataillon/Kgl. Bayerisches Reserve-Infanterie-Regiment Nr. 16*.
05.03.1917–14.10.1918	Again deployed to the Western Front with *Reserve-Infanterie-Regiment 16*.
30.09.1917–17.10.1917	Home leave in Spital.
23.08.1918–30.08.1918	Briefly assigned to duty in Nürnberg.
10.09.1918–27.09.1918	Home leave in Spital.
15.10.1918	Blinded by mustard gas near La Montagne.
21.10.1918–19.11.1918	Hospitalized in the *Preußische Reservelazarett Pasewalk*.
21.11.1918–00.02.1919	Service with *7. Kompanie/I. Ersatz-Bataillon/2. Bayerischen Infanterie-Regiment* (München).
12.02.1919–00.03.1919	Assigned to guard duty at the *Gefangenenlager* (Prisoner of War Camp) Traunstein as a member of *2. Demobilmachungs-Kompanie/2. Bayerisches Infanterie-Regiment*.
00.03.1919–00.05.1919	Stationed in the *Max II.-Kaserne* (München-Oberwiesenfeld). He was sympathetic to the *Unabhängige Sozialdemokratische Partei Deutschlands* (USPD, Independent Social Democratic Party of Germany) during this period and participated in the funeral of the Bavarian *Ministerpräsident* and USPD politician Kurt Eisner (assassinated in München by the right-wing extremist Anton Graf von Arco auf Valley on 21.02.1919), despite the fact that Eisner was a Jew.
00.05.1919	Briefly arrested by troops of *Freikorps "Epp"* in München.
00.05.1919–31.03.1920	"*V-Mann*" (informant, under the cover-name "Wolf") in *1. Bayrischen Schützen-Regiment Nr. 41* (München). He described himself as a *Bildungsoffizier* ("Educational Officer"). In this capacity, on 12.09.1919, he attended a meeting of the obscure *Deutsche Arbeiter-Partei* (DAP, German Workers Party) in München.
16.09.1919–00.00.1919	Member of the *Politischen Arbeiterzirkel* of the DAP (under the chairmanship of Anton Drexler).
18.09.1919	Officially enrolled in the DAP.
18.09.1919–00.00.1920	(seventh) Member of the *Arbeitsausschuss der DAP*.
13.11.1919–00.01.1920	*Werbeobmann der DAP* (Public Affairs Director of the DAP).
00.01.1920–11.07.1921	*Propagandaleiter der DAP* and member of the *Presseausschuss der DAP* (Press Committee of the German Workers Party).
24.02.1920	Redesignation of the *Deutsche Arbeiter-Partei* as the *Nationalsozialistische Deutsche Arbeiterpartei* (NSDAP, National-Socialist German Workers Party). On the same date, a "*25-Punkte-*

Programm" (25-Point Program) for the Party, drafted by Hitler and Anton Drexler, was announced, as follows:

The Program of the German Workers' Party is designed to be of limited duration. The leaders have no intention, once the aims announced in it have been achieved, of establishing fresh ones, merely in order to increase, artificially, the discontent of the masses and so ensure the continued existence of the Party.

1. We demand the union of all Germany in a Greater Germany on the basis of the right of national self-determination.
2. We demand equality of rights for the German people in its dealings with other nations, and the revocation of the peace treaties of Versailles and Saint-Germain.
3. We demand land and territory (colonies) to feed our people and to settle our surplus population.
4. Only members of the nation may be citizens of the State. Only those of German blood, whatever be their creed, may be members of the nation. Accordingly, no Jew may be a member of the nation.
5. Non-citizens may live in Germany only as guests and must be subject to laws for aliens.
6. The right to vote on the State's government and legislation shall be enjoyed by the citizens of the State alone. We demand therefore that all official appointments, of whatever kind, whether in the Reich, in the states or in the smaller localities, shall be held by none but citizens. We oppose the corrupting parliamentary custom of filling posts merely in accordance with party considerations, and without reference to character or abilities.
7. We demand that the State shall make it its primary duty to provide a livelihood for its citizens. If it should prove impossible to feed the entire population, foreign nationals (non-citizens) must be deported from the Reich.
8. All non-German immigration must be prevented. We demand that all non-Germans who entered Germany after 2 August 1914 shall be required to leave the Reich forthwith.
9. All citizens shall have equal rights and duties.
10. It must be the first duty of every citizen to perform physical or mental work. The activities of the individual must not clash with the general interest, but must proceed within the framework of the community and be for the general good. We demand therefore:
11. The abolition of incomes unearned by work. The breaking of the slavery of interest
12. In view of the enormous sacrifices of life and property demanded of a nation by any war, personal enrichment from war must be regarded as a crime against the nation. We demand therefore the ruthless confiscation of all war profits.
13. We demand the nationalization of all businesses which have been formed into corporations (trusts).
14. We demand profit-sharing in large industrial enterprises.
15. We demand the extensive development of insurance for old age.

16. We demand the creation and maintenance of a healthy middle class, the immediate communalizing of big department stores, and their lease at a cheap rate to small traders, and that the utmost consideration shall be shown to all small traders in the placing of State and municipal orders.

17. We demand a land reform suitable to our national requirements, the passing of a law for the expropriation of land for communal purposes without compensation; the abolition of ground rent, and the prohibition of all speculation in land.

[Point 17 was revised by Hitler on 13.04.1928, as follows: "Because of the mendacious interpretations on the part of our opponents of Point 17 of the program of the NSDAP, the following explanation is necessary." Since the NSDAP is fundamentally based on the principle of private property, it is obvious that the expression "confiscation without compensation" refers merely to the creation of possible legal means of confiscating when necessary, land illegally acquired, or not administered in accordance with the national welfare. It is therefore directed in the first instance against the Jewish companies which speculate in land.]

18. We demand the ruthless prosecution of those whose activities are injurious to the common interest. Common criminals, usurers, profiteers, etc., must be punished with death, whatever their creed or race.

19. We demand that Roman Law, which serves a materialistic world order, be replaced by a German common law.

20. The State must consider a thorough reconstruction of our national system of education (with the aim of opening up to every able and hard-working German the possibility of higher education and of thus obtaining advancement). The curricula of all educational establishments must be brought into line with the requirements of practical life. The aim of the school must be to give the pupil, beginning with the first sign of intelligence, a grasp of the nation of the State (through the study of civic affairs). We demand the education of gifted children of poor parents, whatever their class or occupation, at the expense of the State.

21. The State must ensure that the nation's health standards are raised by protecting mothers and infants, by prohibiting child labor, by promoting physical strength through legislation providing for compulsory gymnastics and sports, and by the extensive support of clubs engaged in the physical training of youth.

22. We demand the abolition of the mercenary army and the foundation of a people's army.

23. We demand legal warfare on deliberate political mendacity and its dissemination in the press. To facilitate the creation of a German national press we demand:

(a) that all editors of, and contributors to newspapers appearing in the German language must be members of the nation;

(b) that no non-German newspapers may appear without the express permission of the State. They must not be printed in the German language;

(c) that non-Germans shall be prohibited by law from participating financially in or influencing German newspapers, and that the penalty for contravening such a law shall be the suppression of any such newspaper, and the immediate deportation of the non-Germans involved. The publishing of papers which are not conducive to the national welfare must be forbidden. We demand the legal prosecution of all those tendencies in art and literature which corrupt our national life, and the suppression of cultural events which violate this demand.

24. We demand freedom for all religious denominations in the State, provided they do not threaten its existence not offend the moral feelings of the German race. The Party, as such, stands for positive Christianity, but does not commit itself to any particular denomination. It combats the Jewish-materialistic spirit within and without us, and is convinced that our nation can achieve permanent health only from within on the basis of the principle: The common interest before self-interest.

25. To put the whole of this program into effect, we demand the creation of a strong central state power for the Reich; the unconditional authority of the political central Parliament over the entire Reich and its organizations; and the formation of corporations based on estate and occupation for the purpose of carrying out the general legislation passed by the Reich in the various German states. The leaders of the Party promise to work ruthlessly— if need be to sacrifice their very lives—to translate this program into action.

31.03.1920	Officially discharged from military service.
29.09.1920–11.10.1920	Speaking tour of Austria on behalf of the NSDAP. By this time, he had gradually become the most prominent leader of the Party. This resulted in violent disagreements with the *Parteivorsitzender* (Party Chairman), Drexler.
End of 01.1921	Sentenced to a 1,000 RM fine (*in lieu* of 100 days' imprisonment) for slander against the leader of the *Bayernbund* (a Bavarian separatist organization), Otto Ballerstedt.
11.07.1921	Demonstrative resignation from the NSDAP, but with the help of his supporters (including Hermann Esser, Oskar Körner, and Dietrich Eckart), he defeated his opponents within the Party.
26.07.1921	Reenrolled in the NSDAP.
29.07.1921–09.11.1923	*Erster Vorsitzender der NSDAP (mit diktatorischen Vollmachten)* (First Chairman of the National-Socialist German Workers Party [with dictatorial powers]).
16.11.1921	Became owner of the newspaper *Völkischer Beobachter* and the publishing firm "*Verlag Franz Eher Nachf.*"
12.01.1922	Sentenced to three months' imprisonment for "*Landfriedensbruch*" (public disorder). This conviction resulted from the 09.08.1921 meeting of Ballerstedt's *Bayernbund* at the *Löwenbräukeller*, München during which Hitler, together with Hermann Esser and Oskar Körner entered the hall. During the disturbance that ensued, Hitler physically attacked Ballerstedt (later murdered in the purge of 30.06.1934).
24.06.1922–27.07.1922	Imprisoned at München-Stadelheim (released early for "good behavior").
00.11.1922–00.01.1923	Member of the *Vereinigung der Vaterländischen Vereine* (Union of Patriotic Associations).
04.02.1923–00.11.1923	Member of the *Ausschuss der "Arbeitsgemeinschaft der Vaterländischen Kampfverbände"* (Committee for the "Working Group of the Patriotic Combat Forces").

02.09.1923–00.11.1923	Leading member of the *Deutsche Kampfbund-Kampfgemeinschaft Bayern* (German Fighting League-Fighting Community Bavaria).
25.09.1923–00.11.1923	Political leader of the *Deutschen Kampfbund-Kampfgemeinschaft Bayern*.
08./09.11.1923	Together with *General der Infanterie a. D.* Erich Ludendorff, led a *"Putsch"* in München with the immediate goal of taking control of the Bavarian Government, and ultimately the Reich as a whole. The revolt began when Hitler and an SA contingent of some 600 men surrounded the *Bürgerbräukeller* where the Bavarian *Ministerpräsident* Gustav Ritter von Kahr was making a speech before an audience of 3,000 people. At 20:30 hours, Hitler, together with Hermann Göring, Rudolf Hess, Ulrich Graf, and Alfred Rosenberg stormed through the front door. Hitler fired his pistol into the ceiling and leapt onto a chair, shouting:

The national revolution has broken out! The hall is filled with six hundred men. Nobody is allowed to leave. The Bavarian government and the government at Berlin are deposed. A new government will be formed at once. The barracks of the Reichswehr and those of the police are occupied. Both have rallied to the swastika.

	Hitler then led von Kahr, von Seisser, and von Lossow into a room, threatening to have them shot if they failed to support him in a march on Berlin. Hitler failed to get this support. At about 20:40 hours, General Ludendorff arrived at the *Bürgerbräukeller*, whereupon Hitler telephoned Ernst Röhm (who was the *Löwenbräukeller* with the majority of the München SA), giving him orders to take over key buildings in the city. At approximately 2230 hours, General Ludendorff released von Kahr and the other hostages. By the morning of 09.11.1923, nothing had been accomplished, and a desperate Hitler agreed with Ludendorff's cry of *"Wir marschieren!"* ("We will march!"). The groups under Hitler and Röhm (totaling about 2,000 men) then marched in the direction of the War Ministry. As the Putschists reached the *Odeonsplatz* before the *Feldherrnhalle*, they were met by 100 armed *Landespolizei* men under *Polizei-Oberleutnant* Michael Freiherr von Godin. In the gunfire that followed, four *Landespolizei* men and fourteen Nazis were killed. Hitler, with an injury to his shoulder, was able to escape amidst the chaos.
11.11.1923	Arrested by Bavarian Police at the home of Ernst ("Putzi") Hanfstaengl's sister in Uffing am Staffelsee (Kreis Garmisch-Partenkirchen), then taken to Landsberg Prison where he was held until his trial.
26.02.1924	Formally charged with high treason by the *Volksgericht* in München.
01.04.1924	Sentenced to five years' imprisonment and a 200 *Goldmark* fine in the so-called *"Hitler-Prozess."* In his final statement before the *Volksgericht* on 27.03.1924, he attacked those who had claimed he was motivated solely by personal ambition:

How petty are the thoughts of small men! My aim, from the very first day, was a thousand times more than becoming a minister. What I wanted to become was the destroyer of Marxism. This is my task, and I know when I settle this question—which I will—then the title of minister will become ridiculous.... It was not from modesty that I wanted to become a "drummer" in those days. That was the highest aspiration; the rest is a trifle....

The man who is born to be a dictator is not compelled, he wants it; he does not allow himself to be pushed, he drives himself forward. There is nothing immodest about it!... We face punishment today because the attempt failed. The deed of 8 November did not fail!... I believe that the time will come when the masses which today stand with our swastika flags on the streets will join forces with those who fired on us on 9 November ... that the hour will come when the *Reichswehr* soldiers will stand on our side ... and that the old cockade will be taken from the dirt and the old banners will wave again.... For it is not you, esteemed gentlemen, who pass the ultimate verdict on us ... but the eternal court of history. What verdict you will hand down, I know ... You may pronounce us "guilty" a thousand times over, but the goddess of the eternal court of history will smile and tear to tatters the brief of the state prosecutor and the verdict of this court, for she will acquit us. (Milan Hauser, *Hitler: A Chronology of his Life and Time*, p. 47)

While imprisoned at Landsberg, he wrote the first volume of his book *Mein Kampf*.

00.07.1924–00.12.1924	Relinquished control of the now prohibited NSDAP.
20.12.1924	Released from Landsberg Prison.
01.01.1925	Joined the *Allgemeiner Deutscher Automobil-Club* (ADAC, General German Automobile Club) (with membership number 56180).
27.02.1925	During a nearly two-hour speech to over 2,000 people, officially reestablished the NSDAP at the *Bürgerbräukellar*, München. He closed his speech with, "And I now carry again the complete responsibility for everything that takes place in this movement."
27.02.1925–30.04.1945	*Führer der NSDAP*.
09.03.1925–05.03.1927	Officially forbidden to speak in Bayern.
00.03.1925–00.00.1928	*Gauleiter* of *Gau Bayern der NSDAP*.
00.00.1925–31.12.1937	Editor of the *Völkischer Beobachter*.
27.04.1925	Submitted a request for release from Austrian citizenship.
30.04.1925	Emigration to Germany officially approved by the Austrian government. He remained stateless until 25.02.1932.
11.05.1926	Assumed control of the *österreichischen Nationalsozialisten* (Austrian National-Socialists).
22.05.1926	Elected as *Vorsitzender der NSDAP* (Chairman of the National-Socialist German Workers Party), following a *Generalmitgliederversammlung der NSDAP* (General meeting of the members of the NSDAP) in München.
02.01.1928–27.04.1930	*Reichspropagandaleiter der NSDAP* and acting *Leiter* of the *Propagandaausschuss der NSDAP* (Propaganda Committee of the NSDAP). Succeeded Gregor Strasser. Succeeded by Dr. Joseph Goebbels.

00.07.1929–00.12.1929	Member of the Präsidium of the *Reichsausschuss für das deutsche Volksbegehren* (Reich Committee for the German Referendum).
01.04.1930	Joined the *NS-Automobilkorps* (NSAK, forerunner of the NSKK), with NSAK Nr. 1.
30.08.1930–30.04.1945	*Oberster SA-Führer* (Supreme Leader of the *Sturmabteilung*). Succeeded Franz Pfeffer von Salomon.
00.00.19__–01.12.1933	*Vorsitzender* of the *Nationalsozialistischen Deutschen Arbeitervereins e.V.* (National-Socialist German Workers Association).
01.01.1932	New Year's Command to the SA, SS, HJ, and the NSKK:

The year 1931 strengthened and consolidated the Movement's units combined under the command of the Supreme SA Leadership both internally and in terms of numbers.

The army of Brownshirts has multiplied many times over.

The Movement has had to bear a high number of casualties. Forty-six were killed for the honor and freedom of the Volk; 4,804 were wounded. We wish to commemorate them foremost in loyalty and gratitude.

The victims were not killed in vain. The blood of the fighters shall give the sprout new energy.

Comrades, I thank you at the threshold of the new year for everything you have accomplished in the past year full of renunciation and sacrifices.

I wish to express my unqualified recognition of all the leaders and men of the SA, SS, HJ, and NSKK.

Proud of the accomplishments of 1931, you may enter the new year with cheerful confidence.

You are the hope of the German Volk.

Be worthy of your mission!

Der Oberste SA Führer: Adolf Hitler

(Dr. Max Domarus, ed., *Hitler. Speeches and Proclamations, 1932–1945: The Years 1932–1934*, p. 82)

25.02.1932–04.03.1933	Installed as a *Regierungsrat* in the *Landeskultur- und Vermessungsamt* (State Culture and Surveying Office) of Braunschweig, tasked with serving as a *Sachbearbeiter* (specialist) at the Braunschweig legation in Berlin. With this appointment came the automatic conferment of German citizenship, thus permitting him to run in the upcoming Reich Presidential elections of March 1932.
22.02.1932–13.03.1932	Unsuccessful candidate of the NSDAP in the Reich Presidential elections of 13.03.1932.
00.00.1932	Refused to accept the vice chancellorship in the cabinet of *Reichskanzler* Franz von Papen.
09.12.1932–00.11.1934	(nominal) *Reichsorganisationsleiter der NSDAP*. Succeeded Gregor Strasser. Succeeded by *Reichsleiter* Dr. Robert Ley.
30.01.1933	Charged by *Reichspräsident* Paul von Hindenburg with forming a cabinet from members of the NSDAP, the DNVP, and non-party-affiliated politicians, with himself as *Reichskanzler* (Reich Chancellor).
30.01.1933–30.04.1945	*Reichskanzler*. On the day of his appointment, he proclaimed:

National Socialists! My Party Comrades!

A fourteen-year-long struggle, unparalleled in German history, has now culminated in a great political triumph.

The Reichspräsident von Hindenburg has appointed me, the Führer of the National Socialist Movement, as Chancellor of the German Reich.

National leagues and parties have united in a joint fight for the resurrection of Germany.

The honor witnessed by German history of now being able to take a leading part in fulfilling this task I owe, next to the generous resolve of the Field Marshal, to your loyalty and devotion, my party comrades.

You followed me on cloudy days as unerringly as in the days of good fortune and remained true even after the most crushing defeats, and it is to that fact alone we owe this success.

Enormous is the task which lies before us. We must accomplish it, and we shall accomplish it.

Of you, my party comrades, I have only one major request: give me your confidence and your devotion in this new and great struggle, just as in the past, then the Almighty as well will not deny us His blessings toward reestablishing a German Reich of honor, freedom and domestic peace.

Berlin, 30 January 1933   Adolf Hitler

(Dr. Max Domarus, ed., *Hitler. Speeches and Proclamations, 1932–1945: The Years 1932–1934*, p. 228)

05.03.1933–30.04.1945	Member of the *Reichstag* (*Wahlkreis 24, Oberbayern-Schwaben*).
20.04.1933	Awarded the title of *Ehrenmeister des thüringischen Handwerks* (Honorary Master Craftsman of Thuringia).
25.04.1933–30.04.1945	*Reichsstatthalter in Preußen.*
14.06.1934–16.06.1934	Official visit to Italy for negotiations with Benito Mussolini in Venice. Hitler's hope was that Italy would not intervene in the event of a National-Socialist revolt in Austria. An unsuccessful meeting, as Mussolini vowed to come to Austria's aid if a Nazi coup was to occur in that country.
30.06.1934–02.07.1934	Purge of the SA and selected political figures who had run afoul of Hitler and his lieutenants, orchestrated by Hermann Göring, Heinrich Himmler, and Reinhard Heydrich in connivance with the *Reichswehr*. Among the leading figures murdered in the action, carried out on Hitler's authority by the SS and *Gestapo* on the pretext of a planned *"Putsch"* by the SA, were *SA-Stabschef* Ernst Röhm (personally arrested by Hitler), former *Reichsorganisationsleiter der NSDAP* Gregor Strasser, former *Reichskanzler* and *General der Infanterie* Kurt von Schleicher, and former Bavarian *Ministerpräsident* Gustav Ritter von Kahr. The official number of victims was given as eighty-five, but some sources indicate that as many as 1,000 were slaughtered in this "Night of the Long Knives." On 13.07.1934, speaking before the assembled members of the Reichstag, Hitler sought to justify the violence:

Commissioned thereto by the Government, the Reichstagspräsident, Hermann Göring, has called you together today to give me the possibility of explaining before this best qualified Forum of the Nation events which may well remain for all time in our history as a memory alike of sorrow and of warning. Out of a sum of material causes and personal guilt, from human inadequacy and human defects, there arose for our young Reich a crisis which only too easily might for an incalculable period have produced consequences completely disastrous. To make clear to you and thereby to the nation how this crisis arose and how it was overcome is the aim of my speech. The content of this speech will be of ruthless frankness. Only in its scope do I feel bound to impose upon myself some limitation, and that limitation is on the one side conditioned by the interests of the Reich and on the other side by bounds which are set by the sentiment of shame.

When on 30 January 1933 Generalfeldmarschall and Reichspräsident von Hindenburg entrusted me with the leadership of the newly formed German Government, the National Socialist Party took over a State which both politically and economically was in complete decline. All political forces of the former state of affairs which had just been brought to a close had their share in this decline, and consequently, a share in guilt. Since the abdication of the Kaiser and the German princes the German people had been delivered into the hands of men who, as the representatives of our past world of parties, had either consciously induced this decline or had weakly suffered it to continue. Beginning with the Marxist revolutionaries, and proceeding by way of the Zentrum till one reached the Bourgeois Nationalists—all parties and their leaders were given an opportunity to prove their capacity to govern Germany. Endless coalitions allowed them to put to the test their political arts and their economic skill. They have all failed miserably. 30 January was therefore not the day when our Government formally took over responsibility from the hands of another Government, it was rather the final liquidation, long desired by the nation, of an intolerable state of affairs.

It is essential that this should be clearly stated since, as subsequent events have proved, some individuals would seem to have forgotten that previously they were given full opportunity for demonstrating their political capacities. There is no one in Germany who could have any ground, even did he so wish, to charge the National Socialist Movement with having obstructed or even blocked the way to political forces which offered any hope of success. Fate, for reasons which we cannot fathom, condemned our people for fifteen years to serve as the field on which these politicians could make their experiments—as the rabbit in the hands of the vivisector.

It may have been interesting and pleasurable for the outside world—especially for the world that is ill-disposed towards us—to follow these experiments; for the German people they were as painful as they were humiliating. Look back on this period and before your eyes let all those figures pass who succeeded each other as Chancellors of the Reich. In what land were the scales of Providence more often brought into use, and where more frequently was the verdict passed that the object weighed had fallen short of the due weight? No! We National Socialists have the right to refuse to be counted as members of this line. On 30 January 1933 it was not a case of a new Government being formed as had happened times without number before, but a new regime had superseded an old and sick age.

This historic act of the liquidation of that most melancholy period in our nations life which now lies behind us was legalized by the German people itself. For we have not seized possession of power as usurpers, as did the men of November 1918; we have received power constitutionally and legally. We have not made a revolution as uprooted anarchists, but, as executing the nations will, we have set aside a regime born of rebellion, and we have seen our task to lie not in maintaining power at the point of the bayonet, but in finding that power in the heart of our people, and anchoring it there.

When today I read in a certain foreign newspaper that at the present time I am filled with profound anxieties, and at this moment in particular with economic anxieties, I have only one answer for these scribblers: assuredly that is true, but it is not merely today that anxiety tortures me; it has done so for a long time past. If it was formerly the anxiety for our people which led us to protect our people in the War which, despite its innocence, had been forced upon it, after the collapse it was the far greater anxiety for the future which turned us into revolutionaries. Arid when after fifteen years of struggle at last we received the leadership of the nation this torturing anxiety not only did not loosen its hold upon us, but on the contrary did but embrace us the more closely. I may be believed when I assure you that never yet in my life have I allowed myself to be anxious for my own personal fate. But I confess that from the day when the confidence of the Generalfeldmarschall appointed for me my place I do bear the burden of that heavy anxiety which the present and the future of our people lay upon us all. For on 30 January we did not take over a State which was in good order politically and in a healthy economic condition: we took over a political and economic chaos, which at that time precisely by those who are my critics today was regarded as completely irreparable and was so described by them.

We, however, have had the courage to accept battle in all spheres against these evidences of decline. From days and nights filled with anxieties we have always gained fresh strength for new decisions. For however much hostile critics may carp upon points of detail, even they cannot deny that we have not capitulated before problems, but that we have always striven manfully to solve them and that in numberless cases we have solved them. The result of one and a half years of National Socialist Government lies clear and indisputable before us. Its significance cannot be estimated by comparisons with the conditions with which we were faced on 30 January 1933. No! He who would be just must judge our success by comparing it with that which would have happened if we had not conquered. Only he who in his thought carries on farther the line of development which led up to the 30th of January of last year—only he can measure the greatness of the National Socialist achievement, for we have not only stayed the course of destiny as it was running at that time, but we have in all spheres put destiny on the road to good fortune.

When I as Chancellor of the Reich came into the Wilhelmstrasse, the authority of the Reich had become a worthless phantom. The spirit of revolt and insubordination dominated the German States and communes. The shadows of the most melancholy political past of the German people rose alarmingly before us. Particularism and Separatism insolently proclaimed themselves as the new German conception of the State. From the internal weakness of the Reich sprang its undignified attitude towards the world without. It had once more become a humiliation to confess publicly that one was a German. The spirit of insubordination and of internal revolt within a few months we exterminated and destroyed. While fully respecting the essential character of our German tribes we have strengthened the authority of the Reich as the expression of the common will of our people's life and have made it supreme. The German Reich is today no longer a merely geographical conception: it has become a political unity. We have directed our people's development on to lines which only two years ago were regarded as unattainable. And just as within the Reich we firmly secured the unity and therewith the future of the German people, so in the sphere of foreign policy we have resolutely championed the rights of our people.

It was not enough, however, to overcome the constitutional disunion of the German people, but it appeared to us almost more important to prevent the threatening dissolution in the political life of the people itself. Hardly six months of National Socialist government had passed before the course of our former political life, our party-disunion, was overcome. More and more from month to month the German people separated itself from this period which already today appears to us almost incomprehensible and grew more and more alienated from its characteristic features. There was no need for me to give expression to that fact, for every German feels and knows it to be true; even the bare thought of any return to this confused party-world is ridiculous and absurd.

This great process of the cleansing of the nation's political life was followed by a no less great economic change/ What has been achieved in this sphere during the last eighteen months is shown by the incontestable fact that four and a half million unemployed have been brought back to useful productive work in a period of not quite one and a half years. This is a very simple fact, but the measure of its simplicity is matched only by the greatness of the anxieties which had and still have their roots in this struggle against unemployment It is an embittered fight which we have been waging for more than one and a half years. If you would judge it, you must not start from that which was wrongly done, but rather from the fact of the result which today has been achieved—a result which was precisely that which our critics held to be impossible. And further I would here make one general statement: we have been faced by questions to which those who preceded us have found no answer. In many cases we were quite unable to appeal to the former experience of others. We had to discover our own ways so often that it is naturally easy afterwards to pillory this or that mistake. But I regard it as a greater service to have the courage at least to seek for a way out of misery rather than from fear of choosing the wrong way to remain in misery. We all know that for a government that is truly anxious to do its duty there can never be a time when it is free from anxieties. Always there are new problems to master, new questions to solve, new tasks to fulfil. While we liberated four and a half million men from unemployment and once more made possible for them a different standard of living, we were at the same time increasing their power of consumption: that means that foreign raw materials are consumed to a greater extent. We see difficulties such as these and I can assure the German people of one thing only: We shall solve them.

If our trade balance is unfavorable owing to our exclusion from foreign markets either by economic barriers or by a political boycott, then thanks to the genius of our inventors and chemists and through our own energy we shall find ways to make ourselves independent of the import of those materials which we are in a position ourselves to produce or for which we can discover substitutes. All these problems we shall solve with indomitable resolution, and in that resolution we shall always Ibe inspired by our anxiety to help our people in its struggle for existence. There is hardly a sphere of our national, political, or economic life, hardly a sphere of our life as a whole, in which we have not done pioneering work.

The best proof of the truth of this assertion is the attitude of the German people itself. In all strata of its life it has declared its loyalty to the new regime. The features which marked our former political confusion have not been set aside because we destroyed them, but because the German people removed them from its heart. And I must—today and in this place—confess that assuredly our work would have been utterly vain, and must have been vain, had not the German people given us its confidence and its loyal cooperation in so large a measure. Our success is due to the 41 ½ million men and women from all walks of life who gave us no merely superficial "Yes," but devoted themselves with all their hearts to the new regime.

To them our success is mainly due. Without their confiding trust, without their patient forbearance, without their devotion and readiness for sacrifice the work of German recovery would never have succeeded. They are, as the supporters of the people's rebirth, at the same time the best representatives of the people. They are in truth the German people.

Beginning with the old, true, and unswerving fighters of our Movement and going down to the newly won millions of the working-classes they form the healthy element in our people's life. They have all remained honorable and decent in character. Millions of them still today in Germany fight a hard and bitter struggle for their scanty daily bread. Hundreds of thousands of miners hardly earn the bare necessities of life. Hundreds of thousands of others were ready to share their job with their still poorer fellow-countrymen. And yet they all live looking to the new State with confidence and faith. From millions of hard-working men who earn but little we have been compelled to demand sacrifices to save Germans in other walks of life. And those sacrifices they have made. The words Community of the German people have found precisely in the poorest sons of our people their most lofty and glorious exemplification. Millions of women love this new State, make sacrifices for it, work and pray for it. They sympathize by natural instinct with its mission of maintaining our people to which in their children they have themselves given a living pledge. Hundreds of thousands of members of our former bourgeois society are anxious to seek and find in the new State their way to the German people.

For countless numbers a new life seems to have been opened up, a fairer goal seems to have been set before them for their work and their ceaseless striving and struggling. He who has the good fortune to come amongst this people will himself be seized and carried away by the wave of boundless assurance, of utterly immovable confidence with which they all cling to this new Germany.

And over against this positive world of the German spirit [*Deutschtum*] the incorporation of the true values of our people, there stands also, it is true, a small negative world. They take no part in their hearts in the work of German recovery and restoration. First there is the small body of those international disintegrators of a people who as apostles of the Weltanschauung of Communism alike in the political and economic sphere systematically incite the peoples, break up established order, and endeavor to produce chaos. We see evidence for the activity of these international conspirators all about us. Up and down the countries the flames of revolt run over the peoples. Street riots, fights at the barricades, mass-terrorism, and the individualistic propaganda of disintegration disturb today nearly all the countries of the world. Even in Germany some single fools and criminals of this type still again and again seek to exercise their destructive activity. Since the destruction of the Communist Party we experience one attempt after another, though growing ever weaker as time passes, to found and to sustain the work of Communistic organizations of a more or less anarchistic character. Their method is always the same. While they paint men's present lot as intolerable they praise the Communistic paradise of the future, and thus practically wage a war in Hell's behalf. For the consequences of their victory in a country such as Germany could be nothing but completely destructive. The proof of their capacity and of the effect of their supremacy has by concrete examples already become so clear to the German people that the overwhelming majority even of the German working-classes has recognized the true character of these Jewish-international benefactors of mankind and is no longer seduced by them. The National Socialist State In its domestic life will exterminate and annihilate even these last remnants of this poisoning and stultification of the people, if necessary at the cost of another Hundred Years' War.

The second group of the discontented consists of those political leaders who feel that their political future is closed through the 30th of January, but yet are still unable to accept the irrevocability of this fact. The more time veils with the gracious mantle of forgetfulness their own incapacity, the more do they think themselves entitled gradually to bring themselves back into the people's memory. But since their incapacity was not formerly limited to any special period but was born in them by nature, they are today, too, unable to prove their value in any positive and useful work, but they see the fulfilment of their life's task to lie in a criticism which is as treacherous as it is mendacious. With them, too, the people have no sympathy. The National Socialist State can neither be seriously threatened by them nor in any way damaged.

A third group of destructive elements is formed of those revolutionaries whose former relation to the State was shattered by the events of 1918; they became uprooted and thereby lost altogether all sympathy with any ordered human society. They became revolutionaries who favored revolution for its own sake and desired to see revolution established as a permanent condition. We all formerly suffered under the frightful tragedy that we, as disciplined and loyal soldiers, were suddenly faced with a revolt of mutineers who managed to seize possession of the State. Each of us had been brought up to respect the laws and to reverence authority, we had been trained in obedience to the commands and regulations issued by the authorities, in a subordination of our wills in face of the State's representatives. Now the revolution of deserters and mutineers forced upon us in our thought the abandonment of these conceptions. We could not pay respect to the new usurpers. Our honor, our conscience forced us to withhold our obedience to their orders, our love for the nation and for the Fatherland laid upon us the duty of waging war against them, the absence of any morality* in their laws quenched in us any feeling for the necessity of observing them, and thus we became revolutionaries. But even as revolutionaries we had never cut ourselves loose from the obligation of applying to ourselves just as much as to others the natural laws of the sovereign right of our people; these we were bound to respect.

We did not desire to violate the will of the German people or its right of self-determination: we wanted only to drive out the violators of the nation. And when at last we received our legitimation through the trust reposed in us by this people and drew the conclusions resulting from our fourteen years of fighting, that did not happen in order that we might allow our instincts free rein to vent themselves but only that we might establish a new and better order. For us the Revolution which shattered the second Germany was but the mighty act of birth whereby the Third Reich was called into being. Our desire was to create once more a State to which every German may cling with a loving devotion. Our aim was to establish a regime to which everyone might look up with respect, to devise laws which corresponded with the morality of our people, to make secure an authority to which every man might subject himself in Prussian obedience. For us the Revolution is no permanent condition. When some mortal check is imposed with violence upon the natural development of a people, then the artificially interrupted evolution can rightly by a deed of violence open up the way for itself in order to regain liberty to pursue its natural development. But there can be no such thing as a state of permanent revolution; neither can any beneficent development be secured by means of periodically recurrent revolts.

Amongst the numberless documents which during the last week it was my duty to read I have discovered a diary with the notes of a man who, in 1918, was thrown into the path of resistance to the laws and who now lives in a world in which law in itself seems to be a provocation to resistance. It is an unnerving document- an unbroken tale of conspiracy and continual plotting: it gives one an insight into the mentality of men who, without realizing it, have found in nihilism their final confession of faith. Incapable of any true co-operation, with a desire to oppose all order, filled with hatred against every authority, their unrest and disquietude can find satisfaction only in some conspiratorial activity of the mind perpetually plotting the disintegration of whatever at any moment may exist. Many of them in the early days of our struggle have together with us charged against the State which is now no more, but their inner lack of discipline led most of them, even during the course of the struggle, away from the disciplined National Socialist Movement.

The last remnant appeared to have separated itself from us after the 30th of January [1933]. The link with the National Socialist Movement was severed at the moment when the Movement itself, now representing the State, became the object of their pathological aversion. They are on principle enemies of every authority, and therefore there can be no hope at all of their conversion. Achievements which appear to strengthen the new German State do but increase their hatred, for in general one thing is common to these folk who are from principle in permanent opposition; they do not see before them the German people but the institution which guarantees order, and it is that which arouses their hatred. They are not filled with a desire to help the people, but rather by a hope which severs them from the people—the hope that the Government may fail in its work for the people's salvation. They are for that reason never prepared to admit the benefit resulting from any act: rather they are filled with the determination to deny on principle every success and on every success to trace the failures and the weaknesses which may possibly ensue.

This third group of pathological enemies of the State is dangerous because they represent a reservoir of those ready to cooperate in every attempt at a revolt, at least just for so long as a new order does not begin to crystallize out of the state of chaotic confusion.

I must now mention the fourth group, which often perhaps even against its own will does in fact carry on a truly destructive activity. The group is composed of those persons who belong to a comparatively small section of society and who, having nothing to do, find time and opportunity to report orally everything that has happened in order thus to bring some interesting and important variety into their otherwise completely purposeless lives. For whilst the overwhelming majority of the nation has to earn its daily bread in toilsome work in certain strata of life there are still folk whose sole activity it is to do nothing, only to need afterwards a rest-cure from doing nothing. The more paltry is the life of such a drone, the more eagerly will he seize upon anything which may give some interesting content to the vacuity of his mind. Personal and political gossip is eagerly swallowed and even more eagerly handed on. Since these men as a result of doing nothing do not possess any living relation to the millions which form the mass of the nation, their life is confined in its range to the circle within which they move. Every bit of gossip which strays into this circle reverberates backwards and forwards like figures reflected in two distorting mirrors. Because their whole ego is full of nothingness, and since they find a similar nothingness amongst their like, they look upon the whole world as equally empty; they come to think that the outlook of their own circle is the outlook of everyone. Their anxieties, they imagine, form the cares of the whole nation. In reality this little cloud of drones is but a State within the State; it has no contact with the life, the sentiments, the hopes and cares of the rest of the people. They are, however, dangerous because they are veritable bacillus-carriers of unrest and uncertainty, of rumors, assertions, lies and suspicions, of slanders and fears, and thus they contribute to produce gradually a state of nervousness which spreads amongst the people so that in the end it is hard to find or recognize where its influence stops. Just as in all other peoples, so in Germany they carry on their mischievous activity. For them the National Socialist Revolution was an interesting subject of conversation, and so, on the other hand, was the fight of our enemies against the National Socialist State.

But one thing is clear: the work of reconstruction and indeed the work of our people itself is possible only if the German people in internal calm, order, and discipline follows its leaders and above all if it puts its trust in its leaders. For it is only the trust and the faith in the new State which has enabled us to attack and solve the great tasks which have been set us by our predecessors.

Though it is true that from the outset the National Socialist regime had to take these various groups into account and has in fact taken account of them, yet for some months there has been noticeable a trend of thought which we could not afford lightly to tolerate.

The first idle talk which one heard here and there of a new revolution, of a new upheaval, of a new revolt gradually grew in intensity to such an extent that only an irresponsible statesmanship could afford to ignore it. One could no longer simply dismiss as silly chatter all the information which came to us in hundreds and at last in thousands of reports both orally and in writing. Only three months ago the leaders of the Party were still convinced that it was simply the Irresponsible gossip of political reactionaries, of Marxist anarchists, or of all sorts of idlers with which they had to deal—gossip which had no support in fact.

In the middle of March I took steps to have preparations made for a new wave of propaganda which was to render the German people immune from any attempt to spread fresh poison. At the same time I gave orders to certain departments of the Party administration to trace the rumors of a new revolution which were continually cropping up and to find out, if possible, the sources from which they came. The result was that certain tendencies appeared in the ranks of some of the higher SA-Führer which were bound to cause the gravest anxiety. At first it was a case of general symptoms, the inner connections of which were not at once clear:

1. Against my express order, and in despite of declarations made to me through the Stabschef, Röhm, there had been such an increase in the numbers of the SA, that the internal homogeneity of this unique organization must be endangered.

2. Education in the National Socialist Weltanschauung in the above-mentioned sections of individual higher SA authorities had been more and more neglected.

3. The natural relationship between the Party and the SA began slowly to be weakened. We were able to establish that efforts were being made, as it seemed systematically, to withdraw the SA more and more from the mission appointed for it by me and to use it in the service of other tasks or other interests.

4. Promotions to posts of leadership in the SA when they were tested showed that a completely one-sided valuation had been set on purely external skill or often only on a supposed intellectual capacity. The great body of the oldest and most loyal SA men was always more and more neglected when appointments to the post of leader were made or when vacancies had to be filled, while a quite incomprehensible preference was shown for those who had been enlisted in the year 1933 who were not especially highly respected in the Movement. Often only a few months' membership of the Party, or

even only of the SA, was enough to secure promotion to a higher position in the SA, which the old SA-Führer could not reach after years of service.

5. The behavior of these individual SA-Führer who had for the greater part not grown up with the Movement at all was false to National Socialist standards and often positively revolting. It could not be overlooked that it was precisely in these circles that one source of the unrest in the Movement was discovered, in that their incomplete practical National Socialism sought to veil itself in very unseemly demands for a new revolution.

I drew the attention of the Stabschef, Röhm, to these abuses and to a number of others without meeting with any appreciable help in their removal, indeed without any recognizable concurrence on his part with my objections.

In the months of April and May there was a constant increase in these complaints, and it was then that I received for the first time reports, confirmed by official documents, of conversations which had been held by individual higher SA-Führer and which can only be described as "gross impropriety." For the first time in some official documents we obtained irrefutable evidence that in these conversations, references had been made to the necessity for a new revolution and that leaders had received instructions to prepare themselves both materially and in spirit for such a new revolution. The Stabschef, Röhm, endeavored to maintain that these conversations had not in fact been held and that the reports were to be explained as veiled attacks upon the SA.

The confirmation of some of these cases through the statements of those who had been present led to the most serious ill-treatment of these witnesses who for the most part came from the ranks of the old SA. Already by the end of April the leaders of the Party and a number of State institutions concerned in the matter were convinced that a certain group of the higher SA, leaders was consciously contributing towards the alienation of the SA from the Party as well as from the other institutions of the State, or at least was not opposing this alienation. The attempt to remedy this state of affairs through the normal official channels always remained unsuccessful. The Stabschef, Röhm, promised me personally over and over again that he would inquire into these cases and that he would remove or punish the guilty parties. But no visible change in the situation resulted.

In the month of May numerous charges of offences committed by SA, leaders, both those of high rank and of intermediate position, were received by officials of the Party and of the State; these offences were supported by official documents and could not be denied. Provocative speeches led directly to intolerable excesses. The Ministerpräsident Göring had already previously endeavored, so far as Prussia was concerned, to maintain the authority of the will of the National Socialist State over the self-will of individual elements. In some other German States meanwhile the authorities of the Party and the officials had been compelled to oppose single intolerable excesses. Some of the responsible parties were taken into custody. I have before this always stressed the fact that an authoritarian regime is under special obligations. When one demands of a people that it should put blind confidence in its leaders, then for their part these leaders must deserve this confidence through their achievement and through especially good behavior. Mistakes and errors may in individual cases slip in, but they are to be eradicated. Bad behavior, drunken excesses, the molestation of peaceful decent folk—these are unworthy of a leader, they are not National Socialist, and they are in the highest degree detestable.

I have for this reason always insisted that in their conduct and behavior higher demands should be made of National Socialist leaders than of the rest of the people. He who desires to receive higher respect than others must meet this demand by a higher achievement. The most elementary demand that can be made of him is that in his life he should not give a shameful example to those about him. I do not desire therefore that National Socialists guilty of such offenses should be judged and punished more leniently than are other fellow-countrymen of theirs; rather, I expect that a leader who forgets himself in this way should be punished with greater rigor than an unknown man would be in a like case. And here I would make no distinction between leaders of the political organizations and leaders of the formations of our SA, SS, Hitler-Youth, etc.

The resolution of the National Socialist Government to put an end to such excesses of individual unworthy elements which did but cover with shame the Party and the SA led to a very violent counter-activity on the part of the Stabschef. National Socialist fighters of the earliest days, some of whom had striven for nearly fifteen years for the victory of the Movement and now as high State-officials in leading positions in our State represented the Movement, were called to account for the action which they had taken against such unworthy elements: that is to say that through Courts of Honor, composed in part of some of the youngest members of the Party or even at times of those who were not members of the Party at all, the Stabschef, Röhm, sought to secure the punishment of these oldest Party-combatants.

These disagreements led to very serious exchanges of views between the Stabschef and myself, and it was in these interviews that for the first time doubts of the loyalty of this man began to rise in my mind. Though for many months I had rejected every such idea, though previously through the years I had protected this man with my person in unswerving loyalty and comradeship, now gradually warnings which I received—especially from my deputy in the leadership of the Party, Rudolf Hess—began to induce suspicions which even with the best of will I was not able to stifle.

After the month of May there could be no further doubt that the Stabschef, Röhm, was busied with ambitious schemes which, if they were realized, could lead only to the most violent disturbances.

If during these months I hesitated again and again before taking a final decision that was due to two considerations:
1. I could not lightly persuade myself to believe that a relation which I thought to be founded on loyalty could be only a lie,
2. I still always cherished the secret hope that I might be able to spare the Movement and my SA the shame of such a disagreement and that it might be possible to remove the mischief without severe conflicts. It must be confessed that the last days of May continuously brought to light more and more disquieting facts.

The Stabschef now began to alienate himself from the Party not only in spirit but also in his whole external manner of life. All the principles through which we had grown to greatness lost their validity. The life which the Stabschef and with him a certain circle began to lead was from any National Socialist point of view intolerable. It was not only terrible that he himself and the circle of those who were devoted to him should violate all laws of decency and modest behavior, it was still worse that now this poison began to spread in ever wider circles. The worst of all was that gradually out of a certain common disposition of character there began to be formed within the SA a party which became the kernel of a conspiracy directed not only against the normal views of a healthy people but also against the security of the State. The review which took place in the month of May of promotions in certain SA districts led to the horrible realization that men without regard to services rendered to the National Socialist Party or to the SA had been promoted to positions in the SA solely because they belonged to the circle of those possessing this special disposition. Individual cases with which you are familiar such, for example, as that of the Standartenführer Schmidt in Breslau, disclosed a picture of conditions which could only be regarded as intolerable. My order to proceed against the offenders was followed in theory, but in fact it was sabotaged.

Gradually from amongst the SA-Führer there emerged three groups: a small group of elements which were held together through a like disposition, men who were ready for any action and who had given themselves blindly into the hands of the Stabschef, Röhm. The principal members of this group were the SA-Führer Ernst from Berlin, Heines in Schlesien, Hayn in Sachsen, and Heydebreck in Pommern. Besides these there was a second group of SA-Führer who did not belong to the former group in spirit but felt themselves bound to obey the Stabschef, Röhm, solely from a simple conception of a soldier's duty. Over against these stood a third group of leaders who made no secret of their inner disgust and reprobation and were in consequence in part removed from responsible posts, in part thrust aside, and in many respects left out of account.

At the head of this group of SA-Führer, who because of their fundamental decency had been hardly treated, stood the present Stabschef, Lutze and the leader of the SS, Himmler.

Without ever informing me and when at first I never dreamt of any such action, the Stabschef, Röhm, through the agency of an utterly corrupt swindler—a certain Herr von A—, entered into relations with General Schleicher. General Schleicher was the man who gave eternal expression to the secret wish of the Stabschef, Röhm. He it was who defined the latter's views in concrete form and maintained that

1. The present regime in Germany cannot be supported.
2. Above all the army and all national associations must be united in a single band.
3. The only man who could be considered for such a position was the Stabschef, Röhm.
4. Herr von Papen must be removed and he himself would be ready to take the position of Vice-Chancellor, and that in addition further important changes must be made in the Cabinet of the Reich.

As always happens in such cases there now began the search after the men for the new Government, always under the view that I myself should at least for the present be left in the position which I now hold.

The execution of these proposals of General von Schleicher was bound, as soon as Point 2 was reached, to come up against my unalterable opposition. Both from a consideration of the facts and from a consideration of personal character it would never have been possible for me to consent to a change in the Reich Ministry of War and to the appointment of the Chief of Staff, Röhm, to that Ministry.

Firstly: the consideration of the facts: for fourteen years I have stated consistently that the fighting organizations of the Party are political institutions and that they have nothing to do with the army. On the facts of the case it would be, in my opinion, to disavow this view of mine and my fourteen years of political life if I were now to summon to the head of the army the leader of the SA. In November 1923 I proposed that an officer should lead the army and not the man who was then the Führer of my SA, Hauptmann Göring.

Secondly: the consideration of human character. On this point it would have been impossible for me ever to concur in the proposal of General von Schleicher. When these plans became known to me my picture of the value of the character of the Stabschef, Röhm, was already such that before my conscience and for the sake of the honor of the army I could no longer under any circumstances contemplate admitting him to this post: above all, the supreme head of the army is the Generalfeldmarschall and Reichspräsident. As Chancellor I gave my oath into his keeping. His person is for us all inviolate. The promise which I gave him that I would preserve the army as a non-political instrument of the Reich is for me binding, both from my inmost conviction and also from the word which I have given. But, further, any such act would have been impossible for me on the human side in the face of the War Minister of the Reich. Both I myself and all of us are happy to be able to see in him a man of honor from the crown of his head to the soles of his feet. He reconciled the army with those who were once revolutionaries and has linked it up with their Government today and he has done this from the deepest convictions of his heart. He has made his own in truest loyalty the principle for which I myself will stand to my last breath.

In the State there is only one bearer of arms, and that is the army; there is only one bearer of the political will, and that is the National Socialist Party. Any thought of consenting to the plans of General von Schleicher would be, so far as I am concerned, not only disloyalty to the Generalfeldmarschall and the War Minister, but also disloyalty to the army. For just as General von Blomberg as War Minister in the National Socialist State fulfils his duty in the highest sense of the word, so do, also, the other officers and the soldiers. I cannot demand from them that as individuals each of them should take up a definite position towards our Movement, but not one of them has lost the true position of loyal service to the National Socialist State. And, further, I could not without the most compelling cause have permitted the removal of men who as a united body on the 30th of January gave me their promise to cooperate in the salvation of the Reich and of the people. There are duties of loyalty which one dare not and ought not to violate. And I believe that above all the man who has in his own name unified the nation ought in no circumstances to act disloyally if he would not see both within and without the complete disappearance of all trust in loyalty and good faith.

Since the Stabschef, Röhm, was himself uncertain whether any attempt on the lines which I have described might not well meet with resistance from me, the first plan was devised in order to achieve the desired result by compulsion. Extensive preparations were made: in the first place
1. Psychological conditions which should favor the outbreak of a second revolution were to be systematically created. For this end, by means of the SA propaganda authorities themselves, the assertion was spread through the ranks of the SA that the army intended to disband the SA, and it was later added that unfortunately I myself had been won over to the support of this plan. A wretched and infamous lie!
2. The SA must forthwith anticipate this attack, and in a second revolution must remove the reactionary elements on the one hand and the opposition of the Party on the other. Authority in the State must be entrusted to the SA-Führer.
3. To this end the SA should make as rapidly as possible all the necessary material preparations. Through different pretexts, e.g., by the lying statement that he was anxious to carry through a scheme of social relief for the benefit of the SA, the Stabschef, Röhm, succeeded in collecting contributions running into millions of marks. Twelve million marks were raised for these objects.
4. In order to be in a position to deliver ruthlessly the most decisive blows there were formed under the title of "Stabswache" [Staff Guards] groups of terrorists specially sworn in for the purpose. The old SA man had for more than a decade gone starving in the service of the Movement; now these new formations were paid troops, and the personal character and the purpose for which they were enlisted cannot be more clearly shown than by the truly fearful list of the punishments which they had previously incurred; indeed the old, true SA-Führer and SA-Mann now very quickly were thrust into the background in favor of those elements which had enjoyed no political training but were better qualified for the kind of work for which they were intended. At certain gatherings of leaders as well as on holiday-trips gradually the SA-Führer concerned in the plan were brought together and dealt with individually, that is to say, that while the members of the inner circle systematically prepared the main action, the second and larger circle of SA-Führer was only given general information to the effect that a second revolution was on the way, that this second revolution had no other object than to restore to me personally my freedom of action, and that therefore the new—and this time bloody-rising—"The Night of the Long Knives" was their ghastly name for it—was exactly what I myself desired. The necessity for the initiative of the SA was explained by reference to my own inability to come to any decision: that disability would be removed only when I was faced with an accomplished fact. Presumably it was by means of these untrue pretexts that the preparation for the scheme so far as foreign policy was concerned was given to Herr von Detten. General von Schleicher saw to this aspect of the scheme in part personally, but left the practical side of the negotiations to his intermediary, General von Bredow. Gregor Strasser was brought in.

At the beginning of June I made a last attempt and had yet another talk with Roehm which lasted nearly five hours and was prolonged until midnight. I informed him that from numberless rumors and from numerous assurances and statements of old, loyal comrades and SA-Führer I had gained the impression that by certain unscrupulous elements a National-Bolshevist rising was being prepared which could only bring untold misery upon Germany. I explained to him further that reports had also come to my ears of the intention to draw the army within the scope of these plans. I assured the Stabschef, Röhm, that the assertion that the SA was to be dissolved was an infamous lie and that I refused to make any comment upon the lie that I myself intended to attack the SA, but that I should at any moment be ready personally to oppose any attempt to raise chaos in Germany and that anyone who attacks the State should know from the outset that he will have me for his enemy. I implored him for the last time to oppose this madness of his own accord—let him at the same time use his authority so as to stop a development which in any event could end only in a catastrophe. I raised afresh vigorous protests on the score of the impossible excesses which followed one after another, and demanded the immediate and complete elimination of these elements from the SA in order not to dishonor, through a few unworthy individuals, the SA itself together with millions of decent comrades and hundreds of thousands of old fighters. The Stabschef left this interview after assuring me that the reports were partly untrue and partly exaggerated, and that moreover he would for the future do everything in his power to set things to rights.

The result of the interview, however, was that the Stabschef, Röhm, recognizing that for the undertaking which he was planning he could in no circumstances count on my personal support, now prepared to remove me personally from the scene. To this end it was explained to the larger circle of SA-Führer who had been drawn into the plot that I myself was in thorough agreement with the proposed undertaking, but that I personally must know nothing about it or else that I wished on the outbreak of the rising immediately to be arrested and kept in custody for some twenty-four or forty-eight hours in order thus through the fait accompli to be relieved from an awkward responsibility which must otherwise arise for me in the sphere of our foreign relations. This explanation is conclusively illustrated by the fact that meanwhile care had been taken to bribe the man whose task it was later to carry through my removal. Standartenführer Uhl, a few hours before his death, confessed that he had been ready to execute such an order.

The first plan for the revolution was founded on the idea of granting leave to the SA. During this period of leave, since any plausible excuse was lacking, inexplicable riots were to break out similar to the conditions in August 1932. These would compel me to summon the Chief of Staff, who alone would be in a position to restore order; for this purpose I should have to entrust him with full executive authority. But when meanwhile it had been clearly shown that in no circumstances could my willingness to give such an order be relied upon, this plan was abandoned and direct action was now contemplated.

That action was to begin by a blow struck without any warning in Berlin: there was to be an assault upon the Government building, I myself was to be taken into custody so that further steps, as though ordered by me, could follow without any hindrance. The conspirators calculated that commands given in my name to the SA would immediately call into action the SA throughout the Reich, and also that thereby there would result automatically a division in all the other forces of the State ranged in opposition to the rising.

The Stabschef, Röhm, the Gruppenführer Ernst, the Obergruppenführer Heines, Hayn, and a number of others declared in the presence of witnesses that immediately there was to follow a conflict of the bloodiest kind, lasting several days, with their opponents. The economic side of such a development was dismissed with positively insane irresponsibility: bloody terrorism in one way or another was to provide the necessary means. Here I must deal with the view that every successful revolution provides in itself its own justification. The Stabschef, Röhm, and his followers declared their revolution to be a necessity because only so could the victory of pure National Socialism receive its full justification. But at this point I must assert, both in the interest of the present and of posterity, that these men no longer had any right at all to appeal to National Socialism as their Weltanschauung. Their lives had become as evil as the lives of those whom we defeated in 1933 and whose places we took. The behavior of these men made it impossible for me to ask them to my house or, even if it were once only, to enter the house of the Stabschef in Berlin. It is difficult to conceive what would have become of Germany if these people had won the day. The greatness of the danger could not be fully realized until we received the communications which now reached Germany from abroad. English and French papers began with increasing frequency to speak of an upheaval which would shortly take place in Germany, and from the ever-growing stream of communications it was clear that the conspirators had systematically sought to foster the view in foreign countries that the revolution of the genuine National Socialists was at hand and that the existing regime was now incapable of action. General von Bredow, who as political agent in foreign affairs for General von Schleicher looked after these connections, worked in sympathy with those reactionary circles who—though not perhaps standing in any direct connection with this conspiracy—yet readily allowed themselves to be misused as subterranean purveyors of information for foreign Powers.

Thus at the end of June I had made up my mind to put an end to this impossible development, and that, too, before the blood of ten thousand innocent folk should seal the catastrophe. Since the danger and the tension which oppressed everyone were growing intolerable, and since the authorities both in the Party and in the State were each in duty bound to take measures in self-defense, the extraordinary, sudden prolongation of the period of service of the SA before their leave seemed to me suspicious, and consequently I decided that on Saturday 30 June I would deprive the Stabschef of his office and for the time being keep him in custody and would arrest a number of SA-Führer whose crimes were unquestioned. Since it was doubtful, when things had reached so threatening a climax, whether the Stabschef, Röhm, would have come to Berlin at all, or indeed anywhere else, I decided to go in person to a discussion amongst SA-Führer which had been announced to be held at Wiessee. Relying on the authority of my own personality and on my power of decision which had never failed me in the hour of need, I determined that there at 12 o'clock midday I would deprive the Stabschef of his office, I would arrest those SA-Führer who were principally responsible, and in an earnest appeal to the others I would recall them to their duty.

However, in the course of the 29th of June I received such threatening intelligence concerning the last preparations for action that I was forced at midday to interrupt an inspection of a Workers' Camp in Westfalen in order to hold myself in readiness for all emergencies. At I o'clock in the night I received from Berlin and München two urgent messages concerning alarm-summonses; firstly that for Berlin an alarm-muster had been ordered for 4 o'clock in the afternoon, that for the transport of the regular shock-formations the requisition of lorries had been ordered, and that this requisition was now proceeding, and that promptly at 5 o'clock action was to begin with a surprise attack: the Government building was to be occupied. Gruppenführer Ernst with this end in view had not after all gone to Wiessee but had remained behind in Berlin to undertake the conduct of operations there.

Secondly: in München the alarm-summons had already been given to the SA; they had been ordered to assemble at 9 o'clock in the evening. The SA formations had not been dismissed to their homes, they were already stationed in their alarm-quarters. That is mutiny! I and no one else am the commander of the SA!

In these circumstances I could make but one decision. If disaster was to be prevented at all, action must be taken with lightning speed. Only a ruthless and bloody intervention might still perhaps stifle the spread of the revolt. And then there could be no question that it was better that a hundred mutineers, plotters, and conspirators should be destroyed than that ten thousand innocent SA men should be allowed to shed their blood. For if once criminal activity was set in motion in Berlin, then the consequences were indeed unthinkable. The effect which had been produced by the fact that the conspirators purported to act in my name was proved by the distressing fact that, for instance, these mutineers in Berlin had succeeded through citing my authority in securing for their plot four armored cars from unsuspecting police-officers and further by the fact that the plotters Heines and Hayn in Saxony and Silesia through their appeals had made police-officers doubtful which side they should support in the coining conflict between the SA and the enemies of Hitler. It was at last clear to me that only one man could oppose and must oppose the Stabschef. It was to me that he had pledged his loyalty and broken that pledge, and for that I alone must call him to account!

At 1 o'clock in the night I received the last dispatches telling me of the alarm-summonses; at 2 o'clock in the morning I flew to München. Meanwhile Ministerpräsident Göring had previously received from me the commission that if I proceeded to apply a purge he was to take similar measures at once in Berlin and in Prussia. With an iron fist he beat down the attack on the National Socialist State before it could develop. The necessity for acting with lightning speed meant that in this decisive hour I had very few men with me. In the presence of the Minister Goebbels and of the new Stabschef the action of which you are already informed was executed and brought to a close in

München. Although only a few days before I had been prepared to exercise clemency, at this hour there was no place for any such consideration. Mutinies are suppressed in accordance with laws of iron which are eternally the same. If anyone reproaches me and asks why I did not resort to the regular courts of justice for conviction of the offenders, then all that I can say to him is this: in this hour I was responsible for the fate of the German people, and thereby I became the supreme Justiciar of the German people!

Mutinous divisions have in all periods been recalled to order by decimation. Only one State has failed to make any use of its Articles of War and this State paid for that failure by collapse—Germany. I did not wish to deliver up the young Reich to the fate of the old Reich. I gave the order to shoot those who were the ringleaders in this treason, and I further gave the order to burn out down to the raw flesh the ulcers of this poisoning of the wells in our domestic life and of the poisoning of the outside world. And I further ordered that if any of the mutineers should attempt to resist arrest, they were immediately to be struck down with armed force. The nation must know that its existence—and that is guaranteed through its internal order and security—can be threatened by no one with impunity! And everyone must know for all future time that if he raises his hand to strike the State, then certain death is his lot. And every National Socialist must know that no rank and no position can protect him from his personal responsibility and therefore from his punishment. I have prosecuted thousands of our former opponents on account of their corruption. I should in my own mind reproach myself if I were now to tolerate similar offences in our own ranks. No people and no Government can help it if creatures arise such as we once knew in Germany, a Kutisker for example, such as France came to know in a Stavisky, or such as we today have once more experienced—men whose aim is to sin against a nation's interests. But every people is itself guilty if it does not find the strength to destroy such noxious creatures. If people bring against me the objection that only a judicial procedure could precisely weigh the measure of the guilt and of its expiation, then against this view I lodge my most solemn protest. He who rises against Germany is a traitor to his country: and the traitor to his country is not to be punished according to the range and the extent of his act, but according to the purpose which that act has revealed. He who in his heart purposes to raise a mutiny and thereby breaks loyalty, breaks faith, breaks sacred pledges, he can expect nothing else than that he himself will be the first sacrifice. I have no intention to have the little culprits shot and to spare the great criminals. It is not my duty to inquire whether it was too hard a lot which was inflicted on these conspirators, these agitators and destroyers, these poisoners of the well-springs of German public opinion and in a wider sense of world opinion: it is not mine to consider which of them suffered too severely: I have only to see to it that Germany's lot should not be intolerable. A foreign journalist, who enjoys the privileges of a guest in our midst, protests in the name of the wives and children of those who have been shot and awaits the day when from their ranks there will come vengeance. To this gentleman I can say only one thing in answer: women and children have ever been the innocent victims of the criminal acts of men. I, too, have pity for them, but I believe that the suffering inflicted on them through the guilt of these men is but a minute fraction in comparison with the suffering that perhaps ten thousand German women would have had to endure if this act had been successful. A foreign diplomat explains that the meeting of Schleicher and Roehm was of course of an entirely harmless character. That matter I need not discuss with anyone. In the political sphere conceptions of what is harmless and what is not will never coincide. But when three traitors in Germany arrange and effect a meeting with a foreign statesman which they themselves characterize as "serviceable," when they effect this meeting after excluding every member of their staff, when they give strict orders that no word of this meeting shall reach me, then I shall have such men shot dead even when it should prove true that at a consultation which was thus kept secret from me they talked of nothing save the weather, old coins, and like topics.

The penalty for these crimes was hard and severe. Nineteen higher SA-Führer, thirty-one Führer and members of the SA, were shot, and further, for complicity in the plot, three Führer of the SS, while thirteen SA-Führer and civilians who attempted to resist arrest lost their lives. Three more committed suicide. Five who did not belong to the SA, but were members of the Party, were shot for taking part in the plot. Finally there were also shot three members of the SS who had been guilty of scandalous ill-treatment of those who had been taken into protective custody.

In order to prevent political passion and exasperation venting itself in lynch justice on further offenders when the danger was removed and the revolt could be regarded as suppressed, as early as Sunday 1 July strictest orders were given that all further retribution should cease. Thereby from the night of Sunday 1 July the normal state of affairs was re-established. A number of acts of violence which do not stand in any connection with the plot will be brought before the ordinary courts for judgement.

These sacrifices may indeed be heavy, but they will not be vain if from them once and for all results the conviction that every attempt at treason will be broken down without respect of person. If at some hour or another fate should summon me from my place, then I confidently hope that my successor will not act otherwise, and if he too must give place to another, that the third after us will be ready to protect the security of people and of nation with no less resolution.

If in the two weeks that now lie behind us a part of the foreign press in place of any objective and just report of events has flooded the world with untrue and incorrect assertions and communications, I cannot admit the validity of the excuse that it was impossible to obtain any other information. In most cases it needed only a short telephone call to the authorities concerned in order to show that most of these assertions could not be sustained. When in particular the report was spread that among the victims of the conspiracy there were included even members of the Cabinet of the Reich, it would not have been difficult to establish that the contrary was the case. The assertion that the Vice-Chancellor, von Papen, that the minister Seldte, or other members of the Cabinet of the Reich had been connected with the mutineers is most strongly contradicted by the fact that one of the first intentions of the mutineers was the murder of these men. Similarly all reports of any complicity in the plot on the part of any one of the German princes or of any pursuit of them is free invention. If finally during the last few days an English paper can report that I was at present suffering from a nervous breakdown, it would have needed only a small inquiry to establish the truth. I can only assure these anxious reporters that neither in the War nor after the War have I ever suffered such a breakdown, but this time I have indeed suffered the severest breakdown of the trust and faith which I had placed in a man for whose protection I had done everything in my power, for whom I had actually sacrificed myself.

But at this point I must at the same time confess that my confidence in the Movement and especially in the SS has never wavered. And now, too, my confidence in my SA has been restored to me. Three times they had the misfortune to have leaders—the last time even a Stabschef—whom they believed it was their duty to obey and who have deceived them, to whom I gave my confidence and who betrayed me. But three times over I have had the opportunity of seeing that at the moment when any act was discovered to be treasonable the traitor stood alone, deserted by all. Just as disloyal as was the conduct of this small group of leaders, so great in the decisive hour was the loyalty to me of these two National Socialist organizations. If the SS in these days, although with profound feelings of regret, performed their highest duty, the conduct of the millions of honest SA men and SA-Führer was not less decent: they who stood outside this community of traitors never wavered for a second in their conception of their duty. When I consider this fact I am convinced that at last the present Stabschef [Viktor Lutze]—to whom I am bound by old-time comradeship in our fight—will succeed in rejuvenating the organizations of the SA in accordance with the principles which I have laid down, and will make them a yet stronger member' of the body of our Movement. For never will I consent to the destruction of something which not only remains forever inseparably bound up with the fights and the victory of the National Socialist Movement, but which also has to its credit immeasurable services rendered during the fashioning of the new Reich these days which have been days of severe trial both for me and for its members the SA, has preserved the spirit of loyalty. Thus for the third time the SA, has proved that it is mine, just as I will prove at any time that I belong to my SA men. In a few weeks' time the brown shirt will once more dominate the streets of Germany and will give to one and all clear evidence that because it has overcome its grievous distress the life of National Socialist Germany is only the more vigorous.

When in March of last year our young Revolution stormed through Germany, my highest endeavor was to shed as little blood as possible. To millions of my former opponents, on behalf of the new State and in the name of the National Socialist Party, I offered a general amnesty; millions of them have since joined us and are loyally co-operating in the rebuilding of the Reich.

I hoped that it might not be necessary any longer to be forced to defend this State yet again with arms in our hands. But since fate has now none the less put us to this test, all of us wish to pledge ourselves with only the greater fanaticism to hold fast to that which was formerly won at the price of the blood of so many of our best men and which today had to be maintained once more through the blood of German fellow-countrymen. Just as one and a half years ago I offered reconciliation to our former opponents, so would I from henceforth also promise forgetfulness to all those who shared in the guilt of this act of madness. Let them bethink themselves, and remembering this melancholy calamity in our new German history let them devote themselves to the task of reparation. May they now recognize with surer insight than before the great task which fate sets us which civil war and chaos cannot perform. May we all feel responsible for the most precious treasure that there can be for the German people: internal order, internal and external peace, just as I am ready to undertake responsibility at the bar of history for the twenty-four hours in which the bitterest decisions of my life were made, in which fate once again taught me in the midst of anxious care with every thought to hold fast to the dearest thing which has been given us in this world—the German people and the German Reich! (Translation in Norman H. Baynes, ed., *Hitler's Speeches, Volume 1*, pp. 290-328)

00.08.1934	After the death of *Reichspräsident* von Hindenburg, Hitler united the office of *Staatsoberhaupt* (*Reichspräsident*) with that of *Reichskanzler*, and from that point bore the title *Führer und Reichskanzler*.
02.08.1934–30.04.1945	*Oberster Befehlshaber der Reichswehr* (Supreme Commander of the German Armed Forces; redesignated *Wehrmacht* on 21.05.1935).
01.09.1934	Appointed as *Schirmherr* (Patron) of the *Deutschen Roten Kreuzes* (German Red Cross).
00.00.1934–00.00.1934	*Ehrenpräsident der VII. Internationale Straßenkongresse* (Honorary President of the 7th International Roadways Congress) in München (03.09.1934–09.09.1934).
13.11.1934	Appointed as *Schirmherr* of the *"Olympischen Spiele 1936"* (1936 Olympic Games).
08.04.1935	*Schirmherr* of the *Deutschen Gesellschaft zur Rettung Schiffbrüchiger* (German Society for the Rescue of Shipwreck Victims).
00.04.1935–30.04.1945	*Beauftragter der NSDAP für die Stadt München* (Representative of the NSDAP for the City of Munich).
16.07.1935	*Schirmherr* of the *"Internationaler Gemeindekongress 1936"* (International Municipal Congress) in Berlin and München.
24.09.1937	Appointed by Mussolini as *Caporale Onorario* (Honorary Corporal) of the *Milizia Volontaria per la Sicurezza Nazionale* (MVSN, Voluntary Militia for National Security).
12.03.1938–14.03.1938	Trip to Austria in connection with the German annexation of that country. Flew from Berlin to München, then proceeded by automobile to Mühldorf, Braunau am Inn, Lambach, Wels, and Linz. He spent the night in Linz, then continued on his tour the following day, 13.03.1938. He then visited Wien, staying the night in the Hotel Imperial. On 14.03.1938 he reviewed a parade of German and Austrian troops before flying from Wien back to Germany.
30.01.1939	In a speech before the *Reichstag*, declared:

One thing I should like to say on this day which may be memorable for others as well as for us Germans: In the course of my life I have very often been a prophet, and have usually been ridiculed for it. During the time of my struggle for power it was in the first instance the Jewish race which only received my prophecies with laughter when I said that I would one day take over the leadership of the State, and with it that of the whole nation, and that I would then among many other things settle the Jewish problem. Their laughter was uproarious, but I think that for some time now they have been laughing on the other side of their face. Today I will once more be a prophet: If the international Jewish financiers in and outside Europe should succeed in plunging the nations once more into a world war, then the result will not be the Bolshevization of the earth, and thus the victory of Jewry, but the annihilation of the Jewish race in Europe!

00.10.1939 Issued a decree assigning *Reichsleiter* Philipp Bouhler (head of the *Kanzlei des Führers*) and Dr. Karl Brandt to oversee a program of "Euthanasia" (code-named *"Aktion T4"*) for the mentally and physically disabled. Hitler predated the order to 01.09.1939, the date the war commenced.

Berlin, 1 Sept. 1939
Reichsleiter B o u h l e r und
Dr. med. B r a n d t
sind unter Verantwortung beauftragt, die Befugnisse namentlich zu bestimmender Ärzte so zu erweitern, dass nach menschlichen Ermessen unheilbar Kranken bei kritischster Beurteilung ihres Krankheitszustandes der Gnadentod gewahrt werden kann.
[signed]
Adolf Hitler

Translation: Reichsleiter Bouhler and Dr. med. Brandt are charged with the responsibility of enlarging the competence of certain physicians, designated by name, so that patients who, on the basis of human judgment, are considered incurable, can be granted mercy death after a discerning diagnosis.

08.11.1939 Narrowly escaped assassination while attending the celebration of the sixteenth anniversary of the München *"Putsch."* Shortly after his departure, at 9:20 p.m., a powerful explosion rocked the *Bürgerbräukellar*, killing eight Party members and wounding sixty-three. The would-be assassin was Georg Elser, a thirty-six-year-old carpenter who had hidden a bomb in a hollowed-out pillar behind the speaker's rostrum. While attempting to cross the border into Switzerland about thirty-five minutes before the explosion, Elser was arrested by the *Grenzschutzpolizei* in Konstanz/Baden. He eventually confessed and spent the remainder of the war at the Sachsenhausen and Dachau concentration camps. He was shot to death by SS men at Dachau on 09.04.1945, the order for his execution coming from Gestapo chief Heinrich Müller.

18.12.1941 Meeting with the *Reichsführer-SS* Himmler at *Führer HQ "Wolfsschanze"* in Rastenburg/Ostpreußen. Concerning the first topic of discussion, Himmler noted in his appointment book *"Judenfrage | als Partisanen auszurotten"* (Jewish Question | to be exterminated as partisans). The *Führer* spoke further in this vein in a private conversation on 30.08.1942:

It is here in Russia that Communism shows its true face. We must undertake a campaign of cleaning-up, square metre by square metre, and this will compel us to have recourse to summary justice. The struggle with the terrorists will be savage warfare in the real sense. In Estonia and Latvia these bands have all but ceased to be active; but until Jewry, which is the bandits' Intelligence Service, is exterminated, we shall not have accomplished our task. (*Hitler's Table Talk*, 1941–1944, p. 676)

In the following testimony before the U.S. Military Tribunal, Nürnberg, defendant Dr. Hans Heinrich Lammers (formerly head of the *Reichskanzlei*) stated:

At the beginning of 1942 I asked the Führer for an opportunity to report on the matter [of the "Final Solution"], and this was granted. I wanted to find out what this final solution [*Endlösung*] was all about and whether it was true that he had given corresponding orders, and what their contents were. However, the Führer refused to discuss these matters with me. He only said that he had given Himmler the order for the final solution, namely, for the evacuation of the Jews from Germany. He also said that Himmler was responsible to him alone, and that he would inform me if my participation should turn out to be necessary. (*Trials of War Criminals Before the Nuernberg Military Tribunals Under Control Council Law No. 10. Volume. XIII:* ["The Ministries Case"])

19.12.1941–30.04.1945	*Oberbefehlshaber des Heeres* (Commander-in-Chief of the German Army). He dismissed *Generalfeldmarschall* Walther von Brauchitsch and personally assumed this post.
26.04.1942–30.04.1945	*Oberster Gerichtsherr.*
10.09.1942–21.11.1942	*Oberbefehlshaber* of *Heeresgruppe A* on the Eastern Front.
20.07.1944	Survived an assassination attempt, carried out by *Oberst i. G.* Claus Schenk Graf von Stauffenberg using a bomb, at *Führer HQ* "*Wolfsschanze*" in Rastenburg/Ostpreußen.
29.04.1945	The last will and testament of Adolf Hitler, signed in his *Führerbunker* beneath the *Reichskanzlei* in Berlin:

My Private Will and Testament
As I did not consider that I could take responsibility, during the years of struggle, of contracting a marriage, I have now decided, before the closing of my earthly career, to take as my wife that girl who, after many years of faithful friendship, entered, of her own free will, the practically besieged town in order to share her destiny with me. At her own desire she goes as my wife with me into death. It will compensate us for what we both lost through my work in the service of my people.

What I possess belongs—in so far as it has any value—to the Party. Should this no longer exist, to the State, should the State also be destroyed, no further decision of mine is necessary.

My pictures, in the collections which I have bought in the course of years, have never been collected for private purposes, but only for the extension of a gallery in my hometown of Linz a.d. Donau.

It is my most sincere wish that this bequest may be duly executed. I nominate as my Executor my most faithful Party comrade, Martin Bormann.

He is given full legal authority to make all decisions. He is permitted to take out everything that has a sentimental value or is necessary for the maintenance of a modest simple life, for my brothers and sisters, also above all for the mother of my wife and my faithful coworkers who are well known to him, principally my old Secretaries Frau Winter etc. who have for many years aided me by their work.

I myself and my wife—in order to escape the disgrace of deposition or capitulation—choose death. It is our wish to be burnt immediately on the spot where I have carried out the greatest part of my daily work in the course of a twelve years' service to my people.

Given in Berlin, 29th. April 1945, 4:00 o'clock.
(Signed) A. Hitler.

As Witnesses:
(Signed) Martin Bormann.
(Signed) Dr. Fuhr.
    As Witness:
    (Signed) Nicolaus von Below.

My political Testament
More than thirty years have now passed since I in 1914 made my modest contribution as a volunteer in the first world-war that was forced upon the Reich.

In these three decades I have been actuated solely by love and loyalty to my people in all my thoughts, acts, and life. They gave me the strength to make the most difficult decisions which have ever confronted to mortal man. I have spent my time, my working strength, and my health in these three decades.

It is untrue that I or anyone else in Germany wanted the war in 1939. It was desired and instigated exclusively by those international statesmen who were either of Jewish descent or worked for Jewish interests. I have made too many offers for the control and limitation of armaments, which posterity will not for all time be able to disregard for the responsibility for the outbreak of this war to be laid on me. I have further never wished that after the first fatal world war a second against England, or even against America, should break out. Centuries will pass away, but out of the ruins of our towns and monuments the hatred against those finally responsible whom we have to thank for everything, International Jewry and its helpers, will grow.

Three days before the outbreak of the German-Polish war I again proposed to the British ambassador in Berlin a solution to the German-Polish problem-similar to that in the case of the Saar district, under international control. This offer also cannot be denied. It was only rejected because the leading circles in English politics wanted the war, partly on account of the business hoped for and partly under influence of propaganda organized by international Jewry.

I also made it quite plain that, if the nations of Europe are again to be regarded as mere shares to be bought and sold by these international conspirators in money and finance, then that race, Jewry, which is the real criminal of this murderous struggle, will be saddled with the responsibility. I further left no one in doubt that this time not only would millions of children of Europe's Aryan peoples die of hunger, not only would millions of grown men suffer death, and not only hundreds of thousands of women and children be burnt and bombed to death in the towns, without the real criminal having to atone for this guilt, even if by more humane means.

After six years of war, which in spite of all setbacks, will go down one day in history as the most glorious and valiant demonstration of a nation's life purpose, I cannot forsake the city which is the capital of this Reich. As the forces are too small to make any further stand against the enemy attack at this place and our resistance is gradually being weakened by men who are as deluded as they are lacking in initiative, I should like, by remaining in this town, to share my fate with those, the millions of others, who have also taken upon themselves to do so. Moreover I do not wish to fall into the hands of an enemy who requires a new spectacle organized by the Jews for the amusement of their hysterical masses.

I have decided therefore to remain in Berlin and there of my own free will to choose death at the moment when I believe the position of the Führer and Chancellor itself can no longer be held.

I die with a happy heart, aware of the immeasurable deeds and achievements of our soldiers at the front, our women at home, the achievements of our farmers and workers and the work, unique in history, of our youth who bear my name.

That from the bottom of my heart I express my thanks to you all, is just as self-evident as my wish that you should, because of that, on no account give up the struggle, but rather continue it against the enemies of the Fatherland, no matter where, true to the creed of a great Clausewitz. From the sacrifice of our soldiers and from my own unity with them unto death, will in any case spring up in the history of Germany, the seed of a radiant renaissance of the National-Socialist movement and thus of the realization of a true community of nations.

Many of the most courageous men and women have decided to unite their lives with mine until the very last. I have begged and finally ordered them not to do this, but to take part in the further battle of the Nation. I beg the heads of the Army, the Navy and the Air Force to strengthen by all possible means the spirit of resistance of our soldiers in the National-Socialist sense, with special reference to the fact that also I myself, as founder and creator of this movement, have preferred death to cowardly abdication or even capitulation.

May it, at some future time, become part of the code of honor of the German officer—as is already the case in our Navy—that the surrender of a district or of a town is impossible, and that above all the leaders here must march ahead as shining examples, faithfully fulfilling their duty unto death.

Second Part of the Political Testament

Before my death I expel the former Reichsmarschall Hermann Göring from the party and deprive him of all rights which he may enjoy by virtue of the decree of 29 June 1941, and also by virtue of my statement in the Reichstag on 1 September 1939, I appoint in his place Großadmiral Doenitz, President of the Reich and supreme Commander of the Armed Forces.

Before my death I expel the former Reichsführer-SS and Minister of the Interior, Heinrich Himmler, from the party and from all offices of State. In his stead I appoint Gauleiter Karl Hanke as Reichsführer-SS and Chief of the German Police, and Gauleiter Paul Giesler as Reich Minister of the Interior.

Göring and Himmler, quite apart from their disloyalty to my person, have done immeasurable harm to the country and the whole nation by secret negotiations with the enemy, which they conducted without my knowledge and against my wishes, and by illegally attempting to seize power in the State for themselves.

In order to give the German people a government composed of honorable men—a government which will fulfill its pledge to continue the war by every means—I appoint the following members of the new Cabinet as leaders of the nation:

President of the Reich: Dönitz.
Chancellor of the Reich: Dr. Goebbels.
Party Minister: Bormann.
Foreign Minister: Seyss-Inquart.
Minister of the Interior: Gauleiter Giesler.
Minister for War: Dönitz.
C-in-C of the Army: Schörner.
C-in-C of the Navy: Dönitz.
C-in-C of the Air Force: Greim.
Reichsführer-SS and Chief of the German Police: Gauleiter Hanke.
Economics: Funk.
Agriculture: Backe.
Justice: Thierack.
Culture: Dr. Scheel.
Propaganda: Dr. Naumann.
Finance: Schwerin-Krosigk.
Labor: Dr. Hupfauer.
Munitions: Saur.
Leader of the German Labor Front and Member of the Reich Cabinet: Reichsminister Dr. Ley.

Although a number of these men, such as Martin Bormann, Dr. Goebbels etc., together with their wives, have joined me of their own free will and did not wish to leave the capital of the Reich under any circumstances, but were willing to perish with me here, I must nevertheless ask them to obey my request, and in this case set the interests of the nation above their own feelings. By their work and loyalty as comrades they will be just as close to me after death, as I hope that my spirit will linger among them and always go with them. Let them be hard, but never unjust, above all let them never allow fear to influence their actions, and set the honor of the nation above everything in the world. Finally, let them be conscious of the fact that our task, that of continuing the building of a National Socialist State, represents the work of the coming centuries, which places every single person under an obligation always to serve the common interest and to subordinate his own advantage to this end. I demand of all Germans, all National Socialists, men, women and all the men of the Wehrmacht, that they be faithful and obedient unto death to the new government and its President.

Above all I charge the leaders of the nation and those under them to scrupulous observance of the laws of race and to merciless opposition to the universal poisoner of all peoples, international Jewry.

Given in Berlin, this 29th day of April 1945.   4:00 a.m.
Adolf Hitler.
Witnessed by
Dr. Josef Fuhr.   Wilhelm Burgdorf.
Martin Bormann.   Hans Krebs.
(Translation of Document 3569-PS, in *Nazi Conspiracy and Aggression, Vol. VI*)

PUBLISHED WORKS:
Mein Kampf (1. Band 1924, 2. Band 1927)
Zweites Buch (1928)
Auseinandersetzung mit Brüning. Vortrag vor westdeutschen Wirtschaftlern im Industrieclub zu Düsseldorf (1932)
Reden (1933; edited by Ernst Boepple)
Die Reden des Führers nach der Machtübernahme (1939)
Der großdeutsche Freiheitskampf. Reden Adolf Hitlers vom 16. März 1941 bis 15. März 1942 (3 volumes, 1943)

DECORATIONS & AWARDS:

04.08.1918	*1914 Eisernes Kreuz I. Klasse.* Reportedly awarded on the recommendation of *Leutnant* Hugo Gutmann (*Adjutant* of *Reserve-Infanterie-Regiment 16*), who was Jewish.
02.12.1914	*1914 Eisernes Kreuz II. Klasse*
17.09.1917	*Kgl. Bayerisches Militärverdienstkreuz III. Klasse mit Schwertern*
09.05.1918	*Regimentsdiplom für hervorragende Tapferkeit bei Fontaine* (Regimental Diploma for Extraordinary Bravery near Fontaine)
18.05.1918	*Verwundetenabzeichen, 1918 in Schwarz*
25.08.1918	*Dienstauszeichnung III. Klasse*
04.09.1934	*Ehrenkreuz des Weltkrieges 1914–1918 mit Schwertern*
00.00.1933	*Goldenes Ehrenzeichen der NSDAP*
00.00.1934	*Ehrenzeichen des 9. November 1923 (Blutorden)* (*mit Wirkung vom 09.11.1933*)
00.00.1929	*Nürnberger-Parteitagsabzeichen 1929*
21.06.1935	*Bach-Plakette der Neuen Bach-Gesellschaft*
13.09.1934	*"Deutscher Ring" des Deutschen Auslands-Instituts* (highest award of the DAI)
14.11.1933	*Ehrenbürgerbrief der Stadt Berlin*
21.06.1933	*Ehrenbürgerbrief der Stadt Bischofsheim.*
30.09.1934	*Ehrenbürgerurkunde der Stadt Hameln*
11.04.1935	*Ehrenbürgerbrief der Stadt Braunschweig*
[12?].03.1938	*Ehrenbürgerrecht der Stadt Braunau am Inn/Oberösterreich*
21.03.1938	*Ehrenbürgerrecht der Gemeinde Maria Schmolln in Oberösterreich*
24.03.1938	*Ehrenbürgerrecht der Gemeinde Marktes Haslach an der Mühl/ Bezirk Rohrbach* (status finally revoked, 00.04.2004)
04.04.1938	*Ehrenbürgerrecht der Stadt Klagenfurt/Kärnten*

Adolf Hitler

10.08.1938	*Ehrenbürgerrecht der Gemeinde Sauerbrunn*
20.04.1939	*Ehrenbürgerrecht der Stadt Danzig*
10.05.1939	*Ehrenbürgerrecht der Stadt Graz*
00.10.1934	*Ehrenbürgerrecht der Stadt Neunkirchen/Saar*
07.11.1934	*Ehrenbürgerrecht der Stadt Goslar*
12.11.1934	*Ehrenbürgerrecht der Stadt Mohrungen*
21.04.1933	Awarded the title of *Ehrenbürger* by all 111 Cities in Thüringen.
25.04.1933	*Ehrenbürgerrecht der Stadt Wittenberg*
26.04.1933	*Ehrenbürgerrecht der Landeshauptstadt München*
27.04.1933	*Ehrenbürgerrecht der Stadt Speyer* (status revoked, 21.06.1946)
01.05.1933	*Ehrenbürgerrecht der Stadt Büttelborn/Hessen*
04.05.1933	*Ehrenbürgerrecht der Stadt Braunschweig.* Presented with the *Ehrenbürgerbrief* on 11.04.1935 by *Reichsstatthalter* Wilhelm Friedrich Loeper, *Ministerpräsident* Dietrich Klagges, *Staatsminister* Friedrich Alpers, and *Oberbürgermeister* Dr. Wilhelm Hesse
09.05.1933	*Ehrenbürgerrecht der Stadt Karlsruhe/Baden*
11.05.1933	*Ehrenbürgerrecht der Stadt Vohenstrauss*
11.05.1933	*Ehrenbürgerrecht der Gemeinde Unterschützen/Burgenland*
23.05.1933	*Ehrenbürgerrecht der Stadt Heidelberg*
02.06.1933	*Ehrenbürgerrecht der Gemeinde Unken (Österreich)*
00.00.1933	*Ehrenbürgerrecht der Stadt Pirna*
00.08.1933	*Ehrenbürgerrecht der Stadt Kiel*
15.01.1934	*Ehrenbürgerrecht der Stadt Stadtlohn*
24.03.1934	*Ehrenbürgerrecht der Stadt Deggendorf*
01.05.1934	*Ehrenbürgerrecht der Stadt Saarbrücken*
21.06.1932	*Ehrenbürgerrecht der Stadt Ohrdruf*
12.07.1932	*Ehrenbürgerrecht der Gemeinde Sternberg in Greifswald*
30.01.1933	*Ehrenbürgerrecht der Stadt Schweidnitz*
26.02.1933	*Ehrenbürgerrecht der Gemeinde Gotteszell/Oberpfalz-Niederbayern*
00.03.1933	*Ehrenbürgerrecht der Gemeinde Fürstenzell*
14.03.1933	*Ehrenbürgerrecht der Stadt Passau*
14.03.1933	*Ehrenbürgerrecht der Stadt Hertheim*
24.03.1933	*Ehrenbürgerrecht der Stadt Deggendorf*
24.03.1933	*Ehrenbürgerrecht der Stadt Füssen*
24.03.1933	*Ehrenbürgerrecht der Stadt Nossen/Sachsen*
28.03.1933	*Ehrenbürgerrecht der Stadt Weimar*
01.04.1933	*Ehrenbürgerrecht der Reichshauptstadt Berlin* (presented with the *Ehrenbürgerbrief*, 14.11.1933)
06.04.1933	*Ehrenbürgerrecht der Stadt Hagen/Westfalen*
06.04.1933	*Ehrenbürgerrecht der Stadt Hohenlimburg*
08.04.1933	*Ehrenbürgerrecht der Stadt Potsdam*
12.04.1933	*Ehrenbürgerrecht der Stadt Bochum*
13.04.1933	*Ehrenbürgerrecht der Stadt Hameln* (presented with an *Ehrenbürgerurkunde*, 30.09.1934)
18.04.1933	*Ehrenbürgerrecht der Stadt Trier*
19.04.1933	*Ehrenbürgerrecht der Stadt Göttingen* (status revoked by the *Hauptausschuss der Stadt Göttingen*, 25.08.1952)
20.04.1933	*Ehrenbürgerrecht der Stadt Dortmund*
20.04.1933	*Ehrenbürgerrecht der Freistaat Bayern*

Although he did not wear them, Hitler was eligible for the following awards:

> Medaille zur Erinnerung an die Heimkehr des Memellandes
> Spange "Prager Burg" zur Medaille zur Erinnerung an den 1. Oktober 1938
> Medaille zur Erinnerung an den 1. Oktober 1938
> Medaille zur Erinnerung an den 13. März 1938
> Dienstauszeichnung der NSDAP in Gold
> Dienstauszeichnung der NSDAP in Silber
> Dienstauszeichnung der NSDAP in Bronze
> Deutsches Olympia-Ehrenzeichen I. Klasse
> Deutsche Schutzwall-Ehrenzeichen

NOTES:
* Parents:
  - Father: *k.u.k. Zolloberamtsoffizial* Alois Hitler (*07.06.1837 in Strones, Haus Nr. 13, †03.01.1903 at the Wirtshaus Wiesinger in Leonding bei Linz). Born out of wedlock to Maria Anna Schicklgruber (*15.04.1795 in Strones, †07.01.1847 in Klein Motten bei Strones), who was married in 1842 to Johann Georg Hiedler (*28.09.1792, †00.00.1857), son of Martin Hiedler (*17.11.1762, †10.01.1829) and Anna Maria Grosch (*23.08.1760, †07.12.1854). Alois was raised by his uncle, Johann Nepomuk Hüttler (*00.00.1807, †00.00.1888), in Ort Spital Haus Nr. 36. Alois' first marriage (1873–1880), was to Anna, *née* Glassl-Hoerer (*00.00.1823 in Spital, †06.04.1883); no children were born to this marriage. From in 05/06.1883 he married Franziska (Alois Fanny) Matzelsberger (*00.00.1861, †10.08.1884). Born to this marriage were Hitler's half-siblings, Alois Jr. Matzelsberger (*13.01.1882 in Wien, †20.05.1956), known after 1883 as Alois Hitler, and Angelika (Angela) Hitler (*28.07.1883, †30.10.1949). Alois' third and final marriage was to Hitler's mother, Klara Pölzl.
  - Mother: Klara Hitler, *née* Pölzl (* 12.08.1860 in Spital, Died: 21.12.1907 in Linz of breast cancer). From the marriage of Alois Hitler and Klara were born the following:
    - Gustav (*17.05.1885 in Braunau am Inn, †08.12.1887 of diphtheria).
    - Ida (*23.09.1886 in Braunau am Inn, †02.01.1888 of diphtheria).
    - Otto (*Autumn 1887 in Braunau am Inn, died a few days later).
    - Adolf (*20.04.1889 in Braunau am Inn, †30.04.1945 in Berlin).
    - Edmund (*24.03.1894 in Passau, †02.02.1900).
    - Paul (*21. or 26.01.1896 in Linz, †01.06.1960 in Berchtesgaden)
* On 29.04.1945, Hitler married his long-time mistress, Eva Anna Paula Braun (*06.02.1912 in München; daughter of a teacher) in the *Führerbunker* beneath the *Reichskanzlei*. Witnesses to the marriage were Joseph Goebbels and Martin Bormann.

SOURCES:
Bayerisches Hauptstaatsarchiv, München, Abteilung IV Kriegsarchiv: Excerpts from various *Kriegsranglisten* containing data on the Royal Bavarian Army service of Adolf Hitler.
Baynes, Norman H. (ed.): *The Speeches of Adolf Hitler, April 1922–August 1939, Volume 1.* Oxford University Press, 1942.
Hauner, Milan: *Hitler: A Chronology of his Life and Time.* Palgrave MacMillan, 1983.
Domarus, Dr. Max: Hitler. *Speeches and Proclamations, 1932–1945. The Chronicle of a Dictatorship.* Bolchazy-Carducci Publishers, 1990.
Lilla, Joachim; Döring, Martin; & Schulz, Andreas: *Statisten in Uniform. Die Mitglieder des Reichstags 1933–1945.* Droste Verlag, 2004.

Fournes, April 1915.

Right: With fellow dispatch runners Ernst Schmidt and Anton Bachmann, as well as Hitler's dog, "Fuchsl." (NARA)

Hitler in June 1923, photographed by Heinrich Hoffmann. (NARA, Heinrich Hoffmann Collection)

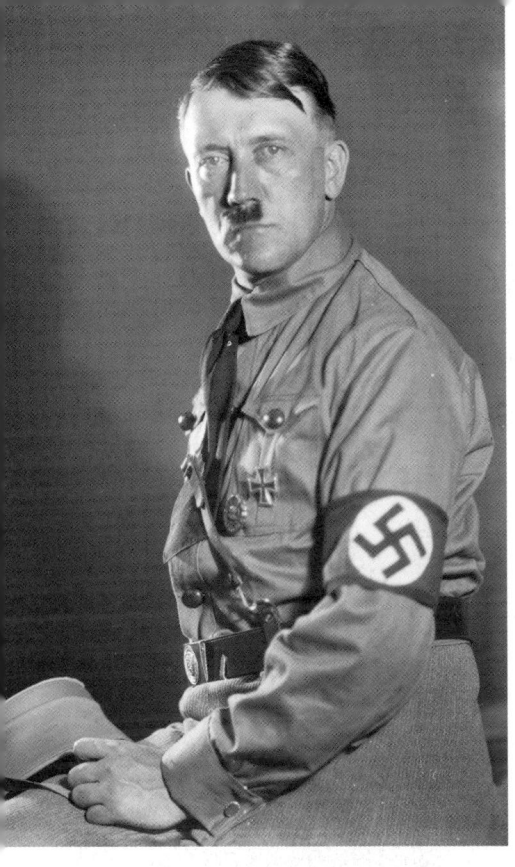

Hitler photographed by Heinrich Hoffmann in January 1928. (NARA, Heinrich Hoffmann Collection)

Above left: Hitler on 19.03.1932. (NARA, Heinrich Hoffmann Collection)

Above right: München, 03.07.1932: *Oberster SA-Führer* Adolf Hitler and *SA-Stabschef* Ernst Röhm during the *Gauparteitag der NSDAP von Oberbayern*. (NARA, Heinrich Hoffmann Collection)

Left: Hitler delivers a speech in 1932. (NARA, Heinrich Hoffmann Collection)

Above: Hitler delivers a radio speech soon after his appointment as *Reichskanzler*, 1933. (NARA, Heinrich Hoffmann Collection)

Right: The *"5. Reichsparteitag der NSDAP"* in Nürnberg (30.08.1933-03.09.1933): The *Oberster SA-Führer* consecrates the banners of *SA-Standarten* (regiments) by touching the *"Blutfahne"*—the blood-spattered flag carried during the march to the *Feldherrnhalle* on 09.11.1923—to them. The official bearer of the *"Blutfahne,"* Jakob Grimminger, stands at far left. (NARA, Heinrich Hoffmann Collection)

Venice, 14.-15.06.1934: Hitler's first official visit with Mussolini. (All NARA, Heinrich Hoffmann Collection)

Above left: Mussolini greets the German leader, accompanied by Reich Foreign Minister Constantin Freiherr von Neurath and Ambassador Ulrich von Hassel.

Above: From NARA, Heinrich Hoffmann Collection.

Right: Hitler in a motorboat with von Hassel and von Neurath. (NARA, Heinrich Hoffmann Collection)

29.06.1934: Hitler and *Reichsleiter* Dr. Robert Ley (behind him at left) tour the *Führerschule der RAD Buddenburg* in Lippolthausen, a district of Lünen in Kreis Unna/Westfalen. The next day, he personally arrested *SA-Stabschef* Röhm and ordered a bloody purge of the SA. (NARA, Heinrich Hoffmann Collection)

The *Reichstag*, 13.07.1934: The *Führer* delivers his speech of justification for the violence of 30.06.–07.02.1934. (NARA, Heinrich Hoffmann Collection)

Above left: A formal portrait of Adolf Hitler, *c.* 1935.

Above right: Hitler delivers a speech during the *"7. Reichsparteitag der NSDAP"* in Nürnberg (10.09.–16.09.1935). (NARA, Heinrich Hoffmann Collection)

Right: Hitler and Göring meet an octogenarian *SA-Führer* during the *"7. Reichsparteitag der NSDAP"* in Nürnberg. (NARA, Heinrich Hoffmann Collection)

August 1936: Hitler at the *Olympiastadion*, Berlin, during the Summer Olympic Games. First row, right to left: Julius Schaub, Dr. Wilhelm Frick, Hitler, and *Generalfeldmarschall* August von Mackensen. Second row, right to left: Viktor Lutze, Dr. Hans Pfundtner, and Richard Walther Darré. Third row, far right: Dr. Hans Frank. (NARA, Heinrich Hoffmann Collection)

20.04.1942: Hitler, with *Reichsminister* Albert Speer and *Generalfeldmarschall* Wilhelm Keitel, receives congratulations on his fifty-third birthday. (Michal Sika)

The Viennese press congratulates the *Führer* on his upcoming fifty-first birthday. (Österreichische Nationalbibliothek)

Führer HQ Reichskanzlei, Berlin, 20.03.1945. Hitler receives *Hitler-Jugend* combat troops decorated with the Iron Cross Second Class. (All NARA, Heinrich Hoffmann Collection)

Above: Left to right: *SS-Obersturmbannführer/HJ-Hauptbannführer* Heinz Lorenz (Press Secretary to the *Führer*), *Reichsjugendführer* Artur Axmann, *SS-Gruppenführer und Generalleutnant der Waffen-SS* Hermann Fegelein, *SS-Obergruppenführer* Julius Schaub, Hitler, *General der Infanterie* Wilhelm Burgdorf, and *SS-Sturmbannführer* Heinz Linge.

Below: With Axmann by his side, the ageing *Führer* congratulates his youngest soldiers.

Above: Second from right: Alfred Zech (aka Czech), age twelve. Third from right: *Oberkameradschaftsführer* Wilhelm (Willi) Hübner, age sixteen, from *HJ-Bann 803* in Lauban, *Gau Niederschlesien*.

At *Führer HQ Reichskanzlei*, Berlin, 20.03.1945. (NARA, Heinrich Hoffmann Collection)

Emil Jules Wilhelm ("Moritzl") Maurice
Organisator und Führer der "Turn- und Sportabteilung" der NSDAP/Organisator der SA
(12.11.1920-00.11.1921)

*	19.01.1897 in Westermoor/Kreis Eckernförde/Harburg/Schleswig-Holstein.
†	06.02.1972 in Starnberg bei München/Regierungsbezirk Oberbayern/Bayern. Gravesite: *Nordfriedhof* in München.
NSDAP-Nr.:	39 (Joined the DAP with Nr. 594, 01.12.1919; Party banned, 09.11.1923-16.02.1925; Officially re-enrolled in the NSDAP with Nr. 39 on 07.01.1926)
SS-Nr.:	2 (Joined 21.09.1925)

PROMOTIONS:

01.12.1917	*Kanonier*
12.11.1920–00.08.1921	*Organisator und Führer der "Turn- und Sportabteilung" der NSDAP* (forerunner of the SA)
00.08.1921–00.11.1921	*Organisator der SA*
21.09.1925	*SS-Anwärter*
00.00.1926	*SS-Mann*
04.05.1933	*SS-Sturmbannführer*
09.11.1933	*SS-Obersturmbannführer*
01.06.1934	*SS-Standartenführer (mit Wirkung vom 01.07.1934)*
00.00.193_	*Unteroffizier d. R. (Luftwaffe)*
00.00.193_	*Leutnant d. R.*
30.01.1939	*SS-Oberführer*
01.01.1940 (?)	*Oberleutnant d. R.*

CAREER:

00.00.1904–00.00.1907	*Volksschule* in Owschlag (Kreis Rendsburg-Eckernförde).
00.00.1907–00.00.1914	*Realschule* in Eckernförde.
14.01.1914–01.10.1917	Served an apprenticeship with the master watchmaker Adolf Christen in Gettorf/Kreis Eckernförde.
00.04.1916	Attempted to join the *Landsturm* (militia) in Eckernförde but deemed unfit due to his generally debilitated physical condition. He remained thus categorized for one year, again attempting to enter service in March 1917; he was again classified unfit for service for a further six months.
00.09.1917	Passed his *Gehilfenprüfung* (assistant's examination) as a watchmaker's assistant.
02.10.1917–30.11.1917	Resettled in München, where he worked as a watchmaker's assistant in a shop on *Sendlinger Straße*.
01.12.1917–25.01.1919	Finally succeeded in entering military service as a *Kanonier* with 4. Ersatz-Batterie/1. Feldartillerie-Regiment "Prinzregent Luitpold."
03.01.1918–23.02.1918	Hospitalized in the *Reserve-Lazarett München* due to influenza.
01.02.1919–01.10.1919	Resumed work as an assistant watchmaker on *Sendlinger Straße*, München.
01.05.1919–01.09.1919	Member of *Freikorps Oberland* in München.

00.00.1919–00.00.1920	Service as a *Freiwilliger* (volunteer) with *Infanterie-Regiment 5* of the *Bayerische Einwohnerwehr* (Bavarian Citizens' Defense).
13.11.1919	Attended a meeting of the *Deutsche Arbeiterpartei* (DAP, German Workers' Party) in the *Münchener Hofbräuhaus*, with Hitler as the featured speaker.
01.12.1919	Joined the DAP.
00.00.1920	Appointed as an *Ordnungsmann der NSDAP* (Nr. 8). He became one of Hitler's few *"Duz-Freunden"* during this period.
12.11.1920–00.11.1921	*Organisator und Führer der "Turn- und Sportabteilung" der NSDAP* (Organizer and Leader of the Gymnastics and Sports Section of the Nazi Party). When these units were redesignated *Sturmabteilung* (Storm Troops) in the autumn of 1921, Maurice was granted the new title *Organisator der SA*. He was succeeded by Hans Ulrich Klintzsch, who was given the new title *Führer der SA*. Konrad Heiden writes of Maurice's contributions as "the spiritual father of the movement's tactics":

He was the first to resort to direct action, in the sense that he roved through the streets at night seeking opponents—especially Jews—that he might beat them up. (Heiden, *Der Fuehrer: Hitler's Rise to Power*, p. 413)

00.00.1921–00.00.1921	Attached, as a member of the *Bund Oberland*, to the *Grenzschutz* (border defense formations) in Oberschlesien.
00.07.1921–00.08.1923	Personal chauffeur to Adolf Hitler.
00.08.1921	Entered NSDAP service as a clerical employee, receiving a monthly salary of 250 RM.
00.08.1921	Joined the SA.
29.10.1921	Arrested for involvement in a 25.10.1921 assassination attempt on the Social Democratic delegate Erhard Auer. Released after just nine days due to lack of evidence.
04.11.1921	Seriously injured in a *"Saalschlacht"* (meeting hall brawl) at the *Münchener Hofbräuhaus*.
00.05.1922	Arrested for burning the national flag of the Reich and for acts of battery against political opponents on the *Münchener Bahnhofsplatz*.
00.06.1922	Rearrested for involvement in a brawl.
14.10.1922–15.10.1922	Member of the SA contingent participating in the "*3. Deutscher Tag*" in Coburg.
00.10.1922–17.01.1923	Arrested and interned in the *Landesgefängnis* (state prison) of Mannheim/Baden for his role in a bomb attack on the *Mannheimer Börse* (Mannheim stock exchange).
00.03.1923–09.11.1923	Member of the *Stabswache Hitler*, an SA company tasked with maintaining Hitler's personal security. The forerunner of the later SS, it was redesignated as the *Stoßtrupp Adolf Hitler* in May 1923.
00.05.1923–09.11.1923	*Adjutant* of the *Stoßtrupp Adolf Hitler* under Joseph Berchtold.
00.08.1923	Resumed work as a watchmaker in München.
08./09.11.1923	Participated in the "*München-Putsch*" as Berchtold's *Adjutant* in the *Stoßtrupp Adolf Hitler*.
29.04.1924	Sentenced by the *Volksgericht München I* to eighteen months' fortress arrest for being an accessory to high treason and three

	months' imprisonment for illegal possession of weapons. He then fled to Pommern where he remained under a false name until turning himself in to the police.
00.00.1924–27.01.1925	Imprisoned with Hitler and other Nazis at the *Staatliche Gefangenenanstalt* in Landsberg am Lech, approximately 65 km west of München.
27.01.1925	Released from Landsberg.
00.02.1925–00.01.1928	Permanent *Begleiter* (escort) to and chauffeur of Adolf Hitler. Succeeded by Julius Schreck.
00.00.1925–00.00.1925	Member of the *Stabswache Hitler*.
21.09.1925	Joined the SS.
21.09.1925–00.01.1928	*1. Inspekteur der SS* (1st Inspector of the SS).
07.01.1926	Officially reentered the NSDAP.
00.12.1927	Break in the friendship between Maurice and Hitler. He had by this time become a member of the innermost circle of the NSDAP and had earned the special affection of his *Führer* (who referred to him as "Moritzl"). In the 1920s, Maurice boasted of being Hitler's best friend. Not even the rumor—constantly flaring up—that Maurice had Jewish ancestors could spoil the friendship. But in the autumn of 1927, Maurice made the mistake of falling in love with Hitler's niece, Angela ("Geli") Raubal (*04.01.1908 in Linz), who had just moved in with her *"Onkel Adolf"* in München; the two had first met in 1926 at an NSDAP function in Weimar. They secretly became engaged, and when Hitler learned of the affair, he flew into a rage that caused Maurice to fear he would be shot. Hitler ultimately prevailed upon Geli to break the engagement and ordered her to separate from Maurice for two years. The matter surely played a role in Hitler's decision to remove Maurice, in January 1928, from all his offices and banish him from the inner circle of the Party. The *Führer* did not fire him outright, but gradually excluded and lapsed in paying him. Maurice ultimately resigned. In April 1928, Maurice brought a lawsuit against Hitler before the *Arbeitsgericht* (labor court) in München, suing his former friend and leader for back pay of 3,000 RM; the *Führer* was ordered to pay the sum of 500 RM. After this trial, Rudolf Hess formally removed Maurice from the SS. Only in April 1933, during a meeting in Hitler's private apartment in München, did the two finally reconcile.
00.00.1928–00.00.1945	Self-employed as a watchmaker and salesman of electrical equipment in München.
00.04.1933–01.10.1935	*Stadtrat* in München.
04.05.1933–01.07.1934	Readmitted to the SS with the status of a *Rangführer z.b.V.* (rank leader for special duties) in *SS-Sturmbann I/1* (München).
01.07.1934–01.10.1934	Assigned as a *SS-Rangführer z.b.V.* to *1. SS-Standarte* (München).
30.06.1934	Participated in the "suppression" of the so-called "*Röhm Revolte*" in München. As a member of a *Sonderkommando* of the *Bayerischen Politischen Polizei* (BPP, Bavarian Political Police), he took part in the arrest of the SA leaders Hans-Peter von Heydebreck and Karl Graf von Spreti. As a reward for this, Hitler promoted him to *SS-Standartenführer*.

01.10.1934–01.04.1936	Assigned as an *SS-Führer z.b.V.* to *1. SS-Standarte* (München).
Spring 1935	In accordance with SS marriage laws, in order to marry on 11.05.1935, Maurice was required to submit proof of his bride's and his own "pure German-blood descent" to the *SS-Rasse- und Siedlungshauptamt*. In the course of the subsequent genealogical investigation, the groom-to-be was found to be of partly Jewish blood. His great-grandfather was the Jewish founder of Hamburg's Thalia Theater, Charles Maurice Schwarzenberger (1805–1896), and this fact prompted the *Reichsführer-SS* to demand that Hitler order his removal from the SS. Hitler refused to do so, as "Moritzl" was one of his earliest assistants and a founding member of the SS. The *Führer* authorized a *Gnadeerlaß* (amnesty) declaring Maurice and his brothers as *Ehrenarier* (honorary Aryans). Hitler's remarkable decision was promulgated via the following official file notice, dated 31.08.1935, by Heinrich Himmler:

1. SS-Standartenführer Emil Maurice is, without doubt, according to his family tree, not of Aryan descent.
2. On the occasion of SS-Standartenführer Maurice's marriage when he had to submit the family tree, I reported to the Führer my position to the effect that Maurice must be removed from the ranks of the SS.
3. The Führer has decided that in this one and only exceptional case Maurice as well as his brothers could remain in the SS, because Maurice had been his very first companion, and because his brothers and the entire family Maurice had served the Movement with rare bravery and loyalty in the first and most difficult months and years.
4. I decree that Maurice must not be entered in the SS-Sippenbuch [Clan Book], and that none of the descendants of the Maurice family may be admitted into the SS.
5. The Chief of the Rasse- und Siedlungshauptamt receives a copy of this Minute with the request for its most strictly confidential treatment; only the Chief of the Sippenamt [Clan Office] is to be informed of the decision.
6. For myself and for all successors as Reichsführer-SS, I state that only Adolf Hitler himself had and has the right to decree such an exception with regard to blood. No Reichsführer-SS has, or will have for all future time, the right to allow exceptions from the requirements of the SS regarding blood.
7. I oblige all my successors to maintain most strictly the position laid down in point 6.
1. Two copies to the Chief of the Race and Settlement Head Office
   A. one closed and sealed for Maurice's marriage file.
   B. one for the information of the Chief of the Sippenamt.
(Peter Hoffmann, *Hitler's Personal Security*, pp. 50-51; translated from the original letter in Maurice's SS file)

17.09.1935	While in Nürnberg, assaulted a seventy-one-year-old Party member from Dresden named Häfner who had the misfortune of getting in the way of his car and not moving aside quickly enough. Charges were brought against Maurice for this assault

but were quashed on Hitler's insistence. On 09.11.1936, the victim wrote the following letter to *Reichsführer-SS* Himmler:

To the Reichsführer SS.
On the 17th of September 1935 I was staying in Nürnberg. Whilst on a road there I had to dismount my bicycle due to heavy traffic and push it. I walked as far to the right as I could. The bicycle was on my right side. I had a fully packed briefcase attached to the handlebar. Behind me, there was a car which was being driven by SS-Standartenführer Maurice from München. There was a woman sitting beside him. The car couldn't overtake me because of the traffic but, he didn't stay at a sufficient distance behind me, but rather he drove so close to me that he hit me in the back of the knees with the bumper, so that I buckled a number of times. I forbade this and told the driver of the vehicle that he could be who he wanted but, he didn't have the right to run people down. After that the vehicle drove even further to the right so that I was trapped between the car and the sidewalk. I obviously felt threatened by this action and shouted to Standartenführer Maurice that he should refrain from such loutish behavior. This phrase escaped me in the commotion. Shortly after this, Standartenführer Maurice overtook me, stopped his car and came directly towards me. Without saying a single word, he hit me on the left side of my face with a rubber truncheon, on which I fell to the ground. I was injured by this blow and the painful swelling is still visible behind my left ear.

Various witnesses were present when this happened, one of them an on duty Feldjäger. He took immediate action and called Standartenführer Maurice to task on his behavior. He let him continue in his journey after he had assured me that he would be reporting this incident to the Braunes Haus Kaserne.

I was directed to a normal police station where I gave a statement on what had happened.

The information that was given to me by a lawyer from Dresden, whom I had asked to investigate the matter, was that the case had been handed to the SS Gericht for further discussion. I was given this information in December of last year. I am now no longer in a position to be able to secure the services of a lawyer and I am of the opinion that this is also not necessary.

According to my reasoning, it should be possible, due to the statements of the witnesses especially that of the Feldjäger, to get to the bottom of this matter. Now I would like to ask you to inform me as to what kind of satisfaction I should receive with regard to the highly incorrect behavior of the SS-Standartenführer Maurice.

I do not believe that it is in line with the will of the Reichsführung when higher leaders of the movement treat other Volksgenossen in this manner. It must have been obvious to SS-Standartenführer Maurice that, due to the traffic situation, I was not blocking his progress on purpose and also that I was an elderly man. I am 71 years of age.

I have never in the whole of my life been subjected to such abuse and I would be deeply offended if I should be at a disadvantage due to the fact that the SS-Standartenführer is in a high position in political life.

> I may also add that my national attitude has never been in question in the past. All the more that I should hope to receive the corresponding satisfaction.
> Heil Hitler
> Häfner.
> (*SS-Personalakte Maurice*)

According to a letter of 24.04.1936 from the *SS-Gerichtsamt* (court office, under *SS-Brigadeführer* Paul Scharfe):

> the criminal proceedings against SS-Staf. Maurice were discontinued on 24.2.36 by the public prosecutor's office due to lack of public interest and that the injured Häfner was referred to a private court. Häfner has filed a private suit against Maurice at the A.G. [*Amtsgericht*] Nürnberg for bodily injury. (*SS-Personalakte Maurice*)

01.10.1935–08.05.1945	*Ratsherr der Hauptstadt der Bewegung München* (Councilman of the Capital City of the [National-Socialist] Movement, München).
01.10.1935–08.05.1945	*Bayerischer Staatsrat*.
01.01.1936–08.05.1945	*Stellvertreter des Reichshandwerkermeisters in der Hauptstadt der Bewegung München* (Deputy to the Reich Craftsmen's Leader in the Capital of the [National-Socialist] Movement, München).
29.03.1936–08.05.1945	Member of the *Reichstag (Wahlkreis 29, Leipzig)*.
01.04.1936–00.05.1945	Attached to *SS-Abschnitt I* (München).
20.09.1936	Appointed as *Landeshandwerksmeister von Bayern* (kommissarisch [acting] until 01.01.1937, then permanent).
01.04.1937	Appointed as *Präsident* of the *Handwerkskammer für München und Oberbayern*.
00.00.193_	Member of the *Vorstand* (board of directors), *Landes-Gewerbebank München*.
00.00.193_–00.00.19__	Member of the *Aufsichtsrat* (supervisory board) of the firm *Lenz*.
11.03.1938–16.03.1938	While participating in reserve training exercises with *3. Scheinwerfer-Abteilung/Flak-Regiment 5*, took part in military operations in connection with the *"Anschluß"* (annexation of Austria).
04.08.1938–18.08.1938	Participated in military training exercises with *Flak-Regiment 5*.
26.09.1938–12.10.1938	While participating in training exercises with *Flak-Regiment 5*, took part in the occupation of the Sudetenland.
01.01.1940–01.10.1942	*Luftwaffe* service as a reserve officer.
00.00.1943–00.05.1945	*Vizepräsident* of the *Gauwirtschaftskammer München-Oberbayern*.
00.00.1943–00.05.1945	*Leiter* of the *Handwerksabteilung* in the *Gauwirtschaftskammer München-Oberbayern*.
00.05.1943–00.05.1945	*Gauhandwerksmeister für den Gau München-Oberbayern*.

Postwar Prosecution:

25.05.1945–00.09.1946	Arrested by U.S. troops in Starnberg and interned there.
00.09.1946	Transferred to Lager Cham bei Regensburg.
18.12.1947	Indicted by the *Spruchkammer* in Regensburg.
13.05.1948	Convicted in de-Nazification proceedings that resulted in his classification as a *"Belasteter"* (incriminated person, in

	de-Nazification *Gruppe II*). Among the charges against him was his role in the murders of SA leaders on 30.06.1934. He was sentenced to four years' labor camp and confiscation of 30 percent of his assets.
[26.03.1951]	Owned a watch shop at *Schumannstraße 5*, München.

DECORATIONS & AWARDS:

00.00.194_	*Kriegsverdienstkreuz II. Klasse ohne Schwerter*
20.08.1934	*Ehrenkreuz des Weltkrieges 1914–1918 mit Schwertern*
c. 1939	*Medaille zur Erinnerung an den 1. Oktober 1938*
c. 1938	*Medaille zur Erinnerung an den 13. März 1938*
00.00.1933	*Goldenes Ehrenzeichen der NSDAP*
00.00.1934	*Ehrenzeichen des 9. November 1923 (Blutorden; Nr. 495, mit Wirkung vom 09.11.1933)*
00.10.1932	*Coburger Ehrenzeichen der NSDAP*
00.00.194_	*Dienstauszeichnung der NSDAP in Gold*
00.00.194_	*Dienstauszeichnung der NSDAP in Silber*
00.00.194_	*Dienstauszeichnung der NSDAP in Bronze*
00.00.193_	*Goldene Ehrennadel des Handwerks*
00.00.193_	*Ehrendolch der SS*
c. 1933	*Ehrendegen des Reichsführers-SS*
00.00.1933	*Totenkopfring der SS*
00.00.193_	*Ärmelband der "Stroßtrupp Hitler"*
16.12.1935	*Julleuchter der SS*
00.02.1934	*Ehrenwinkel für alte Kämpfer*

NOTES:

* Parents:
  - Father: *Karl* (aka Charles) Emil Amandus Maurice (*00.00.1864 in Hamburg), a former factory owner.
  - Mother: Amanda Maurice, *née* Hennings.

* Siblings: Two brothers, both of whom also served in the SS, including:

SS-*Hauptsturmführer* Franz Maurice
  * 17.12.1903 in Westermoor/Kreis Eckernförde/Harburg/Schleswig-Holstein.
  † 04.04.1945 in Breslau/Gau Niederschlesien (killed in action).

NSDAP-Nr.:	6.285 (Joined 25.05.1925)
SS-Nr.:	387

Promotions:

00.00.193_	*Unterführer-Anwärter*
00.00.193_	*Gefreiter d. R. und Reserveoffizieranwärter*
00.00.193_	*Wachtmeister d. R.*
20.04.1934	*SS-Untersturmführer*
09.11.1935	*SS-Obersturmführer*
00.00.193_	*Gauhauptstellenleiter der NSDAP*
30.01.1939	*SS-Hauptsturmführer*

00.00.194_	Leutnant d. R.
01.03.1943	Oberleutnant d. R.
29.11.1944	SS-Obersturmführer d. R. (*mit RDA vom* 01.03.1943)

Career:

c. 1910–c. 1914	*Volksschule.*
c. 1914–c. 1921	*Gymnasium* (?) (graduated *Untersekunda*).
00.00.1923–00.00.1925	*Frontbann* service.
00.00.192_–00.00.192_	SA service.
00.00.19__–00.00.19__	Employed as a salesman and dealer of ironware.
19.05.1937–10.07.1937	Military training exercises with *7.(Ersatz) Batterie/Artillerie-Regiment 48.*
06.02.1939–06.05.1939	Assigned to *10. Batterie/Artillerie-Regiment 12.*
00.00.193_–00.00.19__	*Gauschatzmeisterstellvertreter* (deputy *Gau* treasurer) of *Gau Mecklenburg-Lübeck der NSDAP.*
00.00.19__–00.00.194_	Assigned to the staff of *SS-Abschnitt XXXIII.*
29.11.1944–04.04.1945	Assigned to the *Generalkommando* (Corps HQ) of *V. SS-Gebirgs-Korps.*

Decorations & Awards:

00.00.1940	*1939 Eisernes Kreuz II. Klasse*
00.00.193_	*Goldenes Ehrenzeichen der NSDAP*
c. 1933	*Gauehrenzeichen der Alten Garde von 1923*
00.00.194_	*Dientauszeichnung der NSDAP in Gold*
00.00.194_	*Dientauszeichnung der NSDAP in Silber*
00.00.194__	*Dientauszeichnung der NSDAP in Bronze*
00.00.193_	*Ehrendegen des Reichsführers-SS*
00.00.193_	*Totenkopfring der SS*
00.02.1934	*Ehrenwinkel für alte Kämpfer*
16.12.1935	*Julleuchter der SS*

Notes:

* First married, 18.10.1929. Divorced, 19.01.1939; Remarried, 02.06.1944, to Charlotte Oldachniese, a member of the *NS-Frauenschaft*. Two daughters resulted from his first marriage (*21.08.1931 and 13.09.1935).

* Religion: Protestant until 00.00.1936, then left the church and declared himself *gottgläubig*.
* Became engaged on 31.03.1935 to the medical student (later Dr. med.) Hedwig Maria Anna Ploetz (*26.08.1911 in Aschaffenburg, †00.00.2003; daughter of *Oberst* Rudolf Ploetz [*00.00.1865, †00.00.1942]). They married in München on 11.05.1935, with Christian Weber and Prof. Heinrich Hoffmann appearing as witnesses. Two children resulted from this marriage, including Dr. phil. Klaus Maurice (*00.05.1936 in München), an art historian (specializing in antique clocks), author, longtime director of the *Deutschen Museum* in München, and *Generalsekretär der Kulturstiftung der Länder* (1987–1993) and a daughter (name unknown, *00.00.1937).

SOURCES:

Bayerisches Hauptstaatsarchiv, München, Abteilung IV Kriegsarchiv: Excerpts from various *Kriegsranglisten* containing data on the Royal Bavarian Army service of Emil Maurice.
Dornberg, John: *Munich 1923. The Story of Hitler's First Grab for Power*. Harper & Row, 1982.

Flood, Charles Bracelen: *Hitler: The Path to Power*. Houghton Mifflin Company, 1989.
Gordon, Harold J., Jr.: *Hitler and the Beer Hall Putsch*. Princeton University Press, 1972.
Hamilton, Charles: *Leaders and Personalities of the Third Reich, Volume I*. R. James Bender Publishing, 1984.
Hanfstaengl, Ernst Franz Sedgwick ("Putzi"): *Hitler: The Missing Years*. Arcade Publishing, 1957.
Hayman, Ronald: *Hitler and Geli*. Bloomsbury Publishing USA, 1999.
Heiden, Konrad: *Der Fuehrer: Hitler's Rise to Power*. Houghton Mifflin, 1944.
Höhne, Heinz: *The Order of the Death's Head*. Martin Secker and Warburg, 1969.
Hoffmann, Peter: *Hitler's Personal Security*. Macmillan, 1979.
Kienast, *Ministerialdirigent* Ernst (ed): *Der Großdeutsche Reichstag, IV. Wahlperiode, Beginn am 10.04.1938 verlängert bis zum 30. Januar 1947*. Berlin, November 1943.
Lilla, Joachim; Döring, Martin; & Schulz, Andreas: *Statisten in Uniform. Die Mitglieder des Reichstags 1933-1945*. Droste Verlag, 2004.
Miller, Michael D. and Andreas Schulz: *Leaders of the Storm Troops, Volume 1* (1st Edition). Helion & Co., 2015.
Mitchell, Otis C.: *Hitler's Stormtroopers and the Attack on the German Republic, 1919-1933*. McFarland, 2008.
National Archives and Records Administration, College Park, Maryland: *SS-Personalakte* of Emil Maurice. Microfilm document collection A3343SS.
Ryback, Timothy W.: *Hitler's Private Library: The Books that Shaped His Life*. Random House Digital, 2009.

Landsberg, 1924: The *Führer* and his fellow *Putsch* convicts, photographed by Heinrich Hoffmann.

Above and overleaf: Left to right: Hitler, Maurice, Hermann Kriebel, Rudolf Hess, and Dr. Friedrich Weber.

Below: Kriebel, Hitler, and Maurice. (NARA, Heinrich Hoffmann Collection)

Right: "*Deutscher Tag in Fürth*," 26.09.1925. Maurice at the wheel.

Below: Emil Maurice behind the wheel of Hitler's car—a Selve 6/20—in 1925.

Formal portraits of *SS-Sturmbannführer* Maurice, probably taken in September 1933 by Heinrich Hoffmann. Visible on his left pocket are the *Coburger-Ehrenzeichen,* the commemorative badge of the "*5. Reichsparteitag der NSDAP in Nürnberg,*" and the badge of the *NS-Kriegsopferverband* (NSKOV). (NARA, Heinrich Hoffmann Collection)

Below right: An identification card photo of Emil Maurice, *c.* 1933.

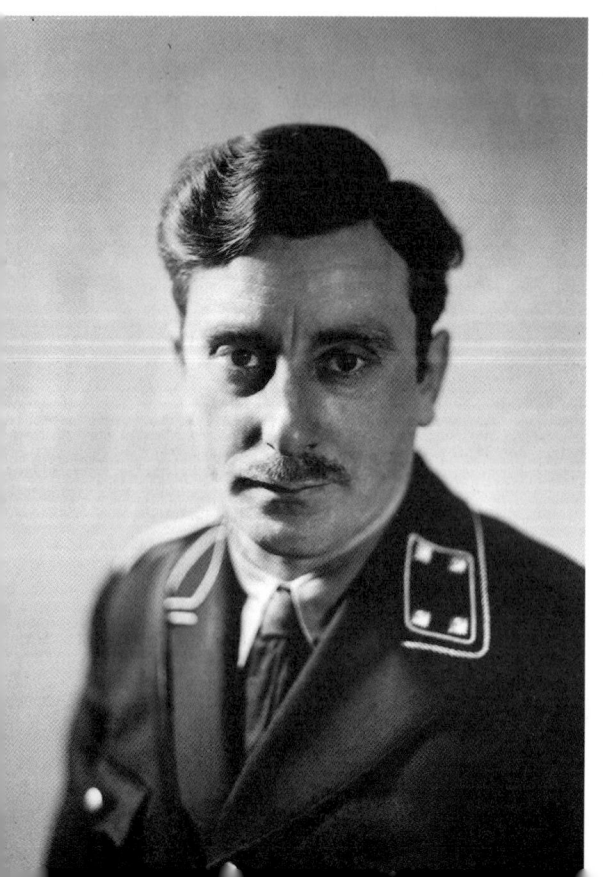

München, 08.–09.11.1933: Commemoration ceremonies for the *"Putsch"* of November 1923.

Maurce (left foreground) stands beside Jakob Grimminger, bearer of the *"Blutfahne"* (Blood Banner). (Michal Sika)

Maurice and Grimminger lead the procession of 1923 Putschists in a recreation of the march to the *Feldherrnhalle*. (NARA, Heinrich Hoffmann Collection)

Hitler revisits Landsberg Prison with Julius Schaub and Emil Maurice, 08.10.1934.

Left: From *Illustrierter Beobachter*, 20.10.1934.

Below: Courtesy of Max Williams.

Bottom: From *Illustrierter Beobachter*, 20.10.1934.

München, 08.–09.11.1933: Commemoration ceremonies for the *"Putsch"* of November 1923.

Right and below: The *Feldherrnhalle* on the *Odeonsplatz*, München, 08.–09.11.1934: Left to right: Karl Wolff, Maurice, Wilhelm Brückner, Rudolf Hess, Christian Weber, Heinrich Himmler, Viktor Lutze, and Julius Schaub. (Michal Sika)

Hitler, accompanied by the rotund Christian Weber and Maurice, reviews his faithful *"Alte Kämpfer"* (Old Fighters). (Michal Sika)

Hitler, Maurice, and Weber inspect units of the *Hitler-Jugend*. (Michal Sika)

Braunschweig, 1934: Left to right: Maurice, Hjalmar Schacht, Wihelm Hesse (*Oberbürgermeister* of Braunschweig), Dr. Robert Ley, Dietrich Klagges (*Ministerpräsident* of Braunschweig), Otto Marrenbach, Kurt Schmalz, and Friedrich Alpers. (NARA, Heinrich Hoffmann Collection)

Above left and middle: SS-*Standartenführer* Emil Maurice, *c.* 1935.

Above right: SS-*Oberführer* Emil Maurice. (Bundesarchiv Bild 146-1980-073-19A)

Hitler shakes hands with veterans of the "*Stoßtrupp Adolf Hitler*," c. 1939. Emil Maurice stands at extreme left. (Roger Bender)

Annual *"Putsch"* commemoration in the *Bürgerbräukeller*, München, 09.11.1937. Seated from left to right: Dr. Joseph Goebbels, Emil Maurice, Dr. Robert Ley, and Philipp Bouhler. (National Digital Archives, Poland)

Left to right: Heinrich Himmler, Goebbels, Maurice, Dr. Robert Ley, and Philipp Bouhler. In the foreground, back to the camera, is *Gauleiter* Julius Streicher. (Michal Sika)

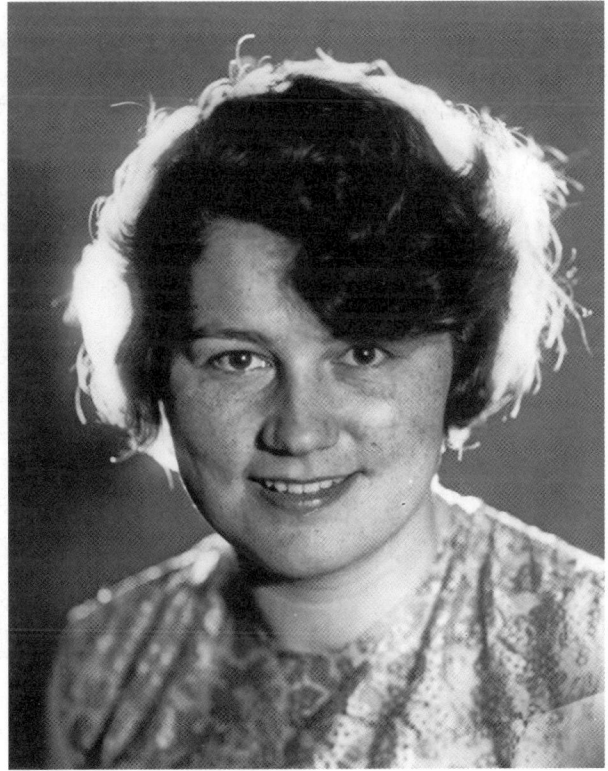

Angela ("Geli") Raubal (1908–1931), Hitler's niece and Maurice's lover.

The return of army regiments to München in late October 1938, after the occupation of the Sudetenland. *SS-Standartenführer* Maurice greets an NCO and fellow *Blutordensträger*. (Max Williams)

Julius *Johann* ("*Hans*") *Ulrich* Klintzsch
Ausbilder der Turn- und Sportabteilungen der NSDAP (20.07.1921–00.11.1921)
Führer der SA (00.11.1921–00.02.1923)

*	04.11.1898 in Lübbenau (Spreewald)/Kreis Calau/Regierungsbezirk Frankfurt/Mark Brandenburg.
†	17.08.1959 in Hamburg while attending the wedding of his son, Fridthjof. Gravesite: *Jüdisches Friedhof Ohlsdorf*, Hamburg.

NSDAP-Nr.: 3.603 (Joined 20.07.1921; Possibly left the Party in Spring 1923)

Promotions:

00.00.1917	*Unteroffizier*
17.09.1917	*Fähnrich zur See (ohne Patent)*
00.00.1919 (?)	*Oberfähnrich zur See* (aka *Säbelfähnrich*, or sub-lieutenant authorized to wear an officer's saber)
00.00.1919	*Vizewachtmeister* (in Freikorps Lützow)
27.09.1919	*Leutnant zur See d. R.* (in II. Marine-Brigade)
10.01.1920	*Leutnant zur See (aktiv)*
20.07.1921–00.11.1921	*Ausbilder der Turn- und Sportabteilungen der NSDAP*
00.11.1921–00.02.1923	*Führer der SA*
Luftwaffe:	
01.10.1936	*Hauptmann*
01.09.1938	*Major*
00.00.1942	*Oberstleutnant*
01.02.1943	*Oberst* (63)

Career:

00.00.1906–00.00.1909	Attended the private *Höhere Töchterschule* in Lübbenau. Of his early schooling, Klintzsch writes:

As I wasn't a very strong child, I did not start school until I was 7 and a half and, in the absence of a Vorschule for the Gymnasium, I attended the Höhere Töchterschule in the town of Lübbenau, a private school usually only attended by the daughters of wealthy citizens.... During my time at the school, there were only two boys amongst all the girls... (Klintzsch, *Lebenslauf* of Spring 1959)

00.01.1910–Easter 1912	*Kgl. Friedrich-Wilhelm-Gymnasium* in Cottbus. Klintzsch continues:

[there] I joined the last quarter of the Sexta, to be transferred to the Quinta at Easter 1910. Going to school was not hard for me but the innate desire for freedom disturbed the continuity of my career. During that time I lived, together with my only brother Heinz, in the Pension Kolshorn, which was in the Vionvillestraße 28. (Klintzsch, *Lebenslauf* of Spring 1959)

Easter 1912–00.00.1916	*Kgl. Joachimsthalische Gymnasium* in Berlin-Wilmersdorf (later in Templin). Klintzsch writes:

After completing an exam, I was admitted to the Alma Mater Joachimica as an *alumnus*, that is, I became a homeschooler with the privilege that

	my father would only have to spend a very small annual allowance for my schooling. Six months later, in the fall of 1912, the school and *alumnus* were moved to Templin in the Uckermark, where a brand-new institution awaited us. (Klintzsch, *Lebenslauf* of Spring 1959)
03.10.1916	Volunteered for service in the *Kaiserliche Marine* (Imperial German Navy). Of the period leading up to his enlistment, he writes:
	Since I was not yet 16 years of age, my father refused to allow me to report as a volunteer. This caused a long feud between my father and me. Finally, in 1916—the Battle of the Skagerrak [Jutland] had just been fought and three of my classmates were already cadets with the Imperial Navy—I managed to soften my father's heart. (Klintzsch, *Lebenslauf* of Spring 1959)
00.10.1916–00.01.1917	Underwent infantry training at the *Marineschule Flensburg-Mürwik*.
00.01.1917–00.03.1917	Received training in seamanship aboard the SMS *Freya* (formerly classed as a cruiser) in Flensburg.
00.03.1917–00.09.1918	Assigned to the *Zerstörerflotte Flandern* (Destroyer Flotilla Flanders).
00.05.1917–00.05.1917(?)	Assigned to the *Große Torpedoboot* SMS *G-95*, commanded by *Kapitänleutnant* Wolf von Eichhorn.
00.05.1917–00.07.1917	Attached to *1. Marine-Artillerie-Regiment*.
00.07.1917(?)–00.11.1917	Returned to Mürwik for officer training, ultimately completing his *Fähnrich* examinations.
00.11.1917–00.01.1918	Participated in a *Fähnrichs-Artillerie-Lehrgang* aboard the *Schulschiff* SMS *Kaiserin Augusta*. He was accommodated aboard the *Hulk Nixe*, a disused sailboat, during this period. Klintzsch continues in his 1959 *Lebenslauf*:
	During this course on 27.01.1918, *the birthday of Kaiser Wilhelm, I received the message that, due to a special order I was to report together with my crewmate Spannagel, once more to the Zerstörerflotte Flandern. This message was the first highlight of my military career. At the beginning of March 1918, I reported to my Halbflottillenchef, Kapitänleutnant Zander.* (Klintzsch, *Lebenslauf* of Spring 1959)
00.03.1918–00.03.1918	Assigned to the *Große Torpedoboot* SMS *V-74*, commanded by *Kapitänleutnant* Junghans. On 25.05.1918, the vessel was sunk in an accidental explosion as mines were being loaded aboard her in the port of Zeebrugge.
00.03.1918–Spring 1918	Assigned to the *Große Torpedoboot* SMS *V-69* (*Kapitänleutnant* Benecke). Of this posting, he writes:
	V 69 was the boat on which my highest soldierly dreams would soon be fulfilled. On 22 March 1918, shortly before midnight, the alarm sounded, and in a few moments the battle for Zeebrugge was underway. In the course of the battle, I was fortunate enough to be able to stand together with my commander at a decisive point in the defense and use my weapon to force a favorable outcome for us. By order of the Kaiser, I received the Iron Cross First Class. (Klintzsch, *Lebenslauf* of Spring 1959)

The action for which he was decorated is described as follows in Heinrich Hoffmann's *Das Braune Heer* (1932):

> As the English attacked Zeebrugge in 1918, this man hunted down a British cruiser with his torpedo boat and, from barely 75 yards away, he slammed explosives into her belly.

Spring 1918–00.09.1918	In anticipation of his assignment as a *Wachoffizier* (watch officer) aboard a destroyer, reported to Kiel to participate in the *Artillerie-Offizier-Lehrgang B*.
00.09.1918–00.11.1918	Resumed service in Flanders through the end of the war.
00.00.1918–17.11.1918	Assigned to the *Große Torpedoboot* SMS *S-53* in Kiel (scuttled in Scapa Flow, 21.06.1919). He writes of this tense period of revolution and mutiny:

> It soon became apparent that the Navy was divided into imperial and revolutionary units. The keyword was: blue piping against red piping. The torpedo boat and boat personnel wore red piping on their uniforms, in contrast to the crews of the "Fat" ships. Of course, we belonged to those loyal to the Kaiser, and after a few days we manage to leave the trouble spot Kiel with our boats.
>
> We first looked for accommodation in Warnemünde, but then, finding that the coast was not clear there, proceeded to Stolpmünde. In this small fishing port in the middle of good-hearted Pommern, we were safe and could wait to see what would happen in peace. The armistice put an end to our stay in Stolpmünde.
>
> The boats had to be transferred to Scapa Flow. Those on board who were not absolutely necessary for the operation of the boats, disembarked.
>
> I finally reached Danzig and in an adventurous way Berlin and from there home. All officers and Fähnriche zur See were transferred to the reserve and so were as good as discharged. (Klintzsch, *Lebenslauf* of Spring 1959)

17.11.1918	Departed *S-53* to go on home leave.
00.12.1918	Transferred to the naval reserves.
00.01.1919	Passed his *Abitur* at the *Joachimsthalische Gymnasium*.
00.02.1919–31.05.1919	Service with *Freikorps Lützow*, with which he commanded a *Maschinenkanonenzug*. In this assignment, he fought in Berlin, Braunschweig, Jena (Thüringen), and München (participating in the "liberation" of the Bavarian capital from the communist "*Räterepublik*" on 01.05.1919).
01.06.1919–Summer 1920	Service with the *Sturmkompanie* of *II. Marine-Brigade* (commanded by *Korvettenkapitän* Hermann Ehrhardt, and also known as the *Marine Brigade Ehrhardt*) in München, with which he went, in August 1919, to Oberschlesien (Upper Silesia) to fight against Polish insurgents. Later, on 13.03.1920, the *Brigade*, with Klintzsch in its ranks, occupied Berlin during the "*Kapp-Putsch*." Following the *Putsch*, *Generaloberst* Hans von Seeckt ordered the dissolution of the *Brigade*, however, it continued to exist under a number of cover organizations. These included *Organisation Consul* (named

	for a *nom de guerre*—"Consul Eichmann"—used by Ehrhardt) established in 1920/21, with which Klintzsch was later to serve.
10.01.1920–02.06.1921	Returned to service as a *Leutnant zur See* in the *Reichsmarine*, assigned to the *Schiffsstammdivision der Nordsee*, then resigned, as he states in his *Lebenslauf* of 16.09.1921, "due to financial and political reasons". Klintzsch continues:

> I could not fulfill the financial standards required of an officer, from my monthly wage of 750 Marks; I had to pay for not only clothing and a share of the catering but also the rent in the barracks, 120 Marks.
> The political reason for my resignation was the impossible feat of bringing the Reichswehr law into line with the old officer's concept of honor and the soldier's national upbringing. (Klintzsch, *Lebenslauf* of 16.09.1921, Landesarchiv Baden-Württemberg [Abteilung Staatsarchiv Freiburg], F 179/4 Nr. 110)

02. or 03.07.1921	Arrived in München, first residing (for three weeks) in the *Pension Quisisana* before moving to a flat in *Hiltensbergerstraße 32/2*. In his 16.09.1921 *Lebenslauf*, he writes:

> I have not attended the university yet as the academic recess ends on the 30th of September and there are no lectures until then.... The time of my departure [from the island of Borkum in Ostfriesland] happened to be in the middle of the semester. I spent July on Borkum and lived in the barracks with comrades. Nevertheless, I was afraid that I would not be able to get by on the money that I received the Navy, around 500 Marks a month.
> I could not return home [to Lübbenau] as my mother was living in humble accommodations. She lives, together with my grandmother and my brother, in a one-room flat on a monthly pension of 500 Marks.
> For this reason, I decided to leave for München at that time. I also considered the fact that it might be easier to obtain a flat during the semester recess. Apart from that, living conditions in München are cheaper than in the city in northern Germany. I spent my time in private studies, amongst other things national economy and art. (Klintzsch, *Lebenslauf* of 16.09.1921, Landesarchiv Baden-Württemberg [Abteilung Staatsarchiv Freiburg], F 179/4 Nr. 110)

In his 1959 *Lebenslauf*, he gave a different reason for his move to München:

> I ... took my leave [from the *Reichsmarine*] on 1 June 1921 and followed the call from Kapitän Ehrhardt to München. With that, I had finally decided on a political career. (Klintzsch, *Lebenslauf* of Spring 1959)

20.07.1921	Joined the NSDAP. Regarding the circumstances of his enrollment, he asserted:

> By chance, I happened upon a meeting of the Nationalsozialistische Arbeiterpartei. I was so impressed with the ideas which were disseminated

there that I concentrated my studies solely on learning about that subject matter. I occupied myself with the Jewish and freemason question. I offered my services and was accepted. For the past six weeks, I have been working in an honorary capacity in the Party office. (Klintzsch, *Lebenslauf* of 16.09.1921)

20.07.1921–00.11.1921 *Ausbilder* (training director) of the *Turn- und Sportabteilungen der NSDAP* (Gymnastic and Sports Sections). Klintzsch's assignment to this post resulted from an agreement between Hitler and Klintzsch's former superior, *Korvettenkapitän* Hermann Ehrhardt. Daniel Siemens writes of the cooperation between the two men:

Those involved in the deal between Hitler and Ehrhardt perceived it as a win-win situation: Hitler would gain further access to the web of military and conservative political leaders in Bavaria, and his young self-defence units would benefit from the military expertise of individuals like Klintzsch. On the other side, Ehrhardt ... hoped to gain in Hitler a public voice and in the NSDAP a new party that would be at his disposal. (Siemens, *Stormtroopers: A New History of Hitler's Brownshirts*, pp. 9-10)

In his new capacity, on 14.08.1921, Klintzsch issued the following appeal, published in the *Völkischer Beobachter*:

To Our German Youth!
Fellow Party members!... The NSDAP has formed a Gymnastics and Sports Section within its organization. It is intended that it should join together our young Party members so that as an iron unit they can place their strength at the disposal of the entire movement as a battering ram. It is to be the symbol of defense of a free people. It should serve as the protective shield for the work of spreading the message that the leaders wish to accomplish. (Translation in Charles Bracelen Flood, *Hitler: The Path to Power*, pp. 209-210)

Of his time in Hitler's service, Klintzsch wrote:

Hitler, to whom the circles of the intelligentsia were initially closed and therefore lacking suitable leaders, turned to Kapitän Ehrhardt, who had been the number one in the national camp since the Kapp Putsch. An agreement was reached, by which Ehrhardt made officers available and organized military training, while Hitler agreed to have the organized young party team join the brigade in the event that it came to any fighting. In "peacetime," this body of men was to serve the party as a Saalschutz. I was the first person to be offered this task by Kapitän Ehrhardt, and since I was fascinated by the name of the party, I agreed immediately.

However, during my two-year tenure with Hitler, I remained committed to Ehrhardt and left Hitler when, in Ehrhardt's absence, he broke his contract. At first, I set up the required units. I divided the units into "Hundertschaften" and called it the Turn- und Sportabteilung. Soon, however, the name Sturmabteilung emerged, and so it happened that I was the founder of S.A. (Klintzsch, *Lebenslauf* of Spring 1959)

Although 05.10.1921 is given in official Party publications as the official date for the organization's redesignation, by Hitler, as *Sturmabteilungen* (SA), a handwritten card found on Klintzsch's person when he was arrested on 13.09.1921 reads:

Die nächster Zusammenkunft der SA findet am 21 am Leiberzimmer der Sterneckerbräu statt. Sturmabteilung der N.S.D.A.P. [The next meeting of the SA will take place on the 21st in the Leiberzimmer of the Sterneckerbräu. Storm Troops of the NSDAP.]

03.08.1921–00.05.1923	Employed as an *Organisationsleiter* (organization coordinator) of the NSDAP.
13.09.1921	Arrested in the late evening as a suspect in the assassination, on 26.08.1921, of Matthias Erzberger. The arrest report read as follows:

Klintzsch Ulrich, born 04.11.98 in Lübenau, Amt Kalau, Prussia, protestant parents: Paul and Dora Kl. nee Schmidtgen, Pastoreheleute (a Pastor couple), mother Living in Lübenau, residing here in the Hiltenbergerstraße No. 32 with Albrecht. His arrest with regard to the murder of Erzberger.

On the 13.09, Kriminal-Assistant Kolmer and myself arrested Freiherr Manfred von Killinger on the Augsburg München train, in relation to the above case.

As we left the train in München with the latter, a young man (Klintzsch) approached us and, as he had no idea of von Killinger's arrest, nor did he know me or Krim. Ass. Kolmer, went directly to Killinger and said, "Watch yourself" and a few other words which I could not understand.

Klintzsch did not manage to say anything else to v. Killinger as he was immediately arrested and, like v. Killinger, taken to the Polizeidirektion.
[Signed] Leonhardt
Kriminal-Assistant
(Staatsarchiv Freiburg F 179/4 Nr. 110; Translation: Gary Costello)

He was held in the *Gerichtsgefängnis München* until 27.10.1921. He was released on that date but immediately rearrested, based on an arrest warrant of 17.10.1921, for *Geheimbündelei* (membership in an illegal secret society). This second period of custody continued until his release on 02.12.1921.

Klintzsch's deputy and fellow *Organisation Consul* member, Dietrich von Jagow (also a retired naval officer) administered the *Turn- und Sportabteilung* during Klintzsch's absence.

A prominent figure in the Catholic *Zentrumspartei*, Erzberger was appointed by President Friedrich Ebert as head of the German Armistice Commission and later served as finance minister until March 1920. The fact that he had signed the Armistice of 11.11.1918 led to his shooting, which occurred in Bad Griesbach (Schwarzwald)/Baden.

The assassins were *Oberleutnant zur See a. D.* Heinrich Tillessen and *Leutnant d. R. a. D.* Heinrich Schulz, retired officers who had gone on to serve in the *Ehrhardt Brigade*. Charles Bracelen Flood writes:

After killing Erzberger they returned to the Organization Consul headquarters in Munich, which was operating under the cover of the offices of the fictitious Bavarian Wood Products Company. Here they immediately received assistance from right-wing sympathizers within the Bavarian police, who issued them false passports, and, while the killers fled to Hungary, obstructed the efforts of the Baden police to find them. In Hungary, which had a right-wing regime, the assassins were arrested and then released on orders from headquarters in Budapest. The Hungarian authorities refused to extradite them for trial to Germany. (Bracelen Flood, Hitler: The Path to Power, p. 217)

In his *Lebenslauf* of 16.09.1921, written at the direction of his interrogators, the young revolutionary officer provided the following glimpses into his ideology:

To the question of the charges against him of 15.09.1921:
As a committee member of the deutsche Arbeiterpartei, I am the chairman of the Turn und Sportabteilung of the Party. The appeal that appeared in the Völkischer Beobachter on the 14.08 which invited people to join an Abteilung built on strict discipline, was only partly written by me but I hereby declare that I agree with every word of the appeal.
To the question of what building an iron formation ["eisernes Organisation"] meant:
Through the destruction of the Wehrmacht, the German people have been robbed of a school that was a guarantee of Germany's national strength.

There is a danger that, without any national pride the coming generation will grow soft and no longer have the will for self-preservation. To form a replacement for this schooling and to strengthen the German youth in mind and body, we have taken things into our own hands and formed the Turn- und Sportverein.
To the question of what he understands by instilling the unrestrained will of action into the young followers:
We are of the opinion that bolshevism which hides behind the mask of a democratic republic as it can be seen in the industrial centers in northern Germany, will one day take off its mask and a surprised Bourgeoisie will be left facing the accomplished fact of a Soviet republic as in 1918.

As in 1918, the people will not have the will to resist.

We national socialists will be the only ones who will be willing to fight an action with a reaction.

The expression, therefore, is not to be understood that we would render political opponents harmless through violence, or by carrying out a murder in an emergency.

For us, the irrefutable facts that we hold against our opponents, are the best propaganda for our ideas.

We will fight our opponents with intellectual weapons as long as he fights back with the same weapons. Should, he however, try to oppress us with violence or terrorize our meetings then we will fight back with violence.

We do not stand firmly on the grounds of the parliamentary constitution in the form found today as we believe that the fate of the people should not be decide by a party majority but rather by the most capable minds who are supported by the majority of the people.

They have emerged from the people. (Klintzsch, *Lebenslauf* of 16.09.1921; Translation: Gary Costello)

00.11.1921–00.02.1923 *Führer der SA*. Resigned and succeeded by Hermann Göring, who assumed command on 01.03.1923. Despite his youth, he proved an innovative organizer with grand designs for the future of the organization. These were laid out in comprehensive guidelines which were the subject of a report by an official named Wegelin in the office of the *Reichskommissar für Überwachung der öffentliche Ordnung* (Reich Commissioner for the Supervision of Public Order):

A recently seized letter from the leader of the Sturmabteilung, Klintzsch, to a National Socialist living outside of Bavaria, as well as the guidelines, attached to this letter, for the formation of a Sturmabteilung, provides information about the character of the National Socialist Sturmabteilung.

We hereby acknowledge receipt of your letter dated 19.11.22. To our delight we learn from this that also in X young people have gathered who, by joining the S.A., have expressed their will to fight for the Party. In order to help you with advice, I am enclosing the guidelines for the formation of a Sturmabteilung, which are, however, in some respects no longer applicable to today's conditions within the S.A.. This is the case with the item: Organization of the S.A. The division into sections a and b, which was mainly due to age differences, has ceased to exist. The present S.A. is composed almost exclusively of younger people whose usability is possible in all cases. Older Party members, who are also well represented, are only admitted on condition that they fulfill all the obligations required of them by the S.A. without reservation. The strength of the S.A. lies not so much in the number of its members as in the unconditional obedience to the orders of the Führer, iron discipline, the most loyal comradeship and the sense of responsibility, which takes full charge of everything that goes on in their section and does not leave the responsibility to any elected, but practically irresponsible, committee. The organization of the S.A. results from all these things. Divided into Gruppen, Züge, and Hundertschaften, each led by a Führer. Führer are always the most capable and loyal, regardless of age and rank. The entire S.A. of Bavaria is subordinate to the München command, from where orders are issued every fortnight, but only to the detachments that are firmly integrated as Hundertschaften within the framework of the organization.

If you wish to be permanently attached to München, please fill in the enclosed enrollment forms and send them to the Kdo [*Kommando*, = Headquarters] as soon as possible, at the same time informing us of the name of your Abteilungsführer (Hundertschaftsführer).

A commitment certificate which is to be submitted to the S.A. is attached. In the hope that the S.A. X will soon become as good a Kampftruppe as the Müncheners, we sign with Deutschen Gruß!

Signed Klintzsch
Führer der Sturmabteilung
(Bundesarchiv, R1507, Reichskommissar für Überwachung der öffentlichen Ordnung; Translation: Gary Costello)

In subsequent pages, Klintzsch outlined the purpose, organization, and activities of the SA:

At the same time as the establishment of a local group, a "Sturmabteilung" must be formed. This initially includes all men of the local group who are fit for military service and is subordinate to a leader to be determined by the committee. At meetings, members of the Sturmabteilung wear a red armband with a black swastika on a white background.

The Sturmabteilung does not represent a separate association, but is part of the Party. All Sturmabteilungen are subordinate to the central leadership, which is located at the party's headquarters in Munich, Corneliusstraße 12.

Purpose of the Sturmabteilung.
The Sturmabteilung has the following purpose:
1.) It provides the order and security service during its own assemblies.
2.) If one's own speakers should speak at opposition meetings, the Sturmabteilung will provide protection for the speaker.
3.) It is used for propaganda purposes in its own meetings and to distribute leaflets on the streets.

Leadership of the Sturmabteilung.
The leader of the Sturmabteilung is not to be elected by the members of the S.A., but is to be determined by the local group chairman. It is desirable that the leader has military training. Otherwise, only efficiency and ability are decisive for the appointment of the leader. The leader of the S.A. appoints the group leaders. The members of the S.A. have to render him unconditional obedience, but he himself is responsible for the recognition of his authority.

Organization of the Sturmabteilung.
The S.A. is divided into Gruppen [squads] of 8 men, headed by a Gruppenführer. If possible, once the Gruppen have been formed, they should not be changed, so that they get to know each other better, so that the feeling of belonging together is promoted and so that each individual group forms a cohesive whole. The Gruppen are always to be used as a single unit.

As the S.A. grows, a division into Abteilungen [sections] "A" and "B" is to be made.

Abteilung "A": In it are all party comrades between the ages of 18 and about 25; these form the active part of the Sturmabteilung, which means that they are also called upon to perform tasks that are not exclusively related to party events. The members of section "A" should be physically fit people who can volunteer their time at any opportunity. Abteilung "A" wears golden numbers on the armbands, which indicate the Gruppe affiliation. Gruppen- and Zugführer [platoon leaders] wear one and two stars respectively.

Abteilung "B": It includes all other members of the S.A., is not divided into groups and wears the armbands without insignia. A leader for each of the two sections is to be appointed by the head of the S.A.

Alarmbezirke [alarm districts]: In larger cities, it is advisable to divide the Sturmabteilung into alarm districts for the purpose of rapid alerting.

The members of the S.A. are grouped according to their residences in sections of 8–10 men. One of the people living in the district is designated as the message bearer. Messages from the leadership are sent to him, while he is responsible for forwarding them. It is desirable that the messengers have a bicycle and can be reached conveniently by telephone or otherwise. They do not hold a leading position.

Sturmabteilung activities.
The Sturmabteilung's activities consist of meetings, sports and excursions.

Meetings: Abteilung "A" meets once a week for the purpose of instruction, to promote comradeship, to discuss important events of the day and to announce the duty roster for the coming week. There is also an urgent need for marching songs to be rehearsed on these occasions.

Sport: From a sporting point of view, the main emphasis is on learning to fight. Therefore, boxing and jiu-jitsu are particularly suitable as compulsory sports.

Excursions: Once a fortnight the S.A. undertakes an excursion to which everyone is obliged to attend. The excursions are also intended to provide opportunities for sporting activities.

General.
The Sturmabteilung is composed of the party's elite. It represents in the most pronounced sense what our movement is: a revolutionary fighting force. This determines which spirit should prevail in the S.A. and which qualities should be cultivated in each individual. That is the most loyal comradeship, the strictest discipline and a battle-hardened bravado. The orders of a leader are to be strictly obeyed, as far as they do not offend a German's honor. Disputes within the S.A. are to be resolved by the leaders using the most radical means. He is also responsible for ensuring that the S.A. remains free of impure elements (informers and the like). Only under these conditions is it possible to make the S.A. the weapon that our leaders require, in order to achieve their lofty goals at the decisive moment.

The above directives are only to be considered as a general guide. The Führers can act independently within this framework and make deviations according to the circumstances, provided they are not of a fundamental nature. In general, S.A. activity will depend on the availability of training staff (sports instructors, etc.). The leadership of the Sturmabteilungen are requested to report from time to time on their activities (also on their strength) and to communicate their experiences to the headquarters. Enquiries are welcome.

(Bundesarchiv, R1507, Reichskommissar für Überwachung der öffentlichen Ordnung; Translation: Gary Costello)

14.10.1922–15.10.1922	Together with Hitler, led a large contingent of SA men to a celebration of the "*3. Deutscher Tag*" in Coburg. They arrived via chartered train, and during a formation march through the city, provoked a street battle with political opponents. In *Mein Kampf*, Hitler wrote of the events in Coburg:

I received an invitation with a note that they wanted me to bring along some supporters from my party.... For my supporters, I designated eight hundred men of the S.A., who were to be transported in fourteen groups by a special train from München to the village that had only recently joined Bavaria. Similar orders were sent to the National-Socialist S.A. groups that had been formed in other cities along the route. It was the first time that a train of this sort traveled in Germany. At each place where new S.A. men boarded, the transport attracted great attention. Many had never seen our flags before and they were very impressed.

When we assembled at the station in Coburg, a representative of the festival committee for "German Day" received us and gave us a signed order which said it was an "agreement" by the local organizations, which meant the Independent Party and the Communist Party. The agreement said that we would not be allowed to enter the city with our flags waving, we would not be allowed to play music—we had brought our own band of forty-two men—and we could not march through the streets in a group or closed ranks. I immediately dismissed these disgraceful conditions and did not hesitate to express to those gentlemen of the festival committee who were present how astonished I was that these kinds of arrangements had been made and that it was disgraceful they had come to any agreement with these people. I explained that the S.A. would immediately march in company formation through the city, and it would be to the sound of music with our flags waving. And that is what happened.

There were already thousands of howling, hooting people to receive us at the depot. "Murderers," "Bandits," "Robbers," "Criminals," were some of the pet names that these outstanding founders of the German Republic graciously showered on us. The young S.A. maintained themselves in perfect order.

The squads of one hundred assembled on the square in front of the railway station and, at first, ignored the abuse. We were unfamiliar with the city streets, so the marching procession was directed by a nervous police escort into the Hofbräuhaus Cellar near the center of the town instead of to our quarters on the outskirts of Coburg like we had previously arranged. On both sides of our troop procession, the noise of the masses constantly increased.

The last squad had barely turned into the courtyard of the beer garden when large crowds, making deafening shrieks, attempted to rush after them. To avoid a confrontation, the police closed the gates. We could not tolerate this situation, sealed in with everyone hollering, so I told the S.A. to reassemble.

I admonished them briefly for breaking ranks and demanded that the police open the gates immediately. After a rather long hesitation, they complied.

We marched back the way we came to reach our quarters and there we finally had to face the mob. After they were unable to disturb the squads using shouts and insults, the representatives of the true socialism, equality, and brotherhood started throwing stones. Our patience was at an end. For ten minutes we attacked furiously on both sides. Fifteen minutes later, nothing Red was to be seen on the streets anymore.

At night, there were more serious attacks. Patrols of the S.A. had found members of the National-Socialist Party who had been attacked and mutilated when they were alone. After that, we quickly took care of our opponents. By the following morning, the Red Terror Coburg had suffered under for years had been smashed.

With typical Marxist-Jewish style, they passed out falsehood-filled flyers and tried again to rally the members of the international laborers into the streets by distorting the facts, saying that our bands of murderers had begun a war to exterminate the peaceful workers in Coburg. At one-thirty, the great "demonstration of the people" was to take place and, according to the flyers, it was hoped that tens of thousands of workers from the area would be present. I was determined to put an end to this Red Terror once and for all, so I had the S.A. assemble at twelve o'clock. The S.A. now numbered nearly fifteen hundred. I marched with them to the Coburg fortress across the large square where the Red demonstration was to take place. I wanted to see if they would be so foolish and attempt to assault us again. As we entered the square, there were only a few hundred present instead of the announced ten thousand. As we approached, they remained quiet, although some ran away. There were a few Red troops present who came from outside of the city and, as yet, did not know what to expect from us. Occasionally, they tried to renew hostilities, but any desire to do so was quickly taken away from them.

As we watched during the speeches, we could see that the population, which was previously so intimidated, slowly awoke, took courage, and ventured out this time to greet us with shouts. When we left in the evening and marched back through the streets, they broke out in spontaneous loud rejoicing at various places along our route.

When we arrived at the train station, we were suddenly told that the workers refused to run the train for us. At that, I informed a few leaders of the mob that if this was the case, I would seize any Red big shots I could find and that my men would operate the train ourselves. I would also take along a few dozen brothers of international solidarity in the locomotive, the supply car, and in each passenger car. I made it very clear to the gentlemen that a trip managed by our own forces would naturally be a very risky journey and that it was quite possible that we would all break our necks. I let them know it would be a pleasure to enter eternity accompanied by the Red gentlemen who advocated equality and fraternity so highly. After that dissertation, the train left very punctually and we arrived in München, safe and sound, the next morning.

00.03.1923–11.05.1923	Member of the *Oberkommando der SA* (SA High Command) under Göring.
00.03.1923–11.05.1923	*Führer* of the *Stabswache* (headquarters guard), established on 05.03.1923 by Joseph Berchtold and Julius Schreck and initially comprised of eight hand-picked SA men who were tasked with providing personal security to Hitler (who appointed Klintzsch to lead them). They wore regular SA uniform with black ski caps bearing a silver *Totenkopf* (death's head) badge. In May 1923, Klintzsch departed to return to the *Brigade Ehrhardt*, and the

	Stabswache was renamed as the *Stoßtrupp Adolf Hitler*, under the dual leadership of Berchtold and Schreck.
00.04.1923–00.05.1923	*I. Adjutant* to the *Kommandeur der SA*, Hermann Göring.
11.05.1923–Fall 1926	Returned to service under Hermann Ehrhardt, serving as a *Bataillonsführer* in the *Bund-Wiking* (successor organization to the *II. Marine-Brigade*). In his postwar writings, Klintzsch recalled:

> Unfortunately, due to Hitler's influence, the S.A. traveled paths that were diametrically opposed to Ehrhardt's intentions. After Hitler's unilateral breach of the agreement in the spring of 1923, I left his circle as I recognized Hitler's behavior as a blatant betrayal and put myself at Ehrhardt's disposal again....
>
> In August I was transferred to Coburg, from where I was to conquer the then communist-ruled Thüringen for the Wikingbund....
>
> From Coburg I traveled throughout Thüringen, where in a short time three Wikinggaue emerged....
>
> As a result of increasing monetary difficulties—the districts of the Wikingbund had to finance themselves—I requested my release from the brigade in order to assume a civilian position. The answer to my request was a transfer to Kiel, where Ehrhardt negotiated a [civilian] position for me with the Navy, which was to give me the economic basis for my continuing "Bundesarbeit." I worked in the intelligence department and at the same time I was assigned to the management of the Wikingbezirk [in] Schleswig-Holstein and Hamburg.
>
> Finally, I was made director of the "Vereinigten Vaterländischen Verbände" [United Patriotic Associations] of Kiel and the surrounding area.
>
> A sudden twist in my destiny occurred in the fall of 1926, when I crashed my motorbike near Laboe and had to stop working for six months. (Klintzsch, *Lebenslauf* of Spring 1959; Translation: Gary Costello)

c. 01.1927–Summer 1927	Briefly worked as an insurance agent and advertising canvasser.
Summer 1927–Spring 1930	Instructor of sports and sailing at the *Hanseatische Yacht-Schule* (Hanseatic Yachting School) in Neustadt (Holstein). Per his own account, he obtained this position with the assistance of a former naval superior, *Kapitän zur See a. D.* Gustav von Stosch (*Führer der Torpedoboote Flandern* during the war). Of his employment there, he writes:

> After a short time at the yachting school, I was placed in charge of a so-called "Fliegerwache." These were students of the Deutschen Verkehrsfliegerschule (D.V.S.), whose nautical training was carried out by the yachting school. Since these courses lasted longer than the school's normal sailing lessons and, as a result, involved more work, they were not very popular with the instructors. So it was only natural, as the newcomer, that I should be handed this task. For me, this had a fateful consequence, because now my further career path was predestined. Following the nautical course in Neustadt, the instructor accompanied his flight students to a "Deutschen Verkehrsfliegerschule" station to teach theoretical navigation there. So it happened that I accompanied my first

year's students to Warnemünde. In the following to Schleißheim and finally, in autumn 1929, back to Warnemünde. This was the way that my connection to aviation was formed and very soon I realized that aircraft navigation required very different tools and methods than the ship navigation which we taught to the students in Neustadt.

I also familiarized myself with aeronautical radio, which was closely linked to navigation. It was therefore inevitable that one day Herr von Gronau, the director of the "Seefliegerschulen" Warnemünde and List on Sylt, asked me if I would like transfer to the D.V.S. full time. (Klintzsch, *Lebenslauf* of Spring 1959; Translation: Gary Costello)

00.00.1927	Proceedings initiated against Klintzsch by the *Landgericht I* in Berlin for his continued work with the government-banned *Bund-Wiking*. The case was dismissed in 1929, in accordance with the *Reichsamnestiegesetz* (Reich Amnesty Law).
Spring 1930–00.00.193_	Instructor in navigation and aeronautical radio at the *Deutschen Verkehrsfliegerschule* in Warnemünde. Klintzsch continues:

During the winter I gave mainly theoretical lessons. In the summer, however, I was in charge of the practical navigation training of the so-called C-students at the List station.

During my time at the D.V.S. I managed to develop several methods and devices for aircraft navigation, that, some of which, were later used by the Luftwaffe.

Whilst lecturing to specialist groups, I became a name in the world of German aviation, especially since I was one of, at most, half a dozen people who had mastered modern flight navigation practically and theoretically.

I acquired an aeronautical radio license and, in 1932, my first airplane license. (Klintzsch, *Lebenslauf* of Spring 1959; Translation: Gary Costello)

Autumn 1933	Severely ill with septic angina and serious heart complications, resulting in six months of detachment from his aviation duties. Of this period, he writes:

During my illness the "Oberste S.A. Führer" [*sic*, *Stabschef*] Röhm, who had been very taken with me in the past, had asked if I would be interested in joining the "Oberste S.A.-Führung." At the same time, the Reichsluftfahrtministerium [RLM, Reich Ministry of Aviation] was showing a great deal of interest in me due to my specialist knowledge, especially as Herr von Gronau had put in a good word for me. (Klintzsch, *Lebenslauf* of Spring 1959; Translation: Gary Costello)

00.01.1934	At the invitation of the OSAF, met with *SA-Sturmbannführer* Hans Erwin Graf von Spreti-Weilbach ("my old friend … with whom I had been in correspondence for some time" [Klintzsch, *Lebenslauf* of Spring 1959]), *Adjutant* to *SA-Stabschef* Röhm, in München. During his visit to the Bavarian capital, he was contacted by the *Reichsluftfahrtministerium* which, he writes,

intervened and asked the "Oberste SA-Führung" to refrain from employing me, as I was needed. The decision was left up to me, but it was recommended that I take up the position with the R.L.M. with the prospect of returning to the S.A. in the event that flying should offer me no further prospects.

After my return from southern Germany, General [then *Oberstleutnant* and *Abteilungsleiter* of *Abt. LC* in the *R.L.M.*] [Hans] Siburg offered me the position of a Gruppenleiter at the Erprobungsstelle (E-Stelle) der Luftwaffe [Air Force Testing Center] Travemünde (at that time it was still called E-Stelle of the Reichsverbandes der deutschen Luftfahrtindustrie). I accepted immediately… (Klintzsch, *Lebenslauf* of Spring 1959)

01.04.1934	*Gruppenleiter* at the *Erprobungsstelle der Luftwaffe* in Travemünde, succeeded by *Kapitänleutnant* and future *Oberst* Friedrich (Fritz) Schily. The head of the *E-Stelle* was *Fregattenkapitän* (later *Generalleutnant*) Hermann Moll. The *Gruppe* headed by Klintzsch "was responsible for the testing of navigation, radio, image, and maritime equipment." (Klintzsch, *Lebenslauf* of Spring 1959.) He soon grew dissatisfied with the *E-Stelle*, however, as he later recalled:

Political developments within the E-Stelle, as well as the annoying competition between us and the Erprobungsstelle Rechlin very soon soured, what had initially appeared to be fruitful work, so that I looked for other job opportunities.

There was no shortage of work to be had; only the good positions were usually the attached to an obligation to join the party. I wanted to avoid that at all costs. Joining the Wehrmacht did not really appeal to me, since the so-called reactivated officers [*reaktivierten Offiziere*] were treated as second-class and badly rated; and yet I this was the way in which I was led. The reason for this was an encounter with Goering at the "Haus der Flieger" in Berlin … he promised me the world. I allowed myself some time before I made my decision to emigrate to the Wehrmacht.

01.10.1936–31.03.1937	Joined the *Luftwaffe*, assigned for training to a *Flieger-Ersatz-Abteilung* in Quedlinburg.
01.04.1937–01.10.1937	Assigned for training as a *Seeflieger* (naval aviator) to a *Mehrzweckstaffel* (multi-purpose squadron) of a *Seefliegergruppe* on the island of Sylt. There he became lead pilot under *Major* Hans ("Bazi") Geiße, *Staffelkapitän* of 3.(M)/*Küstenfliegergruppe 106* at List/Sylt.
01.10.1937–00.08.1939	*Kommandeur* of the *Navigationsschule der Luftwaffe* in Anklam (Pommern).
00.09.1938–00.09.1938	Attended the *"10. Reichsparteitag der NSDAP"* in Nürnberg as a guest of honor of the *Führer*, later writing:

For me, this year had another special meaning. For some reason Hitler remembered me. He arranged for invitation to the Reichskanzlei, to which I was soon on my way. There I had the opportunity to get to know the inner workings of his court at close range and within 12 hours- that was how long my visit lasted- to take a long hard look into the nature of a man who had lost all standards and was preparing to throw the world into the chaos that reigned within his own core. (Klintzsch, *Lebenslauf* of Spring 1959)

00.08.1939–00.09.1939	*Kommandeur* of *Blindflugschule* [BFS] *Brandis* (at Brandis Waldpolenz). Succeeded by *Oberst* Paul Aue.
00.09.1939–00.09.1939	*Kommandeur* of a *C-Schule* (for pilot's licensing), then assigned as a *Gruppenleiter* in the *Reichsluftfahrtministerium*.
31.10.1939–00.08.1940	Assigned to the *Reichsluftfahrtministerium (Luftwaffeninspektion für Flugnavigation* [L.In. 12]).
00.00.1940	Assigned to the *Seenotdienst der Luftwaffe* (Air-Sea Rescue Service of the German Air Force), initially at Norderney and, after 00.04.1941, at the *Seefliegerhorst Schellingwoude* near Amsterdam.
00.08.1940–00.06.1941	*Kommandeur* of the *Seenotgruppe der Luftwaffe* (air-sea rescue group of the German Air Force). On 16.09.1940, he was injured while serving as *Beobachter* (observer) of Heinkel He 59c DA+AG of *Seenotflugkommando 2* when it crashed on takeoff near Ostende.
Spring 1941	Injured, together with his adjutant and a *Staffelkapitän* (squadron leader) when his plane crashed into the harbor of Cherbourg.
00.00.1941–00.00.1941	*Seenotführer* of *Luftflotte 3*, based at Cabourg in Normandy.
05.06.1941–00.11.1942	*Seenotdienstführer West* (redesignated 01.06.1942 as *Seenotdienstführer 3*), based at Cherbourg.
01.12.1942–31.12.1944	*Inspekteur der Seenotdienst (RLM/Luftwaffeninspektion 16 [Seenotwesen,* L.In.16])/*Generalstab der Luftwaffe* (HQ: Wildpark Werder bei Potsdam until 00.00.1944, then Brandenburg an der Havel). From 23.01.1943, he was also *Chef* of *L.In. 16*. End date per Klintzsch's own account, dated Spring 1959; he adds that the inspectorate was dissolved on the same date. Henry L. deZeng IV and Douglas G. Stankey, *Luftwaffe Officer Career Summaries, Section G-K*, give 29.08.1944. In 1959, he wrote of this assignment:

My new position gave me a chance to see many parts of Europe. Frequent inspection trips took me to the Balkans, Crimea, the island of Crete, Italy, North Africa, Russia, Finland, and Scandinavia. My northern-most point I visited was Hammerfest, the southernmost Tripoli. Up until 1943, my inspection activity was very fertile. I was so obsessed with my job and so often absent from my office that my long-awaited promotion was forgotten by both me and my superior, General Seidel. This was remedied in near secrecy in the Spring of 1944.

By 1944 one was forced to improvise continuously due to massive cutbacks. I had to relocate my office and went first to Brandenburg a.d.H. [an der Havel]. Later I moved to Dresden, where we found a nice and reasonably safe accommodation in Schloß Nöthnitz near Bannewitz. For all intents and purposes, we were paralyzed, as communications could only be maintained with great difficulty. In Nöthnitz I was often visited by my wife and the two youngest children, who had been living with my mother in Lübbenau since the end of 1943. My job as an Inspekteur ended on 31 December 1944. On this day the L.In.16 was disbanded. (Klintzsch, *Lebenslauf* of Spring 1959)

00.01.1945–00.02.1945	Hospitalized, due to myocardial damage, in the *Luftwaffenlazarett Riesa* (in *Luftgaukommando IV*, Dresden) where he was treated with the heart stimulant strophanthin.
00.02.1945	After discharge from hospital, ordered to report to *Frontfliegersammelgruppe Quedlinburg*.
00.02.1945	Transferred to a the *Kurlazarett* (spa hospital) in Bad Liebenstein (Thüringen). Fearing capture by the advancing U.S. Army, he requested leave to be with his family in Fürth.
01.03.1945–00.04.1945	*Fliegerführer 6 (Luftflotte 6)*. Succeeded *Oberst* Karl Stockmann. Start date for assignment per Michael Holm, "The Luftwaffe, 1933–45" (www.ww2.dk/air/hq/flfu6.htm). However, in his own account (1959), he writes:

On 1 April 1945 I was ordered to join Luftflotte 6, which was at that time in Treuenbrietzen, allegedly there I was to become the Führer of those units of the Luftflotte operating over the Baltic. A little bird whispered that this was a necessary step on my way to becoming a general. (Klintzsch, *Lebenslauf* of 1959)

Fliegerführer 6 comprised *Seeaufklärungsgruppe 126*, *Bordfliegergruppe 196*, and *Seenotgruppe 60*. Succeeded *Oberst* Karl Stockmann. Formed at Bad Ahlbeck on 26.11.1944, it remained headquartered there until 00.04.1945, when it was transferred to Värlöse (Denmark). During Klintzsch's tenure, it was subordinated to *Luftwaffenkommando Ostpreußen* (24.01.1945–21.04.1945), then to *Luftwaffenkommando Nordost* (21.04.1945–08.05.1945).

POSTWAR CAPTIVITY & ACTIVITIES:

00.04.1945–00.00.1948	Having sent his family to the village of Vach near Fürth, captured by American troops at the *Flugplatz* in Fürth, which had recently been evacuated, then transported to a prisoner collection point at the reception camp near Würzburg before being moved with other officers to Böhl-Iggelheim near Worms. Fourteen years later, he wrote of his years of captivity and its aftermath:

The accommodation was catastrophic, supplies, especially for the sick and wounded, were completely inadequate. I spent whole nights standing in the pouring rain without a roof over my head. The ground was literally knee-deep in mud. I was therefore very happy when, a few days later, a transport for officers left for the south of France. We were crammed together in cattle cars, but at least it was warm and dry. Traveling and suffering companion in my cattle car was pastor Christoph Duncker from Württemberg, whom I had already got to know and learned to appreciate in the camp at Böhl. In the new camp, he became my faithful friend and minister who changed my life.

The train rolled down the Rhône Valley and stopped near Marseille. From there we were taken to camp 404, which became notorious as an American hunger camp.

In Summer 1945 I could have been released from here. But I had set my mind not to being released until the Americans had restored me to the physical condition that I was in before I was imprisoned. This turned out to be a grave mistake. In September there was a release ban for colonels, with this I was now trapped.

We really starved in the camp. This was not the significance and meaning of the time and it is not worth remembering or mentioning it for that reason. More important than that in Camp 404 I experienced my complete inner change to the Christian faith. I joined a small circle of men centered around Father Duncker and thus laid the foundation for my occupation, indeed for my existence after my release from captivity. I was able to leave the camp sooner than expected as it was suspected that I had contracted TB. That made my transfer to a German hospital necessary. This was to be in Idstein am Taunus.

Later I was transferred to the TB hospital in Falkenstein am Taunus. Here again another miracle, the like of which I had I had already experienced in the camp, occurred; my illness turned out to be a misdiagnosis. I had escaped the hell that was camp 404.

In Falkenstein I had the first meeting with my wife and later with the children. The family had gathered in Vach. Only Fritz was missing. We finally learned that he was a prisoner of war of the English in Egypt. After much waiting, I was finally released on 20 April 1946. Together with my wife and two children I travelled to Vach via Frankfurt. Here, after months of living in substandard conditions, my family had been given something that could be called an apartment. Four or five of us lived in two small, damp rooms, sharing the fate of 99% of the population as a totally defeated nation. At the unemployment office, where I felt the communist hatred for the officer class, I was given a job as a construction worker. With a fabulous building contractor, Mr. Steininger from Vach, I spent many a sweaty month. But I was paid, and I received increased food rations.

I later managed to get a job in a toy factory as a painter. Fridthjof worked in arts and crafts, which brought a lot of money back then. He contributed significantly to the maintenance of the family.

In 1948, on Maundy Thursday (29 March), Fritz surprisingly returned from his African captivity. So the whole family was together once more. (Klintzsch, *Lebenslauf* of Spring 1959)

00.00.1948–00.02.1949	Having reconnected with Father Duncker, found employment with the Württemberg *Taunuskirche*, where he passed a brief religion teacher training course. He then worked as a *Religionshilfslehrer* (assistant teacher of religion) in Weiler a. d. Rems (Baden-Württemberg).
00.02.1949–Summer 1951	Completed an advanced religion teacher training course, then held a teaching position in Schorndorf bei Stuttgart until, as he later wrote:

… in the summer of 1951, I collapsed due to complete physical exhaustion. I was no longer able to teach and so I felt compelled to part from the work I had become so fond of. I was dismissed from the church and as at the beginning of our marriage was left with nothing.… A few months before, the so-called 131 law had been passed, which allowed former professional soldiers to claim a pension. So it was that without interruption to my monthly income, I received, albeit from another source, a salary which, together with the payments from the health insurance exceeded my previous income.

Since it was not possible to restore my health to full capacity, I retired in the spring of 1952. Slowly, my desperate condition improved. In order not to remain idle, I tried giving tutoring. Soon I found that I was successful with it. Mathematics, Latin, English, French and German were my main subjects. I was able to quickly refresh my school knowledge and considerably expand it. (Klintzsch, *Lebenslauf* of Spring 1959)

08.11.1955	Moved with his family to Hamburg, where he again worked as a tutor.
00.00.1956	Fell ill with acute kidney disease, which, per his account, "nearly cost me my life."

Decorations & Awards:

31.12.1944 — *Kriegsorden des Deutschen Kreuzes in Silber* as *Oberst* and *Inspekteur der Seenotdienst* (L.In.16)/*Generalstab der Luftwaffe*. Per his own account, written in Spring 1959:

My activity as an Inspekteur ended on 31 December 1944. On this day the L.In.16 was dissolved. General Czech brought me the farewell, the German Cross in Silver. [This is a reference to *Generalleutnant* Hans-Armin Czech—*General des Seewesens der Luftwaffe*, 03.03.1944–04.05.1945.]

00.03.1918	*1914 Eisernes Kreuz I. Klasse*
00.00.1917 (?)	*1914 Eisernes Kreuz II. Klasse*
00.00.194_	*Kriegsverdienstkreuz I. Klasse mit Schwertern*
00.00.194_	*Kriegsverdienstkreuz II. Klasse mit Schwertern*
c. 1921	*Schlesisches Bewährungsabzeichen (Schlesischer Adlerorden) 2. Stufe*
c. 1939	*Medaille zur Erinnerung an den 1. Oktober 1938*
c. 1938	*Medaille zur Erinnerung an den 13. März 1938*
c. 1934	*Ehrenkreuz des Weltkrieges 1914-1918 mit Schwertern*
00.10.1932 (?)	*Coburger Ehrenzeichen der NSDAP*

Notes:

* Parents:
  - Father: Johannes Paul Klintzsch (*00.00.1861, †14.09.1920), a Protestant *Oberpfarrer* (senior pastor).
  - Mother: Johanna Dorothea Klintzsch, *née* Schmidtgen.
* Engaged in Eisenach (Thüringen), 18.03.1923, and married on 08.09.1923 to Marie Emilie Hildegard Friedrichs (*05.01.1906, †24.07.1992). His bride was the sister of *Fähnrich zur See* Friedrichs, with whom he had served in the *Sturmkompanie* of the *Ehrhardt Brigade*. Four children resulted from this marriage— three sons (Fridthjof Ehrhardt, *01.11.1925 [with *Korvettenkapitan* Ehrhardt as godfather], who became an *Oberstarzt* a. D. [dentist] of the *Bundeswehr* and was still living as of 01.11.2015; Friedrich-Wilhelm ["Fritz"], *30.03.1927; and Heidjer, *00.09.1938, who is buried under the same gravestone as his parents) and one daughter (Heidrun, *00.06.1941).

Sources:

Campbell, Bruce: *The SA Generals and the Rise of Nazism*. University Press of Kentucky, 1998.

DeZeng, Henry L. IV and Douglas G. Stankey, *Luftwaffe Officer Career Summaries, Section G-K* at www.ww2.dk/LwOffz%20G-K%202017.pdf, 2020.

Flood, Charles Bracelen: *Hitler: The Path to Power*. Houghton Mifflin Company, 1989.

Gebhardt, Cord: *Der Fall des Erzberger-Mörders Heinrich Tillessen: Ein Beitrag zur Justizgeschichte nach 1945*. Mohr Siebeck, 1995.

Klintzsch, Hans Ulrich: *Lebenslauf* dated Spring 1959, online at http://vikimy.com/l-de/Diskussion:Hans_Ulrich_Klintzsch

Landesarchiv Baden-Württemberg (Abteilung Staatsarchiv Freiburg): F 179/4 Nr. 110. Documents from the file on the investigation (by the *Badischen Landgericht Offenburg, Amtsgericht Oberkirch*) of Hans Ulrich Klintzsch's suspected involvement in the assassination of Matthias Erzberger, 1921.

Miller, Michael D. and Andreas Schulz: *Leaders of the Storm Troops, Volume 1* (1st Edition). Helion & Co., 2015.

Schuster, Peter: *Oberländer: Freikorpskämpfer, Putschisten, NS-Aktivisten, Mitläufer, Geistliche und Widerständler aus dem Freikorps Oberland und dem Bund Oberland. Personalien und Dokumente – Ein Nachschlagewerk*. Nation & Wissen Verlag, 2018.

Siemens, Daniel: *Stormtroopers: A New History of Hitler's Brownshirts*. Yale University Press, 2017.

Steiner, John M.: *Power Politics and Social Change in National Socialist Germany: A Process of Escalation into Mass Destruction*. Moulton Publishers/Humanities Press, 1976.

Leutnant zur See Klintzsch as an officer of *II. Marine-Brigade* (*Marine-Brigade Ehrhardt*), c. 1920.

Mugshots of Hans Ulrich Klintzsch, taken following his arrest by Bavarian police in September 1921. (Landesarchiv Baden-Württemberg)

Berlin, March 1920: *Korvettenkapitän* Hermann Ehrhardt and men of his *II. Marine-Brigade* during the "*Kapp-Putsch*."

Deutschlands erste S.A.
Turn- und Sportabteilung 1921

Name	Geburtszeit	Geburtsort	Eigenhändige Unterschrift	Name	Geburtszeit	Geburtsort	Eigenhändige Unterschrift
Briemann, Wilh. jr.*	3.3.1899	München		Maurice, Emil*	19.1.1897	Westermoor	
Burkhardt, Hugo	1.4.1902	München		Netzer, Paul	29.6.1903	München	
Dietenhauser, Benno	18.9.1904	Wasserburg a. Inn		Pfeiffer, Ernst*	26.11.1893	München	
Dietenhauser, Hans	1.1.1903	Wasserburg a. Inn		Schiller, Rudolf	25.1.1906	München	
Fischer, Karl	14.9.1904	München		Schmid, Gustav	3.6.1904	München	
Gutensohn, Dr. Wilhelm	21.1.1905	München		Schmitt, Karl*	23.1.1895	Bamberg	
Held, Wilhelm	10.8.1900	München		Walti, Ludwig*	23.7.1895	München	
Huber, Josef*	20.3.1891	Siberbach, Obb.		Wagner, Ernst	29.9.1902	München	
Kießling, Heinz	15.6.1903	München		Wagner, Pius	19.11.1903	München	
Klintzsch, Hans Ulrich*	4.11.1898	Lübbenau (Spreewald)		Weiß, Alois	14.10.1906	München	
Küpfer, Adam	11.2.1903	München		Wenng, Christian*	27.3.1892	München	
Langbein, Gerrit	30.9.1903	Coburg		Winkler, Johann	4.11.1900	München	
Lenz, Hans	31.8.1905	Deggendorf					

* Kriegsbeschädigter * Kriegsteilnehmer

Hans Ulrich Klintzsch's name appears in a listing of the first members of the NSDAP's *"Turn- und Sportabteilung,"* forerunner of the SA, from a Party publication.

Above: Hans Ulrich Klintzsch as *Führer* of Hitler's *Stabswache*, Spring 1923. (Heinrich Hoffmann, *Das Braune Heer. 100 Bilddokumente: Leben, Kampf und Sieg der SA und SS,* 1932)

Opposite below: SA-Führer Klintzsch (the tall figure directly directly beneath the swastika flag) stands among other Nazi attendees of the "*3. Deutscher Tag*" in Coburg (14.–15.10.1922).

Hermann Wilhelm Göring
Oberster SA-Führer (01.03.1923-09.11.1923)

*   12.01.1893 at the Sanatorium Marienbad bei Rosenheim/Regierungsbezirk Oberbayern/Bayern.

†   15.10.1946 in Cell #5, Nürnberg Prison at approximately 2245 hours, swallowing a cyanide capsule he had possibly concealed since his arrest.

In 1978, the West German newspaper *Welt am Sonntag* published Göring's suicide note to his wife. It included the following line: "Death by shooting I would have accepted at any time. But the Reichsmarschall of Germany cannot allow himself to be hanged" (*The New York Times*, 21.02.1978). In a statement concerning Göring's final act, Supreme Court Justice Robert H. Jackson, chief United States prosecutor at the Nürnberg Trials, declared:

… When he took his own life, he killed the myth of Nazi bravery and stoicism and deep conviction.… The real significance of this event is its effect on Germany.… If Goering had been made of the stuff that could walk to the gallows voicing some patriotic sentiment such as our Nathan Hale's regret that he had but one life to give to his country, he might well have become a German martyr-hero. The end comes, from the viewpoint of his hero worshipers, as anti-climactic as a burlesque after a Wagnerian overture. Goering could not keep up the part when it began to hurt. The founder of the concentration camps, where death was handed out to millions, could not face the gallows himself. His end betrayed the weakness of his whole life—cunning and crafty, always outwitting somebody, bullying and cowardly. (Associated Press, "Goering Ends 'Martyr Myth,' Jackson Says", 17.10.1946)

In his prison cell on 03.01.1946, after hearing Albert Speer's claim to the court of having plotted to assassinate Hitler by way of poison gas in the *Führerbunker*, a furious Göring shared his thoughts with the prison psychiatrist, Dr. Gustave M. Gilbert:

Tonight Goering looked tired and depressed. "Today was a bad day," he said. "Damn that stupid fool, Speer! Did you see how he disgraced himself in court today? Gott im Himmel! Donnerwetter nochmal! How could he stoop so low as to do such a rotten thing to save his lousy neck! I nearly died with shame! To think that Germans will be so rotten to prolong this filthy life—to put bluntly—to piss in front and crap behind a little longer! Herrgott, Donnerwetter! Do you think I give that much of a damn about this lousy life?" He faced me squarely with blazing eyes. "For myself, I don't give a damn if I get executed, or drown, or crash in a plane, or drink myself to death! But there is still a matter of honor in this damn life! Assassination attempt on Hitler! Ugh! Gott im Himmel!! I could have sunk through the floor!" (Gilbert, *Nuremberg Diary*, pp. 102-103)

NSDAP-Nr.:	23 (Joined 00.12.1922 with unknown Party Nr.; Party banned, 09.11.1923-16.02.1925; Later stricken from the membership rolls during his exile in Italy and Sweden, then readmitted with Nr. 23 on 01.04.1928).

Promotions:

13.05.1911	*Fähnrich*
20.01.1914	*Leutnant (mit Patent vom 22.06.1912)*
18.08.1916	*Oberleutnant*
08.06.1920	*Charakter als Hauptmann (mit Wirkung vom 11.03.1920)*
01.03.1923–09.11.1923	*Oberster SA-Führer*
18.12.1931	*SA-Gruppenführer (NSFK) (per SA-Führerbefehl Nr. 6, 18.12.1931)*
01.01.1933	*SA-Obergruppenführer*
25.03.1933	*DLV-Minister*
05.05.1933–28.04.1945	*Reichsminister der Luftfahrt*
30.08.1933	*Charakter als General der Infanterie (mit RDA vom 01.10.1931)*

The following is excerpted from the 31.08.1933 official notice of appointment by *Reichspräsident* von Hindenburg:

> With effect as per yesterday's date, the Reich President has ... conferred upon the Prussian Ministerpräsident, former Hauptmann Göring, Knight of the Pour le mérite, the rank of General der Infanterie in recognition of his extraordinary merits both in war and peace, by virtue of which he is entitled to wear the uniform of the Reich Army. (Dr. Max Domarus, ed., Hitler. *Speeches and Proclamations, 1932–1945: The Years 1932–1934*, p. 352)

14.09.1933	*General der Landespolizei*
21.05.1935	*General der Flieger*
20.04.1936	*Generaloberst (mit RDA vom 01.04.1936)*
04.02.1938	*Generalfeldmarschall*
19.07.1940–28.04.1945	*Reichsmarschall des Großdeutschen Reiches*

Career:

00.00.1893–00.00.1896	Lived in Fürth with a friend of his mother, Erna Graf. His parents were in the Caribbean during this period as Herr Göring was serving as German *Generalkonsul* in Haiti.
00.00.1896–00.00.1900	Lived in Berlin-Friedenau with his parents.
00.00.1900–00.00.1904	*Volksschule* in Fürth.
00.00.1904–00.00.1905	*Gymnasium* in Ansbach.
00.00.1905–00.00.1909	*Kadettenanstalt* in Karlsruhe.
00.00.1909–20.01.1914	*Haupt-Kadettenanstalt Groß-Lichterfelde*, where, in the spring of 1911, he passed his *Fähnrich* (ensign) examination with the grade *summa cum laude*. Peter Kilduff writes:

> ... he was remarkably successful at Gross Lichterfelde. A sampling of his final grades shows he did "quite good" in English, French and Latin, "good" in map reading, "very good" in German, history, math and physics, and "excellent" in geography. (Kilduff, *Hermann Göring: Fighter Ace*, p. 28)

13.10.1910–26.10.1910	Hospitalized with tonsillitis in the infirmary of the *Haupt-Kadettenanstalt Groß-Lichterfelde*.
20.01.1914–19.08.1914	Entered service, assigned as *Zugführer* (platoon leader) and *Kompanie-Offizier* to *8. Kompanie/4. Badische Infanterie-Regiment "Prinz Wilhelm" Nr. 112* (Mühlhausen [Fr.: Mulhouse]/Elsaß, approximately one mile from the French border). Very early on, the adventuresome young lieutenant demonstrated impulsivity and daring. Kurt Singer writes of Göring's first few days of war:

> Young Göring was at once sent off on patrol at the frontier. It was during a reconnaissance to determine the position in a section of the Vosges that the first shot was fired.
>
> Göring was before Mülhausen. In the evening before the fight for the town he went forward with his company in an armoured train from the right bank of the Rhine towards Mülhausen. The company commander wanted scouts to reconnoitre the position in the town. He ordered Göring to reconnoitre the position with a few men and come back as soon as possible, as the armoured train, owing to its heavy water consumption, had to steam back soon.
>
> Göring drove through the garrison town, where, as it happened, he had once stayed as a cadet, and was told by the people there that an enemy's dragoon patrol had occupied the town hall.
>
> Göring scented a quarry. All his promises to go back quickly were forgotten. With his men he stormed the town hall; but the crowd that gathered hindered him from taking the Frenchmen prisoner. Göring had to satisfy himself with tearing down the French proclamations on the house walls. Then he followed up the patrol, left the armoured train still farther away, got behind Mülhausen, came upon the French beyond Dornach, and once opened fire on them. But this outpost engagement could not stop the French from occupying the town in the evening.
>
> Göring withdrew, found the armoured train was no longer there, but was lucky enough to come up with it when it came out next time. He brought with him four captured dragoon horses.
>
> So Göring had had his first fight, and the young lieutenant was satisfied with himself.
>
> Next day came the fight at Mühlhausen. Göring was under the divisional commander and in charge of patrols; and was ordered to form a cycle patrol from his company. The patrol started out early in the morning…. "Village after village, Sausheim, Illzach, and others were stormed amid cheers," writes Martin Sommerfeldt, Göring's biographer. "This fresh, merry war makes the Göring patrol foolhardy." The young man was drunk with the glory of war. Like one possessed he charged into Mühlhausen. The French general command stood in the midst of a large body of men on a small bridge near the new barracks of the Riflemen; General Pau in command had his young general staff officers around him….
>
> This general must be made a prisoner. But the officers had barely caught site of the cyclist troops when they opened fire.

The only thing now was flight. In a panic the patrol came out of the town and barely got away from the town and their pursuers; racing furiously they reached their regiment, glad to have saved their lives.

That same afternoon Göring's patrol was in the church town of the village of Illzach, which at the time was half in German, half in French hands. Göring had been entrusted with sketching in on the general staff map the movements of the 15th Army Corps from the north....

As German artillery ended by knocking Illzach to pieces, the group fled so as not to be killed by their own side. With some French prisoners they left the ruined village. Information as to troop transports had been got; the task was completed. (Singer, *Göring: Germany's Most Dangerous Man*, pp. 26-28)

20.08.1914–23.09.1914	*Bataillons-Adjutant* of *II. Bataillon/4. Badische Infanterie-Regiment "Prinz Wilhelm" Nr. 112*.
23.09.1914	Fell ill with rheumatic fever in Thiancourt, then hospitalized in the following medical facilities:

23.09.1914: *Feldlazarett Thiancourt*
23.09.1914–24.09.1914: *Festungslazarett Haushaltungsschule Metz-Montigny*
24.09.1914–12.10.1914: *Klinischen Krankenhaus Freiburg in Baden*

While hospitalized, he was visited by a comrade from his regiment, *Leutnant* Bruno Lörzer, who was then receiving advanced flight training with *Flieger-Ersatz-Abteilung 3* in Darmstadt. Lörzer convinced him to volunteer for the flying service and serve as his observer in a two-seat aircraft. Kurt Singer continues:

Headquarters refused his application. Then Göring took things into his own hands, took his seat without leave in Lörzer's plane, and left Freiburg with him. Göring thus appointed himself an airman. The authorities were naturally greatly annoyed at the desertion: the young lieutenant undoubtedly deserved punishment. But then these authorities said no more, for Göring was at the front, and, moreover, airmen in the war did not usually grow old... (Singer, *Göring: Germany's Most Dangerous Man*, pp. 29-30)

13.10.1914–27.10.1914	Training as *Beobachter* (observer) with *Flieger-Ersatz-Abteilung 3* (FEA 3) in Darmstadt.
28.10.1914–29.06.1915	Assigned as *Flugzeugbeobachter* (aerial observer) of *Leutnant* Lörzer in *Feldflieger-Abteilung 25* (FFA 25) at Stenay Airfield. In March 1915, he was decorated with the Iron Cross First Class and granted a period of home leave for actions that prevented the French from bombarding the headquarters of *Generalleutnant* Kronprinz Wilhelm (commanding *Heeresgruppe Deutscher Kronprinz*). The official report of this action read as follows:

On the day of the bombardment Lörzer and Göring circle round at several kilometres behind the enemy's lines. Göring watches the ranging of the batteries and directs the fire by the systematic use of the Verey [flare] pistol. At the same time he makes a careful sketch of where the fire falls. With this sketch he glides back, and Göring throws down the pouch with the report so well that from a height of 600 metres it falls right on the battery's observation post. For another hour he directs the fire before the attack. (Singer, *Göring: Germany's Most Dangerous Man*, p. 32)

Kurt Singer continues:

When he came back [from leave] a surprise was awaiting him: the Crown Prince had learned through whose help the headquarters had been protected, and sent for Göring and Lörzer to come to Stenay. He gave them an audience and congratulated them. At headquarters Göring became personally known to the Hohenzollern prince who later on was to be highly useful to him… (Singer, *Göring: Germany's Most Dangerous Man*, p. 34)

01.07.1915–14.09.1915	Pilot training at *Fliegerschule Freiburg*.
15.09.1915–00.00.191_	Assigned to the *Armeeflugpark* of 5. *Armee*.
15.09.1915–08.07.1916	Assigned as a pilot to *Feldflieger-Abteilung 25*. He flew his first mission as a fighter pilot on 03.10.1915.
09.07.1916–04.08.1916	Attached as a pilot to *Artillerieflieger-Abteilung 203* (under *3. Armee*).
04.08.1916–04.09.1916	Returned to duty with *Feldflieger-Abteilung 25*.
06.09.1916–27.09.1916	Attached to *Kampfstaffel Metz* (*Kampfeinsitzer Kommando* [Kek, single-seat fighter unit] *Metz*).
28.09.1916–27.09.1916	Assigned as pilot to *Jagdstaffel 7* (Jasta 7).
20.10.1916–21.12.1916	Pilot with *Jagdstaffel 5* (Jasta 5) on the Somme.
02.11.1916	While attacking a British Handley-Page bomber, he was severely wounded in the right hip and grazed on the right knuckles by machine-gun fire from a flight of Sopwith Camels over Combles. He was subsequently hospitalized in the following:

02.11.1916–12.11.1916: *Feldlazarett 3/XV. Armee-Korps*
15.11.1916–30.11.1916: *Etappen-Lazarett 6* in Valenciennes
03.12.1916–11.12.1916: *Reservelazarett I* in Bochum
19.12.1916–15.01.1917: *Reservelazarett G* in München

22.12.1916–14.02.1917	Assigned for training to *Fliegerersatz-Abteilung 10* in Böblingen/Württemberg.
15.02.1917–16.05.1917	Pilot with *Jagdstaffel 26* (*Jasta* 26), based in Mühlhausen and commanded by Bruno Lörzer.

Hermann Göring's Aerial Victories, 1915-1918

Nr.	Date & Time	Enemy Aircraft Type & Unit	Location
-	03.06.1915	Unknown and unconfirmed	Stenay
1	16.11.1915	Maurice Farman	Tahure
2	14.03.1916	Caudron G.IV bomber	Forced down and captured intact southeast of Haumont Forest
3	30.07.1916	Caudron G.IV bomber of *Escadrille* C 10 (Pilot: Sergent Girard-Varet)	Mamey, 30 km southwest of Metz
4	23.04.1917, 1720	F.E.2b of 18 Sqn (Pilot: 2Lt. George B. Bate)	Northeast of Arras
5	28.04.1917, 1830	Sopwith 1½ Strutter of Sop 27 Esc	South of St. Quentin
6	29.04.1917, 1945	Nieuport XVII of 6(N) Sqn (Pilot: Sub-Lt. Albert H. V. Fletcher)	Ramicourt
7	10.05.1917, 1505	Airco D.H.4 of 55 Sqn	Northeast of Le Pavé
8	08.06.1917, 0730	Nieuport 23 of 1 Sqn (Pilot: 2Lt. Frank D. Slee)	Near Moorslede
9	16.07.1917, 2005	SE5 of 56 Sqn (Pilot: 2Lt. Robert G. Jardine)	Northeast of Ypres
10	24.07.1917, 2045	Sopwith Triplane of the Royal Naval Air Service (Pilot: Flight Sub-Lt. Theodore C. May)	South of Passchendaele
11	05.08.1917, 2015	Sopwith F.1 Camel of 70 Sqn (Pilot: Lt. Gilbert Budden)	Northeast of Ypres
12	25.08.1917, 0845	Sopwith Camel of 70 Sqn (Pilot: 2Lt. Orlando C. Brideman)	Southwest of Ypres
13	03.09.1917, 1955	Airco D.H.4 (probably of 57 Sqn)	North of Lampemisse
14	21.09.1917, 0905	Bristol BF2B (two-seater, flown by Lt. R. L. Curtis [fifteen victories] and Lt. D. P Fitzgerald-Uniacke [thirteen victories] of 48 Sqn	
15	21.10.1917, 1545	S.E.5 of 84 Sqn (Pilot: 2Lt. Arthur E. Hempel)	Linselles
16	07.11.1917, 0915	Airco D.H.5 of 32 Sqn	Northwest of Poelcapelle
17	21.02.1918, 1000	S.E.5a of 60 Sqn (Pilot: 2Lt. George B. Craig)	Ledeghem
18	07.04.1918, 1250	R.E.8 of 42 Sqn (Pilot: 2Lt. Harry W. Collier)	Southwest of Merville
19	05.06.1918, 1000	A.R.1? (No French loss report for that type reported; Possibly a Bréguet 14 B2)	North of Villers Cotterets
20	09.06.1918, 0845	SPAD S.VII of *Escadrille* Spa 94 (Pilot: *Caporal* Pierre Chan)	South of Coroy
21	17.06.1918, 0830	SPAD of *Escadrille* Spa 93	Ambleny
22	18.07.1918, 0815	SPAD E	Bandry Wood

17.05.1917–06.07.1918 *Führer* of *Jagdstaffel 27* (*Jasta 27*) in Ypres, flying two *Fokker D VII*s (Nr. 278/18 and 324/18). Succeeded by Lothar von Richthofen.

07.07.1918–30.07.1919 *Kommandeur* of *Jagdgeschwader "Freiherr von Richthofen Nr. 1"* (JG 1), appointed via *Befehl des Kommanderenden Generals der Luftstreitkräfte Nr. 178 654 vom 7. Juli 1918*. Succeeded *Hauptmann* Wilhelm ("Willi") Reinhard, who had been killed in the crash of his aircraft on 03.07.1918 after twenty aerial victories. In a letter to his mother, he wrote:

15 July 1918. Staff quarters, Richthofen's squadron. And now to the main business: I have been appointed commander of Baron von Richthofen's fighter squadron and had to go there at once. It is an honorable but at the same time a heavy task to be the great Richthofen's successor in leading

his fighter squadron. God grant that I may duly carry out the hard task. (Kurt Singer, *Göring: Germany's Most Dangerous Man*, p. 45)

In his book *Richthofen Flieger* (1930), one of Göring's former pilots, *Leutnant a. D.* Richard Wenzl (twelve aerial victories), wrote:

Our new commander had arrived during our last days in Beugneux, Oblt. Göring, the former leader of Jasta 27. If there had been some friction now and then during Reinhard's time, Göring understood how to make himself at home in the Geschwader in short order. He was a good comrade to us to the last and a good commander, who upheld the traditions of the Geschwader. (Translation in Norman Franks & Greg VanWyngarden, *Fokker D VII Aces of World War I, Part 1*, p. 15)

Göring flew two D.VIIs during this period: D.VII (F) 294/18 and D.VII (F) 5128/18.

26.07.1918–22.08.1918	On leave.
22.08.1918–00.00.1918	Hospitalized at the *Kriegslazarett Maresolm Deinse* due to tonsillitis.
00.11.1918	In violation of Armistice terms, led *Jagdgeschwader 1* to Darmstadt/Hessen, then formally demobilized the unit at a paper factory in Aschaffenburg. In a local church, he delivered a speech to his men. The following is an excerpt:

The armed struggle is resolved. It will start, that we are determined: the new struggle of principles, morals, character. We have still a long, hard road to travel. Our road is dark, comrades. But our faith shall be our light. We can be proud over what we have carried out, that we did it all and to the last. We must will a new struggle to begin. We must always have it in our thoughts. (Kurt Singer, *Göring: Germany's Most Dangerous Man*, p. 49)

He was later to write of the fall of the German Reich and the country's descent into revolutionary violence:

… And so, on the 9th November, 1918, that vile rising of mutineers took place and Marxist dominance was established. On the same day there began for the poor tormented German people that period of history that may be described as "The Period of German Shame and Tribulation." From the steps of the Reichstag, Scheidemann, a prominent leader of the Social Democrats, proclaimed "Today the German people is victorious all along the line." And at that very moment the German people plunged from proud heights into the abyss. It was not the people which was "victorious" on that day, for all the best elements of the people still stood on all fronts, ready to give their last drop of blood in defence of their country. Only those traitors were victorious for whom the very idea of a Fatherland was non-existent. Those cowards who had deserted from the front were victorious, that human scum that always makes its appearance in times of stress. It was Marxism that was victorious. But wherever Marxism is victorious, at the same moment a nation collapses. Where

Communism raises its head, a people is destroyed... (Göring, *Germany Reborn* [translation of *Aufbau einer Nation*, 1934], pp. 24-25)

... [O]ne will ... be amazed to see what a high percentage of the Social Democratic leaders and agitators were Jews. But now in the days of the post-War rising these Jewish leaders sprouted from the ground like poisonous fungi. Wherever soldiers' councils were formed Jews were the leaders, those very same Jews who had not been seen out at the front but had been employed in the supply departments at the base or had filled indispensable official and military posts at home. In the streets the mob raged. Soldiers had their badges and shoulder-straps torn off. The flag, which for decades had symbolized the greatness of the Reich, was trampled in the mud. On all buildings fluttered the red flag of rebellion; everywhere there was disorder and dissolution. (Göring, *Germany Reborn* [translation of *Aufbau einer Nation*, 1934], pp. 27-28)

In his opening testimony before the International Military Tribunal at Nürnberg on 13.03.1946, Göring stated:

After the collapse in the first World War, I had to demobilize my squadron. I rejected the invitation to enter the Reichswehr because from the very beginning I was opposed in every way to the republic which had come to power through the revolution; I could not bring it into harmony with my convictions. (*Trial of the Major War Criminals Before the International Military Tribunal Nuremberg, 14 November 1945 to 1 October 1946, Volume IX*)

00.12.1918–00.00.1919	Lived in Berlin with fellow air ace Ernst Udet, then with his widowed mother in München.
00.04.1919–00.00.1919	Invited by the *Fokker-Flugzeugwerke* to Denmark to demonstrate their latest aircraft, agreeing on the condition that he be allowed to keep the plane as payment. He was then employed by *Fokker* as a test pilot and aviation advisor, also staging aerobatic displays together with four other veterans of the *"Richthofen" Geschwader*.
Summer 1919	Flew from Denmark to Sweden, selling his *Fokker* at Malmstät. After receiving his license to fly passenger aircraft in Sweden on 02.08.1919, he served as a commercial pilot and flight chief for the fledgling Swedish airline *Firma Svenska Lufttravik AB*, co-owned by Karl Lignell, in Stockholm. He then worked as an aerial chauffeur to wealthy Swedes during this period and received his Swedish license as a passenger aircraft pilot.
13.02.1920	In a letter from Stockholm to Germany, requested demobilization from the Army at the rank of *Hauptmann*, thus forfeiting his pension and disability rights. His application was approved on 08.06.1920, with retroactive effect from 11.03.1920.
Summer 1921	Returned to Germany, eventually buying a villa at *Nr. 30 Döbereinerstraße* in München-Obermenzing which was later seized by Bavarian authorities in the wake of the abortive *München-Putsch*.
00.00.1922–00.11.1923	Sporadic studies in philosophy, political science, and history at the University of München. There, together with Rudolf Hess, he

	attended lectures by the nationalist historian Alexander von Müller, brother-in-law of NSDAP-cofounder Gottfried Feder. He was also employed as a salesman of aircraft equipment during this period.
00.12.1922	Joined the NSDAP. In his courtroom testimony of 13.03.1946, he spoke of how he had come to make this decision:

Then one day, on a Sunday in November or October of 1922, the demand having been made again by the Entente for the extradition of our military leaders, at a protest demonstration in Munich—I went to this protest demonstration as a spectator, without having any connection with it. Various speakers from parties and organizations spoke there. At the end Hitler, too, was called for. I had heard his name once before briefly and wanted to hear what he had to say. He declined to speak, and it was pure coincidence that I stood nearby and heard the reasons for his refusal. He did not want to disturb the unanimity of the demonstration; he could not see himself speaking, as he put it, to these tame, bourgeois pirates. He considered it senseless to launch protests with no weight behind them. This made a deep impression on me; I was of, the same opinion.

I inquired and found that on the following Monday evening I could hear Hitler speak, as he held a meeting every Monday evening. I went there, and there Hitler spoke in connection with that demonstration, about Versailles, the treaty of Versailles, and the repudiation of Versailles.

He said that such empty protests as that of Sunday had no sense at all— one would just pass on from it to the agenda—that a protest is successful only if backed by power to give it weight. Until Germany had become strong, this kind of thing was of no purpose.

This conviction was spoken word for word as if from my own soul. On one of the following days, I went to the office of the NSDAP. At that time, I knew nothing of the program of the NSDAP, and nothing further than that it was a small party. I had also investigated other parties. When the National Assembly was elected, with a then completely unpolitical attitude I had even voted democratic. Then, when I saw whom I had elected, I avoided politics for some time. Now, finally I saw a man here who had a clear and definite aim. I just wanted to speak to him at first to see if I could assist him in any way. He received me at once and after I had introduced myself, he said it was an extraordinary turn of fate that we should meet. We spoke at once about the things which were close to our hearts—the defeat of the fatherland, and that one could not let it rest with that.

The chief theme of this conversation was again Versailles. I told him that I myself to the fullest extent, and all I was, and all I possessed, were completely at his disposal for this, in my opinion, most essential and decisive matter: The fight against the Treaty of Versailles.

The second point which impressed me very strongly at the time and which I felt very deeply and really considered to be a basic condition, was the fact that he explained to me at length that it was not possible under the conditions then prevailing to bring about, in co-operation with only that element which at that time considered itself national—whether it be the political so-called nationalist parties or those which still called themselves national, or the then existing clubs, fighter organizations, the Free Corps, et cetera—with these people alone it was not possible to bring about a reconstruction with the aim of creating a strong national will among the German people, as long as the masses of German labor opposed this idea. One could only rebuild Germany again if one could enlist the masses of German labor. This could be achieved only if the will to become free from the unbearable shackles of the Treaty of Versailles were really felt by the broad masses of the people, and that would be possible only by combining the national conception with a social goal.

He gave me on that occasion for the first time a very wonderful and profound explanation of the concept of National Socialism; the unity of the two concepts of nationalism on the me hand and socialism on the other, which should prove themselves the absolute supporters of nationalism as well as of socialism—the nationalism, if I may say so, of the bourgeois world and the socialism of the Marxist world. We must clarify these concepts again and through this union of the two ideas create a new vehicle for these new thoughts.

Then we proceeded to the practical side, in regard to which he asked me above all to support him in one point. Within the Party, as small as it was, he had made a special selection of these people who were convinced followers, and who were ready at any moment to devote themselves completely and unreservedly to the dissemination of our idea.

He said that I knew myself how strong Marxism and communism were everywhere at the time, and that actually he had been able to make himself heard at meetings only after he had opposed one physical force disturbing the meeting with another physical force protecting the meeting; for this purpose, he had created the SA. The leaders at that time ware too young, and he had long been on the lookout for a leader who had distinguished himself in some way in the last war, which was only a few years ago, so that there would be the necessary authority. He had always tried to find a "Pour le Merite" aviator or a "Pour le Merite" submarine man for this purpose, and now it seemed to him especially fortunate that I in particular, the last commander of the "Richthofen Squadron", should place myself at his disposal.

I told him that in itself it would not be very pleasant for me to have a leading part from the very beginning, since it might appear that I had come merely because of this position. We finally reached an agreement that for 1 to 2 months I was to remain officially in the background and take over leadership only after that, but actually I was to make my influence felt immediately. I agreed to this, and in that way, I came together with Adolf Hitler. (*Trial of the Major War Criminals Before the International Military Tribunal Nuremberg, 14 November 1945 to 1 October 1946, Volume IX*)

00.12.1922	Joined the NSDAP.
01.03.1923–00.11.1923	*Oberster SA-Führer* (on extended leave following the *"München-Putsch"* of 09.11.1923), also known as *Kommandeur der Sturmabteilung*. Succeeded Hans Ulrich Klintzsch. In a discussion with Josef ("Sepp") Dietrich and Göring, on the night of 03./04.01.1942, Hitler recalled his appointment of Göring to the post:

One day I had an opportunity to hear a speech by Göring, in which he declared himself resolutely on the side of German honor. My attention had been called to him. I liked him. I made him the head of my SA. He's the only one of its heads who ran the SA properly. I gave him a disheveled rabble. In a very short time, he had organised a division of eleven thousand men. (H. R. Trevor-Roper, ed., *Hitler's Table Talk 1941–1944*, p. 168)

In his IMT testimony on 13.03.1946, Göring described his primary tasks in leading the early SA:

At first it was important to weld the SA into a stable organization, to discipline it, and to make of it a completely reliable unit which had to carry out the orders which I or Adolf Hitler should give it. Up to that point it had been just a club which had been very active, but which still lacked the necessary construction and discipline. I strove from the beginning to bring into the SA those members of the Party who were young and idealistic enough to devote their free time and their entire energies to it. For at that time things were very difficult for these good men. We were very small in number, and our opponents were far more numerous. Even in those days these men were exposed to very considerable annoyances and had to suffer all sorts of things.

In the second place I tried to find recruits among workmen, for I knew that among workmen particularly I should enroll many members for the SA. At the same time, we had naturally to see to it that the meetings of the Party, which generally were limited at that time to Munich, Bavaria and Franconia, could actually be carried through in a satisfactory manner, and disturbances prevented. In most cases we succeeded. But sometimes we had a strong party of our opponents present. One side or the other still had weapons from the war and sometimes critical situations arose, and in some cases, we had to send the SA as reinforcements to other localities. (*Trial of the Major War Criminals Before the International Military Tribunal Nuremberg, 14 November 1945 to 1 October 1946*, Volume IX)

As of Autumn 1923, the *Oberkommando der SA* was organized as follows:

Oberster SA-Führer.. *Oberleutnant a. D.* Hermann Göring
Chef des Truppenstabes (Ia)..*Major* Adolf Hühnlein
Chef des Organisationsstabes (IIa)................................*Kapitänleutnant a. D.* Alfred Hoffmann
Quartiermeister (Ib) ....*Major a. D.* Hans Streck
Sanitätswesen ....*Oberleutnant d. R. a. D.* Dr. med. Walther ("Bubi") Schultze
Adjutant..*Leutnant a. D.* Walter Baldenius
Stabsfeldwebel.. *Vizefeldwebel* Julius Schreck
Transportabteilung.. Christian Weber

In an article of 30.01.1936, printed in the *Völkischer Beobachter*, Göring wrote:

When the Führer entrusted the SA to me in the first year of the fight, there began for me a period of hard work and proud joyousness.... There grew in the SA a group of men as hard as steel who knew nothing but their Führer and their Fatherland.... We never stood resignedly, we have never appealed to the achievements of the past.... The old SA men were tough fighters, genuine revolutionaries of action.... For them there was.... And still is only one action which is straight as a string: The desire for the Führer. (IMT Nürnberg Document 1856-PS, Translation from *Hermann Göring: Reden und Aufsätze*, pp. 223-225)

Ernst Röhm writes of the early SA leader Göring:

The brisk, carefree dash of this proven German aviator officer—at the end of the war he commanded the Richthofen squadron—always enlivened the already pugnacious mood of our circle. He brought fresh enthusiasm to the SA, if also perhaps raising its self-awareness. I soon won him as a friend and spent many happy hours in the comfortable home near Nymphenburg where he lived with his young Swedish wife. (Röhm, *Die Geschichte eines Hochverräters*; translated by Eleanor Hancock as *Memoirs of Ernst Röhm*)

The early Nazi publicist Kurt Lüdecke writes of a meeting with Hitler in 1923, some months after Göring's appointment to lead the SA:

[T]he reorganization of the SA ... had been begun in January with such swiftness that it was now complete. The Storm Troops were no longer a mere band of political police, but a real, military, fighting unit—armed, drilled, and competently officered.
   I asked about Captain Hermann Göring, the new SA leader.
   "Oh! Göring!" Hitler exclaimed, laughing and slapping his knee with satisfaction. "Splendid, a war ace with the Pour le Mérite—imagine it! Excellent propaganda! Moreover, he has money and doesn't cost me a cent. That's very important, you know." (Lüdecke, *I Knew Hitler*, p. 129)

Ernst ("Putzi") Hanfstaengl and his wife, Helene, developed a close connection to Herr and Frau Göring during this period. Hanfstaengl writes of this relationship in his memoirs:

Goering was a complete *condottiere*, the pure soldier of fortune, who saw in the Nazi Party a possible outlet for his vitality and vanity. Nevertheless, he had a jovial, extrovert manner and I found myself very much at home with him. Before long we were on "thou" (du) terms ... Goering had a certain humorous contempt for the little squad of Bavarians round Hitler, whom he regarded as a bunch of beer-swillers and rucksack-carriers with a limited, provincial horizon ("eine Bande von Biersäufern und Rucksackträgern mit engstirnigem, provinziellem Horizont"). In his over-loud way, he at least brought a whiff of the great outside world with him, and his war record with its *pour le mérite* had given him a much wider set of contacts....
   I remember rebuking Goering once at one of the Munich cafes for screwing a monocle into his eye, and then looking round with the stupid

air of superiority that wearers of such objects usually affect. "*Mein lieber Hermann*," I told him, "This is supposed to be a working-class party and if you go round looking like a Junker we shall never attract their support." Whereupon he looked rather deflated and sheepish and stuffed it in his pocket. (Hanfstaengl, *Hitler: The Missing Years*, p. 72)

Alfred Kube gives the following assessment of Göring's leadership of the SA:

Göring's strongly representative political leadership style met with criticism among his SA subordinates, as can be seen from a letter from a Hundertschaftführer to Hitler, which expressed concern that the leadership was losing contact with the movement and therefore wanted the SA to be directly subordinate to Hitler. The inner-party conflict between the Bavarian and non-Bavarian elements also played a role. Although Göring was a southern German by birth, he considered himself primarily as a representative of the Prussian officer type and took an early stand against the Bavarian core of the Party … Hanfstaengl, who had close contact with Göring in these early days, reports of numerous disputes within the party in which Göring was involved as early as 1923 and some of which continued into the period after the "Machtergreifung." (Translated from Kube, *Pour le mérite und Hakenkreuz: Hermann Göring im Dritten Reich*, p. 9)

01.05.1923	On Hitler's orders, mobilized the SA for a march on München, on the occasion of Marxist "May Day" demonstrations and mass meetings by Social Democrats and Communists in the city. The planned coup did not come to pass, however, as Hitler chose to cancel it when the local *Reichswehr* commander, *Generalleutnant* Otto von Lossow, refused to offer weapons to the right-wing forces.
23.10.1923	Chaired a meeting of the SA leadership, also attended by Hitler, in München. Peter Stachura writes:

[Göring] stressed the need to build up armed resistance against the Republic and to establish a national dictatorship, while Hitler warned the meeting to stand prepared for a national revolution. [Gregor] Strasser was delighted to hear these words, and he later remarked that this meeting "was for me perhaps the most beautiful moment since 1918 because from then on I thought things would change." (Stachura, *Gregor Strasser and the Rise of Nazism*, p. 24)

07.11.1923	Meeting with Hitler and Hermann Kriebel, during which the *Führer* outlined his plans for their coup, which was planned for the 11th of the month. David Irving writes:

Their "troops" would seize the major towns, railroad stations, telecommunications buildings, and city halls throughout Bavaria. It sounded so easy that they brought forward the zero hour. Why not strike the very next day, November 8, 1923? (Irving, *Göring: A Biography*, p. 63)

08.–09.11.1923　　Left the bedside of his wife, who was suffering from pneumonia, then drove his Mercedes-Benz into downtown München for a final meeting with his subordinate SA leaders at 10 a.m. The commander of *SA-Regiment "München,"* Wilhelm Brückner, was ordered to bring his two SA battalions to the *Bürgerbräukeller* in the evening, while other units were to proceed to the beer cellars *Arzbergerkeller* and *Hofbräuhaus*. The 100 men of the *Stoßtrupp Adolf Hitler*, under Joseph Berchtold, were to await orders at the *Torbräukeller*.

At 20:34 hours, Göring, wearing a black leather coat and swastika-emblazoned helmet and brandishing his sword, arrived at the *Bürgerbräukeller* in München. Stepping from the running board of his car, he declared, to SA men arriving in trucks, "The Berlin government—the Reich government—is deposed. We recognize only the dictatorship of Ludendorff-Kahr-Hitler!" (Dornberg, pp. 66-67) He then informed Chief Inspector Philipp Kiefer:

> A new government has been named. Police headquarters has been informed. Herr Doktor Frick will be here soon. Keep your men under control and there'll be no trouble from mine. But do not attempt to leave the building. It is surrounded. (Dornberg, *Munich 1923. The Story of Hitler's First Grab for Power*, pp. 66-67)

Shortly afterward, Hitler and his small entourage (Max Amann, Ulrich Graf, and Alfred Rosenberg) entered the hall, interrupting von Kahr as the latter was delivering a speech. Göring, at the head of twenty-five SA men, stormed into the hall. Hitler then mounted a chair and fired a bullet from his pistol at the ceiling, shouting, "The national revolution has begun!" He continued:

> This hall is occupied by six hundred heavily armed men. No one may leave the hall. The Bavarian and Reich Governments have been removed and a provisional National Government formed. The Army and police barracks have been occupied, troops and police are marching on the city under the swastika banner. (Alan Bullock, *Hitler: A Study in Tyranny*, pp. 106-107)

Hitler directed von Kahr, *Generalleutnant* von Lossow (commander of the Army in Bavaria), and *Oberst* Ritter von Seisser (commander of the *Landespolizei*) to accompany him to a side room for a discussion of his demands. All was pandemonium in the hall, which contained some 3,000 people, and on the orders of *Oberstleutnant* Kriebel, Göring strode to the stage to restore order:

> This [he shouted] is not an assault on Herr von Kahr, the other two gentlemen, the police, or the army, who are already marching out of their barracks with flags waving. It is directed solely against the Berlin government of Jews. It is merely the preliminary step of the national revolution desired by everyone in this auditorium. We have dared this step because we are convinced it will make it easier for the men who lead us to act.

But until the step is completed, you must all stay seated and follow the orders and instructions of the guards. Long live the new Reich government—Hitler, Ludendorff, Pöhner, Kahr! [The crowd thereupon began to sing *"Deutschland, Deutschland über Alles"*.]

Besides, ladies and gentlemen, you've all got your beer. (John Dornberg, *Munich 1923. The Story of Hitler's First Grab for Power*, p. 72)

Early on the 9th, Göring ordered Berchtold and the *Stoßtrupp* to take hostages from the *Ratshaus*. After arriving at the hall, the *Stoßtrupp* member Julius Schaub confronted the assembled aldermen of the city, shouting: "I bring you orders from my commander, Hauptmann Göring, to raise the black-white-red banner immediately." (Dornberg, p. 268)

Eduard Schmid, the Social Democratic *Oberbürgermeister* of München (1919–1924), responded: "You say you have orders for us from Hauptmann Göring? I have never heard of him. But anyway, tell him we shall have to look about first to see if there are any flags in those colors still around." (Dornberg, p. 268)

The rest of the *Stoßtrupp*, led by Berchtold, then arrived in their trucks, and Schaub demanded: "All Marxists and Jews stand up!… All Social Democrats, Independent Socialists, and Communists are under arrest by order of the provisional government." (Dornberg, p. 269)

Nine men, including Schmid, his deputy Hans Küffner (a conservative), and the senior Social Democratic councilor Albert Nussbaum, were brutally taken into custody and loaded aboard one of the *Stoßtrupp*'s trucks, to be transported to the *Bürgerbräukeller*. At the same time, Göring and Ulrich Graf were, on Ludendorff's orders, performing a reconnaissance along the riverfront. Göring contacted *Major* Rudolf von Kramer, whose policemen were confronting the *II. SA-Bataillon* (under Edmund Heines) at the Cornelius Bridge and informed him: "My instructions from Excellency Ludendorff are to tell you that the first dead or wounded in our ranks will mean the death of the hostages we are holding." (Dornberg, p. 271)

By noon, the anti-government forces—over 2,000 men—were assembling on *Rosenheimer-Straße*. Göring, in helmet and black rubber coat, called out to Berchtold: "Get the prisoners—Schmid, Nussbaum, the other councilors. I want them at the rear of the column, and if there is any trouble, shoot them." (Dornberg, p. 283)

At 12:45 p.m., the column of men marching toward the *Feldherrnhalle* behind Hitler and General Ludendorff was ordered by the police to halt. A shot rang out—the man who fired it remains unknown—and struck and fatally wounded police sergeant Friedrich Fink. In the gun battle that followed, fourteen putschists and four policemen were mortally wounded or killed outright. Numerous others suffered severe injury, among them Göring, who was seriously wounded in the groin (where a bullet missed an artery by millimeters) and thigh by police bullets and concrete fragments. In the aftermath of the revolt, he was taken by Wilhelm Brückner and two SA men to the home of the luxury furniture manufacturer, Robert Ballin (born in München on 14.12.1872), whose wife Bella had been a nurse during the war. Frau Ballin was able to stop the blood flow and cared for him until nightfall. Although the Ballins were Jewish and knew the antiemitic party to which Göring belonged, they did not call the police. From the Ballins' home, Göring was carried to the clinic of Professor Alwin Ritter von Ach, who was sympathetic to the Nazi cause. From von Ach's clinic, Göring was driven by his wife to Garmisch-Partenkirchen, 70 miles south of Munich, where he was briefly hidden at the villa of *Major a. D.* Friedrich (Fritz) Schueler van Krieken (*10.10.1885 in Berlin, †12.05.1936 in Freiburg) who had been a staff member of Wilhelm Brückner's *SA-Regiment München* at the time of the *Putsch*. An officer of a *Dragoner-Regiment* who later transferred to the *Fliegertruppe*, he served as an observer in *Feldflieger-Abteilung 23* before his appointment, in 1916, as *Kommandeur der Flieger* (Kofl) of *5. Osmanischen Armee* in Smyrna. In 1934, he was decorated with the *Blutorden* (Nr. 280).

Robert Ballin later benefited from the help he rendered to Göring after the *Putsch*. When his furniture business was "Aryanized" in September 1937, the terms granted to him were more favorable than in most other cases. As a result of Göring's personal intervention, he was also permitted to remain as an employee, and received a monthly pension from the new owner, Edgar Horn. When Ballin and his family were arrested and sent to Dachau after *"Kristallnacht"* in November 1938, Göring ensured their early release after a few days. In March 1942, Robert Ballin and his brother Martin, together with their wives, were able to move to Switzerland where they remained until traveling to Spain in November of that year. They next moved to Argentina (Bella Ballin dying during the voyage on 08.01.1943), then to Paraguay, and finally to the United States in August 1943. In 1958, Robert Ballin returned to his home city of München, where he died on 09.02.1960.

10.11.1923	Arrest warrant for Göring issued by the München police.
10.11.1923	Together with Frau Göring, driven by *SA-Mann* Franz Thanner from Partenkirchen to the Austrian border. An officer of the *Schutzpolizei* station in Garmisch-Partenkirchen, *Leutnant* Nikolaus Maier (a future *Generalmajor* in Göring's *Luftwaffe*), had issued instructions to the frontier post at Mittenwald that Göring was to be arrested if he arrived there. When the car carrying Göring arrived at the border, he and the other occupants were escorted under police guard back to Garmisch. Carin Göring later wrote to her mother:

We drove from München to Garmisch in the car of friends in whose villa we stayed for a few days until it became known where we were and people began to flock to the house, demonstrating and shouting "Hurray." So we thought it best to cross the frontier into Austria. We left by car but were arrested at the border. Police with loaded revolvers drove us back to Garmisch, where the people gathered again, shouting "Heil Göring," and preparing to lynch the police.... The authorities took his passports and

Hermann was taken to a hospital which was surrounded by guards and posts. (Willi Frischauer, *The Rise and Fall of Hermann Goering*, p. 47)

Briefly held at the Wiggers Sanatorium in that city, he soon fled together with his wife. Thanner once again drove him to the Mittenwald frontier post, this time breaking through the barrier into Austria. Once there, Göring was given a false passport, then taken to the Golden Lamb Inn in Seefeld.

12.11.1923 — Checked into the *Tirolerhof* hotel in Innsbruck, owned by a Nazi sympathizer, then given medical treatment by the pediatrician Dr. Soppelsa.

13.11.1923–24.12.1923 — Hospitalized in the clinic of Dr. Soppelsa in Innsbruck. His severe blood loss and pain from infection led to his being treated heavily with opiates, and as a result, he became severely addicted to morphine. Writing to her mother, Carin reported:

Hermann's leg is shattered. The bullet went right through, half a centimeter from the artery; there are a lot of stones and dirt in the long hole the bullet bored. The shot is high up (in the right thigh) and the wound is dreadfully inflamed, since the dirt and so on is trying to come out and in so doing leads to pus forming and to fever and great pain....

We left Munich in such a haste that all I could do was to pack the most necessary things in a small bag as every minute was precious. Our address is: Dr. Soppelsa, 9 Bahnhofsplatz, Innsbruck. Hermann believes that all letters are opened if they have the name Göring on them. So, my dear, write in a double envelope. We are staying here now till Hermann's leg is well. What other plans have we? I have no idea where we shall go.

Heartfelt greetings, Your Carin. (Kurt Singer, *Göring: Germany's Most Dangerous Man*, pp. 76-77)

Ernst Hanfstaengl, who also fled to Austria in the aftermath of the *Putsch*, writes:

Goering I found in hospital in Innsbruck. He really had been badly wounded, although he was over the worst when I saw him. He told me how he had managed to crawl up behind one of the monumental lions in front of the Residenz Palace after he had been hit. Some of the brownshirts had then carried him to the first doctor in the Residenzstrasse, who happened to be a Jew and for many years afterwards Goering spoke warmly of his kindness and skill. Goering was never one of the crazy anti-Semites of the Party, and, as one of the few unmistakably Aryan members of Hitler's entourage, was the least fervent exponent of their racial theories.

From Munich he had been smuggled over the border, and in Innsbruck had to be operated on. He was suffering severe pain and had to be given two morphia injections a day. It was always maintained that he later became an addict. I have no personal and positive proof of this, but this treatment in the Innsbruck hospital very likely provided the inception of the habit....

He simply had no sense of the value of money, and when he finally left Austria via Venice for Sweden, I helped to finance the trip. I received little thanks and never saw my money back. Yet somehow this did not cause offence. He was a very attractive, rollicking fellow, the type that can get away with this sort of thing. In many ways it was a pity that he spent so much time away. He was an intelligent and traveled man, with a much broader fund of common sense that the other Nazis. (Hanfstaengl, *Hitler: The Missing Years*, pp. 110-111)

While in Innsbruck, Göring was also visited by Kurt Lüdecke. A member of the Party since 1922, Lüdecke had been sent on two missions to Italy (September 1922 and again in 1923) where he met with Mussolini on behalf of Hitler and the NSDAP. Lüdecke writes that Göring spoke in great detail of the recent *Putsch*. The historian Michael Palumbo speculates:

They probably also discussed Lüdecke's trips to Fascist Italy and his meetings with Benito Mussolini. In his memoirs Lüdecke gives the impression that his missions to Italy were widely known in Nazi circle, so that Göring was sure to raise the subject. Whether Lüdecke influenced Göring to go to Italy is not known, but the discussion probably left him with the impression that Mussolini's regime was accessible to an emissary from the NSDAP. (Palumbo, "Göring's Italian Exile 1924–1925" in *Journal of Modern History*, Vol. 50, No. 1, March 1978, p. D1035)

24.12.1923	Released from hospital and returned to the *Tirolerhof*. Palumbo continues:

Many of those whom he met in Austria and Italy report that he limped rather badly. He also lost his youthful physique and began to develop the girth that characterized him later on. When his health permitted, Göring took part in various political activities. He established contact with Austrian Nazis and German followers of Hitler who were also in exile. His activities aroused the interest of the authorities—particularly his efforts to raise funds for the National Socialist Movement. When one of his associates was arrested in Vienna, Göring was quietly asked to leave the country. The Nazi exile and his wife were fortunate to receive aid from the Wagner family. As Friedelind Wagner relates [in *Heritage of Fire*, 1945], his bills in Innsbruck were paid by her father and arrangements were made for the Görings to go to Venice to live at a hotel which was owned by a Nazi sympathizer. (Palumbo, "Göring's Italian Exile 1924–1925" in *Journal of Modern History*, Vol. 50, No. 1, March 1978, p. D1036)

22.02.1924	In a letter to his mother-in-law, the Baroness von Fock, Göring wrote hopefully:

We have only got to have a little patience now and then everything will gradually work itself out. Therefore, we have also to look forward to a longish time before we can go back to Germany. While the trial is going on I shall stay here, but if afterwards there is no likelihood of going back for a long time, we shall go to Sweden over Italy by sea, for living there is cheaper and above all nicer than here in Austria. I had already thought of eventually selling our villa and sending the furniture to Sweden, where we should then take a flat, for we cannot go on living for years in hotels. I can also perhaps find some work there, until things allow us to go back to Germany. For I will only go back to a National Germany and not to this Jewish republic. I shall always be ready to fight for my Fatherland's freedom. I do love Sweden above everything else, for I am first and foremost a German and the purest Germans live there....

Gratefully, Your Hermann. (Kurt Singer, *Göring*, pp. 84-85)

05.03.1924	Obtained an Austrian passport in Innsbruck.
24.05.1924	Order issued by the Bavarian government for Göring's arrest on charges of high treason, due to the important role he had played in the *Putsch*.
Early May 1924	Traveled to Venice with *Frau* Göring, with the mission of meeting, on behalf of the imprisoned Adolf Hitler, with Benito Mussolini (of whom he was an admirer) and obtaining from the *Duce* a loan of 2 million lire to rebuild the shattered Nazi Party. The couple stayed briefly in the Grand Hotel Britannia, owned by two Venice-born German brothers, Rudolfo and Carlo Walther. "[Göring's] command of Italian," writes Michael Palumbo, "was substantial, and he decided to utilize his visit to carry on the work of his movement" (Palumbo, "Göring's Italian Exile 1924–1925"). After several days of sightseeing in Venice and Florence, the Görings traveled to Rome, where they stayed at the elegant Hotel Eden from 11.05.1924. Refused an audience with Mussolini, he managed only to meet with the diplomat Giuseppe Bastianini, to whom Dr. Leo Negrelli had introduced him. Negrelli, a journalist for the *Corriere d'Italia* and member of Mussolini's staff, was sympathetic to the Nazi movement and had interviewed Hitler in October 1923. Palumbo writes:

Goering did have considerable dealings with the Fascist government while he was in Rome.... According to Bastianini's memoirs, Goering came to Rome with Giuseppe Renzetti, who was Mussolini's personal agent in Germany. Bastianini met Goering several times in Rome; they talked at length in his office, at restaurants and at certain castles in the Rome area. The Italian diplomat records [in *Uomini, cose, fatti: Memorie di un ambasciatore*, Milan, 1959] that Goering gave him a letter addressed from Hitler to Mussolini concerning the question of South Tyrol, the German-speaking region occupied by Italy after World War I. According to Renzo de Felice [in *Hitler e Mussolini: I rapporti segreti 1922–1933*, Florence, 1975, p. 25] the leading contemporary historian of the Fascist era, no trace of this document has ever been found. However, Goering himself wrote a letter to Mussolini while he was in Rome, which may well be the document referred to by Bastianini. In this memorandum Goering pledges that if the Nazis came to power there would be no quarrel over the South Tyrol. A National Socialist Germany, he said, would guarantee the reparations awarded to Italy by the Treaty of Versailles. Goering also promised that the Nazi press would work for good relations between Germany and Italy. In return, the letter requests Italian help for the Hitler movement which would include favorable press reports, public statements of support, and financial assistance. Mussolini was also asked to adopt an attitude of neutrality in regard to the Treaty of Versailles, including the question of reparations.

The memorandum described by Palumbo was dated 19.09.1924, and included the sentence, "Italy must seek to find strong allies. One such ally would be a National-Socialist Germany under Hitler's leadership" (Charles R. Hamilton, *Leaders and Personalities of the Third Reich, Volume 1*), as well as a sinister reference to the possibility that the NSDAP "might come to power by 'legal or illegal means'" (Palumbo, D1038).

For financial reasons, the Görings eventually had to move to the less luxurious Hotel de Russie. His negotiations with the Fascists failed dismally, with Bastianini ultimately asking him to leave Rome. The Görings departed for Venice on 11.08.1924, returning to the Grand Hotel Britannia. Göring then began a lengthy correspondence with Dr. Negrelli, whom he believed to have the ear of Mussolini. "His letters," writes Palumbo, "are filled with requests which he hoped Negrelli would convey to the Duce" (Palumbo, D1038). Chief among these were his ultimately unsuccessful efforts to help Rudolfo Walther. Palumbo continues:

As a result of the Treaty of Versailles, the Hotel Britannia had been sequestered because it was German-owned. Goering argued that Walther would make an ideal Nazi representative in Italy, and that since he had always been pro-Italian, the property of his family should be spared. No fewer than ten letters written in 1924 and 1925 reflect Goering's constant efforts to gain a favorable judgment for Walther.... Goering's letters on this subject reflect a quite virulent anti-Semitism....

In Rome, Bastianini was unfavorably impressed by Goering's tirades against the evil influence of world Jewry [Bastianini, *Uomini, close, fatti: Memorie di un ambasciatore*, p. 185] He stated that the Jewish-owned Banca Commerciale wished to gain control of the Hotel Britannia and thus form a monopoly of hotels in Venice. On September 23, Goering wrote to Negrelli: "... I have found out that the Jewish Banca Commerciale, behind the scenes and in typical Jewish lowness, wants to seize the hotel." Ironically, the official who had the power to decide in the Walther matter was Guido Jung, the Italian Minister of the Treasury, who was of Jewish origin. Goering in his correspondence displayed a great distrust for Jung because of his Jewish background, and [in a letter dated 15.10.1924] he warned Negrelli against him on that basis....

The Jew above all—out of racial unity—must be against a national movement because he is the final leader of internationalism, so the national groups must form a closed phalanx against them. Most of the national movements today are already anti-Semitic.... [He then lists ten such groups in various countries] ... At this moment anti-Semitism grows everywhere. Why did the Fascists in a great outcry declare the Banca Commerciale to be its greatest enemy? This already displays an unconscious anti-Semitic tendency. (Palumbo, pp. D1039-1040)

Göring also wrote harshly of the Catholic Church, as in this excerpt from a letter to Negrelli dated 23.09.1924: "The Vatican is cunning.... Spiritually and basically, the Vatican is an enemy of fascism." In his letter of 15.10.1924, he wrote:

The Vatican is very deceptive. While in Italy it is apparently very well disposed toward Mussolini, in other countries ... it is entirely against Mussolini.... Mussolini made powerful temporal concessions to the Pope and he may someday regret this ... the large Catholic Party in Germany is expressly anti-Italian and anti-Fascist. (Palumbo, p. D1040)

Göring's efforts to secure a loan for Hitler's movement were expressed in a letter to Negrelli dated 19.09.1924: "... a loan of two million. For this you would have in your press an important speaking trumpet [for pro-Fascist propaganda]. Besides you will get your two million back in five years at the latest." Palumbo continues:

In an undated memorandum to the Directorate of the Fascist Party, Goering made his most serious bid for a loan. He indicated that it would be kept secret and listed several reasons for it. In addition to the plan of building a pro-Fascist press in Germany, the need to fight Communism was also stressed. According to Goering, the large debt incurred by the movement in electoral campaigns necessitated the loan, especially since the Nazi property was under sequesture as a result of the Munich Putsch. The evidence available indicates that Goering never received any money while he was in Italy and gradually dropped the request for a loan. (Palumbo, p. 1041)

Göring tried several times to secure a meeting with Mussolini. On 15.10.1924, he wrote: "Hitler will certainly be released in the next few days and will then perhaps go to Rome with me.... This will happen only if he could be sure of having an audience with Mussolini..." (Palumbo, p. D1043).

And in an undated letter to Negrelli, likely written early in 1925, Göring wrote: "I ask that you do all that you can to arrange an audience [with Mussolini] in the next few days, since I can no longer wait and must soon depart,... I am to write a little book about him and Fascism for propaganda in Germany. It would be stupid to do this if I had never seen him" (Palumbo, p. D1043).

On 25.01.1925, he confidently declared: "Hitler [freed from Landsberg Prison the previous month] will soon have a meeting and an audience with Mussolini. I don't know how this was arranged, but it has been done" (Palumbo, p. D1044).

And on 12.02.1925: "Hitler has commissioned me to speak to an influential member of the Fascist Party who has promised Hitler to take our matter and secure for me an audience with Mussolini" (Palumbo, p. D1043).

These suggestions that Göring was in contact with Hitler during this period remain unsubstantiated, although it is known

	that the *Führer* earnestly wished to meet with Mussolini. The fact that Göring had never met with the *Duce* during his year in Italy did not prevent Göring from claiming that he had. In his diary entry of 04.05.1929, Goebbels writes: "Sat up into the night with Göring… [He] told of Mussolini, whom he personally met at length in his political exile in Rome."
Spring 1925–Summer 1926	Traveled with Frau Göring from Italy to her home country of Sweden and lived in a modest apartment at *No. 23 Odengatan* in Stockholm. He was employed for several weeks as a pilot for *Nordiska Flygrederiet*.
17.04.1925	While in Stockholm, received his membership card (membership Nr. 214) from the *Ehrenbund Deutscher Weltkriegsteilnehmer e. V.* (League of Honor of German World War Veterans), established in München, 13.02.1925.
06.08.1925–30.08.1925	Voluntarily registered himself at the Aspuddens Nursing Home in Stockholm due to his morphine addiction. On 30.08.1925, he broke open a medicine cabinet to obtain Eukodal, a synthetic derivative of morphine, giving himself two injections. On 01.08.1925, he leapt from his bed, demanding more medication. When this was refused, he dressed himself and attempted to leave the building, but found the doors locked. He ran to his room, retrieving a sword cane that he brandished at nursing staff until they gave him the requested injections. When police and firemen came to the nursing home that evening, he vainly attempted to resist but was placed in a straitjacket and transported to the Katarina Hospital.
02.09.1925–07.10.1925	Committed by his wife to the Långbro Asylum near Stockholm. The doctor who attended to Göring described him as depressed, suicidal, egocentric, and a Jew-hater. His condition was seen to improve, resulting in his discharge from Långbro by Prof. Olof Kinberg on 07.10.1925.
12.11.1925	Order for Göring's arrest in Germany officially lifted.
14.05.1926	Indictment against Göring for high treason officially nullified due to an amnesty issued by Reich President Paul von Hindenburg.
22.05.1925–early June 1926	At his own request, returned to the Långbro Asylum to complete their program of detoxification from Eukodal. He was ultimately certified as completely cured by the assistant medical superintendent, Dr. C. Franke.
Summer 1926–00.01.1927	Employed by *Bayerische Motorenwerke* (BMW) as a sales representative for aircraft engines in Sweden.
00.01.1927	Returned to Germany with a commission to sell parachutes for the Swedish firm of *Törnblad*. He soon met with Hitler who dismissively advised him to settle in Berlin and establish contacts with members of society in that city, then rented a hotel room off the *Kurfürstendamm*. He befriended his later adjutant, the wealthy Paul ("Pilli") Körner, during this period. With Körner as chauffeur, Göring attempted to sell parachutes in Germany. The Törnblad company produced a pamphlet described by Kurt Singer as follows:

In Sweden there is a law under which printing presses must send a copy of all their productions to certain State libraries: Thanks to this there is in the Royal Library in Stockholm the following pamphlet:

"Automatic or non-automatic parachutes?
Some points of view in this question based on
Experiences in the World War
by ex-Captain Göring,
finally Leader of Baron von Richthofen's Fighter
Squadron No. 1."

This sixteen-page advertising pamphlet is in the library in three languages: German, English, and Spanish.

In it Göring praises the automatic parachute, mentions that it is used in Germany, but has not yet been introduced into other lands. All the theoretical considerations set forth in the pamphlet have the one purpose of inducing foreign military authorities to buy the German parachute. Göring writes that the German model is absolutely the most reliable.... From the Göring parachute pamphlet we take the following passages:

"Since the general agent for the automatic parachute in the years after the war, the firm of Heinicke, was German, its introduction or trial was out of the question on national grounds for France and England, so that the big-scale American Irving propaganda did not meet with any competition to speak of...." And thus Göring (now no longer representing a State at war but the neutral Sweden) exhorts the various military authorities to use the modern parachute, which had already been introduced into Germany, Russia, Japan, Spain, Italy, Turkey, and the Balkan States. The Swedish automatic parachute of the Törnblad type was a greatly improved form of the Heinicke model. Göring ended with the words: "I am convinced that England also, when the automatic system has been further improved, will come back again to it." (Singer, *Göring: Germany's Most Dangerous Man*, pp. 108-109)

00.05.1927	First meeting with Dr. Joseph Goebbels, *Gauleiter* of Berlin-Brandenburg, who wrote in his diary on 02.05.1927: "Hauptmann Goring. A face like a big baby. Such a hero! I was at first indescribably disappointed. Afterwards he grew on me a lot. He makes intelligent, courageous comments" (Translation in Toby Thacker, *Joseph Goebbels. Life and Death*).
07.09.1927–26.09.1927	Returned to Sweden and readmitted—due to continued morphine abuse—to the Långbro Asylum.
00.01.1928	Returned to Berlin and settled in an office on the *Geisberg-Straße* where he was again engaged in parachute sales. He shared this office with another aviation businessman, Fritz Siebel.
00.00.1928	Hired as a "consultant" to BMW and *Heinkel* and as a paid advisor to the German airline *Lufthansa*.
01.04.1928	Rejoined the NSDAP, having been deleted from the membership files by Alfred Rosenberg.
20.05.1928–23.04.1945	Member of the *Reichstag* (representing *Wahlkreis 4, Potsdam I* from 31.07.1932). He received his parliamentary seat by means

of extortion, threatening a lawsuit against the NSDAP for all monies owed him by the Party back to 1922. He thus forced the Party to include him on its list of candidates for the *Reichstag* in the 20.05.1928 elections. Hitler agreed, guaranteeing him a seat provided at least seven Nazi delegates were selected—the Party won twelve seats in the Social Democratic and Communist-dominated German Parliament, this number rising to 107 in the elections of 14.09.1930. Ernst Hanfstaengl writes of the circumstances preceding Göring's election to the *Reichstag*:

General elections were due in the spring of 1928 and Goering wanted to stand high up on the Party list as one of the candidates, partly from ulterior motives I suspect, as it would not only give him a position and a useful income in Berlin but also the protection of parliamentary immunity should opponents in the Government care to rake up any of his past misdeeds. Hitler put him off and sought excuses and in the end, Goering lost his temper. It was in February or March. I remember there was snow on the ground as we walked together to the Thierschstrasse, where Hitler still maintained his little flat, for the crucial talk. Goering kept asking me to go up with him, but I preferred not to. I only heard afterwards that the two men had a shouting match, with Goering delivering an ultimatum: "This is no way to treat a man who got two bullets in his stomach at the Feldherrnhalle. Either you put me up for the Reichstag or we shall part for ever as enemies." It worked, and Hitler gave way, although it caused much bad blood in the Party and a lot of them went round saying Goering had blackmailed Hitler.

[Goering's] position in the Party was shaky for quite a time. He had grown enormously fat during his years of exile and the old hands considered that this was no advertisement for a working-class party. Even Hitler expressed doubts about his capacity. "I don't know whether Goering is going to make it," he used to say to me. But Goering fooled them all, developing as a speaker, although all he did was to ape Hitler's style and phrases. For some reason Hitler took this as a compliment, a sign of fidelity... (Hanfstaengl, *Hitler: The Missing Years*, pp. 142-143)

In his diary entry of 27.06.1929, Goebbels wrote:

Yesterday: [Spent] the day in the Reichstag. Excited scene with Göring, who is becoming more and more of a faction creep [*Fraktionsekel*]. Yet he is as stupid as straw and as lazy as a toad [*so dumm wie Stroh und so faul wie eine Kröte*]. He treated the others so far *en canaille* and tried that yesterday also with me.

00.11.1928	Moved with Frau Göring into a luxurious apartment on the *Badensche-Straße*, Berlin
01.08.1929–04.08.1929	Participated in the *"4. Reichsparteitag der NSDAP"* in Nürnberg.
00.10.1930	Appointed by order of Hitler as *Reichsschlichter der NSDAP* (Reich Arbitrator of the Nazi Party). In this capacity, he had authority to settle all disagreements between Party leaders at the *Gau* level. Alfred Kube writes:

	This special task was intended to strengthen Göring's position vis-à-vis the party functionaries, to whom his relationship remained problematic, something which even foreign observers did not hide. Above all, he was in rivalry with the Berlin Gauleitung under Goebbels and the Reichsorganisationsleitung of the party under Gregor Strasser. (Translated from Kube, *Pour le mérite und Hakenkreuz: Hermann Göring im Dritten Reich*, p. 17)
14.09.1930–00.01.1933	Personal and political representative of the *Führer* in Berlin. During this period, he was active in raising funds for the Party through his contacts with *Krupp, Thyssen, Lufthansa, Heinkel, Messerschmitt,* the *Deutsche Bank*, BMW, etc.
13.10.1930–04.06.1932	2. *Stellvertreter* (second deputy) to the chairman of the NSDAP Faction and *Schriftführer* (secretary) of the *Reichstag*.
00.11.1930–00.00.1931	*Leiter* of the *Fliegerstaffel* of *NSDAP-Kreisgruppe Frankfurt am Main*.
00.04.1931–00.00.1933	*Politischer Kommissar Oberost der NSDAP* in Berlin.
00.05.1931–00.05.1931	In Rome on Hitler's orders, tasked with meeting Vatican leaders and allaying their fears that the NSDAP was a pagan organization. During the three-week visit, he also met with Mussolini, King Vittorio Emmanuel III, and fellow aviator Italo Balbo, who was to become a close personal friend.
11.10.1931	Participated in the *Tagung der nationalen Opposition* in Bad Harzburg, during which the so-called "Harzburger Front" was established.
00.10.1931–00.00.193_	*Führer* of the *Nationalen Deutscher Luftverband* (National German Air Association).
00.10.1931	Traveled to Sweden for the funeral of his wife, Carin (who had fallen to tuberculosis on 17.10.1931), then returned to Berlin and moved into the Hotel Kaiserhof.
00.12.1931	Appointed to the following posts: * *Inspekteur* of the *Inspektion für Flugwesen der NSDAP* (Aviation Inspectorate of the *NSDAP* * *1. Vorsitzender* (first chairman) of the *NS-Fliegerkorps* * *Vizepräsident* of the *Nationale Deutsche Automobilclub* (NDAC) * *1. Vorsitzender* of the *Abteilung Luftfahrt* in the NDAC
18.12.1931–13.04.1932	Assigned as an *SA-Führer z. V.* to the *Obersten SA-Führung*.
Spring 1932	Vacation on the Isle of Capri.
00.00.1932	Publication of *Halbmast-Heldenbuch der SA und SS*, a tribute to Brownshirts killed in service to the Nazi movement. The book featured forewords by Göring and Röhm, among others. Göring's read as follows:

The men who soaked the German soil with their lifeblood in 1923 erected in their death the tomb of the unknown soldier of the German Revolution.

These men of 1923 were the vanguard of the German Legion, which today is preparing to give face and form to a renewed German Reich. And this Reich will bear the features of their glorified sacrifice.

These men of 1923 remain the only indictment of the betrayal through which violence was inflicted on them. But through their sacrifice they will triumph over this betrayal. And then the day will come when old titles, parchments, institutions will blow away like noise and smoke before the storm of victory and the power of action:

Do what you must-win or die-and let God decide! [*Tu, was Du mußt – Sieg oder stirb – Und laß Gott die Entscheidung!*]
[Signed] Hermann Göring
(Translation: Gary Costello)

10.05.1932 Delivered a lengthy speech before the *Reichstag* attacking the government of *Reichskanzler* Heinrich Brüning and his ban on the SA (13.04.1932–14.06.1932):

Ladies and Gentlemen! When the Brüning cabinet came into being two and a half years ago, great hopes were placed in it from all sides. The bourgeois parties believed that their rule had finally returned, believed they could break away from the politics they had been involved in for a decade alongside the social democrats. The bourgeois newspapers gave the cabinet advanced praise on a large scale. The cabinet modestly called itself the cabinet of the front-line soldiers. At that time we ourselves believed that from this point of view the cabinet would indeed, if it worked in the spirit of the front-line soldiers, carry out purposeful new construction work. It soon became apparent, however, that it was not at all a cabinet of front-line soldiers, but that this cabinet could better be described as the cabinet of illusions. This cabinet has indulged in one illusion after another, and it has had to recognize that step by step this policy has led further towards decline. It did not help at all that the social democrats shirked their responsibility according to the tried and tested parliamentary pattern. This bourgeois cabinet was so strongly aligned with the policy of the Social Democrats, enjoyed such strong support from the Social Democrats from the first moment, that it could not help but continue in the same direction in which the pernicious policy had previously been conducted.

It is therefore a matter of course for us that today, after a final judgement, we must express our censure of this cabinet in its entirety. We do not confine ourselves to splitting hairs as to whether we have to express an extra vote of no confidence in the Chancellor in particular as Chancellor or as Foreign Minister. We believe that the Cabinet has failed so badly in both domestic and foreign policy, as well as in economic policy, that it must receive a vote of no confidence in its entirety, including all its members.

In my further remarks I can, of course, only deal with the policy of the Chancellor and Minister Groener. I know that there are also other ministers present.

Politically, however, they are merely commanding a blind pack and are no longer eligible for their parties' policies. We have also seen that it was quite irrelevant whether the Brüning I cabinet slowly developed into a Brüning II cabinet, whether a minister without portfolio suddenly had something to do. This, too, was of no significance for further decisions.

Why must we now express our strongest mistrust of the Brüning cabinet? Taken as a whole, the Cabinet was the most serious disappointment we have experienced. The cabinet started with big promises, showing high hopes, as we have always been used to from the different cabinets, and disappointed here even more perhaps than its predecessors. In our opinion, this cabinet has completely failed in all areas of public life, in all areas of politics.

I must protest against the attempt being made today to single out one task from the whole group of tasks as having been solved, and thus to hear again and again that even if the Reich Chancellor was not successful in domestic politics, he nevertheless had successes in foreign policy. So far, we have not been able to recognize these foreign policy successes. To date, we do not even see the beginnings of such a successful foreign policy. But we are above all of the opinion that, as I have said, one cannot take one part out of the whole range of responsibilities, but that domestic policy is so interconnected with foreign policy and, dependent on both, economic policy, that they can only be regarded as having an overall effect; and in this overall effect the Cabinet has completely failed.

It is impossible to separate foreign policy from domestic policy. It is impossible to separate economic policy. We have seen: if one really wants to act with strength in foreign policy, a powerful foreign policy requires the awakening of national strength on the domestic front. It is not possible, Chancellor, to take part in international negotiations in order to gain advantages for the German people, but we are of the opinion that only a healthy policy at home and a healthy political force at home create the possibility at all of taking part successfully in international negotiations. We are also of the opinion that a healthy economic policy also needs political strength on the outside and that a healthy national, ethnic basis must also be created on the inside. Bismarck was not merely a brilliant foreign politician, but he was first and foremost an outstanding domestic politician. He first created the instrument at home, first created the power at home, especially against social democracy, in order to be able to pursue a powerful foreign policy.

Once Bismarck had created the instrument at home and was thus able to pursue a powerful foreign policy, it was only then that he brought the state and the economy to the great prosperity that we were able to experience in Germany during the Bismarckian era.

Today we see the opposite. We see how that weak domestic policy dictates foreign policy in its impotence and how these two factors then created this appalling economic situation, which is not merely due to economic crises. If a correct ethnic-national policy were the prerequisite at home, then it would also be possible to confront the world economic crisis, which in itself exists, to a different extent than is the case today. We are convinced that if the global economic crisis had not existed at all, we in Germany would hardly be much better off than we are today.

The latest political development now shows an isolation of France, which we always predicted and which was partly brought about by our movement. In Geneva we now see on one side Italy, England, America and, very weakly represented next to them, Germany in the front against an isolated France. We must emphasize however, that this isolation is not to be understood as a merit of the Brüning cabinet, but that this isolation could be carried out in spite of and against the Brüning cabinet.

We reproach the Brüning cabinet for the fact that the Foreign Minister did not realise this isolation for Germany at all. The Chancellor of the Reich cannot do this, because through his domestic policy and the domestic policy of his cabinet he has made Germany a completely worthless factor in terms of power politics. It is an absurd idea that a nationalistically fractured Germany has any chance in foreign policy. This is a historical fallacy. If you continue to suppress national power at home, you cannot expect to achieve any success in foreign policy.

The real significance of Brüning's foreign policy is not to be seen in the isolation of France which other states were responsible for, but in the low estimation of Germany as a power factor in itself, brought about by the Brüning cabinet and the Herr Foreign Minister, as well as by Herr Groener himself.

I need only pick out two examples here: Danzig and Memel. If these are to be the effective achievements of a foreign policy, if today the threat to our eastern border is stronger than ever, if today we know that Danzig appears to be more threatened than ever by Poland, then we are unable to see in this a foreign policy success. We are also unable to see it in the Memel question.

If today in Memel the German direction has indeed completely asserted itself, if a storm of indignation has indeed shown itself there in the elections, then this is also not a merit of German foreign policy, but it is—we must also say this here—the strong national will that has penetrated beyond the borders of the Reich into all German territories. And this national will does not bear the signature of Brüning, it bears the signature of Hitler.

A long time ago, when people wanted to deny it over and over again, we drew attention to the imminent dangers threatening Danzig, East Prussia and Upper Silesia at the hands of their Polish neighbor. It took a long time, and it was only when the English press presented this danger in an impeccable manner that people were able to slowly, and with still completely inadequate means, get their act together and take a stand against it. We see in this, as in the questions of Danzig and Memel, especially in the way the German representative proceeded there, a foreign policy failure on the part of the government. We immediately demanded that the German representative in Lithuania be recalled, because the direction he took was a complete failure. They covered for him at first and finally had to transfer him anyway, which is tantamount to a dismissal. If today Danzig has not yet been robbed by the Poles, if today Danzig is still held by Germans, then you may rest assured, Chancellor, that this is not the merit of your foreign policy, but here again the merit of that strong moral hold, that strong national will which we have kindled there, which expressed itself most strongly when Adolf Hitler temporarily landed in Danzig and there heard an uplifting declaration of national Danzig to its homeland.

We warn, however, that from this German city, which must remain untouched, there may again be the spark that could set Europe on fire for the second time. We warn the powers that be not to exaggerate and overstretch their demands. As long as we National Socialists are there, Danzig will not fall into Polish hands, no matter what steps are taken in foreign policy.

The Brüning government has not been successful in disarmament either. So far, the Conference on Disarmament has shown no practical result at all. Here, too, we see again and again the domestic political culpability of the cabinet. Here again we see that Germany does not carry the weight it should, because people abroad know what the Brüning government can and must rely on at home. We also know that not only have we not had any success there, but we have even been pushed back on to the defensive. We know that today negotiations are not so much about the disarmament of the enemy's heavy weapons, but that here again a German point has been brought to the fore, that here again France, supported by its vassals, has directed all its energy towards German civil aviation in order to inflict further damage on Germany at the last moment. We have missed the fact that the German representative at the Conference on Disarmament has finally come out of his shell. We do not want an Italian foreign politician to have to represent German policy there and say what a German should have said. The restraint that our delegation is maintaining there is completely misplaced.

Moreover, it is strange that democratic France, of all countries, does not want to know anything about disarmament, that France, which is always so admired by social democracy, is rearming in every direction, while nationalist, fascist Italy, of all countries, has really stood up for disarmament. So, gentlemen of the Social Democrats, you are perhaps more concerned with the armament interests of the French, to a greater extent at any rate than you can speak of nationalist tendencies on our part. There is no national foreign policy if at home one persecutes and suppresses the national forces and relies on pacifist-international organisations which one knows will never be prepared to stand up for their people and fatherland, will never be prepared to uphold the German nation's right to live.

In this direction of suppression of the national forces lies also the banning of our SA. The ban on our SA. represents nothing other than a moral disarmament of the will for freedom by the government. The right of the German nation to live has never been so strongly emphasized over and over again as by this movement in contrast to those destructive elements and organisations which do not want to recognize any fatherland for themselves. The SA. has never been a military organisation; the SA. has never possessed weapons. The government knows that too. The SA. has had to carry out exclusively the political protection against the homicidal terror from the left. It merely carried out the propaganda of the movement.

The Reich Chancellor and the Reich Minister of Defense knew this very well. I will give you proof of this. The last but one emergency decree, the Emergency Decree for the Protection of the Easter Holiday, in itself provided sufficient means to ban the SA. if it had actually acted illegally in any form or had violated it in any direction. However, one thing was necessary for this: the violation had to be proven in court, and you knew, gentlemen, that you would not have been able to prove this in court. That's why you needed a second emergency decree which, again in defiance of the constitution and without a court order, could simply gag the freedom movement again. So why the new emergency decree?

Because the misconduct could not be established in court. However, the findings of the court should have shown that the allegations that are used today as bogus reasons for the dissolution of the SA. are untrue from A to Z. I know that Minister Groener, of course, carried out the ban on the SA. without any influence.

Minister, on a walk in the Harz mountains you had this illustrious idea of banning the SA. We know, however, that other forces were decisive in bringing about this decision on the Easter Walk. The reason given for banning the SA. was that it was military-like.

No, Minister, this expression "military-like" was used, and this expression allows for all kinds of definitions, leaving it to individual subordinates to do as they please.

I would like to inform you that, for example, at a demonstration of the Party—not of the SA., but after the SA. had been dissolved—in Merseburg, the police charged wildly among them, because commands were being given: right turn and left turn, and that these were military commands that were not allowed. I mean, if even the smallest reminiscence of, let's say, military customs is suppressed in this way, I don't know how you want to build up the nation's will to defend itself. On the one hand it is claimed that the SA. must be banned because it is military or military-like, but on the other hand the same SA. is accused of not wanting to protect the German borders; on the one hand it is claimed that it is military and therefore must be banned, on the other hand it is banned because it does not want to carry out military tasks. That is a contradiction which we would like to see clarified in a different way. We also know that when the Leipzig trial material becomes known, the ridiculous action that Herr Severing has allowed himself will collapse completely.

I would like to protest against this movement being accused of treason. I know that we have gradually become so bureaucratic in Parliament that we have to stick to the ministerial departments here: it is you who are responsible for treason here, not us.

Right now, gentlemen, you are objecting to this. You have become very patriotic lately; you suddenly enjoy armored cruisers and the like.

I could, however, present you with a whole mass of material showing that gentlemen of yours have always emphasized that for them the accusation of treason is not an accusation, and that conscientious objection is permissible. The SA. has been accused of treason here by the left, and against this accusation that you have made against us, I have had to make this statement. But I now have a question for the Reich Chancellor. Is it correct, Mr. Reich Chancellor, that the Ambassador von Hoesch repeatedly pointed out in urgent telegrams from Paris before the SA. ban, that the SA. ban would be a necessity both for the disarmament negotiations and for other external political negotiations?

If the banning of the SA. had indeed been necessary for foreign policy reasons, it would really not have achieved any success. What were the foreign policy consequences of the ban? No sooner had the SA. been banned here than Poland, supported by the social-democratic press of Danzig, kept urging and pressing in all its newspapers that the SA. should also be banned in Danzig, because they knew quite well that there perhaps lay the last obstacle to their being able to invade Danzig. In this case, reference was made to measures taken by their own government at home in order to push through the ban of the Danzig SA. by the Polish side at the League of Nations.

Reich Chancellor, you are operating abroad, according to the press, with the argument that in the external political negotiations certain relief must be obtained for Germany, since it is self-evident that otherwise in the future the National Socialist movement would grow stronger and stronger out of its opposition and that then there would be no opportunity at all. I would like to ask you to tell us whether you are really convinced that you can achieve any relief for Germany with this argument, or whether it would not have been more expedient to proceed the other way round and to emphasize precisely the strong national content of the movement, in order to show foreign countries that this movement must necessarily be there in order to be able to initiate a different foreign policy.

But if, on the one hand, you dissolve the SA., you are demonstrating to foreign countries that the national uprising for self-assertion and for the protection of the right to life should no longer be an option in the future. Only through this, believe me, has the danger, which has now become so acute, intensified in the East. It goes without saying that if the enemy in the East wants to take action against Germany, he can only agree to it if those organisations are suppressed which he regards as the incarnation of the nation's will to live. On the other hand, he knows that the present cabinet is based on Social Democracy and thus on the Reichsbanner, a pacifist-democratic organisation which has included conscientious objection as a special point in its programme. You can say that ten times, it is always the same. I therefore do not understand how the Reichswehr Minister, of all people, was able to support the Reichsbanner, although he must know that the Reichsbanner is home to those destructive forces which can never be reconciled with soldierly feeling and thinking, and that the Reichswehr therefore regards it as an intolerable burden.

It is known that today the SA. is the sharpest instrument in the struggle for enlightenment, in the moral struggle against the Treaty of Versailles. It is known that, on the other hand, the Reichsbanner repeatedly advocated the Treaty of Versailles.

The legal side of the SA. ban will have to be discussed in court. There we will smash and destroy the arguments that you, Minister, put forward in favor of the ban. You know that this decision cannot be upheld in court in any way. Certainly, Herr Breitscheid—I cannot go into his speech any further, because it was the swan song of a dying party—whistled very mildly. He spoke of the fact that the judges had taken an oath to the Republic, that they received their salary from the Republic, and that for these reasons a different administration of justice had to be expected from them. I was surprised that the President did not intervene here after a deliberate bending of the law was to take place from this rostrum. The judge did not take his oath to the Republic, but to the German people and to the law of the German people.

When your agitation speakers used to travel around the country and declare that it was contrary to a sense of decency that civil servants who were against this state, who were National Socialists, should take salary from this state on the first of every month. I can tell you this once: To our regret, Herr Severing has not yet personally paid the police, nor does the Republic pay them, nor does the state pay them, but the German people pay the civil servants, and we are too are among these taxpayers. It might contradict our sense of decency if today ministers, civil servants and police officers, who are suppressing and terrorizing this movement over and over again, accept their money on the first of the month from the German people, 14 million of whom are also provided by us as taxpayers.

Incidentally, the ban on SA. also has one good side. Hopefully, it has shown the center parties once and for all where complete adherence to this cabinet leads. In the end, gentlemen, the ban on SA. has completely destroyed your parties. You already know that better than we do, if you have received the necessary rejections. You see here the unfortunate entanglement that you have brought about time and again by supporting this cabinet. Again and again it is the fear of dissolution with which Herr Brüning is forcing you into the Kaudinian yoke today to support him. You know that the majority on which this cabinet is based would never exist, that the differentiation of the parties on which it is based is so great that not once would a common decision be reached if today the basis of the Brüning cabinet were not solely the fear of National Socialism. I hope that the bourgeois parties will now finally realize that if they really want to disappear for good politically, they only need to identify themselves completely once more—for the last time-with the cabinet of the Reich Chancellor.

The right of the SA. is in no way affected by this ban, and I would like to say from this very place, where the SA. has so often been reviled: If we had not had the SA., then no order at all would be possible in Germany today.

The SA. has made it possible that national politics can still be pursued today. The time will come when the bourgeois parties will also thank the SA. for having had the courage to stand up against this red plague, for having had the courage to take back the streets from your terror. We know that the SA made sacrifices, as no other movement does today. We know that these young people died out of ardent love for their people and for their fatherland, slaughtered under your murderous terror.

By the way, Minister, don't think that when you take the brown shirt off the SA. you also take off the spirit. Even if other parties change their attitudes as often as their shirts, here the spirit and attitude will remain the same, despite the ban. You will not be able to eradicate the spirit from this SA. I know that loyalty and comradeship have perhaps gradually become a phantom in certain circles, just as the oath of allegiance was once regarded as such. For us, however, loyalty, comradeship and the oath of allegiance still have the same value, they still form the foundation of the union of German men who want to stand up together for their country and their people. Here I would also like to address for the second time the accusation that the SA. is not prepared to protect the German borders. Our SA. is ready, and has been ready at all times, to be cut to pieces as the most loyal guard in defense of Germany.

You, however, only want to live from Germany, but do not want to stand up for it. At the same time, however, we emphasize that the SA. will never be used to set itself up as a truncheon guard for Versailles like the *Reichsbanner*, under whatever sporting guise it may be. You will not have the SA. for that.

Thus, as positively as foreign policy is weakened by the destruction of the German will to resist, it is negatively influenced in an unfavorable sense by the preservation of pacifist, democratic decomposition organisations of an international hue. I will pick out just one thing here from the numerous material that we could read out to you for hours: "No, you gentlemen of the Reichswehr, if you should once again unleash a defensive war, then a new enemy will arise for you who will first of all break your neck, the Reichsbanner."—Mr. Kraschutzki in the October 1929 issue of the magazine *Junge Menschen*.

You have allowed this organisation, which is responsible for this destruction of the military spirit, to exist, Minister Groener, while you ban an organisation of which—and we are proud of this—Prime Minister Tardieu declared that within it the spirit of the old army is alive. We are proud that the Prime Minister of an enemy state declares that in the SA. there is the spirit of the best of all armies and of all times.

We do not understand, Minister, how you can protect such pacifist organisations. Rest assured: the *Reichswehr* will not understand this either. But we know one thing: This eternal yielding to Social Democracy, especially in defense matters, these eternal bows to the organisations of Marxism, which have only had a destructive effect, must in the end only recall to the troops the memory of that time when this same party, and organisations similar to it, raised the red flag of betrayal at the back of the fighting army.

We know: a National Socialist Minister of Defense would not discuss the defense concerns of the German nation at all with the Social Democrats who proclaimed conscientious objection.

We do not believe that Germany's interests can be represented to the outside world as long as these un-German and anti-Christian organisations persist, which fundamentally undermine the morals of the German people. No matter how Hitler's Lauenburg speech may be twisted and distorted, it will be clearly and unambiguously understood by every German in its actual version.

Following this remark, I would like to read out a passage which our Führer said there: "It is quite understandable to me that there can be no salvation of the German border unless the whole nation stands behind the formations that want to protect a border. Germany will lose nothing more, and no border area will be sacrificed on the day when, behind Silesia and East Prussia, 25 million Germans will stand behind the National Socialist conception."

In the end, there can be no salvation of German borders at all as long as there is a leadership and a base that cannot defend Germany at all because of its inner ideological attitude. It does not even have the possibility to do so because it cannot bring the forces behind it that could perhaps be used for the defense alone. This can only be done by a government that clearly and unequivocally renounces the trajectories of the previous course and stands behind or in front of the forces on which it alone can rely.

We are told and reproached for promising so much. Chancellor, you had the opportunity two years ago to get your bearings. There the German people had spoken for the first time in their new formation of will. At that time, it would have been time to finally abandon the course with the left-wing parties. At that time, you could have earned yourself a historic merit. But not today. Two years have now passed in which so much has been destroyed, in which the national will has been suppressed again and again, that we cannot now follow this cabinet, but are virtually obliged, out of our innermost attitude to the people and the nation, to express our censure of this cabinet.

I would like to draw an analogy to the year 1919: Upper Silesia. At that time, gentlemen, volunteers also defended the German borders, but these volunteers were not your people, they were our people. Afterwards, however, these volunteers were imprisoned and persecuted as criminals by your people.

We don't want to risk that a second time.

A national Germany will protect its borders above all by first eliminating the traitors within. We will not tolerate the fact that millions of young Germans are being asked to put everything on the line at the border, while at the same time, in the background, the will to resist is being sabotaged and destroyed by organisations which have so far practiced nothing but national sabotage.

In summary, then, I say: weak and impotent in foreign policy, anti-national in domestic policy, oppression and violations of law against our movement, in which the national will of Germany to assert itself is indisputably solely represented. We have endured oppressions that are truly rare in the history of nations.

I don't have the time to explain everything that happened during the election in terms of repression and terror. I don't have time to talk about the outrageous injustice that was perpetrated against the largest movement. Not once did our presidential candidate receive radio broadcasting, it was considered a political matter alone, although the broadcasting is not paid for by the government alone, but also by the taxpayers and we therefore had the same right. Assemblies have been banned on the most ridiculous grounds, because there were not enough traffic police.

But if a National Socialist bureau had to be cleared somewhere, they arrived in armored cars and with machine guns. They have banned demonstrations, they have issued bans on public speaking.

My party comrades! We have been provoked so often that this provocation by Mr. Weiß no longer matters. Speech ban upon speech ban has been issued. They have suppressed and banned our entire press, they have even forced the press to record untrue official statements, they have simply imposed them upon them. The police exercised a terror that no longer knew any arbitrary limits. Truly a shining example of democracy and parliamentarism. An abuse of democracy! We did not create democracy, we did not wish for it. You lifted it into the saddle, you destroyed an old empire so that you could bring us the blessings of democracy.

Today, you deny this democracy more than anyone else. When Mr Breitscheid sang his gentle swan song here yesterday and complained that terror was being practiced on our side—gentlemen of the Social Democrats, who actually invented the saying: And if you don't want to be my brother, then I'll smash your head in?

This is how you initiated the terror at the time. Alongside the oppression and the terror, there is also the murderous incitement, against which there was no sufficient protection. We also demand for our relatives, hundreds of whom have now been murdered, that they too receive full state protection.

To date, we have lost several hundred of the best young Germans as sacrifices for the future freedom of Germany, truly a testimony to a will for freedom that no other organisation or movement could even come close to.

Incidentally, there is no example in world history of a government that so systematically suppressed the national strength of the people and then still wanted to have political success externally. Gentlemen of the government, you can also talk and explain what you want, the verdict on you, the justification for us, was pronounced by the German people on the 24th of April and will continue to be pronounced in our favour in the future.

A government that has governed a people so unhappily in terms of foreign and domestic policy can of course only lead to disaster in terms of economic policy. The promises of the cabinet to stimulate the economy, the promises on job creation and settlement have all stalled. Gentlemen of the government, you are not in a position to carry out this task. Your whole economic programme from the Young Plan until today is a straight line in the decline of the German economy. Foreclosures, expropriations on the one hand, handouts and waste on the other. What is unfortunate is the way taxes are announced and collected. Also unfortunate in every direction are the government's other measures, which further weaken the economically weak and further protect the strong. I will take just one example, the standstill agreement. This standstill agreement applies to the German banks, but not to the debtors of these banks; the German debtors have nothing to gain from the standstill agreement. The way in which the taxes were tendered and implemented caused a general outrage. My party comrade Straßer has already explained today in excellent words what we mean by an economic construction programme. I can therefore pass over the economic policy issues in a few words, after this issue has been dealt with in such detail this morning.

We know very well that if we take on the responsibility, we will inherit a terrible legacy. The entire economy is so overburdened and sucked dry by the mammoth state that the entire nation is in danger of going under. Above all, the last years of the current cabinet's term in office, with their hesitant measures that impose ever greater sacrifices on the economy and the people, but without steering towards a clear goal, have destroyed the last vestige of substance in the German economy. We compare, as we have always pointed out, the economy in the state with the circulation of blood in the human body, and we must firmly oppose the fact that attempts are still being made to continue to drain blood from this body and thus slowly but surely bring the body to a standstill. The programme which the Reich Chancellor allegedly started with good will and perhaps also with the best of intentions for the elevation of the economy, above all of agriculture, has, precisely as a result of the hesitant measures, the half-measures, gradually led to an appalling shrinkage of the entire productive power of Germany, essentially, however, to the disadvantage of the working masses in particular. 6 million unemployed are a staggering testimony to this.

It is therefore incomprehensible to us how representatives of this government, and unfortunately also the Reich Chancellor himself, can still claim and express today that, if we took responsibility, it is certain that chaos in Germany is to be expected.

In contrast, we have to note that since the present government took office, the situation has almost turned into chaos. We should not be accused of irresponsibility when we see that the present government, which the overwhelming majority of the German people no longer want, is endeavoring to squeeze the last remnants out of the economy and the creative classes, and then to leave the chaos to us in the parliamentary-democratic system.

If we keep calling for responsibility today, it is not because we, like the others in charge of the government, long for ministerial chairs and party officials' posts, but because we have seen in the course of the last two years that every day that keeps us away from responsibility must bring us closer to economic and thus state chaos.

The sacrifices made so far have been made uselessly, and sacrifices that could have saved the situation two years ago are now also doomed to uselessness. It is clear that the youth occupies a large space in our movement, and this only because it sees that the exponents of the older generation are managing the state and the national economy, which they took over after the lost war, in the most insane way, and that with the youth every possibility of development and every space for development is being narrowed increasingly. Young people find it unacceptable that the present generation wants to live at the expense of the young, only to leave them with nothing. They cannot expect that these young people, who are following after them and who have a clear understanding of these things, will put up with it any longer. It is willing with all its vigour and inherent tenacity to correct today, even at the greatest sacrifice, in order to regain, albeit in the long term, the possibility of serious activity, work and existence.

The most irresponsible agitation, which even prominent members of the system are not afraid of, is to claim that we are creating a new inflation. What is not mentioned is that Herr Hilferding, as an expert on inflation, must feel very offended by this. That is your territory, not ours. It is there (to the left) that the inflationists sit and not here (to the right).

I don't want to go into the tone that is common in your ranks (to the left). A government which, in our view, has lost and continues to lose every battle in domestic, foreign and economic policy can no longer claim trust. We see every additional day of these methods of government as a national calamity and the costs incurred are in no way justified by the successes. Even if, on your forays into the intellectual heritage of National

Socialism, you pick out something trivial, it will be completely ineffective, because the people's lack of confidence will not allow it to have any effect. It is always the case in history that if a commander loses every battle, he must disappear. The troops are not there to bleed themselves to death for a commander, and the people are not there to ruin themselves for governments that are not able to cope with the situation.

Here I recall a great historical example from recent German history. When in autumn 1916 the situation was almost desperate—all of Germany desperate, the army hopeless, the French attacks at Verdun and the Somme, the impression made by the English offensive, the Austrian failure in the south, the Brussilov offensive in the east, Romania's declaration of war— only new men could help, the old men had to go and men with new names had to restore confidence. We are in the same situation today.

Thus, at that time, a new hope gripped every soldier because two new names had arrived who had the fullest confidence. But let us also learn the lesson from the situation at that time. We are convinced that if it had been possible to call the commanders Hindenburg and Ludendorff to the spot perhaps a year earlier, the beginning of the world war, apart from the revolt of the Social Democracy, would have been different. And so we also declare today: Herr Reichskanzler: perhaps there can soon be a too late for the whole nation, as there has already been a too late for your cabinet today. The cabinet no longer enjoys the confidence of the people; it demands new men today, as it clearly stated in the election on the 24th. Every day longer on this unfortunate path will only increase the shambles that has been created here.

We also cannot believe that the emergency decrees will somehow master the situation. We do know that a vast number of emergency decrees have been issued to date, but that they were created more to bridge one's own need to govern than to actually alleviate the need of the German people. It is not acceptable that such emergency decrees should very often shift the blame. If you come and say that you are going to change the stock corporation law or some other things, then you are trying to create an opinion among the people as if these people were to blame, whereas in reality the government alone is to blame, because this government did not recognize in time where the forces on which it must rely are to be found. We therefore declare once again that the situation cannot be mastered with these emergency decrees, which are also constitutionally questionable and unsuitable.

We turn to all parties that consciously want to work on the construction of Germany. Especially now, after we have emerged so strong from the elections, we offer our hand for joint construction. But you must know that a new course must be steered. We are not in favour of somehow adding beauty patches to old patchwork. A completely new course must be steered. Whoever is ready for this, may receive our hand. On the other hand, we declare and leave no doubt that our struggle continues relentlessly!

It has been repeatedly claimed that our movement has already passed its peak. That's what they said after every election: "Now the National Socialists will decrease." This was also one of the fundamental illusions that this cabinet indulged in. Our peak has not yet been passed; it will be reached on the day when the entire German people, apart from its seducers, stands behind our cause of freedom and the opportunity to exist.

We will therefore continue to fulfil our historical mission to reconcile the classes, to make it clear to the ranks that the questions of the fate of the nation must be placed above the small questions of everyday life and that the ranks, classes, confessions must subordinate themselves to this one question of the fate of the German nation. However, in order to be able to fulfil this historic mission for which this power center has been formed, the first precondition is that the Brüning cabinet disappears. The Brüning cabinet must be eliminated so that Germany can live. (*Verhandlungen des Reichstags, V. Wahlperiode 1930, Band 446*; Translation: Gary Costello)

05.06.1932	Participated in the *"Gau-Sturmtag"* in Linz (Oberösterreich), together with Franz Ritter von Epp. Members of the NSDAP from all over Austria and Germany were in attendance, with Göring and Epp giving speeches before large crowds. The events were held in three major locations, as follows:

Volksgartensaal (c. 2,000 participants, 200 in uniform)
Parteiheim Märzenkeller (c. 1,800 participants, 1,400 in uniform)
Restaurationsgarten (c. 1,600 participants, 900 in uniform)

The *"Gau-Sturmtag"* culminated in a march through the city of Linz and returning to the *Märzenkeller* and involving 5,191 men (3,717 SA, 343 SS, and 627 HJ) as well as forty cars, 134 motorcycles, six musical bands, seventy-two flags, and four standards. (Data from Thomas Dostal, *Das "Braune Netzwerk" in Linz: Die illegalen nationalsozialistischen Aktivitaten zwischen 1933 und 1938*, p. 36)

01.07.1932–26.01.1934	Assigned to the *Stab der Obersten SA-Führer*.
15.07.1932	One month after the lifting of the government ban on the SA, delivered a speech in the Berlin *Sportpalast* in which he called for the arming of the SA:

The murdering rabble still counts on the discipline of the SA. It also knows that there is an order that no SA man is allowed to carry a gun. I tell you: this is the end. When the Führer returns from East Prussia in the next few days, I will ask him together with other leaders of the Party—and I know that the request will be fulfilled—that this order be revoked. Three times twenty-four hours the right of self-defense is established, and the Brown Shirts are given freedom, and the cowardly rabble crawls into the last hole. (Hans Klering, et al., *Weissbuch über die Erschiessungen am 30. Juni 1934*, p. 34)

30.08.1932–23.04.1945	*Präsident des Deutschen Reichstages* (President of the German National Parliament). Succeeded Paul Löbe (SPD). Dieter Hoffmann provides an example of Göring's behavior in this role:

On 12 September 1932, a sensational incident occurred in the Reichstag. Even foreign countries reported about it extensively. In France, it was said that Germany was no longer governable. At the beginning of the

plenary session, the communist deputy Ernst Torgler moved to change the agenda and to express a vote of no confidence in the Government. But before the Parliament could decide, Reichskanzler Franz von Papen asked to take the floor. Thereupon, Reichstagspräsident Hermann Göring, one of the best-known National Socialists, refused to grant it to him because voting had already begun. Now von Papen rose, but Göring ignored him once more. Finally, the Chancellor took out a document from his red folder and went to the President of Parliament to hand it over. When the latter refused, the head of government put the document on his desk and left the chamber with the ministers. The vote that followed produced the most negative vote against state leadership in all of German history, with 513 votes against only 32 for the government. However, it should never have taken place, because according to the Constitution of the Weimar Republic, "representatives of the Reich Government had to be heard in the Reichstag even outside the agenda." Apart from that, it had come about through the interaction of the two extreme parties. Göring, as the representative of the strongest party, brought the KPD's motion to the floor. The paper presented by Papen and disregarded by the Nazi politician was a decree by Reichspräsident Paul von Hindenburg for the immediate dissolution of Parliament. The result of the vote had been foreseeable, since the presidential government supported by Hindenburg was backed only by the small right-wing conservative Deutschnationale Volkspartei (DNVP). All other parties in the Reichstag were against the so-called Cabinet of the Barons [Kabinett der Barone], in which ministers of noble origin formed the majority. With the vote, Göring clearly violated the Constitution. If he had given the Chancellor the floor, the Reichstag would have been dissolved immediately. According to a report in the respected *Vossische Zeitung*, Göring gloated at a dinner with Adolf Hitler, Joseph Goebbels, former Italian Interior Minister Luigi Federzoni, and representatives of his country's embassy that same evening, that he had known the content of the document von Papen wanted to give him from the begging. He had been aware that the Government wanted to stop the vote with its motion, "he had therefore been determined not to let the Reich Chancellor have his say under any circumstances." The Reichstagspräsident's disregard for the Constitution testifies not only to his will to bring about a loss of face for the government at all costs, but also to the National Socialists' treatment of the Republic and its institutions. (Hoffmann, *Der Skandal*, pp. 9-10; Translation courtesy of Gary Costello)

02.10.1932	Participated in the *"Gauparteitag der NSDAP"* in Wien, accompanied by Ernst Röhm, Julius Streicher, Joseph Berchtold, and others.
Mid-November 1932	Sent by Hitler to Rome to meet with Benito Mussolini (possibly to raise funds for the NSDAP, which had lost 2 million votes in the *Reichstag* elections of 06.11.1932 and was therefore reduced from 230 seats to 196).
22.01.1933–30.01.1933	*Bevollmächtigter für weitere Verhandlungen* (Plenipotentiary for Further Negotiations [toward the establishment of a Hitler-led coalition government]) of the NSDAP.

30.01.1933–05.05.1933	*Reichsminister ohne Geschäftsbereich* (Reich Minister without Portfolio).
30.01.1933–11.04.1933	*Reichskommissar für das preußische Innenministerium* (Reich Commissioner for the Prussian Ministry of Interior). On 11.04.1933, he was formally appointed as *Preußischer Minister des Innern*. Succeeded Dr. Franz Bracht. Succeeded by Dr. Wilhelm Frick. Soon after his appointment, he began a wide-ranging purge of the Ministry. Volker Ullrich writes:

Fourteen police presidents in Prussian cities as well as numerous other senior municipal officers were sent into retirement in February 1933 alone. "Goebbels is cleaning house," Goebbels declared [in his diary] on 16 February. "We are gradually enmeshing ourselves in governmental administration." (Ulrich, *Hitler: Ascent: 1889–1939*, p.)

Göring himself later wrote:

... The Führer gave me the Prussian Ministry of the Interior, above all things in order that I should overthrow and crush Communism in this, the greatest State of the Reich. He wished me to root out this destructive and traitorous party, and to inspire the State officials with the austere philosophy of National Socialism in place of the existing corrupt Marxist-bourgeois idea....

An enormous task lay before me.... And now, on the 1st of February 1933, amidst the deafening applause of a crowd of several thousands, the victorious swastika was hoisted to the main flagstaff, before a guard of honor consisting of police, SS and Stahlhelm and a band playing the Prussian ceremonial march....

I had taken on a heavy responsibility, and a vast field of work lay before me. It was clear that I should be able to make little use of the administrative system as it then was. I should have to make great changes. To begin with, it seemed to me of the first importance to get the weapon of the criminal and political police firmly into my own hands. Here it was that I made the first sweeping changes of personnel. Out of 32 police chiefs I removed 22. Hundreds of inspectors and thousands of police sergeants followed in the course of the next month. New men were brought in, and in every case these men came from the great reservoir of the SA and SS. My task was to inspire the police with an entirely new spirit. Previously the police had been degraded to the role of whipping-boy for the Republic, partly by compelling them to belabour the Republic's opponents and partly by always shifting the responsibility on to the shoulders of minor officials, the leaders being too cowardly to stand up for their subordinates. Now that was all going to be changed. Authority would be in the right place. After a few weeks one could already notice how the bearing of the police had changed, how they had become more assured and self-confident, how the embittered officials gradually became valuable officers and police-sergeants.... Devotion to duty, loyalty and obedience were demanded of them, and above all that they should pledge themselves unreservedly to serve the National Socialist State and the new Germany. (Göring, *Germany Reborn* [translation of *Aufbau einer Nation*, 1934], pp. 119-122)

30.01.1933–05.05.1933	*Reichskommissar für den Luftverkehr* (Reich Commissioner for Air Transportation; redesignated as *Reichskommissar für die Luftfahrt* [Reich Commissioner for Aviation] on 02.02.1933).
07.02.1933	In his capacity as *Reichskommissar für das preußische Innenministerium*, issued the following proclamation to officials of the Prussian government:

I call upon you to reform Prussia together with me, in accordance with the true ideals of the old Prussian administration, making this once more the citadel of cleanliness, economy and a devoted sense of duty. I am firmly convinced that for the main part the Prussian civil service has not yet been touched by the philosophy that in past years has placed the false gospel of class warfare above the unity of the nation.

If, therefore, you are willing to cooperate with me in sincerely and devotedly rebuilding the Fatherland, you will always find me the promoter of your interests. Should there, however, be officials who do not feel able to ride in the same direction with me on the ship whose wheel I have taken, I expect that as honest men they will leave before the voyage starts. ("Nazis Belabor Foes While Asking Unity" in *The New York Times*, 08.02.1933)

17.02.1933	Issued his *"Schießbefehl"* (shooting order) which contained the following:

[Police are] to use all the means in their power to support every activity undertaken in the national interest, whereas acts of Communist terror and similar attacks are to be rigorously resisted, if necessary with the use of weapons. Police officers who use their weapons when carrying out their duties will be protected by me without regard for the consequences of their use of those weapons. Conversely, anyone who out of a misguided sense of consideration fails to use his weapons will face disciplinary proceedings. (Thomas Friedrich, *Hitler's Berlin: Abused City*, p. 323)

And:

Each bullet which now leaves the barrel of a policeman's revolver is my bullet. If you call that a murder, it is I who am the murderer. These are my orders and I give them my full support. I assume the responsibility and I am not afraid. (Jacques Delarue, *Gestapo: A History of Horror*, p. 34)

20.02.1933	Delivered a speech to Prussian Police officials from which the following is excerpted:

I believe I can spare myself special reference to the fact that the police must refrain from even a mere semblance of an antagonistic attitude toward organizations, such as the Nazi storm troops and the Stahlhelm of the Nationalist parties. I expect, on the contrary, that the police will establish and maintain a cordial accord with the organizations mentioned, which contain the most important forces for reconstruction of the State.

Going beyond that, every manifestation for a Nationalist purpose and Nationalist propaganda must be supported with full vigor. With respect to them, police restrictions or instructions must be resorted to only in the most urgent cases.

On the other hand, the activities of organizations inimical to the State must be countered with the greatest rigor. The police must proceed against Communist acts of terrorism with the utmost severity and must use their arms ruthlessly when necessary. I will protect every policeman who makes use of firearms in the exercise of his duty, regardless of results. Police officers who from false consideration fail to act may count on disciplinary penalties.

For the protection of the Nationalist population, often hampered in its expression, there must be the most rigorous application of the statutory provisions against prohibited demonstrations, unlicensed meetings, incitement to treason, mass strikes, delinquencies of the press and other activities of disturbers of the peace.

Every police officer must always bear in mind that failing to act is a graver fault than errors made in action.

I expect and hope that all the police feel at one with me with respect to the goal of saving the fatherland from threatened ruin by the consolidation of all nationalist forces. ("Police in Prussia Told To Shoot Reds" in *The New York Times*, 21.02.1933)

22.02.1933 — Established the *Hilfspolizei* (Hipo, auxiliary police), composed of approximately 25,000 SA, 15,000 SS, and 10,000 *"Stahlhelm"-Bund* men. Among other duties, the Hipo rounded up political opponents and sent them to the *Oranienburg* and *Papenburg* concentration camps which had also been set up on Göring's orders. By October 1933, some 700 political prisoners had been murdered in these and other *"wilde Lager"* ("wild camps") of the SA. The following are excerpts from Göring's order establishing the *Hilfspolizei*:

The growing excesses of the Left radicals, especially in Communist quarters, have produced a constant and intolerable threat to public security as well as to the lives and property of the State-conscious populace. The available police forces are far overtaxed. It is therefore no longer possible to renounce the voluntary support, in case of emergency, of helpers fit to act as auxiliary police....

Only honorable Germans entitled to vote and standing on nationalistic ground may be sworn in as auxiliary policemen. They must be provided with authorization by the police and must wear officially stamped white arm-bands, otherwise wearing their own clothing, which may also be the uniform of organizations... (Frederich T. Birchall, "Hitler Arms Nazis as Prussian Police" in *The New York Times*, 25.02.1933)

The following is excerpted from the cross examination of Göring by Justice Robert Jackson, chief prosecutor of the International Military Tribunal at Nürnberg, on 18.03.1946:

JACKSON:	The principles of the authoritarian government which you set up required, as I understand you, that there be tolerated no opposition by political parties which might defeat or obstruct the policy of the Nazi Party?
GÖRING:	You have understood this quite correctly. By that time we had lived long enough with opposition and we had had enough of it. Through opposition we had been completely ruined. It was now time to have done with it and to start building up.
JACKSON:	After you came to power, you regarded it necessary, in order to maintain power, to suppress all opposition parties?
GÖRING:	We found it necessary not to permit any more opposition, yes.
JACKSON:	And you also held it necessary that you should suppress all individual opposition lest it should develop into a party of opposition?
GÖRING:	Insofar as opposition seriously hampered our work of building up, this opposition of individual persons was, of course, not tolerated. Insofar as it was simply a matter of harmless talk, it was considered to be of no consequence.
JACKSON:	Now, in order to make sure that you suppressed the parties, and individuals also, you found it necessary to have a secret political police to detect opposition?
GÖRING:	I have already stated that I considered that necessary, just as previously the political police had existed, but on a firmer basis and larger scale.
JACKSON:	And upon coming to power you also considered it immediately necessary to establish concentration camps to take care of your incorrigible opponents?
GÖRING:	I have already stated that the reason for the concentration camps was not because it could be said, "Here are a number of people who are opposed to us and they must be taken into protective custody." Rather they were set up as a lightning measure against the functionaries of the Communist Party who were attacking us in the thousands, and who, since they were taken into protective custody, were not put in prison. But it was necessary, as I said, to erect a camp for them—one, two, or three camps.
JACKSON:	But you are explaining, as the high authority of this system, to men who do not understand it very well, and I want to know what was necessary to run the kind of system that you set up in Germany. The concentration camp was one of the things you found immediately necessary upon corning into power, was it not? And you set them up as a matter of necessity, as you saw it?
GÖRING:	That was faultily translated-it went too fast. But I believe I have understood the sense of your remarks. You asked me if I considered it necessary to establish concentration camps immediately in order to eliminate opposition. Is that correct?
JACKSON:	Your answer is "yes," I take it?
GÖRING:	Yes.
JACKSON:	Was it also necessary, in operating this system, that you must not have persons entitled to public trials in independent courts? And you immediately issued an order that your political police would not be subject to court review or to court orders, did you not?
GÖRING:	You must differentiate between the two categories; those who had

committed some act of treason against the new state, or those who might be proved to have committed such an act, were naturally turned over to the courts. The others, however, of whom one might expect such acts, but who had not yet committed them, were taken into protective custody, and these were the people who were taken to concentration camps. I am now speaking of what happened at the beginning. Later things changed a great deal. Likewise, if for political reasons- to answer your question- someone was taken into protective custody, that is, purely for reasons of state, this could not be reviewed or stopped by any court...

JACKSON: ... You did prohibit all court review and considered it necessary to prohibit court review of the causes for taking people into what you called protective custody? [...]

GÖRING: In connection with your question that these cases could not be reviewed by the court, I want to say that a decree was issued through me and Frick jointly to the effect that those who were turned over to concentration camps were to be informed after 24 hours of the reason for their being turned over, and that after 48 hours, or some short period of time, they should have the right to an attorney. But this by no means rescinded my order that a review was not permitted by the courts of a politically necessary measure of protective custody. These people were simply to be given an opportunity of making a protest.

JACKSON: Protective custody meant that you were taking people into custody who had not committed any crimes but who, you thought, might possibly commit a crime?

GÖRING: Yes. People were arrested and taken into protective custody who had not yet committed- any crime, but who could be expected to do so if they remained free, just as extensive protective measures are being taken in Germany today on a tremendous scale. (*Trial of the Major War Criminals Before the International Military Tribunal, Nuremberg, 14 November 1945–1 October 1946, Volume IX*)

In his memoirs, the former British ambassador in Berlin, Sir Neville Henderson, wrote:

I once did my best to persuade Goering to use his influence with a view to their abolition. His answer was typical. After listening to all I had to say, he got up without a word and went to a bookcase from which he took a volume of the German Encyclopaedia. Opening it at Konzentrationslager (concentration camps) he read out, "First used by the British, in the South African War." He was pleased with his own retort; but the truth of the matter was that, though it was he who had originally formed these camps when he was Minister of Police for Prussia, he had no longer anything to do with them. They were entirely under the control of Himmler. (Henderson, *Failure of a Mission. Berlin 1937–1939*)

In an interrogation report of 23.05.1945, Major Paul Kubala (commander of the 7th Army Interrogation Center in Augsburg) wrote of Göring's claims with regard to what had occurred in the camps:

Although Goering openly admitted that he knew of the "existence" of concentration camps, he claimed that he never realized that they were particularly bad institutions. "I always thought that they were places where people were employed for some useful work." After seeing some of the pictures taken at Dachau Concentration Camp, Goering said "all this must have happened in the last few weeks." He said that he could not "understand" that there are some people in Germany who could commit such atrocities. ("Interrogation Records Prepared for War Crimes Proceedings at Nuernberg, 1945–1947/OCCPAC Interrogation Transcripts and Related Records: Göring, Hermann"; Publication Number M1270, Record Group RG238)

25.02.1933	Established the *Polizeiabteilung z.b.V.* "*Wecke,*" an elite 414-man police unit designed to seek out and destroy "enemies of the State" (principally communists). It was named for its commander, *Polizei-Major* (promoted to *Polizei-Oberstleutnant* on 21.03.1933 and eventually to *General der Luftwaffe*—equivalent to *General der Flieger*—on 01.12.1942) Walther Wecke, who led the unit until 05.06.1934 (he was succeeded on 06.06.1934 by *Oberstleutnant der Landespolizei* Friedrich Wilhelm Jakoby). On 17.07.1933, the unit was redesignated *Landespolizeigruppe Wecke z.b.V.*, and on 22.12.1933 it became *Landespolizeigruppe General Göring*. Further redesignation, as *Regiment General Göring*, took place on 01.04.1935.
27.02.1933	The "*Reichstagsbrand*" (Reich Parliament Fire) in Berlin. The building was largely gutted, however, Göring's office remained intact. A mentally troubled ex-communist Dutchman, Marinus van der Lubbe, twenty-four years of age, was discovered by firefighters as they attempted to douse the flames, and he thus became the chief suspect. Göring was advised of the fire at 09:30 hours and raced to the scene. The following day, at Göring's command, some 4,000 communists were arrested, and all Social Democratic and Communist newspapers banned. Hitler issued the "*Verordnung des Reichspräsidenten zum Schutz von Volk und Staat vom 28. Februar 1933*" (Decree of the Reich President for the Protection of the People and State of 28 February 1933), signed by *Reichspräsident* von Hindenburg, which stated:

On the basis of Article 48, Section 2, of the German Constitution, the following is decreed as a defensive measure against Communist acts of violence that endanger the state:

§ 1

Articles 114, 115, 117, 118, 123, 124, and 153 of the Constitution of the German Reich are suspended until further notice. Thus, restrictions on personal liberty, on the right of free expression of opinion, including freedom of the press, on the right of assembly and the right of association, and violations of the privacy of postal, telegraphic, and telephonic communications, and warrants for house searches, orders for confiscations as well as restrictions on property are permissible beyond the legal limits otherwise prescribed.

§ 2

If any state fails to take the necessary measures to restore public safety and order, the Reich government may temporarily take over the powers of the highest state authority.

§ 3

State and local authorities must obey the orders decreed by the Reich government on the basis of § 2.

§ 4

Whoever provokes, appeals for, or incites the disobedience of the orders given out by the supreme state authorities or the authorities subject to them for the execution of this decree, or the orders given by the Reich government according to § 2, can be punished—insofar as the deed is not covered by other decrees with more severe punishments—with imprisonment of not less than one month, or with a fine from 150 to 15,000 Reichsmarks.

Whoever endangers human life by violating § 1 is to be punished by sentence to a penitentiary, under mitigating circumstances with imprisonment of not less than six months and, when the violation causes the death of a person, with death, under mitigating circumstances with a penitentiary sentence of not less than two years. In addition, the sentence may include the confiscation of property.

Whoever provokes or incites an act contrary to the public welfare is to be punished with a penitentiary sentence, under mitigating circumstances, with imprisonment of not less than three months.

§ 5

The crimes which under the Criminal Code are punishable with life in a penitentiary are to be punished with death: i.e., in Sections 81 (high treason), 229 (poisoning), 306 (arson), 311 (explosion), 312 (flooding), 315, paragraph 2 (damage to railways), 324 (general public endangerment through poison).

Insofar as a more severe punishment has not been previously provided for, the following are punishable with death or with life imprisonment or with imprisonment not to exceed 15 years:

1. Anyone who undertakes to kill the Reich President or a member or a commissioner of the Reich government or of a state government, or provokes such a killing, or agrees to commit it, or accepts such an offer, or conspires with another for such a murder;

2. Anyone who under Section 115, paragraph 2, of the Criminal Code (serious rioting) or of Section 125, paragraph 2, of the Criminal Code (serious disturbance of the peace) commits these acts with arms or cooperates consciously and intentionally with an armed person;

3. Anyone who commits a kidnapping under Section 239 of the Criminal Code with the intention of making use of the kidnapped person as a hostage in the political struggle.

§ 6

This decree enters into force on the day of its promulgation.
Berlin, 28. February 1933

The Reich President von Hindenburg
The Reich Chancellor Adolf Hitler
The Reich Minister of the Interior Frick
The Reich Minister of Justice Dr. Gürtner
(Translated from *Reichsgesetzblatt 1933, Teil 1, Nr. 17*)

As a result of the decree, Göring's *Hilfspolizei* were free to terrorize all real and perceived enemies of the new regime, and numerous "wild" concentration camps were set up for their detention and torture. Within a week of the fire, accusations arose in Germany and abroad that it had been a clever ploy devised by Hitler, Göring, and other Nazis to permit their unchallenged dictatorship over the Reich. Also, on the 28th, Hitler wrote the following letter to Göring:

In yesterday's dastardly attack on the Reichstag building bearing the signature of a criminal Communist hand, the prompt action of the Berlin Fire Department, the circumspect direction of its leadership, and the self-sacrificing duty performed by individual firemen aided in averting, within the space of a few hours, the immediate danger of the complete destruction of the building and in holding the fire in containment.

It was also the active initiative of the police which made it possible to go about the work of extinguishing the fire without disruption and to conduct a successful investigation into the crime.

I am glad to take this opportunity to extend my special thanks and my warmest appreciation to all those who took part in the rescue operation, and I request that you, Herr Minister, bring this gratitude to the attention of the Berlin Fire Department and Police.
Adolf Hitler
(Dr. Max Domarus, ed., Hitler. *Speeches and Proclamations, 1932–1945: The Years 1932–1934*, p. 259)

On 1 March, Göring delivered a speech alleging a massive Communist plot against the new regime:

The communists recruited militant workers through leaflets and passes to form a mass Red self-defense. This institution was a cover to mobilize the masses of revolutionary communists and use them in the struggle against the people and the state.

I would like to state openly that we do not want to wage a defensive struggle but want to go on the attack on the whole front. It will be my foremost task to eradicate communism from our population. That is why we have also mobilised those nationalist forces in Germany whose main task must be to overcome communism.

On the 15th of February it was established that the KPD was busy forming terrorist groups of up to 200 men. The task of these groups was to put on SA uniforms and then to attack cars, department stores, shops, etc. Such raids were also to be carried out on allied associations, such as the Stahlhelm and nationalist parties. The intention was to disrupt the unity of the nationalist Movement. On the other hand, terrorist groups in Stahlhelm uniforms were to carry out similar acts. When arrested, false identity cards were to be shown. Furthermore, numerous forged orders were found from SA and Stahlhelm leaders in which the SA was mysteriously ordered to be ready on the night of the 6th of March in order to occupy Berlin and to do so with ruthless use of weapons, suppression of all resistance, etc. These forged orders were then disseminated to authorities and citizens in order to raise the spectre of a National Socialist coup d'état and to create the necessary confusion among the workers. Police orders were also forged, according to which armored cars were to be delivered. In a meeting of the KPD on the 18th of February, there was talk of an explicit attack pact of the united proletarians against the bourgeoisie and against the fascist states. On the same day, the leader of a bridge demolition squad, who became a suspect due to the absence of large quantities of explosives, was arrested. Soon afterwards, an organisation of the KPD was discovered which was to employ poison. Through the uncovering of such a poison plan in Köln am Rhein it became apparent that the poison was to be used in communal meals of the SA as well as the Stahlhelm. Another document proves that not only the wives and children of leading personalities were to be held hostage, but also the wives and children of police officers, who were to be used as a living barricade during demonstrations. The leadership of this murder organisation was in the hands of the communist leader Münzenberg. On the 22nd of February, the Central Committee issued the call to arm the workers. The corresponding order said: "Every means and every weapon are to be used for the application of terror." Mass strikes were ordered. Solidarity strikes were to be prepared. All people who knew how to handle a gun were to report in, everything was to change to illegality....

I would say to the Communists that I have not lost my nerve yet, and I feel strong enough to stand up to their criminal activities! (*"Den Kommunisten darf ich sagen Meine Nerven sind bisher noch nicht durchgegangen, und ich fühle mich stark genug, ihrem verbrecherischen Treiben Paroli zu bieten!"*)
(*Braunbuch über Reichstagsbrand und Hitler-Terror*, pp. 60-61; Translation: Gary Costello)

In postwar years, the ex-police officials Rudolf Diels and Hans Bernd Gisevius each placed the blame for the conflagration squarely on the Nazi leadership, in Diels' case Göring ("Göring knew exactly how the fire was to be started [and ordered me] to prepare, prior to the fire, a list of people who were to be arrested immediately after it.") and according to Gisevius, Goebbels ("... it was Goebbels who first thought of setting the *Reichstag* on fire"). The following is excerpted from the cross-examination of Göring by Justice Robert Jackson at Nürnberg (18.03.1946):

GÖRING: That accusation that I had set fire to the Reichstag came from a certain foreign press. That could not bother me because it was not consistent with the facts. I had no reason or motive for setting fire to the Reichstag. From the artistic point of view I did not at all regret that the assembly chamber was burned—I hoped to build a better one. But I did regret very much that I was forced to find a new meeting place for the Reichstag and, not being able to find one, I had to give up my Kroll Opera House, that is, the second State Opera House, for that purpose. The opera seemed to me much more important than the Reichstag.

JACKSON: Have you ever boasted of burning the Reichstag building, even by way of joking?

GÖRING: No. I made a joke, if that is the one you are referring to, when I said that, after this, I should be competing with Nero and that probably people would soon be saying that, dressed in a red toga and holding a lyre in my hand, I looked on at the fire and played while the Reichstag was burning. That was the joke. But the fact was that I almost perished in the flames, which would have been very unfortunate for the German people, but very fortunate for their enemies.

JACKSON: You never stated then that you burned the Reichstag?

GÖRING: No. I know that Herr Rauschning said in the book which he wrote, and which has often been referred to here, that I had discussed this with him. I saw Herr Rauschning only twice in my life and only for a short time on each occasion. If I had set fire to the Reichstag, I would presumably have let that be known only to my closest circle of confidants, if at all. I would not have told it to a man whom I did not know and whose appearance I could not describe at all today. That is an absolute distortion of the truth.

JACKSON: Do you remember the luncheon on Hitler's birthday in 1942 at the Kasino, the officers' mess, at the headquarters of the Fuehrer in East Prussia?

GÖRING: No.

JACKSON: You do not remember that? I will ask that you be shown the affidavit of General Franz Halder, and I call your attention to his statements which may refresh your recollection. I read it.

"On the occasion of a luncheon on the Fuehrer's birthday in 1942, the people around the Fuehrer turned the conversation to the Reichstag building and its artistic value. I heard with my own ears how Goring broke into the conversation and shouted: 'The only one who really knows the Reichstag is I, for I set fire to it.' And saying this he slapped his thigh."

GÖRING: This conversation did not take place and I request that I be confronted with Herr Halder. First of all, I want to emphasize that what is written here is utter nonsense. It says, "The only one who really knows the Reichstag is I." The Reichstag was known to every representative in the Reichstag. The fire took place only in the general assembly room, and many hundreds or thousands of people knew this room as well as I did. A statement of this type is utter nonsense. How Herr Halder came to make that statement I do not know. Apparently that bad memory, which also let him down in military matters, is the only explanation. (*Trial of the Major War Criminals Before the International Military Tribunal, Nuremberg, 14 November 1945–1 October 1946, Volume IX*)

On 04.11.1933, Göring and Goebbels were called as witnesses to the "*Reichstagsbrandprozeß*" (*Reichstag* Fire Trial) before the *Reichsgericht* in Leipzig. On trial in addition to van der Lubbe were the Bulgarian communist leaders Georgi Mikhaylovich Dimitrov, Vasil Kontantionov Tanev, and Blagoi Simeonov Popov, as well as Ernst Torgler (chairman of the KPD in the *Reichstag*), all of whom were alleged to have plotted the destruction of the German parliament building. Dimitrov, who was ultimately acquitted along with all of his co-defendants, made a particularly strong impression as he relentlessly interrogated Göring:

DIMITROV: On 28 February, the morning papers published a statement or an interview by Ministerpräsident Göring on the Reichstag fire. This report alleged—I remember its general sense very clearly—that the fire had been started by the Communist Party, that Torgler was one of the culprits, and that the arrested Dutch Communist. van der Lubbe carried his passport and a membership card of the Communist Party on his person. I should like to know how Ministerpräsident Göring could have known at the time that van der Lubbe had a Communist Party membership card on him?

GÖRING: I must admit that, so far, I have not bothered unduly about this trial, that is, I haven't read all the reports. I did gather, however, that you are an exceptionally bright fellow and hence I should have expected even you to know the correct answer to this question, which was given long ago. I have already testified that I don't rush round pulling things out of people's pockets. In case you don't know, I have a police force to do that sort of thing and—in case you don't know that either—the police search every criminal and in case you don't know even that they report their findings to me. The whole thing is really quite simple.

DIMITROV: Herr Ministerpräsident...

COURT PRESIDENT DR. WILHELM BÜNGER (hereafter PRESIDENT): Dimitrov!

DIMITROV: If I may speak quite freely...

PRESIDENT: First listen to what I have to say. I should like to draw your attention to the fact that this question has been fully answered.

DIMITROV: If I may speak quite freely...

PRESIDENT: The question has been answered I tell you. If you want to ask a further question then please do so, but in such a way as to make its purport quite clear from the start.

DIMITROV: Yes, quite clear. I should like to put it to the Herr Ministerpräsident that the three police officers who arrested and searched van der Lubbe all agreed that no Communist Party membership card was found on him. I should like to know where the report that such a card was found came from.

GÖRING: I can tell you that very easily ... [DIMITROV: Please do!] I was told by an officer. Things which were reported to me on the night of the fire, particularly those which cropped up in the course of explanations by officials, could not all be tested and proved. The report was made to me by a responsible official and was accepted as a fact. As it could not be immediately tested, it was announced as a fact. When I issued the first report to the press on the morning after the fire, the interrogation of van der Lubbe was not concluded. In any case, I do not see that anyone has anything to complain of, because it seems to have been proved in the trial that van der Lubbe had no such card on him.

DIMITROV: As Prussian Ministerpräsident and Minister of the Interior, did you order an immediate police investigation?

GÖRING: I could not understand a word of what you were saying, so please repeat the last sentence.

DIMITROV: I was saying, did Herr Göring, as Prussian Ministerpräsident, as Minister of the Interior and as Speaker of the Reichstag, give immediate orders for the apprehension of van der Lubbe's accomplices? [GÖRING: Yes, of course.] After all, he is the one—and he has said so himself—who bears the full responsibility, for his department and for his police. Is that not so? [GÖRING: Quite so!] I would like to ask the Minister of the Interior what steps he took on 28 and 29 February or on the following days to make sure that van der Lubbe's route to Henningsdorf, and his stay and meetings with other people there, were investigated by the police in order to assist them in tracking down van der Lubbe's accomplices?

PRESIDENT: Your question is quite long enough!

DIMITROV: Quite clear enough!

GÖRING: I have already acknowledged my responsibility. You didn't even have to ask your question. If you had only paid attention, you would have heard me say that, as a Minister, I don't have to track criminals like a detective, and that I leave it to the police to make detailed investigations. I merely gave orders to carry out the investigation with the utmost speed and with the utmost care. Of course, I, too, was fully aware that van der Lubbe must have had accomplices. [DIMITROV: Quite true!] and I ordered their speedy arrest.

DIMITROV: When you, as Prussian Ministerpräsident and Minister of the Interior, let it be known in Germany and abroad that the Communists burned the Reichstag. [GÖRING: Exactly!] that the Communist Party [GÖRING: Quite so!] was responsible, that the Communist Party of Germany conspired with van der Lubbe and other alleged foreign Communists, did you not, in fact, influence the police and judicial investigations in a particular direction, thus preventing the apprehension of the real incendiaries?

GÖRING: I know what you are getting at, but there is really no problem at all. The police were from the start given orders to pursue their investigations in every possible direction, no matter where these investigations led them. But as I am not a detective myself but a responsible Minister, it was not important that I should trouble myself with trifling details. It was my business to point out the Party and the mentality which were responsible for the crime. All I had to determine was: Is this a civil offence, or is it a political offence? Now it was clearly a political offence and at the same time it became clear to me, and it remains just as clear today, that your Party were the criminals.

PRESIDENT [to Dimitrov]: Regarding your reference to influencing the judges, you did refer to that, didn't you? To influencing the judges?

DIMITROV: No. What I said, Herr President, was that the police inquiry and later the preliminary examination could have been influenced by these political directives, and mainly in one direction. That is why I am asking my question.

GÖRING: Herr Dimitrov, that, too, is admitted. If the police were allowed to be influenced in a particular direction, then, in any case, they were only influenced in the proper direction.

DIMITROV:	That is your opinion. My opinion is quite different.
GÖRING:	But mine is the one that counts.
DIMITROV:	I am only the accused, of course.
PRESIDENT:	You may only ask questions.
DIMITROV:	I am doing that, Herr President. Does Herr Ministerpräsident Göring realize that those who possess this alleged criminal mentality are today controlling the destinies of a sixth part of the world, namely the Soviet Union? [GÖRING: Unfortunately.] The Soviet Union has diplomatic, political and economic contacts with Germany. Her orders provide work for hundreds of thousands of German workers. Does the Minister know that?
GÖRING:	Yes, I do. [DIMITROV: Good!] I also know that the Russians pay with bills and I should prefer to know their bills are met. In that case Russia's orders would really provide work for our workers. But that is not the point here. I don't care what happens in Russia. Here, I am only concerned with the Communist Party of Germany and with the foreign Communist crooks who come here to set the Reichstag on fire. [Loud bravos from the public.]
DIMITROV:	Yes of course, bravo, bravo, bravo! They have the right to fight against the Communist Party, but the Communist Party of Germany has the right to go underground and to fight against your Government; and how we fight back is a matter of our respective forces and not a matter of law.
PRESIDENT:	Dimitrov, I will not have you making Communist propaganda here. [DIMITROV: But he is making National Socialist propaganda!] I most emphatically order you to desist. I will not have Communist propaganda in this courtroom!
DIMITROV:	Herr President, arising out of my last question, there is just one further question that needs explaining in any case: The question of party and philosophy. Herr Ministerpräsident Göring has stated that he is not concerned with what happens in the Soviet Union, but only with the criminal mentality of the Communist Party. Is the Minister aware that this criminal mentality rules the Soviet Union, the greatest and best land in the world?
GÖRING:	Look here, I will tell you what the German people know. They know that you are behaving in a disgraceful fashion. They know that you are a Communist crook who came to Germany to set the Reichstag on fire, and who now behave yourself with sheer impudence in the face of the German people. I did not come here to be accused by you. [DIMITROV: You are a witness.] In my eyes you are nothing but a scoundrel, a crook who belongs to the gallows. [DIMITROV: Very well, I'm most satisfied...]
PRESIDENT:	I have repeatedly warned you not to make Communist propaganda. [Dimitrov tries to speak on.] If you continue in this vein, I shall have you put outside. I have told you not to make Communist propaganda, and you cannot wonder that the witness gets angry when you continue to do so. I order you most emphatically to desist from doing so. If you have any questions, then let them be purely factual and nothing more.
DIMITROV:	I am highly satisfied with Herr Göring's explanation.
PRESIDENT:	Whether or not you are satisfied is a matter of complete indifference to me. [DIMITROV: Most satisfied. I am merely asking questions.] After

DIMITROV:	your last comment, I must ask you to sit down. [DIMITROV:.I'm asking questions.] I am asking you to sit down. Do so!
DIMITROV:	I am asking a purely factual question.
PRESIDENT:	I have asked you to sit down
DIMITROV:	You are greatly afraid of my questions, are you not, Herr Minister?
GÖRING:	You will be afraid when I catch you. You wait till I get you out of the power of this Court, you crook!
PRESIDENT:	Dimitrov is expelled for three days. Out with him! [Dimitrov is hustled out.]

(Fritz Tobias, *The Reichstag Fire*, pp. 84-86)

Göring's failure in this battle of wits with Dimitrov was a great propaganda victory for the Left. Anson Rabinbach writes:

Dimitrov's triumph over Göring was instantly turned into a media event. Brochures and fly sheets appeared immediately, and a second *Brown Book* titled *Dimitrov against Göring* sported on its jacket another [John] Heartfield photomontage—reproduced hundredfold—depicting the monumentally enlarged Dimitrov towering over a diminutive Göring sputtering epithets like "Red tramp, criminal, scum swindler, to the gallows!" In his photomontage Heartfield rearranged images of the courtroom, the defendant, and Göring, radically altering their position and the scale, and inverting the courtroom hierarchy (prisoner *vs*. witness). (Rabinbach, "Staging Antifascism: The Brown Book of the Reichstag Fire and Hitler Terror")

On 23.12.1933, van der Lubbe was sentenced to death. He was beheaded on 10.01.1934. Seventy-four years later, on 06.12.2007, the verdict was nullified and van der Lubbe granted a posthumous pardon by Germany's attorney general, Monika Harms, on the basis that the sentence by the *Reichsgericht* had been politically motivated and rendered on behalf of an unjust regime.

03.03.1933   Delivered a speech ("We Bear the Responsibility") in Frankfurt am Main in which he declared:

Fellow Germans, my measures will not be crippled by any judicial thinking. My measures will not be crippled by any bureaucracy. Here I don't have to give Justice, my mission is only to destroy and exterminate, nothing more! This struggle, fellow Germans, will be a struggle against chaos and such a struggle I shall not conduct with the power of any police. A bourgeois state might have done that. Certainly, I shall use the power of the state and the police to the utmost my dear Communists, so that you won't draw any false conclusions but the struggle to the death, in which my fist will grasp your necks, I shall lead with those down there— those are the brown shirts. (Partial Translation of Document 1856-PS, in *Nazi Conspiracy and Aggression, Volume III*)

11.03.1933   Stated the following in a speech at Essen:

I have only just begun my purge; it is far from finished. For us the people are divided into two parts: One which professes faith in the nation, the other which wants to poison and destroy. I thank my Maker that I do not know what objective is. I am subjective. I repudiate the idea that the police are a defense force for Jewish department stores. We must put an end to the absurdity of every rogue shouting for the police. The police are not there to protect rogues, vagabonds, usurers, and traitors. If people say that here and there someone has been taken away and maltreated, I can only reply: You can't make omelets without breaking eggs. Don't shout for justice so much, otherwise there might be a justice that is to be found in the stars and not in your paragraphs! Even if we make a lot of mistakes, we shall at least act and keep our nerve. I'd rather shoot a few times too short or too wide, but at least I shoot. (Translation from Johannes Hohlfeld, ed., *Deutsche Reichsgeschichte in Dokumenten, Vol. IV*, in Joachim C. Fest, *The Face of the Third Reich*, p. 77)

17.03.1933 Delivered a speech to farmers in Pommern, from which the following is an excerpt:

We have cleaned things up and settled accounts with the damnable criminals of German history, settled accounts for that damnable November 1918 and this cleansing will and must be carried out.... The Government of National Concentration will, with an iron fist, destroy those conflicts of interest which in the last fourteen years have grown artificially so large between individual groups of our people, and force them into that harmony which is so necessary for the well-being of [Germany].

If the previous speaker has said, Marxism must never be allowed to return, I will say something more: Not only with they never return, we will exterminate them! I will BEAT these creatures so long throttling their necks with my hands, until they are finished. We will not only exterminate these pests, we will rip out the very word Marxism from every book in the country. In fifty years, a person in Germany will not even know what that word means. (Webpage of John L. Heineman [1935–2017], Professor Emeritus of History at Boston College)

23.03.1933 In a speech before the *Reichstag*, boasted of the alleged lenience toward Jews and other perceived enemies of the new regime since Hitler's assumption to power:

But for the rest, ladies and gentlemen, each of you know: you can walk through Germany today in the North or the South, in the East or the West, there is not a looted or wrecked shop, not a shop in the whole of Germany that cannot exist today, where sales and purchases are not going on quietly, not a department store that has been destroyed or robbed or obstructed! Just walk through all the merchandise palaces: you will see that the gentlemen can still make a killing, that business is still going on there. It is not true that trade and commerce are disturbed here. Go past the Synagogues, walk through the Jewish cemeteries—you will not be able to show me one place where there is even one word against the Jew, where even one stone has been defiled. To smear the dead, that is reserved for your press abroad, not ours. Go on through the prisons; ask Herr Thälmann, Herr Torgler if the slightest thing has happened to them. If Herr Thälmann seems depressed that his followers are running away by the thousands, it is not our fault. After all, I cannot take special care in cheering him up....

The Chancellor was right. I hope that, as the responsible minister in Germany's largest state, I have made it clear that all these atrocity reports are lies, that all these representations are untrue. Germany has never been more peaceful. It can never have been more uplifting for a foreigner to walk through Germany than it is today; for he finally sees again a people full of hope, a people full of faith and a people full of pride, and we owe that to the men who have now taken charge of the country's affairs. That is why the National Socialist faction has only one thing to say about the Enabling Act: There have been years of talk; now we have a leader at the head of the German government, now there is no more talk, now there is action! (*Verhandlungen des Reichstags, VIII. Wahlperiode 1933, Band 457*; Translation: Gary Costello)

09.04.1933   Speech to members of the *NS-Betriebszellenorganisation* (NSBO, National Socialist Factory Cells Organization) in Berlin's *Sportpalast*:

German women and German men! I have spoken at numerous meetings and have taken repeated positions on many issues. But today is something very special for me: it is special because today I stand before Germans who work hard every day or who must live in dire poverty, and who have therefore learned from their own experiences what National Socialism is and what its victory means for productive citizens.

My dear citizens! We are living through a National Socialist revolution. We emphasize the term "socialist" because many speak only of a "national" revolution. Dubious, but also wrong. It was not only nationalism that led to the breakthrough. We are proud that German socialism also triumphed. Unfortunately, there are still people among us today who emphasize the word "national" too strongly and who do not want to know anything about the second part of our worldview, which shows that they have also failed to understand the first part. Those who do not want to recognize a German socialism do not have the right to call themselves national.

Only he who emphasizes German socialism is truly national. He who refuses to speak of socialism, who believes in socialism only in the Marxist sense, or to whom the word "socialism" has an unpleasant ring, has not understood the deepest meaning of nationalism. He has not understood that one can only be a nationalist when one sees social problems openly and clearly. And on the other hand, one can only be a socialist when he clearly sees that nationalism must triumph to protect the living space of a people from outside forces.

Just as nationalism protects a people from outside forces, so socialism serves a people's domestic needs. We want the people's strength to be released within the nation, forging the people once more into a strong block. The individual citizen must again have the sense that, even if he is finds himself in the simplest and lowest position, that his life and opportunities are assured. He should see that his own existence is rooted in the existence of his people and that he must serve his people will all his strength. If I want to ensure that each individual has the ability to survive, that each individual German can be active, can work, can support himself once more, I must also work to ensure that conditions beyond our borders make that possible.

We did not make a national revolution in the sense of a barren, outdated hyper-patriotism, but rather this revolution is in the truest sense of the word a National Socialist revolution. Previously the two fought each other, divided by hatred and unfortunate enmity. Nationalism and socialism stood opposed: the bourgeoisie supported nationalism, the Marxists socialism. The bourgeoisie fell into a barren hyper-patriotism, lost in pacifistic cowardice. On the other side, a Marxist layer of the people, a Marxist class, wanted nothing to do with the Reich or a people. There was no bridge between them.

Marxist socialism was degraded to a concern only with pay or the stomach. The bourgeoisie degraded nationalism into barren hyper-patriotism. Both concepts, therefore, must be cleansed and shown to the people anew, in a crystal-clear form. The nationalism of our worldview arrived at the right moment. Our movement seized the concept of socialism from the cowardly Marxists, and tore the concept of nationalism from the cowardly bourgeois parties, throwing both into the melting pot of our worldview, and producing a clear synthesis: German national Socialism. That provided the foundation for the rebuilding of our people. Thus this revolution was National Socialist.

Our idea grew out of the people. And because it grew from the people, led by the unknown corporal of the World War, this idea was destined to bring an end to fragmentation and forge once more a unity among our people.

Outwardly, the Reich was weak, existing only on paper. Inwardly, the people were torn apart, bleeding from a thousand wounds. At home, strife dominated between parties, occupations, groups, classes, and religions. Our Führer Adolf Hitler saw that the Reich could survive and grow strong only if one achieved unity within the German people. That was the work of our party over the last fourteen years: to make once more one German people from a people of competing interests, from a people of differing religions, occupations, groups and classes.

My German citizens! How often have we stood in this place, how often elsewhere in Germany, today in this city, tomorrow in another one! We raced from place to place, spoke, raising the spirits, even of those who despaired. Ever again we hammered at the masses, a hundred times, a thousand times, ten thousand times: A German people must rise up! We tore one after another from the despair of the parties, classes and groups, making them into the bricks, the pillars of this new Reich. We worked hard for years. Today, amidst the jubilation of victory, we may quietly remember the hard struggle, the terrible poverty, which often we no longer believed we could master, yet which always drove us to new inner strength, to one more attempt. The movement collapsed, hardly born, splintered, yet climbing upward once more.

What enormous effort, what huge sacrifice, what devotion! That is why, in the midst of our meetings and celebrations that demonstrate the powerful awakening of our people, we must always remember those who gave everything they had. Countless of them are no longer alive. Others are crippled, still others left alone. They fought, they sacrificed everything. Their only motto was battle and work. And when the Reds claim that we are now the bigwigs, we answer, fellow citizens, as follows: We have not had the time to become bigwigs. We had no time, and too much work and too many battles to fight, which hardened us. We want only to be workers in German construction, masons on German projects. In exhausting labor and through great exertion, we have slowly built that which has risen up.

The parties are finished! They tremble in cowardice. They were cowards because they were born of cowardice. The System was cowardly, and it left in a cowardly way, because it also grew from cowardice. How miserably they went, fetched by a lieutenant and two officers. It did not even take a dozen men. How these labor leaders betrayed the workers! I can tell you this. If I had the time and opportunity to let German worker look at the files of their so-called leaders, at the countless and many requests to their bosses for support, even when they themselves held the highest posts, he would learn the truth about those leaders. One could show the German worker the attempt by a top Red party bigwig to get credit toward his pension for the time which he betrayed the German people and our fatherland as editor of a Social Democratic newspaper. Thirty or forty years of pension credit were not enough for these gentlemen. They wanted to start at eighteen with their military service. That is how those Red gentlemen were! They lost their followers because they thought only about themselves, no longer about their followers. No one demanded of them that they live in poverty themselves, but they were not expected to forget about those for whom life was hard. One expected that they would work for others, not for themselves, the expectation Germans have always had of labor.

We have slowly begun to create unity from the chaos of parties. Today these old parties play only a comic role. Today when one says something political about certain parties, a speaker can hardly do it. As soon as he names certain parties, laughter breaks out in the meeting, since people no longer take them seriously. Who today knows anything about all these ridiculous parties and party splinter groups? Everyone laughs at these leftovers from former times, rather as one looks at antediluvian animals. One shakes one's head that such things ever existed in the German Reich.

Only after Adolf Hitler had established the first foundations of domestic unity could we begin to think about strengthening the Reich internationally. For centuries, it had been only a hope, a dream, in Germany: He reestablished the unity of the Reich with a single law from the ruler of the Reich. Where are all those party leaders who a few months ago were saying: Herr Hitler will soon learn that south of the Main River his day is over. This law achieved what generations had longed for: the Reich, the scepter of the Reich, governs all the German provinces. The variety, the uniqueness, the ethnic heritage, all that will be maintained.

Now that the Reich once more firmly controls the individual provinces, the German people must be forged into a similar unity. Now, my national comrades, you members of factory cells are the blacksmiths who are forging our German people. You must work toward this in your cells, in your factories. You must constantly explain, constantly educate, constantly attempt to make clear to your fragmented national comrades what is at stake.

Comrades, for years we struggled for the German soul, to win over each individual, to transform him, to free him from all the filth of a corrupt system, to make him again into a German fighter, a German person. Now you must continue this in your factories. You must continually fight for each individual German soul. You must raise them from their lethargy, and you must educate and persuade those who have been misled.

To be sure, we have won a great victory, and each victory has certain consequences. One such consequence is competition. We know that there are many who really have no deep support for us, who have no understanding at all for National Socialism, yet today they have suddenly become the best National Socialists around. They have spread like mushrooms. We must be cautious! Clothing is not enough to make a National Socialist, nor the badge for which we were persecuted for a decade, nor the *Heil* greeting. The heart alone determines whether one is a National Socialist. We want no fighter, no National Socialist, of the mind! No, only he who is one from the heart; he must come to us from his own feelings and senses, and become ours. We therefore must look clearly and sharply, with ice-cold vision, into their hearts, not into their brains, to see if they have become National Socialists. But on the other side, citizens, we also should be generous. We do not want to take petty revenge. We are, after all, the victors. What difference does it make if someone once called us criminals, or brown bandits, or something else! Years have passed, and now they have come to us with real conviction. And we, too, were not National Socialists from birth. So let us be generous, remembering that we also once thought differently, and are thankful to those who led us to this splendid goal! The more we are ourselves National Socialists, the stronger and freer we feel it, the more we can forget the past and warmly extend the hand of reconciliation. But on the other hand, where real crimes were committed against the people, there must be pitiless and just revenge. That is the prerequisite if we are to forgive the others. The big ones must be caught, not the little ones. We want to let the little ones alone, but we must settle accounts with the big ones who know how to juggle things back and forth, doing their business here and there. They must receive just revenge with pitiless hardness.

This is the context in which we have to understand the new civil service law, as everything is being cleansed, purified, and rebuilt. Citizens, we cannot deny it: This is a hard law. It affects the individual with, when necessary, great force. It shatters careers if falsely applied. Since it is so hard, and must be that hard, I have ordered that no one except a minister himself can decide the career of a subordinate. Whether it concerns the fate of a worker, a porter, or a state secretary makes no difference. Everyone is affected equally. We want to be clear about this: The law may not be used by anyone who wants to apply his personal instincts, who wants to settle old scores with someone he has been unhappy with since his schooldays. That may not happen. The sole factor is whether the person in question is for the state or against his people. That is the only factor that may be considered. The individual civil servant with a good conscience can proudly hold his head high. Nothing will happen to him or any other employee. As much as a person can be just, justice will be the policy here. Be aware of the great responsibility here, for you have this responsibility too, not only the minister.

I know that today denouncers are appearing, almost a pile of them, complaining about someone or another, mostly from envy, since they perhaps want to have someone's job, or because they do not like someone. People are ostracized, gossiped about, or denounced. Volksgenossen [People's Comrades], he who denounces someone else reveals his true character. He who openly says: "I accuse" will be listened to, but he must be willing to stand by his accusation. Denouncers are those who carry on their filthy business at night, with anonymous letters with the worst sort of accusations. Mostly, this consists of lies. We must keep our state and our people pure. Anyone has the right to make an accusation, but if his charges are false, if they are lies, the laws of libel apply. If we follow this guideline, I am sure that this law will be a blessing for our people despite all the difficulties.

Volksgenossen, we have spoken of those all too eager to accuse others, who are driven by envy. But let me assure you that not everyone who comes to us today does so out of envy. Believe me: Despite the busybodies, despite all the excess, these people are, thank God, a tiny minority. Other motives and other reasons explain the thousands and ten thousands of others who have come to us. In part, as you know, the pressure, the force was so heavy that many could hardly do anything, even if they wanted to. That is not the most important point. Do not forget something else—something about which we can be proud and happy: Millions of Germans throughout Germany over these years had no idea what National Socialism was. They saw the brown columns, they read terrible things about those columns each day in the Jewish press, they read how bad National Socialism was, they read that it would destroy everything, that it would ruin everything, that it could lead to anarchy, to collapse. They did not know us. In part, they had become too dulled to worry about the nation's fate. There was no point to it. Everything was too dismal, too tragic, the desperation was too great. And then, suddenly, the movement came, tearing through the clouds, suddenly there was light again, the sun shone. Hundreds of thousands, even millions, of people suddenly woke up. The scales fell from their eyes, and they saw something wonderful. They suddenly saw how a movement that had been insulted, outlawed, estranged, took the light in its hands. They were happy to see a new spring coming that would change everything. There was new joy, new hope. A faith that had been buried, that had been soiled, came alive. Those are the ones coming to us today, the ones who say: "We did not know it. Accuse us of being too weak. But we were not bad. We did not know. Everything that we only dreamed about, what was in our subconscious, has become true. Let us in!" The number of these Volksgenossen is growing! These are good people who may be fighters tomorrow. You must further awaken them, strengthen their sentiments. They should become a great army, so that one day Germany will think and feel only in National Socialist ways. Then this people's unity will be eternal.

Men and women of the factory cells! You should certainly handle economic and social problems in your factory cells. You should certainly be an economic support for your comrades. But that is not the main task! No, the material is not the prime goal, rather the ideals. The factory cells, too, are called first of all to train the German worker, the German employee, in worldview matters, to form him, to educate him, until he has become a German National Socialist. That is your main task. You must make clear to the former Marxist or communist that work is no curse, but rather a blessing.

That is how we want to build the state once more. Slowly, with exhausting effort, we must reestablish the right to work. We want to give German people work again so they can earn their own bread. We want to sow once more and show that a person can live from his own efforts, not depending on some kind of support, that no one starves because someone has stolen from him the right to work. The whole nation must demand that. On the other hand, I demand that each individual puts his whole strength in service of this people and this nation.

Volksgenossen! Much has happened in the past weeks. We have seen and experienced new things. In the past few weeks, Marxism apparently collapsed, outwardly, at least. Through laws, through regulations, and other such things, one can destroy Marxism's external organization. But that is only external. The state, the police, the government can only deal with the external forms. You, however, must smash and destroy the idea of Marxism. One cannot destroy and eliminate an idea with outward means, but rather the strength to overcome an idea must come from another idea, a better idea. It must be clear, more active, more energetic, if it is to drive the other idea from the world. The National Socialist worldview smashed Marxist insanity in this way. The factory cells have to keep attacking Marxism. You can do that only from within. The strength you need must be found in your confidence in what we preach, in what we do, in what we want to build. And furthermore, it requires blind loyalty, loyalty to the Führer who has created everything, without whom there would be nothing that we see today. They strength grows with discipline. A military unit can have everything it needs. It can have the best position, better material, great superiority, the best leadership—it can have all this, but without iron discipline it will be defeated, it will be destroyed. A small but disciplined unit will always overcome and defeat a larger undisciplined mob. That is why inner discipline is necessary, first the inner discipline of the individual, which then shines from the group, from the movement to which he belongs.

There are two more sources of strength, and they above all will help you to bring our idea to victory and the other idea to defeat. That is this unshakable faith: Germany must live, German will live, because we want it, because it is necessary. This idea will give you strength. And from this faith will come hope, the home, the longing, that always helps a person to win, even when he wants to despair. Night may surround us, but as long as the torch of our hope shines, no one will be defeated. Action must come from these inner sources of strength. You must bear the idea and help it to victory.

Confidence, loyalty, discipline, faith, and hope: These are the pillars on which this movement must rest, because this movement has become the bearer of this powerful idea.

We want to live, and therefore we will live. There is a vast field of ruins before us. Everything has collapsed. Wherever one looks, things have been undermined, hollowed out, broken, become rotten. Small steps have already been taken. A little has been cleared away, here and there is the start of firm ground on which one can build. But the destruction extends far, far to the horizon, with wasteland everywhere, everything in ruins. My Volksgenossen, you are used to working, and therefore in the coming days there is but one slogan: work, work, and still more work for our people, and for our fatherland that must be rebuilt. Get to work, and may God bless our labors!
(Göring, "Nationalismus und Sozialismus: Rede auf der NSBO. Im Berliner Sportpalast am 9. April 1933", in *Hermann Göring: Reden und Aufsätze* [Zentralverlag der NSDAP, 1941], pp. 36-49; Translation at Prof. Randall Bytwerk's German Propaganda Archive—research.calvin.edu/german-propaganda-archive/goering1.htm)

10.04.1933 — Establishment by Göring of the *"Forschungsamt"* (FA, Research Office), a powerful and ultrasecret intelligence and wiretapping agency; among its targets were *SA-Stabschef* Röhm and other SA leaders. Initially a component of Göring's Prussian State Government under Paul Körner's general management, but by 1937 it had been transferred to his *Reichsluftfahrtministerium*. Under postwar interrogation, Albert Speer stated:

The Reichsforschungsamt was under Goering and was directed by Staatssekretaer Koerner. Its function was the tapping of telephone conversations. The results were reported in the so-called "brown sheets" (Braune Blaetter). These were circulated to all Ministers, but each of them would only receive an assortment of relatively insignificant matter bearing on his jurisdiction. Hitler had issued a strict ban on the tapping of conversations by the Reich Ministers themselves, but I do not know if this was observed. Most of the listening-in was done on big industrialists and businessmen, but it was said that embassies and legations were also tapped … "Reich Research Bureau" was only a cover name. It had nothing to do with the Reich Research Council (Reichsforschungsrat). I did not learn about this institution until 1942. Sometimes the reports were very instructive. There were occasions when they conveyed to me the views of sensible industrialists who, for some reason or other, did not care to talk to me, or had been unable to secure an appointment. Sometimes I learnt of justified complaints against my departmental chiefs, who then were very much surprised that I knew about these matters. (Interrogation Records Prepared for War Crimes Proceedings at Nuernberg, 1945–1947/ OCCPAC Interrogation Transcripts and Related Records: Speer, Albert; Publication Number M1270, Record Group RG238)

10.04.1933–20.04.1933 Mission to Rome to strengthen relations between Germany and Italy, during which he and Franz von Papen met three times with Mussolini and once, on 12.04.1933, with Pope Pius XI. The itinerary for the visit was as follows:

10.04. Arrival in Rome
11.04. First conversation with Mussolini; in the evening dinner at the German Embassy with Mussolini
12.04. Audience with the Pope and Cardinal Secretary of State Eugeno Pacelli; afterwards breakfast with Mussolini
13.04. Joint press reception of Göring and Pope; wreath-laying; dinner at Balbo's in the evening
14.04.–17.04. Flight to Naples and Sicily for sightseeing
17.04. Evening dinner at the German Embassy to the Holy See
18.04. Audience with King Vittorio III; Göring and Mussolini together at the parliamentary trade conference; in the evening, Göring and Papen together as guests
Guest at the "Deutsche Vereinigung Roms" (German Association of Rome)
19.04. Flight to Milan; visit to a sample fair
20.04. Return flight to Germany (Alfred Kube, *Pour le mérite und Hakenkreuz: Hermann Göring im Dritten Reich*, p. 36)

Upon his departure from Rome, he wrote:

His Excellency, Signor Mussolini, Rome.
Aboard my airplane, and flying over the Italian Frontier, I utter my most heartfelt thanks and those of my companions to Your Excellency. I shall never forget the days in Italy. The Italian people's hospitality and interest have left the deepest impression.

With admiration we have witnessed the mighty achievements of Fascism and its Duce. National Socialist Germany hails Fascist Italy with all its heart.

Long live Fascism! Long live the Duce! Long live Italy!
With all my respect,
Hermann Göring. (Kurt Singer, *Göring: Germany's Most Dangerous Man*, p. 173)

To his friend General Italo Balbo, he telegrammed:

His Excellency, General Balbo, Rome.

As we leave your magnificent country, once more the heartiest thanks from us all for the wonderful days we have lived, thanks to your hospitality.

Sincere greetings to the minister, comrade, and friend.

Hermann Göring (Kurt Singer, *Göring: Germany's Most Dangerous Man*, pp. 173-174)

Despite the warm tone of these messages to Italian leaders, the meeting had not gone smoothly, and resulted in friction between the two nations. Göring had been strident in demanding that Italy immediately cease financial support of the *Heimwehr* organization in Austria, the greatest impediment to Nazi efforts to take over that country. He alarmed Mussolini through his belligerent statements on other European nations, particularly Great Britain, ultimately prompting the *Duce* to order Italian delegates to the World Disarmament Conference in Geneva to halt cooperation with their German counterparts. Mussolini also resolved to provide greater moral and financial support to the *Heimwehr*.

11.04.1933–23.04.1945 *Preußischer Ministerpräsident* (Prussian prime minister). Succeeded *Vizekanzler* Franz von Papen, who served as *Reichskommissar für Preußen* from 30.01.1933 to 10.04.1933. Göring was appointed as *Ministerpräsident* via the following telegram from Hitler, dated 11.04.1933:

With effect as per today's date I hereby appoint you Ministerpräsident of Prussia. I may request that you be so kind and assume the duties of this office on 20. April in Berlin.

I am happy for this opportunity to demonstrate to you my trust and my gratitude for the services which you have rendered in support of the new uprising of the German Volk for over ten years as a fighter in our Movement; for the victorious execution of the National Revolution as temporary Minister of the Interior in Prussia; and, last but not least, for the unique loyalty with which you have bound your destiny to mine.

Reich Chancellor Adolf Hitler (Dr. Max Domarus, ed., *Hitler. Speeches and Proclamations, 1932–1945: The Years 1932–1934*, p. 307)

In his memoirs, von Papen recalled the difficulties he and others experienced as a result of his successor's style of leadership:

During February, and particularly after the Reichstag fire, I agreed with Goering that the Prussian police should take active steps to deal with Communist elements. There was, in fact, good reason to suppose that Moscow had instructed them to engage in open revolt. Goering always excused the excesses of the Brownshirts and the S.S. by claiming that they had been provoked by the Communists. A decree dated February 28 legalized the numerous arrests that had taken place. Hitler and Goering seized the opportunity, while their non-Nazi colleagues were still in the dark about their real intentions, to take complete administrative control of the police, so that they might use them for their own purposes to even greater effect after the Reichstag elections. Prussia was only one State, albeit the largest. In the other States the judiciary and the police were still in the hands of Weimar ministers and officials. But they too were swept up in the current of events, which followed the same pattern throughout the country. Between March 5 and April 7, 1 retained my position as Reich Commissioner for Prussia. I had daily disputes with Goering in the Cabinet over his high-handed activities. I insisted that none of the senior posts in the Prussian administration and police should be made the subject of new appointments without my express permission. Goering disregarded my objections whenever he could, but it was possible to ensure that a number of the police commissioner posts went to trustworthy men, such as Admiral von Levetzow in Berlin and Colonel von Heydekampf in the Ruhr. I received less support than I expected from the senior officials in the Prussian Prime Minister's office. [Dr. Erich] Gritzbach, for example, my chef de cabinet, very soon joined the "winning side" and deferred to Goering more than he did to me. His reward was that he continued to remain in office for many years. (Von Papen, *Memoirs*, p. 293)

The businessman and early financial supporter of the NSDAP, Fritz Thyssen, writes of Göring's leadership and corruption in this post:

Goering, field marshal and prime minister of Prussia, incarnates the corruption of the regime. He practices graft on a scale commensurate with government operations rather than private or business deals. Goering is the sovereign of Prussia; he administers its state domains (the former crown properties). The Prussian state grants him free disposal over its lands for his own personal use. He distributes those lands as compensations for services rendered to him. Old President von Hindenburg did not disdain to accept a castle and several thousand hectares of lands and forests from the hands of Goering, whom he had just made a general. This looked like a gift of gratitude. But the old field marshal, and, above all his son, Oscar, land-greedy like all Junkers, considered this quite normal, as though Goering had been king of Prussia....

But Goering is generous especially to himself. He accumulates various public salaries; he receives a field marshal's pay, a salary as president of the Reichstag, another as minister for air, and another as prime minister of Prussia. I mention only in passing his titles of Great Master of the Forests and Chief Huntsman of the Reich and of Prussia: in connection with these, too, Goering is not the man to refuse a monthly salary. The revenues he derives from his public functions certainly exceed two million marks a year, paid out of the budgets of the Reich and the state of Prussia....

But Goering is not content with merely depleting the budget by his salaries. As prime minister he is virtually proprietor of the Prussian state.... It is the domain which he exploits, and never has any king of Prussia lived on his subjects as magnificently as the field marshal! Whatever belongs to Prussia belongs to him. He made himself a present—for his private use—of several thousand hectares of wooded lands in the beautiful forest of Schorfheide north of Berlin. This forms a superb natural park, where Goering breeds elks and aurochs....

A new residence has been built for him in the gardens of the old Prussian House of Lords, next to the new Air Ministry. A whole section of Berlin at the very centre of the city forms a regular "Goering City," with his private palace, the Herrenhaus, the House of Aviators, and the impressive building of the Air Ministry, completed in 1935....

Being the second most important man in Germany, Goering felt he owed it to himself to own, like the Führer, a villa in the Bavarian Alps. The prime minister of Bavaria, knowing his desire, offered him land at Obersalzberg, facing the Führer's property... (Thyssen, *I Paid Hitler*, pp. 200-201)

21.04.1933–30.04.1934	*Preußischer Staatsminister und Minister des Innern* (Prussian minister of interior), an expansion of the powers he already held as *Reichskommissar für das preußische Innenministerium* (see entry of 30.01.1933–11.04.1933, above). Succeeded by Dr. Wilhelm Frick. On 01.05.1933, Hitler wrote the following letter to Göring:

My dear Göring,
As early as 17 March of this year, you proposed to me that the Reich Minister of the Interior, Dr. Frick, be entrusted with performing the duties of the office of Prussian Minister of the Interior. Placing your own personal interests secondary to those of the great work of the Reich reform, you expressed the desire to be released from your duties as Prussian State Minister and Minister of the Interior.

I have now complied with your wishes. Please find enclosed a certificate of dismissal from your post as Prussian State Minister and Minister of the Interior. I feel compelled in this context to express my sincere and heartfelt gratitude for everything which you have accomplished in this post. You yourself have correctly pointed out that you have now solved the special problems involved in the administration of internal Prussian affairs, a task which I had assigned to you at the beginning of the National Socialist Revolution. You have accomplished this task with great circumspection and vigor. If now, retaining your office as Prussian Minister-President, you retire—corresponding to your own wish—from your post as Prussian Minister of the Interior and allow Dr. Frick, the Reich Minister of the Interior, to take your place, I know that this will serve—corresponding to your own wishes—to promote the great goals of the Reich reform in a particularly fitting way.
In true friendship and grateful regard,
Your Adolf Hitler
(Dr. Max Domarus, ed., Hitler. *Speeches and Proclamations, 1932–1945: The Years 1932–1934*, p. 454)

11.04.1933–30.04.1934 26.04.1933	*Chef der Preußischen Polizei* (chief of the Prussian police). Issued the following "Law on the Organization of a Secret State Police Office" (*Geheime-Staatspolizeiamt* [*Gestapa*]) under the *Preußische Ministerium des Innern* (i.e., under his personal control).

The State Ministry has resolved on the following law:
Article 1

(1) The Geheime Staatspolizei, with headquarters in Berlin, is organized in order to carry out the duties of political police with or in place of the ordinary police authorities (Article 2, paragraph 1 of the Code of Police Administration of June 1, 1931, Gesetzsammlung, p. 77) The Geheime Staatspolizeiamt has the rank of a higher police authority and is subordinate only to the Minister of the Interior.

(2) The Minister of the Interior determines the functional and territorial jurisdiction of the Geheime Staatspolizeiamt.

(3) The regulations of the Code of Police Administration of June 1, 1931 concerning appeals against orders of the higher police authorities are applicable in so far as the Administrative Court in Berlin has exclusive jurisdiction over court appeals against orders of the Geheime Staatspolizeiamt.

Article 2 Within its jurisdiction, the Geheime Staatspolizeiamt can make requests for police action to all police authorities.

Article 3 The Minister of the Interior is entitled to issue administrative orders for the execution of this law. He acts in agreement with the Minister of Finance in regard to the number and type of officials and employees who should be employed by the Geheime Staatspolizeiamt.
Article 4 The law goes into effect on the day of its promulgation.
Berlin 24 April 1933
The Prussian Staatsministerium
/signed/ Göring and by Popitz and for the Minister of the Interior

The above law, resolved by the Prussian Staatsministerium, is herewith promulgated.
Berlin 26 April 1933
(signed) For the Reichskanzler:
The Prussian Ministerpräsident
Göring
(1933 *Preußische Gesetzsammlung*, p. 122; Translation of Document 2104-PS, in *Nazi Conspiracy and Aggression, Volume IV*)

As *Gestapa* director, Göring appointed Rudolf Diels, head of *Abteilung Ia* (*Politische-Polizei*, Political Police) of the Prussian Interior Ministry. Diels was dismissed at the end of September 1933 and succeeded as acting head of the *Gestapa* by the former *Gauleiter* Paul Hinkler. During the fifteen days that Hinkler led the office, rumors spread in SA circles that he was mentally weak and dependent on alcohol. At the end of November or start of December 1933, Diels returned from his exile in Czechoslovakia at Göring's request and reassumed the post (see entry for 29.11.1933, below). In his 1934 memoir detailing the first year of the Third Reich, Göring described his work in establishing the Gestapo:

… [F]or weeks I was personally engaged in the work of reorganization. Finally, I alone created, on my own initiative, the "Secret State Police Department." This is the instrument which is so much feared by the enemies of the State, and which is chiefly responsible for the fact that in Germany and Prussia today there is no question of a Marxist or Communist danger. Without taking seniority into consideration, I put the ablest men I had into this "Secret State Police Department," and put it under the command of the most capable of my younger officials. Every day I am further strengthened in my opinion that I chose the right men. The achievements of Diels and his men will always remain one of the glories of the first year of German recovery. I was most actively supported by the SS and SA. Without their help and support I should never have mastered the enemies of the State so quickly and effectively. I have now reorganized the Secret Police once more and placed it under my direct control. By means of a network of centres in the provinces, with Berlin as the headquarters, I am kept daily, I might almost say hourly, informed of everything which happens in the vast Prussian State. The last refuge of the Communists is known to us. However often they change their tactics and change the names of their couriers, a few days later they are tracked down, reported, watched and arrested. We had to proceed against these enemies of the State with complete ruthlessness. It must not be forgotten that at the moment of our taking over the Government there were, according to the March election figures, about fourteen million supporters of Communism and Marxism. These people were indeed not all of them enemies of the State. The greater part of them, countless millions, were good Germans, led astray by insane theories and by the emptiness and spinelessness of the Middle-Class Parties. It was therefore all the more urgent that these people should be rescued from error and brought back once more into the community of the German people. But it was also just as necessary to take strong action against the deceivers, agitators and chiefs themselves. And so, the concentration camps were set up, to which we had sent first of all thousands of officials of the Communist and Socialist Democratic parties. It was only natural that in the beginning excesses were committed. It was natural that here and there beatings took place; there were some cases of brutality. But if we consider the greatness of the occasion and all that had preceded it, we must admit that this German revolution for freedom was one of the most bloodless and most disciplined of all revolutions in history. (Göring, *Germany Reborn* [translation of *Aufbau einer Nation*, 1934], pp. 126-129)

27.04.1933–28.02.1935   *Mit dem geheimen Aufbau der Luftwaffe beauftragt* (charged with the secret building of the *Luftwaffe*). Future *Generalleutnant* Adolf Galland, who was to experience great frustration and total disillusionment at Göring's wartime mismanagement of the *Luftwaffe*, writes of Göring's role in the creation of the German Air Force:

It was unquestionably thanks to Hermann Göring, the creator of the Luftwaffe, that it was at all possible for the German air force to develop while such a vast program of construction and enlargement was taking place at the same time in all fields. It was estimated that the reconstruction of the Luftwaffe represented 40 per cent of the total German rearmament capacity during those years. With great energy and a passionate love for his arm, Göring knew how to create for it the place which in his mind was its due in the structure of a Continental military power. In any case, the importance of the air force in a future war had been recognized in Germany in good time, accurately, and fundamentally.

Without doubt, mistakes were made during the period of development. Doubtless everything suffered from undue haste and overoptimism. The effect of an air force and of its combat potential in those days was exaggerated, although of course the concept anticipated later technical developments. But the principles on which Hitler, advised and encouraged by Göring, based the creation of an independent Luftwaffe were sound and correct. (Galland, *The First and the Last*)

29.04.1933 Established the *Reichsluftschutzbund* (RLB, Reich Air Raid Protection League). In a statement issued that date, Göring declared:

Since the end of the war universal disarmament has been promised to the German people. The facts, however, are that the world today bristles with more arms than ever before. Thousands of military aircraft surround Germany, who has seen herself completely defenseless in the air and has had defense from the ground almost entirely taken from her....

Intelligent cooperation by the whole populace is essential for success. This cooperation should be obtained if the newly founded Reich Luftschutzbund to avoid the spreading of efforts has sole charge of the pertinent matters.

This organization shall instruct and propagandize the populace. Above all it shall awaken among the masses the moral forces that inspire unselfish labor and sacrifice.

I call upon all patriotic men and women to give their utmost support to this organization. Whomever joins it, works in it, or promotes it financially contributes to the protection of himself, his family and his property. At the same time, he fulfills a solemn patriotic duty.

A people that surrenders to the arbitrariness of the enemy forfeits its existence. But a people imbued by iron will to exist as a nation will also be able to successfully defy danger from the air. ("Reich Forms Body for Air Defense" in *The New York Times*, 30.04.1933)

The RLB was under the control of Göring's *Reichsluftfahrtministerium* until 1940, when it was formally placed under *Luftwaffe* jurisdiction. By 1938, the RLB, organized into fifteen *Landesgruppen* throughout the Reich, numbered 13 million members. This increased by the Spring of 1943 to 22 million. The organization was led by an *RLB-Präsident*, with the following officers successively holding that post:

29.04.1933–30.04.1936	*Generalleutnant* Hugo Grimme
30.04.1936–30.05.1939	*Generalleutnant* Karl von Roques
30.05.1939–03.06.1941	*General der Flakartillerie* Ludwig von Schröder
30.05.1939–03.06.1941	*General-Hauptluftschutzführer* Hermann Sautier (RLB chief of staff, in acting command following the death of von Schröder)

01.08.1942–31.01.1945	*General der Flakartillerie* Friedrich Hirschauer

On 23.09.1933, Göring announced his ruling that Jews would not be admitted to the RLB, stating:

The [*Reichsluftschutzbund*] can perform its task only if it can rely on the cooperation of the widest and most important sections of the population. But this comprehensive task could not be safeguarded if the association were to admit non-Aryans to membership.

Furthermore, I am concerned to avoid the unpleasantness that might develop for the Jews were they to attend public meetings of the association attended by representatives of all sections of our nation. (Hugh Jedell, "Reich Bars Jews from Air Defense" in *The New York Times*, 24.09.1933)

03.05.1933	Letter to Göring from a certain A. Müller in Bonn. It is unlikely the author received a reply:

Dear Ministerpräsident!

The incomparably beautiful course of the May Day celebrations throughout Germany is a new highlight in the wonderful achievements of our venerable Reichskanzler. He has achieved so many beautiful and good things through the unification of the German people, which was previously thought to be impossible, that one cannot imagine that it could ever be otherwise again, but it is precisely the concern that this could happen that prompts me to write the following.

I will be very brief; it is the Jewish question. I am a genuine "Aryan," I also voted nat.soz., but I cannot agree with the solution of the Jewish question (in agreement with most of my compatriots).

The "people" actually do not know of any Jewish question, but only the authorities, who unfortunately carry it into the people. There was also persecution of Jews in the Middle Ages, but it had an ideal purpose, namely the complete expansion of Christianity. Once the Jew had become a "Christian", his persecution ceased. Today, however, it is no longer religion that is being fought, but race. The Catholics reject this as un-Christian, we should love all people, also the other races, Negroes, Japanese, Chinese and Jews, there is no difference. In the case of the Jewish race, however, it is particularly important to remember that Christianity originated in Judaism. The Son of God did not become man among the ancient Germanic peoples, but among the Jews. His mother, his foster father and his relatives also belonged to the Jewish nation. How is it possible for a Christian to hate the Jewish nation? The mass prayers of the Catholic Church, the vestments of its priests, the "commandments" are of Jewish origin. So, in short: we Catholics reject this hatred....

Now the practical side of the Jewish question:

The Jews are not allowed to become "civil servants," they are only allowed to study to a limited extent and to exercise "learned professions," but no Aryan is allowed to make use of them or to buy anything from them, indeed what are the people supposed to live on? They are not allowed to emigrate either, at least not to take their assets with them, besides, the other states would probably oppose mass immigration, so what is to happen to them? So, they end up forming a state within a state, as was the case in the worst times of the Middle Ages, a state that has certainly not stood the test of time.

This standpoint is unworthy of the German people and also attracts the enmity of foreign countries. If Jews have done wrong, they should be punished, but most of the Jews in Germany are small, quite harmless people whom we might not choose as our friends and for personal intercourse, but who have done nothing wrong other than being Jews. That is not acceptable, we must put an end to it.

I ask you, Ministerpräsident, to see to it that this is done.

With the greatest respect
(Götz Aly, et al., eds, *Die Verfolgung und Ermordung der europäischen Juden durch das nationalsozialistische Deutschland 1933-1945, Teil 1: Deutsches Reich 1933-1937*; Translation: Gary Costello)

05.05.1933–23.04.1945	*Reichsminister der Luftfahrt* (Reich Minister of Aviation).
19.05.1933	Arrived in Italy for further discussions with his Italian counterpart, Air Minister General Balbo. The official reason given for the visit was to discuss the creation and employment of civil airlines between Germany and Italy.
29.05.1933	Issued the following order, "Re: SA and SS Questioning of Prisoners Currently Held by Police Authorities":

Experience has shown in many cases that when persons arrested on suspicion of punishable political offenses or actions inimical to the state are questioned by the regular police the results are not nearly as successful as when the questioning of these same persons is carried out by members of the SA and SS. In view of the extraordinary situation prevailing, it appears advisable, to empower for the time being all police authorities, in suitable cases, on their own initiative or in response to requests from the national organizations [i.e. SA, SS, or Stahlhelm] to turn certain prisoners under arrest over to auxiliary police officials for responsible questioning in their own offices [i.e. outside the police station], including confrontation with other guilty parties or witnesses who are to be temporarily released or transferred for this purpose. Against such procedures, no objections are to be raised especially if the involved prisoners are transported to the outside office by police officials who again retrieve them after the questioning.

I request that you provide all your subordinate officials as soon as possible with instructions to this effect. Within a month, you are to report to me the results of this new procedure, with an accompanying recommendation on whether or not the process should continue.
(Webpage of John L. Heineman [1935-2017], Professor Emeritus of History at Boston College)

00.06.1933(?)   Issued an order to combat "defeatism" in the Reich. The following are excerpts:

> I have recently been notified repeatedly that officials, employers and workers in talking with others have made remarks that were likely to create dissatisfaction with the government's measures and sow suspicion. Such persons may be designated as killjoys.
>
> I wish to point out to all officials, employers and workers that henceforth such methods will be regarded as a continuation of Marxist agitation and killjoys will be treated as camouflaged Marxists who are still active in the Marxist manner.
>
> I further request all officials, employers and workers who are responsible for personnel to watch for such cases and report the respective persons. Failure to make such charges will be regarded as a demonstration of solidarity with such agitators. ("Nazis Determined to End 'Defeatism'" in *The New York Times*, 02.07.1933)

Göring defined a "Killjoy" as:

> [one who] is always in bad humor, who spreads an atmosphere of discomfort and jealousy around him, who has no joy in men, animals and plants, who finds no recreation in sea or mountain, who is irritated by a waterfall, who dislikes the sun, who knows everything better than others but usually knows it wrong, who spoils every party, who accompanies everything with spiteful remarks and paints everything black in black. ("Nazis Determined to End 'Defeatism'" in *The New York Times*, 02.07.1933)

00.07.1933   Excerpt from a statement made by Göring at a press conference:

> … Whoever in the future lifts his hand against a representative of the National Socialistic movement or of the State, must know that he will lose his life in a very short while. Furthermore, it will be entirely sufficient, if he is proven to have intended the act, or, if the act results not in a death, but only in an injury. (Partial Translation of Document 2494-PS [excerpt from the *Völkischer Beobachter*, Berlin Edition, 23./24.07.1933], in *Nazi Conspiracy and Aggression, Volume V*)

08.07.1933–23.04.1945   *Präsident der Preußische Staatsrat* (president of the Prussian State Council).

15.09.1933   Official opening ceremony for the *Preußische Staatsrat* under the presidency of Göring, who stated in his speech, "I alone bear the responsibility for it under the authority conferred on me by my Führer; no one can deprive me of this responsibility, nor dare I share it with anyone else." In his diary entry of 15.09.1933, the U.S. Ambassador in Berlin, William E. Dodd, wrote:

> One of the amusing days! The Prussian authorities had invited the diplomatic corps to attend the formal opening of the new Council of State, substitute for the former German Upper House. As the thing was

purely official, I decided to go. On the way, vast masses of Brown Shirt soldiers lined the streets on both sides from the Victoriastrasse to the university, about a mile—perhaps 100,000 uniformed men....

Slowly the officials of the new Nazi state filed into their seats in the middle of the room. Hermann Goering, a fat ridiculous looking man according to my taste, came towards his centrally located chair with a score of men behind him. He stopped and gave the Hitler salute, a click of shoe-heels, a raise of the right hand and a sharp Prussian bow....

The Prussian Minister, Goering, in Hitler uniform, began a long harangue which, not being in front of him, I could understand only in broken snatches here and there It was a passionate oration on the meaning of the new state, the Third Reich, in which three or four times I discerned contemptuous remarks about the discarded parliamentary system. It is curious: next week they are trying three or four men in Leipzig on a charge of treason for burning the old Reichstag building, and yet this man, next in authority to Hitler himself, denounces parliamentarianism as a betrayal of Germanism.

The meeting adjourned about 12.30 and the diplomatic corps took its place on the terrace in front of the university to witness the marching of thousands of Prussian police. Brown Shirts and Stahlhelm troops... (Dodd, *Ambassador Dodd's Diary, 1933–1938*, pp. 51-52)

08.07.1933–23.04.1945	*Protektor der Preußischen Akademie der Künste* (Guardian of the Prussian Academy of the Arts), Berlin.
16.08.1933	Issued an order banning vivisection in Prussia, in order, as he stated, to end the "unbearable torture and suffering in animal experiments." The law stated that "Anyone presuming to practice vivisection henceforth will be taken to a concentration camp" ("Order by Goering Bans Vivisection in Prussia" in *The New York Times*, 17.08.1933). In a radio broadcast of 28.08.1933, he declared:

An absolute and permanent ban on vivisection is not only a necessary law to protect animals and to show sympathy with their pain, but it is also a law for humanity itself.... I have therefore announced the immediate prohibition of vivisection and have made the practice a punishable offense in Prussia. Until such time as punishment is pronounced the culprit shall be lodged in a concentration camp. (Kathleen Marquardt, *Animalscam: The Beastly Abuse of Human Rights*, p. 124)

The following day, he continued to discuss the ban:

Germans are differentiated from any other nation, particularly those of the Asiatic races, by their attitude toward animals. The puzzling circumstance that German law has not hitherto expressed the German love of animals is to be ascribed to the fact that the framing of Germany's laws had passed into the hands of men of an alien race....

[The measures are intended] not only for the protection of dumb animals but to combat human brutality and cruelty. ("Explains Vivisection Ban. Goering Says it is to Combat Human Cruelty" in *The New York Times*, 30.08.1933)

	The law was revised on 05.09.1933 by a decree which permitted the Reich Interior Minister to authorize animal experimentation in a limited number of essential cases by designated research institutes and universities, provided anesthesia was administered.
30.08.1933	Appointed to the *Generalsynode der Evangelischen Kirche* (General Synod of the Evangelical Church).
20.10.1933–24.10.1933	Visit to Sweden to visit the grave of his wife at Lovö Kyrka in Lovön.
06.11.1933–07.11.1933	Visit to Rome, ostensibly to observe German cultural institutions in the city. The real purpose was to meet with Mussolini concerning Germany's withdrawal from the League of Nations and World Disarmament Conference.
29.11.1933	Announced, via the following letter, that he was taking personal control of the Gestapo:

As of today, I am assuming the leadership of the political police. I have forwarded the attached law to the Staatsministerium for approval.

I am thus taking into my own hands the reorganization of the Geheime Staatspolizei as ordered by the decree of the Prussian Minister of the Interior of the 15 November 1933 -I G. 1150/74-. The special order given to the Polizeipräsident Hinkler in Altona will expire. I request that Polizeipräsident Hinkler, after handing over the affairs, return to his previous office and report to me that this has been done. I further request that you express my thanks and appreciation to Polizeipräsident Hinkler for the services he has rendered and instruct him to summarize his experiences as head of the Staatspolizeistelle under his authority in a memorandum and to submit it to me.

I hereby appoint Ministerialrat Diels as Inspector of the Geheime Staatspolizei, temporarily leaving him in his position as kommissarischer Polizei-Vizepräsident in Berlin. In this position, he is to gather the expert knowledge necessary for the reorganization of the Berlin political police and to prepare this reorganization. At the same time, Ministerialrat Diels will assume his new position as of today. He is instructed to submit to me within the shortest possible time the organisational plan drawn up by Polizeipräsident Hinkler, taking into account the guidelines provided for in the attached draft law.

I hereby disband the "politische Gruppe" (Abt. II G) that exists within the framework of the police department of the Ministry of the Interior. I am transferring their responsibilities to the Geheime Staatspolizeiamt. Ministerialdirigent Fischer will leave the political police with immediate effect. Details of his further use will be provided soonest. For the time being, the remaining case officers of the "politische Gruppe" will continue to work as part of the Geheime Staatspolizeiamt. The right is reserved to regulate the matter in greater detail. They will also decide on the more detailed division of individual special areas between the Ministry of the Interior and the Geheime Staatspolizeiamt. For the future, I expressly reserve the right to appoint the heads of the Staatspolizeistellen as well as all senior officials of the Geheime Staatspolizei.

I request that the attached decree to the officials of the Geheime

Staatspolizeiamt and all Staatspolizeistellen be published in the Ministerial Gazette of the Internal Administration after the promulgation of the law.
Signed Göring
(Bundesarchiv R 43-II-395-0077, R 43-II-395-0079, and R 43-II-395-0081; Translation: Gary Costello)

The following is the text of Göring's *"Erlass über die Umorganisation der Geheimen Staatspolizei"* (Decree on the Reorganization of the Secret State Police), signed 30.11.1933:

The State Ministry has resolved the following law:
    Article 1
(1) The Geheime Staatspolizei is an independent branch of the Administration of the Interior. The Prime Minister is its chief. He appoints an Inspector of the Geheime Staatspolizei as acting manager of the affairs.
(2) In case of absence, the Staatssekretär of the Staatsministerium acts as deputy of the Ministerpräsident in his capacity as Chief of the Geheime Staatspolizei.
(3) The Inspector of the Geheime Staatspolizei is also chief of the Geheime Staatspolizeiamt.
    Article 2
The jurisdiction of the Geheime Staatspolizei covers all political police matters of the general and interior administration. The Ministerpräsident as Chief of the Geheime Staatspolizei, will issue the regulations regarding the matters which must be transferred to the Geheime Staatspolizei.
    Article 3
(1) With the enactment of this law the Geheime Staatspolizeiamt takes over matters of a political nature which were previously handled by the Ministry of the Interior.
(2) The district, county and local police authorities [*Landeskreis und Ortspolizeibehörden*] are subject to the directives of the Geheime Staatspolizeiamt.
    Article 4
The Minister of Finance is empowered to make changes in the budget of the State in order to carry out this law.
    Article 5
Provisions of the law of 26 April 1933 (Gesetzsammlung 1933, p. 122) which conflict with this law are superseded by this law.
    Article 6
This law goes into effect with its promulgation.
Berlin, 30 November 1933
The Prussian State Ministry,
[signed] Göring and by Popitz
and for the Minister of Interior
(*1933 Preußische Gesetzsammlung*, p. 413; Translation of Document 2105-PS, in *Nazi Conspiracy and Aggression, Volume IV*)

In an accompanying announcement to the police officials impacted by the reorganization, Göring wrote:

To all officials, auxiliary officials, employees of the Geheimen Staatspolizeiamt and all Staatspolizeistellen.

With the elections of 12th of November 1933, an epoch of the work of the Geheime Staatspolizei has reached a preliminary conclusion. The result of the elections was the visible expression that a considerable number of enemies of the state and opponents of the National Socialist government no longer exist in Prussia and Germany. Freed from the pernicious influence of leaders who incited the people, the masses, hitherto hostile to the National Socialist idea, have declared their support for the National Socialist government and for the aims of the Führer. A considerable part of this great historical success is due to the work of the Geheime Staatspolizei.

During the establishment of the Geheimen Staatspolizei, I entrusted particularly reliable and proven civil servants, employees and members of the National Socialist Combat Units with the honorable task of promoting the National Socialist Revolution in its objectives and, after its implementation, of ensuring the order of the state. The work of the Geheime Staatspolizei has not disappointed me. Together with the S.A. and the S.S., every civil servant, assistant civil servant and employee has devoted himself to carrying out my instructions, using all his strength and in keeping with an old Prussian sense of duty. I thank you for this also on behalf of the Führer. Even if the visible organisations of the enemies of the state have been crushed, the result of the Reichstag election will not hide from you the fact that the law-breaking and anti-state activity has not ceased. Although the supporters of communist and Marxist ideas have shrunk to a small group, there are still seducers of the people in freedom who now continue their hustle and bustle with other invisible, but therefore not less dangerous methods, with the support of high traitors who have fled the country. The change in the underground work of the police opponents also requires a change in the methods of persecution. I now intend to adapt the organisation of the Geheimen Staatspolizei to the new situation. Therefore, as of today, I have taken over the leadership of the Geheimen Staatspolizei. I have appointed the previous head of the Geheimen Staatspolizei, Ministerialrat Diels, to the position of Inspector of the Geheimen Staatspolizei. I have instructed him to carry out this reorganization. For the time being, I am leaving Ministerialrat Diels in his position as Police Vice-President in Berlin in order for him to gain the experience necessary for the reorganization of the Berlin political police and to prepare the reorganization.

I expect all officers and employees of the political police to be aware, also for the future, of the honorable task before which I have placed them and to continue to do their duty in the service of the Fatherland. (Bundesarchiv R 43-II_395-0085 and R 43-II_395-0087; Translation: Gary Costello)

02.12.1933-26.06.1936	*Chef der Preußische Geheime Staatspolizei* (chief of the Prussian Secret State Police [*Gestapo*]).
07.12.1933	Announced the planned release of 5,000 prisoners from the concentration camps. In his instructions to the police, he stated:

"The prisoners are to be left in no doubt that if they repay the generosity of the National Socialist State with new hostile activities, I shall eliminate them ruthlessly and forever" ("Goering Will Free 5,000 from Camps" in *The New York Times*, 08.12.1933).

31.12.1933 Letter from Hitler to Göring:

My dear Göring:
When in November 1923 the Party tried for the first time to conquer the power of the State, you as Commander of the SA created within an extraordinarily short time that instrument with which I could bear that struggle. Highest necessity had forced us to act, but a wise providence at that time denied the success. After receiving a grave wound, you again entered the ranks as soon as circumstances permitted as my most loyal comrade in the battle for power. You contributed essentially to creating the basis for, the 30th of January. Therefore, at the end of a year of the National Socialist Revolution, I desire to thank you wholeheartedly, my dear Party Comrade Göring, for the great values which you have for the National Socialist Revolution and consequently for the German people. In cordial friendship and grateful appreciation.
Yours,
(signed) Adolf Hitler! (Translation of Document 3259-PS, in *Nazi Conspiracy and Aggression, Volume II*)

27.01.1934 Appointed as *Ehrenführer* of SA-Standarte 1, Berlin.

07.03.1934 Issued the following instructions to the German Foreign Ministry concerning "Exclusion of unauthorized persons from Saar politics and from the Saar intelligence service":

I have been forced to note that the instruction of the Minister of Interior dated 11 September 1933—II G 1901-II SG 2210—concerning the exclusion of unauthorized persons from Saar politics and from the Saar intelligence service is not being universally observed.

The plebiscite campaign for reincorporation of the Saar Territory [*Saargebiet*] into the Reich has entered its final and crucial stage. The campaign is therefore being conducted by the opposition with added intensity and larger means. The opposition is concerned not only with the fate of the Saar Territory and its population, but equally with administering a stinging defeat to the idea of Greater Germany, to the new German Reich and its government.

The employment of considerable numbers of émigrés in the civil service of the Governing Commission, where they are active as bitter opponents of the new Germany and the idea of reunion, the complaints lodged by the Governing Commission with the League of Nations about alleged encroachments of the NSDAP and German "nefarious informers" are samples of the intensified campaign methods of the opposition. Occupation by French troops or at least strong French gendarmerie units is desired by influential circles close to the Governing Commission, as it is undoubtedly the objective of the efforts by some of its members themselves.

It is the clear duty of Germans to meet the oppositions anti-German machinations and widely ramified network of informers with resolute and coordinated countermeasures.

The direction of German countermeasures, where these involve political police functions, must be centralized in one authority. Any duplication, confusion, or working at cross-purposes can only cause considerable harm. The opposition is better informed about some of the German intelligence agencies than the responsible Prussian headquarters.

In addition to government authorities other than those of Prussia, a number of private, official, and party organizations are active in intelligence work in the Saar. This harms the NSDAP of the Saar Territory and the entire German countereffort; in particular, the livelihood and freedom of loyal German civil servants in the Saar Territory are being seriously threatened.

With reference to the instruction of the Minister of Interior referred to earlier, I therefore expressly order as follows:

(1) Within the territory of the Free State of Prussia the Gestapo has exclusive direction over political police functions and over the intelligence service in matters concerning the Saar.

(2) Intelligence services in the Saar Territory may be operated only by those commissioned to do so by the Gestapo.

(3) Intelligence services which have existed heretofore shall be immediately disbanded. Intelligence reports are to be communicated to the Gestapo, with precise identification and personal evaluation of the informants. Material in the possession of informants is to be called in and, if necessary, seized.

(4) Authorities having knowledge of unauthorized intelligence services must immediately inform the Gestapo to this effect.

Strict measures will be taken in future against any unauthorized meddling in political affairs of the Saar.
[Signed] Göring
(*Documents on German Foreign Policy 1918–1945, Series C [1933–1937], The Third Reich: First Phase, Volume II, October 14, 1933–June 13,1934*, pp. 569-570)

11.03.1934   Signed the "Order concerning protective custody" [*Schutzhaft*]:

Effective immediately I order the following:

1. The regulations which so far dealt with competence with regard to the application of protective custody for political reasons are cancelled. In future restrictions of personal freedom in accordance with article 1 of the Decree for the Protection of the People and State, dated 28 February 1933, may be ordered with effect on the entire state territory [of Prussia] by the Geheime Staatspolizeiamt only, and within their local fields of jurisdiction by the Oberpräsidenten, Regierungspräsidenten, the Polizeipräsident in Berlin and the local state police offices.

The district police authorities, especially the Landräte, are no longer competent for such measures. The measures hitherto ordered by them will be rescinded as per 31 March unless they have been extended by order of the competent police authorities of the constituent states.

Offices of the Party and the affiliated organizations may not carry out arrests on their own initiative. In case of disobedience to this order the competent authority will interfere, and report to me, at once.
(*Trials of War Criminals Before the Nuernberg Military Tribunals*, Volume III, "The Justice Case")

00.03.1934–00.03.1934	Visited the Polish State Hunting Ground at Bialowiéza, at the invitation of József Lipski (Polish Ambassador in Berlin).
09.04.1934	Appointed as *Präsident* of the *Reichsklub (Kameradschaft) vom 30. Januar 1933*.
20.04.1934	Appointed *Reichsführer-SS* Heinrich Himmler as inspector and deputy head of the *Geheime-Staatspolizei* (*Gestapo*), in succession to Rudolf Diels, with Reinhard Heydrich as director of the *Geheime-Staatspolizeiamt*. During the change of command ceremony, Göring asserted that prior to his taking control of it, the Prussian police was suffering from an infestation of Marxism. "There was no model in all the world," he explained, "on which I could fashion the political police of the new Reich and I was compelled to build up an organization along wholly new lines- one that would be free of all bureaucracy" ("Secret Police Get One Chief In Reich" in *The New York Times*, 21.04.1934). Göring relinquished directive functions over the *Gestapo* to Himmler in November 1934 (see entry of 20.11.1934, below). He retained titular command until 26.06.1936, when the *Gestapo* was placed under Heydrich in his capacity as *Chef* of the *Sicherheitspolizei* (composed of the *Gestapo* and *Kriminalpolizei*).
02.05.1934	Appointed as *Oberster Leiter der Landespolizei in Preußen* (Supreme Head of the State Police in Prussia).
15.05.1934–27.05.1934	"Vacation" in southeastern Europe (accompanied by Paul Körner, Erhard Milch, Prince Philipp of Hessen, Hanns Kerrl, and his future wife, Emmy Sonnemann). The actual purpose of this tour, during which he made stops in Belgrade, Athens, and Budapest, was to convince the southeastern European countries of Germany's intention to safeguard them from Italian territorial ambitions. On the 25th, he met in Budapest with Hungarian Premier Gyula Gömbös and Admiral Miklós Horthy, Regent of the Kingdom of Hungary.
00.00.1934–00.00.1936	Co-chairman (together with *Generaloberst* Werner von Blomberg) of the *Deutschen Olympia-Komittees für Reiterei* (German Olympic Committee for Equestrian Events).
18.06.1934	In a speech to the *Preußische Staatsrat*, declared:

The application of new and perhaps still more radical revolutionary methods will scarcely produce an improvement. It is not up to us to determine whether a second revolution is necessary. The first revolution was ordered by the Führer and it has been ended by the Führer. If the Führer wishes a second revolution, then we will be on the streets tomorrow. If he does not wish it, then we will crush everybody who tries

	to make such a revolution against his will. (Joseph Nyomarkay, *Charisma and Factionalism in the Nazi Party*, p. 131)
23.06.1934	Sharing the stage with *Gauleiter* Julius Streicher, delivered a speech at the "*2. Frankentag*" on the Hesselberg near Wassertrüdingen (*Kreis Ansbach* in *Gau Franken*), about 60 km from Nürnberg. The event was described in the American press:

"If ultra-cautious politicians contend that our anti-Semitic policy needs breaking we can only tell them they do not understand the problem," General Goering told a mass meeting in Franconia.

He declared that Herr Streicher's district was the only thoroughly National Socialist region in Germany, that the Jewish question must be fought out ruthlessly, that intellectuals were at best Laodiceans and that Christianity as a whole had drained the strength of the Nordic race and its culture.

Herr Streicher followed General Goering, stating: "We must wage a religious war against the Jews and we have come here to swear our oath for prosecuting it." (Otto D. Tolischus, "Nazi Row Spreads; Chiefs Warn Foes" in *The New York Times*, 26.06.1934)

26.06.1934	Delivered a speech at an NSDAP gathering in Hamburg in which he railed against "interest cliques" and "unproductive critics" (i.e., Kurt von Schleicher and Gregor Strasser, both of whom were snuffed out in Göring's and Himmler's organized bloodbath of 30.06–01.07.1934):

When one day the cup runneth over, I will strike! We have worked as no one has ever worked before, because we have behind us a Volk which trusts us. Anyone who gnaws away at this trust is committing a crime against the Volk, he is committing treachery and high treason. He who designs to destroy this trust, destroys Germany. He who sins against this trust has put his own head in the noose. (Dr. Max Domarus, ed., *Hitler. Speeches and Proclamations, 1932–1945: The Years 1932–1934*, p. 466)

28.06.1934	Together with Hitler, served as a witness to the wedding of his friend *Gauleiter* Josef Terboven in Essen. He returned that afternoon to Berlin.
30.06.1934–01.07.1934	Presided over the purge of the SA leadership and others from his villa on the *Leipzigerplatz* in Berlin. Together with Himmler, Heydrich, *Generalmajor* Walter von Reichenau, and others, Göring decided who would live and who would be shot for their part in an alleged conspiracy to make Kurt von Schleicher (murdered in his home together his wife) Chancellor and *SA-Stabschef* Ernst Röhm (shot by Theodor Eicke at Stadelheim Prison near München) Defense Minister. At shortly after 10:00 hours on Saturday the 30th, Goebbels, who had just spoken with Hitler at Party headquarters in München after the arrest of Röhm and other SA leaders, phoned Göring in Berlin. He said only one word: "*Kolibri*" (hummingbird), the signal for Göring to begin

action against the "traitors" in Berlin on what became known as the "*Nacht der langen Messer*" ("Night of the Long Knives"). A witness to Göring's role in the purge was the *Kripo* official (and later member of the conspiracy to assassinate Hitler), Hans Bernd von Gisevius, who recalled:

Suddenly loud shouting reached us from the adjoining room. This room was Göring's study, and here the execution committee was meeting. Now and then couriers from the *Gestapo* rushed into and out of this room, slips of white paper in their hands. Through the door we could see Göring, Himmler, Heydrich, and little Pilli Koerner, under-secretary to Göring in his capacity as minister-president. We could see them conferring, but naturally we could not hear what was being said. Occasionally, however, we could catch a muffled sound: "Away!" or "Aha!" or "Shoot him!" For the most part we heard nothing but raucous laughter. The whole crew of them seemed to be in the best humor.

Göring radiated cheerful complacency. It was easy to see that he was in his element. He swaggered about the room, his long hair waving, in a white military tunic and blue-gray military trousers, with high black boots that reached over his fat knees. There goes Puss-in-Boots, I thought suddenly. The epithet seemed appropriate, not so much because of the spiteful, catlike attitude of the man as because there was something puffed-up, counterfeit, and ridiculous about him.

But to continue—we suddenly heard loud shouting. A police major, his face flaming, rushed out of the room, and behind him came Göring's hoarse, booming voice: "Shoot them ... take a whole company ... shoot them ... shoot them at once!" The written word cannot reproduce the undisguised blood lust, fury, vicious vengefulness, and, at the same time, the fear, the pure funk, that the scene revealed... (Gisevius, *To the Bitter End*, p. 152)

Another who had occasion to see Göring in action that day was Hitler's Vice Chancellor, Franz von Papen, who testified at Nürnberg on 17.06.1946:

On the morning of 30 June, I received a telephone call from Minister Göring, asking me to come to have a talk with him. I went to see Göring; he told me that a revolution had broken out in the Reich—an SA revolution—that Hitler was in München to put down this uprising there, and that he, Göring, was charged with restoring law and order in Berlin. Herr Göring asked me, in the interests of my own safety, as he said, to return to my apartment and stay there. I protested quite vehemently against this demand, but Herr Göring insisted. On my way back to my apartment, I went first to my office in the Vice Chancellery. On arriving there, I found my office occupied by the SS, and I was permitted only to enter my own room and get my files. I went on home to my apartment, where I found a large number of SS. The telephone was disconnected; the radio was disconnected; and I was completely cut off from the outside world for 3 whole days....

I naturally did not hear about the measures taken against my staff until 3 July, after I had regained my freedom. I learned that my press adviser, Herr

Von Bose, had been shot in his office. I further learned that two of my male secretaries, Herr von Tschirschky and another gentleman, had been taken to a concentration camp and a few days later, I learned of the death of my friend and colleague—a private colleague of mine—Herr Edgar Jung.

I finally succeeded, on the third day of my arrest, in contacting Goring by telephone. I demanded to be set free at once. Herr Goring apologized and said that it was only a mistake that I had been kept under arrest for this long period of time… (*Trial of the Major War Criminals Before the International Military Tribunal, Nuremberg, 14 November 1945–1 October 1946, Volume IX*)

On 02.07.1934, Reich President von Hindenburg sent the following telegram to Göring:

I may express to you my thanks and appreciation for your vigorous and successful action in crushing the attempt to commit high treason.
With comradely regards, von Hindenburg (Dr. Max Domarus, ed., *Hitler. Speeches and Proclamations, 1932–1945: The Years 1932–1934*, p. 480)

An interview with Göring published in the 03.07.1934 issue of the Swedish newspaper *Nya Dagligt Allehand* quoted him as follows:

… the action became necessary not only due to the plans for a putsch. Röhm's private life as well as that of the other persons who have now been arrested was such that it meant a scandal for the entire SA. They were a moral cancer which had to be cut out. (Dr. Max Domarus, ed., *Hitler. Speeches and Proclamations, 1932–1945: The Years 1932–1934*, p. 482)

According to Hitler's *Reichstag* speech of 13.07.1934, seventy-four deaths had resulted from the purge (postwar research indicates the minimum figure was probably eighty-five, including twelve members of the *Reichstag*; Göring cynically conceded that "in the general excitement some mistakes were made." According to official reports, 1,124 people had been arrested on Göring's orders). In his lengthy speech, in which he sought to justify the purge, Hitler gave special recognition to Göring: "Meanwhile Minister President Goering had previously received my instructions that in case of a purge, he was to take analogous measures at once in Berlin and in Prussia. With an iron fist he beat down the attack on the National Socialist State before it could develop." (Excerpt from Document 3442-PS, in *Nazi Conspiracy and Aggression, Volume II*)

Following the speech, Göring stood and addressed his *Führer*:

You have succeeded! You have the trust and, based upon this trust, it is possible for you to do what is required for Germany's reconstruction. However, this trust is also the platform upon which Germany stands today. He who seeks to shake and destroy it is guilty of more than treason to the internal and external security of the State. That is the most colossal crime imaginable, and he who commits it must be destroyed—for he is knocking down the very foundation upon which Germany stands today.

The fact that the Reichstag has today resolved: "The Reichstag grants its approval to the statement of the Reich Government and thanks the Reich Chancellor for his energetic and resolute salvation of the Vaterland from civil war and chaos," is merely an outward expression of what the entire Volk—man for man and woman for woman—would declare today. And if foreign countries presently believe that chaos is descending upon Germany, the German Volk's reply is the single cry: "We will all always approve of everything our Führer does." (Dr. Max Domarus, ed., *Hitler. Speeches and Proclamations, 1932–1945: The Years 1932–1934*, p. 502)

The Prussian *Ministerpräsident* celebrated the successful conclusion of the operation with a crab feast to which were invited Werner von Blomberg, Himmler, Erhard Milch, and Paul Körner. A second celebration took place at *Carinhall* on 07.03.1934, with Göring playing host to Reinhard Heydrich and his *Gestapo* staff. On 12.07.1934, Göring delivered a speech to the Public Prosecutors of Prussia, declaring: "The action of the Government in the days of the Röhm revolt was the highest realization of the legal consciousness of the people. Later the action which itself was justified, now has been made legal by the passage of a law." (Translation of Document 2496-PS, in *Nazi Conspiracy and Aggression, Volume V*)

In his testimony of 14.03.1946, Göring gave his version of the events of June–July 1934:

The main controversy between Röhm and us was that Röhm, like his predecessor Pfeffer, wanted a stronger revolutionary way to be adopted, whereas the Führer, as I said earlier, had ordered a legal development, the final victory of which could be expected.

After the seizure of power Röhm desired, under all circumstances, to get hold of the Reich Defense Ministry. The Führer refused that point-blank, as he did not wish the Armed Forces to be conducted politically in any way, or to have any political influence brought to bear on the Armed Forces.

The contrast between the Armed Forces and the Röhm group am intentionally not speaking of a contrast between the Armed Forces and the SA, since there was none, but solely of this leadership group, which called itself at that time the SA Leadership and it actually was-was that Röhm wanted to remove the greater number of the generals and higher officers who had been members of the Reichswehr all this time, since it was his view that these officers did not offer a guarantee for the new State, because, as he expressed it, their backbone had been broken in the course of the years and they were no longer capable of being active elements of the new National Socialist State.

The Führer, and I also, had exactly the opposite point of view in this connection.

Secondly, the aims of the Röhm-minded people, as I should like to call them, were directed in a different direction, towards a revolutionary act; and they were opposed to what they called reaction. They definitely desired to adopt a more Leftist attitude. They were also sharply opposed to the Church and also very strongly opposed to the Jews. Altogether, and I refer only to the clique consisting of certain persons, they wished to carry out a revolutionary act.

That Röhm placed all his people in leading positions in the SA and removed the decent elements, and misguided the decent SA people without their knowledge, is a well-known fact. If encroachments did occur at that time, they always involved the same persons, first of all the Berlin SA leader, Ernst, secondly the Breslau leader, Heines, the Munich and Stettin leaders, et cetera.

A few weeks before the Röhm Putsch a low-ranking SA leader confided in me that he had heard that an action against the Führer and his corps was being planned to replace the Third Reich as expeditiously as possible by a final Fourth Reich, an expression which these people used.

I myself was urged and begged to place outside my house not only guards from a police regiment but also to appoint an SA guard of honor. I had agreed, and later on I heard from the commander of these troops that the purpose of that guard of honor was to arrest me at a given moment. I knew Röhm very well. I had him brought to me. I put to him openly the things which I had heard. I reminded him of our mutual fight, and I asked him to keep unconditional faith with the Führer.

I brought forward the same arguments which I have just mentioned, but he assured me that he naturally was not thinking of undertaking anything against the Führer. Shortly afterward I received further news to the effect that he had close connections with those circles who also were strongly opposed to us. There was, for instance, the group around the former Reich Chancellor Schleicher. There was the group around Gregor Strasser, the former member of the Reichstag and organizational leader of the Party, who had been excluded from the Party. These were groups who had belonged to the former trade unions and were rather inclined to the Left. I felt it my duty to consult the Führer now on this subject. I was astonished when he told me that he, too, already knew about these things and considered them a great threat. He said that he wished, however, to await further developments and observe them carefully.

The next event occurred just about as the witness Körner described it here, and therefore I can skip it. I was given the order to proceed immediately against the implicated men of the Röhm group in northern Germany. It was decided that some of them were to be arrested. In the course of the day the Führer ordered the execution of the SA leader of Pomerania, Ernst, and two or three others. He himself went to Bavaria where the last meeting of a number of Röhm leaders was taking place and personally arrested Röhm and these people in Wiessee.

At that time this matter presented a real danger, as a few SA units, through the use of false passwords, had been armed and called up. At one spot only a very short fight ensued, and two SA leaders were shot. I deputized the police, which in Prussia was then already under Himmler and Heydrich, to make the arrests. Only the headquarters of Röhm, who himself was not present, I had occupied by a regiment of the uniformed police subordinated to me. When the headquarters of the SA leader Ernst in Berlin were searched, we found in the cellars of those headquarters more submachine guns than the whole Prussian police had in its possession.

After the Führer, on the strength of the events which had been met with at Wiessee, had ordered who should be shot in view of the state of national emergency, the order for the execution of Ernst, Heydebreck, and some of the other Röhm collaborators was issued. There was no order to shoot the other people who had been arrested. In the course of the arrest of the former Reich Chancellor Schleicher, it happened that both he and his wife were killed. An investigation of this event took place and it was found that when Schleicher was arrested, according to the statements of the two witnesses, he reached for a pistol, possibly in order to kill himself, whereupon the two men raised their pistols and Frau Schleicher threw herself upon one of them to hold him, causing his revolver to go off. We deeply regretted that event.

In the course of that evening, I heard that other people had been shot as well, even some people who had nothing at all to do with this Röhm Putsch. The Führer came to Berlin that same evening.

After I learned this, later that evening or night, I went to him at noon the next day and asked him to issue an order immediately, that any further execution was under any circumstances forbidden by him, the Führer, although two other people who were deeply involved and who had been ordered by the Führer to be executed, were still alive. These people were consequently left alive. I asked him to do that because I was worried lest the matter should get out of hand—as, in fact, it had already done to some extent—and I told the Führer that under no circumstances should there be any further bloodshed. This order was then given by the Führer in my presence, and it was communicated at once to all offices. The action was then announced in the Reichstag, and it was approved by the Reichstag and the Reich President as an action called for by the state of national emergency. It was regretted that, as in all such incidents, there were a number of blunders. The number of victims has been greatly exaggerated. As far as I can remember exactly today, there were 72 or 76 people, the majority of whom were executed in southern Germany. (*Trial of the Major War Criminals Before the International Military Tribunal, Nuremberg, 14 November 1945–1 October 1946, Volume IX*)

To the psychologist Dr. G. M. Gilbert, he was more brutally candid about the "Night of the Long Knives":

At the mention of Roehm's name, Goering hit the ceiling. "Roehm! Don't talk to me about that dirty homosexual swine! That was the real clique of perverted bloody revolutionarists! They are the ones who first made the Party look like a pack of hoodlums, with their wild orgies and beating up Jews on the street, and smashing windows! They set out to do right in the beginning what actually took place later under the pressure of war. They would have given you a real demonstration of a bloody revolution! They were bent on wiping out the whole generals' corps, the whole Party leadership—all the Jews, naturally—everything, in one grand blood bath! What a gang of perverted bandits that SA was! It is a damn good thing I wiped them out, or they would have wiped us out!" The ruthless-gangster side of his personality stood clearly revealed as the jovial mask fell completely away, even as he strode up and down the cell in breeches, shirt, and bedroom slippers, gesticulating wildly, hatred flashing out of his eyes. "I made no bones about it. I went to that SA captain and said, 'Do you have any weapons?' 'Why no, Herr Polizeichef,' the swine says to me, 'none except the pistol for which you gave me a permit.' Then I found an arsenal in the cellar bigger than the whole armament of the Prussian police force! I just told my men to take the bastard out and shoot him. That was a gang of double-crossing cutthroats for you! Do you think good old Hindenburg would have sent me a message of congratulations the next day, if he hadn't realized like a flash that I had averted a catastrophe?" (Gilbert, *Nuremberg Diary*, p. 79, entry of 15–16.12.1945)

03.07.1934–23.04.1945	*Reichsforstmeister* (Reich Master of Forests).
03.07.1934–23.04.1945	*Preußischer Landesforstmeister* (Prussian State Master of Forests).
03.07.1934–23.04.1945	*Reichsjägermeister* (Reich Master of the Hunt). In his memoirs, Albert Speer quoted Hitler on the topic of Göring's "passion for hunting":

How can a person be excited about such a thing[?] Killing animals, if it must be done, is the butcher's business. But to spend a great deal of money on it in addition.... I understand, of course, that there must be professional hunters to shoot sick animals. If only there were still some danger connected with hunting, as in the days when men used spears for killing game. But today, when anybody with a fat belly can safely shoot the animal down from a distance.... Hunting and horse racing are the last remnants of a dead feudal world. (Speer, *Inside the Third Reich*, p. 97)

20.07.1934	In Halle an der Saale, delivered a fawning and fanatical speech, exhibiting a doglike devotion to Adolf Hitler. The following is an excerpt:

Always the Führer is the strongest. For that reason the people love him. The people know that he is just and charitable but also has an iron hand. For that reason the people trust the Führer. This trust is the bond that holds Germany together.

The Führer accomplishes great deeds out of the greatness of his heart, the passion of his will and the goodness of his soul. Trust in him is alone the basis for our life. When anyone dares to touch our faith in him then he must be destroyed. Such a one has ceased to be a German.

Storm Trooper or Minister, we are all the creation of the Führer. Only one thing matters—that the Führer has faith in us. His faith makes us the most powerful of men. If he removes his confidence we are nothing, we are plunged into darkness and lost to the memory of man, for Germany is Adolf Hitler. ("Goering Reaffirms Loyalty to Leader" in *The New York Times*, 21.07.1934)

18.10.1934	Attended the funeral of King Alexander of Yugoslavia in Belgrade (assassinated, together with French Foreign Minister Louis Barthou, by Bulgarian and Croatian terrorists in Marseilles on 09.10.1934).

13.11.1934	Delivered a speech to Dr. Hans Frank's *Akademie für Deutsche Recht* at the *Stadthalle* in Berlin. U.S. Ambassador William Dodd describes the occasion:

> This morning I violated my usual rule and went to the City Hall to hear General Goering address the Academy for German Justice, a kind of German bar association. The wonderful hall was crowded to utmost capacity when I arrived....
>
> Goering entered the hall in a Brown Shirt uniform, his chest covered with medals and badges of honor. He turned towards the audience as he approached the platform, raised his right hand, bowed and shouted "Heil Hitler." I did not enjoy these demonstrations. They have always seemed so absurd to me....
>
> The audience sat down and Goering read an address which re-emphasized the absolute dependence of every German citizen upon the Fuehrer. There was to be no sort of resistance at any time. When the speaker briefly explained the murders of June 30, he showed no sign whatever of any consciousness of error on that occasion. All foreign peoples had denounced the acts of the Fuehrer although he pretended he was saving the German people from disaster, but this was stupid. "We needed to have no indictments, proofs or trials. We were killing enemies of the people."
>
> Everybody knew Goering had ordered the killing of men and women against whom there was no feeling or evidence anywhere that they were guilty of treason. At one place the fat general said heads will simply be chopped off if men do not obey the inspired Hitler and submit to his decrees. A good many of these statements were interjected. They did not appear in the printed copy when it came out in the papers. (Dodd, *Ambassador Dodd's Diary, 1933-1938*, pp. 198-199)

During the same speech, Göring declared: "Gentlemen, for the German nation this matter was settled by the words of the judge in this hour, the Führer, who stated that in this hour of uttermost danger he alone, the Führer elected by the people, was the supreme and only judge of the German nation." (*Trials of War Criminals Before the Nuernberg Military Tribunals, Volume III, "The Justice Case"*)

20.11.1934	In his capacities as *Preußische Ministerpräsident* and *Chef der Geheimen Staatspolizei*, relinquished directive functions over the *Gestapo* to Heinrich Himmler via the following order:

> For organizational reasons, I have seen fit to entrust the Inspector of the Geheimen Staatspolizei, Reichsführer-SS Himmler, with my representation also in the matters of the Geheimen Staatspolizei, which were previously dealt with by the Prussian Staatsministerium. The Inspector of the Geheimen Staatspolizei will now conduct the business of the entire Prussian Geheimen Staatspolizei with sole responsibility towards me. The correspondence will take place in the matters I have reserved for myself under the name of: "Preußische Geheimen Staatspolizei. The Deputy Chief and Inspector".
>
> In informing you of this, I request that correspondence in all matters of the Prussian Geheimen Staatspolizei now be addressed

	directly and exclusively to the Geheime Staatspolizeiamt, Berlin SW 11, Prinz-Albrecht-Straße 8.
	[signed] Göring
	(Bundesarchiv R 43-II-395-0105; Translation: Gary Costello)
07.12.1934–23.04.1945	*Stellvertreter des Reichskanzlers in allen Angelegenheiten der Staatsführung* (deputy to the Reich chancellor in all aspects of national government), appointed via *Führer* decree.
27.01.1935–31.01.1935	Official visit to Poland where he participated in a hunting party and conversations with Marshal Józef Piłsudski, Foreign Minister Józef Beck, and deputy Foreign Minister Jan Szembek. The primary purpose of the visit was to investigate Poland's readiness to work with Germany in the event of conflict with the Soviet Union.
30.01.1935–23.04.1945	*Reichsstatthalter in Preußen.*
01.03.1935–24.04.1945	*Chef der Reichsluftwaffe* (Chief of the Reich Air Force; redesignated *Oberbefehlshaber der Luftwaffe* on 01.06.1935). The Treaty of Versailles had forbidden Germany an air force. Göring countered that prohibition with pronouncements such as the following:

As long as I am Minister for Air, I shall not cease to tell the world again and again, that so long as Germany is debarred from development in the air, so long she will remain defenceless. We demand equality of rights and nothing less. When the other nations are prepared to disband their military air fleets, then Germany will also agree to do the same. But as the other nations are arming for war in the air, we also reserve to ourselves the right to make similar technical preparations, so that the necessary measure of safety may be assured to the German people… (Erich Gritzbach, *Hermann Goering: The Man and His Work*, p. 93)

In Berlin on 20.05.1935, he swore in 1,000 newly commissioned *Luftwaffe* officers and delivered a speech in which he declared: "I repeat: I intend to create a Luftwaffe which, if the hour should strike, shall burst upon the foe like a chorus of revenge [*wie ein Chor der Rache*]. The enemy must have a feeling of being lost already before even having fought…." (Translation from Erich Gritzbach, ed, *Hermann Göring, Reden- und Aufsätze*)

01.04.1935	Appointed as *Oberbefehlshaber der Flakartillerie* (commander-in-chief of anti-aircraft artillery).
04.04.1935	In Danzig as lead spokesman of the German government for the parliamentary elections in the Free City, to be held on the 7th of the month. The NSDAP ultimately won 59 per cent of the vote and forty-three of seventy-two seats in the Danzig *Volkstag*. Prior to his speech, he was honored by a parade of some 10,000 uniformed men. In his speech, Göring denounced as traitors all who would vote against the NSDAP, and stated:

Now I have something to say to both Germans and foreigners. The German Government will recognize the status quo here. It does not need to take Danzig by force of arms for nature will assert itself. The hour will come when the rest of the world will recognize this fact and perhaps aid in the fulfillment of the inevitable. Danzig recognizes its duty. It regards firstly the interests of the Reich, then its own. Danzig will remain German. Hope for the hour of reunion and it will certainly come. ("Nazi Chiefs Stage Military Display for Danzig Voters" in *The New York Times*, 05.04.1935)

18.05.1935–19.05.1935	In Warsaw for the funeral of Marshal Piłsudski and talks with the Polish Foreign Minister, Józef Beck.
24.05.1935–08.06.1935	"Political Honeymoon" in southeastern Europe, accompanied by his new wife, Emmy, and an eight-member entourage. On the afternoon of the 24th, he landed his red-painted Junkers Ju 52 *"Manfred von Richthofen"* (which he had personally flown from Berlin) at the airport in Budapest. Later that day, he had a lengthy private meeting with Regent Miklós Horthy and Premier Gyula Gömbös. On the 26th at 11:00 hours, Göring departed Budapest and proceeded to Bulgaria, his reception in Sofia being far more subdued. After landing in Sofia at 15:00 hours, the Görings were greeted by Minister of Education Todor Radeff and Minister of Communications Todor Kojoukaroff. They were then driven to the Hotel Bulgarie. Despite the presence of some friendly crowds, there were also protests by Bulgarian Communists still angry at Göring's treatment of Dimitroff at the time of the *Reichstag* Fire Trial in October 1933. A meeting of communists in Sofia's Central Park resulted in eight arrests by police with revolvers drawn. While in his general's uniform, Göring laid a wreath at the German war cemetery and observed a parade of the Sofia garrison. Between 17:40 and 19:00 hours, Göring spoke at length with King Boris and was later treated to a dinner at the Hotel Bulgarie by Prime Minister Andrew Tocheff.

After departing Sofia, Göring and his entourage proceeded to Yugoslavia, where the reception was not a warm one, and visited Dubrovnik, Sarajevo, and Mostar before flying to Belgrade.

On his arrival in the Yugoslav capital, which his *Luftwaffe* would devastate six years later, he was received by the German minister as well as leading members of the German community and representatives of the Yugoslav government. The following day, he met for a long conference with the Yugoslav Premier Bogoljub Jevtić and General Petar Živković, minister of the Yugoslav Armed Forces. During this meeting, he pressed the Yugoslav leaders to join Germany in a proposed "anti-Soviet bloc to include Germany, Austria, Italy, Poland, Bulgaria, Hungary, and Yugoslavia." Göring stressed that in joining such a union, Yugoslavia would protect itself from potential attack by Bulgaria, Hungary, and Italy. The plan evoked little if any enthusiasm on the part of the Yugoslavs, due to the feelings of Slavic kinship between Yugoslavia and Russia and the impression that it would be a speculative gamble. |
| 23.06.1935 | Again attended and spoke at the "*3. Frankentag*" on the Hesselberg near Wassertrüdingen, accompanied by *Gauleiter* Julius Streicher. During his speech before an audience of 200,000, the red-faced Göring shouted: |

The next time that a Communist writes with chalk on a road "Death to Hitler," I'll let my Storm Troops loose on him. No State's Attorney will have anything to do with the procedure. No court will prevent him from receiving his just punishment. Let me tell you that anyone who thinks that a term in a concentration camp is a vacation is very much mistaken....

It is perhaps a wholly inevitable result that the [British] people which itself possesses Germanic blood is the first to grant to Germany its respect [A reference to the recently concluded Anglo-German Naval Agreement of 18.06.1935/MdM]. We are happy to recognize this respect, for only respect grows into friendship and only respect and friendship combined develop genuine peace.

Germans were profoundly cheered by the declaration of the British heir apparent. He can be sure the German front soldier and the German people grasp gladly the hand offered them. ("Anti-Semitic Views Voiced by Goering" in *The New York Times*, 24.06.1935)

The following are additional excerpts from the speech:

When on such a place as the old cult as this solstice fires are lighted and we assemble here, that, too, is a sacred act. For we have rediscovered the voices of our blood. Our opponents may call our ancient forefathers heathen. That is not decisive. It is decisive only that they were of Germanic and Nordic blood like we are.

If our opponents think it is neo-paganism when we espouse the greatness of our ancestral history, then let them call it that. If they call our pilgrimage to these old cult places heathenism, let them. But let them not object if we prefer to stream together here in the unity of our people to lift up our hearts to the idea of our Fuehrer rather than listen to the chattering of quarrelsome clerics.

It is better that we demonstrate how to make in God's free nature the unity of our people than to permit a denominational quarrel to drive our people apart....

No church has been built so beautiful, so great, so mighty and so strong in faith as the dome of God over this mountain. If others say we have cast aside our faith, then we ask them when has there been in Germany deeper or more passionate faith than today? When has there been stronger faith than the present faith in our Fuehrer? It is better to be strong in faith in one's nation than to have forgotten passages of the catechism....

When people cease to have faith, churches are futile. Decisive is not faith in this or that dogma, or in this or that interpretation. Decisive is how strong is the faith of a people in its future. This faith is not contrary to God, for the Almighty has created our people that they may make their place on this earth. And by believing in my people and their future I believe in the Almighty.

We do not permit ourselves to be fascinated by disbelief or revealed miracles, for there never has happened a greater miracle than in our time. This miracle of the Almighty has been performed through Adolf Hitler—a miracle of resurrection of the German people. Today our shining armor is filled with strength again and guarantees the security of the nation. That is merely the result of this miracle. ("Germanism Soars at Pagan Festival" in *The New York Times*, 25.06.1935)

16.07.1935 | Issued a decree on the "Struggle Against Political Catholicism." The Austrian *Allgemeiner Tiroler Anzeiger* reported on the decree in its 20.07.1935 issue:

Göring's campaign decree [*Kampferlaß*]
As has already been briefly reported, General Göring, in his capacity as Preußischer Ministerpräsident and head of the Gestapo (Geheime Staatspolizei), addressed a decree to the Oberpräsidenten and Regierungspräsidenten, drawing their attention to the "rejectionist attitude of certain circles of the Catholic clergy against National Socialism and its institutions" and instructing them to "put a stop to these abuses". The decree states, among other things:

"The times when the will and the power of the state were not sufficient to effectively protect the Church from the inciting influences of the godless movement are over. For the church, this means that there is no need to maintain political influences beyond the area of religious activity or to find new ones. It may therefore neither invoke God against this state, a monstrosity that we experience in open and hidden form every Sunday, nor may it organize its own political forces under the flimsy justification that it must ward off threatening dangers from the state. We do not tolerate aspirations that used to be supported by the Zentrum, we fight them, even if they appear under the guise of religious activity. We fight them all the more decisively the more they clothe themselves in deceitful and mendacious forms. This includes when clerics who do not want to come to terms with the political totality of National Socialism recently transfer more and more the language, expressions and symbols of the National Socialist struggle to their alleged 'struggle'. They apply abbreviations that have become second nature to every member of the people, such as 'H.J.' to 'Herz Jesu Jugend' and 'B.D.M.' to 'Bund der Marienmädchen' and a variation of the German greeting to 'Jesus Christ'. They do not confine themselves to the traditional church events, but they increase the number of large demonstrative processions and church festivities and use a form of presentation for these events that is unprecedented. From the pulpit, they unabashedly disparage state institutions and policies. It has come to such a point that the only impression that believing Catholics take away from attending the service is that the Catholic Church rejects institutions of the National Socialist state because the sermons continue to allude to political issues and daily events in a polemical manner. The ecclesiastical superiors, according to the oath they have taken as bishops, owe respect to the government and are obliged to have it respected by the clergy as well. According to their statements, they also condemn the described goings-on. But apparently they are powerless against certain parts of the clergy. Since all warnings have only led to abuse of the previous leniency, the Ministerpräsident now expects all law enforcement agencies to apply the full rigor of the existing provisions."

The decree then claims that "the so-called confessional Catholic youth associations were moving further and further away from their exclusively religious activities." If there is not a complete changeover in this regard, the associations should be regarded as political and banned. The wearing of uniforms and popular sporting activities are reserved exclusively for the state youth and the other branches of the party. The decree makes it obligatory for all state authorities to resolutely stop the abuses, but to be aware of the seriousness of the responsibility in the application of the procedures given by law.

The decree concludes: "The faith in God and the religion of the Catholic people will not be tampered with. We leave the complete freedom of faith and doctrine to the Catholic Church just as we do to the Protestant Church. Politically, however, only one conception of the state exists and is conceivable in Germany: the National Socialist idea." (Translation: Gary Costello)

On 20.07.1935, Franz Schlegelberger (*Staatssekretär* in the Reich Justice Ministry) sent the following letter to Germany's chief and senior public prosecutors:

Subject: Struggle against political Catholicism
For your confidential information and notice, I enclose a copy of the Prussian Ministerpräsident's decree of 16 July 1935—St.M.1. 7905—to the Oberpräsidenten and Regierungspräsidenten, etc.

I decree it to be the duty of all prosecuting authorities to cooperate closely with the competent State Police and administrative authorities in taking action—with the deliberation necessary to avoid mistakes but also with the severity necessitated by the dangerous nature against all manifestations of the efforts of political Catholicism to undermine the unity of the State and create discord among the people, wherever they appear without regard for the person or rank of the perpetrator....

The cases must be investigated with the utmost rapidity, so that the punishment will follow the crime as quickly as possible. The penalties called for at the trials shall be such as the national sense of justice deems appropriate to the dangerous nature of these intrigues against the State and people and the unscrupulous-ness of the perpetrators.

A report must be made to me in quintuplicate in all cases where proceedings of this type are initiated. At the close of the investigation a concluding report on the incidents indicating the measures to be taken will be submitted to me. In case of an indictment, the bill of indictment, and later the sentence, will be submitted, each in quintuplicate. If the sentence imposed is made the subject of an appeal, a report must be made to me immediately, indicating the probable result.

This circular decree will be published in the next number of "Deutsche Justiz," together with an extract from the decree communicated below, issued by the Prussian Ministerpräsident Göring on 16 July 1935.
[Signed] Dr. Schlegelberger
(Prosecution Exhibit 428, in *Trials of War Criminals Before the Nuernberg Military Tribunals Under Control Council Law No. 10, Volume III*)

18.08.1935–21.08.1935	*Schirmherr der "23. Deutschen Ostmesse"* (patron of the 23rd Eastern Exhibition) in Königsberg.
10.09.1935–16.09.1935	Participated in the *"7. Reichsparteitag der NSDAP"* in Nürnberg, during which, on the 15th, he announced the enactment of the *"Nürnberger-Gesetze"*—the antisemitic and racist laws that stripped German Jews of their civil rights. Reading from the preamble of the laws to a large audience Göring loudly declared: "A citizen of the Reich can only be a person of German or related blood who demonstrates by his behavior that he is willing and suited to loyally serve the German people and Reich. Marriages between Jews and citizens of German or related blood are forbidden."

He went on to say:

[The swastika is a] symbol of our struggle for our own species-specific race, it is a sign to us of the struggle against the Jews as racial wreckers....

[The Laws are] a declaration of faith in the strengths and blessings of the Germanic-Nordic spirit. We know that to sin against the blood is to sin against the inheritance of a people. We ourselves, the German people have had to suffer greatly because of this hereditary sin. We know that the final root of all Germany's decomposition came in the last analysis from these sinners against heredity. So we have to try to make a connection again to the chain of heredity that comes to us from the greyness of prehistory.... And it is the duty of every government, and above all it is the duty of the people themselves, to ensure that this purity of the race can never again be made sick or filled with rottenness. (Translation of excerpt from "Göring begründet die Gesetze", *Berliner Tageblatt* of 16.09.1936, in Richard J. Evans, *The Third Reich in Power*, p. 544)

God has created the races. He did not want equality and therefore we energetically reject any attempt to falsify the concept of race purity by making it equivalent with racial equality. We have experienced what it means when a people have to live in accordance with the laws of an equality that are alien to its kind and contrary to nature. For this equality does not exist. We have never acknowledged such an idea and therefore must reject it also, as a matter of principle, in our laws, and we must acknowledge that purity of race which Nature and Providence have destined. (Translation of Document No. 3458-PS, Office of U.S. Chief of Counsel, International Military Tribunal, Nürnberg)

In an interrogation report of 23.05.1945, Major Paul Kubala (Commander of the 7th Army Interrogation Center in Augsburg) wrote of Göring's claims with regard to Nazi racial policy:

Goering's explanation for the racial policy in Germany was as follows: The persecution was not intended to take on the aspects which it did later on. It was originally intended to squeeze only those Jews who were in leading positions, since they "represented a serious danger for the German nation". "After all, those Jews who fought in the World War and received the Iron Cross 1st class, were allowed to remain. We even encouraged their emigration to Palestine, and helped them to leave Germany." Goering made no attempt to hide the fact that he was very much in favor of the "aryanization" of Germany, it was just the "methods" with which he was not quite in accord. "Anyway, during the first few years of National Socialism we did not persecute the Jews." He admitted that the pogroms of 1938 were "pretty bad" (recht schlimm), but claimed that this was the first instance of persecution of the Jews in Germany. "It was never intended that the "Aryanization" of Germany should take on such forms" (es war nie vorgesehen dass die Sache solche Formen annehmen sollte). ("Interrogation Records Prepared for War Crimes Proceedings at Nuernberg, 1945–1947/OCCPAC Interrogation Transcripts and Related Records: Göring, Hermann"; Publication Number M1270, Record Group RG238)

10.02.1936	Issued a "Decree for Execution of the Law on the Secret State Police", Article 1 of which read: "The Gestapo is authorized to carry out police investigations in high treason, treason, and explosive cases, as well as other punishable aggressive actions against Party and State." (*1936 Preußische Gesetzsammlung*, p. 22-24; Partial Translation of Document 2108-PS, in *Nazi Conspiracy and Aggression, Volume IV*)
01.03.1936–00.00.1936	Member of the *Ehrenausschuss* (Committee of Honor) of the "*Deutschen Kulturausstellung in Finnland*" (German Cultural Exposition in Finland).
00.00.1936	Appointed as *Generalbevollmächtigter für die Kraftstoff-Verteilung* (General Plenipotentiary for the Allocation of Fuel).
04.04.1936–23.04.1945	*Reichskommissar für Rohstoffe und Devisen* (Reich Commissioner for Raw Materials and Foreign Exchange; later redesignated *Reichsbeauftragter für Rohstoff- und Devisen-Fragen* [Reich Representative for Raw Materials and Foreign Exchange Questions]). Under interrogation on 24.07.1945, Göring spoke of his appointment to this post and his role in the assignment:

In 1934 started the Rearmament. With it business got a tremendous boost. I for example started to build my Air Force. Engine factories suddenly got big orders. I had to build armories and landing fields, etc. Due to our lack of gasoline, I had to build large hydrogenation plants. All in all it gave trade, business and commerce a big momentum. Unemployment diminished and disappeared rapidly. After a year and a half, a lack of workers started to appear and difficulties arose to finish the planned program on time.

When the worker had money again, he was able to buy better food, and clothes which in turn enlivened the food and clothing industries. At the same time, the worker could see himself much better protected and a lot has been done for him. Measures were taken to secure vacations and proper insurance. KdF came into function. Hotels were built, Kindergartens, and a series of new social measures were passed to the workers' benefit. This time brought extraordinary prosperity, but also a certain disorder:
1. Everybody was eager to further the progress in his own field. This caused certain competition in hiring workers away, which was not good.

2. We needed more foodstuffs. There was a tremendous demand for consumer goods. Foreign exchange was needed to buy wool, grains, etc. All this caused some difficulties. What we needed from foreign countries stood in greater proportion to what we could buy until now through the "Clearing."

A new commercial policy had to be formed. We had to determine which goods had to be manufactured for export in order to get valuable foreign exchange.

It also happened that foreign exchange was used for not too important imports, etc. This development of arbitrary imports of raw materials, and expenditures of foreign exchange led to difficulties as early as the end of 1934, beginning of 1935. Foreign exchange streamed out, raw materials came in, without being regulated according to urgency. All this led to difficulties with Schacht (President of the Reichsbank), Schmidt [sic, Schmitt] as Minister of Economics, War Minister Blomberg, etc.

So one day all three of them came to see me, and asked me to take over a sort of position whereby I would—standing above the various interests—establish coordination and a balancing of their various demands. Since I had never anything to do with commerce or finances, I was skeptical as to my ability to handle such a job. But what they wanted was just that. Not an expert, but a man with authority to balance diversified interests. Well, so I became Commissar for Raw Materials & Foreign Exchange.

Of course, Schacht thought that I was only the shield who should parry all attacks of the party. But very soon I had to make interventions, not of a technical nature, but as to the policy of how, and for what type of imports, foreign exchange may be spent. The importance and urgency were ironed out in mutual understanding at meetings. (Institut für Zeitgeschichte, ZS-42812-43)

01.05.1936–06.07.1936	*Leiter* of the *Dienststelle "Ministerpräsident Generaloberst Göring-Rohstoff- und Devisenstab"* (Raw Materials and Foreign Exchange Staff).
15.05.1936	Appointed as *Vorsitzender* of the *Gutachterausschuss für Exportfragen* (Committee of Experts on Export Questions).
26.07.1936	Ordered the establishment of *Sonderstab W*, named for *Generalleutnant* Hellmuth Wilberg and tasked with overseeing the transportation of military aid to General Francisco Franco's nationalist rebellion in Spain. This followed a three-hour meeting, from 22:30 hours to 1:30 hours on 25–26 July, between Hitler and a delegation from Franco consisting of the Germans Johannes Bernhardt and Adolf P. Langenheim, accompanied by two Spanish officers. Bernhardt and Langenheim were German businessmen based in Spanish Morocco; Langenheim was also *Ortsgruppenleiter* of the *Auslandsorganisation* in Tetuán while Bernhardt, a personal friend of Franco, was local manager of the import-export firm H. & O. Wilmer, chief representative of the foreign trade organization of the *Auslandsorganisation* in the territory, and an *SS-Obersturmbannführer* (later *Oberführer*). Both men had joined the NSDAP in April 1933 (Langenheim

with Nr. 1.572.863 and Bernhardt with 1.572.819). They had been dispatched by Franco on the 22nd with a letter requesting that Hitler provide military assistance in the form of aircraft and weapons for the coming nationalist coup. Although likely destroyed shortly after its delivery to Hitler, it was reconstructed from memory by Bernhardt after the war, and published in a book by his friend, Wilfred von Oven. Goebbels' press adjutant (1943–45), von Oven had earlier served as a war correspondent with the *Legion Condor*. The letter read approximately as follows:

Your Excellency,
Our national and military movement has as its objective the struggle against the corrupt democracy of our country and against the destructive forces of communism, organized under the command of Russia.

I take the liberty of addressing you with this letter, which will be delivered to you by two German gentlemen who share with us the current tragic events.

All good Spaniards have firmly decided to begin this great struggle, for the good of Spain and of Europe.

There are severe difficulties in transporting quickly to the peninsula well-proven military forces from Morocco due to lack of loyalty in the Spanish Navy.

In my capacity as superior commander of these forces, I beg you to provide me with the means of air transport: 10 transport planes of the largest possible capacity; I also ask you for 20 anti-aircraft pieces of 20 mm. and 6 Heinkel fighter planes.

The maximum number of machine guns and rifles with plenty of ammunition.

In addition, aerial bombs of various types, up to 50 kgs.

Excellency:

Spain has throughout its entire history fulfilled its commitments. With Germany it feels more united than ever in these hours of its crusade against communism.

Francisco Franco Bahamonde

Supreme Chief of the Military Forces in Morocco (von Oven, *Hitler y la Guerra Civil Española. Misión y Destino de la Legión Cóndor*, p. 123; Translation by Michael Miller)

Franco's emissaries had initially flown to Berlin, where Rudolf Hess and Ernst Wilhelm Bohle (head of the *Auslandsorganisation*) secured them an audience with Hitler. The *Führer* and Göring were attending the Bayreuth Wagner Festival and Franco's delegates promptly reported to that city. Robert H. Whealey writes:

… the Führer asked them about Franco's chances of winning the war. Bernhardt apparently presented favorable prospects for victory, even convincing the Führer of the need to set up an economic organization in Spain to demonstrate that the Germans would not try to run the show from afar. Hitler then decided to send Franco twenty tri-motor Junkers transports, together with six escort fighters. (Whealey, *Hitler and Spain: The Nazi Role in the Spanish Civil War, 1936–1939*, p. 7)

After the meeting, Hitler conferred with Göring, Reich War Minister Werner von Blomberg, and Admiral Wilhelm Canaris (head of the *Abwehr*). Canaris strongly supported and advocated for the Spanish general "as a 'tested man'" who "deserved full trust and support." (Dr. Karl Abshagen, *Canaris*, p. 112) Regarding Göring's assessment of the matter, Raymond L. Proctor writes:

… Hermann Goering objected strongly, noting that Germany itself lacked military equipment and that at the same time any assistance from the Reich might precipitate difficult international problems. Hitler's position was that it would be wise to run the risk of international complications; Franco did not need men, but he must have equipment and aircraft to move the troops from Africa to the mainland. Hitler, surprisingly, took the view that where Germany's help could not be extended as a gift, it could be granted on credit.

Air Minister Goering immediately shifted his position of objections to one of enthusiasm for the idea. Whether this was because of his desire to please his *Führer* or indeed to test his new *Luftwaffe* as he was to proclaim after the war is open to debate.…

Possibly fearing that the movement of aircraft and personnel would dilute his very small air force, as well as still being concerned about precipitating an international incident, Goering suggested that the planes and crews should come from Lufthansa. Hitler followed this with the order that they should be camouflaged so as not to be recognizable as property belonging to the German government. And importantly, absolute secrecy was to be maintained. To remove the German government further from involvement, a private company [eventually named, at Franco's suggestion, *Hispano-Marroqui de Transportes, S.L.*, or HISMA] would be established through which the material would be moved… (Proctor, *Hitler's Luftwaffe in the Spanish Civil War*, pp. 18-19)

Formation of the *Sonderstab W* began on the 27th, planned jointly by Wilberg and Göring's *Staatssekretär*, Erhard Milch. On the 29th, twenty Ju 52 transports were airlifting Franco's troops from Spanish Morocco to Spain as part of what Hitler designated Operation *Feuerzauber* ("Magic Fire"). Soon after, German pilots were sent to Spain. Whealey continues:

After the expected speedy Nationalist victory failed to materialize, Hitler made a second basic commitment on August 28, when he authorized the German fighter pilots in the original contingent to engage in combat. By late September, Hitler again expanded his intervention with Operation Otto, which supplied twenty-four tanks, flak, and radio equipment. In addition, [*Major* Alexander von] Scheele converted the Ju 52 transports into bombers, and Berlin transferred fifteen additional fighters to his command. By mid-October, the Germans probably had 600 to 800 men in Spain. Later that month Hitler decided on the biggest escalation of German participation in the war. The Legion Condor, with an initial strength of 3,786 men, 37 officers, and 92 all-new planes, joined the Spanish conflict in November 1936. This legion, with replacements, was destined to fight for Franco until the surrender of Madrid and the end of the civil war. Not until May 26, 1939, would Hitler bring it home. (Proctor, *Hitler's Luftwaffe in the Spanish Civil War*, p. 8)

Göring used Spain as a proving ground for his *Luftwaffe*, an opportunity to test its effectiveness and provide his men with valuable combat experience. On 13.04.1946, he testified:

When the Civil War broke out in Spain, Franco sent a call for help to Germany and asked for support, particularly in the air. One should not forget that Franco with his troops was stationed in Africa and that he could not get the troops across, as the fleet was in the hands of the Communists, or, as they called themselves at the time, the competent Revolutionary Government in Spain. The decisive factor was, first of all, to get his troops over to Spain.

The Führer thought the matter over. I urged him to give support under all circumstances, firstly, in order to prevent the further spread of communism in that theater and, secondly, to test my young Luftwaffe at this opportunity in this or that technical respect.

With the permission of the Führer, I sent a large part of my transport fleet and a number of experimental fighter units, bombers, and antiaircraft guns; and in that way I had an opportunity to ascertain, under combat conditions, whether the material was equal to the task. In order that the personnel, too, might gather a certain amount of experience, I saw to it that there was a continuous flow, that is, that new people were constantly being sent and others recalled. (*Trial of the Major War Criminals Before the International Military Tribunal, Nürnberg, Volume IX*, pp. 280-281)

	All told, 19,000 Germans served for various periods of time in Spain and 298 lost their lives.
29.07.1936–23.04.1945	*Präsident* of the *Deutsche Akademie für Luftfahrtforschung* (German Academy for Aviation Research).
29.07.1936	Appointed as a member of the Committee for the *Braune Band von Deutschland* (an organization set up to maintain the quality of horses for sporting activities and to control the quality of such stock for mounted units of the SS and other organizations).
18.10.1936–23.04.1945	*Beauftragter des Führers für den Vierjahresplan* (representative of the *Führer* for the Four-Year Plan) and *Vorsitzender* of the *Generalrate der Vierjahresplan* (General Council of the Four-Year Plan). He was appointed to this post by the *Führer* via the following decree of 18.10.1936:

For the realization of the Four-Year Plan announced by me at the Nürnberg Parteitag der Ehre [Party Congress of Honor], there must be one uniform leadership to control all Germany's resources and to bring about the closest amalgamation of all the component departments in the Party and the State. I nominate *Ministerpräsident* Göring as Commissioner for the Four-Year Plan. General Göring has full powers for the execution of the task allotted to him, and is authorized to issue Decrees of State and to formulate general administrative laws. He is further authorized to summon all authorities, including high officers of State and all official Party functionaries of the Party and to furnish them with instructions.

Berchtesgaden, 18 October 1936.
The Führer and Reichskanzler,
Adolf Hitler
(Dr. Erich Gritzbach, *Hermann Goering: The Man and His Work*, pp. 103-104)

Under interrogation on 27.07.1945, Göring spoke of his appointment and service as Germany's economic and industrial supremo:

In order to rearm we had to become self-sufficient. We had to rearm, since our proposals to France and England to limit armament and armies were unsuccessful.

So the Fuehrer came to me one day, and said that this being Commissar for Raw Materials & Foreign Exchange was in his opinion not the right thing. He wanted Germany to gain self-sufficiency, be it for the eventuality of war, or peace. We simply could not reach economic order without being self-sufficient. So the Fuehrer wanted a plan of four years, in which time the first step to self-sufficiency was supposed to be reached. Thus I became Head of the Four-Year Plan.

Two all-important steps had to be made:
1. In the field of food production. (By adequate guidance, a lot could be improved).
2. In the field of national economy. (Here we could not spend the little we had on foreign exchange for unnecessary things, but had to satisfy the military aspects of our economy.

In the Fuehrer's opinion there were great possibilities to produce a lot of raw materials within Germany, a process which had been neglected so far, because private economy couldn't see a profit in it.

Since we had no gasoline or rubber, we tried to find substitutes by scientific discovery. So I put scientists and inventors to work on this field.

There were also other things, like new main highways, the salvaging of all waste, etc., to be taken care of. All these aspects I had to organize within the Four-Year Plan.

Initially I directed my attention to agriculture. Everything had to be tried and done to increase production. Decisions had to be made as to which products are more important, which products can be raised on German soil, and how can we change and modify sowing, so that we don't have to rely on imports. How far can we increase production through cultivation of new land in Germany. What can be done in the field of synthetic production of artificial fertilizer. All these things had to be worked out, and I had experts to make the necessary studies and proposals.

Of course, I had to be prepared also for the eventuality that England may cut us off from certain raw materials. New treaties were prepared, especially with the Balkan Countries, to promote increased production in these countries. I was willing to buy for ten years the surpluses from Romania or Yugoslavia. At the same time, I tried to stock up goods and grain in Germany. Up to 1939 I was able to stock up 7 million tons of bread grains.

It seemed to me that everything was dependent upon our food production. In the end that was also the reason that with the exception of the last 6 months of the war, the food supply in Germany was adequate.

The whole livestock economy was put on a new basis. I ordered a price-reduction of fertilizer, and many other things. Commercial treaties were influenced by me. All, in order to put the Four-Year Plan over with the least amount of difficulties, the greatest speed, and the utmost efficiency. I only could do all these things, because of the vast powers which were vested in me as Head of this Plan.

In the field of large and small industry and the crafts it was necessary to secure coal and iron.

We had coal all right, but it was important to direct coal production in a way that it could be increased with the use of more labor. I had to stimulate private interest with tax reductions, etc. to get more production. We had good results afterwards, so that our coal production during the war could be increased, contrary to England, where it suffered a decrease.

With coal almost anything could be done. It was fantastic. We even made butter out of coal. Lumber was such a product too. Since we didn't have enough of it, we had to make trade agreements with Finland and Sweden. (Lumber was a basis for many other products—textile fiber, etc.).

During the last war (1914–18) we based our whole production upon iron and consequently, upon iron imports from Sweden. Therefore our whole mining industry relied on high grade Swedish iron, and never thought of it to occupy itself with lower grade iron from Germany. Iron and steel were most important to become self-sufficient in an economy geared for rearmament.

I did not consider that the Swedish ore was under all circumstances securely available to us, not because I saw a danger from Russia, but I had to figure that England could in case of war reach these Swedish ores.

I tried to spur our own industry to prepare for mining in Germany proper. There were rich ore regions in Salzgitter, but that ore was acid and not very high in its iron content. Then there was the reason of Amberg in northern Bavaria and the Blumberg region. The prospecting rights were mainly in the hands of the Vereinigte Stahlwerke and other Ruhr [companies]. I explained to them that it was their patriotic duty to start smelting these ores. They always explained that these ores had no value and were "just a lot of muck." So I waited for a whole year, then I just took the mines away from them, basing myself on their own statements that they were a lot of muck. Immediately I started opening up these mines. But not much could be gained by open working. It was hard to smelt these acetous ores. So I got in touch with Brassert, an English-American concern, which developed a new method to smelt acetous ores, and he also was given by me the technical supervision of the building of the Hermann Goering Werke. His new process of smelting acetous ores proved very satisfactory, and we planned to build the works in four steps, to have 32 blast furnaces at the end.

Afterwards, I forced the Ruhr industrialists to mix their own ores with acetous ores and smelt them. Later on we began to produce also in the Amberg region. In 1938 Austria was incorporated into the Reich, and the Alpine Montangesellschaft was made part of the Hermann Goering Werke. (Linz)....

Well, the particular question of iron ores was solved. But we had to find new ore deposits....

I tried to reach an agreement with Sweden. I offered them to make long term contracts with me, in case they wanted to increase their own production. In [this?] I succeeded, and could also buy on credit. With Finland an agreement on nickel was made.

As head of the Four-Year Plan I had vast powers, and practically could do anything to get this plan going and to succeed....

Well, slowly I was able to accumulate adequate reserves of foreign exchange for the eventuality of war, despite the added demand for goods within Germany. I could also accumulate a big enough gold reserve....

The entire economic life of Germany was greatly influenced by the Four-Year Plan....

All in all the Four-Year Plan proved to be very successful. In a second Four-Year Plan, the well started work could have been brought to an ultimate conclusion, by which our railroads, etc., could have been improved.

After the incorporation of Austria, its economy was influenced the same way as Germany. The happened with Sudeten Germany.

The Czech economy had to be differently treated. There we tried to exercise control through the medium of a common interest. After all, the geographical position alone lead to certain ties. But of course, when Czechoslovakia became a German Protectorate, the Four-Year Plan was introduced there too, although not with the same energy as in Germany.

The Hermann Goering Werke bought a considerable amount of shares from the Skoda works. We also got part of the French shares of Wittkowitz and Poldi Huette....

When we occupied countries during the war, the Four-Year Plan was made part of our decrees. The Four-Year Plan was directed by my staff in Berlin but executed by the administration which was in an occupied country....

In the first year of the plan, I had my own administrative office for the Plan. But later on the work was done by the respective ministries, based on directives from my staff. The state-secretaries in these ministries were at the same time the officials for the Four-Year Plan....

The Four-Year Plan did not form a ministry. I used my own Prussian State Ministry for the handling of administrative matters....

After the Russian campaign started, I was too busy with the war, so that I couldn't devote practically any time to the Four-Year Plan since 1942. The economic part I handed over to Speer, whereas the agricultural field was handed over to the respective minister [Herbert Backe]. Later on Sauckel was appointed for manpower questions. Since 1943 I hardly gave any directives, because I just didn't have the time. (Institut für Zeitgeschichte, ZS-42812-43)

Fritz Thyssen wrote scornfully of the "Four-Year Plan" in his memoirs:

The pet enterprise of the regime was the famous Four-Year Plan. I have always wondered why it was called a "plan." Government regulation of commerce and industry in Germany had led to total state control; Hitler picked up the Russian idea of the Five-Year Plan. Yet the difference is considerable. The Russians desired to create large-scale industrial production in a country where it was as yet non-existent. Hitler's Four-Year Plan, on the contrary, had no aim except its demagogical effect.... When Hitler announced the Four-Year Plan at Nuremberg, German industrialists were greatly surprised. He had consulted nobody and no one knew what he meant.

Highways, uniforms, rearmament, large-scale building enterprises, and the leaders' luxury caused vast expenditures. German exports did not suffice to afford the import of the necessary supplies. German exports decreased. They did not bring in sufficient foreign exchange to provide food for the German people and raw materials for industry.

"This shall not embarrass us," Hitler said to himself. "Germany shall produce all she needs. She has scientists, technicians, and inventors. Germany will be explored in its depths. It is a question of will power, intelligence, and energy. The National Socialist regime will overcome all difficulties." And he commissioned Goering with the carrying out of the plan.

Goering knows nothing about economic problems. He is the first to admit it. But he has recipes which he thinks infallible. The first of these is to order. Goering says, "Build a factory that produces a hundred thousands of tons of gas per year!" And the factory must be built. Suddenly he declares, "Production must be doubled!" And he thinks that it is enough to will in order to succeed.... (Thyssen, *I Paid Hitler*, pp. 178-179)

One day, Goering declared: "Copper? Why, we have plenty of copper in Germany. For years we have imported it; consequently, we have considerable stocks."

This is the kind of reasoning that guides the leader of German economy. It is true, no doubt, that there are thousands of tons of copper in Germany. But they are being used. After the war broke out, Goering confiscated all copper utensils that were not essential. This, however, represents very little. The copper is in the machines, in the factories, in electric wires, etc., and to recapture it, all the electrical plants of Germany would have to be demolished.... (Thyssen, *I Paid Hitler*, pp. 182-183)

Goering is an army man. He imagines that it is enough to give orders for industry to carry them out. If the industrialists declare that it is impossible, they are accused of sabotage. (Thyssen, *I Paid Hitler*, p. 187)

18.10.1936–23.04.1945	*Vorsitzender der Kleine Ministerrat* (Chairman of the Small Ministerial Council).
28.10.1936	Delivered his infamous *"Kanonen statt Butter"* (Guns Instead of Butter) speech at the *Sportpalast*, Berlin:

My dear German Volksgenossen and Volksgenosseninnen, my dear Kampfkameraden!

First of all, I want to express my heartfelt thanks for the honor that has just been bestowed upon me by the Gauleiter of the capital, my old comrade-in-arms, Party comrade Dr Goebbels. I received this badge [the *Goldenes Gauehrenzeichen des Gaues Groß-Berlin der NSDAP*] with very special pride, it will always connect me to the most difficult, but also most beautiful and glorious work of our struggle here in Berlin. Back then, we fought from the Sportpalast, from here we crushed the enemy. So let this tradition flow out to everyone today, to give them strength for the struggle that we are also announcing anew today, the struggle for a great goal that is to be achieved after the second four years. In Nürnberg, the Führer explained in an unambiguous and clear manner what it is all about, why he has tasked the German people with a second four-year plan. The Führer has now entrusted the implementation of this plan to me, and I want to explain to the German people how we can best solve this task collectively.

What is the second four-year plan? I will summarize it in one fundamental sentence: the safeguarding of German honor and the safeguarding of German life. A clear goal, but clear above all since we know today how far the safeguarding has progressed and since we know that this safeguarding in the Second Four-Year Plan consists in further strengthening and expanding Germany's economic power. The purpose of the powers that the Führer has given me is to unite all forces, to direct all forces uniformly towards a single goal.

We must take today's situation as our starting point. The first four-year plan has shown tremendous achievements. All of us and the whole world are aware of the importance of regaining the freedom to defend ourselves. Just as in the past four years the external strength has been restored by regaining freedom of arms, so it was a second tremendous achievement which restored to the German people the most necessary foundations for their nourishment and for their lives: When the Führer called for the enormous production drive by the German farmers, this second mighty achievement of the past four years took place. Once again, the farmer now sits securely on his land. Alongside this mighty production drive there went the greatest of all labor struggles. Today, this task has been almost completely solved. German freedom and German honor were restored! The saddest chapter of German history has been closed, the pages of shame and disgrace, German misery and impoverishment have been torn out, and the new chapter has been according to the principle: Freedom and honor are the foundation of the Third Reich.

Just as the successes of the Führer and the movement came one after the other, just as we became a great power in foreign policy, so above all we became a Volksgemeinschaft in our domestic policy. From 60 million energies striving against each other, a single energy has been created, clenched in the fist of the Führer, ready to be used where the power of the nation demands it.

Great achievements have been achieved in the economic sector. Here, it is necessary to create even greater things, it is necessary to further strengthen Germany's economic power, it is necessary to make Germany independent. The work in the economic sector is so difficult because perhaps in no other area has the past sinned as much as it did through the destruction of the German economy. This must be said again and again so that each individual realizes. What massive accomplishments did the Führer and the movement, make in order to bring about such a difference? And now I ask you and I ask through the airwaves all the German people: What did the movement promise and what did it deliver in these first four years? Above all else, what has it achieved? That alone is the decisive factor. And we can say it again and again and make it clear at home and abroad.

Yes, a miracle, a great German miracle has taken place in these past four years. For there lies a world between the past and the present, a world, however, for which we no longer wish to yearn. When we see what has been achieved in these four years through the ingenious hand of our Führer, through the combined strength of the German people, through the cohesion of the leadership of Party and State, this does not give us the right to rest on our laurels, but only the obligation more than ever to get to work now.

The past of the four years only means that we must all continue to bundle our strength to the maximum. Both the global political and the global economic situation did not allow Germany any rest. We must understand that no one will help us forward if we do not want to help ourselves. Through our own strength we have become, through our own strength we will continue to progress.

That is why nothing can prevent desolate and false reporting and slander from so often misrepresenting things here in Germany. Yes, one can read that the German people are now in a very bad way because another four-year plan has been announced. One can read that we are reproached for not having all the raw materials in Germany, the raw materials that we Germans would also like to have, that we Germans would like to have a share in the treasures of the world. Then I say: Yes, we want a share and we will have a share. Is that grounds for reproach? Or even that we ourselves cannot produce enough food! Is it a disgrace that we do not have all the raw materials in our soil? The world should be grateful that we are trying to peacefully compensate for what we have been deprived of.

We will be told: Yes, if you want raw materials, then buy them, pay for them with gold. Yes, we would have been prepared to pay in gold if we had not been deprived of all our gold by the reparations.

If we work honestly and peacefully today to produce the raw materials that are being withheld from us, if that is a sign that today Germany is once again at the end of the road and a sign of Germany's weakness, then in four years' time one will have to get used to correcting one's judgement in the same way as one has already had to do time and again.

We Germans have tried to work during these four years, to feed our people, although we have no colonies. Although we lack raw materials, Germany has become a country of peace, an island of order, contentment and construction.

You know, my dear Volksgenossen, the Führer also said in Nürnberg that in spite of all attempts to secure our food supply, not all foodstuffs can be fully supplied from Germany, in spite of all the efforts being made. There are 136 people living on one square kilometer in Germany. In England, 137 people live on one square kilometer. In total, this England owns a third of the world as colonies for these 137 people on one square kilometer, and we have nothing! If we had a fraction of these colonies, we would not need to talk about the fact that there is a shortage of foodstuffs and raw materials.

But what can now be done? Why have there been increasing shortages now and then in recent years? Why were not all foodstuffs available in abundance during this period? The Führer has also told you this. Because we were so infinitely happy to get 5½ million people back into work and bread, that they should have earnings again and that they should want and be able to buy food for their earnings on the foodstuffs market again.

What can and must be done now? We will only be able to produce a few things on our own soil in the agricultural sector. Of course, we will be demanding a further increase in production. We will call upon the Reichsnährstand to do its utmost to extract the maximum from German soil. We will continue to try to increase production by improving the already parched and exhausted German farmland. We continue to try to improve the organisation and to get the goods from the producer to the consumer in a faster and more efficient way. This is also necessary to a certain extent today. The existing gap will still not be closed by these measures. Of course, one of the most important measures will be to secure the German harvest at all times. The concentration of responsibilities in these matters made it possible for the labor service to be deployed for the harvest overnight.

The German farmer must understand one thing: It is necessary that the farmer understands what a sacred good he holds in his hand in the form of German bread grain, that he knows that with it he is providing food for his people. German farmers, be careful with this most sacred good of our German earth!

We hear there are meat shortages here and there. Certainly there will be tension here and there, but here too everything will come to pass. We will try to lay further foundations for breeding more livestock. But above all, my dear Volksgenossen, there is also something very good apart from meat. There are fish! And if you do not get meat, we will ensure that there will be enough fish in such times of tension. In this way, everything that is conceivable in any way will be done. And yet, we know that the greatest strain exists in the area of fat. This is where the greatest foreign demand is necessary, and so here too the greatest restriction of all will be required. Nevertheless, we will also increase production here. If all the Volksgenossen help and if everyone understands that today Germany is not rich enough to throw waste aside, but that this waste must be collected in order to supply it the large feedlots in the cities, etc., then you will also see that the fat situation will improve. We are now in a fortress. This means: Use all, and everything.

The most important and decisive thing, however, is that under all circumstances, we secure for the less well-off and above all for the hard-working population, what they need for their strength and their work. The Führer's proclamation that under all circumstances cheap and sufficient fats must be available for the less fortunate, will be a sacred command to me, which will be carried out under all circumstances. We will be able to do this in a rationing organisation without cards if everyone adopts enough common sense. The bottom line is, Volksgenossen: Every German should be sated, no German should go hungry. That's all you can ask of me at this time. That is the decisive thing!

It goes without saying that one has to accept certain restrictions if one wants to achieve great things. And now I turn to you, my German housewives. A great responsibility lies on your shoulders. Remember that the first food on your menu should always be that which is seasonal, that which is available, that which Germany's own national production is producing at that moment. It is a sin to always want to buy and have what is not being produced by nature at that moment. May the wealthier households in particular also be aware of this. First and foremost, we adhere to what the German soil gives us. By informing them in good time about the current supply situation, we will help to ensure that housewives know from the outset which foodstuffs are now available. Then they will not need to queue outside for hours.

My dear Volksgenossen! To summarize once again: Consume those foodstuffs primarily which we can satisfy from our own national production. Because that after all, makes it easier to bear the stresses. Of course, these stresses are often purely seasonal. They cannot be bridged in any other way. Eggs, butter, milk-these are things whose production we cannot influence in any other way! There are certain times when the hens lay a lot of eggs, and other times when they lay few; and this is the case in the other areas as well.

Above all, the important thing is that the broad masses of our people get enough food so that they can work and create at full strength, and I take responsibility for that, I will bring it about.

The situation is similar in the raw materials sector. Here, too, we have a shortage of raw materials and, again, mainly due to the fact that we do not have any colonies. Therefore, we have to consider which raw materials we can now make ourselves by virtue of our ingenuity as Germans. This will be one of the main tasks that I and the men responsible with me will have to perform and question. And here we can do great work in many areas.

I would like to do justice to my duty of gratitude and emphasize that a great deal has already been done here, some of it great indeed, both by the responsible Minister for Economic Affairs, Schacht, and by the Führer's former Commissioner for Economic Affairs, Dr Keppler. Great things have been done by both men and I will build upon their work.

In the end, however, it is important that we get out of this stage of trials and preliminary tests and that we now use all our strength and energy to put this into practice and to establish Germany's security as quickly and as extensively and as far as possible. In the coming times, new factories will be built, factories in which we will make our own rubber, factories in which we will create our own clothes from cellulose fiber, in which we will no longer need the cotton that costs us millions in foreign currency today.

We would gladly take them, we would do without all that, if foreign countries understood that we cannot be enclosed, that we cannot be bound.

We will now create petrol and mineral oils from German coal, and the Führer's promise: "In 18 months German petrol will be ready—we will be independent with petrol"—I will redeem it! We will extract mineral oils of all kinds from German coal. We will develop our own iron and ores and, above all, we have not yet sufficiently explored Germany. From now on, we will not be content with the fact that only one tenth of Germany has been geophysically investigated. The decisive thing here is just the will to shape things and to do things. In the field of light metals, of aluminum, we have an inexhaustible supply base at our disposal. Coal, wood and German ores will be the basis on which the factories of Germany's own production of raw and other materials will be built in the future.

A massive program! Large structures, mighty factories are to be built to show the world: Germany will not capitulate. Germany insists on its existence and will shape it.

Thus, a huge economic boom will be added to the previous one. But remember this: everyone is to be involved, not for individuals, not for a few, but for all, for the whole population! But, my dear Volksgenossen, this can only happen if you too, each and every one of you, break with old ideas, if you finally eliminate this old, eternal timidity towards the new, inherited from the past centuries. This was already the case with our ancestors when they at one time did not want to plant potatoes.

But there was at that time already a National Socialist on the Prussian throne who taught the Prussian people to plant this fruit. Now, even if I don't want to compare myself to this great man—the willpower to teach the German people to be proud of their own produce—I have that, I promise you! Be proud of your produce!

But I would like to say one thing to the economy: it has a great, great responsibility. The individual businessman and industrialist should only not wait for what the state suggests, what the state demands, but he should seek ways and means on his own and spare no effort to support this work. Dear entrepreneurs! You always talk about the free initiative of the economy. Now you have the free initiative. Use it!

The mission! Above all, I would now like to emphasize one thing. Without the entire united and passionate commitment of our German workers, the task will be impossible from the outset. Because today I have to rack my brains about how to make up for the shortage of workers. So it follows that the nations have different concerns. We are worried about getting enough workers, the others are worried about how to accommodate their workers. But I believe that our concern that we do not have enough workers is the more pleasant and smaller one.

So that is the question today: How do I get the necessary workers? And this can only be done if the German worker understands that he can only help me, only support the plan of the Führer, if he works and works again and again, if he does not quarrel, but rather when there is peace in the factories and if work is done from morning to evening. I therefore ask that it be understood that today it is important to have the necessary peace and quiet at work, that it be understood that joy and the desire to create must reign in the factories, that all denunciation, all slander must be banished. That has no place in Germany.

To be able to build this vision, we cannot raise the wage level at this moment; it is impossible. I shall read out the words of the Führer [of 9 September 1936]: "It would have been possible for the state and economic leadership to increase wages by 20, by 40 or by 50 per cent without further ado. The wage increase alone without an increase in production is a self-deception that the German people have already gone through once. According to the National Socialist conception of economics, it is madness to increase wages and at the same time, if possible, to shorten working hours, that is, to limit production. This is because the total wage income of the people is distributed over the total production that can be consumed. If, therefore, the total wage income increases by 15 per cent, but the total production decreases by 1 per cent, this wage increase will not only be without result in the livelihood of the individual, but on the contrary, because of the decrease in production, will lead to a complete devaluation of money." And that would be the same dance that we have already gone through once to our detriment. That is why we have to enlighten our German worker. Just as it is now the task of the trustees appointed by the state to lead and balance in wage matters, under all circumstances, to be responsible for the company and its tranquility, so the German Labor Front must place itself with its whole powerful organisation wholeheartedly at the service of this plan. That is why I want us all to remain in that wonderful, determined community. That is why I oppose all the destructive forces, all that is likely to destroy the trust between the factory leader and the followers, all that is likely to bring back old Marxist habits. If we demand fixed and stable wages from the worker, then the German worker can demand fixed and secure prices from us. Here too, we will commit ourselves with all the passion of our will.

The Führer has today appointed a Price Commissioner [*Preiskommissar*, *Gauleiter* Josef Wagner], once again an old National Socialist fighter; I will give him the necessary guidelines and provide him with powers to prevent price hikes and price increases under all circumstances and, where necessary, to reduce high prices.

Looking ahead, I now issue a reminder to all. The signs of the situation will be a good indicator here and a good opportunity to intervene wherever necessary. We will have our eyes open everywhere. Only then will we recognise the signs of an approaching difficulty in time, and once this difficulty is recognised, it will also be overcome.

This Price Commissioner will be endowed with such powers that he will be able, above all, to get to grips with an epidemic, an epidemic which has shown itself to be fatal for every nation which is in a situation like that of Germany. This epidemic—and I can promise you this—we will try to eradicate it with root and branch: hoarding! I am not only targeting the hoarders, but especially those who are guilty of price fixing. For they are even greater criminals against the people. They only know their own ego.

It will be the task of the Price Commissioner to determine again and again whether the price is justified or springs from selfishness and egoism. If the latter is the case, then ruthless action will be taken. I will intervene with draconian measures against all those who try to exploit Germany's economy and recovery, and against parasites.

The same applies to the black marketeers and all those who immediately hold the goods when fixed and maximum prices come. We will not only take their goods from them, but also smash their existence, because they do not want to do anything for the existence of Germany.

The task must succeed! It will succeed because we want it to and because we are National Socialists, because we have the strength to accomplish what we want! If someone still wants to grumble: please do, there's nothing to say about it, it doesn't have any bearing on the matter. We also grumbled and still worked, and that alone is what counts. We have to approach things with a healthy and fresh optimism, because only optimism provides us with the fresh and cheerful energy, we need to form things. We believe in our nation. We know that it has a great future, and that is why we must take this path.

This brings me to a very crucial point. I am taking over the implementation of this plan today. Today we are at a kind of starting point. So today the shortage of raw materials is at its greatest. In six months, however, the situation will already improve, because by then a number of measures that we are implementing will already have had a practical effect. And these measures will continue to have an increasing impact. The decisive thing is the clear goal: we have to get through here, and if we get through here, we will reach the liberating heights. This can be calculated with mathematical certainty, and that is why I am not making empty promises, but showing the positive goal towards which we are all striving. It is my task and that of all my colleagues that we do not resign ourselves to the fact that today Germany does not have certain raw materials and foodstuffs in sufficient quantities. No, we make an effort, we think and work and worry about how we can create what is missing for the German people. Our people should not be worse off than the other peoples of this earth. In order to achieve this, we will calmly accept temporary restrictions.

Once again I appeal to all: Follow my orders and measures! It is necessary that they be followed by all with a joyful heart. Every individual must have the feeling that he is helping, he is helping the Führer, it is him, his help, that is decisive. Do not think that we are making orders and taking measures to torment you or to harass you. We can't do that! You are going to believe me, that nothing is dearer to my heart than the German people. If something has to happen, it will happen for the good of the whole.

And one more thing: The Führer and all of us are not asking anything of you that we are not prepared to do ourselves every hour. We want to create a strong, independent nation, and we are now using all our strength to achieve this.

First and foremost, I appeal for complete cooperation to all inventors, to the men of science; to all entrepreneurs and economists. Don't think of your profits, think of a strong, independent German economy.

I appeal to the German workers. On you, on you above all, depends success. I appeal to the farmers of Germany: You farmers of Germany sustain the life of the nation. Your responsibility is to feed the people. It is the greatest. Safeguard the food, safeguard the bread!

I turn with particular passion to the National Socialist Workers' Party and all its elements. It is about your Reich, it is your Nation that you have conquered, that you have created. From you I expect commitment as it was in the greatest times the struggle. The Old Guard in front, the leaders of the party, at the head their Gauleiter. Sweep the people along, march, and the work will be done.

But I call upon the whole Nation: Forward with all your might! Thank the Führer for having created for you a new people, a new empire, a new nation! After the Führer has entrusted me with this difficult office, I will do my utmost. Not as a professional. I say that quite openly. Not as a great economic mind and even greater entrepreneur, but with an irrepressible will, with an ardent belief in the greatness of my people, and with a passionate heart from which alone great things can be created.

The Führer sends me as a National Socialist. As a National Socialist fighter, as his representative, as the representative of the National Socialist Party, I will stand here and complete the task. Nothing in the world collapses unless the will collapses. Behind me, Volksgenossen, sit the men of the state, sit the leaders of the party, there sit the old fighters, the Gauleiter and bearers of our movement, not divided, as the foreign press reports, but united and united in the will for action.

And then understand one thing: we do not work for ourselves alone, but for the happiness and security of those who come after us, for the peace and happiness of our children. They should have it better. Trust in the Führer—and this is perhaps the most decisive thing, Volksgenossen—trust in the Führer, trust in each other, that is the greatest capital we have.

The Führer is not asking you to do anything impossible. What he is asking is achievable. He has always proved that. He always kept his promise. Behold, Volksgenossen, when many of you believe that you have to work hard and suffer and have great worries, and perhaps you are becoming weak, then look at the Führer, see how the man works, think of what a life this man leads, our Führer! He works for us. Think of his worries! Think of his gigantic responsibility for the future of the nation! The man carries a huge burden for you; be prepared to carry a small burden for him! What has he made of us, of Germany before the seizure of power! How he has brought us up from the darkest night! How his faithfulness to the people has uniquely helped overcome all difficulties! It is a great time in which we live. Be unspeakably proud that you can be part of it. Away with everything small, away with all selfishness! A great time demands a great people. Prove that you are the great people! Be worthy of our great leader Adolf Hitler!

Once again, let each person examine himself every day to see what he can do himself and what he can contribute to the success of the mission.

Proves that our thanks should be our trust in the Führer, our faith in him. He has taught us, he has taught the German people to believe again out of unbelief, out of despair, and has thereby made us unspeakably strong. We believe in the tremendous mission of the German nation. We passionately believe that under the Führer there will arise an empire of strength, a nation of honor and a people of freedom. Let this be the watchword in this hour, and therefore, as we begin the work, we implore the Almighty with fervent faith: "Almighty God, bless the Führer, bless his people and bless his work!" (*Dokumente der deutschen Politik, Band 4*; Translation: Gary Costello)

12.01.1937–23.01.1937	Official visit to Italy, accompanied by Frau Göring, for meetings with Mussolini and the Italian Government. He arrived by train in Rome on the 13th and held a series of meetings with the *Duce* and other Italian statesman over the following ten days, primarily discussing German and Italian contributions to the Nationalist effort in the Spanish Civil War.
12.01.1937	Appointed as *Chef* of the *SA-Standarte* "Feldherrnhalle" (München).
14.07.1937–00.04.1945	*Protektor der Preußischen Akademie der Künste* (Guardian of the Prussian Academy of Arts), Berlin.
15.07.1937–23.04.1945	Founder and *Hauptleiter* of the *Reichswerke AG für Erzbergbau und Eisenhütten* "Hermann Göring" in Salzgitter.
27.11.1937–15.01.1938	*Reichs- und Preußische Wirtschaftsminister* (m.d.F.d.G.b.). Given responsibility for the business of the Reich and Prussian Ministries of Economics in the interim between the dismissal of Hjalmar Schacht and the appointment of Walter Funk.
04.02.1938–23.04.1945	Member of the *Geheime Kabinettsrat* (Secret Cabinet Council).
17.03.1938–18.03.1938	Chairman of the *Ehrengericht* (Court of Honor) against *Generaloberst* Werner Freiherr von Fritsch (*Oberbefehlshaber des Heeres*) who had been accused of homosexual conduct. These charges were later dismissed, but von Fritsch never recovered from them and was to be killed in action during the siege of Warsaw, on 22.09.1939, as honorary colonel of *Artillerie-Regiment 12*.
22.03.1938	Letter to *Generalfeldmarschall* August von Mackensen, in response to that venerated military leader's attempt to intercede on behalf of Pastor Martin Niemöller, a decorated U-boat officer during the Great War. Niemöller's criticism of the Nazi regime had resulted in his arrest on 01.07.1937, followed on 02.03.1938 with trial before a *Sondergericht* and a sentence of 7 months' "*Sonder- und Ehrenhaft*" (special and honorable detention). Although released due to time already served in pre-trial detention, he immediately found himself in Gestapo custody and spent the next eight years as an inmate of KL-Sachsenhausen and Dachau:

Dear Generalfeldmarschall.

As a result of historical events, I have only today had the opportunity to reply to your letter of the 7th of March. Things are briefly as follows:

1. the court, in all conviction, pronounced an absolutely wrong judgement, because it did not deal with what Niemöller was accused of, but it was more a council about the confessional church, Christianity, National Socialism, etc. In this, Niemöller understood in an extraordinarily skillful way how to lead the judges around by the nose, so that this completely impossible miscarriage of justice could be handed down, which was simply a mockery of any state security. I would like to expressly emphasize that Niemöller committed a serious offence against this state by making inflammatory speeches. If the court underlay a noble motive, the court would also have to do so with very many communists, who would then have the completely same claim: because they also do it on the basis of their conviction. However, this would establish that attacks against the state and its worldview can be a noble and worthwhile act nowadays. Unfortunately, it has been shown time and again that some of our judges have not understood at all what is at stake and are in no way up to their task in a political perspective. The state must defend itself against all these destroyers and must not resign itself even if an incompetent panel of judges reaches wrong decisions. Above all formal law, which is represented here by only three small judges, stands the security of the nation.

2. Niemöller was re-arrested for security reasons, because during the trial and through statements after the trial he made it known that he would continue to stand by his position and act as his conscience dictated, i.e., hostile to the state. He shows no remorse, on the contrary a heightened will to attack. Every state that puts up with such things must capitulate in the long run. We have seen this in all clarity in the downfall of Imperial Germany. Here, too, the formal law did not understand how to defend the existing state out of complete misjudgment. I would remind you of the countless wrongful convictions against the enemies of the state at that time. But the National Socialist state will never capitulate, not even to Herr Niemöller. Just as a thief, although he has served his sentence for the crime he has committed, is nevertheless placed in security custody if it is believed that when he is released he will immediately resume his trade—so the State must take precautions in cases where it knows for certain and has documentation that the adversary, even if he has served his sentence, will again begin the fight against it. That is what happened here. Niemöller has been taken into protective custody, as his statements and attitude clearly reinforce the conviction that he is more willing than ever to work against the state. Where would a state end up if it allowed its existence to be challenged by formal court rulings. One must remember that judges are nothing more than human beings—just as capable but just as incapable as others. Where here formal criminal law fails, the higher law of the state takes precedence.

I hope I have explained in detail the reasons that absolutely justify the re-arrest of Niemöller. Personally, I consider anyone who attacks this state to be a criminal to whom noble motives must never be imputed; because the attacker is attacking a state that saved the German people from the deepest misery, led them up from shame and disgrace, created Europe's first great power again from an impossible empire and only now, through an act of world-historical significance, has completed a work that other Germans have not yet had the strength to do, the reunification of the

Germans. A state that has the greatness and power to accomplish this must not be interfered with, even under a cover of so-called religious conflicts.

With Heil Hitler
Your very humble

Hermann Göring
Generalfeldmarschall
(Bundesarchiv N 39-439-0051, N 39-439-0052, and N 39-439-0053; Translation: Gary Costello)

Mackensen's letter of 07.03.1938 to Göring, sent from Falkenwalde bei Stettin:

Honorable Herr Ministerpräsident and Generalfeldmarschall.
The Niemöller case has prompted numerous citizens of all walks of life to ask me verbally and in writing to intercede for the arrested man. Intervening in the court proceedings was out of the question. But since the court made its decision on the 2nd of this month and revoked the arrest warrant, I have been virtually besieged to make representations against the renewed arrest of Pastor Niemöller to the most authoritative places.

I know very well that this is an overestimation of my word; but the fact that a sentence issued by an appointed court is immediately disregarded by another authority and answered with the transfer of the released prisoner to a concentration camp seems so contradictory and so fatal to my thinking that I can no longer remain silent.

Your personality, dear Sir, and your office as Prime Minister are held in such high trust and esteem by me that, in view of the events in question before and after the judgement, I must also ask you, as Generalfeldmarschall, all the more to attend to Pastor Niemöller, as he is a former naval officer and Knight of the Order Pour Le Mérite [sic, he was not in fact a recipient of this award], whose patriotic deeds in the World War have made him a name beyond the borders of our fatherland.

I ask you to regard my letter as the outpouring of a mind and legal consciousness seized by the case in question and to consider helping the sorely tested arrestee and his family.

I am grateful for a benevolent examination,

Mit deutschem Gruß
Yours sincerely
Mackensen.
(Bundesarchiv N 39-439-0039 and N 39-439-0040; Translation: Gary Costello)

26.03.1938　　In a speech delivered in Wien on that date, shortly after Austria's incorporation into the Reich, made the following statements:

May everybody, friend or foe, know that in Germany a man is put to death only after the court has sentenced him to death and the Führer has confirmed the sentence. In Germany only one man decides over life and death: The Führer. Nobody else has such a right. Anybody, any agency, whether of state or Party, intrudes upon the most sacred right of the Führer if it would intrude here.

Where there are 300,000 Jews, one cannot speak of a German city... [Wien must again become a German city by means of] the elimination of the Jews.... As Commissioner of the Four-Year Plan, I ... commission the Reich Governor in Austria [Dr. Seyss-Inquart] together with the Reich Plenipotentiary to take quietly all measures necessary for the expert transformation of the Jewish economy, i.e., the Aryanization of business and economic life, and to execute this program according to the laws but without mercy. (Translation from Erich Gritzbach, ed., *Hermann Göring, Reden- und Aufsätze*)

11.04.1938 Received the following telegram from the *Führer*:

Dear Generalfeldmarschall Göring,
Five years ago today you entered office as Ministerpräsident of Prussia. With heartfelt gratitude, I honor your loyal cooperation in the rebuilding of Germany. The feats you have accomplished within the past five years in the service of strengthening Germany belong to history. It is my sincere desire that I may continue to count upon your loyal assistance for many years to come.
Yours in old friendship, Adolf Hitler
(Dr. Max Domarus, ed., *Hitler. Speeches and Proclamations, 1932–1945: The Years 1935–1938*, p. 1091)

26.04.1938 Signed the *"Verordnung über die Anmeldung des Vermögens von Juden"* (Ordinance for the Registration of Jewish Assets, *Reichsgesetzblatt*, Part I, p. 414), which read:

On the basis of the Decree for the Execution of the Four-Year Plan of 18 October 1936 (RGBl I, 887) the following is hereby decreed:

Article 1

1. Every Jew (Article 5 of the First Regulation under the Reich Citizenship Law of 14 November 1935 (RGBl I, 1333) shall report and evaluate in accordance with the following instructions his entire domestic and foreign property and estate on the day when this decree goes into force. Jews of foreign citizenship shall report and evaluate only their domestic property.

2. The duty to report holds likewise for the non-Jewish marital partner of a Jew.

3. Every reporting person's property must be given separately.

Article 2

1. Property in the sense of this law includes the total property of the person required to report, irrespective of whether it is exempt from any form of taxation or not.

2. It does not include movable objects used by the individual or house furnishings as far as the latter are not classed as luxury objects.

Article 3

1. Every part of the property shall be valued according to the usual value it has on the elective date of this regulation.

2. No report is necessary when the total worth of the property to be reported does not exceed 5000 marks.

Article 4

The report is to be presented on an official form by 30 June 1938, to the administrative official responsible at the place of residence of the reporting individual. When such a report is not possible by this date the responsible office can extend the period. In such case, however, an estimate is to be presented by 30 June 1938, together with a statement of the grounds of delay.

Article 5

1. The reporting individual must report, after this decree goes into force, to the responsible office, every change of said individual's total property as far as it exceeds a proper standard of living or normal business transactions.

2. The reporting requirement applies also to those Jews who were not required to report on the effective date of this regulation, but who have acquired property exceeding 5000 Reichsmarks in value, after this date. Article 1 (1) clause 2, shall apply respectively.

Article 6

1. The administrative offices responsible under this regulation are in Prussia—Regierungspräsident (in Berlin the Polizeipräsident); Bavaria—Regierungspräsident; Saxony—The Kreishauptmann; Württemberg—The Minister of the Interior; Baden—The Minister of the Interior; Thüringen—Reichsstatthalter; Hessen—Reichsstatthalter; Hamburg—Reichsstatthalter; Mecklenburg—Ministry of the State, Interior Department; Oldenburg—Minister of Interior; Braunschweig—Ministry of Interior; Bremen—Senator for Administration of Interior; Anhalt—Ministry of State Interior Department; Lippe—Reichsstatthalter (Land Government); Schaumburg-Lippe—Land Government; Saarland—The Reichskommissar for the Saar.

2. Austria—The Reichsstatthalter has jurisdiction. He may transfer his authority to another board.

Article 7

The Deputy for the Four-Year Plan is empowered to take such necessary measures as may be necessary to guarantee the use of the reported property in accord with the necessities of German economy.

Article 8

1. Whoever willfully or negligently fails to comply with this reporting requirement, either by omitting it, or making it incorrectly, or not within the time specified, or whoever acts contrary to any instruction issued pursuant to Article 7 by the Deputy of the Four-Year Plan shall be punishable by imprisonment and by a fine or by both of these penalties, in particularly flagrant cases of willful violation the offender may be condemned to hard labor up to ten years. The offender is punishable notwithstanding that the action was in a foreign country.

2. Any attempt to commit such actions is punishable.

3. In addition to the imposition of the penalties under (1) the property may be confiscated, insofar as it was involved in the criminal action. In addition to hard labor confiscation may be made. Where no specific individual can be prosecuted or convicted, confiscation may be decreed independently, where the prerequisites for confiscation warrant it.
Berlin, 26 April 1938
The Deputy for the Four-Year Plan
Göring
Generalfeldmarschall
The Reich Minister of the Interior
Frick
(Translation of Document 1406-PS, in *Nazi Conspiracy and Aggression. Volume III*)

19.04.1938	Appointed as *Ehrenmeister des deutschen Handwerks* (Honorary Master of German Craftsmanship).
12.11.1938	In the wake of "*Kristallnacht*," convened an inter-ministerial meeting (from 11:00 to 14:40 hours) on "the Jewish Question" at the *Reichsluftfahrtministerium* in Berlin. Göring, outraged by the extent of the damage caused by Goebbels' "spontaneous" pogrom, opened the meeting as follows: "Today's meeting is of a decisive nature. I have received a letter written on the *Führer*'s orders by the Stabsleiter of the *Führer*'s deputy Bormann, requesting that the Jewish question be now, once and for all, coordinated and solved one way or another. And yesterday once again did the *Führer* request by phone for me to take coordinated action in the matter." The other participants were:

Reichsminister Dr. Joseph Goebbel (Ministry of Popular Enlightenment and Propaganda)
Reichsminister Dr. Walther Funk (Ministry of Economics)
Reichsminister Dr. Wilhelm Frick (Ministry of Interior)
Reichsminister Lutz Graf Schwerin von Krosigk (Ministry of Finance)
Reichsminister Franz Gürtner (Ministry of Justice)
Reichsminister Hanns Kerrl (Ministry of Church Affairs)
Staatssekretär Ernst Woermann (Foreign Office)
Staatssekretär Fritz Reinhardt (Ministry of Finance)
Staatssekretär Dr. Wilhelm Stuckart (Ministry of Interior)
Staatssekretär Rudolf Brinkmann (Ministry of Economics)
Hans Fischböck (Austrian Minister of Economics, Labor, and Finance)
SS-Obergruppenführer und General der Polizei Kurt Daluege (Chief of *Hauptamt Ordnungspolizei*)
Reichskommissar and *Gauleiter* Josef Bürckel
Eduard Hilgard (Leader of the Reich Association for the Insurance Industry)
Ministerialdirektor Rudolf Schmeer (Ministry of Economics)
Reichsbankdirektor Karl Blessing

During the conference, the following exchange concerning passenger train accommodations for Jews took place between Göring and Goebbels:

Goebbels: ... Furthermore, I advocate that the Jews be eliminated from all positions in public life in which they may prove to be provocative. It is still possible today that a Jew shares a compartment in a sleeping car with a German. Therefore, we need a decree by the Reich Ministry for Communications stating that separate compartments for Jews shall be available; in case where compartments are filled up, Jews cannot claim a seat. They shall be given a separate compartment only after all Germans have secured seats. They shall not mix with Germans, and if there is no more room, they shall have to stand in the corridor.

Goering: In that case, I think it would make more sense to give them separate compartments.

Goebbels: Not if the train is overcrowded!

Goering: Just a moment. There'll be only one Jewish coach. If that is filled up, the other Jews will have to stay at home.

Goebbels: Suppose, though, there won't be many Jews going on the express train to Munich, suppose there would be two Jews in the train and the other compartments would be overcrowded. These two Jews would then have a compartment all themselves. Therefore, Jews may 'claim a seat only after all Germans have secured a seat.

Goering: I'd give the Jews one coach or one compartment. And should a case like you mention arise and the train be overcrowded, believe me, we won't need a law. We'll kick him out and he'll have to sit all alone in the toilet all the way!

Goebbels: I don't agree. I don't believe in this. There ought to be a law...
(Translation of Document 1816-PS, in *Nazi Conspiracy and Aggression, Volume IV*)

On the same date, he signed the following decrees (published in *Reichsgesetzblatt, 1938*, I, p. 1580):

Decree relating to the payment of a fine by the Jews of German nationality of 12. November 1938:
The hostile attitude of Jewry towards the German people and Reich, an attitude which does not even shrink from committing cowardly murder, makes decisive defensive action and harsh atonement necessary. I order, therefore, by virtue of the decree concerning the execution of the Four-Year Plan of 18. October 1936 as follows:

1 On the community of Jews in Germany the payment of a contribution of 1,000,000,000 RM to the German Reich is imposed.

2 Provisions for the implementation will be issued by the Reich Minister of Finance in agreement with the Reich Ministers concerned.
Berlin, 12. November 1938
The Commissioner for the Four-Year Plan
Göring, Generalfeldmarschall (Translation of Document 1412-PS, in *Nazi Conspiracy and Aggression, Volume IV*)

Order eliminating Jews from German economic life of 12. November 1938:
On the basis of the Decree of 18. October 1936 for the execution of the Four-Year Plan, the following is ordered:

ARTICLE 1

1 From 1. January 1939 operation of retail shops or mail order houses as well as independent handicrafts businesses is forbidden to Jews …

2 Moreover from the same date it is forbidden to Jews to offer goods or services in markets of any kind, fairs, or exhibitions, or to advertise such or accept orders therefor.

3 Jewish shops operated in violation of this order will be closed by police …

ARTICLE 2

1 No Jew can manage a firm according to the interpretation of the term "manager" under the Law for National Labor of 20. January 1934.

2 If a Jew is an executive in a business concern he may be dismissed with notice of six weeks. At expiration of this period all claims resulting from the employee's contract, especially claims for severance pay or pensions, become null and void.

ARTICLE 3

1 No Jew can be a member of a cooperative society.

2 Jewish members of cooperatives lose membership from 21. December 1938. No notice is necessary.

ARTICLE 4

The Reich Economic Minister in consultation with other Reich ministers whose competencies are involved are empowered to issue regulations required by this decree. They may permit exceptions insofar as this is necessary for the transfer of Jewish firms into non-Jewish hands, the liquidation of Jewish businesses, or in special cases to insure the availability of supplies.

Berlin, 12. November 1938

The Commissioner for the Four-Year Plan

Göring, Generalfeldmarschall (Translation of Document 1662-PS, in *Nazi Conspiracy and Aggression, Volume IV*)

Sometime in the weeks following the nationwide pogrom, Göring spoke privately to the assembled *Gauleiter*. The following are the recollections of Dr. Siegfried Uiberreither (*Gauleiter* of Steiermark):

H.G. called the Gauleiter a few weeks after 9 November 1938 to Berlin and in a temperamental manner strongly condemned the occurrences a) because of the occurrences in themselves, b) because of their effect upon the world public. The Reich had other possibilities of reacting to the kind of attack the murder of the ambassador [sic] represents. Wild individual actions should never be allowed. What happened did not correspond to the dignity of the Reich. He granted that, with few exceptions, the Gauleiter did not participate and to a large part were not in their districts during the period in question, but he pointed out expressly that it was the duty of the Gauleiter to use their whole influence so that similar occurrences would not be repeated.

[Signed] Uiberreither

(Letter of 22.02.1946 to Göring's attorney, Dr. Otto Stahmer; Exhibit Goering Nr. 19 in "Excerpts from Goering speeches and articles", Thomas J. Dodd Papers, University of Connecticut)

14.12.1938	Issued the following order to the *Obersten Reichsbehörden* (Supreme Reich Authorities):

In order to ensure the necessary unity in the treatment of the Jewish question, which most strongly affects all economic matters, I request that all decrees and other important orders affecting the Jewish question be forwarded to me before they are issued and that my consent be obtained. I ask you to inform all departments and authorities in your area of responsibility that any independent action on the Jewish question must be refrained from. (Confidential memorandum re: *"Behandlung der Judenfrage"* [Treatment of the Jewish Question] of the *Reichsstatthalter in Hessen*, Darmstadt, 07.01.1939)

28.12.1938	Secret memorandum on the Jewish Question:

Upon my proposal, the Führer made the following decisions concerning the Jewish problem:

A

I. Housing of Jews

1. a. The tenant protective law, as a rule, is not to be abrogated for the Jews. On the contrary, it is desired, if possible, to proceed in particular cases in such a way that the Jews are quartered together in separate houses insofar as the housing conditions allow that.

b. For this reason the aryanizing of the house ownership is to be postponed until the end of the total Aryanization, that is to say, for the present the aryanizing of houses has to be carried out only where in individual cases urgent reasons exist. The aryanizing of industries, businesses, agricultural estates forests, etc., is to be considered as urgent.

2. Use of sleeping and dining cars is to be forbidden to the Jews. At the same time, no special Jewish compartments to be established. As well, the use of trains, street cars, suburban railways, underground railways, buses, and ships cannot be prohibited to the Jews.

3. Only the use of some public establishments, etc., is to be prohibited to the Jews. In this category belong the hotels and restaurants visited especially by Party members (for instance: Hotel Kaiserhof-Berlin; Hotel Vierjahreszeiten-Munich; Hotel Deutscher Hof-Nürnberg; Hotel Drei Mohren-Augsburg, etc.). The use of bathing establishments, some public places, bathing resorts, etc. can be prohibited to the Jews; also medicine baths, so far as they are prescribed in particular cases by physicians, may be used by Jews, but only in such ways that no offense is created....

11. Jews who were officials and have been pensioned are not to be denied their pensions. Investigations though have to be made as to whether these Jews can get along with a reduced allowance.

III. The Jewish welfare organizations are not to be aryanized or abolished so that the Jews do not become a public charge, but may be supported by Jewish welfare organizations.

IV. Jewish patents are property, and as such have to be aryanized. (A similar procedure toward Germany was carried out by U. S. A. and other countries during World War I).

B Mixed Marriages.

I. 1. With children (part Jews 1st class)

a. If the father is a German and the mother a Jewess, this family may stay in the future in its present lodging. The regulations for exclusion of Jews are not to be applied to such families as far as their housing is concerned.

In these cases, the property of the Jewish mother can be transferred to the German husband, or to the mixed children.

b. If the father is a Jew and the mother a German, such families also, are not to be moved for the present into Jewish quarters, because the children (part Jews 1st class) in the future, must serve in the labor service and the armed forces, and must not be exposed to Jewish propaganda. Concerning the property, one must for the present proceed in such a way that it can be completely or partly transferred to the children.

2. Without children.

a. If the husband is a German and wife a Jewess, the provisions of Ia are valid accordingly.

b. If the husband is a Jew, and the wife a German, these child-less couples are to be proceeded against as if they were full-blooded Jews. The husband's property cannot be transferred to the wife. Both, husband and wife can be moved into the Jewish houses or Jewish quarters.

Especially in case of emigration such married couples are to be treated as Jews, as soon as an increased emigration is gotten under way.

11. If a German wife divorces a Jew, she reenters the German racial community and all disadvantages for her discontinue.

Signed: GÖRING

(Partial translation of Document 841-PS, in *Nazi Conspiracy and Aggression*, Volume III)

00.01.1939   Appointed as *Beauftragter für die Regelung der Judenfrage* (representative for the Settlement of the Jewish Question). In this capacity, he appointed Heydrich as *Leiter der Reichszentrale für jüdische Auswanderung* (Head of the Reich Central Office for Jewish Emigration) within the *Reichsministerium des Innern* on 24.01.1939 (see entry of 31.07.1941, below). In the following letter to Reich Interior Minister Dr. Wilhelm Frick, dated 24.01.1939, Göring outlined the anticipated tasks of this *"Reichszentrale"*:

The emigration from Germany of Jews is to be advanced by all means. A Reich Central Office for Jewish Emigration is established within the Reich Ministry of the Interior from the representatives of the agencies concerned. The Reich Central Office has the mission to uniformly within the whole territory of the Reich

1. Take all measures for the preparation of an increased emigration of the Jews, among other things to create a Jewish organization which is qualified to prepare all steps to make available and utilize the internal and foreign funds, and to determine, in collaboration with the Reich Bureau for Emigrant Matters, countries suitable for emigration.

2. Direct the emigration; and to favor among other things, particularly, the emigration of the poorer Jews.

3. Expedite emigration in individual cases by central coordinated processing of the necessary applications, State certificates and vouchers needed by the individual emigrant and by the controlling of the course of the emigration.

The Chief of the Sicherheitspolizei [Heydrich] is in charge of the Reich Central Office. He appoints the manager and regulates the management of the Reich Central Office.

I will be currently informed of the work of the Reich Central Office. My decision must be requested before measures of fundamental importance are taken.

In addition to the other agencies concerned, Ambassador Eisenlohr as Delegate for Official International Negotiations and Ministerialdirektor Wohlthat as Delegate for the Negotiations on the Rublee Plan, are to be members of the executive committee.

Signed: GÖRING

(Translation of Document NG-258b-A2, in *Trials of War Criminals Before the Nuernberg Military Tribunals Under Control Council Law No. 10. Volume. XIII ["The Ministries Case"]*)

In 1934, Göring had summed up his attitude toward the Jews:

Altogether the Jew had for long taken the lead in the fight against us. It was he who pulled the strings behind all our various opponents. At times he would appear as a reactionary, as a supporter of the German Nationalists, at times he was to be found as the soft and hypocritical and, on that account, craftier member of the Centre Party; and then again he would be the peaceful bourgeois of the People's Party. At other times he would look at us with the satiated middle-class face of a Marxist politician; and then again he would stare at us with the hate-distorted features of a Communist from the underworld. However different the masks might be, the face behind was always the same—Ahasuerus, the Wandering Jew, always burrowing and agitating and considering every means legitimate. (Göring, *Germany Reborn* [English translation of *Aufbau einer Nation*], pp. 73-74)

By spreading these stories [of Nazi atrocities], the Jews of Germany have proved more conclusively than we could do in our speeches and attacks how right we were in our defensive action against them. Here the Jew is in his element, lying and concocting atrocity stories, from a safe distance throwing buckets full of mud at the people and country whose hospitality he had enjoyed for decades. The decent Jews have only the members of their own race to thank that they are now treated all alike. They can send their protests to the Jewish organizations abroad which play the chief part in the atrocity campaign. Our case against the Jews is not merely that the part they played in every profession was out of all proportion to their total numbers; it is not merely that they had made themselves masters of finance, capital; it is not merely that they carried on usury and corruption on a vast scale and that they exploited Germany and sucked the blood from her veins; it is not merely that they were primarily to blame for the crime of the inflation, that they pitilessly strangled their economically weaker German hosts. Our chief accusation against the Jews is that it was they who provided the Marxists and Communists with their leaders, and it was they who occupied the editorial offices of those subversive and defamatory newspapers which besmirched with their venom and hatred all that to us Germans was sacred; they it was who cynically distorted and ridiculed the words "German" and "National," and the ideas of honor and freedom, marriage and loyalty. No wonder, then, that the German people was at last seized with a righteous anger and was at last unwilling to allow these parasites and oppressors to play the part of master any longer. Only he who has observed the activities of the Jews in Germany, only he who knows the Jew from his behavior in Germany, can fully understand the necessity of what has now been done. The Jewish question has not yet been completely solved. All that has happened up to the present has simply been defence of the people, a reaction against the ruin and corruption produced by the Jewish race… (Göring, *Germany Reborn* [English translation of *Aufbau einer Nation*], pp. 130-132)

30.01.1939	In response to Hitler's *Reichstag* speech of 30.01.1939, declared:
	My Führer!
	Your comrades of the first hour are seated before you willing to follow your lead loyally as one united whole; to stride forth at your side in the future also, suffused by the single desire to follow you blindly toward the attainment of the greatest of victories: the victory of our great German Volk. You have led us onward to victories unfathomable. You have restored to us a life worth living, a life splendid and magnificent. It was you who created Greater Germany. How feeble are our expressions of gratitude; words to express our gratitude to you simply defy us! The cries with which we jubilantly hail you presently, my Führer, these shouts of Heil sum up everything we feel within ourselves in respect to inspiration, dedication, love, and loyalty.
	Comrades! To our dearly beloved Führer, the creator of Greater Germany: Sieg Heil! Sieg Heil! Sieg Heil!
	(Dr. Max Domarus, ed., *Hitler. Speeches and Proclamations, 1932–1945: The Years 1935–1938*, p. 1459)
07.04.1939–12.04.1939	Departed Naples aboard the *Hamburg-Amerika* liner *Monserrat* for a visit to Libya. On arrival in Tripoli, he met with his old friend and Governor-General of the colony, Italo Balbo and spent several days sightseeing before returning to Italy.
15.04.1939–18.04.1939	Meeting with Mussolini in Rome, then returned to Berlin.
00.00.1939	Appointed as *Schirmherr* of the *Lilienthal-Gesellschaft für Luftfahrtforschung* ([Otto] Lilienthal Society for Aviation Research).
00.00.1939	Appointed as an *Ehrensenator* (honorary senator) of the *Technischen Hochschule Braunschweig*.
30.08.1939–23.04.1945	*Vorsitzender des Ministerrates für die Reichsverteidigung* (chairman of the Ministerial Council for Reich Defense), established via the following *Führer* Decree:

For the period of the present foreign political tension, I decree the following for the uniform leadership of administration and economy:

I

(1) A Ministerial Council for Reich Defense shall be established as a standing committee out of the Reich Defense Council.

(2) The standing members of the Ministerial Council for Reich Defense shall include: Generalfeldmarschall Göring as chairman, Führer's Deputy, Commissioner General for Reich Administration, Commissioner General for the Economy, Reichsminister and Chief of the Reich Chancellery, Chief of the High Command for the Armed Forces.

(3) The chairman may draw on other members of the Reich Defense Council including further personalities for advice.

II

The Ministerial Council for Reich Defense may issue decrees with statutory effect, in so far as I have not provided for the passing of a law by the Reich Government or the Reichstag.

III

The authority of Generalfeldmarschall Göring under the Decree for the Administration of the Four-Year Plan of 13 October 1936 (RGBl. I 887) including his power to issue instructions shall remain unaffected.

IV

The Reichsminister and Chief of the Reich Chancellery shall supervise the business of the Ministerial Council for Reich Defense.

V

I shall determine the period for the expiration date of this decree.
Berlin, 30 August 1939.
The Führer
Adolf Hitler
Generalfeldmarschall
Göring
The Reichsminister and Chief of the Reich Chancellery
Dr. Lammers
(Translation of Document 2018-PS [*1939 Reichsgesetzblatt*, Part I, p. 1539], in *Nazi Conspiracy and Aggression, Volume IV*)

01.09.1939–06.10.1939	"*Fall Weiß*" (Case White), the German invasion of Poland. Two *Luftwaffe* air fleets—*Luftflotte 1* (807 aircraft under *General der Flieger* Albert Kesselring, with assistance from an additional ninety-two seaplanes under the *Fliegerführer der Seeluftstreitkräfte*) and *Luftflotte 4* (627 aircraft under *General der Flieger* Alexander Löhr, as well as thirty machines of the Slovak Air Force) were deployed over Poland as key components of this Blitzkrieg campaign. An additional 333 reconnaissance planes were allocated to the Army. Within the first two weeks of the campaign, the Polish Air Force was reduced from 397 to fifty-four aircraft. The *Luftwaffe*, and most notably its Ju 87 (*Stuka*) dive bombers, were thus able to destroy Polish ground targets at will. German bombers dropped some 3,000 tons of explosives on Poland. According to Cajus Bekker's postwar research of *Luftwaffe* documents and interviews

01.09.1939	with pilots, German aerial losses in Poland were 285 planes destroyed, 379 planes damaged, and 734 airmen killed. (Bekker, *Angriffshohe 4000. Ein Kriegstagebuch der deutschen Luftwaffe*) Officially named as Hitler's first deputy and designated successor as *Reichskanzler*. In his speech before the *Reichstag* on that date, the *Führer* declared:

Should anything happen to me in this war, my first successor shall be Party member Göring. Should anything happen to Party member Göring, his successor shall be Party member Hess. To these men as your leaders you would then owe the same absolute loyalty and obedience that you owe to me. (Translation of Document 2322-PS, in *Nazi Conspiracy and Aggression, Volume IV*)

03.01.1940–23.04.1945	*Leiter der gesamten Kriegswirtschaft* (Coordinator of the Entire War Economy).
12.02.1940	Chaired a meeting "on questions concerning the East," also attended by *Reichsminister* Lutz Graf Schwerin von Krosigk (Reich Ministry of Finance), *Generalgouverneur* and *Reichsminister* Dr. Hans Frank, *Gauleiter/Reichsstatthalter* Albert Forster, Arthur Greiser, Erich Koch, and Josef Wagner; *Reichsführer-SS* Heinrich Himmler; *Staatssekretäre* Paul Körner, Erich Neumann, Dr. Fritz Landfried, Herbert Backe, Dr. Friedrich Syrup, Dr.-Ing. Wilhelm Kleinmann, and Friedrich Alpers; and the head of the *Haupttreuhandstelle Ost* (Main Trusteeship Office East), Max Winkler. The official minutes read as follows:

By way of introduction, the Generalfeldmarschall [Göring] explained that the strengthening of the war potential of the Reich must be the chief aim of all measures to be taken in the East. Therefore it is necessary, that the conditions be stabilized as soon as possible, even if this means that the type and methods of administration will be different in the new Eastern Gaus from those in the General Government. From this it is obvious that, with the possible exception of the Beskiden Gau no part will be finally included within the German frontiers.

If all measures must serve the chief purpose of strengthening the economic power, we must refrain, within the area, from the attempt of Germany to bring it up to the standard of the Old Reich (Altreich) immediately. The process assimilation in the new Eastern Gaus will, therefore, be much slower than was possible in Austria and in the Sudeten Gau in times of peace. It will be the task of the Reich to carry out the reconstruction of the East with all its power *after the end of the war*. With this chief purpose in view, the following principles for individual problems are to be observed:

1. Agriculture:

The task consists of obtaining the greatest possible agricultural production from the new Eastern Gaus disregarding questions of ownership. The Minister of Food and Agriculture has the sole responsibility for this, regardless of when, where and how they will later be settled. Transfer of property can be considered only for the Baltic Germans and for the Wolhynien Germans. * * *

2. *Trade economy:*

In the Reich Gaus, all essential industrial concerns of importance to the war, are to be reinstated. The examination of the raw material stovehouses is to continue; no great results will, however, be achieved by this. It is possible that the investigation of raw materials will have better success in the General Government. The main thing here is the petroleum which must be exploited and transported into the Reich regardless of how the payment for it is to be arranged. The mining of iron ore also must be pressed forward.

4. *Special questions concerning the Government General:*

* * * The General Government will have to receive the Jews who are ordered to emigrate from Germany and the new Eastern Gaus. However, it must not occur again that transport trains are sent into the General Government without notification of the General Governor in the regular way and at the right time.

The following reported on the situation in the Eastern Territories:

1. *Reichsstatthalter and Gauleiter:*

* * * There have been no evacuations. The Jews are employed on road construction and are needed for this purpose for a time. The Poles are employed in agriculture and in factories. Should the prisoners of war, employed in agriculture in East Prussia, be removed, as intended, into the interior of the Reich, East Prussia will need 115–120,000 Polish farm workers.

2. *Reichsstatthalter Gauleiter Forster:*

The population of the Danzig/West Prussia Gau (newly acquired territories) is 1,5 million, of whom 240,000 are Germans, 850,000 well-established Poles and 300,000 immigrant Poles, Jews and asocials (1,800 Jews). *87,000 persons have been evacuated, 60,000 of these from* Gotenhafen. From there, also the numerous shirkers, who are now looked after by welfare, will have to be deported to the General Government. Therefore, an evacuation of 20,000 further persons can be counted on for the current year.

* * *

3. *Reichsstatthalter Gauleiter Greiser:*

The Gau has approximately 4½ million inhabitants, of whom 400,000 are Germans and 400,000 Jews. *So far, 87,000 persons have been evacuated.* Among these are no workers, except those who were politically tainted; agricultural workers have not been deported.

4. *Lord Lieutenant Gauleiter Wagner:*

Agriculture is in good shape. Industry could increase its output by 30 to 50% if it were possible to eliminate the transportation difficulties. No evacuations have taken place so far. However, for the future the deportation of 100–120,000 Jews and 100,000 unreliable Polish immigrants is being considered.

The Reich Commissar for the consolidation of the German race, Reichsführer-SS Himmler, reports that 40,000 Reich Germans had to be accommodated in Gotenhafen, and that room had to be made for 70,000

Baltic Germans and 130,000 Wolhynien Germans. Probably not more than 300,000 persons have been evacuated so far (the Polish population being 8 Mill.)

On the other hand, it will probably be necessary to transfer into the Eastern Gaus 30,000 Germans from the Lublin area east of the Weichsel *which is to be reserved for Jews.* (Partial translation of Document EC-305, in *Nazi Conspiracy and Aggression, Volume VII*)

08.03.1940 Issued the following directive concerning Polish forced laborers in the Reich:

To the supreme Reich authorities
Subject: Treatment of male and female civilian workers of Polish nationality in the Reich.

The mass employment of male and female civilian workers of Polish nationality in the Reich necessitates a comprehensive ruling on treatment of these workers.

The following orders are to be executed at once:

1. The Poles are to be provided with a specially marked labor permit card with photo. This card will serve also for the purpose of police registration. The necessary orders will be issued by the Reich Labor Minister in agreement with the Reichsführer-SS and Chief of the German Police at the Reich Ministry of the Interior.

2. The Poles have to wear a badge firmly attached on their clothing. Regulation will be issued by police decree of the Reich Minister of the Interior (Reichsführer-SS and Chief of the German Police).

3. Poles are not to be employed in those areas where special national political dangers would be caused thereby. The Reichsführer-SS in his capacity as Reich Commissar for the Consolidation of the German race in agreement with the Reich Labor Minister will determine the definitions and limits of these areas. If necessary, foreign workers of non-Polish nationality are to be employed in these areas.

4. The blameless conduct of the Poles is to be assured by special regulations. The legal and administrative regulations necessary for this will be issued by the Reichsführer-SS and Chief of the German Police at the Reich Ministry of the Interior.

5. The orders apply to the territory of the Greater German Reich with the exception of the eastern territories incorporated into the Reich.

6. Attention is drawn to the explanations enclosed as appendix.
[signed] Göring
(Partial translation of Document R-148, in *Nazi Conspiracy and Aggression, Volume VIII*)

10.05.1940–00.06.1940 "*Fell Gelb*" (Case Yellow), the invasion of France and the Low Countries (Belgium, The Netherlands, and Luxembourg). The numbers of aircraft deployed in the campaign—in *Luftflotten* 2 (Kesselring) and 3 (Hugo Sperrle)—were as follows: 1,482 bombers, 1,016 single-engined fighters, and 248 twin-engined fighters (Messerschmitt Bf 110s). On 09.05.1940, Hitler left Berlin in Göring's hands and entrained for the newly opened Western Front. Göring remained for the next six days on his new *Sonderzug Asien* (Special Train "Asia") at his headquarters in Kurfürst near Berlin. On the 15th, he departed for the Western Front, arriving in the west of Germany, in the Eiffel mountains, the following day. He remained in the West until 30.05.1940, then returned to the Reich.

21.06.1940 Accompanied Hitler to the Forest of Compiègne outside Paris for the presentation of German armistice terms to a delegation of French military leaders. The same train carriage in which representatives of Imperial Germany signed the armistice ending the First World War was used for this occasion. The other members of the German delegation were Joachim von Ribbentrop, Rudolf Hess, Wilhelm Keitel, Walther von Brauchitsch, and Erich Raeder. The German press release on the event read:

At 3:30 p.m. on 21 June 1940, the Führer and Supreme Commander received the French delegation to accept the armistice conditions in the presence of the Commanders in Chief of the Wehrmacht branches, the Chiefs of the High Command of the Wehrmacht, the Reich Foreign Minister, and the Deputy of the Führer.

The French delegation consisted of: General Huntziger, member of the Supreme French War Council; Air Force General Bergeret; Vice Admiral LeLuc; and Ambassador Noël.

In the Forest of Compiègne, the Führer conducted the state act of the presentation of conditions in the same wagon in which, on 11 November 1918, Marshal Foch dictated the terms of the armistice to the German delegates under the most dishonorable circumstances.

Today's act in the Forest of Compiègne has erased injustice perpetrated against the German military honor.

The dignity of the behavior toward an honorably defeated adversary stood in striking contrast to the eternal hatred sown by the monuments on this site at which Gallic deceit disparaged the unbeaten German Army. (Dr. Max Domarus, ed., Hitler. *Speeches and Proclamations, 1932–1945: The Years 1939–1940*, p. 2026)

The following day, Keitel and General Huntziger met again in the same train carriage and the latter, as authorized representative of the French Government, signed the armistice agreement.

19.07.1940–23.04.1945 *Reichsmarschall des Großdeutschen Reiches* (Reich Marshal of the Greater German Reich). In his lengthy speech to the *Reichstag* on 19.07.1940, Hitler acknowledged the contributions to victory of Göring and his *Luftwaffe*:

At dawn on the morning of 10 May, thousands of fighter planes and dive bombers, under the cover of fighters and destroyers, descended on enemy airfields. Within a few days uncontested air superiority was assured. And not for one minute in the further course of the battle was it allowed to slip.

Only where temporarily no German airplanes were sighted, could enemy fighters and bombers make short appearances. Besides this, their activities were restricted to night action. The Field Marshal had the Luftwaffe under his orders during this mission in the war.

Its tasks were:

1. to destroy the enemy air forces, i.e., to remove these from the skies;
2. to support directly or indirectly the fighting troops by uninterrupted attacks;
3. to destroy the enemy's means of command and movement;
4. to wear down and break the enemy's morale and will to resist;
5. to land parachute troops as advance units.

The manner of their deployment in the operation in general, as well as their adjustment to the tactical demands of the moment, was exceptional. Without the valor of the Army, the successes attained should never have been possible. Equally true is it that, without the heroic mission of the Luftwaffe, the valor of the Army should have been for naught. Both Army and Luftwaffe are deserving of the greatest glory!

The deployment of the Luftwaffe in the West took place under the personal command of Field Marshal Göring. His Chief of Staff: Generalleutnant Jeschonnek....

Generalfeldmarschall Göring as creator of the German Luftwaffe, and as an individual man, has made the greatest contribution to the rebuilding of the German Wehrmacht. As the leader of the German Luftwaffe he has, in the course of the war up to date, created the prerequisites for victory. His merits are unequaled!

I name him Reichsmarschall of the Greater German Reich and award him the Grand Cross of the Iron Cross. (Dr. Max Domarus, ed., Hitler. *Speeches and Proclamations, 1932–1945: The Years 1939–1940*, pp. 2053-2054 and p. 2056)

A witness to Göring's appointment was the American journalist William Shirer, who wrote in his diary:

Under one roof I have never seen so many goldbraided generals before. Massed together, their chests heaving with crosses and other decorations, they filled a third of the first balcony. Part of the show was for them. Suddenly pausing in the middle of his speech, Hitler became the Napoleon, creating with the flick of his hand (in this case the Nazi salute) twelve field-marshals, and since Göring already was one, creating a special honour for him—Reichsmarshal. It was amusing to watch Göring. Sitting up on the dais of the Speaker in all his bulk, he acted like a happy child playing with his toys on Christmas morning. (Only how deadly that some of the toys he plays with, besides the electric train in the attic of Karin Hall, happen to be Stuka bombers!) Throughout Hitler's speech Göring leaned over his desk chewing his pencil, and scribbling out in large, scrawly letters the text of his remarks which he would make after Hitler finished. He chewed on his pencil and frowned and scribbled like a schoolboy over a composition that has got to be in by the time class is ended. But always he kept one ear cocked on the Leader's words, and at appropriate moments he would put down his pencil and applaud heartily, his face a smile of approval from one ear to the other. He had two big moments, and he reacted to them with the happy naturalness of a big child. Once when Hitler named two of his air-force generals [as] field-marshals, he beamed like a proud big brother, smiling his approval and his happiness up to the generals in the balcony and clapping his hands with Gargantuan gestures, pointing his big paws at the new field-marshals as at a boxer in the ring when he's introduced. The climax was when Hitler named him Reichsmarshal. Hitler turned around and handed him a box with whatever insignia a Reichsmarshal wears. Goring took the box, and his boyish pride and satisfaction was almost touching, old murderer that he is. He could not deny himself a sneaking glance under the cover of the lid. Then he went back to his pencil-chewing and his speech. I considered his popularity—second only to Hitler's in the country—and concluded that it is just because, on occasions like this, he's so human, so completely the big, good-natured boy. (But also the boy who in June 1934 could dispatch men to the firing squad by the hundreds.) (Shirer, *Berlin Diary*, pp. 455-456)

08.08.1940–30.10.1940	The Battle of Britain, known to the Germans as the "*Kanalkampf.*" It took part in three phases, as follows:

First Phase (08.08.1940–18.08.1940):
2,800 aircraft, including 1,300 bombers and 900 fighters distributed among three *Luftflotten* (2 [*Generalfeldmarschall* Albert Kesselring, based in northern France]; 3 [*Generalfeldmarschall* Hugo Sperrle, with bases in Belgium and The Netherlands]; and 5 [*Generaloberst* Hans-Jürgen Stumpff, in Norway]). *Luftwaffe* forces were opposed by just 650 fighters of Air Marshal Sir Hugh Dowding's RAF Fighter Command. The *Luftwaffe* made 1,485 sorties on the first day (08.08.1940), and most attacks consisted of strafing runs against fighter bases and seaports, the aim being to lure British fighters into combat and shoot them down. With the aid of radar, a recent British innovation, Dowding was able to determine the areas most in need of protection and concentrate his units accordingly. As a result, the RAF maintained dominance of the skies over Britain.
Second Phase (24.08.1940–05.09.1940):
The focus of *Luftwaffe* bombing changed to main inland bases of the RAF, and substantial damage was done by large bomber formations abundantly protected by fighters. The *Luftwaffe* enjoyed noteworthy success during this period, downing 450 RAF fighters and bringing Fighter Command to the brink of collapse.
Third Phase (07.09.1940–30.09.1940):
Target: London. A non-stop wave of attacks was launched against the British capital, culminating with a great and extremely destructive raid by over 1,000 bombers and approximately 700 fighters on the 15th of the month. The British refused to give in, however, and the high losses of *Luftwaffe* aircraft resulted in discontinuance of daytime bombing raids (the last of these took place 30.09.1940). In a series of attacks conducted 14.–15.09.1940, |

RAF Bomber Command destroyed some 200 barges in the ports of France, Belgium, and the Netherlands, leading Hitler to suspend his plans for *Unternehmen Seelöwe* (Operation Sea Lion), the invasion of Great Britain planned for 27.09.1940.

Final Phase (01.10.1940–30.10.1940):

Luftwaffe attacks became sporadic, but London was hit hard by a bombing raid on 10.10.1940. The *Führer* cancelled *Seelöwe* on the 12th. German losses were horrendous: 1,733 aircraft destroyed, with enemy losses numbering 915. The following month, however, a renewed air offensive—known as the "Blitz"—began, and continued through May 1941, by which time over 43,000 British civilians had been killed and 51,000 severely wounded. Among the most devastating attacks were those against Coventry (almost completely destroyed by approximately 500 bombers on 14.–15.11.1940) and London (set aflame in a raid on 29.12.1940).

In a letter of 21.11.1940, sent from his hunting estate *Reichsjägerhof Röminten* in East Prussia to his brother-in-law, Eric von Rosen, Göring gave the following defense of his air force's performance in the Battle of Britain and the "Blitz":

Dear Eric,
I thank you for your letters and the attached items. I am sorry to learn from it that insidious and untrue reporting of the great Swedish newspapers gave you the impression too that the air warfare and the destruction caused by it are about the same in England as in Germany. I should like to point out that England has suffered terrible blows from my Luftwaffe and that a city such as the important armament town of Coventry, was actually completely levelled, while London shows immense destruction and earthquakelike annihilation of entire districts. On the other hand, Mary will be able to tell you that with the exception of a few burnt attics and a few destroyed houses, nothing at all has been destroyed in Berlin. The exaggerations of the British are simply grotesque. A comparison will be able to show how different the achieved results are. Until 1 November 1940 the British have dropped 31 tons on Berlin, while we have dropped during the same period 15,872 tons of bombs on London. Up to that date (1 November 1940) the British have dropped a total of 130 tons of bombs over Germany while we have dropped 21,500 tons of bombs over England. It is also to be considered that the heaviest type of bombs dropped by the British was a bomb of 250 kg which until now has been dropped in a very few instances only, while the majority of the high explosive bombs weighed 100 kg. The greater part of bombs used were incendiary bombs of the 25 kg type. On the other hand, the heaviest German bomb weighs 1800 kg, while the bulk of the bombs which we have dropped, consisted of bombs weighing 250 to 500 kg.

While the British fly with 60 to 90 aircraft per night over Germany, and do not dare to come at all during daytime with a single plane with the exception of three instances when they attacked with one plane, the German Luftwaffe sends on the average four to five hundred planes to England per night and attacks without interruption during the day.

A further comparison may be derived from the fact that until now London had almost 350 air raid alarms while Berlin had not even one tenth this number. During many nights when the British did not send any planes at all because of the weather, such as just tonight, the German planes were over England in all sorts of weather.

Since the attack on London on 7 September, London was not bombed for one night only and was spared during daytime on six days. Otherwise bombs are thundering day and night in London without interruption, while during the war Berlin was never attacked in daytime and had one to two nightly air raid alarms per week, on the average.

Alone from the amount of bombs dropped by either side you can see the tremendous difference between the German and British Air Forces. Until now in no part of the entire German Reich were damages caused which could not have been repaired within a few hours, while in England photographs prove that important armament factories, etc. were completely levelled. Besides, I have not even mentioned the innumerable ships which have been sunk by the Luftwaffe.

It is especially easy for Sweden to investigate the ridiculously small damage which the British Air Force has caused in Germany. Time and again opportunity was offered to Swedish reporters for this purpose, the more so as we here in Germany are outraged at the impossible attitude of especially the large Swedish bourgeois newspapers. I do not make any single exception; even though the Stockholm Tidningen may be slightly better, even this paper is far away from an attitude which could be called friendly or even strict neutrality.

I have done everything to point to this fact time and again and to warn. I did not leave any ways unexplored. If Sweden believes that its freedom of press, i.e., its lack of discipline is more important than its future, then we have to accept such an attitude. But Sweden should not be surprised later on if Germany's attitude will take the consequences from these facts one day. However, I would like to tell something more pleasant, namely, the fact that your Finnish friends can be completely reassured as to their future, even after the visit of Molotov. In this matter I have sent my confidential agent to Mannerheim months ago and am doing it right now again. The Finns were clever enough to realize their completely wrong policy towards Germany, which nearly cost them their existence and to change their attitude radically in the sense of a pro-German attitude. A friendly Finland can and will never be deserted by Germany.

Furthermore, I am quite prepared to give to a small Swedish group to which you could belong too, an opportunity to personally inspect the so-called damage caused by the British and, on the other hand to show to this commission how the German Luftwaffe dealt with Holland, Belgium and France, as we are not in the position right now to prove the damages caused in England by our side. But I am completely convinced that this will become possible one day. Unfortunately, the British government has a completely different attitude, because it exercises a rigorous censorship in order to prevent that anything should become known about German destructions in England. Nevertheless, we have received sufficient reports from neutral side, particularly from Americans, partly with photographic

evidence, and we ourselves have made enough air photos in order to prove how terribly severe the destructions are in England.
With kindest regards I remain
Your faithful brother-in-law
(signed) Hermann Göring
(Translation of Document 3775-PS, in *Nazi Conspiracy and Aggression, Volume VI*)

15.12.1940 Issued the following decree concerning Jewish-owned artwork:

In conveying the measures taken until now, for the securing of Jewish art property by the Chief of the Military administration Paris and the Einsatzstab Rosenberg (The Chief of the Supreme Command of the Armed Forces 2 f 28.14.W.Z.Nr 3812/40 g), the art objects brought to the Louvre will be disposed of in the following way:
1. Those art objects about which the Führer has reserved for himself the decision as to their use.
2. Those art objects which serve to the completion of the Reichsmarschall's collection.
3. Those art objects and library stocks the use of which seem useful to the establishing of the higher institutes of learning and which come within the jurisdiction of Reichsleiter Rosenberg.
4. Those art objects that are suited to be sent to German museums, of all these art objects, a systematic inventory will be made by the Einsatzstab Rosenberg; they will then be packed and shipped to Germany with the assistance of the Luftwaffe.
5. Those art objects that are suited to be given to French museums or might be of use for the German-French art trade, will be auctioned off at a date yet to be fixed; the profit of this auction will be given to the French State for the benefit of those bereaved by the war.
6. The further securing of Jewish art property in France will be continued by the Einsatzstab Rosenberg in the same way as heretofore in connection with the Chief of the Military Administration Paris.

Paris, 5 November 1940

I will submit this proposal to the Führer. Those instructions are in effect until he has reached a decision.
Signed: GÖRING
(Translation of Document 141-PS, *Nazi Conspiracy and Aggression, Volume III*)

00.11.1940–10.01.1941 Convalescent leave at Röminten, during which he consulted with the heart specialist Prof. Dr. Siebert. He left Erhard Milch in command of the *Luftwaffe* during this period.

18.02.1941 Sent the following top-secret letter, with the subject "Measures of population policy for the Auschwitz Buna Plant in Ost-Oberschlesien", to *Reichsführer-SS* Himmler:

I request that the following steps be taken in order to assure the supply of laborers and the billeting of these laborers needed for the construction of the Auschwitz Buna Plant in Ost-Oberschlesien, which will commence in the beginning of April and which has to be carried out with the highest possible speed.

1. The Jews at Auschwitz and in the surrounding area must be quickly expelled especially for the purpose of clearing their lodgings in order to billet the construction workers of the Buna Plant.

2. Preliminary permission for the Poles in Auschwitz and the surrounding area who may be used as construction workers, to stay in their present lodgings until the termination of the construction works.

3. Availability of the largest possible number of skilled and unskilled construction workers from the adjoining concentration camp for the construction of the Buna Plant.

4. The total requirement for construction and fitting workers will be 8,000 to 12,000 men, on the construction lot, according to the speed of work which can be reached.

I request you to inform me as soon as soon as possible about the orders which you will issue jointly in this matter with the GB-Chemie [*Generalbevollmächtigter für Sonderfragen der Chemischen Erzeugung*, Plenipotentiary for Special Problems of the Chemical Production, Dr. Carl Krauch].
[Signed] GÖRING
(Translation of Document NI-1240, Office of Chief of Counsel for War Crimes, at the Harvard Law School Nuremberg Trials Project, nuremberg.law.harvard.edu/documents/4218)

00.03.1941	Established the *Wirtschaftsführungsstab Ost* (Economic Executive Staff East), responsible for the economic exploitation of the occupied eastern territories, in anticipation of Operation Barbarossa. On 30.07.1941, he issued the following "Directives for the Operation of the Economy in the Newly Occupied Eastern Territories" (also known as the *"Grünen Mappe"* [Green Folder]):

Part I (2nd edition) Functions and Organization of the Economy Berlin, July 1941....
THE ECONOMIC ORGANIZATION
A. In General

For the uniform direction of the economic administration in the area of operations and in the areas of the future political administration, the Reichsmarschall has created the *"Wirtschaftsführungsstab Ost"* which is responsible directly to him and which, in the absence of the Reichsmarschall, is directed by State Secretary Körner. The Chief of the Wehrwirtschafts- und Rüstungsamts, General der Infanterie Thomas, in his capacity as a member of the Wirtschaftsführungsstab Ost, acts as a representative of the military interests during the preparation and execution of the military operations. The orders of the Reichsmarschall cover all economic fields, including nutrition and agriculture. They are to be executed by the subordinate economic offices (infra under B). The

orders of the Wirtschaftsführungsstab Ost are transmitted for execution by the Chief Wi Rü Amt to the *"Wirtschaftsstab Ost"* which is proceeding into the occupied territory and which, during operations, is located in the immediate vicinity of the OKH/Gen Qu.
B. *Economic Organization in the Area of Operations*

* * * * * * *

IV. *The particulars of the organization of the economic offices.*
1. *Wirtschaftsstab Ost*

The Wirtschaftsstab Ost, as the advance command offices of the Wirtschaftsführungsstab Ost, is located in the immediate vicinity of the OKH/Gen Qu. It has the function of representing, at the OKH/Gen Qu, the commands directed to it by the Reichsmarschall via the Wirtschaftsführungsstab Ost and the Chief Wi Rü Amt; and it has the function of securing their execution through the channels stated supra under B 111.

The Wirtschaftsstab Ost is sub-divided into: Chief of the Wirtschaftsstab, together with the group of leaders (function: questions of leadership; in addition, assignment of work).

Group La (functions: nutrition and agriculture, the economy of all agricultural products, provision of supplies for the army, in co-operation with the army groups concerned).

Group W (functions: industrial economy, including raw materials and public utilities, forestry, finance and banking, enemy property, trade and commodity transactions.) The special staff of the Plenipotentiary for Motor Transportation is a member of Group W.

Group M (functions: needs of the Army, military economy, transportation of economic goods).
(Partial translation of Document EC-472, in *Nazi Conspiracy and Aggression, Volume VII*)

22.06.1941　　Opening of *"Unternehmen Barbarossa,"* the German invasion of the Soviet Union on a 2,780-mile front stretching from the Barents Sea in the north to the Black Sea in the south. As in the previous Blitzkrieg campaigns, Göring's *Luftwaffe*—including *Luftflotten 1, 2, 4,* and *5*—played a key role in supporting the advancing ground units and decimating the Red Air Force. 2,598 frontline aircraft were deployed to the new Eastern Front. 1,489 Soviet aircraft were reported destroyed on the ground and 322 in the air during the first day of Barbarossa, compared to German losses of just thirty-five aircraft. By 29.06.1941, the *Luftwaffe* reported the destruction of 4,990 enemy aircraft in the air and on the ground, while Germany's well-trained and equipped squadrons lost only 179 in the first week of the campaign. These happy and successful days were not to last long, as the Russian winter would cause considerable setbacks to the invasion, both on the ground and in the air.

Early in June 1941, shortly after the defeat of British and Commonwealth forces during the costly assault on Crete, Göring informed his top fighter commanders, Adolf Galland and Werner Mölders, of the coming invasion of the Soviet Union. Galland writes of the meeting:

Göring spoke ... in Paris at a briefing of the commanders of all the units stationed in France. He left us in no doubt that the Battle of Britain had only been an overture to the final subjection of the British enemy. This was to be effected by an immensely increased rearmament of the air force, an intensification of the U-boat war, and would be brought to a conclusion by the actual invasion itself. I must say that the plans Göring unfolded before us were convincing and that we took it for granted that the necessary war-industrial capacity was available. At the end of the discussion Göring took Mölders and me aside. He beamed. He wanted to know what we thought of his speech. He chuckled softly and rubbed his hands with glee. "There's not a grain of truth in it," he said. Under the seal of greatest secrecy he disclosed to us that the whole discussion was part of a well-planned bluff, the aim of which was to hide the real intentions of the German High Command: the imminent invasion of the Soviet Union. It was a paralyzing shock! The dread which had been hanging over us like the sword of Damocles since the beginning of the war would now become a reality: war on two fronts. I could think of nothing else but the dark and sinister vision of starting a war with the Soviet Union, so tremendously strong in manpower and natural resources, while our strength had already proved insufficient to conquer the British in the first assault.

Now we were to turn against a new, unknown, and in any case gigantic enemy, without having first cleared our rear. We thought, in view of our experiences, that to attack England again was a hard decision. But, after all, we knew our opponent and his potential power. It was no easy task but we knew how to hit him, and we could do it if we concentrated all our forces on this one aim. It went against the grain, it was contrary to the German concept of purpose and duty, to be satisfied with a half-measure of success when a task had to be accomplished, and worse to turn to a new aim while the first had not yet been achieved. It was absolutely contrary to what Hitler had told me personally and to what he said in his Christmas speech to our squadron: to avoid war on two fronts and to eliminate one enemy after another. I had admired that concept. This new one which Göring expounded to us filled me with the greatest mistrust, even with horror. I was stunned by the idea and did not hide my scruples. But no one shared my opinion. To my amazement not only Göring but Mölders was excited and enthusiastic. In the east, said Göring, the Luftwaffe would win new laurels. The Red air force was numerically strong but, from a point of machines and personnel, hopelessly inferior. It would only be necessary to shoot down the leader of a flight for the remaining illiterates to lose themselves on the way home. We could shoot them down like clay pigeons.

I listened to Göring, neither convinced nor sharing his enthusiasm in the slightest. "And what about England?" I asked. Göring merely waved his hand disdainfully. In two months or at the latest in three, the Russian colossus would be crushed. Then we would throw against the west all our strength, enriched by the inexhaustible strategic resources of Russia. The Führer, he said, could not wage war against England with the full weight of our forces so long as the rear was threatened by a power which undoubtedly had offensive and hostile intentions toward us. (Galland, *The First and the Last*)

29.06.1941	*Führer* Decree confirming Göring as his designated successor: "In the event that I am impeded in the discharge of my duties by sickness or other circumstance, even temporarily ... I denote as my deputy in all my offices the *Reichsmarschall* of the Greater German Reich, Hermann Göring."
29.06.1941	*Führer* decree "on the Economy in the Newly Occupied Eastern Territories":

(1) In the newly Occupied Eastern Territories Reichsmarschall Hermann Göring as Plenipotentiary for the Four-Year Plan and within his competency as such will order all measures which will serve towards the highest possible utilization of the supplies found and of the economic capacities and for the development of the economic capacities for the benefit of the German war industry.

(2) For this purpose he can also give direct instructions to the offices of the armed forces in the Occupied Eastern Territories.

(3) This decree becomes valid as of today. It is only to be published on special order.

The Führer
[Signed] Adolf Hitler
(Excerpted from Partial Translation of Document NG-1280, in *Trials of War Criminals Before the Nuernberg Military Tribunals*, Volume XII ["The Ministries Case"])

00.07.1941	Meeting chaired by Göring and attended by Ulrich Scherping (*Preußischer Forstmeister und Oberjägermeister*) and *Oberforstmeister* and *Hauptmann d. R.* (artillery) Walter Frevert, the *Reichsmarschall's* former estate forester. Göring spoke of his wish to declare the Białowieża Forest a *Reichsjagdgebiet* (Reich Hunting Reserve), expanded from 160,000 to 260,000 hectares. Scherping and Frevert subsequently established the *Oberforstamt Bialowies* to administer the region, following which Göring, on the 14th of the month, "ordered the forest cleared of all 'Jews and partisans.'" (Philip W. Blood, "Securing Hitler's Lebensraum: The Luftwaffe and Białowieża Forest, 1942–1944" in *Holocaust and Genocide Studies 24*, no. 2 [Fall 2010], p. 251.) Philip Blood writes:

Acting under Göring's direct command between July 1, 1941, and April 1, 1942, Frevert was in charge of "pacification" and "resettlement." Working alongside [SS-*Gruppenführer* Erich von dem] Bach-Zelewski's SS troops and a police bicycle battalion, and in charge of his own company (Hundertschaft) from the FSK [*Forstschutzkorps*], Frevert directed "anti-partisan" and anti-Jewish actions. Between July 24 and 31, 1941, he thus oversaw the deportation of upwards of 7,000 people from thirty-four villages. The Germans subsequently pillaged the villages. The Germans kept all of the Poles' livestock, causing economic chaos in the region. On August 9 Himmler's men slaughtered at least 584 male Jews over fifteen years of age. Women and children were deported to the ghetto in Kobryn, near Brest-Litovsk, ninety kilometers south of Białowieża. Some Jews fled to the forest, to live by poaching or to join the partisans... (Excerpted from Partial Translation of Document NG-1280, in *Trials of War Criminals Before the Nuernberg Military Tribunals, Volume XII ["The Ministries Case"]*)

31.07.1941   Signed an administrative directive which authorized Reinhard Heydrich to implement a "Solution of the Jewish Question" in Europe. The document was drafted by *SS-Sturmbannführer* Adolf Eichmann at Heydrich's instruction, submitted to Göring for signature, and read as follows:

Complementing the task already assigned to you in [my] directive of 24.01.1939, to undertake, by emigration or evacuation, a solution of the Jewish question as advantageous as possible under the conditions at the time, I hereby charge you with making all necessary organizational, functional, and material preparations for a complete solution of the Jewish question in the German sphere of influence in Europe.

Insofar as the jurisdiction of other central agencies may be touched thereby, they are to be involved.

I charge you furthermore with submitting to me in the near future an overall plan of the organizational, functional, and material measures to be taken in preparing for the implementation of the aspired final solution [*Endlösung*] of the Jewish question. (Translation of Document 710-PS, in *Nazi Conspiracy and Aggression, Volume II*)

26.08.1941   Letter from Göring to Himmler concerning economic exploitation of the occupied eastern territories:

Dear Party Comrade Himmler:
In order to fulfill the task given to me by the Führer, namely to exploit the economic capacities of and the stocks found in the newly occupied Eastern territories to the utmost in the interest of the German war economy, I see myself forced to centralize and direct strictly all the economic power of the Eastern territory. Even if, in individual cases, I quite understand the demand to leave certain individual plants or agricultural estates to private enterprise, this would, considering the number of such requests, lead to complete disruption and result without doubt in decreased output of the entire economic system.

Supplies for German labor sent to the newly occupied Eastern territories will therefore also have to be handled through the competent economical authorities.

I have already sent appropriate instructions to the authorities concerned.

I know, dear Party Comrade Himmler, that you will certainly have complete understanding for my views as stated above as far as your requests for a cessation of economic undertakings are concerned and I would as you not to secure the necessary supplies within your sphere of responsibility directly but by establishing the appropriate close contact with the economical authorities concerned, especially considering that I have effected the addition of a liaison officer with you to the staff of each Reichskommissar.

I have, however, issued further instructions that according to your wishes you will remain in charge as Commissioner of the following:

China factory "Kusneszow", Riga
Furniture factory "Janis Prikulis", Riga
Automobile repair shop, Riga
The pottery in Wenden

I have furthermore requested the Reichskommissar for the Ostland to show an appropriate appreciation of your request to secure and supply the necessary articles of daily use and consumer goods.

With comradely greetings and
Heil Hitler!
Yours
[Signed] GÖRING
(Translation of Document No. 10-1019, Office of Chief of Counsel for War Crimes, at the Harvard Law School Nuremberg Trials Project, nuremberg.law.harvard.edu/documents/4299)

16.09.1941	Chaired a meeting of the *Wirtschaftsstab Ost* in Berlin, during which he announced the following:

First come the fighting forces, then the remaining troops in enemy countries, and then the troops at home. The daily rations are feed accordingly. Next the German nonmilitary population is supplied. Only then comes the population in the occupied territories. Basically, in the occupied territories only those people who are working for us should be assured of appropriate food supplies. Even if one wished to feed all the rest of the inhabitants, one could not do so in the newly occupied eastern territory. As for issuing food to Bolshevik prisoners, we are, in contrast to the situation with other prisoners, not bound by any international obligations. Provisions for them can therefore only be determined according to the work they do for us. (Memorandum on the meeting by *Generalmajor* Hans Nagel, in translation of Document 003-99EC [*Trial of the Major War Criminals Before the International Military Tribunal, Nürnberg, Volume XXXVI*])

01.12.1941	Three-hour meeting with the Vichy French Chief of State Marshal Henri Philippe Pétain and Admiral François Darlan at Saint-Florentin-Vergigny. Robert O. Paxton writes:

Darlan and the cabinet ministers prepared an enormous dossier of economic, social, and political steps that would normalize Franco-German relations. Each minister prepared a list of concessions needed in his area of responsibility. Petain tried to deliver this memorandum to Goering, who wanted only to discuss the ways in which France could help the beleaguered Afrika Korps if Rommel had to retreat as far west as Tunisia.

The meeting was a complete fiasco, and on December 4 the French government quietly withdrew the memorandum. (Paxton, *Vichy France. Old Guard and New Order, 1940–1944*, p. 128)

04.12.1941 Issued a "*Verordnung über die Strafrechtspflege gegen Polen und Juden in den eingegliederten Ostgebieten*" (Ordinance on the Administration of Criminal Justice Against Poles and Jews in the Incorporated Eastern Territories), issued on 16.12.1941 and effective 30.12.1941:

The Council of Ministers for the Defense of the Reich [*Ministerrat für die Reichsverteidigung*] decrees with the authority of the law:

1. Substantive criminal law

I

(1) Poles and Jews shall conduct themselves in the incorporated eastern territories in accordance with German laws and the orders issued for them by the German authorities. They shall refrain from everything that is detrimental to the sovereignty of the German Reich and the reputation of the German people.

(2) They shall be punished by death if they commit an act of violence against a German on account of his belonging to the German nationality.

(3) They shall be punished by death or, in less serious cases, by imprisonment, if they manifest anti-German sentiments through spiteful or inflammatory activity, in particular if they make anti-German statements or tear down or damage public notices of German authorities or offices, or if they disparage or damage the reputation or welfare of the German Reich or the German people through their other conduct.

(4) They shall be punished by death, in less serious cases by imprisonment,
1. if they commit an act of violence against a member of the German armed forces or their entourage, the German police including their auxiliary forces, the Reich Labor Service, a German authority or an office or branch of the NSDAP;
2. if they willfully damage facilities of the German authorities or services or property serving their work or the public good;
3. if they incite or encourage disobedience of a regulation or order issued by the German authorities;
4. if they agree to commit an offense punishable under subsections 2, 3 and 4 nos. 1 to 3, enter into serious negotiations about it, offer to commit it or accept such an offer, or if they obtain credible knowledge of such an offense or their intention at a time when the danger can still be averted and fail to report it in good time to the authority or to the person threatened;
5. if they are found to be in unlawful possession of a firearm, hand grenade, cutting or thrusting weapon, explosives, ammunition or other war material, or if they receive credible knowledge that a Pole or Jew is in unlawful possession of such an object and fail to report it to the authorities without delay.

II.

Poles and Jews shall also be punished if they violate German penal laws or commit an act which, according to the basic idea of a German penal law, deserves punishment under the state necessities existing in the incorporated eastern territories.

III.

(1) The penalties imposed on Poles and Jews shall be imprisonment, fines or confiscation of property. Imprisonment in a penal camp from three months to ten years. In severe cases, imprisonment in an enforced penal camp from two to fifteen years.

(2) The death penalty shall be imposed where the law provides for it. Even where the law does not provide for capital punishment, it shall be imposed if the offense is of a particularly low character or is particularly serious for other reasons; in such cases capital punishment shall also be permissible against juvenile felons.

(3) The minimum duration of a sentence specified in a German penal law and a mandatory sentence may not be decreased, unless the offense is directed exclusively against the offender's own nationality.

(4) A non-enforceable fine shall be replaced by imprisonment for a period of one week to one year.

2. criminal proceedings

IV.

The public prosecutor shall prosecute criminal offenses committed by Poles and Jews, the punishment of which he deems necessary in the public interest.

V.

(1) Poles and Jews shall be sentenced by the special court or the district judge.

(2) The public prosecutor may file the charges in all cases at the special court [Sondergericht]. He may file the charges with the district judge if no more severe punishment than five years' imprisonment or three years' aggravated imprisonment is to be expected.

(3) The jurisdiction of the People's Court [Volksgerichtshof] shall remain unaffected.

VI.

(1) Every judgment is immediately enforceable; however, the public prosecutor may appeal against judgments of the district judge to the Higher Regional Court. The time limit for appeal is two weeks.

(2) The public prosecutor shall also have the sole right of appeal; the Higher Regional Court [Oberlandesgericht] shall decide on the appeal.

VII.

Poles and Jews cannot reject German judges as being biased.

VIII.

(1) Arrest and provisional detention are always permissible if there is urgent suspicion of an offence.

(2) In the pre-trial proceedings, the public prosecutor may also order the arrest and other permissible means of coercion.

IX

Poles and Jews shall not be sworn as witnesses in criminal proceedings; the provisions on perjury and false oath shall apply mutatis mutandis to an untrue unsworn statement in court.

X.

(1) Only the public prosecutor may apply for a retrial. The special court shall decide on applications for a retrial against a judgment of the special court.

(2) An appeal for annulment shall be available to the Attorney General; the Higher Regional Court shall decide on it.

XI.

Poles and Jews can file neither private nor accessory charges.

XII.

The court and the public prosecutor shall conduct the proceedings on the basis of German criminal procedural law according to their dutiful discretion. They may deviate from provisions of the Judicature Act and the Imperial Criminal Procedure Act where this is expedient for the speedy and emphatic conduct of the proceedings.

3. summary proceedings

XIII.

(1) The Reichstatthalter (Oberpräsident) may, in the incorporated Eastern territories, with the consent of the Reich Minister of the Interior and the Reich Minister of Justice, order for his administrative area or individual parts thereof that Poles and Jews may, until further notice, be tried by summary courts for serious outrages against Germans as well as for other offences which seriously endanger the German reconstruction work.

(2) The penalty imposed by the summary courts shall be the death penalty. The summary courts may also refrain from imposing punishment and instead pronounce referral to the Geheime Staatspolizei.

(3) The Reichsstatthalter (Oberpräsident), with the consent of the Reich Minister of the Interior, shall regulate the details of the composition of the courts of criminal jurisdiction and their procedures.

4. Extension of the scope of application

XIV.

(1) The provisions of Nos. I to IV of this Ordinance shall also apply to Poles and Jews who on 1 September 1939 had their domicile or permanent residence in the territory of the former Polish state and committed the offence in an area of the German Reich other than in the incorporated eastern territories.

(2) The court of the place of residence or domicile at the time shall also have local jurisdiction; the provisions of Nos. V to XII shall also apply to it.

(3) Paragraphs 1 and 2 shall not apply to offences tried by the courts of the Generalgouvernement.

5. final provisions

XV.

Poles within the meaning of the Ordinance are protected persons and stateless persons of Polish nationality.

XVI.

Article II of the Ordinance on the Introduction of German Criminal Law in the Incorporated Eastern Territories of 6 June 1940 (Reichsgesetzbl. I p. 844) no longer applies to Poles and Jews.

XVII.

The Reich Minister of Justice is authorized, in agreement with the Reich Minister of the Interior, to issue the legal and administrative provisions necessary for the implementation and supplementation of this Ordinance and to decide on questions of doubt by administrative means.

XVIII.

The Ordinance shall enter into force on the fourteenth day after its promulgation.

Berlin, 4 December 1941.

Der Vorsitzende des Ministerrats für die Reichsverteidigung
Göring
Reichsmarschall

Der Generalbevollmächtigte für die Reichsverwaltung
Frick
Der Reichsminister und Chef der Reichskanzlei
(*Deutsches Reichsgesetzblatt Band 1941* Teil I, Nr. 140, pp. 759–761)

23.01.1942	Assigned by Hitler as chairman of a *Sondersenat* (special senate) of the *Reichskriegsgericht* (Reich court-martial) at *Führerhauptquartier* in the trial of *Generalleutnant* Hans Graf von Sponeck. Charged with disloyalty for making an unauthorized withdrawal of his forces from the Kerch Peninsula on the Russian Front, von Sponeck was reluctantly sentenced to death, at Göring's urging, by this court. Hitler later commuted the sentence to fortress arrest, but he was executed on 23.07.1944.
00.01.1942–00.02.1942	Visit to Rome to meet with Mussolini.
21.03.1942	Diary entry of Dr. Goebbels:

In the afternoon I had a more than three-hour talk with Göring, which came off in an atmosphere of the greatest friendliness and cordiality. I was happy we could let our hair down. We surveyed the overall situation, and I was gratified to note that we agree 100 per cent on all important problems. Without having consulted each other we have arrived at almost exactly the same appraisal of the situation.

Göring is in exceptionally good condition physically. He works hard, achieves enormous successes, tackles problems with a healthy common sense, without much theorizing, and for this reason is pretty skeptical about certain trends in the Party. I can't blame him for this. He has the rare good fortune of not being dependent on the Party in his work, so that he can risk being more independent. In many respects he is to be envied....

We are in complete agreement about the Wehrmacht. Göring has nothing but abysmal contempt for the cowardly generals.... Generalfeldmarschall Keitel, he said, was not tough enough. He was probably responsible for the fact that the plan of campaign in the East did not function properly. He carried the Führer's commands to the OKH with trembling knees. While he bore a great part of the responsibility he was not told sufficiently plainly [by Keitel] that he must obey the Führer, and that if he did not do so, he would soon feel the consequences....

> Göring spoke in terms of highest praise about our [the Propaganda Ministry's] work. We resolve to meet more frequently and have frank talks about everything.... The result of my talk with Göring is exceptionally satisfactory and favorable... (Louis P. Lochner, ed., *The Goebbels Diaries 1942–1943*)

00.04.1942–23.04.1945	*Vorsitzender der Zentrale Planungsrat* (chairman of the Central Planning Council). The other members were Reich Armaments Minister Albert Speer and Göring's *Staatssekretär*, *Generalfeldmarschall* Erhard Milch. The council first convened on 27.04.1942.
09.06.1942–23.04.1945	*Präsident der (neue) Reichsforschungsrat* (*RFR*, president of the [new] Reich Research Council).
06.08.1942	Chaired a conference attended by *Reichskommissare* and military commanders of the occupied territories. The following is excerpted from the minutes of the meeting (N.B. The transcript addresses Göring as "REICHMARSHALL GÖRING" but his rank has been omitted here for space):

GÖRING: Yesterday the Gauleiter expressed opinions here. Although there may have been variations in emphasis and demeanor, it was evident that they all feel that the German people have too little to eat. Gentlemen, the Führer has given me general powers exceeding any hitherto granted within the Four-Year Plan. He gave me additional authorities, pertaining even to the remotest links of our economic structure, whether they be within the State, the Party, or the Wehrmacht. I am, therefore, at this moment shouldering the final responsibility toward the Führer and the nation for the food situation; the mere thought that the German workers are bound to slacken in their output, that above all, German mothers and German women are already showing critical symptoms, is a challenge to my full sense of responsibility.

There are two more things to be taken into consideration. The Führer repeatedly said, and I repeated after him: If anyone has to go hungry, it shall not be the Germans, but other peoples. The second thing is—as I have already said yesterday—Germany at present commands the richest granaries that ever existed in the European area, from the Atlantic Ocean to the Volga and the Caucasus; lands more highly developed and fruitful than ever before, even if there are certain countries included which cannot be regarded as granaries. I need only to refer to the fabulous fertility of the Netherlands, the unique paradise that is France; Belgium too is extraordinarily fruitful, as is also the province of Poznan. Then, above all, what is to a large extent Europe's storehouse of rye and other grains, the Government General, to which are attached such tremendously fruitful regions as Lvov and Galicia where the harvest is exceptionally good. Then there comes Russia, the black earth of the Ukraine on either side of the Dnepr, the area of the Don-bend, with its remarkably fertile and only slightly damaged districts. Our troops have now already occupied, or are in the process of occupying, the excessively fertile districts between the Don and the Caucasus. Also in the East we are controlling some fertile regions; and in the presence of all these facts, the German people are starving. These are regions, gentlemen, such as we never had during the last World War, and yet I have to give a bread ration to the German people, which is no longer to be justified. I have had foreign workers brought to Germany from all regions, and these foreign workers, regardless of where they come from, declared that they had better food at home than here in Germany. This proves to me, that even in the occupied regions, the official rations on paper do not provide the basis of the nutrition, but rather the black market. In every one of the occupied territories, I see the people fed to bursting point and among our own people there is starvation. God knows, you are not sent out there to work for the welfare of the people in your charge, but to get the utmost out of them, so that the German people can live. That is what I expect of your exertions. This everlasting concern about foreign peoples must cease now, once and for all.

I have here before me reports on what you are expected to deliver. It is nothing at all when I consider your territories. It makes no difference to me in this connection if you say that your people will starve. Let them do so, as long as no German collapses from hunger. If you had been present when the Gauleiter spoke here, you would understand my boundless anger over the fact that we conquered such enormous territories through the valor of our troops, and yet our people have really almost been forced down to the miserable rations of the First World War.

In the Ruhr region, German cities have been raided very heavily. The people have suffered enormously. At the gates of the Ruhr district lies wealthy Holland. It could send much more vegetables into this stricken area than it has done up to now. What the Dutchmen think about it is all the same to me. It would not be quite without advantage, if the Dutch population were considerably weakened in their powers of resistance; they are, after all, nothing but one whole nation of traitors to our cause; I don't hold that against them; maybe I would not act differently myself. But it is not our job to feed a people which is against us at heart. If this people is so weak that it can no longer raise its hand, if we do not need its labor, so much the better. Once it is so weak, it will also not revolt against us at the time when we might be threatened from the back. In general, I am interested only in those people in the occupied regions who work in armament and food production. They must receive just enough to enable them to continue working. It is all one to me whether Dutchmen are Germanic or not. If they are, they are only all the greater blockheads, and it has already been demonstrated in the past by greater personages how Germanic numbskulls often have to be treated. Even if you are abused from various quarters, you will have acted right-for it is the Reich alone that counts.

As for Belgium, I'll admit that a great proportion of the Belgian population is working for the German interests. Whether or not they are actually working for German interests everywhere, I shall have checked carefully. For, if for example, a factory produces goods to supply everyday needs which disappear in the Belgian economy, these are not goods produced for Germany. I am interested only in those goods that go from there to Germany....

With regard to France, I maintain that it is still not cultivated to the utmost. France can be cultivated far differently if the peasants there are forced to work in a different manner.

Secondly, right in France itself the population is eating so well that it is a dirty shame. I saw villages where columns of people walked with their long loaves of white bread under their arms. In small villages, I saw oranges by the basketful, fresh dates from North Africa. Yesterday someone said: It is true, the normal food in these regions comes from the black market; on their ration card they only draw additional food. That is the only way, how the people in France can be so gay, otherwise they would not be....

I would say nothing at all—on the contrary, I would think ill of you—if we didn't have a fabulous restaurant in Paris where we can provide ourselves properly with the best food; but I don't want the French to be able to saunter into it. Maxime's must have the best food for us. Three or four absolutely first-class restaurants for German officers, German civilians; but not for the French. They don't need to eat that way. The people who sit there at lunch and dinner time are the black-market operators. They are richer than ever because they make us pay through our noses. It is like seeing the Berlin of 1919 rise again before one's eyes. The same types in those few amusement places, while the whole nation outside is starving, the only difference being that the French are not starving.

But we are not concerned with food here. I have expressed myself so many times on the fact that I regard all of France, which is now occupied by us, as conquered territory. In former times the matter appeared to me to be comparatively simpler. Then one called it plundering. It was the right of the person concerned to take away that which was conquered. Well, practices have become more humane. I intend to plunder, nevertheless, and on a large scale; in such a manner that, starting with Holland and Belgium, I shall send a great number of buying agents with extraordinary powers also to France. They will then have time until Christmas to buy up more or less everything which is to be found in the nice stores and warehouses; and this I will display in the store windows here for the German people; for the German people to buy. It is not my concern to see that every French woman runs about like a dressed-up prostitute. They shall not buy anything new for some time to come. They have anyway too many clothes to wear; on the other hand, too little. I shall show them what it means to represent the interests of the German Reich.

Furthermore, we must keep like bloodhounds on the track of anything that German people can still use. That stuff should be brought here out of the warehouses with lightning speed. Whenever I have issued a decree, I stated repeatedly: soldiers may buy as they please, whatever they please, whatever they can carry. But already it is said: in such and such a store one cannot buy, because it is a Jewish-owned business. Formerly that would not have bothered these people. Then it was the Party that kept on the tail of the Jews, not the economic administration. All at once it was twisted around like this. have stated: this is out of the question. Then someone thought of something else. An order was issued: as much as a soldier can carry and still salute, *and similar rubbish*. It was said that, for heaven's sake, one could not give the servicemen his monthly pay in cash, etc., otherwise there would be inflation in France. I don't want it otherwise! There shall be such an inflation that everything goes bang! The franc shall be worth no more than a well-known type of paper used for certain purposes. *Only then, perhaps, will France be hit in the way in which we want France to be hit.*

Collaboration is a thing which only Mr. Abetz does. Mind my words; I don't deal in collaboration. I visualize collaboration on the part of the Frenchman in the following manner only: If they deliver to us until they are exhausted, if they do this voluntarily, I shall say, I collaborate with them. If they stuff themselves, then they don't collaborate; that must be clear to France.

Now you will tell me—Laval's foreign policy. Mr. Laval calms down Mr. Abetz, and for all I care Mr. Laval may enter Maxime's although it is off limits. But, as far as everything else is concerned, the French must be taught that very quickly. They show an impudence of which you can have no idea.…

For example the scrap metal collection. I just got very interesting comparative figures on this. *France has previously by no means been squeezed dry like the German Reich.*

You must not forget how many scrap metal collections we have had previously, during the World War and later. A population of 44 millions turned in 11,750 tons of copper, 800 tons of tin. That makes *0.28 tons* [handwritten: "kg"] per head of population; Belgium turned in 3,400 tons of copper, 28 tons of tin, that makes *0.28 t.* [handwritten "kg"] per head. The Netherlands with 8 millions of inhabitants have delivered 2,900 tons of copper. They are a point better than France with 0.38 tons per head. Take away their old milk pots, they are made from copper. The German Reich delivered 55,500 tons of copper, 6,000 tons of tin. That makes 0.77 per head. You see it again and again-as long as Germans are concerned, they are squeezed to the utmost, while Frenchmen, etc., are being handled with kid gloves.

I have here the comparative figures for the import and export surpluses in France for 1938. I won't read them to you, gentlemen, for I am not interested in this. I am not a statistician. I soon forget figures. That is not what I am interested in. It is all the same to me, what they imported and exported, for the circumstances were different. The Frenchmen lived like God in France. The only point that interests me is, what can be squeezed out of the territory now under our control, with utmost application and by straining every nerve, and how much of that can be channeled into Germany. I don't give a damn about import and export statistics of former years.

Now as for shipments to the Reich. Last year France shipped 550,000 tons of bread grain, and now I demand 1,200,000 tons. Two weeks from now a plan will be submitted how it can be handled. There will be no more discussion about it. What happens to the Frenchmen is a matter of indifference to me; 1,200,000 tons will be delivered. Feed grain last year 550,000; now 1 million. Meat last year, 135,000; now 350,000. Fats last year, 23,000; this year 60,000. Cheese—last year they did not deliver anything, so they will supply 25,000 this year. Potatoes last year, 125,000; this year, 300,000. Wine—nothing last year; 6 million hectoliters this year. Vegetables, 15,000 last year; this year 150,000. Fruit last year 200,000; this year 300,000. These are the shipments from France.

Now to the Netherlands. Bread grain 40,000; grain fodder 45,000; meat 35,000; fats 20,000; potatoes 85,000; leguminous vegetables 45,000; sugar 30,000; cheese 16,000; vegetables 1 million; vegetable seeds 10,000 (Exclamation by Seyss-Inquart.)

1 million should be easy for you. Well, take the entire harvest. You can substitute, after all-a little less vegetables, a little more fats. I don't mind.

Belgium is a poor country. But even so, she is not as poor as you say. She doesn't have to supply bread grains, but because of that she won't receive any either. But in this connection don't forget to supply me with 50,000 tons of grain fodder. They won't get any meat, and I don't want any either. Fats they won't get and I don't want any either. I want 20,000 tons of sugar, 50,000 of potatoes, 15,000 tons of fruit. Now for Norway. Here is a question of the fish supply—400,000 tons.

TERBOVEN: We shipped more last year!
GÖRING: 500,000 tons.
TERBOVEN: Then I must ask that the Navy return the fishing boats to me!
GÖRING: I know. We must discuss that with the Navy. You must give me some meat. How much?
(Exclamation: None whatever!)
GÖRING: Don't you have any grain fodder either?
(Exclamation: None either!)
TERBOVEN: The Army, too, is largely being fed by me....
GÖRING: In general, that takes care of the West. Concerning the buying agents: the clothes, shoes, etc., everything there is, buy it up—a special order is to be issued.

Now comes the East. Here I agree with the Wehrmacht. The Wehrmacht renounces the requirements it ordered from the home country. What was it for, hay?
BACKE: 1.5 million tons; straw over 1 million; oats 1.5 million tons. We can't deliver that (?).
GÖRING: Well, there you can take barley after all....

It is a matter of course that the Wehrmacht in France will be supplied with food by France. That is a matter of course, and I did not even mention it before. But now Russia. About her fertility there is no doubt. I cannot but pay tribute to the fact that in the southern area—so far I have only seen the southern area—it was possible, in spite of enormous difficulties, to cultivate the land in conjunction with the Wehrmacht; one cannot help marveling at it, despite everything. I must say this—for one who is responsible for these things, it is a feeling of elation to drive through the entire area from Vinnitsa up to Poland. There all the crops stand of unimaginable quality, and I should never have thought it possible to cultivate the land so extensively. Also in Wehrmacht circles we agree that all emergency measures must be taken. This is a matter of course, and I should also like to ask you, Riecke, to take all emergency measures so that aid is given even now, and that the matter is perfectly safe, as it would be a crying shame if this crop got lost. In this land of Russia, however, there is an unbelievable quantity of hay. The straw is short, but plentiful.

BACKE: But it is still there from the preceding year....

GÖRING: Why from the preceding year? Because the straw and hay were taken there from Germany and rotted there. We did not have any trains running regularly. War feeds war! That is now written in capital letters. The Wehrmacht is to be given in addition only what is considered as supplementary matter, chocolate and such things....

SAUCKEL: I may be permitted to clarify the following for the Reichsmarschall and the Reichskommissar. It is not for fun that I take the people out of these territories, but because a strict and bitter order exists to this effect. German agriculture alone had to be provided with more than 600,000 workers—today, the figure is already 700,000—because in the last years, more than a million farmers have been called away from German agriculture to the colors.

GÖRING: I must say one thing to this. I do not want to praise Gauleiter Sauckel, he does not need that. But what he has accomplished in this short period to get with such rapidity, workers from all of Europe—this is unique. I want to tell this to all gentlemen: if each, in his respective field, would use only one tenth of the energy which Gauleiter Sauckel has used, then it would really be an easy thing to accomplish the tasks requested from you. This is my holy conviction, and not a manner of talking.

KOCH: I have sent over half a million. After all, he got the people from me, it was I who gave them to him.

GÖRING: But Koch, these are not only Ukrainians. Your ridiculous 500,000 people! And how many did he [Sauckel] bring? Almost two million! From where did he get the others?...

LOHSE: I can also answer this. Only a small fraction of Jews are still alive. Many thousands of them are gone. I may state however, what the local population gets; they get, according to your instruction, 15 percent less than the Jewish population.

GÖRING: But we don't want to go into this little milk bill. What is on your lists is one thing, and what grub the people get is another....

Now we will see what Russia can deliver. I think, Riecke, we must succeed in obtaining 2 million tons of bread grain and grain fodder from the whole Russian area.

RIECKE: They will be obtained.

GÖRING: We must therefore obtain 3 million apart from the Wehrmacht.

RIECKE: No, what is there is only for the Wehrmacht.

GÖRING: Then get 2 million.

RIECKE: No.

GÖRING: Then get 1 million.

RIECKE: Yes. All right.

GÖRING: Then oilseed, that is quite open.

RIECKE: That will improve still more.

GÖRING: Meat is improving?

RIECKE: Yes.

(Excerpted from Partial Translation of Document NG-1280, in *Trials of War Criminals Before the Nuernberg Military Tribunals, Volume XIII* ["The Ministries Case"])

04.10.1942 — Delivered a speech at the *Sportpalast* in Berlin on the occasion of *Erntedankfest* (Harvest Thanksgiving Festival). The following are excerpts:

National comrades, men and women! Germans on the land! We are at the beginning of the fourth year of the war, and today we celebrate the German harvest thanksgiving. Today we cannot celebrate the nation's festivals in the scope and manner to which we were formerly accustomed.

Today great masses of the German countryfolk cannot appear before the Führer through their deputations, to bring him a harvest wreath and fruits of the last harvest, because we are in a war, in the most difficult war of the German people, and in this war there is only one thing: Work, work, fighting and work, and again fighting and work.

The last three harvest years, in particular the first two of them, were by no means favorable. Quite unexpectedly, three terribly hard and severe winters broke upon us and destroyed much of the labor that had previously been put into the ground.

But, nevertheless, it was possible, first of all, to guarantee nourishment of the people absolutely; for at that time, when I spoke in this same hall on taking over the responsibility of carrying out the Four-Year Plan, many a compatriot will still be able to remember how, right at that time, I laid very strong emphasis on the concept and the term "enemy blockade."

When the third harvest had such a bad outlook I did everything to avoid rationing, but there was no alternative. We did not only have to worry about bread. There was also the question of potatoes. The transport system increased our worries, as it had constantly to supply our forces in the East.

These problems have been solved and will never recur. The conquered territories are the most fertile in Europe. Most of the talk about the seriousness of the food situation in occupied countries is just propaganda. I am firmly resolved that while I do not want to see the populations of occupied countries suffer hunger and privation, if through enemy measures privation is unavoidable it will in no circumstances affect Germany.

German workers and German agricultural laborers will be fed better than any others. The German peasant goes out to fight, leaving his work to women. Children are helping as soon as they are able.

There should be no difficulty feeding Germany, but there are over six million foreign workers in Germany and over five million prisoners of war who have to be supplied.

Now that the future is clearer, the meat ration is to be increased by another fifty grams in the raid-threatened areas.

The German people come before all other peoples for food.

The whole German Army is fed from conquered countries.

By no means let us forget that when it is a question of raw materials for armament, there are two raw materials which are just as fundamental for feeding our people as for their subsistence as a whole. And these raw materials are coal and iron, and both raw materials we ourselves possess in sufficient quantities, and we have also—thank God—won enormous additional quantities by conquest.

Bear in mind, therefore, that since we do not have a sufficient surplus of this valuable material, coal, we should not waste it unnecessarily. And everyone who turns on a single light or other electrical appliance unnecessarily, or who leaves it on longer than necessary, is committing a sin.

Anyone who uses too much gas should remember that this gas comes from coal, and that a worker has to slave for it by the sweat of his brow hundreds of meters underground. Anyone who uses too much power should also consider that fact.

But, my dear German comrades, one thing more I should like to say here quite plainly. When a national community is being created, and when an entire nation as a totality and a single entity, must win a victory and must secure its freedom, then the individual, too, must be ready to submit to more or less stringent limitations on his personal freedom.

This limitation of personal freedom is necessary even in peacetime. In democracy, to be sure, there is always one thing only—freedom of the individual. That is what we National Socialists call license. If every one may do as he likes, if no one has to have any consideration for his neighbors or his relatives, and even gets ahead by doing so, then you can imagine how such a community gets along.

And if you tear down the splendid façade of dollar-rich America and look behind it, you will also see what such a country—where, as in "God's own country," democracy is particularly cherished—what such a country and nation really looks like. In front it is splendid façade, with an infinite misery behind it. Even the fool, Mr. Roosevelt, cannot deny that misery is at home in his capital, and that there are only a few who swim around on top, like fat-flecks on top of bouillon, as dollar millionaires.

I should like now to broach a topic that indeed concerns me very especially as the Commander in Chief of the Luftwaffe and Reich Air Minister. It is about the heavy enemy air attacks on German cities. Here, too, my dear fellow countrymen, there must often be a very great restriction of personal freedom.

I am far from belittling these attacks or anything like that. I know how it is. I am an expert. I know what it means when a hundred or two hundred planes drop their bomb load. I know that many innocent people must die, in this way, absolutely to no purpose.

The Führer told our enemies in his Reichstag speech some time ago that one should at least stop attacking absolutely harmless people where there is no war industry. And today they cannot get out of it by saying that they just accidentally missed, they were aiming at industrial plants, because we are in possession of their original orders.

Mr. British Air General instructed his fliers that war industry was not the important thing to destroy, but residential sections ... terrorizing the German population, dropping bombs on children and women. That is the main thing for these gentlemen, even though a few decent fliers have protested against being assigned again and again to this slaughter.

So I know how hard all this is and how terrible and how senseless this destruction of cultural values. It that fool would reflect on the virtues of German culture, and that German culture exists not only for Germans—it has made endless contributions to Europe and the world- that simple respect for it should keep the wretches from destroying German seats of culture.

Our seats of culture are not valuable for the German people only, they are valuable for the whole world, which can derive unending benefits from them. And the German has always been the greatest leaven of cultural progress.

You may be sure—I am now speaking to our fellow-countrymen of those regions that are subject to the threat of air raids—that everything humanly possible is being done in my efforts to alleviate the situation and to prevent such attacks, first of all by active counter-defense.

But in this regard let no one forget that at present I have to fight hardest on the Eastern Front and cannot provide defense on a full scale, which will definitely someday be provided.

Nevertheless, the enemy always loses out very heavily in these raids. And although Mr. Churchill declared a few weeks ago that he would make a little excursion with a thousand airplanes over Germany every night, then I can say, first of all, that he has not as yet made a single such excursion with a thousand planes, and he will never make one either, and in any case these planes—these excursions will have to be paid for so heavily that he has already greatly restricted them.

And finally, I have only one more thing to say to that gentleman. In the East, too, the enemy will be conquered, and then we'll see each other in England again.

But it is now the all-important thing to fight where the center of gravity is, and they will not prevent us from doing so by these air raids.

Today the German Luftwaffe is fighting day after day on a scale that you cannot imagine, at Stalingrad and where the decisive victories are to be won. Once that is finished there, we will meet again at Philippi!

I shall see to it myself that steadily increasing and additional camps shall be prepared that will take care of the victims of the air raids. I have purchased supplies in all countries to which I had access, on a tremendously large scale.

And, my dear fellow-citizens, everything is in our favor when we consider the situation. Just how are our enemies going to be able to carry out their continued assertions and declarations that they are going to win this war?

They have some hope or other in the astronomic figures of American production. Now, I would be the last person to underestimate American production. In certain field the Americans have made colossal achievements in technique and in production.

We know they have done a stupendous amount with the auto. They have also won special merit with the radio and the razor blade. In these three fields they have undoubtedly wrought ever colossally, but these things are, nevertheless, something else yet than what one needs for war.

And if I do not by any means underestimate them, nevertheless I know by first-hand acquaintance what enormous difficulties there are in the matter of armament production. And even over there, if Roosevelt constantly makes two times two equal five or six or eight, nevertheless, even in America two times two is and remains four, and he can't change that a bit.

And even in America nothing gets done faster than with us, but slower rather, and even in America raw materials are necessary, workers are necessary. You can't at the same time build up an army of several million, and on the other hand triple the number of workers. That doesn't work in America, either.

You must realize that the gentlemen are very hard to teach; they are democrats. So the hope of internal German decay—in spite of everything that many newspapers are beginning to write that they will be disappointed, that the nation will not collapse and so forth—is still their hope today.

And they still continue to believe that they could do that primarily through hunger, as they did in 1918 by the blockade, although they are gradually being obliged to understand that the blockade is only working in reverse. What price a blockade when one possesses the whole—as I have already explained previously—vast Ukrainian fertile lands and so on?

War is the last process of selection, and it assesses values; and only there can in be seen how one comes up to the mark, this one remains; the other cannot quite make it, this one is given a less important task; the third understands nothing at all, he is sent home.

Generals shot? And our [Führer] has already said recently, "None has been shot at all."

But there is one thing about which I wish to leave no doubt. It was not just because one does not shoot a general, for that, too, has changed fundamentally since the World War.

Equal discipline for all, from Reich Marshal to the last recruit, equal obedience and loyalty to the Führer, equal distinctions and also equal punishment.

Today, if a man is a coward and deserts his company, he is shot. If a general abandons his company through cowardice, he is shot, too. ("Excerpts From Goering's Speech" in *The New York Times*, 05.10.1942)

00.10.1942–00.10.1942	One-week visit to Rome to meet with Mussolini.
26.10.1942	Issued the following order concerning actions to be taken in the aftermath of anti-partisan operations:

Simultaneously with the intensified combating of gang activities, [*Bandentätigkeit*] ordered by the *Führer*, and with the cleaning up of the hinterland, in particular that behind Heeresgruppe Mitte, I request that the following aspects are taken into consideration and that the deductions drawn therefrom are put into practice.

1. During combating of the underground and the combing through of the areas contaminated by them, all the available cattle stock there, must simultaneously be driven off to safe areas. Food supplies are to be evacuated and protected similarly, so that they will no more be accessible to the bands.

2. All masculine and feminine labour which can be considered for some kind of employment, must be seized by force and transported to the plenipotentiary Chief of the Labor Exchange who will employ them in the safe areas of the hinterland or at home. The accommodation of the children in the hinterland camps is to be regulated separately.

permitted German engineers to visit their arms factories and they had proved to be larger than we could have ever imagined....

Historians will consider that the decision of 22 June 1941 was the most important decision in all history and was taken by a strong soul. The German Army stormed the Russian enemy. Victory followed victory. One army after another was annihilated. But, with these victories, distances and difficulties of supply began to increase....

Not the enemy, but the elements themselves, arose and for the first time called a halt to the victorious troops. The icy Russian winter descended on us with unimaginable strength and fury. I need not tell you that. Many of you experienced it. Neither will I speak of the weakness of many of your commanders. It was the Führer who, against all the weaklings who whined around him, with all his strength held the front in the east alone. Thanks to his strength and genius, the German Army stepped forward to a new gigantic push....

This enemy is hard, and his commanders are barbarically hard. If we blew up a railway line, the Soviet Commissar just drew a circle around an area of twenty kilometers and in this area every old man, every woman and every child was whipped into work—with their bare hands if necessary. The Commissar did not worry about food or transport. His transport was the whip. If a man fell by the way, he was shot. A nation so dominated is a stern foe....

Russia is now mobilizing her last reserves. But I am convinced that these last reserves that could be squeezed out are possible only because Russian ruthlessness has been raised to the level of crime. The Russians have ceased to respect human life. Russian leadership is of the utmost brutality, but we have beaten them again. What we are doing is to frustrate their plan to reconquer their raw material areas....

But the battle is hard. The battle has taken on gigantic proportions. We are fighting from the Bay of Biscay to the deserts of Africa and, in the east, from the North Cape to the Volga. Like a gigantic monument there looms up amid this mammoth fighting the name of Stalingrad. Someday it will be called the greatest battle of heroism in history. Historians will remember that it was there that Germany put the seal on her victory because a nation that can fight like this must be victorious....

You all know the law that you must die for Germany if Germany's life requires it. This is not only a duty for our soldiers. It is a duty for every German....

The Führer has ordered the mobilization of all German men and women. The German people understand that times are hard and demand hardness. It is a disgrace if any German today grumbles at having to work. I appeal to everyone for his utmost effort. Let everyone give what he can. Not because, as the enemy claims, we are on our last legs. No. It is because the fight has reached its peak and everyone, both at home and at the front, must regard himself as a fighter. Not for one moment shall we weaken....

Let me, as Oberbefehlshaber of the Luftwaffe, assure the people that every morning when I hear of the destruction done, of the women and children killed, it touches me very deeply. But it is unavoidable and must in no way affect the will of the people to resist. Perhaps many of you will be saying,

(Saxon, *The German Side of the Hill: Nazi Conquest and Exploitation of Italy, 1943-45*, pp. 52-53)

30.01.1943

On the day before the surrender of *Generalfeldmarschall* Paulus and his *6. Armee* at Stalingrad, delivered a speech from which the following is excerpted:

My comrades, you are standing here as a delegation of the entire German Wehrmacht.

This is an appeal that is addressed at the same time to all comrades of the Wehrmacht, no matter where they are at present.

It is an appeal to think of that day ten years ago when the fate of the German Reich underwent a fundamental change. It was exactly at this hour that the Führer, then Chancellor, and his closest collaborators took the oath to Hindenburg....

We have only to look into the mirror presented by the leaders. Up to ten years ago we see a rotten gang of leaders capable of destroying even the best in the German people. The collapse of 1918 was brought about by lying promises from the outside and the cowardice of the people's leaders. Times were hard, but in no way so hard as to justify capitulation....

Today we are united, and we shall fight to the very last for our way of life. One of our enemies is also united and conditioned by its way of life.

Russia would long ago have collapsed had it not been for the strength this gives her.

We stand again on the same platform on which we stood at the time of our internal struggle. This time it is a struggle against an external enemy. The same issues are at stake. Those ridiculous bourgeois parties and their followers were not even worth fighting. There was only one opponent then. There is only one today—communism....

I need not remind you of the gigantic battles that we have fought, on our own unique victories in Poland, Norway and France. In Yugoslavia, in the air, on the sea and under the sea—everywhere are victories of German arms. The German people began to think that victory as a whole was a foregone conclusion, a matter of course.

Fate, however, does not give such gifts easily—particularly the gifts of big things. It submits people to a test. At one time we, and perhaps the whole nation, thought we had won the war everywhere—that the war would soon end. The east was not regarded as a danger; we even had an economic understanding with Russia.

We had just seen a small but gallant nation [Finland] fight heroically for many months against this vast empire and we though, "What danger can possibly come from the Empire in the east?" It required all the hardships of last winter for us to realize that Russia's war against Finland was perhaps the cleverest and greatest camouflage in world history....

What would our position have been if the Führer in his political genius had not clearly realized the Russian danger? True, there were weaklings who said: "Russia has three, four or five times as many tanks and ten times as many planes as we thought she had." The Russians had just

A few days later I was back at the Führer's headquarters. Zeitzer was now giving a daily report on the tons of rations and munitions the Sixth Army was receiving by air. They came to only a fraction of the promised quantities. Göring, repeatedly called to account by Hitler, had excuses: The weather was bad, fog, freezing rain, or snowstorms had so far prevented commitment of as many planes as planned. But as soon as the weather changed, Göring said, he would be able to deliver the promised tonnage. (Speer, *Inside the Third Reich*, p. 249)

Hitler was infuriated with the *Luftwaffe* and its leader, and his relationship with Göring would never recover. Regarding losses, David Irving writes: "Göring's air force had airlifted into Stalingrad 8,350 tons of supplies, a daily average of 116 tons. But he had lost 266 Junkers 52 transports, 165 Heinkel 111 bombers, and 42 Junkers 86 bombers—virtually an entire air corps." (Irving, *Göring: A Biography*, p. 558)

28.11.1942 Meeting at *Führer HQ "Wolfsschanze"* with Hitler and *Generalfeldmarschall* Erwin Rommel, who had come to Rastenburg to request the evacuation of German forces from North Africa to Italy. Timothy D. Saxon writes:

Given that Axis shipping could not supply forces already there, withdrawal from North Africa was urgent. Supported by Göring Hitler sharply rebuked the exhausted Field Marshal. Blind to conditions in North Africa, Hitler upbraided Rommel as a defeatist. "I no longer want to hear such rubbish from your lips," he declared. "North Africa will be defended as Stalingrad will…"

Göring blithely promised that his air forces, already stretched to the limit airlifting supplies into besieged Stalingrad, would also supply Tunis. Hitler indulged Göring's fantasy that North Africa could be supplied by air. Hitler proclaimed that the Reichsmarschall had assured him the air trip to Tunis was merely "a short hop" for his flyers. The Führer rejected outright Rommel's entreaties to withdraw German forces.

Hitler ordered the departing Rommel to accompany Göring to Rome. (Saxon, *The German Side of the Hill: Nazi Conquest and Exploitation of Italy, 1943–45*, pp. 51-52)

30.11.1942 Visit to Rome, together with Rommel, to meet with Mussolini concerning the status of the North African campaign. Saxon continues:

The duo was to reassure Mussolini's worried government of German support. Rommel, however, [had] left Hitler's headquarters a changed man. The Desert Fox departed Rastenburg enraged at his leader's incompetence and unwilling ever again to trust Hitler's "strategic genius." The ensuing visit to Rome only further unsettled Italian officials. Göring blamed the "inadequate Italian organization" for the defeats in North Africa, which did little to reassure Italian leaders. As the Italians feared, promises of air support for Mediterranean operations proved illusory.

3. In the execution of the directives outlined under paragraphs 1 and 2, no regard is to be paid to whether the agricultural or any other production in these areas will suffer or succumb owing to these measures. Since up to now these band infested areas have nothing to show in the way of production anyway, but were directly or indirectly useful to the bands. I request all authorities concerned, in as far as it is necessary, in mutual agreement, to effect the requisites within their spheres of competence, in order to act according to the directives outlined by me.

About the detailed delimitation of areas an Agreement must be reached between the various head groups of agriculture of the Economy Offices [*Wirtschaftsdienststellen*].
[signed] Göring
(Translation of Document 1742-PS, in *Nazi Conspiracy and Aggression, Volume IV*)

23.11.1942 Meeting with Hitler at Rastenburg regarding the Soviet encirclement of Friedrich Paulus's 300,000-man 6. *Armee* at Stalingrad. Albert Speer writes:

Depressed, with a beseeching note in his voice, Hitler asked him: "What about supplying Stalingrad by air?" Goering snapped to attention and declared solemnly: My Führer! I personally guarantee the supplying of Stalingrad by air. You can rely on that." As I later heard from Milch, the Luftwaffe General Staff had in fact calculated that supplying the pocket was impossible. [General] Zeitzler, too, instantly voiced his doubts. But Göring retorted that it was exclusively the business of the Luftwaffe to undertake the necessary calculations. Hitler … did not even ask for an accounting of how the necessary planes could be made available. He had revived at Göring's mere words, and had recovered his old staunchness. Then Stalingrad can be held! It is foolish to go on talking any more about a breakout of the Sixth Army. It would lose all its heavy weapons and have no fighting strength left. The Sixth Army remains in Stalingrad. (Speer, *Inside the Third Reich*, pp. 248-249)

He gave the *Führer* his promise that he would mobilize all the *Luftwaffe*'s transport aircraft, and the following day, the airlift began. It was a failure, largely due to the fact that it gave Hitler the false impression that 6. *Armee* could survive in the Stalingrad cauldron, when in fact the best course of action at this early stage would have been for Paulus to lead a breakout from the Soviet encirclement. Wolfram von Richthofen's *Luftflotte 4*, despite being very shorthanded and using every type of aircraft that could be scavenged, dropped approximately 5,300 tons of cargo into the city. The planes were subjected to attack by Soviet fighters, anti-aircraft fire, a shortage of fuel, and extreme challenges to their effective ranges, and the operation—like 6. *Armee*'s attempt to take Stalingrad—was a miserable failure. Speer continues:

"Why are we always getting bombs dropped on the Ruhr and elsewhere and why do we not retaliate?" You must not forget that we have so vast a battlefront that the weight of the Luftwaffe is spread all over the north, east and south. The day will come when the last remnant of Bolshevik resistance will break down and then the avenging hand will strike. I promise you that....

In conclusion, I ask you to accept one declaration of faith from me—my unshakable faith in German victory. This faith comes from a most profound recognition of facts and my inner faith in justice. I see the heroism of our fighters, I see the heroism of our fighters, I see the strength of our National Socialist philosophy and I see the Führer and his strength, which penetrates all things. I see how, in these ten years, from a tattered and divided nation has come a strong united army....

These are the facts that give me my unshakable faith in victory. In these ten years, Hitler has led us from poverty and impotence to victory and is now leading us to the greatest of all victories. He must have our devotion and our absolute loyalty. Our leader—our beloved leader—Sieg Heil! ("Excerpts from Speeches by Goering and Goebbels at Party Rally" in *The New York Times*, 31.01.1943)

01.03.1943 — Lengthy meeting (nearly four hours) with Goebbels at *Carinhall*, during which the two discussed the war situation and their mutual displeasure with other senior members of the Reich leadership (notably Reich Ministers Rosenberg and von Ribbentrop and the so-called *Dreimännerkollegium*, or "Committee of Three" [Martin Bormann, Dr. Hans Heinrich Lammers, and Wilhelm Keitel]). The following is an excerpt from Goebbels' diary entry of 02.03.1943:

The little dissensions that have crept into our work in the course of time were not even mentioned. They seem quite unimportant compared with the historic tasks that we have to discuss....

Göring evidenced the greatest concern about the Führer. To him too, the Führer seems to have aged fifteen years during three-and-a-half years of war. It is a tragic thing that the Führer has become such a recluse and leads so unhealthy a life. He doesn't get out into the fresh air. He does not relax. He sits in his bunker, fusses and broods. If one could only transfer him to other surroundings! But he has made up his mind to conduct this war in his own Spartan manner, and I suppose nothing can be done about it.

But it is equally essential that we succeed somehow in making up for the lack of leadership in our domestic and foreign policy. One must not bother the Führer with everything. The Führer must be kept free for the military leadership.... As was always the case during crises of the Party, the duty of the Führer's closest friends in time of need consists in gathering about him and forming a solid phalanx around his person....

Göring realizes perfectly what is in store for all of us if we show any weakness in this war. He has no illusions about that. On the Jewish question, especially, we have taken a position from which there is no escape. That is a good thing. Experience teaches that a movement and a people who have burned their bridges fight with much greater determination than those who are still able to retreat....

I introduce my proposals. I express the opinion that we'd be 'over the hump' if we succeeded in transferring the political leadership tasks of the Reich from the Committee of Three to the Ministerial Council for the Defense of the Reich. This Ministerial Council would then have to be composed of the strong men who assisted the Führer in the Revolution. These will certainly also muster the strength to bring this war to a victorious conclusion....

While talking I gained the spontaneous impression that my presentation visibly pepped up Göring. He became very enthusiastic about my proposals and immediately asked how we were to proceed specifically....

I am very happy that a clear basis of mutual trust was established with Göring. I believe that the Führer, too, will be very happy about this. I hope we shall render him the very greatest service possible. (Louis P. Lochner, ed., *The Goebbels Diaries 1942–1943*)

Goebbels' grand plans of heightening his power and realizing his dreams of totalizing the war with Göring's help faded quickly. The *Reichsmarschall*'s stock had plummeted in all quarters, owing mainly to the many failures of his *Luftwaffe* to adequately defend the Reich from Allied bombing and to provide sufficient aerial supply and support to the doomed 6. *Armee* at Stalingrad. In testimony before the International Military Tribunal at Nürnberg on 08.03.1946, Göring's friend and former liaison officer to *Führer HQ, General der Flieger* Karl Bodenschatz, stated:

According to my personal opinion and conviction, Hermann Göring began to lose influence with Hitler in the spring of 1943.... That was the beginning of large-scale air attacks by night by the R.A.F. on German towns, and from that moment there were differences of opinion between Hitler and Göring which became more serious as time went on. Even though Göring made tremendous efforts, he could not recapture his influence with the Führer to the same extent as before. The outward symptoms of this waning influence were the following: First, the Führer criticized Göring most severely. Secondly, the eternal conversations between Adolf Hitler and Hermann Göring became shorter, less frequent, and finally ceased altogether. Thirdly, as far as important conferences were, concerned, the Reich Marshal was not called in. Fourthly, during the last months and weeks the tension between Adolf Hitler and Hermann Göring increased to such a degree that he was finally arrested... (*Trial of the Major War Criminals Before the International Military Tribunal Nuremberg, 14 November 1945 to 1 October 1946, Volume IX*)

07.09.1943   Issued the following secret order:

Concerning: The evacuation of the Harvest Crops and the Destruction of the Means of Production in the Agricultural and Food Economy in Parts of the Occupied Eastern Territories
By direction of the Führer, I give the following order:

1. In the territories east of the line fixed by the highest military command, the following measures are to be taken gradually, according to the military situation at the time. The measures are to be determined by the Oberbefehlshabers of the Army Groups:

i. All agricultural products, means of production and machines of enterprises serving the agricultural and food economy are to be transported away.

ii. The factories serving the food economy, both in the field of production and of processing, are to be destroyed.

iii. The bases of agricultural production, especially the records and establishments (storage plants, etc.) of the organizations charged with seizing the food economy are to be destroyed.

iv. The population engaged in the agricultural and food economy is to be transported into territory west of the fixed line.

2. The Chief of the Economic Staff, East, General der Infanterie Stapf, is charged with the direction of the measures, as representative of the Economic Executive Staff. Execution takes place under the responsibility of the highest military command offices which are bound by the substantive orders of the pertinent departments of the Economic offices.

3. In the performance of his task, General Stapf is bound by the directives of the chief of the department of my office dealing with "Food", State Secretary Backe. He is entitled to give binding orders to all military and non-military offices for the purpose of executing his task and of receiving the transported goods in the occupied territories and in the war theater of Germany.

[signed] GÖRING

(Translation of Document EC-317, in *Nazi Conspiracy and Aggression, Volume VII*)

31.12.1943   Delivered the following New Year's appeal to the German people:

German Volksgenossen!

In the past year, the demands of war have once again increased. The heaviest material battles have been fought and the fiercest defensive struggles have been mastered. In this year of war, in self-sacrificing fulfilment of duty, the German soldier on land, at sea and in the air has once again demonstrated the highest heroism on all fronts and kept the hostile masses away from the German borders and the heartland of mainland Europe.

The homeland, too, has endured the highest burdens and shown itself worthy of the fighting front and the selfless sacrifice of the fallen. It is working with all its strength in extreme concentration and under difficult conditions to secure the defense of the country. Hundreds of thousands of formerly non-working women have taken on additional duties in the struggle for the existence of our nation in addition to their domestic tasks, which were already difficult during the war. Day and night, work races in the huge armament factories; and the rural population has again provided for the daily bread with toil and diligence.

The strong labour force of those working in the war effort has not been broken even under the enemy's air terror. On my fact-finding journeys over the last few months, I have visited the cities most severely affected by the brutal attacks by British and American planes. There I spoke with laborers of all professions and especially with women.

Never have I been prouder to be a German, never happier to be able to devote all my strength to this people. With a brave heart it endures the cruelly heavy blows of such barbaric warfare against women and children, against home and farm, against culture and morality. Courageous and tenacious, they always go to work undeterred and also to repair the damage. This shows that the spirit of the front is also alive at home. Such a people can never perish. It will, that is my sacred conviction, also defy all coming dangers and hold its own in the storms of this time.

Hardened by destiny and inwardly strengthened in our community, we enter the year ahead, a new year of the most difficult struggles and the greatest efforts. We are not under any illusions and do not deceive ourselves about the fact that much, very much is still required of us. Each and every one of us is prepared to do our utmost to preserve our freedom and to shatter the plans of our enemies who seek to destroy our fatherland and plunge us all into the abyss of endless suffering and bitter misery. Only in our sword lies our salvation! We will only lay it down when nation and empire are secured for all future.

In this hour, let us look ahead fearlessly and courageously. Ahead of us lies the great task set before us by destiny. We cannot evade it. We must and we will solve it. With perseverance and certain of victory, we will continue to fight and work and break the terror of the enemies with the hardest of blows. In loyalty and obedience to our beloved leader, who stands before us unflinchingly as a shining example, we will fulfil our duty until the goal is reached and the longed-for peace is won.

The slogan for the New Year is: All strength and every sacrifice for freedom and victory!

Hermann Göring
Reichsmarschall des Großdeutschen Reiches und Beauftragter für den Vierjahresplan.
("Alle Kräfte und jedes Opfer für den Sieg!" in *Der Führer: Das Hauptorgan der NSDAP Gau Baden*, 01.01.1944; Translation: Gary Costello)

21.07.1944 — While at *Führer HQ "Wolfsschanze"* in Rastenburg/Ostpreußen in the aftermath of the 20 July bomb attack on Hitler's conference room, delivered the following announcement to the men of his service:

Comrades of the Luftwaffe!
An unimaginable, vile assassination attempt was carried out against our Führer on Thursday by an Oberst Graf Stauffenberg on behalf of a wretched clique of former generals who had to be hounded away because of their equally cowardly and bad leadership. The Führer was miraculously saved by Almighty Providence.

These criminals, as usurpers, are now trying to cause confusion among the troops by means of false orders. I therefore order: In the Reich, on my behalf, Generaloberst Stumpf, as Oberbefehlshaber Luftflotte Reich, commands all units of the Luftwaffe within the territory of the Reich.

Only my orders and his orders are to be obeyed. The Reichsführer-SS Himmler is to be actively supported by all services of the Luftwaffe upon request. Courier flights, regardless of the aircraft, may only be carried out with my permission or his permission.

Officers and soldiers of any rank, as well as civilians, who promote these crimes and approach you in order to persuade you on behalf of their wretched scheme, are to be arrested and shot immediately.

Where you yourselves are deployed to exterminate these traitors, you must act ruthlessly. These are the same wretches who are trying to betray and sabotage the front.

Officers who participate in these crimes place themselves beyond their people, beyond the Wehrmacht, beyond any soldierly honor, beyond oath and loyalty. Their destruction will give us new strength. Against this betrayal, the Luftwaffe places its sworn loyalty and fierce love for the Führer and its wholehearted commitment to victory. Long live our Führer, whom the Almighty God blessed so visibly today.

("Hermann Goring an die Luftwaffe!" in the *Mährisch-Schlesische Landeszeitung*, 21.07.1944; Translation: Gary Costello)

24.07.1944

Just days after the 20.07.1944 assassination attempt, the following announcement was made from *Führer HQ "Wolfsschanze"*:

Reichsmarschall Göring, as the most senior officer of the German Wehrmacht, has in his name and in the names of Generalfeldmarschall Keitel and Großadmiral Dönitz reported to the Führer that all parts of the German Wehrmacht on the occasion of the Führer's escape have asked for the German Salute to be introduced in the Wehrmacht as a sign of unbreakable loyalty and closest attachment between the Army and Party.

The Führer has complied with the request and given his approval. With effect at once the salute of lifting the right hand to the military headgear is replaced by the German Salute. The new regulations apply to all Officers and Men of the German Wehrmacht both when on and off duty and the act of outstretching the right arm must be accompanied by the greeting "Heil Hitler."

07.10.1944

Letter from Göring to Albert Speer, *Reichsminister für Rüstung und Kriegsproduktion* (Reich Minister for Armaments and War Production):

Dear Speer,

I have been told that, at the suggestion of the Heereswaffenamt, your Ministry is also considering combining the ordering of ammunition for the three Wehrmacht branches at the Heereswaffenamt Wa I Rü Mun.

In a letter dated 08.03.1943, the *Führer* ordered:

"To carry out joint procurement of the same and similar equipment from different branches of the Wehrmacht and the Waffen-SS to the last consequence. The procurement of the same and similar equipment (weapons, ammunition, communications equipment, optics and the like) is to be carried out by only one branch of the Wehrmacht."

In his decree of 23.06.1944, Generalfeldmarschall Keitel, responsible for the ammunition procurement of the OKW, stated that the Wehrmacht unit with the greatest need would be in charge of processing ammunition commonly used by several Wehrmacht branches. I also consider it necessary that the branch of the Wehrmacht which has the decisive influence over the development and use of the devices peculiar to it should also be in charge of the ordering of these devices, because only this branch of the Wehrmacht can coordinate the constantly changing demands resulting from use and development with the production centers. According to our agreements, industrial production and production control are the responsibility of the Rüstungsministerium.

I therefore consider it inexpedient to hand over the ordering of Luftwaffe-owned equipment such as on-board weapons, on-board weapon ammunition, air-dropped weapons, air mines, air torpedoes, remote-controlled bodies, anti-aircraft missiles, etc. to the Heereswaffenamt since it cannot possibly represent the special interests of the Luftwaffe in dealings with the production.

Heil Hitler
[Signed] Göring. (Bundesarchiv RL3/2569; Translation: Gary Costello)

17.10.1944   *"Reichsmarschall Befehl Nr. 3"* issued to the *Luftwaffe* that date:

In the difficult battles in the East and in the West, in addition to exemplary conduct and outstanding bravery, there have also been shameful failures on the part of individuals and entire units.

In shameful flight, individual cowards—indeed, even squads and headquarters—have surrendered their weapons undestroyed to the enemy.

But anyone who gives up his weapon also gives up his soldier's honor.

Only the severely wounded who can no longer wield his weapon in combat has the right to surrender his weapon.

On the other hand, anyone found unwounded on the battlefield without his weapon is to be treated as a marauder. Every honorable soldier has the right and the duty to arrest a coward who has surrendered his weapon and to present him to the nearest superiors for sentencing. I make it the duty of superiors of all ranks to immediately sentence such dishonorable cowards who have obviously abandoned their weapons and to have the punishment carried out without delay.

Even the implementation of the death penalty does not require prior authorization by me.

The implementation is to be reported retrospectively to the Chief of the Lw. Rechtspflege.

I leave no doubt that in future I will remove all decorations from entire units and staffs which have dropped their weapons into the hands of the enemy without compelling reasons or, if it is not possible to take them, have not destroyed them, and after punishing those responsible I will announce the disgraceful failure of the unit concerned to the entire Luftwaffe.

I expect officers of all ranks to make scrupulous enquiries about every weapon that is lost and, when reporting the loss, to report whether and how the culprits have been brought to justice.

[Signed] Göring.

(Bundesarchiv Rl 1/4 007; Translation: Gary Costello)

17.03.1945 "*Reichsmarschall Befehl Nr. 3*" issued to the *Luftwaffe* that date:

The German Volksgenossen from the evacuated Reich territories require the special protection of the German soldier. Anyone who misappropriates their belongings, whether carried along or left behind, not only undermines manly discipline in the ranks, but also shakes the confidence of the homeland, which is prepared to make every sacrifice, in its Wehrmacht through their collective behavior.

Every soldier must respect, treat and protect the belongings of his fellow Germans as if they were his own property.

I therefore order:

1.) The troops are to be instructed in detail by officers immediately and in future on a weekly basis about appropriate behavior in the homeland.

2.) In the case of any suspicion of looting of property carried by or left behind by German Volksgenossen from the evacuated territories of the Reich, court martial investigations are to be conducted on an expedited basis, unless the circumstances require a trial by summary court martial on the spot.

Such looting must be punished with the most severe penalties; only under special circumstances will it be possible to refrain from the death penalty.

Summary court martial death sentences against looters shall be carried out by hanging, on the spot.

For further deterrence, the reason for the execution is to be announced through a placard next to the hanged individual.

3.) The appropriation or operation of articles of war use, even within the scope of urgent need, is permitted only by order of a disciplinary superior or local commander. Without such an express order, collection may be made only in cases of real emergency.

4.) In all cases of looting, the judicial officer shall determine whether the responsible supervisors have violated their duty of supervision. If this is the case, the strongest possible action must be taken.

[Signed] Göring

(Bundesarchiv RL 1/4 0047; Translation: Gary Costello)

16.04.1945 "*Reichsmarschall Befehl Nr. 18*" issued to the *Luftwaffe* that date:

Time and again it has been shown that German attacks against the Russians came to an early halt because the Russians had an extensive system of positions and trenches at their disposal. As soon as the Russians had established themselves somewhere for only a few days, 4, 5 and 7 positions were created in succession.

On the other hand, I continually find that the German troops are almost afraid of digging in. The man does not dig in more than is absolutely necessary, hence very often the high casualties in the face of concentrated fire from the enemy.

In the First World War it was different. Here, every soldier, whether in position or in reserve, spent several hours a day digging in. I therefore order that all superiors down to the squad leaders be constantly reminded to take advantage of every free minute to dig in. One trench after the other, connecting trenches, barricade positions, dugouts, etc., are to be laid out and extended again and again one after the other.

The procedure is to be followed accordingly. The positions must be difficult for the enemy to see. It is a madness when the excavated yellow sand is thrown up on green or black soil, so that the positions can be seen shining from afar. First the surface must be lifted off, then the extraction takes place; this is then covered again with the lifted off upper part. The positions are to be offset in the terrain in such a way that they are difficult to see. All camouflage options must be used. Especially important is the dug-in and camouflage of forward observers. All these are long recognized truisms, preached again and again and not followed.

It is the task of the higher superiors to constantly convince themselves of the state of development of the positions and to apply the necessary pressure behind their orders.

The artillery and Flak, especially the latter, also still have a lot of work to do to improve their positions and keep them out of sight of the enemy. I have seen Flak positions, visible at 40 to 50 km in good visibility, standing completely uncamouflaged free in a field in the usual circular earthworks. The flak positions are also to be expanded by trench systems suitable for close combat.

I will once again issue a brief instruction on the most appropriate method of building positions , but it is not necessary to wait for it, but rather to work on the construction of the positions now with all possible vigor. Neglect in the construction of positions due to convenience, recklessness and lack of interest will be severely punished in the future. A superior who does not assert himself here proves that he is not fit to lead a troop unit and must be relieved.

In the artillery the mock and alternative positions are also particularly important. Here it is necessary to work with the utmost imagination and improvisational skills.

Units that excel at this will receive special praise from me, and their zeal will be rewarded by the allocation of sutler goods. Remember always and everywhere: the better the position, the more position systems in a row, the less losses and the more successful the resistance. The same applies to the installation of anti-tank obstacles, lurking positions with the Panzerfaust and the like.

Where experience and ability are lacking, an attempt must be made to borrow suitable officers or men from neighboring sections who can assist with the installation.

The solution must be: dig in and dig in again, so that unnecessary losses are avoided and every weapon carrier can be put to full use at the decisive moment of battle.

[Signed] Göring

(Bundesarchiv RL 1/4 0051; Translation: Gary Costello)

20.04.1945	Visited Adolf Hitler for the last time in the *Führerbunker* on the occasion of the *Führer*'s fifty-sixth birthday.

Albert Speer writes: |

As soon as the situation conference was over and the generals dismissed, Goering turned to Hitler.... He had urgent tasks awaiting him in South Germany, he said; he would have to leave Berlin this very night. Hitler gazed absently at him.... With a few indifferent words, he shook hands with Goering. (Speer, *Inside the Third Reich*, pp. 474-475)

After departing the Bunker, he made one last visit to his *Carinhall* estate, then fled by air to Berchtesgaden.

20.04.1945	*"Reichsmarschall Befehl Nr. 20"* issued to the *Luftwaffe* that date:

No period of this gigantic struggle so imperatively requires the uniting of the troops through firm leadership. It is necessary to give agile, clear orders that are appropriate to all situations that may arise.

The nature of mobile warfare no longer allows for everything to be dictated down to the last detail by the top leadership. In accordance with a development of the situation, middle and lower leadership must be given more opportunities to take the initiative.

If, after diligent examination, it becomes apparent that the prerequisites of an order received or given have been overtaken by the situation or time, then all leaders have the duty to act independently.

Soldierly leadership is particularly based on the joy of responsibility. Taking responsibility means giving orders in the spirit of the best German soldiering. Those who do not have a sense of responsibility and cannot bear responsibility do not belong in a leadership position. I demand from every officer of my Luftwaffe the highest degree of responsibility and energetic commitment of his whole person.

The action of the fighter pilots, for example, must increasingly be led by the squadrons. For this purpose, clear instructions are necessary from the higher troop leadership, which are implemented through orders from the squadron commanders.

I expect every leader to be aware of the plight of our fatherland at every moment and to act independently when the situation demands, no orders have been received or when given orders are outdated. Those who believe they are not up to their task must act according to the Führer's orders and transfer the power of command to those who are willing to take on the responsibility.

[Signed] Göring

(Bundesarchiv RL 1/4 0061; Translation: Gary Costello)

21.04.1945	Arrived at the Obersalzberg, Berchtesgaden (approximately 11:00 p.m.), joining his wife and daughter who had fled there from *Carinhall* in January 1945 due to the advance of Soviet forces. After removing several trainloads of innumerable art treasures and other belongings, Göring had *Carinhall* destroyed.
23.04.1945	In reaction to reports that Hitler had suffered a nervous collapse in Berlin, Göring (at the Berghof) consulted with *Reichsminister* Dr. Hans Heinrich Lammers and *Reichsleiter* Philipp Bouhler and drafted a telegram to Hitler. The message read as follows:

My Führer:
General Koller gave me a briefing today, based on communications that Generaloberst Jodl and General Christian had made to him, according to which you had referred to me in certain decisions, emphasizing that if negotiations became necessary, I would be in a better position than you in Berlin. This statement was so surprising and serious to me that I felt it was my duty, if there is no reply by 2200 hours, to assume that you are deprived of your freedom of action. I will then consider the conditions of your decree as given and will act for the good of the people and the fatherland. What I feel for you in these most difficult hours of my life, you already know, and I cannot convey this through words. May God protect you and nevertheless allow you to come here as soon as possible.
Your loyal Hermann Göring
(Translation from the original telegram by Gary Costello)

Hitler's reply, sent by radio to the Berghof on the 25th, read:

The Führer decree of 29 June 1941 is herewith declared null and void. Your behavior and your measures constitute a betrayal of my person and the National Socialist cause. I am in complete possession of my freedom of action and forbid any further measures.
Adolf Hitler
(Translation by Gary Costello)

Shortly afterward, the following announcement was issued on the *Führer*'s order:

Reichsmarschall Hermann Göring has become acutely ill due to a chronic heart problem which has long troubled him. He himself has requested to be relieved of the command of the Luftwaffe and the connected tasks in view of the current situation, which demands the deployment of all forces. The Führer has granted this request. He has appointed Generaloberst [Robert] Ritter von Greim as the new commander in chief of the Luftwaffe and promoted him to Generalfeldmarschall.
(Translation by Gary Costello)

24.04.1945	Arrested on Hitler's orders by *SS-Obersturmbannführer* Dr. Bernhard Frank at 5:00 p.m. and detained at the Berghof, the *Führer*'s residence on the Obersalzberg. The Berghof was destroyed

on the 25th by a USAAF bombing raid which dropped 1,232 tons of bombs, but Göring was unharmed, having sat out the raid in a bomb shelter. The following is "Annex III: Goering's Arrest" (22.10.1945), from the interrogation report of *SS-Brigadeführer und Generalmajor der Waffen-SS und Polizei* Ernst August Rode:

On the morning of 23 Apr 45 Rode was visited by one of Goering's adjutants, with the request that he transmit the following message to Himmler:
"Mein Fuehrer, nach Vortrag des Generals Koller befurchte ich, dass Sie nicht mehr die volle Handlungsfreiheit besetzen, sondern in Berlin eingeschlossen sind. Ich nehme deshalb an, dass meine Vollmacht in Kraft tritt, falls ich bis 22 Uhr keine Antwort habe. GOERING."
[My Führer, according to the report of Gen Koller, I am afraid that you no longer have a free hand, but are encircled. Therefore, unless I hear from you by 10:00 p.m., I shall assume full power. GOERING.]
On the following night Rode received a phone call from O/Stubaf Frank, summoning him immediately. Frank informed Rode that Hitler, through ... Bormann (under Landes Gericht Praesident Mueller) had ordered Goering's arrest. Additional messages expelled Goering from the NSDAP and ordered him to relinquish all his duties. Goering complied by wire. Goering was put under house arrest by guards of the Waffen SS. Dr. Lammers was also arrested in Bischofswiesen. Later an order arrived from Bormann to shoot Goering and his associates in the event that Berlin surrendered. Rode ordered Frank to shoot no one under any circumstances. Rode visited Gen Koller in Berchtesgaden, 28 Apr 45, in order to ask if any further instructions regarding Goering had been received from Gen/FM von Greim, Goering's successor. [On 28.04.1945,] Goering was transferred to [Schloß] Mauterndorf [in Taunach-Tal] by order of Kaltenbrunner because of air attacks on Obersalzberg. ("Interrogation Records Prepared for War Crimes Proceedings at Nuernberg, 1945–1947/ OCCPAC Interrogation Transcripts and Related Records: Rode, Ernst August"; Publication Number M1270, Record Group RG238)

29.04.1945   Formally expelled from all posts by Hitler, who wrote in his final testament:

Before my death, I expel the former Reichsmarschall Hermann Göring from the Party and strip him of all his rights that might be derived from the decree of 29. June 1941, and my Reichstag declaration of 1. September 1939. In his place, I appoint Großadmiral Dönitz as Reich President and supreme commander of the Wehrmacht....

Göring and Himmler, by their secret negotiations with the enemy, which took place without my knowledge and contrary to my will, as well as by attempting to usurp power in the state in violation of the law, have done immeasurable damage to the country and the entire *Volk*, not to mention their disloyalty to my person. (Excerpt from translation of Document 3569-PS, in *Nazi Conspiracy and Aggression, Volume VI*)

Under cross examination by Chief Prosecutor Jackson at Nürnberg on 18.03.1946, Göring asserted:

> I neither betrayed the Führer, nor did I at that time negotiate with a single foreign soldier. This will, or this final act of the Führer's, is based on an extremely regrettable mistake, and one which grieves me deeply—that the Führer could believe in his last hours that I could ever be disloyal to him. It was all due to an error in the transmission of a radio report and perhaps to a misrepresentation which Bormann gave the Führer. I myself never thought for a minute of taking over power illegally or of acting against the Führer in any way. (*Trial of the Major War Criminals Before the International Military Tribunal, Nuremberg, 14 November 1945–1 October 1946, Vol. IX*)

In testimony before the International Military Tribunal at Nürnberg, Göring's former chief adjutant, *Oberst* Bernd von Brauchitsch, described the *Reichsmarschall*'s arrest:

> … [O]n 23 April at 1900 hours we were surrounded. The Reichsmarschall was led to his room and from that moment on he was kept closely guarded; later we were Separated and put into solitary confinement. Finally we were separated from him altogether by SS troops stationed at the Berghof. (*Trial of the Major War Criminals Before the International Military Tribunal, Nuremberg, 14 November 1945–1 October 1946, Vol. IX*)

On 06.05.1945, on orders of *Generalfeldmarschall* Albert Kesselring (*Oberbefehlshaber Süd*), Göring was released by his final captor, the SS legal officer *SS-Standartenführer* Ernst Brausse.

On the day of his release, he sent the following message to Dönitz seeking a role in peace negotiations with the western Allies. Dönitz filed it away without responding and authorized the unconditional surrender of Germany on 7 May.

> Are you, Admiral, familiar with the intrigues, dangerous to the security of the State, which Reichsleiter Bormann has carried on to eliminate me? All steps taken against me arose out of the request sent by me in all loyalty to the Führer, asking whether he wished that his order concerning his succession should come into force…. The steps taken against me were carried out on the authority of a radiogram signed "Bormann." I have not been interrogated by anybody in spite of my requests and no attempt of mine to justify my position has been accepted. Reichsführer-SS Himmler can confirm the immense extent of these intrigues.
>
> I have just learned that you intend to send Jodl to Eisenhower with a view to negotiating. I think it important in the interests of our people that, besides the official negotiations of Jodl, I should officially approach Eisenhower, as one marshal to another. My success in all the important negotiations abroad with which the Führer always entrusted me before the war is sufficient guarantee that I can hope to create the personal atmosphere appropriate for Jodl's negotiations. Moreover, both Great Britain and America have proved

through their press and their radio, and in the declarations of their statemen during the last few years, that their attitude toward me is more favorable than toward other political leaders in Germany. I think that at this most difficult hour all should collaborate and that nothing should be neglected which might assure as far as possible the future of Germany.

Göring, Reichsmarschall

Göring also wrote the following letter to General Eisenhower. After he fell into American captivity, it was translated from the original German by the G-2 Translation Section, Headquarters 7th Army on 08.05.1945:

The Reich Marshal
of the
Greater German Reich   6 May 1945.
Your Excellency!

On the 23rd of April, after I had tried for many months, unfortunately without success, to make my influence felt in this direction, I decided, as the highest ranking officer of the German Army [probably *"Wehrmacht"* in the original/MdM/], to place myself in personal communication with your Excellency to do everything on my part to provide a basis for the prevention of further bloodshed.

On that day I was arrested with my entire entourage and family by the SS in Berchtesgaden. The order to shoot me and my household, including my family, was not carried out by my guards. At the same time, I was expelled from the Nazi Party. The story given forth on the radio was that I had been relieved of my command of the Luftwaffe because of a serious heart disease. Because of the close ties which bind me to the German people and its soldiers, this account was given little credence and the majority of the people believed that I had been forcibly removed from the scene. Because of my arrest, I am today still unable to understand fully on what basis the whole procedure against me was carried out, especially since I had right on my side being the decreed successor. Through recent developments and the arrival of some of our own Luftwaffe units, I have just succeeded in regaining my freedom at the place of my arrest, after having previously been removed from Berchtesgaden together with my entourage.

In spite of all the events which occurred during my arrest, I submit to you, your Excellency, the same request, to receive me personally without any obligations on your part and to allow me to talk to you as one soldier to another. I request of you to grant me free passage for this interview and to place my entourage and family under American protection. Although my house there has been completely destroyed there is a sufficient number of rooms in the house of my adjutant's office.

Would you please inform me where we can meet for this interview. If, for reasons of time or technical reasons, it is impossible for your Excellency to receive me in the near future, I would ask you to appoint a plenipotentiary to whom I could convey what I wish to tell you personally. My request may possibly seem very strange to your

Excellency; nevertheless I made it, remembering the time when the aged Marshal of France, Petain, in a situation equally difficult for his country, asked me for a similar interview which then actually took place.

I wish to emphasize again that it would be an interview entailing absolutely no personal obligation on the part of your Excellency. It would be a conversation purely on a human and soldierly level.

I ask you Excellency to let me have your reply through my personal adjutant, Colonel von Brauchitsch, the bearer of this letter. If you agree to my suggestion, please inform the American commander in the Salzburg-Berchtesgaden area of my request to have my household placed under American protection at Berchtesgaden or at another locality within his command. Your Excellency will understand how I feel in this, my most difficult hour, and how much I have suffered through my disability, due to my arrest, to do everything possible a long time ago in order to prevent further bloodshed in a hopeless situation.

With the expression of my soldierly respect, I remain

yours truly
HERMANN GÖRING

Unfortunately for Göring, Eisenhower was not to be swayed. As the American commander wrote after the war:

> ... as far as I was concerned, I was interested only in those who were not yet captured. None of them would be allowed to call on me. I pursued the same practice to the end of the war. Not until Field Marshal [sic, *Generaloberst*] Jodl signed the surrender at Reims in 1945 did I ever speak to a German general, and even then my only words were that he would be held personally and completely responsible for the carrying out of his surrender terms. (Eisenhower, *Crusade in Europe*, pp. 173-174)

POSTWAR PROSECUTION:

07.05.1945 — That evening, Göring sent a note from his location—Schloß Mauterndorf—to the headquarters of the U.S. 7th Army in Kitzbühel. He stated he would surrender at Schloß Fischhorn in the town of Bruck near Zell am See, approximately 100 miles away.

08.05.1945 — According to his sworn testimony of 20.05.1945, Brigadier General Robert I. Stack, Assistant Commander of the 36th (Texas) Division and a platoon of 636th Tank Destroyer Battalion, drove to Schloß Fischhorn, which was still in German hands (held by troops from *8. SS-Kavallerie-Division "Florian Geyer"*). There they were told that the *Reichsmarschall* had not yet arrived. The *Waffen-SS* men were ordered by the Americans to make contact with Göring and learned that his travel was impeded by snow and roadblocks. In an interview conducted many years later, Lieutenant-Colonel Rufus Lester Leggett, Jr. (U.S. Army [Ret.]; 1923–2008), then a sergeant and reconnaissance platoon commander with 636th Tank Destroyer Battalion, recalled:

Göring was not at the castle. General Stack got a hold of Göring's senior aide [*Oberst* Bernd von Brauchitsch] and said, "Can you find him?" Brauchitsch said: "I'm making phone calls. I think I've found him on the road between here and Mauterndorf. He's somewhere on the road trying to get here [to Fischhorn]." Göring was cluttered up on the road someplace.... General Stack—and this is one of the things that gripes me—wrote that he went forward from the castle at about 4 o'clock in the afternoon looking for Göring. I'm going to tell you, Snell and I were the only ones that knew who left and who came into that castle.... General Stack did not leave.... The general [Stack] called 2nd [*sic*, 1st] Lt. [Jerome N.] Shapiro in and asked 1st Lt. Sill to leave the room. Evidently Stack told Shapiro to take his sedan and his driver and let Göring's senior aide go forward in that vehicle to find Göring on the road. And that's what they did. That Plymouth station sedan and one jeep with two of Shapiro's men left with von Brauchitsch. Stack was still in the castle. (David Lesjak, Interview of Lester Leggett, in "Bagging a Bigwig", *World War II Magazine*, January/February 2006, pp. 34-40)

The *Reichsmarschall* was found stranded by the roadside in his Mercedes-Benz near Radstadt, some 30 miles from Schloβ Mauterndorf and 35 miles southeast of Salzburg, together with his wife, daughter, and members of his staff. He was reportedly located and arrested by First Lieutenant Shapiro (1918–1968), a Jewish officer of the Infantry Intelligence and Reconnaissance Platoon (of 142nd Infantry Regiment), attached to the 636th Tank Destroyer Battalion. Göring was then driven back to Fischhorn, arriving at around midnight. Göring was then introduced to the Commanding General of 36th Division, Major General John E. Dahlquist and Brigadier General Stack. Stack and Dahlquist were subsequently accused of fraternizing with Göring and an investigation of the matter was conducted by Lieutenant Colonel Joseph W. Whitaker (assistant inspector general, Seventh Army). Whitaker's report included Stack's statements on the arrest of Göring, including his claim of having personally taken the *Reichsmarschall* into custody, denied by Leggett's statement (above):

Q   In the course of handling such German personnel through this division have you at any time had contact with them upon a basis of familiarity?
A   No.
Q   I understand you made one of the first contacts with Goering.
A   I did....
   On May 8th, before the surrender was accomplished, I went to a castle or estate near Breucht which at that time was occupied by troops of the Waffen SS Florian Geyer. They had not been disarmed, although they knew about the arrangements for surrender. Goering was supposed to come there. I waited about three hours while members of his household staff—staff officers—were trying to get contact with him. They finally said that he was held up due to German roadblocks or physical conditions—snow on the roads—so I took off [sic] with a German Major [Karl-Heinz Sandmann], my aide, Lieutenant Bond, to find him.

We drove about forty-five miles through the German lines. There were German roadblocks, but they lifted them when I arrived. I finally found Goering with his household on a country road a few miles from Radstadt. He and his outfit were stopped there; for what reason, I do not know. I told this German major who was with me that I would accomplish the surrender there. I had an interpreter although this German major spoke some English. Goering got out of his car, and I did. Goering came up to the point in the road where I was standing and salute with the German army salute. I returned his salute. I asked him if he spoke English. He said no but that he understood it fairly well. I told him that his letters had been forwarded and that I would accept his surrender and would take him to Breucht that night. It was then about eight-thirty, I think, in the evening. I told him that he would be sent forward to the Seventh Army Headquarters either that night or the next day and that his family and staff would be put under American guard in the vicinity of Breucht. He agreed cheerfully to these terms. I then told him that we would get started immediately, that I would lead the way, that my aide in a jeep would follow his car, and that the rest of his staff would follow behind that. It took a little time to explain these matters to Goering and to his headquarters commandant, or whatever he was. My driver turned my car around and we started back. There were thousands of German troops in the immediate vicinity, and my personal opinion is that was the reason he was stopped there. I don't know; I didn't ask him.

Q   After you arrived at Breucht what contact did you have with Goering?

A   We drove back to this house near Breucht. We passed through many German roadblocks who gave us no difficulty. We passed through an American or British roadblock at St. Johan who stopped us. I told them who I was, that I had a German convoy behind me and to let the German convoy come through. This roadblock was released prisoners, I believe. By that time it was pretty dark. We arrived at this castle about eleven or twelve o'clock at night. The American lines then were about twenty miles further on.

Q   That is, you were twenty miles behind the American lines, or in front of the American lines?

A   In front of the American lines; in the German lines. This castle was still occupied by troops of the Florian Geyer Division of the German army, but there was a platoon of the reconnaissance company of the 636th Tank Destroyer Battalion there that I had brought with me. I told Goering through an interpreter that he and his staff would spend the night there, that I wanted the arms—the weapons—of all his people delivered to me personally in a room that I would select. There was a photographer there who requested that pictures of Goering be taken at that time. I agreed. The pictures were taken.

Q   Did those pictures show you with Goering?

A   The pictures showed me with Goering but at a distance of two or three feet. There was not then, nor previously, nor later any question of any shaking hands or being friendly with Goering. I went to the room that Lieutenant Shapiro had selected for me and got contact with the division commander whose orders were to bring Goering on to Kitzbuhel. The arms of Goering's household guards were delivered to me in my room. At that time his headquarters commandant said that Goering and he were very much afraid that these SS troops who were in the vicinity might kill Goering that night. I permitted four members of Goering's staff to have pistols that night; those four soldiers slept in front of the room occupied by Goering. The next morning I had the SS German troops in the vicinity disarmed and took up the weapons from these four Luftwaffe soldiers. I had breakfast on the morning of the 9th of May with Lieutenant Shapiro, Lieutenant Bond, and another American officer whose name I cannot remember. Goering was fed by his own people. Two of these SS officers struck me as dangerous so I ordered them to accompany me to Kitzbuhel. About ten o'clock in the morning I took off in my car for Kitzbuhel. Again Goering in his car followed me and my aide, Lieutenant Bond, followed Goering's car. By this time division headquarters was at Kitzbuhel, and I delivered Goering to the division commander at the Grand Hotel in Kitzbuhel, which was the division CP....

Q   What was the necessity of your going personally to contact Goering?
A   At the time it seemed a dangerous mission. There might have been difficulties with American troops, with German troops, or with released Allied prisoners of war. I thought, and presumably the division commander thought, that a general officer could take care of those problems easier than a junior officer.

   Goering's surrender to me was accomplished before the fighting was over with, fifty miles at least inside the German lines and I treated him as a German general. There was certainly no question of friendship or familiarity. On the other hand, I did not treat him as a criminal because it would not be very tactful. He had thousands of soldiers there, and I wanted to get him back to the American lines as quickly as I could. That was all I was interested in. (NARA, "Fraternization by General Officers of 36th Division", report by Lt. Col. Joseph Whitaker, IGD, Investigating Officer, Kaufbeuren, Germany, dated 20.05.1945)

According to then-Sergeant Lester Leggett, who was on guard duty at the gate of Schloß Fischhorn:

At about 11:30 [p.m.] we saw all these vehicles with lights on approaching. There were about 13 followed by the Plymouth. The first vehicle was one of our jeeps. The second was Göring's Mercedes 770 150-W, better known as the 7.7-liter Mercedes. He had his driver, his wife, his daughter, a nurse and an officer with him.... Sill later wrote to me that he and the general [Stack] walked out of the castle and into the clearing and that was the first time the general had laid eyes on Göring. That is not what Stack wrote later. That's the way that Göring surrendered. (David Lesjak, Interview of Lester Leggett, in "Bagging a Bigwig", *World War II Magazine*, January/February 2006, pp. 34-40)

The following is from Lt. Col. Whitaker's interview with Major General Dahlquist, who was accused of shaking hands with Göring:

Q   Have you at any time with any such personnel [high-ranking German officers] treated them in other than an official manner?

A   No, I have not.
Q   Have you at any time with any such personnel had dinner with them or drinks with them?
A   I had lunch with Marshal Goering. He arrived at my command post at 1230. I fed him lunch in my room and then dispatched him to Seventh Army Headquarters.
Q   Who else was present at that lunch.
A   General Hess and General Stack. (David Lesjak, Interview of Lester Leggett, in "Bagging a Bigwig", *World War II Magazine*, January/February 2006, pp. 34-40)

The favorable treatment given to Göring led General Eisenhower to issue official reprimands to Dahlquist and Stack, and to make the following remarks:

My attention has been called to press reports of instances of senior United States officers treating captured Nazi and high German officials on a "friendly enemy" basis. Any such incident has been in direct violation of my express and long-standing orders.

Drastic measures have been set in motion to assure termination of these errors forthwith.

Moreover, any past instances of this nature are by no means indicative of the attitude of this army, but are results of faulty judgment of individuals concerned, who will be personally acquainted with expressions of my definite disapproval.

In the name of this great force and on my own, I regret these occurrences. ("Ike Attacks Friendliness to Prisoners" in *The Austin American*, 15.05.1945)

It is regrettable that Jerome Shapiro's important role in the capture of Göring is neglected in many accounts. However, in January 2006, and thanks to the efforts of his daughter, he was honored during a session of the United States Senate. Senator Carl Levin, Democrat from Michigan, spoke as follows:

Mr. President, this week, as we observe Holocaust Remembrance Day, Yom Hashoah, I would like to take a moment to recognize Stephanie Mellen of Troy, MI, for her tireless and enduring efforts to honor the memory of her father and help ensure that the horrific events of the Holocaust will never be forgotten. On May 7, 1945, Ms. Mellen's father, 1Lt Jerome N. Shapiro, led the team that captured Air Marshal Hermann Goering, the de facto leader of Nazi Germany following Adolf Hitler's suicide. Eighty miles behind enemy lines in Austria, Lieutenant Shapiro and three others caught Goering and his entourage of 78 people. Goering calmly surrendered his weapon to Lieutenant Shapiro, a Jewish American, and was held under Lieutenant Shapiro's command at Fischhorn Castle in Zell Am See, Austria, until he was transferred to Allied headquarters 2 days later. Hermann Goering was the principal defendant at the Nuremberg Trials the following year, and Lieutenant Shapiro continued as part of his guard detail during the trial.

Lieutenant Shapiro was hesitant to talk about his role in Goering's capture, but Stephanie Mellen began to understand the importance of his story even as a young girl. She saw the gun that her father was carrying when Goering surrendered and recalls using Goering's field typewriter to type her school assignments. Stephanie was 13 years old when she saw her father named as "Goering's guard" in a television documentary. These memories helped her to understand and appreciate what her father accomplished.

Lieutenant Shapiro passed away on April 4, 1968, but his legacy lives on through the committed actions of his daughter. Stephanie Mellen has spent countless hours writing and speaking to educate people on the importance of what her father did to bring Hermann Goering to justice. She shares her father's story to honor the courage and resolve of Lieutenant Shapiro and all those members of America's "greatest generation"' who fought and defeated the Axis Powers in one of humanity's most critical moments. But most of all, she shares the story of her father to remind all of us that the cause of universal human freedom and dignity is our own. ("Honoring Army Lieutenant Jerome N. Shapiro" in Congressional Record [Bound Edition], Volume 152 [2006], Part 5, pp. 6074-6075)

Shapiro, a graduate of the City College in New York, died of a heart attack in Dover Delaware on 05.04.1968. He had spent the postwar years as operator of a number of retail merchandise shops and as a state social service worker.

09.05.1945	At approximately 10:00 a.m. that morning, driven to the U.S. 7th Army Headquarters in the Grand Hotel at Kitzbühel where he met with General Carl F. Spaatz, Commander of U.S. Strategic Air Forces in Europe, and was treated to a party by his captors. Upon hearing of this affair, General Eisenhower ordered that Göring was to be treated as an ordinary prisoner of war.
10.05.1945	Flown from Kitzbühel to Augsburg in a Piper L5 piloted by Captain Mayhew "Bo" Foster, arriving at 5:00 p.m. Upon initial processing, he was forced to give up the awards he was wearing (*Pour le Mérite*, Knight's and Grand Crosses of the Iron Cross, 1914 Iron Cross First Class and 1939 Clasp, and his Combined Pilots and Observers Badge with Diamonds) as well as his Smith & Wesson Police Model K .38 caliber revolver, *Reichsmarschall*'s baton, and a hunting dagger given to him by his brother-in-law, Erik von Rosen.
10.05.1945–20.05.1945	Held at the 7th Army Interrogation Center (SAIC) in Augsburg. Shortly after his arrival, he was interrogated on the subject of *Luftwaffe* strategy and organization by General Spaatz, Lieutenant General Hoyt Vandenburg (Commander, 9th Air Force), Lieutenant General Alexander M. Patch (Commanding General, U.S. 7th Army), Brigadier General Edward P. Curtis (Chief of Staff, U.S. Strategic Air Forces [USSTAF] in Europe), Bruce Hopper (USSTAF historian), and the Russian-American aviation pioneer and Special Consultant to the Secretary of War Major Alexander P. de Seversky. Among his most noteworthy statements during this two-hour interview (5:00 p.m. to 7:00 p.m.) were the following:

In the early years when I had supreme command of the Luftwaffe, I had definite plans, but in 1940 Hitler began to interfere, taking air fleets away from our planned operations. That was the beginning of the breakdown of the Luftwaffe efficiency....

[In response to Spaatz's question "When did you know that the Luftwaffe as losing control in the air?"] When the American long-range fighters were able to escort the bombers as far as Hannover, and it was not long until they got to Berlin. We then knew we must develop the jet planes. Our plan for the early development of the jet was unsuccessful only because of your bombing attacks....

[Spaatz: "When you conquered France in 1940, why didn't you go on through to Spain and Gibraltar?"] Germany had saved Spain from the Bolsheviks. Spain was in the German camp. I insisted on going to Spain but to no avail. We could have battled the British Fleet in the Mediterranean, but no—the Fuehrer wanted to go to Russia. My idea was to close both ends of the Mediterranean ... I am positive we could have taken Gibraltar. The Luftwaffe was ready and we had two divisions of parachutists ready and trained, but Mussolini objected. Part of our pain—the Italians....

My intention at first was to attack only military targets and factories, but after the British attacked Hamburg [July/August 1943] the people were angry and I was ordered to attack indiscriminately....

[T]he Russians are no good [in the air], except on undefended targets. You need only three or four Luftwaffe airplanes to drive off a twenty-plane Russian attack. The Americans are superior technically and in production. As for the personnel, the English, German and American are equal as fighters in the air....

You might find around Germany some jet airplanes equipped with anti-tank guns. Don't blame me for such monstrosities. This was done on the explicit orders of the Fuehrer. Hitler knew nothing about the air. He may have known something about the Army or Navy, but absolutely nothing about the air. He even considered the ME 262 to be a bomber; and he insisted it should be called a bomber....

I always believed in strategic use of air power. I built the Luftwaffe as the finest bomber fleet, only to see it wasted on Stalingrad. My beautiful bomber fleet was used up for transporting munitions and supplies to the army of 200,000 at Stalingrad. I always was against the Russian campaign. (Top Secret report on the interrogation of Göring, Donovan Nuremberg Trials Collection, at the Cornell University Law Library)

In a report dated 24.05.1945, the commander of SAIC, Major Paul Kubala, provided the following statements—fraught with half-truths, omissions, and outright lies—made by Göring during his brief time there:

IV. CONCENTRATION CAMPS

These pictures (of Dachau) which you showed me yesterday must depict the activities of the last few days. It is beyond me, just what was behind all that. Himmler must have suddenly gotten a fiendish pleasure out of such things. I have heard such stories before, for example that a large load of Jews left for Poland during the winter, where some of the people froze to death in their vehicles. I heard of these things mostly from the ranks of my employees and from the people. When I made inquiries, I was told that such things would not happen again—it was claimed that the trains had been sent on the wrong route. Then there was some talk about what you call "VERNICHTUNGSTRUPPEN" (Extermination troops). It was claimed that there were many diseased people in these camps and that many died of pestilence. These troops had the job of bringing the corpses to a crematorium where they would be burned....

All cruelty was repulsive to me. I can name may people whom I have helped, even Communists and Jews. My wife was so kind—I really have to be grateful for that. I often thought, if only the *Fuehrer* would have had a sensible wife who would have said to him: "Here is a case where you can do some good, and here another, and this one...." that would have been better for everyone.... It was very depressing for me. In some cases I had to write to Himmler, that he should release this one and that one. And he would reply, that he was very sorry, but that he could not do it, or perhaps that he didn't want to do it. But there were quite a few cases, where he did it anyhow.... But now it is pretty clear to me that all my efforts were wasted. Whoever attacked Himmler, was eliminated. On top of that, he lied to me. Not a single report was read to the Fuehrer....

I wanted the foreign workers to be rounded up so that they could be turned over to the advancing enemy troops at some central point instead of being allowed to run around loose. And then I told him (Hitler) that the concentration camps should be guarded if at all possible, until the British and Americans arrived, because we were detaining quite a number of criminals there which neither we nor they would want to release. You surely can't be interested in freeing a lot of criminals. And the same thing goes for workers from foreign territories—that was my biggest worry. I told him that something would have to be done about them, as well as about prisoners of war. We also mentioned Russian prisoners of war—but there we knew what would happen if they broke loose. The French were very decent.... They were mainly employed as farmhands....

These Nuremberg laws came as a great surprise to me [see entry of 10.09.1935–16.09.1935, above, in which he personally announced the laws during the *"7. Reichsparteitag der NSDAP"* in Nürnberg/MdM]. I am still wondering today, where they could have originated. I knew only too well that they would cause bad feelings abroad.... I was in charge of the Four-Year Plan. At that time Schacht came to see me and said: "Sir, these incidents will cause us serious economic difficulties abroad." So I went there, and they showed me the laws, saying that they had not been approved yet. Some of the clauses were being changed, but there were no major changes. And from then on the Jew-baiting really started. The United States responded with a most disagreeable boycott. And I was given a lecture, that from now on it would be very difficult to maintain any kind of commercial relation with America. But all this was temporarily forgotten in the excitement over the Sudeten incident in Sep 38. The war started in '39. For the time being, all was well. Then, early in '40 they went to it again—paying particular attention to the Jews in the occupied countries. I have to admit that things kept getting worse, and that they were sanctioned by various groups. All sorts of impossible excesses occurred. I didn't approve of them, but unfortunately I couldn't do anything against them. I didn't have too good a name with the party myself. The first time when they really attacked me was in '38. They didn't say anything about the wedding, but when I had my child christened in the first year of my marriage [sic, he was married in 1935 and his daughter was born in 1938/MdM], I was attacked vehemently. It was claimed by the party, that the christening of my child would put the Fuehrer into a terrible dilemma if it ever became known. They wanted me to name my child without a religious ceremony. That may all be well and good, except that the Fuehrer had been put up to this—particularly by the Minister of the Interior and Goebbels. Then Lutze, chief of the SA, started to reproach me, saying that such a step against the Nazi Party was intolerable. And from then on there was no end of trouble—someone would always point out this incident. Later on we had some serious arguments. It was intended to merge the two religions.... Next we had these terrible days in Tirol—there were some uprisings when these silly Hitler Youth boys started trouble in a church [Hanns] Kerrl, who is a smart man, said: "I am a catholic myself, I do not want to have anything to do with that." [Adolf] Wagner of Munich had the same attitude. The whole thing was just plain madness. (Central Intelligence Agency Information Report, "Miscellaneous 1945 Seventh Army Reports on Germany," 22.09.1950)

In his report of 19.05.1945, Kubala wrote the following summary of Göring:

Source is by no means the comical figure he has been depicted so many times in newspaper reports. He is neither stupid nor a fool in the Shakespearian sense, but generally cool and calculating. He is able to grasp the fundamental issues under discussion immediately. He is certainly not a man to be underrated. Although he tried to soft-pedal many of the most outrageous crimes committed by Germany, he said enough to show that he isas much responsible for the policies within Germany and for the war itself, as anyone in Germany. Goering took great pride in claiming that it was he who was responsible for the planning and successful execution of the paratroop landing in Crete, that it was he who had drawn up the plans for a capture of Gibraltar, a plan which was never carried out because Hitler was opposed to it at the last minute, that it was he who was responsible for the development of the Luftwaffe. On the other hand, he denied having had anything to do with the racial laws and with the concentration camps, with the SS and the atrocities committed both in Germany and outside. Goering is at all times an actor who does not disappoint his audience. His vanity extends into the field of the pathological, as is exemplified by the pearl-grey uniform, the heavy, solid gold epaulettes and an enormous diamond ring on his right hand, even though his medals were limited to two, including the Grand Cross of the Knight's Cross with Swords and Diamonds [sic]. Just as much a part of Goering are two of his aides, Obst (Col) von Brauchitsch, son of the Field

Marshal, and Hptm (Capt) Klaas. Goering was only too pleased to be able to discuss the history of the past 12 years, and he gave all information more than willingly to a group of interrogators. ("Interrogation Records Prepared for War Crimes Proceedings at Nuernberg, 1945–1947/OCCPAC Interrogation Transcripts and Related Records: Göring, Hermann"; Publication Number M1270, Record Group RG238)

In a report of 23.05.1945, Kubala continued:

The cause for which Goering stood is lost—but the canny Hermann, even now, thinks only of what he can do to salvage some of his personal fortune, and to create an advantageous position for himself. He condemns the once beloved Fuehrer without hesitation. Up to now he has not made a plea in favor of any of his former henchmen, alive or dead. Yet, behind his spirited and often witty conversation, is a constant watchfulness for the opportunity to place himself in a favorable light. ("Interrogation Records Prepared for War Crimes Proceedings at Nuernberg, 1945–1947/OCCPAC Interrogation Transcripts and Related Records: Göring, Hermann"; Publication Number M1270, Record Group RG238)

20.05.1945–00.09.1945 Held at the Central Continental Prisoner of War Enclosure No. 32 (CCPWE No. 32)—known as "Ashcan"—located in the Palace Hotel in Mondorf-les-Bains, Luxembourg. The facility was commanded by Colonel Burton C. Andrus, a U.S. Army cavalry officer who went on to command Nuremberg Prison during the trials of Göring and other senior defendants. First Lieutenant (later Captain) John E. Dolibois, the Luxembourg-born future U.S. Ambassador to Luxembourg, served as an interrogator at "Ashcan" under the pseudonym "John Gillen". By a show of sympathy toward the prisoners, playing "good cop/bad cop" in collaboration with other interrogators, he succeeded in manipulating them to confide valuable information to him. Göring held him in such high esteem that he presented the American officer with one of his *Reichsmarschall* epaulets (*Schulterklappen*) and a personally inscribed portrait of himself. Dolibois writes of Göring's stay at Ashcan:

Reichsmarschall Hermann Goering brought not only eleven suitcases but also his valet [Robert Kropp] to the CCPWE number 32. Captain Sensenig said it took a whole afternoon to list his valuables and search his luggage. It took an equally long time to pacify him. His hand shook so he could barely sign his name. The shaking was from his addiction to narcotics. On his person and in his luggage were found large quantities of small white pills which were identified as paracodin, the chemical name for which is Dihydrocodeine. Goering was in the habit of taking twenty in the morning and twenty in the evening. The German doctor among the labor PW, Dr. Ludwig Pfluecker, started at once in getting Goering to cut down on his intake. As I got to know Goering better, I found it interesting that he took great pride in cooperating in this endeavor. Later on, our own American doctor, Captain William J. Miller, took charge of the program. The prisoner of war rations and the routine the doctors prescribed resulted in Goering's losing considerable weight and becoming healthier than he had been for some time. It was the one development about which the former Reichsmarschall did not complain. His vanity was being aroused... (Dolibois, *Pattern of Circles*, p. 88)

Goering considered himself the number one personage at the detention center, so he attempted to be the chief spokesman, with or without their consent. He fancied himself the captain of the team. He tried to organize a joint defense, to be the aggressive cheerleader. But feelings were bitter. Judgment was passed by one on the other. Thus Goering was, after all, alone, sitting by himself during mealtimes or reading in his favorite cane chair on the Palace Hotel veranda. (Dolibois, *Pattern of Circles*, p. 93)

Everybody who came to Ashcan wanted to interview Goering. Sometimes he would be very cooperative and turn on all his charm. On other occasions he would balk, pouting, protesting at being at everyone's beck and call. Then it would be necessary to stroke his ego. "No wonder, Herr Goering, after all, you are the highest ranking of all officials in this prison. You are the official spokesman for the Third Reich, the most knowledgeable...." He would eat it up; his chest swelling. Thoughtfully, he would nod in agreement. But I also sensed he was chuckling to himself. I don't think we fooled him one bit. (Dolibois, *Pattern of Circles*, p. 103)

00.09.1945	Sent to Nürnberg Prison to stand trial as lead defendant before the International Military Tribunal (IMT).
20.11.1945–01.10.1946	Tried by the IMT in Nürnberg, with Dr. Otto Stahmer as defense counsel. He was charged with all four counts of the IMT indictment: Count 1, Conspiracy to Commit Crimes Alleged in Other Counts; Count 2, Crimes Against Peace; Count 3, War Crimes; and Count 4, Crimes Against Humanity. Early in the trial, he said to the prison psychologist, Gustave M. Gilbert:

As far as the trial is concerned, it's just a cut-and-dried political affair, and I'm prepared for the consequences. I have no doubt that the press will play a bigger part in the decision than the judges. And I'm sure that the Russian and French judges, at least, already have their instructions. I can answer for anything I've done, and can't answer for anything I haven't done. But the victors are the judges ... I know what's in store for me. I'm even writing my farewell letter to my wife today... (Gilbert, *Nuremberg Diary*, p. 13, entry of 11.11.1945)

His codefendant, former Vice Chancellor and Reich Commissioner for Prussia Franz von Papen, writes of Göring's performance during the trial:

He was probably the outstanding personality of the whole trial. Hitler, the principal actor, had committed suicide. So had his main supporters, Goebbels and Himmler. Those who now appeared to answer for their actions were, with the exception of Goering, not of the first rank. He completely outclassed these dei minores, and was the only one who had the courage to defend what he had done and what he had tried to do. "Not a word against Hitler," he said to us on one occasion when the guards' attention was elsewhere. He seemed to think that loyalty to the regime should continue even within the walls of a prison; or it may have been pride which prevented him from admitting to the enemy what his own intelligence had probably grasped in the meanwhile. At least it was to his credit that he was the one man who really tried to defend his beliefs.

In the conversations I had with Goering during the period between the end of the trial and the pronouncement of the sentences, I found him the same uninhibited and jovial character I had always known. Completely unconcerned at his certain fate, he often discussed with Neurath, Keitel and myself certain phases of the past. At one period l had tried to find out why this "crown prince" of the Third Reich had not intervened when he saw that Hitler's policies must lead to war and the collapse of Germany. Now I tried again, but on this point it was still not possible to pin him down. "I have accepted full responsibility for everything that happened," he answered. "I could not prevent the war, even though I regarded it as a great mistake. You or Neurath could probably have made peace, but Ribbentrop was incapable. All he did was to blabber what he thought was in Hitler's mind." He told me that in the latter years of the war he felt that Hitler was probably insane, but he was unable to do anything about it. As a person, Goering had many virtues. He was a man of open, masculine nature, with great personal charm. This he retained to the end. (Von Papen, *Memoirs*, pp. 554-555)

31.08.1946 Delivered his final statement to the Tribunal:

The Prosecution, in the final speeches, has treated the defendants and their testimony as completely worthless. The statements made under oath by the defendants were accepted as absolutely true when they could serve to support the Indictment, but conversely the statements were characterized as perjury when they refuted the Indictment. That is very elementary, but it is not a convincing basis for demonstration of proof.

The Prosecution uses the fact that I was the second man of the State as proof that I must have known everything that happened. But it does not present any documentary or other convincing proof in cases where I have denied under oath that I knew about certain things, much less desired them. Therefore, it is only an allegation and a conjecture when the Prosecution says, "Who should have known that if not Göring, who was the successor of the Führer?"

Repeatedly we have heard here how the worst crimes were veiled with the most secrecy. I wish to state expressly that I condemn these terrible mass murders to the utmost, and cannot understand them in the least. But I should like to state clearly once more before the High Tribunal, that I have never decreed the murder of a single individual at any time, and neither did I decree any other atrocities or tolerate them, while I had the power and the knowledge to prevent them.

The new allegation presented by Mr. Dodd in his final speech, that I had ordered Heydrich to kill the Jews, lacks every proof and is not true either. There is not a single order signed by me or signed in my behalf that enemy fliers should be shot or turned over to the SD. And not a single case has been established where units of my Luftwaffe carried out things like that.

The Prosecution has repeatedly submitted some documents which contain alleged statements, reported and written down at third and fourth hand, without my having previously seen these statements in order to correct erroneous ideas or to preclude misunderstandings.

How easily completely distorted reports can arise from third hand notes is also proven, among other things, by the stenographic transcript of these court sessions, which often needed correction when checked.

The Prosecution brings forward individual statements over a period of 25 years, which were made under completely different circumstances and without any consequences arising from them at the time, and quotes them as proof of intent and guilt, statements which can easily be made in the excitement of the moment and of the atmosphere that prevailed at the time. There is probably not one leading personage on the opposing side who did not speak or write similarly in the course of a quarter of a century.

Out of all the happenings of these 25 years, from conferences, speeches, laws, actions, and decisions, the Prosecution proves that everything was desired and intended from the beginning according to a deliberate sequence and an unbroken connection. This is an erroneous conception which is entirely devoid of logic, and which will be rectified someday by history, after the proceedings here have proved the incorrectness of these allegations.

Mr. Jackson in his final speech points, out the fact that the signatory states are still in a state of war with Germany, and that because of the unconditional surrender merely a state of truce prevails now. Now, international law is uniform. The same must apply to both sides. Therefore, if everything which is being done in Germany today on the part of the occupying powers is admissible under international law, then German was formerly in the same position, at least as regards France, Holland, Belgium, Norway, Yugoslavia and Greece. If today the Geneva Convention no longer has any validity so far as Germans are concerned, if today in all parts of Germany industry is being dismantled and other great assets in all spheres can be carried away to the other states, if today the property of millions of Germans is being confiscated and many other serious infringements on freedom and property are taking place, then measures such as those taken by Germany in the countries mentioned above cannot have been criminal according to international law either.

Mr. Jackson stated further that one cannot accuse and punish a state, but rather that one must hold the leaders responsible. One seems to forget that Germany was a sovereign state, and that her legislation within the German nation was not subject to the jurisdiction of foreign countries. No state ever gave notice to the Reich at the proper time, pointing out that any activity for National Socialism would be made subject to punishment and persecution. On the other hand, if we, the leaders as individuals, are called to account and condemned—very well; but you cannot punish the German people at the same time. The German people placed their trust in the Fuehrer, and under his authoritarian government they had no influence on events. Without knowledge of the grave crimes which have become known today, the people, loyal, self-sacrificing, and courageous, fought and suffered through the life-and-death struggle which had broken out against their will. The German people are free of guilt.

I did not want a war, nor did I bring it about. I did everything to prevent it by negotiations. After it had broken out, I did everything to assure victory. Since the three greatest powers on earth, together with many other nations, were fighting against us, we finally succumbed to their tremendous superiority.

I stand up for the things that I have done, but I deny most emphatically that my actions were dictated by the desire to subjugate foreign peoples by wars, to murder them, to rob them, or to enslave them, or to commit atrocities or crimes.

The only motive which guided me was my ardent love for my people, its happiness, its freedom, and its life. And for this I call on the Almighty and my German people to witness. (*Trial of the Major War Criminals Before the International Military Tribunal Nuremberg, 14 November 1945 to 1 October 1946, Volume XXII*)

01.10.1946

Sentenced to death by hanging. In a postwar communication with the author Ben E. Swearingen, Colonel Bud Jones, who had been present as a second lieutenant and marshal of the court when Göring was sentenced, stated:

Goering was the first defendant to emerge from the elevator, followed by two guards. I handed him the headset so that he might hear his sentence. The judge started to read the sentence. Goering said nothing but raised both hands in a gesture of despair. At first, I did not know what was wrong, but then Goering put his hands to the headset and shook his head. It was obvious that he could hear nothing. I took the headset from him and put it to my ear. There was no sound. When I attempted to adjust the control knob, I succeeded only in breaking the wire. The judge had stopped reading the sentence and was waiting. I spotted Captain Valentine, the court communications officer, sitting near the dock. All it took was a look from me, and Captain Valentine vaulted over the dock and quickly replaced the headset. There was no further problem, and Goering reacted well to the minor mishap. He stood motionless with a calm expression on his face. (Swearingen, *The Mystery of Hermann Goering's Suicide*, p. 221)

The American prison psychologist G. M. Gilbert writes of Göring's reaction to the sentence:

Goering came down first and strode into his cell, his face pale and frozen, his eyes popping. "Death!" he said as he dropped on the cot and reached for a book. His hands were trembling in spite of his attempt to be nonchalant. His eyes were moist and he was panting, fighting back an emotional breakdown. He asked me in an unsteady voice to leave him alone for a while. (Gilbert, *Nuremberg Diary*, p. 431)

Indignant at the prospect of the gallows, Göring sent the following statement, dated 11.10.1946, to the Allied Control Council:

I would have allowed myself to be executed by a firing squad. But the German Reichsmarschall should not die on the gallows. I simply cannot allow that for the sake of Germany. Furthermore, I have no moral obligation to submit myself to the punishment fixed by my enemies. Therefore I choose the manner of death of the great Hannibal.

I was aware from the beginning that I would be sentenced to death, because I viewed the entire trial as a political stunt of the victors. I was willing to endure the trial for the sake of my people, and I expected that I would be granted the right to die like a soldier. Before God, my people and my conscience, I consider myself not guilty of the crimes of which an enemy court has convicted me.

Hermann Göring
(John Dolibois, *Pattern of Circles*, p. 208)

The question of how he was able to conceal the cyanide capsule with which he took his own life has never been conclusively answered. It is possible he received it from a U.S. Army lieutenant, Jack G. ("Tex") Wheelis (1913–1954), whom he had befriended at Nürnberg.

The following is the full text of the tribunal's judgment:

Göring is indicted on all four counts. The evidence shows that after Hitler he was the most prominent man in the Nazi Régime. He was Commander-in-Chief of the Luftwaffe, Plenipotentiary for the Four-Year Plan, and had tremendous influence with Hitler, at least until 1943 when their relationship deteriorated, ending in his arrest in 1945. He testified that Hitler kept him informed of all important military and political problems.
Crimes against Peace
From the moment he joined the Party in 1922 and took command of the street-fighting organisation, the SA, Göring was the advisor, the active agent of Hitler and one of the prime leaders of the Nazi movement. As Hitler's political deputy he was largely instrumental in bringing the National Socialists to power in 1933, and was charged with consolidating this power and expanding German armed might. He developed the Gestapo, and created the first concentration camps, relinquishing them to Himmler in 1934, conducted the Röhm purge in that year, and engineered the sordid proceedings which resulted in the removal of von Blomberg and von Fritsch from the Army. In 1936 he became Plenipotentiary for the Four-Year Plan, and in theory and in practice was the economic dictator of the Reich. Shortly after the Pact of Munich,

he announced that he would embark on a five-fold expansion of the Luftwaffe, and speed rearmament with emphasis on offensive weapons.

Göring was one of the five important leaders present at the Hossbach Conference of 5th November, 1937, and he attended the other Important conferences already discussed in this Judgment. In the Austrian Anschluss, he was indeed the central figure, the ringleader. He said in Court: "I must take 100 per cent responsibility. I even overruled objections by the Führer and brought everything to its final development." In the seizure of the Sudetenland he played his role as Luftwaffe chief by planning an air offensive which proved unnecessary and his role as a politician by lulling the Czechs with false promises of friendship. The night before the invasion of Czechoslovakia and the absorption of Bohemia and Moravia, at a conference with Hitler and President Hacha he threatened to bomb Prague if Hacha did not submit. This threat he admitted in his testimony.

Göring attended the Reich Chancellery meeting of 23rd May, 1939, when Hitler told his military leaders "there is, therefore, no question of sparing Poland," and was present at the Obersalzburg briefing of 22nd August, 1939. And the evidence shows he was active in the diplomatic maneuvers which followed. With Hitler's connivance, he used the Swedish businessman, Dahlerus, as a go-between to the British, as described by Dahlerus to this Tribunal, to try to prevent the British Government from keeping its guarantee to the Poles.

He commanded the Luftwaffe in the attack on Poland and throughout the aggressive wars which followed. Even if he opposed Hitler's plans against Norway and the Soviet Union, as he alleged, it is clear that he did so only for strategic reasons once Hitler had decided the issue, he followed him without hesitation. He made it clear in his testimony that these differences were never ideological or legal. He was "in a rage" about the invasion of Norway, but only because he had not received sufficient warning to prepare the Luftwaffe offensive. He admitted he approved of the attack: "My attitude was perfectly positive." He was active in preparing and executing the Yugoslavian and Greek campaigns, and testified that "Plan Marita," the attack on Greece had been prepared long beforehand. The Soviet Union he regarded as the "most threatening menace to Germany," but said there was no immediate military necessity for the attack. Indeed, his only objection to the war of aggression against the U.S.S.R. was its timing; he wished for strategic reasons to delay until Britain was conquered. He testified: "My point of view was decided by political and military reasons only."

After his own admissions to this Tribunal, from the positions which he held, the conferences he attended, and the public words he uttered, there can remain no doubt that Göring was the moving force for aggressive war second only to Hitler. He was the planner and prime mover in the military and diplomatic preparation for war which Germany pursued.

War Crimes and Crimes against Humanity

The record is filled with Göring's admissions of his complicity in the use of slave labor. "We did use this labor for security reasons so that they would not be active in their own country and would not work against us. On the other hand, they served to help in the economic war." And again: "Workers were forced to come to the Reich. That is something I have not denied." The man who spoke these words was Plenipotentiary for the Four-Year Plan charged with the recruitment and allocation of manpower. As Luftwaffe Commander-in-Chief he demanded from Himmler more slave laborers for his underground aircraft factories: "That I requested inmates of concentration camps for the armament of the Luftwaffe is correct and it is to be taken as a matter of course."

As Plenipotentiary, Göring signed a directive concerning the treatment of Polish workers in Germany and implemented it by regulations of the SD including "special treatment." He issued directives to use Soviet and French prisoners of war in the armament industry; he spoke of seizing Poles and Dutch and making them prisoners of war if necessary, and using work. He agrees Russian prisoners of war were used to man anti-aircraft batteries.

As Plenipotentiary, Göring was the active authority in the spoliation of conquered territory. He made plans for the spoliation of Soviet territory long before the war on the Soviet Union. Two months prior to the invasion of the Soviet Union, Hitler gave Göring the over-all direction for the economic administration in the territory. Göring set up an economic staff for this function. As Reichsmarschall of the Greater German Reich, "the orders of the Reichsmarschall cover all economic fields, including nutrition and agriculture." His so-called "Green" folder, printed by the Wehrmacht, set up an "Economic Executive Staff, East." This directive contemplated plundering and abandonment of all industry in the food deficit regions and, from the food surplus regions, a diversion of food to German needs. Göring claims its purposes have been misunderstood but admits "that as a matter of course and a matter of duty we would have used Russia for our purposes," when conquered.

And he participated in the conference of 16th July, 1941, when Hitler said the National Socialists had no intention of ever leaving the occupied countries, and that "all necessary measures—shooting, desettling, etc." should be taken.

Göring persecuted the Jews, particularly after the November, 1938 riots, and not only in Germany where he raised the billion mark fine as stated elsewhere, but in the conquered territories as well. His own utterances then and his testimony now show this interest was primarily economic—how to get their property and how to force them out of the economic life of Europe. As these countries fell before the German army, he extended the Reich's anti-Jewish laws to them; the Reichsgesetzblatt for 1939, 1940, and 1941 contains several anti-Jewish decrees signed by Göring. Although their extermination was in Himmler's hands, Göring was far from disinterested or inactive, despite his protestations in the witness box. By decree of 31st July, 1941, he directed Himmler and Heydrich to bring "about a complete solution of the Jewish question in the German sphere of influence in Europe."

There is nothing to be said in mitigation. For Göring was often, indeed almost always, the moving force, second only to his leader. He was the leading war aggressor, both as political and as military leader; he was the director of the slave labor program and the creator of the oppressive

program against the Jews and other races, at home and abroad. All of these crimes he has frankly admitted. On some specific cases there may be conflict of testimony, but in terms of the broad outline, his own admissions are more than sufficiently wide to be conclusive of his guilt. His guilt is unique in its enormity. The record discloses no excuses for this man.
Conclusion
The Tribunal finds the defendant Göring guilty on all four counts of the Indictment.
(Judgment of the International Military Tribunal for the Trial of German Major War Criminals)

PUBLISHED WORKS:
Aufbau einer Nation (1934). The following are noteworthy excerpts:

> [Pages 86-87] I declared at that time before thousands of fellow Germans, each bullet which leaves the barrel of a police pistol now, is my bullet. If one calls this murder, then I have murdered; I ordered all this, I back it up; I assume the responsibility, and I am not afraid to do so. Through a network of outer offices converging into the headquarters in Berlin, I am daily, one could almost say hourly, informed about everything that happens in widespread Prussia.
>
> [Page 891] Against the enemies of the State, we must proceed ruthlessly. It cannot be forgotten that at the moment of our rise to power, according to the official election figures of March 1933, six million people still confess their sympathy for Communism and eight million for Marxism....
>
> Therefore, the concentration camps have been created, where we have first confined thousands of Communists and Social Democrat functionaries.
>
> [Page 921] The Gestapo deserves a great deal of credit for the success of the revolution and for the consolidation of its achievements. Right in the middle of this constructive work occurred the blaze that destroyed the high cupola and the auditorium of the Reichstag. Criminal hands had set this fire, had put the German Reichstag in flames, in order to give a last beacon to dying Communism, so that it could make one last desperate thrust before the Hitler government was consolidated. The blaze was to be the signal for the Communist party for general terror, for a general uprising and for civil war. That it did not have these consequences, Germany and the world owe not to the noble motives of Communism, but solely to the iron resolution and the hard fist of Adolf Hitler and his closest collaborators, who struck more quickly than the enemy had expected, and harder than he could imagine, and with the first blow suppressed Communism once and for all. That night, when I ordered the arrest of 4,000 Communist functionaries, I knew that by dawn Communism had lost a great battle. (Partial Translation of Document 2324-PS, in *Nazi Conspiracy and Aggression. Volume III*)

Der Geist des neuen Staates (1934)
Reden und Aufsätze (1938, edited by Erich Gritzbach)

DECORATIONS & AWARDS:

<u>German</u>

19.07.1940	*Großkreuz des Eisernes Kreuzes.* Awarded to recognize the *Luftwaffe*'s achievements in the Western Campaign of May–June 1940. He was the first and only Third Reich recipient of this award.
30.09.1939	*Ritterkreuz des Eisernes Kreuzes* (for his command of the *Luftwaffe* in the Polish Campaign)
02.06.1918	*Orden Pour le Mérite* as *Oberleutnant* and *Führer* of *Jagdstaffel 27*, Western Front.
20.10.1917	*Ritterkreuz mit Schwertern des königlich Preußischen Hausordens von Hohenzollern* as *Oberleutnant* and *Führer* of *Jagdstaffel 27*
02.06.1918	*Ritterkreuz des Großherzoglich Badischen Militär Karl-Friedrich-Verdienstordens* as *Oberleutnant* and *Führer* of *Jagdstaffel 27*
15.04.1916	*Ehrenbecher für den Sieger im Luftkampf.* Awarded for his second aerial victory, a Maurice Farman MF.11 Shorthorn reconnaissance and light bomber of the French *Armée de l'Air*, shot down over Tahure on 16.11.1915.
18.07.1915	*Orden vom Großherzoglich Badischen Ordens vom Zähringer Löwen, Ritterkreuz II. Klasse mit Schwertern*
00.09.1939	*1939 Spange zum 1914 Eisernes Kreuz I. Klasse*
00.09.1939	*1939 Spange zum 1914 Eisernes Kreuz II. Klasse*
22.03.1915	*1914 Eisernes Kreuz I. Klasse* as *Leutnant* and *Flugzeugbeobachter* in *Feldflieger-Abteilung 25*.
15.09.1914	*1914 Eisernes Kreuz II. Klasse* as *Leutnant* and *Bataillonsadjutant* of *II. Bataillon/4. Badische Infanterie-Regiment "Prinz Wilhelm" Nr. 112*.
00.00.193_	*Großkreuz des Herzoglich Sachsen-Ernestinischen Hausordens*
00.00.1918	*Verwundetenabzeichen, 1918 in Schwarz*
12.10.1915	*Königlich Preußische Militär-Flugzeugführer-Abzeichen*
15.11.1914	*Königlich Preußisches Flugzeugbeobachter-Abzeichen*
00.00.1935	*Gemeinsames Flugzeugführer- und Beobachter-Abzeichen in Gold mit Brillanten* (Combined Pilot's and Observer's Badge in Gold with Diamonds)
00.00.194_	*U-Boot-Kriegsabzeichen Modell 1939 in Gold mit Brillanten.* Presented as a gift by *Großadmiral* Karl Dönitz.
19.01.1935	*Fliegerschaftsabzeichen*
00.00.1939	*Medaille zur Erinnerung an die Heimkehr des Memellandes*
c. 1939	*Spange "Prager Burg" zur Medaille zur Erinnerung an den 1. Oktober 1938*
c. 1939	*Medaille zur Erinnerung an den 1. Oktober 1938*
00.00.1938	*Medaille zur Erinnerung an den 13. März 1938*
00.00.19__	*Deutsche Ehrendenkmünze des Weltkrieges mit dem Kampfabzeichen*
01.09.1934	*Ehrenkreuz des Weltkrieges 1914-1918 mit Schwertern*
00.00.1936	*Wehrmacht-Dienstauszeichnung I. Klasse*
00.00.1936	*Wehrmacht-Dienstauszeichnung II. Klasse*
00.10.1935	*Luftwaffen-Ärmelband "Jagdgeschwader Frhr. v.Richthofen Nr. 1 1917/1918"* (Commemorative cuff title for his service with that unit)
08.09.1940	*Namentliche Nennung im Wehrmachtbericht* (Named reference in the daily armed forces communiqué)

21.01.1938	*Amtskette des Präsidenten und der Präsidiumsmitglieder der Deutsche Akademie der Luftfahrtforschung*
01.12.1933	*Goldenes Ehrenzeichen der NSDAP*
00.00.1934	*Ehrenzeichen des 9. November 1923 (Blutorden)* (Nr. 4, *mit Wirkung vom 09.11.1933*)
00.00.1929	*Nürnberger Parteitagsabzeichen 1929*
28.10.1936	*Goldenes Gauehrenzeichen des Gaues Groß-Berlin der NSDAP.* The presentation of this award was described in the German press as follows:

Berlin 29 October.
The entire German nation awaited with extraordinary excitement last night's rally in Berlin's Sportpalast, where Ministerpräsident Hermann Göring was to speak on the second Vierjahresplan. Half an hour after the doors of the Sportpalast opened, the huge hall was already filled to the highest tiers. The old, honorable memorial to the fierce battle for the Reich capital was resplendent with swastika flags and fresh fir greenery. After the standards were marched in, the Gauleiter of Berlin, Reichsminister Goebbels took the floor.

In an introductory speech, the Minister stated:

["]Today, the second Vierjahresplan proclaimed by the Führer at the Nürnberg Parteitag der Ehre is to be launched before the German and the world public. It is no coincidence that this starting signal is being given before the movement and before the people, and also that it is taking place in the Berlin Sports Palace. For this site is perhaps the most traditional of our National Socialist struggle. From this podium we conquered the Reich capital; From this podium, we proclaimed the ideas and projects that have now, in the course of four years of government and state activity, to a large extent already become reality.

["]And that is why our Parteigenosse Göring, who has been entrusted with the implementation and thus also the responsibility for the new Vierjahresplan, is appearing before the public to call on them to cooperate in this grandiose undertaking.

["]And with that in mind, I address my own Parteigenosse. It has been ten years since we first took up the fight for a National Socialist Berlin on a broad front. In the past days, hundreds of thousands of Berliners and fellow citizens have taken to wearing the symbol of remembrance of these ten years of National Socialist struggle. This is not the first time that we have stood together on this podium, but from the very first day that you returned to Berlin from political exile, you have ruthlessly worked once again for the rise and implementation of the National Socialist movement, especially here in Berlin. For me, it is perhaps one of the most pleasant memories of the time of struggle, which was difficult at the time but is all the more uplifting today, when I remember how often we appealed to the nation together from this podium and in all the major cities in Germany. The symbol, which hundreds of thousands are wearing in Berlin at this time, is made of gold and reserved for the 30 best and most loyal and reliable Parteigenossen of the Berlin movement and will be presented to them tomorrow in a ceremonial act. But this number of 30 would be incomplete if our Parteigenosse Göring did not appear in it. And I would therefore like to ask you, dear Parteigenosse Göring, to accept from my hands this token of remembrance that unites us all, in memory of this time we lived through and fought through together, and I may well say suffered through together. It should also be an eternal reminder for you that when we National Socialists have set ourselves a great goal, there is never one person alone who strives for this goal, but that the whole movement stands around him and fights and struggles with him. I am a firm believer: Just as our common struggle succeeded in recapturing for Germany a city that was almost Bolshevik at the time, so will your and our common struggle succeed in actually achieving the great goal that the Führer has charged you with achieving.["]

When, after these words, Reich Minister Dr Goebbels presented the commemorative badge to the Ministerpräsident, Generaloberst Göring, and the latter strode to the lectern, a cheer erupted in which the entire confidence of the German people in the man to whom the Führer had entrusted with the implementation of the great edification of the Vierjahresplan was expressed.

In the closing words of the great, powerful rally, Reichsminister Rudolf Hess emphasized that Hermann Göring could rely on the movement behind him to tackle his difficult task. They were all ready with comradely loyalty for full commitment and passionate dedication to the new task. (*Sorauer Tageblatt verbunden mit Der Beobachter. Amtliches Mitteilungsblatt für den Kreis Sorau der NSDAP, Gau Kurmark*, Nr. 254, Jg. 126, 29.10.1936; Translation: Gary Costello)

20.04.1937	*Gauehrenzeichen "Silberner Gauadler" des Gaues Thüringen der NSDAP*
00.00.194_	*Dienstauszeichnung der NSDAP in Gold*
00.00.194_	*Dienstauszeichnung der NSDAP in Silber*
00.00.194_	*Dienstauszeichnung der NSDAP in Bronze*
00.10.1939	*Kreuz von Danzig I. Klasse*
00.10.1939	*Kreuz von Danzig II. Klasse*
00.00.1939	*Deutsches Schutzwall-Ehrenzeichen*
20.04.1938	*Luftschutz-Ehrenzeichen 1. Stufe*
00.00.1936	*Deutsches Olympia-Ehrenzeichen I. Klasse*
00.00.1934	*Großkreuz des Ehrenzeichens des Deutschen Roten Kreuzes*
00.00.1934	*Ehrenzeichen des Deutschen Roten Kreuzes I. Stufe*
12.01.1937	*SA-Ehrendolch für Führer der SA-Standarte "Feldherrnhalle"*
00.00.1943	*Ehrenring der Stadt Wien*
14.01.1939	*Ehrenring der Stadt des Deutschen Handwerks* (Frankfurt am Main)
00.00.193_	*Sportkranz in Gold-Ring der nationalen Kraftfahrt- und Luftfahrtbewegung* (Association of the National Motoring and Aviation Movement)
05.05.1934	*Ehrenurkunde des Internationalen Jagdrates* (Honor Certificate of the International Hunting Council)
05.05.1933	*Ehrenmitgliedsurkunde der vereinigten Flieger-Verbände Bayerns "in dankbarer Anerkennung seiner großen Verdienste um das Flugwesen"* (in grateful recognition of his great services to aviation)

06.05.1939	*Ehrenbürgerrecht der Universität Göttingen*
01.03.1937	*Ehrenbürgerrecht der Stadt Saarbrücken*
30.01.1937	*Ehrenbürgerrecht der Stadt Hamburg*
26.03.1936	*Ehrenbürgerrecht der Stadt Karlsruhe* (revoked, 00.04.1946)
00.00.1936	*Ehrenbürgerrecht der Stadt Wesermünde* (revoked, 00.00.1949)
26.10.1933	*Ehrenbürgerrecht der Stadt Stettin*
13.09.1933	*Ehrenbürgerrecht der Kreisstadt Ottweiler im Saar*
28.08.1933	*Ehrenbürgerrecht der Stadt Allenstein*

Foreign
Kingdom of Bulgaria

27.05.1935	Order of Saints Cyril and Methodius, the Small Collar (Малко огърлие на ордена "Св. св. равноапостоли Кирил и Методий"). Personally presented by King Boris III of Bulgaria
00.00.19__	Order of Saint Alexander, Grand Cross with the Breast Star with Diamonds (Велик кръст на ордена "Свети Александръ", звезда с брилянти)
00.00.19__	Order of Saint Alexander, the small collar (Малко огърлие на ордена "Свети Александръ")
00.00.19__	Order of Bravery, I Grade, 1st Class (Орден "За храброст" I степен 1 клас)

Independent State of Croatia (Nezavisna Države Hrvatska, NDH)

06.04.1942	Order of the Crown of King Zvonimir, Grand Cross with the Breast Badge with Oak Wreath (*Red krune kralja Zvonimira 1. stupnja sa zvijezdom i hrastove grančice*)
00.00.194_	Military Pilot Badge (*Oznaka Zrakoplovstva Nezavisne Države Hrvatske*)

Democratic Republic of Georgia (refugee government, reestablished in the castle of Leuville-sur-Orge in France)

00.00.19__	Order of Saint Tamara

Kingdom of Denmark

06.08.1938	Order of the Dannebrog, Grand Cross with Diamonds (*Storkorset af Dannebrogordenen med bryststjeme i diamanter*)

Republic of Finland

25.03.1942	Order of the Cross of Liberty, Grand Cross with Swords (*Vapaudenristin suurristi miekkojen kera*)
27.08.1941	Pilot Badge with diamonds (*Suomen lentomerkki briljantein koristeltuna*)
00.00.1941	Order of the White Rose of Finland, Grand Cross with Swords (*Suomen Valkoisen Ruusun suurristi miekkojen kera*)
00.04.1935	Order of the Lion of Finland, Grand Cross with Swords (*Suomen Leijonan suurristi miekkojen kera*). Presented by President Pehr Evind Svinhugvud. Bestowal of the award upon Göring stirred controversy in the Finnish press. According to a report of *The New York Times* (26.05.1935):

The honor had been conferred at the time of General Goering's wedding in April and he wore it above his other decorations. But no official notification of the bestowal was made. This secrecy is severely criticized. It is said that such honors should be conferred by the whole nation and it is entitled to know whom it honors. The leading labor organ takes occasion to censure the authorities for indiscriminate conferring of honors and says that in this instance the award has caused painful attention. It remarks that it does not know what General Goering has done for Finland and demands official explanations. One newspaper calls the incident a scandal. Referring to certain well-known events in the Nazi record, it doubts that other bearers of this decoration will enjoy his company. (26.05.1935), his bestowal of this award caused controversy in Finland, with Göring.

Kingdom of Hungary

00.00.1941 (?)   Royal Hungarian Order of Saint Stephen, Grand Cross (*Nagykeresztje Magyar Királyi Szent István-rend*)

00.00.1938 (?)   Royal Hungarian Order of Merit, Grand Cross with the Crown of Saint Stephen (*Nagykeresztje Magyar Érdemrend a koronát a Szent István*)

Kingdom of Italy

26.05.1933   Order of Saints Maurice and Lazarus, Grand Cross (*Gran Croce dell'Ordine dei Santi Maurizio e Lazzaro*)

27.11.1941   Military Order of Savoy, Grand Cross (*Gran Croce dell'Ordine militare di Savoia*)

10.01.1943   Military Order of the Roman Eagle, Grand Cross (*Gran Croce dell'Ordine Militare dell'Aquila Romana*)

22.05.1940   Supreme Order of the Most Holy Annunciation, the small collar (*Piccola Collare dell'Ordine Supremo della Santissima Annunziata*). Göring was highly indignant when the Reich Foreign Minister Joachim von Ribbentrop, whom he despised, was presented the award on the day the "Pact of Steel" was signed in Berlin (22.05.1939). In the year that followed, a petulant Göring continuously pestered Italy's foreign minister, Count Galeazzo Ciano, about what he perceived as a terrific snub. The following entries from Ciano's diary detail the absurd saga:

23.05.1939: Göring, whose standing is always very high, but no longer in the ascendency, had tears in his eyes when he saw the collar of the Annunziata around the neck of Ribbentrop. Von Mackensen told me that Göring had made a scene, complaining that the collar really belonged to him, since he was the true and only promoter of the alliance. I promised Mackensen that I would try to get Göring a collar.

06.02.1940: I see the Prince of Hesse. He wants to confer with the Duce on behalf of Hitler, but has nothing special to say. He informs me that Göring is more than ever incensed against Italy, and apparently against me personally. That won't keep me awake. The real reason must be sought in the collar of the Order of the Annunziata given to von Ribbentrop when he expected it for himself. He blames me for it. He will calm down when he gets his.

23.04.1940: Renzetti has spoken to me again about what might be called Göring's tragicomedy of the collar of the Annunziata. It seems that the heart of the big marshal is still as filled with desperate sadness as when he saw the picturesque, glittering scenes of the Annunciation hanging from von Ribbentrop's neck. I speak of it to the Duce. We must not let the voluminous quasi-dictator of the Reich suffer any longer. And Mussolini, who has a sincere scorn for these honors, authorizes me to write the King a letter of appeal to describe the pitiful situation of the tender Hermann and to propose that a suitable pendant be given him on the twenty-second of May, the sad anniversary of the Alliance. Let's hope the King will accede to the proposal, because in the matter of the collar of the Annunziata he is cautious and reserved.

29.04.1940: Mussolini relates that the King was against granting the collar of the Annunziata to Göring, but that, willy-nilly, he will do it in the end.

06.05.1940: [The King] has decided to give the collar of the Annunziata to Göring, but rather unwillingly. Mussolini, who conferred with him about the matter, said: "Your Majesty, it's perhaps a lemon that you must gulp down, but everything advises us to make such a gesture at this moment."

12.05.1940: The King sends word that he will give the collar of the Annunziata to Göring, but, nevertheless, wants to avoid sending him a telegram of congratulations and the notification. I shall try to find a way out. His Majesty desires that his wish be kept secret from Mussolini.

17.05.1940: [German Ambassador Hans Georg von Mackensen] speaks of the bestowal of the collar of the Annunziata on Göring; this can be presented by Alfieri. But Marshal Göring insists on a telegram from the King. I fear that the present situation will not allow any alternative. The King must do it.

21.05.1940: The King almost attacked me on the question of the collar of the Annunziata for Göring. He said, "This thing has gone all wrong. To give Göring the collar is a gesture that displeases me, and to send him a telegram is distasteful for a hundred thousand reasons."

20.07.1940: In the afternoon a visit to Göring. He looked feverish, but as he dangled the collar of the Annunziata from his neck he was somewhat rude and haughty toward me. (Ciano, *The Ciano Diaries, 1939–1943*)

Empire of Japan

29.09.1943	Order of the Rising Sun, Grand Cross with Paulownia Flowers (*Kyuokujitsu sho Guddokōdon Kiri no hana*)
00.00.194_	Order of the Rising Sun, Grand Cross with the Grand Cordon (*Kyuokujitsu sho*, 1st Class)
00.00.194_	Honorable Samurai Sword of the nationalist organization *Shochoku Seishin Shinkokai* (詔勅精神振興会), awarded in recognition of Göring's "loyalty to the Great Germany and exceptional military merit"

Ottoman Empire

c. 1916	War Medal (aka *Eiserner Halbmond*, or "Gallipoli Star" (*Harb Madalyasi*)

Kingdom of Romania
21.10.1941 — Order of Michael the Brave, Model 1941, 1st, 2nd and 3rd Classes (*Ordinul Mihai Viteazul, Clasele I-III*), per Royal Decree Nr. 2868 dated 14.10.1941.
11.10.1941 — Order of Aviation Merit, Commander Cross with Military Decoration and Swords (*Ordinul Virtutea Aeronautică în grad de comandor, cu însemne de război și cu spade*)
00.00.19__ — Order of Carol I, Grand Collar (*Ordinul Carol I, Colan*)
00.00.19__ — Order of Carol I, Grand Cross (*Ordinul Carol I, Mare Cruce*)
00.00.194_ — Military Pilot Badge (*Insignă de pilot brevetat*, Model 1941)

Slovak Republic
00.00.194_ — Slovak War Victory Cross, Grand Cross (*Velký kříž Slovenského válečného vítězného kříže*)
c. 1943 — Slovak War Victory Cross, 1st Class without Swords (personally presented by President Jozef Tiso)

Republic of Spain
00.00.1939 — Imperial Order of the Yoke and Arrows, the Large Collar (*Gran collar de la Orden Imperial del Yugo y las Flechas*)
c. 1939 — Nationalist Pilot Badge (*Placa de Piloto*)

Kingdom of Sweden
02.02.1939 — Royal Order of the Sword, Grand Cross (*Kungliga Svärdsorden, Kommendör med stora korset*)

Kingdom of Yugoslavia
00.06.1935 — Order of the White Eagle, Grand Cross (*Велики крст Ордена Белог Орла*)

NOTES:
* Parents (Married in London, 26.05.1885):
 - Father: Dr. jur. Ernst *Heinrich* Göring (*31.10.1839 in Emmerich, †06.12.1913 in München), son of the *Landgerichtsdirektor* Wilhelm Göring (*09.08.1791 in Of/Trabzon Province, Turkey, †09.12.1874 in Emmerich am Rhein/Kreis Kleve) and his wife Caroline Maria Anna Francesca Huberta, *née* de Nerée (*23.07.1815 in Rheinland-Pfalz, †30.09.1886 in Emmerich). Peter Kilduff writes of his family background:

He was descended from a line of civil servants among who include a *commissarius loci* [administrative district commissioner] appointed by the eighteenth-century Prussian King Frederick the Great. Born in 1649 at Rügenwalde in Brandenburg Province and christened Michael Christian Gering, this ancestor changed the family name—which, as an adjective, means "small, trifling, petty"—to Goring. Under the name of Michael Christian Goring, he became so successful at his work that he was appointed to be royal tax collector for the Ruhr industrial area, and thus his descendants lived in western Germany, where they prospered as officials and officers. (Kilduff, *Hermann Göring: Fighter Ace*, p. 16)

 - Mother: Franziska (Fanny) Tiefenbrunn (*21.04.1859 in München, †15.07.1923 in München; daughter of Peter Paul Tiefenbrunn from Reit/Tirol and his Elisabeth, *née* März).

A Prussian cavalry officer (rising to the rank of *Hauptmann der Landwehr*) during the Austro-Prussian War of 1866 and the Franco–Prussian War of 1870–1871, Heinrich Göring later became the *Kaiserlicher Kommissar* (imperial commissioner) of *Deutsche Südwest-Afrika* (German Southwest Africa, today Namibia), serving as *Reichskommissar* and official representative resident in that German colony. He arrived there in May 1885, and in August, together with his secretary Dr. Nel and a police superintendent named von Goldammer, established his headquarters in the mission school building at Otjimbingwe (which became the capital of Namibia). Concerning his role in Namibia, the following is excerpted from the *House of Commons publication Papers by Command, Volume 17* (1918):

Goering was a kind of commercial agent, with certain limited powers and jurisdiction over German settlers in the country, but with not the slightest authority to promise the protection of Germany to the natives. Aided by the missionary, Carl Büttner, Dr. Goering immediately proceeded, however, to make "Protection Agreements" with such native chiefs as he had persuaded to ask for the protection and good will of the Emperor. In return for such protection the chiefs were required to give Germans favoured-nation treatment, and they undertook to give no facilities or rights to others that Germans, without the Emperor's consent. Amongst these, Kamaherero, the chief of the Okahandja Hereros, styled "Chief Captain of the Hereros in Damaraland," entered into such an agreement on 21st October 1885. Writing of these agreements ... Governor [Theodor] Leutwein remarks, "those persons who promised the protection in the name of the German Emperor had not the slightest authority to do so." (*Elf Jahre Gouverneur*, page 13)

In 1888, leaders of the Ovaherero tribe succeeded in expelling Dr. Göring from the colony. David Killingray writes:

In October 1888—only three years after it had been concluded—the Herero in South-West Africa unilaterally withdrew from the protection agreement. Their reason was that the *Deutsche Kolonialgesellschaft für Südwestafrika* (DKGfSWA, German Colonial Society for Southwest Africa, of which Göring was director) was unable to effectively honour their guarantee them against attack from their neighbours. Heinrich Goering, the local director of the company and representative of the Reich, immediately withdrew to [Walvis Bay on] the coast. He then asked the Chancellor [Otto von Bismarck] to send 400–500 troops, the number he thought were necessary to re-occupy the lost territories... (Killingray, *Guardians of Empire: The Armed Forces of the Colonial Powers, c. 1700–1964*, p. 92)

Dr. Göring departed Africa in August 1890, and became German consul in Haiti and San Domingo, a post he held until his retirement in 1895. He was twice married, first at Neuwied-Heddesdorf on 24.07.1869 to *Ida* Friederike Remy (*26.09.1847 in Rasselstein, †23.04.1879 of "maternity fever," in Devant les Ponts, near Metz). From his first marriage were born the following older half-siblings of Hermann Göring:
- Friedrich Wilhelm Göring (*29.10.1870 in Heddesdorf bei Neuwied, †14.12.1959 in Wiesbaden). Joined the *Schutztruppe für Deutsch-Ostafrika* 1901–1905, *Stations- und Bezirkschef*; 1906, *Kompaniechef* in Deutsch-Ostafrika; 1908: Promoted *Hauptmann*; 1910: Appointed as *Resident für Urundi*; 1911: Retired; At the start of World War I, he was assigned to *Ersatz Bataillon/Infanterie-Regiment Nr. 87*; Start of October 1914: Attached to the *Kommando der Schutztruppen* in the *Reichskolonialamt*; 22.03.1915: Promoted char. Major.
- Ida Göring (*13.09.1872, †30.09.1872)
- Ernst Albert Göring (*05.10.1873 in Metz, †21.04.1909 in Berlin), a lawyer.
- Friederike (Frieda) Wilhelmine Clara Göring (*16.07.1875 in Metz, †09.10.1929 in

Kiel). Married to *Korvettenkapitän* Otto Burchardt (*06.09.1865 in Rostock, †10.01.1904 in Kiel), that marriage producing one daughter (Ilse Burchard, *28.04.1898 in Kiel).
- Dr. med. Heinrich Carl Göring (*17.04.1879 in Devant les Ponts). Director of the *Augenklinik* (eye clinic) in Wiesbaden. He was married twice, first to Dora Barth (*15.02.1881 in Berlin) and later to Edith Zambona (*17.08.1898 in Hildesheim). His son, and Hermann Göring's eldest nephew, was Dr. jur. Heinz Göring (*04.09.1907 in Wiesbaden, killed in action 29.07.1944 near Pogorzel, east of Warsaw as *Hauptmann* and *Kompaniechef* of *10. Batterie/III.(Stug)Abteilung/Panzer-Regiment "Hermann Göring"*; he completed his law studies in Wiesbaden on 20.07.1936).

In London on 26.05.1884, Dr. Heinrich Göring remarried, to Franziska (Fanny) Tiefenbrunn. From this marriage Hermann and the following were born:
  - Karl-Ernst Göring (*03.08.1885 in Rosenheim, †04.10.1932 in Hannover). He also served in the *Deutsch-Ostafrika Schutztruppe* and was *Adjutant* in Daressalaam in 1914. In November of that year, he took command of *4. Feldkompanie* of the *DOA-Schutztruppe* and was promoted *Hauptmann* by Lettow-Vorbeck on 25.02.1915. He was appointed an *Abteilungsführer* in 1916 and was severely wounded on 30.08.1918. On 06.09.1918, he was captured by British troops near Lioma. In the postwar years, he served as a police officer, rising to the rank of *Polizei-Oberstleutnant*. Married to Ilse Burchard (*28.04.1898 in Kiel), he had one son, Peter Göring (*4.04.1922 in Weissenfels, killed in action as a *Leutnant* with *Stab/Jagdgeschwader 26 "Schlageter"* over Hubersent, France, 13.10.1941).
  - Olga Therese Sophie Göring (born 16.01.1889 in Walvis Bay, Deutsch-Südwestafrika, died 00.00.1970). Married on 27.05.1912 to Dr. jur. Friedrich (Fritz) Rigele (born 12.08.1878 in Wolkersdorf, died from injuries sustained in a mountain climbing accident in Bad Reichenhall near Berchtesgaden, 10.10.1937), a notary public in Saalfelden (Salzburg) and later in Linz. From 1931 to 1935, Dr. Rigele administered Göring's personal budget.
  - Paula Elisabeth Rosa Göring (born 08.05.1890 in Rosenheim, died 00.00.1960). Married 06.09.1920 to Dr. jur. Franz Hueber (*10.01.1894 in Untergrünberg/Oberösterreich, †10.07.1981 in Salzburg), a notary public in Mattsee (Salzburg) and later in Wels (Oberösterreich). He served as Austrian Minister of Justice [1930 and 1938-1939] and rose to the rank of *SA-Brigadeführer*.
  - *Albert* Günter Göring (*09.03.1895 in Berlin-Friedenau, †12.12.1966 in München), a businessman. A signals *Oberleutnant* in the Bavarian Army during World War I, he subsequently worked as an engineer in Wien. He ultimately rose to become director of the Skoda armaments works, a post he held from 1938 to 1945. On 10.05.1945, he voluntarily reported to the U.S. CIC in Salzburg and was arrested on 13.05.1945. Eventually released, he was, at the request of Czech authorities, rearrested by the Americans in Germany on 15.11.1945, and extradited to Czechoslovakia. Held at Pankrác prison, Prague, to await prosecution for war crimes, he was released due to lack of evidence in March 1947. Married 16.03.1921 to Maria von Ammon; later divorced and remarried 02.10.1923 to Ernestine Mathilde Emma Buchlmeyer *01.11.1886 in München). One daughter was born to this marriage (*c.* January 1945). Disgusted by the Nazi regime and its crimes, he used his family connection to the *Reichsmarschall* and his position at Škoda to save numerous Jews, members of the Czech resistance, and others from Nazi persecution.
* Godfather to all the Göring children was Dr. med. Hermann Louis Epenstein, Ritter von Mauternburg (*08.01.1850 in Berlin, †05.06.1934 in Mauterndorf/Salzburg/Österreich), a

wealthy landowner, former Prussian Army surgeon, and friend of Hermann's father from his years in Africa. He had been granted the title "Ritter von Mauternburg" by Emperor Franz Joseph I in 1908. Although Roman Catholic, his father was a Jew. Von Epenstein provided his castle, Veldenstein, near Neuhaus an der Pegnitz/Franken (which he had purchased on 29.11.1897) to the Göring family, and Hermann spent his boyhood there beginning in 1901. Von Epenstein retained a room of the castle and was to take Fanny Göring as his mistress for fifteen years before marrying Elisabeth (Lilly) Schandrovich, Edle von Kriegstrue (1887–1939) in 1913.

* Religion: Protestant (confirmed in 1908). With regard to his religious views, he declared the following in a 1935 speech:

… We have told the churches that we stand for positive Christianity. Through the zeal of our faith, the strength of our faith, we have once again shown what faith means, we have once again taken the *Volk*, which believed in nothing, back to faith.…

Naturally there are always people at work who represent a type of provocateur, who have come to us because they imagine National Socialism to be something other than it is, who have all kinds of fantastic and confused plans, who misunderstand National Socialist racial thought and overstate their declaration to blood and soil, and who in their romantic dreams, are surrounded by Wotan and Thor and the like.

Such exaggerations can harm our movement, since they make the movement look ridiculous, and ridiculousness is always something most harmful. When I hear that a "Germanic wedding" is to be celebrated, I have to ask: my God, what do you understand to be a Germanic wedding? What do you understand to be National Socialist? (*Positives Christentum*, 03.11.1935; Translation in Richard Steigmann-Gall, *The Holy Reich: Nazi Conceptions of Christianity, 1919–1945*, pp. 119-120)

* *First Marriage*: After flying Count Carl Gustaf Bloomfield *Eric* von Rosen (*02.06.1879 in Stockholm, †25.04.1948 in Stockhold, later cofounder of the Swedish *Nationalsocialistiska Blocket* [National Socialist Bloc]) to his castle at Rockelstad, Sweden on 20.02.1920, Göring met the beautiful sister of the Swedish explorer's wife (Countess Mary von Rosen, née Fock [*05.02.1886, †26.02.1967]), Carin [aka Karin] von Kantzow, *née* Freiin von Fock (born Carin Axelina Hulda Fock in Stockholm on 21.10.1888, †17.10.1931 in Stockholm of a myocardial infarction resulting from tuberculosis). Born into a family which had emigrated from Westfalen to Sweden, she was the fourth of five daughter of the Swedish Army Colonel Karl Alexander Freiherr Fock (*29.06.1854 in Stockholm, †12.10.1938 in Stockholm) and his wife Huldine, *née* Beamish [*27.10.1859 in Ashbourne, Ireland, †25.09.1931 in Stockholm]). On 07.07.1910, Carin married the Swedish Army officer Captain Niels Gustav von Kantzow (*1885, †1967), and by this first marriage had a son, Thomas (*01.03.1913, †27.05.1973). An affair soon developed between Göring and Carin, and she divorced Niels von Kantzow on 13.12.1922. Göring and Carin were married in a civil ceremony in Stockholm on 25.01.1923, and the marriage was solemnized at München-Obermenzing on 03.02.1922. Willi Frischauer writes:

The wedding party at the Park Hotel in Munich was in the true Goering style. Goering's mother, his sisters and brothers attended. Karin's eldest sister had come from Sweden; many airmen of the Richthofen Squadron, Goering's war comrades, were among the guests. Karin wore a white dress with a wreath of red roses in her hair; Goering's decorations were pinned to his civilian suit. Major Bodenschatz, Goering's former adjutant now a Reichswehr officer and company commander in Nuremberg, led the chorus in the singing of a mixed programme of old solders' ditties and new nationalist songs. The union of Hermann and Karin Goering was sealed to the strains of "Deutschland ueber Alles." The next day dawned as the young couple left the party to drive to their new home. Hermann carried his bride over the threshold of Hochkreuth, the little hunting lodge at Bayrischzell near Munich, which he had bought with part of Karin's dowry. (Frischauer, *The Rise and Fall of Hermann Goering*, pp. 36-37)

A virulent antisemite and anti-Communist who equated Judaism with Bolshevism, Carin soon became an ardent National-Socialist. Fiercely loyal to her Nazi husband, she was his primary supporter throughout his troubled years in the 1920's. Frischauer continues:

> Twice [while Hermann was in exile] Karin travelled to Munich to organise help for her husband. She saw Ludendorff, who was polite and sympathetic but obviously no longer interested in Goering or the Hitler movement. She visited Hitler in Landsberg, but the Party had no funds to help the exiled comrade. Hitler gave Karin his picture inscribed, "To the honoured wife of my S.A. Commander, Frau Karin Goering, in memory of her visit to the Fortress of Landsberg on 15 April, 1925. Adolf Hitler." (Frischauer, *The Rise and Fall of Hermann Goering*, p. 53)

Carin's death in 1931 left Göring inconsolable. On 20.06.1934, he had her remains brought from Stockholm to Germany, where he reinterred them at a massive country lodge, named *Carinhall*, built in her honor.

* *Second Marriage*: In Weimar in 1932, Göring became romantically involved with a stage actress, Emma Johanna Henny ("Emmy") Köstlin, née Sonnemann (*24.03.1893 in Hamburg, †08.06.1973 in München [stomach cancer]; daughter of the Hamburg chocolate factory owner Johann *Heinrich* Friedrich Sonnemann and his wife Emmy, née Sagell, *01.08.1858, †00.00.1935 in Hamburg), who had been separated from her husband, the actor and director Karl Köstlin (*13.01.1886, †00.00.1960; married in Trieste on 13.01.1916, they divorced in 1926). Sir Neville Henderson, British Ambassador in Berlin (1937–1939), described her as follows: "I liked *Frau* Goering as much as her husband, and possibly for better moral reasons. Absolutely unaffected, she was all kindness and simplicity" (Henderson, *Failure of a Mission. Berlin 1937–1939*).

    Göring married her, in one of the most elaborate ceremonies of any kind ever arranged in the Third Reich, in Berlin on 10.04.1935, with Hitler as his best man. At the christening of their only child (a daughter, *Edda* Carin Wilhelmine Göring, *02.02.1938, †21.12.2018 in München) on 04.11.1938, Hitler presented Frau Göring with a Golden Party Badge engraved with NSDAP-Nr. 744.606. Emmy Sonnemann-Göring was arrested by Allied authorities on 25.10.1945, and Edda was cared for by farmers until eventually joining her mother in Straubing Prison. Emmy and Edda were released from Straubing on 19.02.1946 and met with Hermann for the last time on 07.10.1946. Rearrested by German authorities as the result of a warrant issued 29.05.1947, she was held at an internment camp in Göggingen and was charged at the internment camp in Garmisch-Partenkirchen on 20.07.1948 with having benefited from the Nazi regime. Placed in de-Nazification Group II, she had 30 percent of her assets confiscated, was prohibited from practicing as an actress for five years and was sentenced to one year in a labor camp, with credit for time served. She was immediately released. In 1967, she published her memoirs, *An der Seite meines Mannes* (*By My Husband's Side*), a shameless whitewash of her late husband which was ghostwritten by her lawyer, Dr. Erich Ebermeyer, and Alfred Muhr, neither of whom were acknowledged in the book.

* Hermann Rauschning was president of the Danzig Senate from 20.06.1933 until his resignation and succession by Arthur Greiser on 23.11.1934. He eventually became disillusioned with the Nazi regime and fled to Poland in 1936 (later finding his way to Switzerland, France, and Great Britain before immigrating to the United States in 1941). As an émigré in Great Britain, he wrote several books on the National Socialist revolution and epoch, in one of which he wrote at length of Göring's character and personality:

I have never been in close touch with Goring, though there were things that might have made it possible for me to work with him. [A]fter the seizure of power, ... I heard him talking to some of the Gauleiter at the Chancellery, outside Hitler's door.... The words he shouted to the Gauleiter, with stentorian brazenness, "I have no conscience. My conscience is Adolf Hitler", gave me the first great shock which set me in doubt whether not to abandon the National Socialist path at once....

Goring's boast that he had no conscience hit the nail on the head. He is the least problematical, perhaps the only uncomplicated, individual among the party comrades who came to the fore. His unscrupulousness is not a product of speculation and reflection. It is a completely naive lack of the inhibitions which are a matter of course for other people. In many things he has remained a youth who has failed to grow up, with all the irresponsibility and adventurousness of that type. There is certainly no perverse lust at the back of his cruelty and brutality. They are the natural reaction of a human beast of prey....

This natural, uncomplicated consciencelessness is, perhaps, in a way less shocking than the reasoned, deliberate brutality and stifling of scruple which a man like Hitler has forced upon himself for the sake of certain dark doctrines, overcoming his natural plebeian sentimentality. Göring's character has been imposed on him by his past as a famous flying officer of the last war, a man who could never settle down to any humdrum occupation in civil life. There are things about him that were certainly the inevitable outcome of his special fighting qualities, which at one time were highly valued. Even when he was harsh and cruel, Goring retained traces of chivalry and a naive youthfulness, which do not diminish his share in the responsibility for war and revolution, but help to explain some of the sympathy with which he has been regarded by a good many people both in Germany and abroad. His politics were similarly simple and unproblematical. He was no thinker; he left it to others to rack their brains about high policy. This does not mean that he had no interest in home and foreign politics.

In declaring that he had no conscience, in the ordinary moral sense, Göring was certainly speaking the truth. But in the rest of his confession, his declaration that his conscience was Adolf Hitler, he spoke, consciously or unconsciously, an untruth. Goring has certainly a measure of respect for Hitler and devotion to him. But, so far, at all events, as I learned in my experience of the inner processes of the party, Goring has never recognized Hitler as the great and preeminent leader. He regarded him as a necessary interim phase, as the trumpeter, the mouthpiece, the colporteur of a coming new age, never as the hero who was to determine Germany's fate for the next thousand years. Not that he was jealous of Hitler—the idea never entered his mind. His opinion of Hitler was far too low and of himself far too high for that. It was the deep differences in the instincts and the conscious aims of these two main figures of the German revolution that inevitably brought them into disagreement.

He loved pomp and possessions. And he could enjoy life with all the coarse broadness of his nature. He had none of the twinges of conscience, in doing so, of other men whom National Socialism had raised to eminence. He never gave a thought to the broken promise to return to Spartan simplicity. He moved amid all his luxury as a matter of course, without giving it a thought. It was not an unfamiliar style of living for him, as it was for Hitler and Hess and Himmler and the rest. In all his uniforms and his comic fancy costumes the fat man moved about with astonishing liveliness. He was of a robust type. He had in him something of Danton. His naive robbing of shopkeepers who had jewelry, antiques, paintings, and other luxury articles to sell was almost disarming in its complete unscrupulousness....

Göring had no programme. He has no Weltanschauung, no philosophy of life. He was not even a revolutionary. He loved power and magnificence....

Goring is more than the mere corrupt profiteer that a one-sided press calls him. This man is a primitive force. He is the Bull. He was given that high title, amid howls of approval from the party comrades, at a great meeting in the Sports Palace in Berlin by no other than the Führer's Deputy, Rudolf Hess. He is the bull who can lift with his horns things that are too heavy for anyone else. He has little real understanding of the great majority of the tasks he tackles. He frankly admits it. But with his ruthlessness he beats to the ground all the opposition which, in many cases, perhaps most, is no more than red tape. He acts as the battering-ram for the experts behind him. He enables them to overcome interested or prejudiced opposition and to cut through the snares of passive resistance. If he takes up a problem he settles it. For better or worse. Often for worse rather than better. But it is not always his fault that commissions are entrusted to him with the result of irreparable destruction in Germany's economic or political fabric. Sometimes he achieves wonders. His forest administration and his hunting regulations are in some sense masterpieces....

He liked to assume an air of simple respectability, but he could never free it from a suggestion of trickery and malice. He was fond of addressing intelligent people in the style in which officers used to address recruits in the time of William II—with a genial gruffness, and with a downrightlitness that ignored difficulties of the most serious nature. He never really rose above the level of the cadet or the young officer... (Rauschning, *Makers of Destruction*, pp. 343-345, 347)

* The following are excerpts concerning Göring from the "Final Interrogation Report—Five Years of Nazi Germany 1933–1938—A Report by Former *Reichswehrminister* (Minister of War) Marshal [Werner] von Blomberg" (Prepared by Seventh Army Interrogation Center, Augsburg, 13.09.1945):

... (3) Association With the Party...

... The Fuehrer could use this man, who turned out to be adept at public speaking, had a stentorian voice, and knew how to become popular. In addition to that he was still a Pour le Merite flier and a gentleman. Hitler welcomed Generals Litzmann and Epp for similar reasons. He gave Goering preferential treatment, however. As soon as the National Socialist Party had grown sufficiently strong to nominate a President for the German Reichstag, Goering was the man chosen to fill this place. He was also chosen to act as Hitler's personal political negotiator on many occasions. At that time Goering was diligent and ambitious.

His sole connecting link with the Party was the Fuehrer himself. He told me once that he had never quite finished reading the Party program. For Goering, the whole National Socialist Party was embodied in that one person, in Hitler. As a result of this belief, he was an independent member of the Party, apart from all others.

(4) The Rise to Power

After the National Socialists gained control over Germany, Goering wanted all sorts of privileges and offices for himself. He wanted to be top man in the army first of all—his command over the GAF [German Air Force] was a mere consolation prize. He also wanted to become a statesman—thus his position of Ministerpraesident of Prussia. But above all, he wanted power, recognition, and a life of luxury and popularity.

Goering was not cut out to be a great soldier. He did not have the necessary ability of decision, and he lacked the background of knowledge and talent. His knowledge was limited to a few pertinent facts about the Luftwaffe, which he had picked up in his conversation with competent men. His statesmanship in Prussia was little more than an act. He created a council which had no functions except to spend money. His ministries should have been incorporated in those of the central government at Berlin.

As long as I have known Goering, he was absolutely subservient to his chief. He was actually afraid of him. I remember times when Hitler spoke quite sharply to him, even in my presence, reprimanding him for very minor misbehaviors. It always has been a puzzle to me why Hitler should put this man in any important positions. Immediately after my departure, Goering was promoted to Field Marshal without any reason at all. When, after the campaign in the west in 1940, many other Field Marshals were appointed, he was advanced to Reichsmarschall. This was a position which had never been heard of before in the history of Prussia or Germany. Goering immediately made it ridiculous by creating a uniform to go with it which looked as though it had been designed for an operatic fantasy.

(5) Observations on the Goering Mentality

Goering's behavior was most likely conditioned by emotions and appetites rather than by deliberate thought. He was a man who lived just for the moment, a man lacking education and maturity. His was a primitive nature. Reading and self-education were foreign to him. If he had not teamed up with Hitler, his career would probably have turned out to be that of a small-time adventurer, or a stumble-bum and parasite. But even that might not have phased him a lot, because he cared little for matters of respectability. He had but one important interest, the person of Hermann Goering.

He loved to receive gifts, even to the extent of soliciting them. This custom began with his second marriage, getting worse from year to year at the celebration of his birthdays. It was a well disguised form of corruption. There was not reticence either on the part of the donor, nor on that of the recipient.

Goering liked to play the part of a "good fellow", freely dispensing gifts and favors, whenever he found suitable company. He shared the "live and let live" doctrine of most of his men, as long as he could get enough for himself first. He was an unscrupulous egotist, undaunted by the victims who had to fall on his way. Gossip has it that he was responsible for the suicides of Generals Udet and Jeschonnek. When necessary he would make a tearful show of sentimentality, which was coupled with inhuman brutality.

(6) Failure

'I have no idea whether Goering contributed anything to our entry into the war. He would have found it difficult, however, to give sound advice on this subject, since he was ignorant of foreign affairs. Nevertheless he contributed greatly to Germany's defeat. He failed miserably in his position as head of the Luftwaffe. He also failed to dissuade Hitler from continuing to fight when it became clear that our defeat was inevitable. But this was not his greatest fault. No man on earth could have changed the Fuehrer's mind.

Hitler's final gesture towards his admirer of long standing, of sentencing him to death, was no more than an additional piece of evidence showing the degraded relationship between Germany's leading personalities. ("Interrogation Records Prepared for War Crimes Proceedings at Nuernberg, 1945–1947/OCCPAC Interrogation Transcripts and Related Records: Von Blomberg, Werner Eduard Fritz"; Publication Number M1270, Record Group RG238)

* Assessment of Göring by his codefendant, former *Großadmiral* Karl Raeder (*Oberbefehlshaber der Marine*, 01.06.1935–30.01.1943), excerpted from his statement to the International Military Tribunal, Nürnberg:

The person Göring had a disastrous effect on the fate of the German Reich. His main peculiarities were unimaginable vanity and immeasurable ambition, running after popularity and showing off, untruthfulness, impracticability and selfishness, which were not restrained for the sake of state or people. He was outstanding in his greed, wastefulness, and soft unsoldierly manner. Only in the course of years of war did I realize fully that clear picture. During the only visit we, my wife and I, paid to Karinhall in February 1940 we were shown the picture of a simple and absolutely wartime-based household. According to my conviction, Hitler realized very soon his character but took advantage of him if it served his purposes and burdened him with ever new tasks in order to avoid his becoming dangerous to the Führer. Göring places utmost importance on outwardly appearing particularly loyal to the Führer, but despite that was very often unbelievably tactless and mannerless in his behavior to Hitler, which was deliberately overlooked by the Führer. I don't know whether there existed a certain relationship between them on the basis of their former common experiences. Anyway, it was impossible in spite of all the continual requests and accusations, to achieve anything against Göring in negotiations with Hitler, no matter how correct according to facts it would be (for example, Marine flying corps—see Part I ["The Development of German Naval Policy, 1933–1939"]). In the beginning he posed outwardly as full of comradeship and friendship for the Navy; soon, however, he began to show an intense jealousy and the ambition to imitate the best the Navy could offer or to take it away in order to apply it to his "Aircorps". But behind their backs he minimized and degraded the Navy. That came to light during the partition of the Navy air corps (Part I ["The Development of German Naval Policy, 1933–1939"]). The absolutely unobjective treatment of this question is responsible to a great extent for the failure of the German merchant—sea warfare against England, as explained in Part I ["The Development of German Naval Policy, 1933–1939"]. Göring further injured the Navy due to news about sea warfare events (battles, etc.) which he received first through his organization of the air-report-service [*Flugmeldedienst*] and which he, as the first, telephoned the Führer, usually in a distorted and untruthful manner (because he himself had no clear impression at all). Therefore the Führer was from the very beginning prejudiced and unfavorably inclined, thereby causing the great difficulties. Goering dropped unfavorable remarks about the Navy or me in the presence of the Führer when no one was at hand immediately to contradict him, whether it be in connection with some failure of new weapons (magneto ignition, 1940) or about personal affairs. For instance: "Raeder has his Navy in good shape but he attends church." That remark of course wasn't effective because I told the Führer quite clearly my position in this respect and attended church services quite openly. Concerning other cases which were the causes of the Führer's dissatisfaction I could realize without any doubt Goering's instigations.

It shows the correct situation that at the time I resigned from the High Command I told the Führer: Will you please protect the Navy and my successors from Goering, which he understood very well. (Translation of Statement IX, in *Nazi Conspiracy and Aggression, Volume VIII*)

* Göring got along quite well with Sir Neville Henderson (1882–1942), British ambassador to Germany (28.05.1937–03.09.1939), a mutual admirer and believer in a policy of appeasement toward Hitler's Germany. In his memoir of service as ambassador in Berlin, Henderson devoted an entire chapter to his German friend. The following are some of his remarks:

As usual Goering was very outspoken and at times bellicose. Yet our many talks, in spite of complete frankness on both sides, were never conducted on any but mutually friendly lines. He suffered comparatively little from the personal resentments which so often inspired Hitler and Ribbentrop, and up to the last I was inclined to believe in the sincerity of his personal desire for peace and good relations with England. He laid stress on this at Nuremberg [in 1937], though at the same time he added that, if the British Empire refused to collaborate with Germany, there would be nothing for the latter to do but to devote herself to the destruction of that Empire instead of to its maintenance. In that connection he mentioned to me, and was the first German to do so, the possibility of the Reich being compelled to revise the Anglo-German Naval Agreement. I told him then, and again some months later, that such a step would inevitably lead in the end once more to war with Britain. He regretfully admitted that this might be so and added that it was against his advice that Hitler had insisted, when he did, on the conclusion of that Agreement.

Of all the big Nazi leaders, Hermann Goering was for me by far the most sympathetic. He may have been the man who was chiefly responsible for the firing of the Reichstag in 1933; and he certainly was the one to whom, as his most trusted adherent, Hitler confided the task of cleaning up Berlin at the time of the Roehm purge in 1934. In any crisis, as in war, he would be quite ruthless. He once said to me that the British whom he really admired were those he described as the pirates, such as Francis Drake; and he reproached us for having become too "debrutalized." He was, in fact, himself a typical and brutal buccaneer; but he had certain attractive qualities; and I must frankly say that I had a real personal liking for him.

He was the absolute servant of his master, and I have never seen greater loyalty and devotion than his to Hitler. He was admittedly the second power in the land, and had always given me to understand that he was Hitler's natural successor as Führer. Seconds are often inclined to lay stress on their own importance. In all the very frank talks which I had with Goering, he never once spoke of himself or of the great part which he had played in the Nazi revolution. Everything had been done by Hitler, all the credit was Hitler's, every decision was Hitler's, and he himself was nothing. Inasmuch as the enumeration of the posts which Goering filled in the Nazi regime took about five minutes to read aloud, this self-effacement before his leader was all the more remarkable; and the more so, since, without Goering, Hitler would never have reached where he was. Hitler's brain might conceive the impossible, but Goering did it. The building up of the German Air Force was in itself a striking achievement, and that of which Goering was probably, and legitimately, proudest. However vain he may have been in small ways and however much he loved pomp and uniforms and decorations, jewels and pictures, and the applause of his fellow men, he was quite without braggadocio over the big things which he had accomplished....

[B]ehind all the ruthlessness and brutality which led Goering to shrink from nothing to obey an order or to achieve an end and behind his harmless vanity and love of display, there were agreeable qualities. However little compassion he may have had, like so many Germans, for his fellow men, he loved animals and children....

Goering was also a keen sportsman and a first-class shot with a rifle. His game laws for Germany were a model for the protection and improvement of animal life. All kinds of steel traps were, for instance, absolutely prohibited in Germany, where rabbits are not the scourge that they are in England. He had successfully introduced elk into the 100,000-acre estate at Karinhall in spite of the unfavorable advice of all his foresters. He was also endeavoring to reintroduce there not only the European bison but also the original wild horse, such as is represented on the old Greek friezes. Sportsmen all over the world should in fact be ready to recognize the services which he rendered to international sport in general; and his great hunting exhibition of 1937 was quite the finest ever held of its kind....

Goering was also supreme head of the Ministry of Economy, and Commissioner for the Four Years' Plan for making Germany economically independent of other countries. It was a curious combination for an air-force leader, but those who worked with him commented on his great ability to study files of documents and rows of figures and to extract everything which was essential out of them. He was, in fact, much more the able administrator of the Mussolini type than Hitler could ever be; and he owed his indisputable position as second-in-command chiefly to these organizing abilities. Hitler might turn to others in order to win approval of his foreign policy or of his other schemes, but Goering was indispensable when it came to action and administration. His loyalty and devotion could always be counted upon in any crisis, and his personal popularity with the public was an asset to the regime. So far as I was able to judge, none of the Nazi leaders except Goering had any sort of hold on the people....

He was a man to whom one could speak absolutely frankly. He neither easily took nor lightly gave offense and he was quick to seize the point at which one was driving. I do not flatter myself that in the long conversations which I had with him I ever modified his opinions, but he was always ready to listen and eager to learn. He was always, for instance, asking questions about England and English personalities, about whom he was very fully, though often incorrectly, informed, but in respect to whom he often also expressed shrewd judgments. Nor, except on the last occasion on which I ever saw him, did he ever make those long and tiresome oratorical speeches to which one had sometimes to listen from others. Brutal he was and "just as bad as the others" according to anti-Nazis, but away from politics he had many good points. I spent two hours in his company on August 31st last while the Polish Ambassador was seeing Ribbentrop and a few hours before the advance of the German Army into Polish territory and the dispatch of his airmen at dawn to bomb the Polish airdromes. At that moment the order for the aggression had not yet finally been signed by Hitler, and everything was believed to hang upon the nature of the interview between Lipski and Ribbentrop. Goering, though absolutely ready to press the button, still seemed at least half-hopeful of a peaceful issue. Incidentally, he gave me the most categorical assurances that, in the event of war with Britain, his airmen would not bomb anything except definitely military objectives. When I pointed out that, owing to the height and speed of modern aircraft, that would not prevent bombs, aimed supposedly at a military target, falling in residential London and that I would much object to being hit on the head by "any such present from Hermann Goering," his immediate answer was that, if that did happen, he would certainly send a special airplane to drop a wreath at my funeral. And, if it did happen, I have no doubt he would do so. (Henderson, *Failure of a Mission. Berlin 1937–1939*)

* Another foreign diplomat who had frequent occasion to meet with Göring was the French ambassador in Berlin, André François-Poncet, who described him in his memoirs:

Goering ... loved publicity, decorum, etiquette. He enjoyed society. He liked to appear in his glory, his pomp, and his bulk and to observe what interest and curiosity greeted his resplendent uniforms, his wide ribbons, his medals and his jewels. (François-Poncet, *The Fateful Years. Memoirs of a French Ambassador in Berlin, 1931–1938*, p. 207)

Goering was, by origin, more bourgeois than most of his fellows. His father had been a colonial governor; he himself had attended the Cadet School and in 1914 was a career officer. His position in the hierarchy of the Third Reich was above the rest; he exerted a prerogative of which he was very jealous and which he defended vigorously against rivals he suspected of plans to supplant him. One day, he asked me point-blank: "Do you know what would happen if the Führer disappeared?" I afforded him vast pleasure by replying as though the issue were automatic and indubitable: "Why, of course. Goering would succeed him."

Indeed he was the heir designate, the *Kronprinz* of the regime. He possessed all the classic features of this position. He was devoted body and soul to Hitler, he proclaimed himself the Führer's "first peer," and nothing on earth could make him betray the Führer's cause. But he did criticize and find fault and, deep in his heart, he considered that Hitler had been reigning somewhat too long. The two often quarreled. Goering, sensitive and easily hurt, would withdraw to his tent like Achilles: but Hitler would soon call him back and pat him on the shoulder, saying, "Good old Goering!" At which Goering flushed with pleasure, and everything was all right again.

The heir apparent to the Third Reich had a noble head, regular features, an open brow, light and cold eyes with a hard, disquieting expression. Unfortunately for him he was obese and tortured by his obesity. From time to time he would undergo a strict cure, and soon take off seventy pounds, then, a month later, put on eighty. He had a more serious infirmity, namely his addiction to morphine. He tried periodically to cure himself and would succeed, but here, too, he suffered relapses....

He was not a man of wide culture but his intelligence was prompt and elastic. Clearsighted, he appreciated the mediocrity of certain of the Führer's collaborators. He did not hesitate to tell me that Rosenberg was a blunderer, Bishop Müller a starveling, and Prince August Wilhelm a puppet. Yet first time we ever conversed he spent two hours explaining the fundamental principles of racism to me with the most profound conviction.

Goering was shrewd, skillful, tricky, cool and collected. His audacity knew no bounds; he had a will of iron. No scruple stopped him; a cynic, not without moments of chivalry, he could be implacably cruel. He was the real inventor of the Gestapo and the concentration camps.

Hitler valued him and made no decision without him. The accomplishment of tasks Hitler considered most important he placed in Goering's hands. Thus Goering went on missions to Poland, Italy, Yugoslavia, and Greece. It was Goering who gave the Reich a powerful air force. It was Goering that the Fuehrer entrusted with direction of the second Four-Year Plan, in other words the economic preparation for World War II.

Yet there were weaknesses, enormous weaknesses in his make-up. He was not only ambitious but vain, and beyond vanity, greedy for money. He could never collect enough decorations or titles. He gathered the most diverse offices into his lap: he was Premier of Prussia, Reich Minister of Aviation, President of the Reichstag, Director of National Economy, President of the Hermann Goering Factories, and Reich Grand Master of the Hunt. He had been a captain; he was promoted general, then field marshal, but as there were other field marshals, he asked for unique ranking: he would be a supermarshal, a Reich marshal, subordinate to Hitler alone.

[There followed a lengthy description of Göring's lavish lifestyle.]

To us diplomats Goering offered a valuable advantage. Far from seeking to avoid us he actually sought to establish contacts with us. He accepted and returned our invitations. Appreciating the arrangement and brilliance, the rich far and the fine wines of these soirees, he would converse familiarly and reply to indiscreet questions. Disdaining precautions and circumlocutions, he spoke out bluntly and freely, raising for us one corner of the veil which the Wilhelmstrasse and the Goebbels press had cast over reality. We were grateful to him for it and we cheerfully obtained for him satisfactions of the vanity to which he was susceptible....

In the bosom of his family Goering was kindly, affectionate, and attentive. This cynic and adventurer, who in earliest youth ran away from school to seek his fortune afar, this *condottiere* and pirate chief, fierce in action, had but to return from his expeditions to meet his family in the shelter which housed his treasures, and forthwith he became a candid, goodhearted soul. (François-Poncet, *The Fateful Years*, pp. 213-218)

Sources:

Aly, Götz, et al., eds, *Die Verfolgung und Ermordung der europäischen Juden durch das nationalsozialistische Deutschland 1933-1945, Teil 1: Deutsches Reich 1933-1937*. Oldenbourg Wissenschaftsverlag, 2008.

Angolia, LTC John: *For Führer and Fatherland- Military Awards of the Third Reich*. R. James Bender Publishing, 1976.

—*For Führer and Fatherland: Political and Civil Awards of the Third Reich*. R. James Bender Publishing, 1978.

—*On the Field of Honor: A History of the Knight's Cross Bearers* (2 volumes). R. James Bender Publishing, 1979, 1980.

Anonymous: *Braunbuch über Reichstagsbrand und Hitler-Terror*. Universum-Bücherei, Basel, 1933.

Barnett, Correlli (ed): *Hitler's Generals*. Grove-Weidenfeld, 1989.

Bekker, Cajus: *Angriffshohe 4000. Ein Kriegstagebuch der deutschen Luftwaffe*. G. Stalling Verlag, 1964.

Bender, Roger James & Petersen, George A.: Hermann Göring: From Regiment to Fallschirmpanzerkorps. *R. James Bender Publishing, 1975.*

Bennecke, Dr. phil. Heinrich: *Hitler und die SA*. Günter Olzog Verlag, 1962.

Blood, Philip W.: "Securing Hitler's Lebensraum: The Luftwaffe and Białowieża Forest, 1942-1944", in *Holocaust and Genocide Studies 24*, No. 2 (Fall 2010).

Bradley, Dermot/Hildebrand, Karl-Friedrich/Rövekamp, Markus: *Die Generale des Heeres 1921-1945*. Biblio Verlag, 1993-1999.

Browning, Christopher R.: *The Origins of the Final Solution*. University of Nebraska Press & Yad Vashem, 2004.

Bullock, Alan: *Hitler: A Study in Tyranny*. Harper & Row, 1962.

Bundesarchiv, Berlin-Lichterfelde: *Personalunterlagen von SA-Angehörigen: SA-Personalakte* of Hermann Göring.
Campbell, Bruce: *The SA Generals and the Rise of Nazism*. University Press of Kentucky, 1998
Ciano di Cortellazzo, Conte Galeazzo: *The Ciano Diaries, 1939–1943*. Doubleday & Co., 1946.
United States Congress: *Congressional Record* (Bound Edition), Volume 152 (2006).
Davidson, Eugen: *The Trial of the Germans. Nuremberg, 1945–1946*. MacMillan 1966.
Delarue, Jacques: *The Gestapo: A History of Horror*. Macdonald & Co., 1964.
Deschner, Günther: *Reinhard Heydrich*. Stein and Day, 1981.
Deutsche Hochschule für Politik: *Dokumente der deutschen Politik, Band 4*, 1937.
Dodd, William E.: *Ambassador Dodd's Diary, 1933–1938*. Victor Gollancz, Ltd, 1945.
Dolibois, John E.: *Pattern of Circles: An Ambassador's Story*. Kent State University Press, 1989
Dornberg, John: *Munich 1923. The Story of Hitler's First Grab for Power*. Harper & Row, 1982.
Evans, Richard J.: *The Third Reich in Power*. Penguin Press, 2005.
Fest, Joachim: *The Face of the Third Reich: Portraits of the Nazi Leadership*. Weidenfeld & Nicholson, 1970.
Flood, Charles Bracelen: *Hitler: The Path to Power*. Houghton Mifflin Company, 1989.
François-Poncet, André: *The Fateful Years. Memoirs of a French Ambassador in Berlin, 1931–1938*. Harcourt, Brace and Company, 1949.
Franks, Norman L.R.; Bailey, Frank W.; & Guest, Russell: *Above the Lines: A Complete Record of the Fighter Aces of the German Air Service, Naval Air Service and Flanders Marine Corps, 1914–1918*. Grub Street, 1993.
Franks, Norman & VanWyngarden, Greg: *Fokker D VII Aces of World War I, Part 1 (Aircraft of the Aces 53)*. Osprey Publishing, 2003.
Friedrich, Thomas: *Hitler's Berlin: Abused City*. Yale University Press, 2012.
Frischauer, Willi: *The Rise and Fall of Hermann Goering*. Houghton Mifflin Company, 1951.
Galland, Generalleutnant a. D. Adolf: *The First and the Last*. Henry Holt, 1954.
Gilbert, Dr. Gustave M.: *Nuremberg Diary*. Farrar, Straus and Giroux, Inc., 1947.
Gisevius, Hans Bernd: *To the Bitter End*. Houghton Mifflin Company, 1947.
Goebbels, Dr. Paul Joseph: *The Goebbels Diaries 1942–1943* (ed. by Louis P. Lochner). Doubleday, 1948.
Göring, Hermann: *Aufbau einer Nation*. Ernst Siegfried Mittler und Sohn Buchdruckerie G.m.b.H., 1934.- *Germany Reborn* [translation of *Aufbau einer Nation*]. Elkin Mathews & Marrot Ltd, 1934.
Great Britain. Parliament. House of Commons: *Papers by Command, Volume 17*. His Majesty's Stationery Office (HMSO), 1918.
Gritzbach, Dr. Erich: *Hermann Göring. Werk und Mensch*. Zentralverlag der NSDAP, Franz Eher Nachf., 1938.
Hamilton, Charles: *Leaders and Personalities of the Third Reich, Volume I*. R. James Bender Publishing, 1984.- *Leaders and Personalities of the Third Reich, Volume II*. R. James Bender Publishing, 1996.
Hanfstaengl, Ernst Franz Sedgwick ("Putzi"): *Hitler: The Missing Years*. Eyre & Spottiswoode, 1957.
Heiden, Konrad: *Der Fuehrer: Hitler's Rise to Power*. Houghton Mifflin, 1944.
Henderson, Sir Neville: *Failure of a Mission. Berlin 1937–1939*. G. P. Putnam's Sons, 1940.
Hett, Benjamin Carter: *Burning the Reichstag. An Investigation into the Third Reich's Enduring Myth*. Oxford University Press, 2014.
Hilberg, Raul: *The Destruction of the European Jews*. (Revised and definitive edition—3 Volumes). Holmes & Meier, 1985.
Höhne, Heinz: *The Order of the Death's Head*. Martin Secker & Warburg, 1969.
Hoffmann, Dieter: *Der Skandal. Hindenburgs Entscheidung für Hitler*. Donat Verlag, 2019.

International Military Tribunal, Nürnberg: *Trial of the Major War Criminals Before the International Military Tribunal Nuremberg*, (multiple volumes). 1948.

Irving, David: *Göring: A Biography*. Avon Books, 1990.

Jablonsky, David: *The Nazi Party in Dissolution: Hitler and the Verbotzeit, 1923-1925*. Psychology Press, 1989.

Kay, Alex J.: *Germany's Staatssekretäre, Mass Starvation and the Meeting of 2 May 1941*. In: *Journal of Contemporary History*. Vol. 41, 2006, No. 4, pp. 685-700.

Kershaw, Ian: *Hitler: 1936-1945- Nemesis*. W.W. Norton, 2000.

Kienast, *Ministerialdirigent* Ernst (ed): *Der Großdeutsche Reichstag, IV. Wahlperiode, Beginn am 10.04.1938 verlängert bis zum 30. Januar 1947*. Berlin, November 1943.

Kilduff, Peter: *Hermann Göring-Fighter Ace*. Grub Street, 2010.

Killingray, David: *Guardians of Empire: The Armed Forces of the Colonial Powers, c. 1700-1964*. Manchester University Press, 1999.

Knopp, Guido: *Göring: Eine Karriere*. C. Bertelsmann Verlag, 2009.

Kube, Alfred: *Pour le mérite und Hakenkreuz: Hermann Göring im Dritten Reich*. Oldenbourg Verlag, 1987.

Lange, Eitel: *Der Reichsmarschall im Kriege*. Curt E. Schwab, 1950.

Lilla, Joachim; Döring, Martin; & Schulz Andreas: *Statisten in Uniform. Die Mitglieder des Reichstags 1933-1945*. Droste Verlag, 2004.

Lyne-Gordon, David: *"And yet you have conquered"- Notable recipients of the Blood Order, Volume I*. Galago Publishing, 2000.

Miller, Michael D.: *Leaders of the SS & German Police, Volume I: Reichsführer-SS-SS-Gruppenführer (Georg Ahrens to Karl Gutenberger)*. R. James Bender Publishing, 2009.

—and Andreas Schulz: *Leaders of the Storm Troops, Volume 1* (1st Edition). Helion & Co., 2015.

Mosley, Leonard: *The Reich Marshal: A Biography of Hermann Göring*. Doubleday, 1974.

National Archives & Records Administration, College Park, Maryland: *SA-Personalakte* of Hermann Göring.

—"Interrogation Records Prepared for War Crimes Proceedings at Nuernberg, 1945–1947/ OCCPAC Interrogation Transcripts and Related Records: Göring, Hermann"; Publication Number M1270, Record Group RG238.

—"Interrogation Records Prepared for War Crimes Proceedings at Nuernberg, 1945–1947/ OCCPAC Interrogation Transcripts and Related Records: Von Blomberg, Werner Eduard Fritz"; Publication Number M1270, Record Group RG238.

—"Interrogation Records Prepared for War Crimes Proceedings at Nuernberg, 1945–1947/ OCCPAC Interrogation Transcripts and Related Records: Rode, Ernst August"; Publication Number M1270, Record Group RG238.

Noakes, Jeremy & Pridham, Geoffrey (Eds): *Nazism 1919-1945: A History in Documents and Eyewitness Accounts, Volume II-Foreign Policy, War and Racial Extermination*. Schocken Books, 1990.

Nyomarkay, Joseph: *Charisma and Factionalism in the Nazi Party*. University of Minnesota Press, 1967.

Office of United States Chief Counsel for Prosecution of Axis Criminality: *Nazi Conspiracy and Aggression (11 volumes)*. U.S. Government Printing Office, District of Columbia, 1946.

Padfield, Peter: *Himmler*. Henry Holt & Company, 1990.

Palumbo, Dr. Michael: "Goerings Italian Exile 1924–1925". *Journal of Modern History*, Vol 50, No 1, March 1978.

Papen, Franz von: *Memoirs*. Andre Deutsch, 1952.

Paxton, Robert O.: *Vichy France. Old Guard and New Order, 1940-1944*. Columbia University Press, 1972.

Payne, Robert: *The Life and Death of Adolf Hitler*. Praeger Publishers, 1973.
Proctor, Raymond L.: *Hitler's Luftwaffe in the Spanish Civil War*. Greenwood Press, 1983.
Rabinbach, Anson: "Staging Antifascism: The Brown Book of the Reichstag Fire and Hitler Terror", in *New German Critique No. 103, Dark Powers: Conspiracies and Conspiracy Theory in History and Literature* (Winter, 2008), pp. 97-126, Duke University Press.
Reitlinger, Gerald: *The SS. Alibi of a Nation 1922–1945*. Viking Press, 1968.
Rentsch-Roeder, F. Karl (ed): *Halbmast-Heldenbuch der SA und SS*. Braune Bücher, 1932.
Saxon, Timothy D.: *The German Side of the Hill: Nazi Conquest and Exploitation of Italy, 1943–45*. PhD Dissertation presented to the Graduate Faculty of the University of Virginia, January 1999.
Schirach, Baldur von: *Die Pioniere des Dritten Reiches*. Zentralstelle fur der deutschen Freiheitskampf, 1933.
Schulz, Andreas & Zinke, Dr. Dieter: *Die Generale der Waffen-SS und Polizei 1933–1945, Band 1 (Abraham-Gutenberger)*. Biblio-Verlag, 2003.
Schuman, Frederick L.: *Hitler and the Nazi Dictatorship. A Study in Social Pathology and the Politics of Fascism*. Robert Hale & Company, 1934.
Sereny, Gitta: *Albert Speer: His Battle with Truth*. Vintage Books, 1995.
Shirer, William L.: *The Rise and Fall of the Third Reich*. Simon and Schuster, 1960.
—*Berlin Diary. The Journal of a Foreign Correspondent, 1934–1941*. Alfred A. Knopf, 1942.
Siemens, Daniel: *Stormtroopers: A New History of Hitler's Brownshirts*. Yale University Press, 2017.
Sigmund, Anna Maria: *Women of the Third Reich*. NDE Publishing, 2000.
Singer, Kurt: *Göring: Germany's Most Dangerous Man*. Hutchinson & Co., Ltd, 1940.
Speer, Albert: *Inside the Third Reich*. Macmillan, 1970.
Stachura, Peter D.: *Gregor Strasser and the Rise of Nazism*. Routledge, 1983.
Stargardt, Nicholas: *The German War: A Nation Under Arms, 1939–1945*. Basic Books, 2015.
Steigmann-Gall, Richard: *The Holy Reich: Nazi Conceptions of Christianity, 1919–1945*. Cambridge University Press, 2003.
Swearingen, Ben E.: *The Mystery of Herman Goering's Suicide*. Harcourt Brace Jovanovich, 1984.
Taylor, Blaine: *Hermann Goering in the First World War*. Fonthill Media, 2014.
—*Hermann Goering: Beer Hall Putsch to Nazi Blood Purge 1919–34*. Fonthill Media, 2015.
—*Hermann Goering: From Secret Luftwaffe to Hossbach War Conference 1935–37*. Fonthill Media, 2016.
—*Hermann Goering: Blumenkrieg, From Vienna to Prague*. Fonthill Media, 2017.
Thacker, Toby: *Goebbels. Life and Death*. Palgrave Macmillan, 2009.
Thyssen, Dr. jur. e. h. Fritz: *I Paid Hitler*. Hodder & Stoughton, Ltd, 1941.
Tobias, Fritz: *The Reichstag Fire*. Martin Secker & Warburg, Ltd, 1963 (English translation of *Der Reichstagsbrand*, published by G. Grotesche Verlagsbuchhandlung).
Trevor-Roper, Hugh Redwald: *Hitler's Table Talk 1941–1944*. Translation of Dr. Henry Picker and Gerhard Ritter, *Tischgespräche im Führerhauptquartier 1941–1942*. Weidenfeld and Nicolson, 1953.
Ullrich, Volker: *Hitler. Ascent: 1889–1939*. Alfred A. Knopf, 2016.
U.S. Department of State: *Documents on German Foreign Policy 1918–1945* (various volumes). U.S. Government Printing Office, 1959)
Whealey, Robert H.: *Hitler and Spain: The Nazi Role in the Spanish Civil War, 1936–1939*. University Press of Kentucky, 1989.

Above left: *Kadett* Göring at the *Kadettenanstalt* in Karlsruhe, 1907. (Bundesarchiv Bild 183-R25668)

Above right: *Leutnant* Göring as aerial observer to Bruno Loerzer (left) in 1915.

Right: *Leutnant* Göring in 1916.

Left: *Leutnant* Göring in the map room of his squadron, *c.* 1916.

Below: *Leutnant* Göring (fourth from left) as a pilot of *Feldflieger-Abteilung 25*, *c.* 1916. Second from left is Lothar von Richthofen (forty aerial victories by the war's end), younger brother of Manfred von Richthofen (the "Red Baron"). (Hermann-Historica, Auctioneers, München)

Opposite above: Göring in the cockpit of his Albatros D.III 2049.

Opposite below: *Oberleutnant* Göring in the cockpit of his Fokker D.VII.

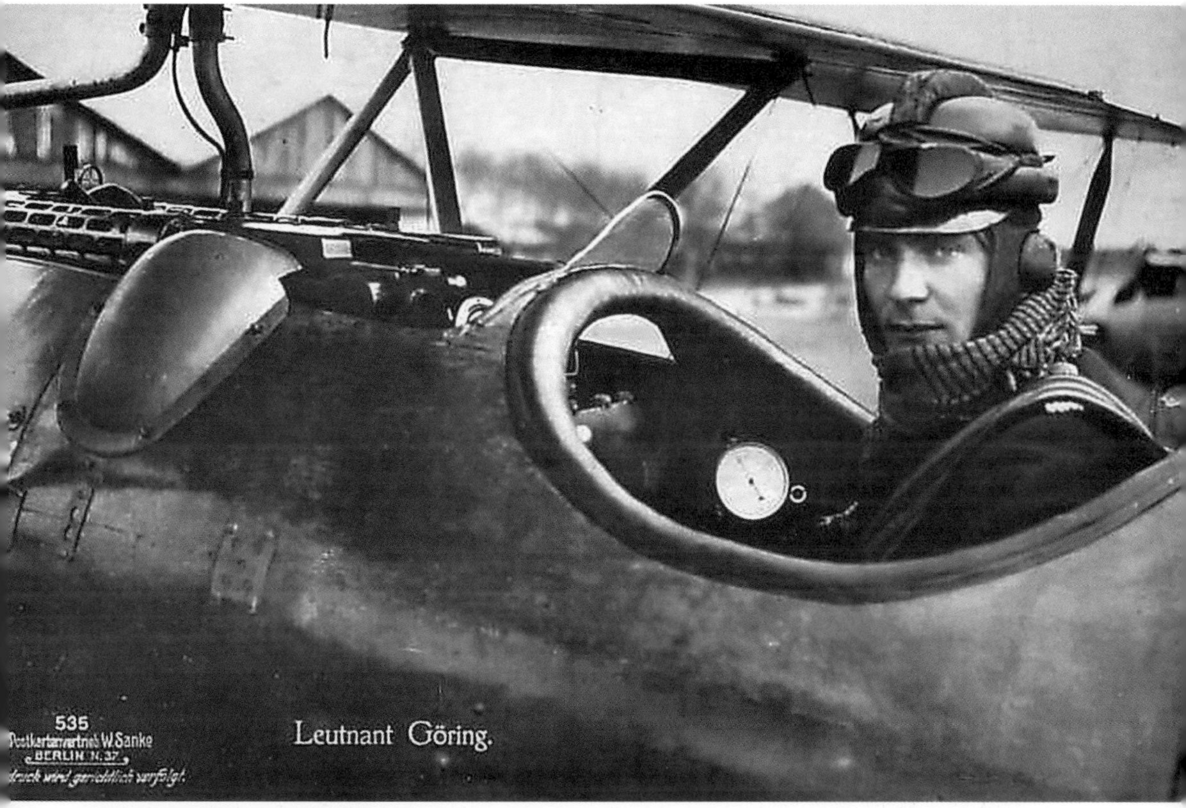
535
Postkartenvertrieb W. Sanke
BERLIN N. 37
druck wird gerichtlich verfolgt.
Leutnant Göring.

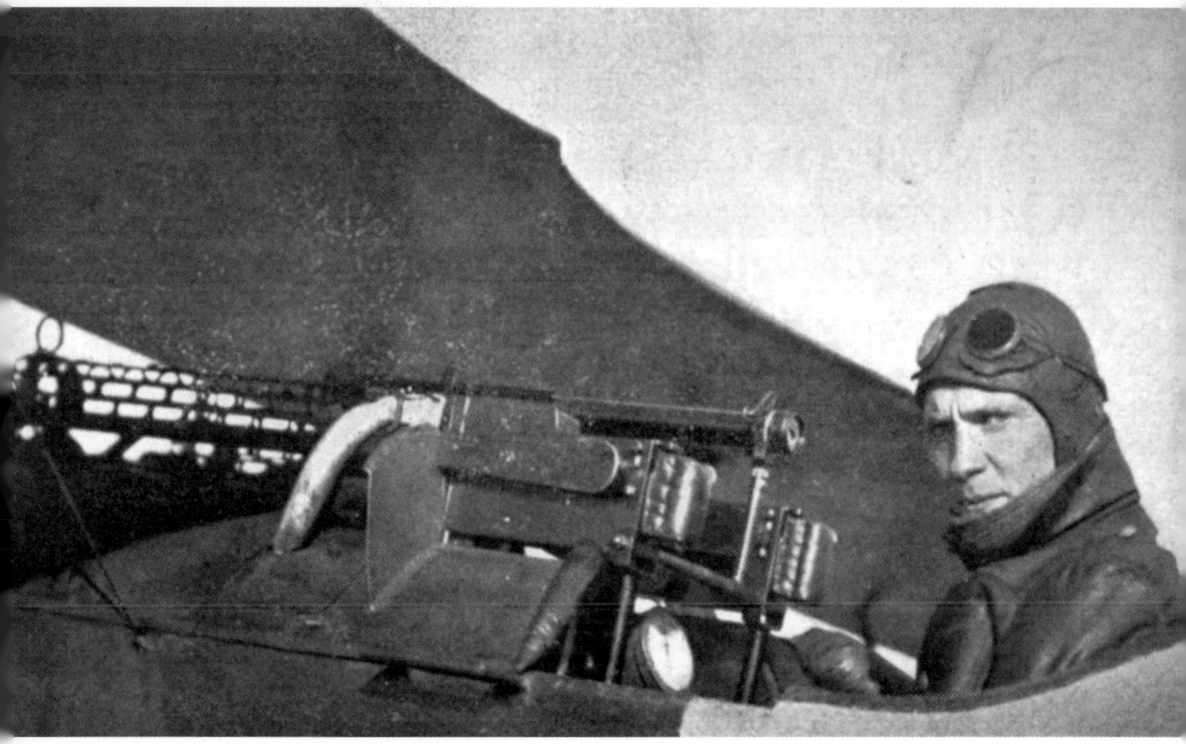

Left: Oberleutnant Göring wearing his *Pour le Mérite* in 1918.

Below: Stills from a film of Göring and Loerzer, 1918.

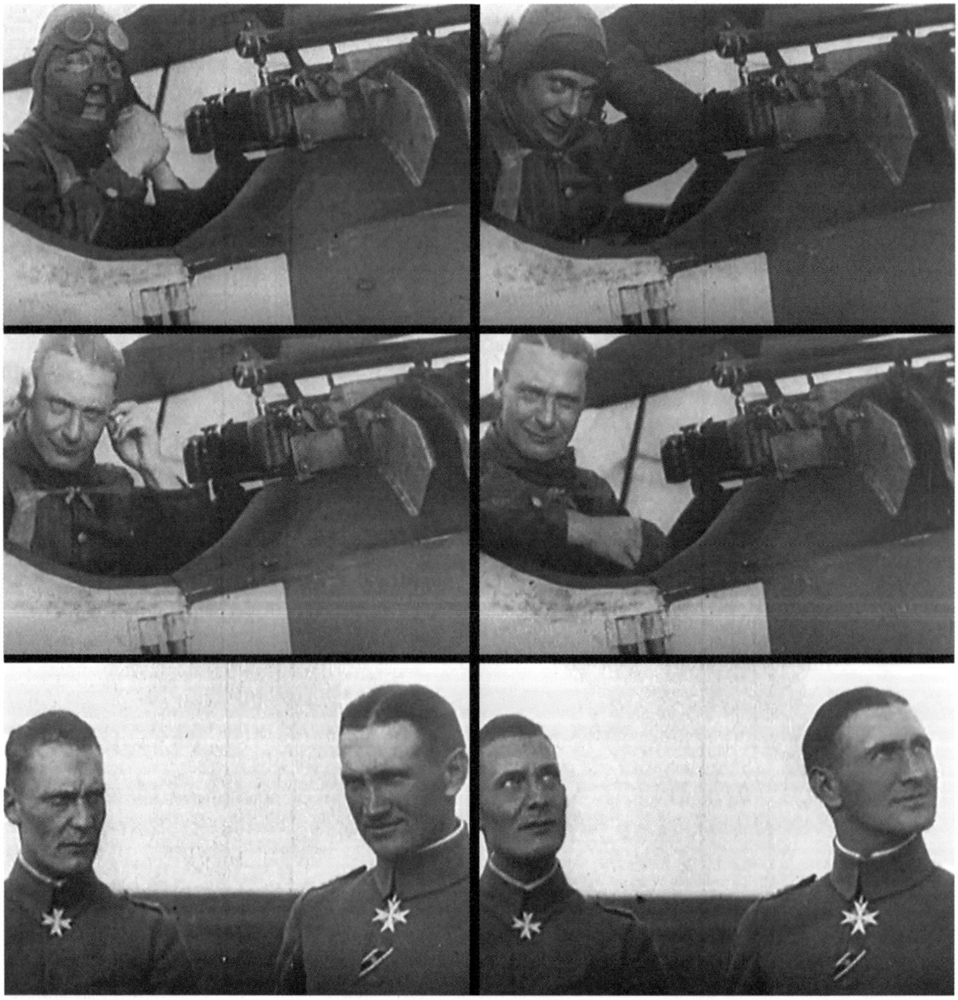

Above: *Oberleutnant* Göring poses beside his Fokker D.VII.

Right: A studio portrait of *Oberleutnant* Göring.

Sanke postcards of Hermann Göring, captioned "Our successful combat flier *Oberleutnant* Göring."

Both from Adalbert Gimbel, *So kämpften wir! Schilderungen aus der Kampfzeit der NSDAP*, 1941.

Left: Göring and Loerzer pose with the young Dutch aircraft designer Anthony ("Tony") Fokker in 1918.

Below: A group photo of some of the highest scoring German aviators of the First World War, with a combined victory tally, in enemy airplanes and balloons, of 259. Seated, left to right: Hermann Göring, Bruno Loerzer, and Oskar Freiherr von Boenigk. Standing, left to right: Hans Klein, Joseph ("Seppl") Veltjens, Ernst Everbusch (who designed the Pfalz D.III), Ernst Udet, and Josef Carl Peter Jacobs. All of these pilots were recipients of the *Pour le Mérite*, survived the war, and went on to serve in the *Luftwaffe*.

Right: Heinrich Hoffmann's portrait of Göring, taken shortly before the *"München-Putsch"* in 1923. Note the armband unique to his position as *Oberster SA-Führer*. The original caption for this photo, which appeared in Hoffmann's book, *Das Braune Heer. 100 Bilddokumente: Leben, Kampf und Sieg der SA und SS* (1932), read:

"This man is known both at home and abroad. Abroad he's known for having shot down French and English aircraft, as one of the bravest aces of our air force. At home, however, we've learned to know him as commander of an S.A. unit which, in 1923, tried to cut the German knot with a single stroke. A fighter from head to foot, valiant and loyal! Today he is President of the German Reichstag. What he will be tomorrow, only God knows. An iron fist of the Führer: HAUPTMANN GÖRING."

Below: Studio portraits of *Oberster SA-Führer* Göring taken by Heinrich Hoffmann in 1923. (NARA, Heinrich Hoffmann Collection)

Schliersee (Oberbayern), 30.09.1923: *Oberster SA-Führer* Göring with General Erich Ludendorff during the inauguration of the *Oberlanddenkmal* (Oberland Memorial), honoring the fifty-two men of *Freikorps Oberland* killed fighting Polish insurgents Oberschlesien in 1921.

Above left: Far left: Ludendorff.

Above right: Left to right: Göring's chief of staff, Alfred Hoffmann, Göring, Ludendorff, and Dr. Friedrich Weber, leader of the *Bund Oberland*.

Below right: Right to left: Göring, Weber, Ludendorff, and General a. D. Adolf Ächter (military leader of the *Bund Oberland*).

Another view of Göring as *Oberster SA-Führer* in 1923.

The "*4. Reichsparteitag der NSDAP*" in Nürnberg, August 1929.

Above left: Göring and Hinrich Lohse (*Gauleiter* of Schleswig-Holstein).

Above right: Left to right: Ulrich Graf, Göring, Hitler, and (in cap at right) Gottfried Feder. (NARA, Heinrich Hoffmann Collection)

Stills from the official NSDAP film of the "*4. Reichsparteitag.*" In the lower frames Göring speaks with Franz Ritter von Epp.

Weimar, 12.04.1931: Göring participates in the "*Gauparteitag Thüringen der NSDAP.*" Outside of the car, from left to right, are Dr. Hans Severus Ziegler, Hitler, and Adolf Wagner.

Hitler and Göring in Berlin, 1931.
(National Digital Archives, Poland)

Bad Harzburg in the Freistaat Braunschweig, 11.10.1931: Formation convention for the right-wing, anti-democratic alliance known as the "*Harzburger Front*."

Above: Hitler salutes his SA men from his car. Standing in front of him are, from left to right, Gerret Korsemann, Viktor Lutze, Ernst Röhm, Hermann Göring, Curt von Ulrich, and Dietrich Klagges.

Below: Right to left: Wilhelm Friedrich Loeper, Otto Telschow, Christian Mergenthaler, Dr. Bernhard Rust, Theodor Oppermann, Hermann Göring, Adolf Hühnlein, Franz Ritter von Hörauf, Curt von Ulrich, Karl Leon Graf Du Moulin-Eckart, Ernst Röhm, Heinrich Himmler, and Gerret Korsemann.

Hoffmann postcard photos of Göring in brown shirt. Courtesy of Roger Bender (left) and NARA, Heinrich Hoffmann Collection (right).

In Linz together with Franz Ritter von Epp, to participate in the "*Gauparteitag Oberösterreich der NSDAP,*" 06.06.1932. The two Party representatives delivered speeches in the city's *Volksgartenhalle* and inspected local SS and SA units.

Right to left: Alfred Proksch, Adolf Hühnlein, Franz Ritter von Hörauf, Walter Turza, Göring, Ritter von Epp, and an unknown *SA-Standartenführer*.

The new *Reichstagspräsidium*, 30.08.1932: Göring as *Reichstagspräsident*.

Above: Left to right: *2. Vizepräsident* Walther Graef (*Deutschnationale Volkspartei*, DNVP), *1. Vizepräsident* Thomas Esser (*Deutsche Zentrumspartei*), and *3. Vizepräsident* Hans Rauch (*Bayerische Volkspartei*, BVP).

Below: Left to right: Graef, Göring, Esser, and Rauch. (National Digital Archives, Poland)

Above: Berlin, 05.09.1932: Göring and Gregor Strasser leaving the *Reichstag* after its temporary dissolution.

Right: Berlin, 12.09.1932: Göring and Himmler walking to the *Reichstag*.

Two views of Göring *en route* to the *Reichstag*. (National Digital Archives, Poland)

"*Gauparteitag der NSDAP in Wien*", 02.10.1932.

Göring, in SA uniform, inspects Austrian NSDAP leaders together with the local *Gauleiter*, Alfred Eduard Frauenfeld.

Göring and Röhm salute from their car. In the foreground, from left to right: Theo Habicht, Frauenfeld, and Karl Leon Graf Du Moulin-Eckart.

Göring, with Frauenfeld beside him, delivers a bellicose and impassioned speech.

Above left: *SA-Gruppenführer* Göring in full regalia, 1932. (NARA, Heinrich Hoffmann Collection)

Above right: A postcard photo of *SA-Gruppenführer* Göring.

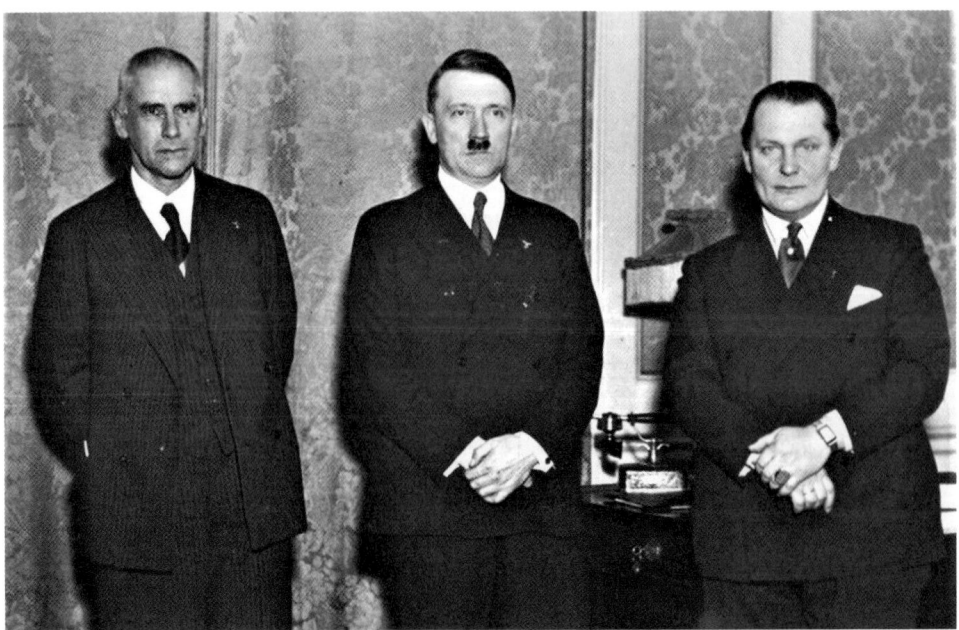

Hotel Kaiserhof, Berlin, 30.01.1933: Göring, Hitler, and Dr. Wilhelm Frick celebrate the *Machtübergreifung* (Seizure of Power).

The *Berliner Dom*, 02.02.1933. Hitler attends the funeral of *SA-Sturmführer* Hans Maikowski and *Oberwachtmeister* Josef Zauritz. Left to right: Bruno Gesche, Wolf Heinrich Graf von Helldorff, Göring, Hess, Goebbels, "Sepp" Dietrich, Hitler, Wilhelm Brückner, and an unidentified *SS-Sturmführer*.

Berlin, 28.02.1933: Hitler inspects the *Reichstag* shortly after the fire. Right to left: Wolf-Heinrich Graf von Helldorff, unknown, Göring, Josef ("Sepp") Dietrich, Hitler, Prinz August Wilhelm, Julius Schaub, Goebbels, and Karl Hanke.

Göring delivers a speech over the radio, 28.02.1933.

The *Reichskanzlei*, Berlin, 24.03.1933: The four men of the *Reichstagspräsidium* before a meeting with *Reichspräsident* von Hindenburg. Left to right: Ernst Zörner, Walther Graef, Göring, and Thomas Esser. (NARA, Heinrich Hoffmann Collection)

Göring's official visit to Rome, 10.04.1933. Right to left: Göring, Marshal Italo Balbo, and Ulrich von Hassel, the German Ambassador.

Göring photographed at an airport in *Deutsche Luftsportverband* (DLV) uniform, 1933. (NARA, Heinrich Hoffmann Collection)

Flugplatz Tempelhof, Berlin, 1933: Göring inspects the newly introduced Heinkel He 70 *Blitz*, a mail plane and fast passenger aircraft later utilized by the *Luftwaffe* as a bomber and aerial reconnaissance plane.

Above: Left to right: Dr. Heinrich Sahm (*Oberbürgermeister* of Berlin), Göring, Paul Körner, and Erhard Milch.

Below: Left to right: Körner, unknown, Milch, Dr. Sahm, Friedrich Christiansen, Göring, and an unidentified pilot. (NARA, Heinrich Hoffmann Collection)

Right: Hitler's letter declaring Göring's appointment as Prussian Minister of the Interior. (Bundesarchiv R43/I-2282-0505, courtesy of Gary Costello)

Below: Göring at his desk.

31.08.1933: Göring at the *Ehrenmal* on the *Unter den Linden*, Berlin, after being granted the rank of *General der Infanterie* by *Reichspräsident* von Hindenburg.

The "*5. Reichsparteitag der NSDAP*" in Nürnberg (30.08.1933-03.09.1933).

Above left: Göring chats with Goebbels. Visible in the background are *Reichsleiter* Max Amann, Franz Xaver Schwarz, and Dr. Wilhelm Frick. (NARA, Heinrich Hoffmann Collection)

Above right: Left to right: Franz Ritter von Epp, Ernst Röhm, and Göring. (Michal Sika)

Berlin, *Unter den Linden*, 15.09.1933: Göring, flanked by Ernst Röhm and Heinrich Himmler, attends the opening ceremony for the *Preußische Staatsrat* (Prussian State Council). Also present, on the left, are *General a. D.* Karl Litzmann and *Generalfeldmarschall a. D.* August von Mackensen. On the right are *Gauleiter* Dr. Bernhard Rust (Prussian Minister of Education) and the bespectacled Johannes Popitz (Prussian State Minister of Finance, who was to be executed on 02.02.1945 as a member of the German resistance).

The *Tannenberg-Nationaldenkmal* near Hohenstein/Ostpreußen, 27.08.1933: *Reichspräsident* Paul von Hindenburg and Hitler at a ceremony commemorating the Battle of Tannenberg (26.–28.08.1914).

Above left: Behind von Hindenburg, left to right: Hitler, Walter Funk, Göring, Dr. Erich Gritzbach, and *Gauleiter* Erich Koch.

Above right: Göring delivers a speech in memory of the dead at Tannenberg.

Göring appearing as a witness during the "Reichstag Fire Trial."

Two versions of John Heartfield's collage—as a news magazine illustration and book cover—depicting the Bulgarian Communist leader Georgi Dimitrov as a giant during his dramatic courtroom debate with *Ministerpräsident* Göring.

Above left: Göring in his uniform as a *General der Infanterie* of the *Reichswehr*.

Above right: *General der Infanterie* Göring observing maneuvers of *5. Reichswehr-Division* in Ulm (05.–06.09.1933).

The *Reichsjägermeister* in his hunting attire. (NARA, Heinrich Hoffmann Collection)

The "*Berliner Pressefest,*" 03.02.1934. At left: French Ambassador to Berlin, André François-Poncet.

Göring attends the opening of the "*Jagdausstellung*" (hunting exposition) in Berlin's *Europahaus*, 04.05.1934. At far left is his friend, the zoologist and director of the Berlin Zoological Garden, Lutz Heck. Also present, from right to left, are Peter Menthe, Dr. Hans Posse, Lutz Graf Schwerin von Krosigk, and Franz von Papen.

Portraits of *General der Flieger* Göring in DLV uniform, 1934.

Above right: This photo was presented as a gift to the actor Werner Krauss (1884–1959).

The *Tannenberg-Nationaldenkmal*, 07.08.1934: The funeral of *Reichspräsident* Paul von Hindenburg. Left to right: Walther von Brauchitsch, unknown adjutant, Göring, Friedrich Hoßbach, Hitler, Wilhelm Brückner, Werner von Blomberg, unknown DLV officer, Julius Schaub, Karl Bodenschatz, and Paul Körner.

Göring delivers an antisemitic speech at the "*2. Frankentag*" on the Hesselberg in Julius Streicher's Gau Franken, 23.06.1934. (NARA, Heinrich Hoffmann Collection)

Above left: Left to right: Hanns-Günther von Obernitz, Hanns Koenig, Karl Holz, Karl Bodenschatz, and Dr. Benno Martin.

Above right: Right to left: Hanns Koenig, Karl Bodenschatz, Göring, Dr. Erich Gritzbach, and an unidentified police officer.

Göring and his future Nürnberg co-defendant Joachim von Ribbentrop in 1934. (NARA, Heinrich Hoffmann Collection)

General der Flieger Göring with his faithful adjutant and Great War comrade, Karl Bodenschatz, in 1935. (NARA, Heinrich Hoffmann Collection)

Göring, in his rarely seen *Landespolizei* uniform, attends a gathering of senior police officers. Left to right: Paul Körner, *Polizei-Generalmajor* Heinrich Niehoff (later a *Generalleutnant* in the *Luftwaffe*), Göring, and Kurt Daluege. Dr. Erich Gritzbach looks on in the background. (NARA, Heinrich Hoffmann Collection)

Göring shakes the hand of an *SS-Brigadeführer* and *Staatssekretär* Ludwig Grauert of the Reich Ministry of Interior, 1935. (NARA, Heinrich Hoffmann Collection)

"*Tag der Nationalen-Solidarität*" (Day of National Solidarity), 08.12.1934. Himmler and Göring sporting collection tins for the annual *Winterhilfswerk* (WHW) charity drive.

Above: Left to right: Gritzbach, Bodenschatz, Göring, Himmler, and Hitler.

Below: Left to right: Gritzbach, Göring, Bodenschatz, an unknown woman, Himmler, and Hitler. (NARA, Heinrich Hoffmann Collection)

Göring represents the German Reich at the funeral of Poland's Marshal Józef Piłsudski.

Above left: Göring prepares to depart Berlin. At left is his adjutant, *Major* (later *General der Fallschirmtruppe*) Paul Conrath. (NARA, Heinrich Hoffmann Collection)

Above right: From NARA, Heinrich Hoffmann Collection.

Below left: Right to left: *General der Infanterie* Fedor von Bock, Ambassador Hans-Adolf von Moltke, Göring, and Polish Minister for Foreign Affairs Józef Beck

Below right: Warsaw, 18.05.1935: Göring and *Generalmajor* Walther Wever (*Chef des Generalstabes* of the *Luftwaffe*). (National Digital Archives, Poland)

Above: Budapest, May 1935: Göring meets with Hungarian officers. Behind him are Hans Georg von Mackensen (German Ambassador to Hungary), Paul Körner, and Bruno Loerzer.

Right: A postcard image of Göring attending a public event with Hitler. (Michal Sika)

23.06.1935: Hermann Göring is the guest of honor during celebrations of "*Frankentag*" on the Hesselberg near Wassertrüdingen.

Above: Left to right: Hanns-Günther von Obernitz, Karl Holz, Göring, and Streicher. (NARA, Heinrich Hoffmann Collection)

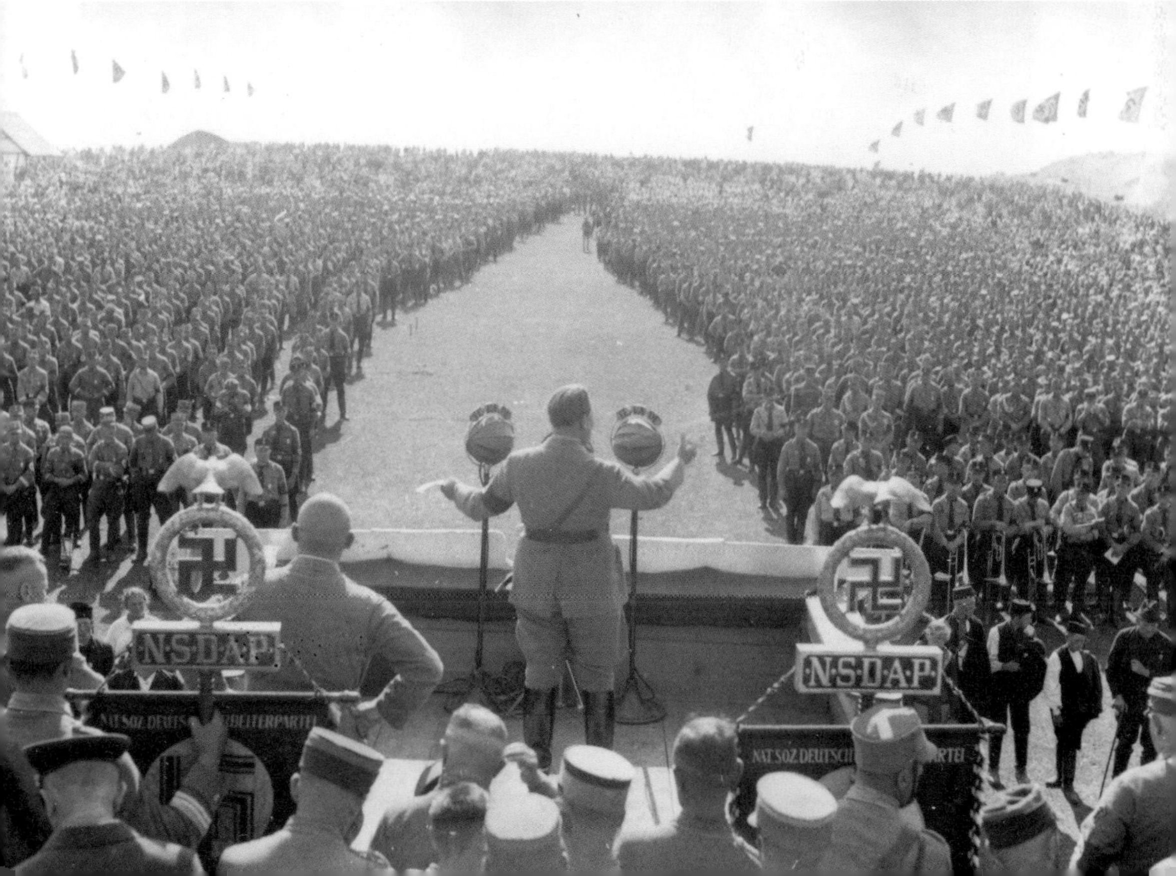

The *7. Reichsparteitag der NSDAP* (10.09.1935–16.09.1935).

Above left: Göring and Goebbels. (NARA, Heinrich Hoffmann Collection)

Above right: Göring shakes the hand of an unidentified *SA-Standartenführer*. (Michal Sika)

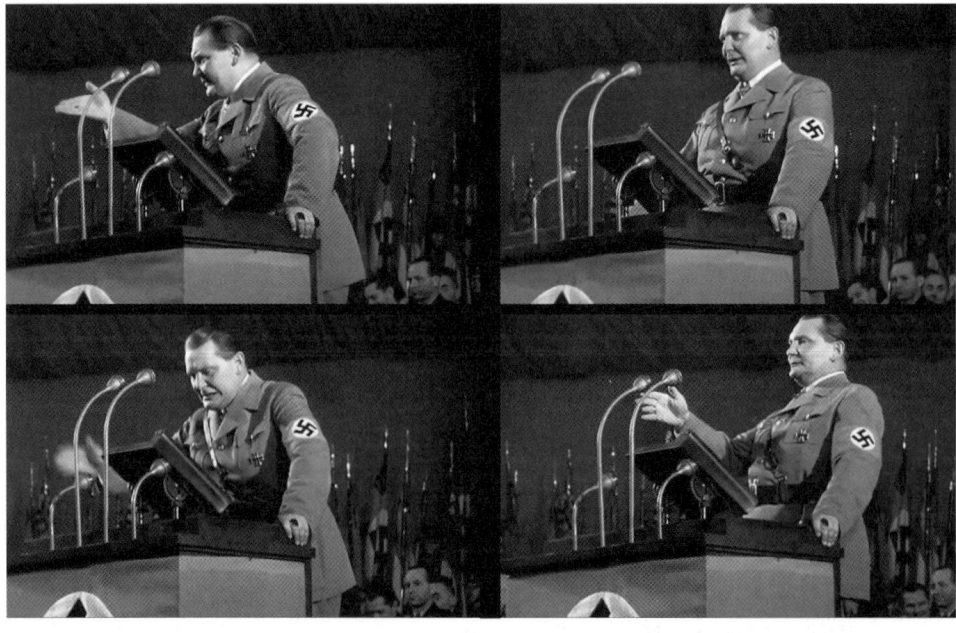

The *Sportpalast*, Berlin, 28.10.1936: Göring delivers his "*Kanonen statt Butter*" (Guns Instead of Butter) speech.

Above left: General der Flieger Göring poses with his wedding sword, a gift from the firm of Carl Eickhorn and designed by the graphic artist Paul Casberg, in 1935. (*Illustrierter Beobachter*, 09.01.1936)

Above right: A rare image of Göring in his uniform as a *General der Landespolizei*, with Kurt Daluege at right. (Roger Bender)

Berlin, August 1936: Göring with the eldest sons of Benito Mussolini during the Summer Olympic Games. Left to right: Vittorio Mussolini, Dr. Erich Gritzbach, Göring, and Bruno Mussolini.

The *Messegelände* (fairgrounds) in Berlin, 03.11.1937: Göring, as *Reichsjägermeister*, opens the "*Internationale Jagdausstellung*" (International Hunting Exposition). (Roger Bender)

The "*9. Reichsparteitag der NSDAP*" in Nürnberg (06.–13.09.1937).

Above left: Göring in conversation with Julius Streicher. Erhard Milch and Paul Körner stand in the background.

Above right: Göring wears the gorget of *SA-Standarte* "*Feldherrnhalle.*" Note that he wears two armbands- the standard/plain SA band as well as the one bearing three gold stripes from his time as *Oberster SA-Führer* in 1923. (NARA, Heinrich Hoffmann Collection)

A formal portrait and signature of *Generaloberst* Göring, c. 1937.

Göring departing Berlin for newly annexed Austria, 24.03.1938, flanked by *SA-Oberführer* Fritz Görnnert (left) and *SS-Gruppenführer* Paul Körner (right). (Todd Gylsen)

Göring arrives in Wien, 26.03.1938. Visible through the windshield, at center, is *Gauleiter* Josef Bürckel.

Right: Göring, in his leather hunting vest, relaxes in his study at *Carinhall*, 1938.

Below: *Generalfeldmarschall* Göring grasps his baton of rank. (NARA, Heinrich Hoffmann Collection)

Above left: Berlin, February 1939: Göring with King Gustaf V of Sweden (right) and his son, Prince Gustaf.

Above right: 28.04.1939: Göring in his assigned seat as *Reichstagspräsident* as Hitler speaks to the assembled members of the Reichstag.

Left: April 1939: Göring's official visit to Tripoli. He is accompanied by Marshal Balbo, Governor-General of Italian Libya (01.01.1934–28.06.1940).

Above: Berlin, 31.05.1939: Göring and *Generalmajor* Wolfram von Richthofen review the *Legion Condor* on its triumphal return from Spain.

Right: Berlin, 03.06.1939: Göring with Prince Regent Paul of Yugoslavia during an operatic performance.

Göring examines a map while visiting a *Luftwaffe* air unit during the Polish Campaign, September 1939. At left is Bruno Loerzer and behind him, Hans Jeschonnek.

30.09.1939: Göring receives the Knight's Cross of the Iron Cross for the successes of his *Luftwaffe* in the Polish Campaign.

Hermann Göring wearing the white summer tunic of the *Luftwaffe*, with rank insignia of *Generalfeldmarschall*, 1940. On his top left breast he wears the Spanish Nationalist Pilot Badge. (Roger Bender)

July 1940: Göring in discussion with staff officers. To his right is *Generaloberst* Erhard Milch. To his left stands *Generalmajor* Hans Jeschonnek.

The *Reichskanzlei*, Berlin, 04.09.1940: Reception for the *Generalfelsmarschälle* of the *Luftwaffe*. Left to right: Erhard Milch, Hugo Sperrle, Hitler, Göring, and Albert Kesselring. (NARA, Heinrich Hoffmann Collection)

Above left: *Generalfeldmarschall* Göring wears the officer's *Fliegerbluse* in 1940.

Above right: A formal portrait of *Reichsmarschall* Göring, 1940. (NARA, Heinrich Hoffmann Collection)

Above left: *Reichsmarschall* Göring smokes an ornate pipe, probably during an inspection tour of *Luftwaffe* units in France during the fall of 1940. (Roger Bender)

Above right: Göring inspects the Maginot Line on 05.12.1940.

Formal portraits of *Reichsmarschall* Göring. (Left and center: NARA, Heinrich Hoffmann Collection; right: Roger Bender)

A Röhn postcard photo of *Reichsmarschall* Göring.

12.01.1941: Göring's forty-eighth birthday.

Above left: Reinhard Heydrich congratulates the *Reichsmarschall*. Right to left: Walter Schmitt, unknown, Heydrich, Erich Hilgenfeldt, Karl Hanke, Göring, and Philip Bouhler.

Above right: Goebbels shakes Göring's hand.

Right: Walter E. Herbst's woodcut portrait of *Reichsmarschall* Göring, *c.* 1942. (Roger Bender)

Below: Göring is visited by Marshal Slavko Kvaternik on the Eastern Front. The Croatian military leader presents him with multiple gifts and a proclamation of thanks on behalf of the Croatian people. Also present is the German Minister to the Independent State of Croatia, *SA-Obergruppenführer* Siegfried Kasche. (Stills from *Die Deutsche Wochenschau Nr. 569*, 30.07.1941)

Der Reichsmarschall des Großdeutschen Reiches
Beauftragter für den Vierjahresplan
Vorsitzender des Ministerrats für die Reichsverteidigung

Berlin, den 7.1941

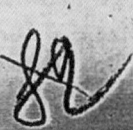

An den
Chef der Sicherheitspolizei und des SD
SS-Gruppenführer H e y d r i c h

B e r l i n.

    In Ergänzung der Jhnen bereits mit Erlaß vom 24.1.39 übertragenen Aufgabe, die Judenfrage in Form der Auswanderung oder Evakuierung einer den Zeitverhältnissen entsprechend möglichst günstigsten Lösung zuzuführen, beauftrage ich Sie hiermit, alle erforderlichen Vorbereitungen in organisatorischer, sachlicher und materieller Hinsicht zu treffen für eine Gesamtlösung der Judenfrage im deutschen Einflußgebiet in Europa.

    Soferne hierbei die Zuständigkeiten anderer Zentralinstanzen berührt werden, sind diese zu beteiligen.

    Ich beauftrage Sie weiter, mir in Bälde einen Gesamtentwurf über die organisatorischen, sachlichen und materiellen Vorausmaßnahmen zur Durchführung der angestrebten Endlösung der Judenfrage vorzulegen.

[signed] Göring

Göring's letter directing Reinhard Heydrich to implement a "Final Solution of the Jewish Question" in Europe (see entry for 31.07.1941).

Above left: Führer HQ "Wolfsschanze," September 1941: Göring meets with *Generalfeldmarschall* Walther von Brauchitsch.

Above right: Berlin, 28.11.1941: Hitler and Göring attend the state funeral of *Oberst* Werner Mölders (*General der Jagdflieger*, 114-victory fighter ace, and recipient of the Diamonds to the Oak Leaves and Swords of the Knight's Cross). (National Digital Archives, Poland)

Führer HQ "Wolfsschanze," 24.09.1941: Göring with the Hungarian Regent and head of state Admiral Miklós Horthy de Nagybánya. Right to left: Josef ("Beppo") Schmid, Horthy, Göring, Hans Jeschonnek, and the Hungarian Prime Minister László Bárdossy de Bárdos.

Saint-Florentin-Vergigny, 01.12.1941: Göring meets with Marshal Henri Philippe Pétain.

Above: Left to right: Paul Schmidt (Hitler's personal interpreter), Pétain, and Göring.

Below: Left to right: Admiral François Darlan, Secretary of State Fernand de Brinon, Pétain, Schmidt, Göring, and Fritz Görnnert.

Göring with Mussolini, 11.04.1942.

Portraits of *Reichsmarschall* Göring by Prof. Heinrich Hoffmann, *c.* 1942. (NARA, Heinrich Hoffmann Collection)

Above left: Göring chats with *Luftwaffe* personnel during an inspection tour of the Eastern Front, Summer 1942.

Above right: Göring examines a map on the Eastern Front in 1942. (Michal Sika)

Left: Göring in conversation with Herbert Backe at *Führer HQ* "*Wehrwolf*," Vinnitsa, 24.08.1942.

Above left: The *Sportpalast*, Berlin, 04.10.1942: *Reichsmarschall* Göring delivers his speech during the celebration of "*Erntedankfest*" (Harvest Thanksgiving). (NARA, Heinrich Hoffmann Collection)

Above right: A moment of levity between Hitler and his *Luftwaffe* commander. Also present are Prof. Dr. Ferdinand Porsche, Dr. Karl Brandt, and Albert Speer. (*Illustrierter Beobachter*, 11.04.1943)

Right: Göring wears his double-breasted *Reichsmarschall* tunic, 00.12.1942. (NARA, Heinrich Hoffmann Collection)

20.04.1943: Göring congratulates Hitler on his fifty-fourth birthday.

20.04.1944: Göring congratulates the *Führer* on his fifty-fifth birthday.

Führer HQ "Wolfsschanze" at Rastenburg/Ostpreußen, 20.07.1944, shortly after the attempt on the *Führer's* life.

Above: Left to right: Benito Mussolini, Bormann, Friedrich Dollmann, Karl Dönitz, Hitler, Göring, unknown, Hermann Fegelein, unknown, and Bruno Loerzer.

Below: Left to right: Wilhelm Keitel, Göring, Otto Günsche, Alfred Jodl, Hitler, Nikolaus von Below, Martin Bormann, Heinrich Himmler, Hermann Fegelein, and Ferdinand Schörner.

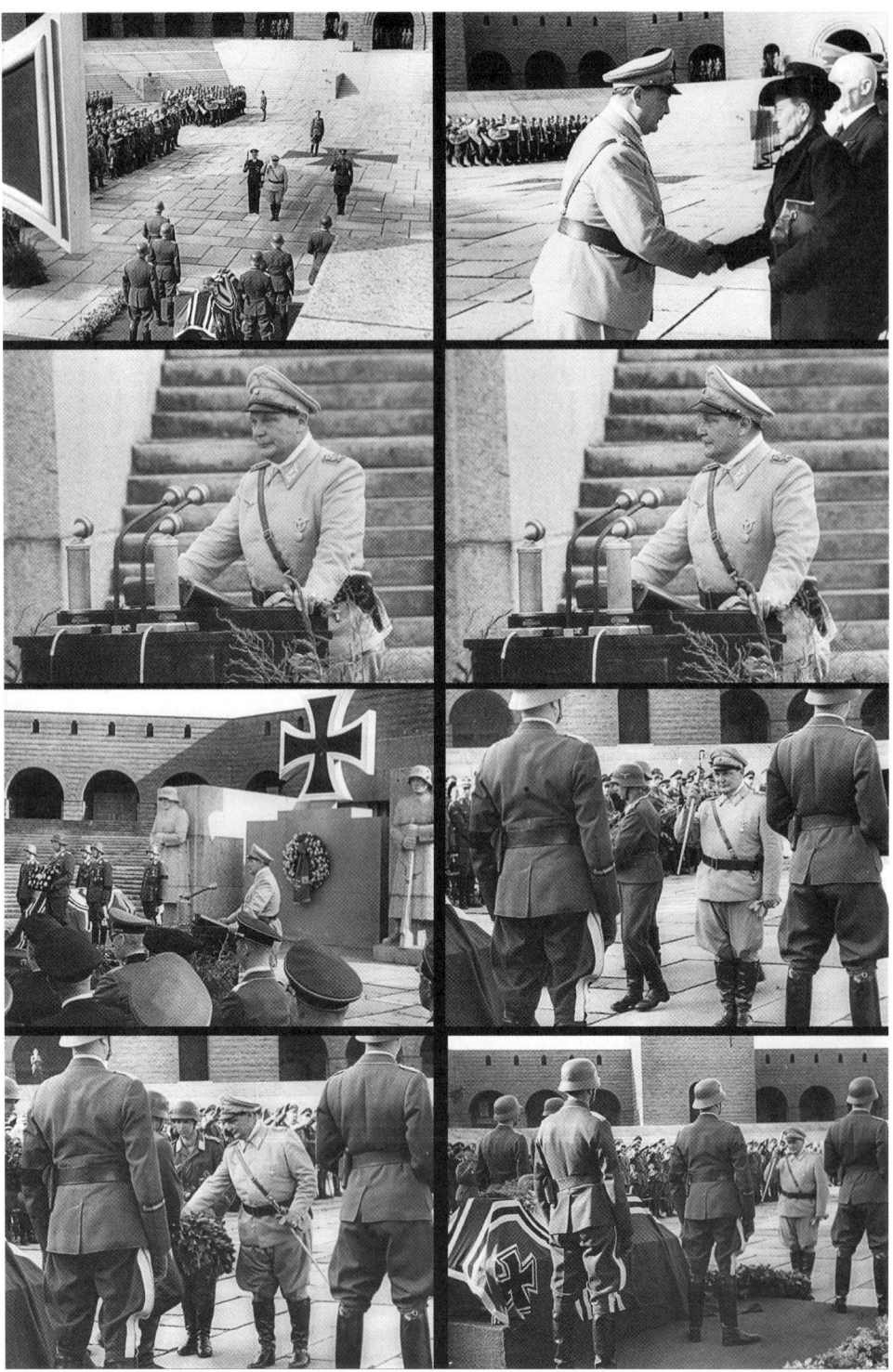

The *Tannenberg-Nationaldenkmal*, 03.08.1944. Göring officiates at the state funeral for his *Luftwaffe* chief of staff, *Generaloberst* Günther Korten, who died on 22.07.1944 of wounds sustained in the bombing of Hitler's conference room at Rastenburg. (Stills from *Die Deutsche Wochenschau Nr. 726*, 03.08.1944)

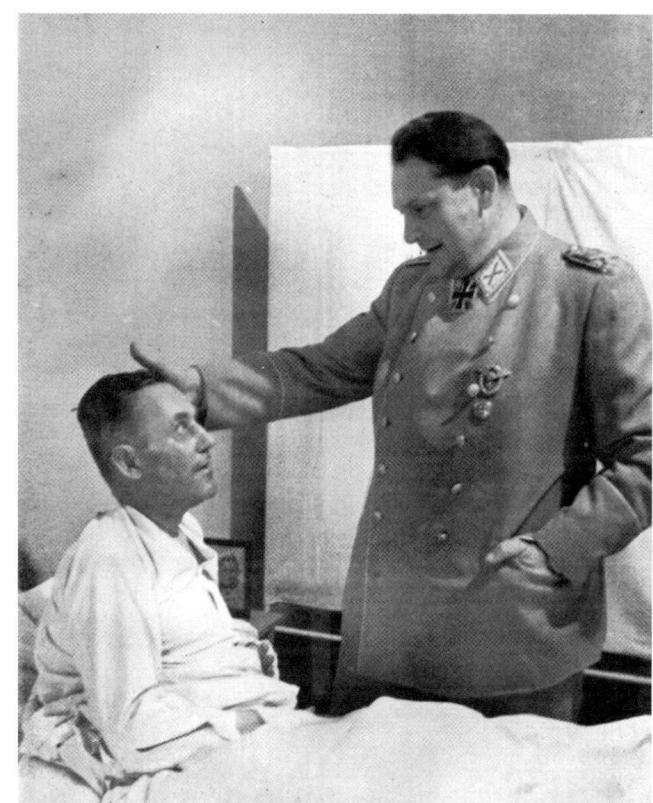

Right: Göring visits Bodenschatz, injured on 20.07.1944, in the hospital. (Eitel Lange, *Der Reichsmarschall im Kriege*)

Below: Göring and Loerzer with young *Luftwaffe* recruits training with the *Panzerfaust* anti-tank weapon at the end of 1944. (Eitel Lange, *Der Reichsmarschall im Kriege*)

12.01.1945: Göring looks skyward on the morning of his fifty-second birthday. The strain is evident as the end nears. (Eitel Lange, *Der Reichsmarschall im Kriege*)

Göring in East Prussia early in 1945. (Eitel Lange, *Der Reichsmarschall im Kriege*)

Göring shortly after his capture. (Alexander Historical Autographs)

Göring at the Grand Hotel in Kitzbühel, command post of the 36th Infantry Division.

Göring in conversation with Major General John E. Dahlquist (left) and Brigadier General Robert J. Stack, commander and assistant commander, respectively, of the U.S. 36th Infantry Division.

Göring awaits his flight from Kitzbühel to Augsburg, 10.05.1945.

Above: Göring and Brigadier General Walter W. Hess, artillery commander of 36th Infantry Division. (United States Holocaust Memorial Museum, Provenance: Phyllis Adler)

Below: Left to right: Göring, Captain Mayhew ("Bo") Foster (pilot of the Piper L5), and an unidentified USAAF officer. (United States Holocaust Memorial Museum, Provenance: Phyllis Adler)

Left to right: Captain Foster, Göring, and *Hauptmann* Friedrich Klaas (Göring's adjutant). (United States Holocaust Memorial Museum, Provenance: Phyllis Adler)

Left to right: Göring, *Hauptmann* Klaas, and Brigadier General Hess. (United States Holocaust Memorial Museum, Provenance: Phyllis Adler)

Major General Dahlquist speaks for the last time with Göring.

Above and next three pages: 09.05.1945: Hermann Göring, accompanied by his aide-de-camp *Oberst* Bernd von Brauchitsch, on arrival and during his initial processing at the 7th Army Interrogation Center (SAIC) in Augsburg. (U.S. Army)

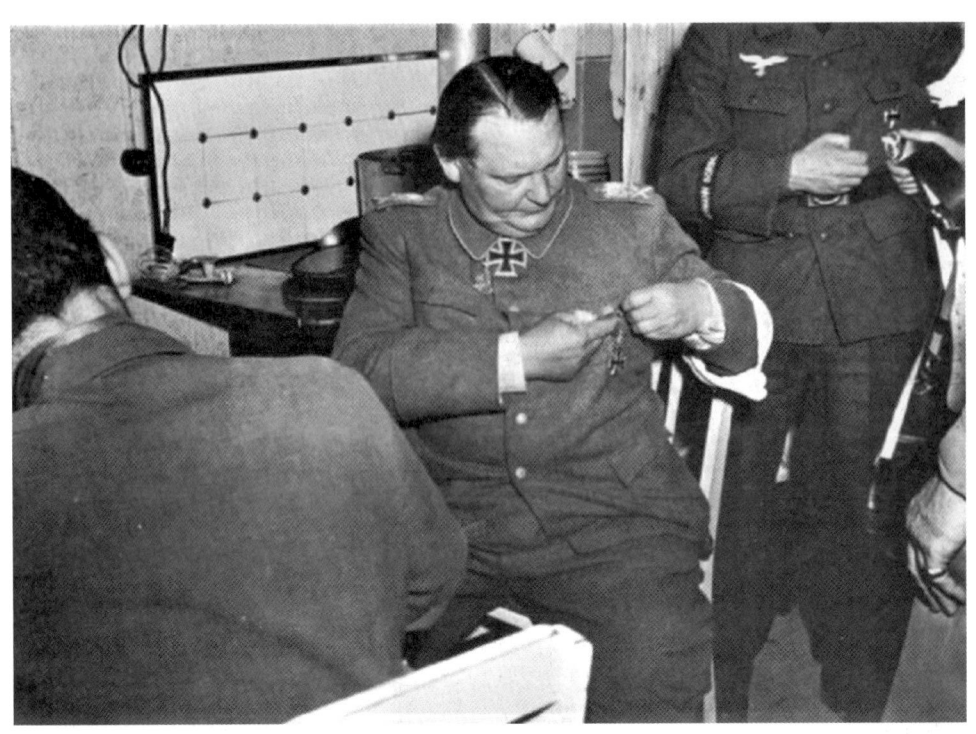

Above: First Lieutenant Rolf Wartenberg escorts Göring on the grounds of the SAIC. A German-Jewish émigré who had come to the United States in the 1930s, Wartenberg went on to serve as chief interrogator for the trial of *Einsatzgruppen* defendants before the U.S. Military Tribunal at Nürnberg. (United States Holocaust Memorial Museum, Provenance: Thomas Wartenberg)

Right: POW Göring speaks to the press in Augsburg. The facility's commanding officer, Major Paul Kubala, is seated to his left.

Göring waits to board the plane from Augsburg to Mondorf-les-Bains, Luxembourg. (Credit for all photos: United States Holocaust Memorial Museum, courtesy of Family of Paul Gordon)

Above: Mug shots of Prisoner of War "Goering, Hermann," taken from his U.S. Army Detention Report. (U.S. Army Signal Corps)

Right: 24.11.1945: Military Police Staff Sergeant Peter Misko peers into Göring's cell. (NARA)

Göring in his cell. (U.S. Army Signal Corps; Michal Sika)

Göring dines with his fellow defendants in the prison mess hall at Nürnberg.

Below: Counter-clockwise from left: Göring, Karl Dönitz, Walther Funk, Baldur von Schirach, and Rosenberg.

Göring in consultation with his lawyer, Dr. Otto Stahmer.

Defendant Göring enters the courtroom at Nürnberg, 26.11.1945. (Michal Sika)

Göring testifies before the IMT, Nürnberg, 1946.

Above left: Göring in the dock as senior-ranking defendant before the IMT.

Above right: Göring with Karl Dönitz and Rudolf Hess during a break in the proceedings.

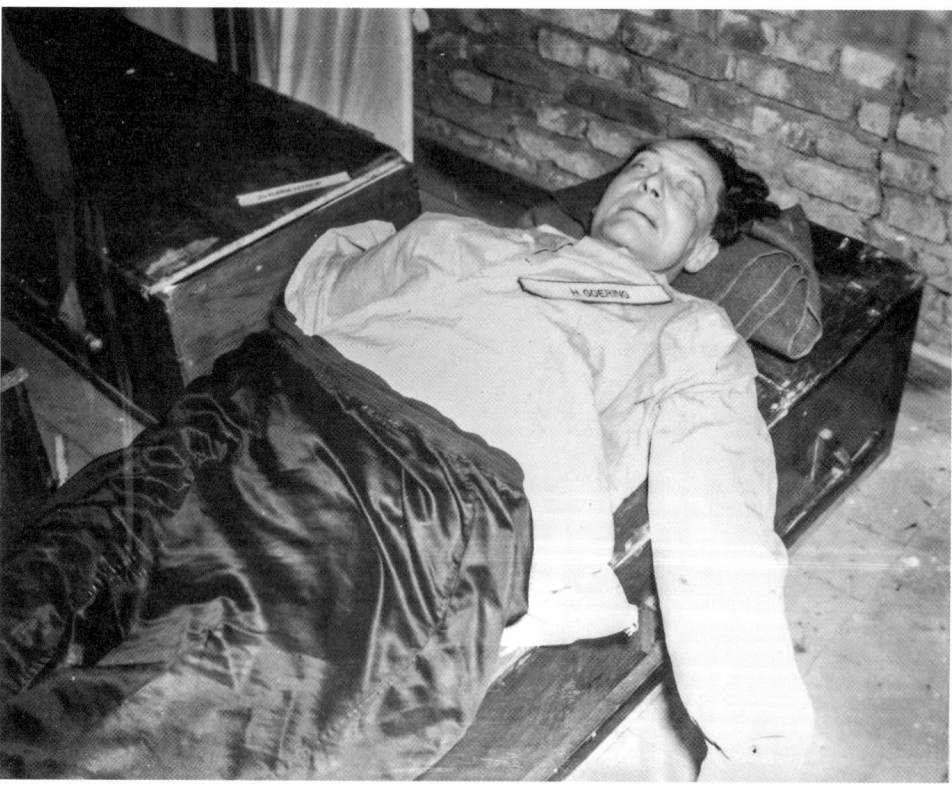

The end of *Reichsmarschall* Hermann Wilhelm Göring, 16.10.1946. (U.S. Army Signal Corps)

Above left: Dr. Heinrich Ernst Göring, *c.* 1890. (Emil Zimmerman, ed., *Unsere Kolonien, unter Mitwirkung hervorragender Afrikaner*, 1912)

Above right: Dr. Heinrich Ernst Göring, *c.* 1895. (*Übersee- und Kolonial-Zeitung*, Berlin, 01.09.1935)

Right: Göring's parents, *c.* 1910.

Above left: Göring with his mother and siblings in 1899.

Above right: The first Frau Göring, Carin, on the cover of her biography (written by her sister, Fanny Gräfin von Wilamowitz-Moellendorf).

Below: Carin von Kantzow as a young woman.

Above left: Carin Göring in December 1927.

Above right: A painting of Carin Göring by *Studienrat* Arthur Stein, 1937. (Derek Gloster)

The Görings in Stockholm.

Above: Publicity photos of Emmy Göring, Hermann's second wife (left and center), and a candid view (right).

Below: Göring and his bride pose with the *Führer,* April 1935.

Berlin, 10.04.1935: The most extravagant wedding in the history of the Third Reich. (NARA, Heinrich Hoffmann Collection)

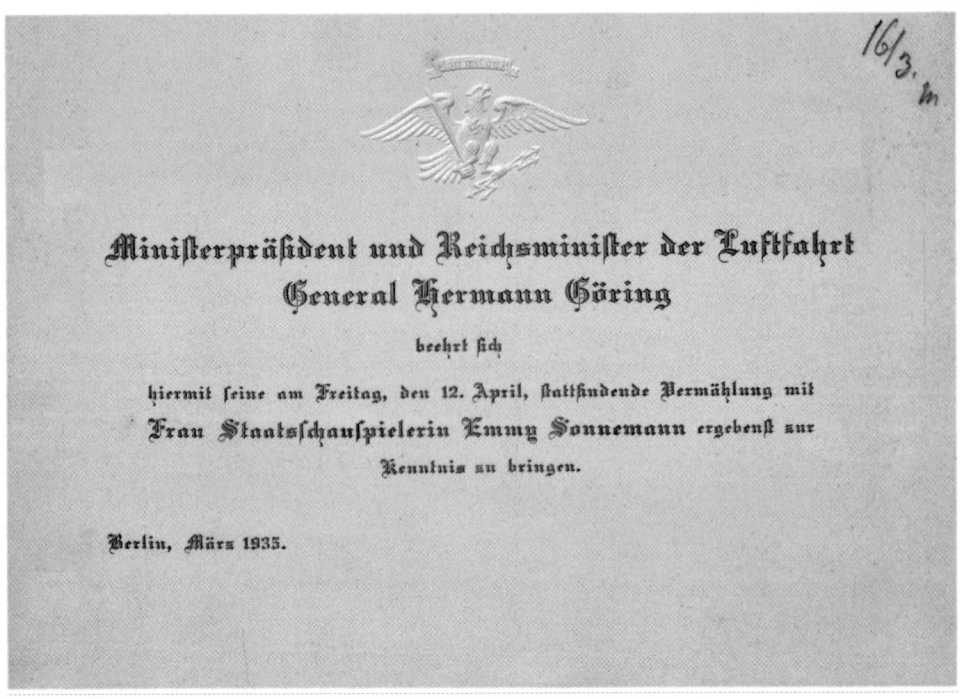

Above: An official invitation to a meeting with Hermann and Emmy Göring, two days after their wedding. (Bundesarchiv N39/62-0036)

Below left: An official portrait of Hermann and Emmy Göring. (Michal Sika)

Below right: Hermann and Emmy Goring pose in fur-lined coats, 1935. (Michal Sika)

Above left: The *Staatstheater*, Berlin, 00.04.1935: Emmy Goring's last stage appearance (as the title character in a performance of Gotthold Ephraim Lessing's 1767 play "Minna von Barnhelm"). (NARA, Heinrich Hoffmann Collection)

Above right: The Görings attending a public event in 1935.

Below: The newly wed Görings meet with a delegation of farmers offering their products and congratulations. Visible between the *Luftwaffe* chief and Frau Göring is *SS-Brigadeführer* Wilhelm Meinberg. (NARA, Heinrich Hoffmann Collection)

Edda Göring's baptism at Carinhall, 04.11.1938.

Right: Göring with his infant daughter.

Below: Emmy and Edda Göring on Hermann's birthday, 12.01.1939. At left is Karl Bodenschatz.

Above: The Göring family in 1940.

Below: Wartime images of Hermann Göring with his daughter. From NARA, Heinrich Hoffmann Collection (left), and Eitel Lange, *Der Reichsmarschall im Kriege* (right).

Above: Schloβ Fischhorn, May 1945: Emmy and Edda Göring under U.S. Army guard.

Below: The widowed Frau Göring lies ill in the hospital barrack at the internment camp at Augsburg-Gögging, 06.06.1947.

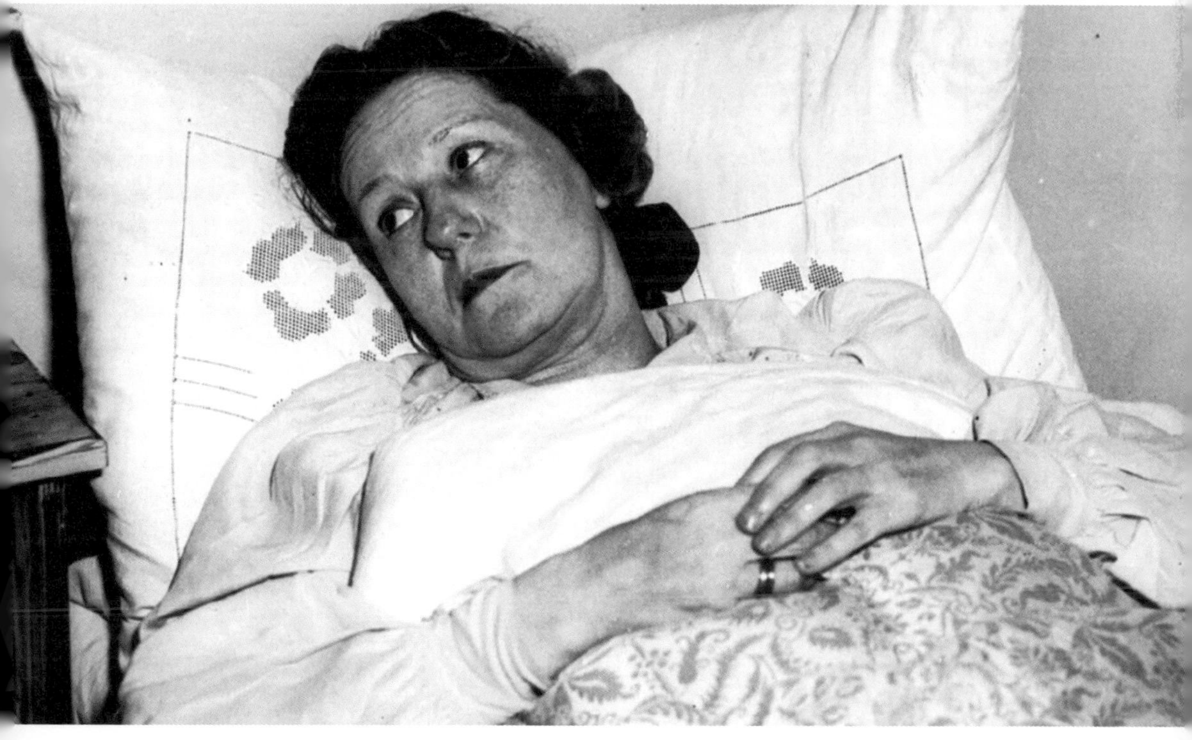

Above left: Emmy Göring in München, November 1950. (Willy Frischauer, *The Rise and Fall of Hermann Goering*)

Above right: Edda Göring as a teenager, 1958.

Left: The *Reichswehrministerium*, Berlin, 21.09.1934: *Generaloberst* Werner von Blomberg sits at his desk beneath a large painting of *General der Infanterie* Hermann Göring. (NARA, Heinrich Hoffmann Collection)

Right: The cover of Dr. Erich Gritzbach's biography of his chief, featuring a portrait of Göring by Prof. Conrad Hommel.

Below: Portraits of *Reichsmarschall* Göring by H. R. Sander, 1942.

Above left: Göring's shoulder boards as *Reichsmarschall* of Germany. (Hermann-Historica, Auctioneers, München)

Above right: One of Göring's *Reichsmarschall* collar tabs. (Hermann-Historica, Auctioneers, München)

Above: John Heartfield collages depicting Göring as "The Hangman of the Third Reich" and a global arsonist.

Opposite: The second pattern *Reichsmarschall* standard used by Göring in the years 1941–1945, today housed in the *Musée de la Guerre in Les Invalides*, Paris.

Göring was a frequent subject for the covers of periodicals throughout Germany and occupied Europe. (All Österreichische Nationalbibliothek)

Wien, 31. März 1938 — Österreichische Woche — 6. Jahrgang, Nr. 13

Generalfeldmarschall Göring in Wien

Hermann Göring, der in diesen Tagen zu unseren Volksgenossen in Österreich spricht, wird bei seiner Ankunft in Wien von Reichsstatthalter Dr. Artur Seyß-Inquart begrüßt.

Salzburger Zeitung

Tagblatt mit der illustrierten Beilage „Österreichische Woche"
Schriftleitung und Verwaltung:
Salzburg, Bergstraße 12 / Fernruf 2000–2003

Nr. 76 — Samstag, 2. April 1938 — 74. Jahrgang

Generalfeldmarschall Ministerpräsident Hermann Göring

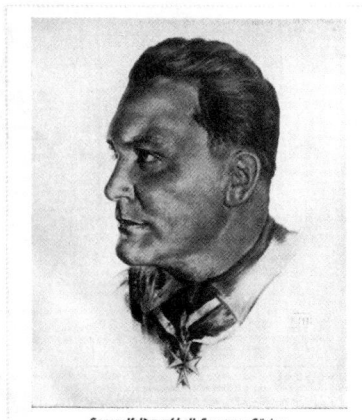

G.K.B.-Zeitung
für Eisenbahn u. Bergbau

9. Jahrg. — Mai 1938 — Heft 5

Generalfeldmarschall Hermann Göring

Das Interessante Blatt

Preis für Großdeutschland 30 Rpf.

Der Führer begrüßt einen Ritterkreuzträger.

Der Staatsakt in der Neuen Reichskanzlei.

Above:
The *Anerkennungsplakette für ausgezeichnete Leistungen im technischen Dienst der Luftwaffe* (Plaque of Recognition for Outstanding Achievements in the Technical Service of the Luftwaffe), a non-portable award established by a decree of 30.06.1941.

Right: Göring thanks *Generalfeldmarschall* August von Macksensen for congratulating him on his promotion to *Generaloberst*. (Bundesarchiv N39/62-0056)

Hans *Walter* Buch
"mit der Führung der illegalen SA beauftragt"
(13.11.1923–00.01.1924)

*	24.10.1883 in Bruchsal/Landeskommissariat Karlsruhe/Baden.
†	Friday, 09.09.1949 in Schondorf am Ammersee/Kreis Landsberg am Lech/Regierungsbezirk Oberbayern/Bayern. The *Langener Zeitung* of 16.09.1949 reported: "According to the Bavarian state police [*bayerische Landespolizei*], his body was found on the shore of the Ammersee. Buch had cut his wrists and then plunged into the lake." The official cause of death was given as "death by drowning". He was buried on 12.11.1949 in the Friedhof St. Johannes Baptist in Inning am Ammersee . Most publications give his date of death as 12.09.1949 but this was the date the police officially announced his death, not the actual date thereof. German historian Claus Strobl writes of Walter Buch's motivations for ending his life:

Condemned "Hauptschuldiger" [major offender], impoverished, old, physically ill, mental depressed, one daughter dead (Gerda Bormann), rather little contact with his other children, no contact with his grandchildren in South Tyrol, bad relations with his stepchildren- Buch was a broken man.

NSDAP-Nr.:	7.733 (Joined 09.12.1922 with Nr. 13.726; Party banned, 09.11.1923–16.02.1925; Reenrolled 15.06.1925)
SS-Nr.:	81.353 (Joined 01.07.1933)

Promotions:

30.09.1902	*Fahnenjunker*
27.01.1904	*Leutnant*
27.01.1913	*Oberleutnant*
24.12.1914	*Hauptmann*
20.11.1918	*Major a. D.*
13.11.1923–00.01.1924	*"mit der Führung der illegalen SA beauftragt"* (Charged with leadership of the illegal SA)
18.12.1931	*SA-Gruppenführer z. V.* (per *SA-Führerbefehl Nr. 6*, 18.12.1931)
02.06.1933–08.05.1945	*Reichsleiter der NSDAP*
01.07.1933	*SS-Gruppenführer*
09.11.1934	*SS-Obergruppenführer*

Career:

c. 1889–c. 1893	*Volksschule* in Bruchsal.
c. 1893–00.09.1902	*Humanistische Gymnasien* in Karlsruhe and Konstanz (passed his *Abitur* in Konstanz).
30.09.1902–00.00.1915	Entered service as *Fahnenjunker*, assigned to *6.(badische) Infanterie-Regiment "Kaiser Friedrich III" Nr. 114* (Konstanz). Assigned as *Regiments-Adjutant*, 00.09.1914–00.00.1915.
27.01.1904–00.00.19__	Commissioned and assigned as a *Lehr-Offizier* (instructional officer).
[00.00.1912–00.00.1914]	Assigned to the *Unteroffizierschule* in Biebrich (wearing the uniform of *Infanterie-Regiment Nr. 114*).

00.00.1915–00.00.191_	Assigned to *8.(westfälisches) Infanterie-Regiment* "Herzog Ferdinand von Braunschweig" Nr. 57, then 47. Infanterie-Brigade.
00.00.191_–00.00.191_	*Kompaniechef* in *4.(badische) Infanterie-Regiment* "Prinz Wilhelm" Nr. 112.
00.00.191_–00.12.1918	*Kommandeur* of 23. *Maschine-Scharfschütze-Gewehrabteilung* (Machine-Gun Sharpshooter Detachment) in *6. (badische) Infanterie-Regiment* "Kaiser Friedrich III" Nr. 114.
00.03.1918–00.09.1918	*Kommandeur* of the *Offiziers-Aspiranten-Bataillon* and machine-gun instructor at the *Infanterie-Lehrschule* in Döberitz.
00.09.1918–00.11.1918	Assigned to the *Kriegsministerium* in Berlin as a specialist in the employment of machine gun units.
20.11.1918	Retired from service as *Major a. D.*, having refused to swear the oath of loyalty to the new German republic. In a letter of 02.11.1931 to William Fanderl, editor of *Der Angriff*, Buch wrote that he "did not want to work in the new command under the flag of [Weimar Republic President Friedrich] Ebert" (Donald M. McKale, *The Nazi Party Courts: Hitler's Management of Conflict in His Movement, 1921–1945*, pp. 53-54). He was declared 50 percent *"Kriegsbeschädigt"* (war-disabled).
00.00.1918–00.00.1923	Owned a small chicken farm in Scheuern bei Gernsbach/Schwarzwald, near the estate of his father.
00.03.1920	First meeting with Adolf Hitler, as described in an interrogation report of 13.06.1945:

Buch's father, an Amtsrichter, had written a book entitled *Vom Internationalen zum Nationalen Arbeitsstaat*, published by Lehmann Verlag in Munich. Through correspondence with Lehman, the older Buch became vitally interested in Hitler, and ordered his son to take a copy of the book he had written to Hitler personally. In this manner, in Mar 1920, Walter Buch met Hitler, and became one of his followers. He corresponded with Hitler on several occasions, and followed his efforts through hearsay and newspapers... ("Special Report on Walter Buch, Reichsleiter and Oberster Parteirichter", Special Detention Center "Ashcan"—Detailed Interrogation Report, in "Interrogation Records Prepared for War Crimes Proceedings at Nuernberg, 1945–1947/ OCCPAC Interrogation Transcripts and Related Records: Buch, Walter Hans"; Publication Number M1270, Record Group RG238)

In a letter to his colleague Willi Grimm, Buch wrote: "My political work began in 1920 through my father with the *Deutschnationalen* and had to end there immediately when I was expected to make a secret of my position on Judaism. I imbibed my aversion to foreigners with my mother's milk, so to speak. So it is only natural that I came to Hitler..." (Buch to Grimm, 24.07.1930, Bundesarchiv NS 26/1374)

00.12.1918–00.00.19__	Member of the *Deutschen National Schutz- und Trutzbund*.
c. 1919–00.00.19__	Member of *Badische Verband ehemaliger Kriegsteilnehmer* (Baden Organization of War Veterans).
00.00.1919–00.00.1923	Member of the *Deutschnationale Volkspartei* (DNVP, German Nationalist People's Party). He rose to become Party Secretary in Karlsruhe by 1923.

00.00.1920–00.00.192_	Member of the *Bund Oberland*.
00.00.1921–00.00.19__	Co-editor of the *Badische Wochenzeitung*, a small *völkisch* newspaper in Karlsruhe.
14./15.10.1922	Participated in the violent demonstration march of some 700 SA men to the third annual *Deutschen Tag* of the *Deutschvölkischer Schutz- und Trutzbund* in Coburg.
09.12.1922	Joined the NSDAP. Around this time, he wrote to Max Amann, business manager of the Party, regarding possible employment in the NSDAP or SA. Above all other reasons, Buch enrolled in the NSDAP because its platform mirrored his own virulent antisemitism (which had been instilled in him by his own father). Donald M. McKale writes:

> Buch's anti-Semitic philosophy represented a synthesis of German völkisch thought with the ideology of a new "revolutionary nationalism" that began to develop among far-right elements at the beginning of the 1920s. Thus, he despised Jews not so much for religious or cultural reasons but on biological and racial grounds. For Buch, whose anti-Semitism was typically Nazi, the Jew had been Germany's enemy throughout history.... [H]e saw [the] "decay" brought about by Jews] most clearly in the decline of the German family and of the Germanic concepts of "honor" and "justice." Supposedly, the destructive characteristics of Jewish blood had been allowed to mix with pure Aryan blood during the nineteenth century, and this fateful development had led to Germany's collapse in World War I. The reason for this, Buch argued [in *Ehre und Recht*, 1932], had been the liberal Enlightenment and the French Revolution, whose sole aim was "the emancipation of Judaism, The result was the defeat of a superior people (that is, the Germans), whose destiny in the world was unlike that of other peoples." [In *Niedergang und Aufstieg*, he wrote:] "There is no race with an equal or even similar depth of soul to the German.... The assertion that the French Revolution was contrived as a conspiracy by the Jewish enemy for the destruction of Germanic-Nordic blood can be proven with little difficulty today." (McKale, *The Nazi Party Courts: Hitler's Management of Conflict in His Movement, 1921–1945*, p. 55)

In an article that appeared in the 21.10.1938 issue of *Deutsche Justiz*, Buch wrote:

> National Socialism recognized: The Jew is not a human being. He is a rottenness. Just as the fission-fungus first settles in the rotting wood and destroys its tissue, so the Jew could only creep into the German people and cause mischief when it began to rot internally, weakened by the blood loss of the Thirty Years' War, and had eagerly offered its ulcers to the influences of the French Revolution.
> [The original German text: *Der Nationalsozialismus hat erkannt: Der Jude ist kein Mensch. Er ist eine Fäulniserscheinung. Wie sich der Spaltpilz erst im faulenden Holz einnistet und sein Gewebe zerstört, so konnte sich der Jude erst im deutschen Volk einschleichen und Unheil anrichten, als es geschwächt durch den Blutverlust des 30-jährigen Krieges*

innerlich zu faulen begann und seine Schwären begierig den Einflüssen der der Französischen Revolution dargeboten hatte.] (Quoted in "Die Diskriminierung, Ausschaltung und Ermordung jüdischer Juristen aus Koblenz und Umgebung," a presentation by Joachim Hennig, Judge of the *Oberverwaltungsgericht* in Koblenz, delivered there on 14.11.2008)

In the 02.01.1940 issue of *Der Parteirichter. Amtliches Mitteilungsblatt des Obersten Parteigerichts der NSDAP* (München), he wrote: … For what else did we struggle, take upon us want and deprivation, for what else did the courageous men of the SA and the SS, the boys of the Hitler Youth fall, if not for the possibility that one day the German people might start its struggle for liberation against its Jewish oppressors? In this struggle we are now involved.… Neither Jew nor freemason will finish the war with treaties that bear in them new mischief. Victory will be attained by Adolf Hitler and he will bring Europe the peace that forever takes away from the Jewish sub-man the opportunity to decompose men and peoples and play them off against each other. (S. Mendelsohn, *The Polish Jews behind the Nazi Ghetto Walls*)

00.00.1922–00.09.1923	*Ortsgruppenleiter* of the *Ortsgruppe Karlsruhe der NSDAP*.
01.08.1923	Joined the SA.
01.08.1923–09.11.1923	*Bezirksführer der SA* for Franken and *Führer* of *SA Sturmregiment 3* (also known as *SA-Regiment "Frankenland"* and *SA-Kommando Franken*) in Nürnberg. The SA force over which he assumed command from Walter Steinbeck (dismissed in July 1923 due to conflicts with Julius Streicher) numbered some 275 men as of July 1923, a number that grew to about 800 by October. Buch was succeeded by *Oberleutnant* Freund.
08./09.11.1923	Played a peripheral role in the "*München-Putsch*." In the wake of the failed coup, he successfully eluded the police in Nürnberg and succeeded in transferring the files of the Nürnberg SA to Erlangen. Buch also called for a pogrom against the Jews, although there was no evidence that Jews had given any attention—positive or negative—to the Nazi bid for power in München. He issued the following order of the day for 11.11.1923:

The first period of the National Revolution is over. It has brought the desired clearing [of the air]. Our highly revered leader, Adolf Hitler, has again bled for the German people. The most shameful treachery that the world has ever seen has victimized him and the German people. Through Hitler's blood and the steel directed against our comrades in München by the hands of traitors the patriotic Kampfverbände are welded together for better or for worse. The second phase of the National Revolution begins [now]… (Harold J. Gordon, Jr., *Hitler and the Beer Hall Putsch*, pp. 432-433)

00.11.1923–00.04.1924	Employed as a wine and cigar salesman in München.
00.00.1924–01.01.1928	*Gau-SA-Führer Oberbayern-Schwaben*.
13.11.1923–00.01.1924	"*mit der Führung der illegalen SA beauftragt*" (charged with leadership of the illegal *SA*), leading the SA during the ban

	imposed in the wake of the "*München-Putsch.*" Appointed by Alfred Rosenberg, Max Amann, and Anton Drexler who jointly led the Party following Hitler's arrest. He succeeded Hermann Göring who had been severely wounded during the *Putsch*. During this period, he and his adjutant, Emil Danzeisen, worked diligently to reorganize and camouflage the SA, setting up rifle clubs and choral societies as a cover for illegal SA activities. He was succeeded by Wilhelm Freiherr Marschall von Bieberstein.
00.00.1924–01.01.1928	*Gau-SA-Führer Oberbayern-Schwaben.*
00.02.1924	Arrested in München, charged with attempting to reestablish the NSDAP (released after submitting a statement to the Police).
00.02.1925–23.11.1927	*SA-Führer in München.*
15.06.1925	Officially reenrolled in the NSDAP.
c. 1925–00.00.192_	*Vorsitzender* of the *Ehrengericht "Deutsche Vaterländische Orden"* (Court of Honor of the German Patriotic Order).
27.11.1927–01.01.1928	Acting *Vorsitzender* of the *Untersuchungs- und Schlichtungsausschuss* (USCHLA, Investigation and Arbitration Committee) in the *Reichsleitung der NSDAP.* Succeeded *Generalleutnant a. D.* Bruno Heinemann who had retired due to differences with Hitler, and possibly also due to age and frequent illness-related absences from office. Buch worked closely with Hitler, whom he worshipped, on every significant matter dealt with by the Party courts. Donald M. McKale writes:

[H]e did not always agree with Hitler on matters involving the *Reichs-Uschla*, but he was willing to subordinate his own ideas to those of the *Führer* and to carry through the latter's decisions at any cost.... [T]he Führer apparently had an extraordinary talent for convincing Buch in private discussions. Yet at the same time, Buch recognized early a fateful trait in Hitler that was eventually to cost the world dearly[:] Hitler's "contempt for humanity" (*Menschenverachtung*)... (McKale, *The Nazi Party Courts: Hitler's Management of Conflict in His Movement, 1921–1945*, pp. 61-62)

On 01.10.1928, Buch wrote a remarkable letter to Hitler, the handwritten original—in pencil—of which is found in the *Bundesarchiv* (NS 26/Folder 1375); however, it is uncertain if it was ever sent:

I have recently acquired an impression about a number of things and feel it is my difficult duty to tell you, Herr Hitler, that you have a contempt for humanity that fills me with grave uneasiness. I do not believe, Herr Hitler, that a person who is filled with human contempt from recent experiences can continue to fulfill a task that has burdened a people's fate for centuries.... It is quite clear to me that for some time you have believed yourself capable of building on the bitter disappointments of people and that during the past months you have received such a vote. I hope, however, these votes will be permanent. (McKale, *The Nazi Party Courts: Hitler's Management of Conflict in His Movement, 1921–1945*, p. 62)

01.01.1928–01.01.1934	*Vorsitzender* of the USCHLA in the *Reichsleitung der NSDAP*.
01.01.1928–09.12.1933	*Gau-SA-Führer* of Oberbayern-Schwaben. Succeeded by Friedrich Karl Freiherr von Eberstein.
20.05.1928–18.07.1930	Member of the *Reichstag (Wahlkreis 24, Oberbayern-Schwaben)*.
00.00.1930	Involved in a conspiracy to murder Ernst Röhm and certain members of his staff (including Graf Spreti, Graf du Moulin-Eckart, and Georg Bell). The originator of this plan, Emil Traugott Danzeisen, a former *SA-Standartenführer* and adjutant to Buch, was tried and sentenced to six months' imprisonment. Charges were not brought against Buch and the other conspirators due to lack of evidence.
14.09.1930–14.10.1933	Member of the *Reichstag*.
11.06.1930–00.10.1931	*Leiter* of the *Jugendamt* (Youth Office) in the *Reichsleitung der NSDAP*. McKale writes:

He felt especially strongly about the value of military education for German youth. Such an education, he maintained, taught the young the virtues of "loyalty, trust, obedience, courage, bravery, and comradeship." Buch firmly believed that without these, Germany could never survive in the future. Consequently, once he entered the NSDAP, he continually urged the party's Hitler Youth … to adopt an educational program that would indoctrinate its members in such ideals. Only then would it be possible, he emphasized, "to make the young people immune to the Jewish poison in all areas of public life." (McKale, *The Nazi Party Courts: Hitler's Management of Conflict in His Movement, 1921–1945*, p. 54, citing Buch's essay "Referent für Jugendfragen: Hitler Jugend," undated, BA, NS 26/Folder 1374)

00.00.193_–00.00.1933	Assigned as an editor of the *Völkischer Beobachter*.
03.01.1931–00.00.1931	Cruise from Hamburg to Genoa aboard the *Hamburg-Amerikanische* liner *Njassa*.
11.10.1931	Participated in the *Tagung der nationalen Opposition* in Bad Harzburg, during which the so-called "Harzburger Front" was established.
17.10.1931–18.10.1931	Participated in the "SA-Aufmarsch in Braunschweig."
01.06.1932–10.10.1935	*Vorsitzender* of the *I. Kammer der Reichs-USCHLA* (redesignated *I. Kammer des Obersten Parteigerichts der NSDAP*, 01.01.1934). He resigned from this post and was succeeded by Johannes Schneider.
30.08.1932–12.09.1932	Member of the *2. Ausschuss (Auswärtige Angelegenheiten) der Reichstag* (Second Committee [Foreign Affairs] of the *Reichstag*).
06.12.1932–01.02.1933	Member of the *2. Ausschuss (Auswärtige Angelegenheiten) der Reichstag*.
01.07.1933–01.10.1934	Joined the SS, assigned as *Ehrenführer* to 63. SS-Standarte.
30.08.1933–03.09.1933	Participated in the "5. Reichsparteitag der NSDAP" in Nürnberg.
04.11.1933	Appointed as *Ehren-Gauführer* for *Oberen Murg-Gau (Baden)* of the *Reichsbund Kyffhäuser*.
12.12.1933–28.03.1936	Member of the *Reichstag (Wahlkreis 15, Osthannover)*.
01.01.1934–08.05.1945	*Vorsitzender des Obersten Parteigerichts der NSDAP* (chairman of the Supreme Party Court of the NSDAP, also known as *Oberster*

Parteirichter [Chief Party Judge] *der NSDAP*), München. Buch fervently believed that National Socialism should represent a revolution in morality as well as politics and power. He naively expected Adolf Hitler to be a champion of law and decency, spearheading a crusade against vice and corruption. "For Buch," writes Dietrich Orlow, "morality consisted primarily of a series of negatives, chief among them anti-Semitism, anti-freemasonry, and anti-pornography." (*History of the Nazi Party: 1933–1945*, p. 67) But Buch was given little power or direction by his *Führer* in overseeing the preservation of moral rectitude among the Party membership, and it did not help that neither Buch nor his judges were trained in law. "Moreover," continues Orlow, "Buch had little control over disputes within the *PO* [*politische Organisation* of the NSDAP]. In quarrels between *Reichsleiter* and *Gauleiter*, for example, his role was restricted to that of a mediator…" (*History of the Nazi Party: 1933–1945*, p. 67) Under interrogation at Nürnberg by Lt. Col. Thomas S. Hinkel, Buch made the following statements concerning his role in this assignment:

05.09.1945: I was charged with the administration of all party courts in the different states and I was in charge of higher court methods in cases of higher party members. In other words, when higher party members stood before the court, I took charge of the court procedure. The higher court I divided in different departments, and they have independently without my influence handled the different cases…. I myself was only a judge in the case of higher party officials….

31.10.1945: … I would like to ask you to consider the position of a man who for seventeen years was forced to do against his will, a job which he didn't like. I kept asking that I be relieved of my functions, and be permitted to return to my original profession as a regular army officer. This was particularly true during the war when my boys were out in the field, and my mind was not on my job as much as it was on the military situation. This is why the things that I may have done, which had to be done in the execution of my functions, are not as clear in my memory as they would have been if I had taken more interest in my job, which I had to do against my own will.

Another interrogation report, dated 18.07.1945, states:

Buch tried to organize the party courts along the lines of the Ehrengerichte of the old German Army. He was a member of the Army himself, and a passionate soldier. His father who was a judge of the Supreme Court (Oberlandesgericht) in Baden, had warned the boy to stay away from the study of law. Buch had followed this advice, and apparently kept a deep-rooted distrust of all legal procedures. Just the same, he was always fascinated by the problem of justice. He found the highest expression of justice in the army, and consciously organized his party justice so as to be similar to that of the army. Even the punishments of the party courts were the same as the punishments in the military court of honor, viz. Verweis, Verwarnung (after 1933 Verwarnung mit Aberkennung der Fähigkeit, ins Amt zu bekleiden) (reprimand with the prohibition of holding an office), Entlassung [discharge], Ausschluss [dismissal], and Ausstossung [expulsion]. The latter punishment involved the prohibition for any party offices or organizations to employ the culprit in [the] future. He became an outcast of the party. Private firms or private parties, however, were not bound by this prohibition. The Ausstossung … was generally pronounced only when a criminal act had been committed, and was followed, as a rule, by a trial before a regular civilian court.

It was, however, not the only task of the party courts to take disciplinary action against party members who had sinned against the spirit of the party. A vast sector of the party judiciary was concerned with arbitration between party members. In all cases, the party courts were entitled to conduct investigations. In no case could the party courts pronounce a sentence which had effect outside the party proper; it could not impose punishments other than disciplinary actions which only affected the defendant within the party.

If a case involved any criminal acts, the party court would notify the regular courts, and even furnish the material of its findings. Regularly, according to Buch, an action of the party courts would precede a trial before the regular courts.… A pronouncement of the party court did not bind the regular courts, e.g., if a man was expelled from the party because he had embezzled party funds, a regular court was not compelled to sentence this man; he might have refunded the embezzled money, or might be acquitted before the regular court for other reasons. By the same token, a man who was acquitted by a party court might yet be prosecuted before a regular court. However, Buch is not sure whether it happened in practice that cases that were dismissed by the party courts were prosecuted further by regular courts.

The jurisdiction of the party courts was not based upon any codified law. Hitler ordered Buch in 1933 to draft a codified criminal law for offenses of party members which would be prosecuted by party justice. For that purpose Buch was to get in contact with the Reichsjustizminister Gürtner. Buch stalled all during 1933, because he was opposed to the use of codified laws; finally, in December 1933 he found his way to Gürtner, with whom he had a long conversation. The result of this conversation was that both men agreed that such a law would be against the spirit of the institution of party courts. Buch reported this agreement to Hitler who let himself be convinced.…

Buch tried to avoid choosing professional lawyers as party judges. He tried to fill these positions with old members of the party who had partaken in the fight of the party for power, because he trusted these men to maintain the spirit of the party. Most of the judges worked on an honorary basis, only those of the Supreme Court and the Gaugerichte were full time judges and paid as such. They numbered, all in all, about 100 men.

When the war broke out, Buch insisted that his judges become soldiers for a limited time. He wanted them to experience the life of a front-line soldier, so as to be better fitted for their job when they returned from the war. 150 full time judges were killed in the war, which lead to a degeneration of the party court system. More professional lawyers infiltrated into the courts, and the best judges were absent or dead. At the same time, the expulsions pronounced by party courts took a sharp increase (proportionally), because the better elements of the party were at the front, and the new party members who were accepted into the party, largely under pressure from the party treasurer, were no longer carefully selected to represent the elite of the nation....

The Oberste Parteigericht needed the confirmation of Hitler himself to make its decisions effective. Since 1941, the Chief of the Parteikanzlei, Bormann, achieved the power of confirming the decisions of the Supreme Party Court. He became, by Hitler's delegation, the party's Supreme Justice (Oberster Gerichtsherr). As such, he not only was able to nullify sentences pronounced by the Supreme Court, but also inform the court that a certain decision was expected in an individual case. Buch tried to main his independence of decision, but since he was in practice unable to judge according to his personal convictions, he refused to preside in court sessions, and more or less retired from his position. This interference of Bormann, however, only applied when the court was sitting in first instance, e.g., proceedings against Gauleiter, but not in cases where the Supreme Court was judging an appeal from a lower court... (Institut für Zeitgeschichte, München, Akte 4637/71)

In his postwar memoirs, the former Hamburg *Gauleiter* Dr. Albert Krebs described Buch as follows:

I had frequent dealings with Buch and in the process always found him to be an honorable man of the best intentions. Without a doubt he had the goodwill to operate his office in such a way as to keep out or remove all corrupt elements. But it is equally without doubt that he did not succeed in doing so. His concept of what constituted behavior injurious to the party differed from Hitler's so frequently that it was impossible for Buch to effectuate it. As a dry, somewhat pedantic man in his ideas and needs, Buch possessed neither the wit nor the charm that was needed to resist or even convince Hitler. That is, Buch presented opinions and proposals but then simply obeyed when Hitler held contrary opinions and ordered decisions in accordance with them.... On [one] occasion ... Buch openly admitted to me his attitude and his method, saying it was caused by his military training in obedience. "You just click your heels together and say 'yes, sir!'" (Dr. Krebs, *The Infancy of Nazism*)

Buch's relevance in the NSDAP steadily waned as a result of a crusade against immorality within the Party that backfired. In his official publication, *Der Parteirichter* (issues of 10.04.1935; 10.06.1935; 10.08.1935; 10.10.1935; 10.01.1936; and 10.06.1936) he stated that scrupulous marital fidelity and the maintenance of family stability were National-Socialist cornerstones. His greatest mistake was to demand the punishment by party courts of moral offenses by senior Party leaders. In a Party where marital infidelity was rather commonplace at all levels of the chain of command, this won Buch no friends (notable examples of those who would theoretically be affected by Buch's morality campaign were the powerful *Reichsminister* Dr. Goebbels, as well as two philandering *Gauleiter*, Wilhelm Kube and Julius Streicher. Hitler himself disapproved of Buch's statements and writings, as it was loyalty to *Führer* and Party that concerned him—not the amorous adventures of his otherwise stalwart satraps. It was likely only after being called to meet with an angry Hitler on 14.11.1935 that Buch learned that he was acting against the will of his *Führer*. His significance as a Party leader all but disappeared following that meeting.

01.01.1934–10.10.1935 *Vorsitzender der I. Kammer des Obersten Parteigerichts der NSDAP* (chairman of the First Chamber of the Supreme Party Court of the NSDAP).

23.02.1934–00.00.1934 Cruise aboard the *Hamburg-Südamerikanische* liner *Cap Arcona* together with Frau Buch, departing Hamburg and visiting Southampton, Vigo, Lisbon, Las Palmas, Rio de Janeiro, Santos, and Montevideo.

00.06.1934–00.07.1934 Played an important role in the purge of the SA leadership. He had amassed a large quantity of incriminating material against the SA from *Gauleiter* and other NSDAP officials and collected hundreds of complaints from SA men and parents of Hitler Youth members. Also in his possession were "love letters" to male friends sent by Röhm to Bolivia. Buch demonstrated great zeal and brutality during the purge of 30.06.–01.07.1934, with unconfirmed accounts accusing him of personally directing the execution of SA leaders by SS men at Stadelheim Prison near München. The following is excerpted from a report of Buch's postwar interrogation:

The Purge of 1934

Sometime in 1933, PW Walter Buch received numerous letters and official complaints about the homosexual activities of the Leader of the SA, Roehm. Because Buch was the Party Judge, it was only right that he should be the one to whom such complaints from the mothers, wives, etc. of Roehm's subordinates, would be addressed. Buch immediately sought audience with Hitler and informed him of the complaints, also showing the written proof. But Hitler, who was always frantically loyal to his friends, refused to listen to Buch's advice and did not believe the charges brought against Roehm....

On the 30th of June 1934, Buch was working in his office in Munich when Hess called on him and told him that Roehm had been arrested. Together with Hess, Buch went to a gathering of Party leaders whom Hitler addressed at that time. In his speech, Hitler told the assembly that Roehm was guilty of conspiracy, and that he had ordered his arrest. He then went on to say that Buch had warned him about Roehm a year before, but that he, (Hitler) had not listened to Buch's advice. (PW says that since this day, Hitler and he were estranged, because Hitler bore a grudge against him for making him admit his mistake).

Although the case of Roehm should have come before the Supreme Party Judge, this was not done, and the entire Purge was handled by the SS in a very secretive fashion. Buch was told several days later that Roehm had been killed. ("Special Report on Walter Buch,

Reichsleiter and *Oberster Parteirichter*" [13.06.1945], Special Detention Center "Ashcan"—Detailed Interrogation Report, in "Interrogation Records Prepared for War Crimes Proceedings at Nuernberg, 1945–1947/ OCCPAC Interrogation Transcripts and Related Records: Buch, Walter Hans"; Publication Number M1270, Record Group RG238)

05.09.1934–16.09.1934	Participated in the "*6. Reichsparteitag der NSDAP*" in Nürnberg.
01.10.1934–01.04.1936	Assigned as an *SS-Führer z.b.V.* to the *Reichsführer-SS*.
00.09.1934–30.04.1945	Member of the *Sachverständigenbeirat für Bevölkerungs- und Rassepolitik* (Council of Experts for Population and Racial Policy) attached to the *Reichsministerium des Innern*.
03.10.1934–00.00.1944	Member of the *Akademie für Deutsches Recht*, München.
10.09.1935–16.09.1935	Participated in the "*7. Reichsparteitag der NSDAP*" in Nürnberg.
05.02.1936	At a press conference in München on 05.02.1936, declared: "Right is what benefits the German people, and wrong is what would be harmful. To establish the limits between right and wrong is the task of the highest party court of justice." (Rolf Tell, *Sound and Fuehrer*, p. 128)
01.04.1936–30.04.1945	Assigned to the staff of the *Reichsführer-SS*.
08.09.1936–14.09.1936	Participated in the "*8. Reichsparteitag der NSDAP*" in Nürnberg.
30.01.1937–08.05.1945	Member of the *Reichstag (Wahlkreis 29, Leipzig)*.
06.09.1937–13.09.1937	Participated in the "*9. Reichsparteitag der NSDAP*" in Nürnberg.
00.00.193_–00.00.19__	Member of the Committee for the *Braune Band von Deutschland* (an organization set up to maintain the quality of horses for sporting activities and to control the quality of such stock for mounted units of the SS and other Party organizations).
05.09.1938–12.09.1938	Participated in the "*10. Reichsparteitag der NSDAP*" in Nürnberg.
13.02.1939	Submitted the following secret report on his investigation into the "*Reichskristallnacht*" pogrom to Hermann Göring:

Dear Party Comrade Göring!
I enclose the report of my special senate about the procedure hitherto concluded concerning the excesses on the occasion of the anti-Jewish operations of 9. and 10. November 1938. Heil Hitler!
[signed] Walter Buch…

Report about the events and judicial proceedings in connection with the antisemitic demonstrations of 9. November 1938.

On the evening of 9. November 1938, Reich Propaganda Minister Party Comrade Dr. Goebbels told the Party leaders assembled at a social evening in the old town hall in München, that in the Gaue of Kurhessen and Magdeburg-Anhalt it had come to demonstrations against Jews, during which Jewish shops were demolished and synagogues were set on fire. The Führer, at Goebbels' suggestion, had decided that such demonstrations were not to be prepared or organized by the Party, but so far as they originated spontaneously, they were not to be discouraged either. In other respects, Party Comrade Dr. Goebbels carried out the purport of what was prescribed in the teletype of the Reich Propaganda Administration of 10. November 1938 (12:30 to 1 o'clock) (Enclosure 2). It was probably understood by all Party leaders present, from the oral instructions of the Reich Propaganda Minister, that the Party should not appear outwardly as the originator of the demonstrations but in reality should organize and execute them. Instructions in this sense were telephoned immediately (thus a considerable time before transmission of the first teletype) to the bureaus of their Gaue by a large part of the Party members present.... At the end of November 1938, the Oberstes Parteigericht, through reports from several Gau courts, heard that these demonstrations of 9. November 1938 had to a considerable extent gone as far as plundering and killing of Jews and that they had already been the object of investigation by the police and the state prosecutor. The deputy Führer [Rudolf Hess] agreed with the interpretation of the chief Party Court, that known transgressions in any case should be investigated under the jurisdiction of the party. Because of the obvious connection between the events to be judged and the instructions which Reich Propaganda Minister Party Comrade Dr. Goebbels gave in the town hall at the social evening. Without investigation and evaluation of this connection, a just judgment did not appear possible. This investigation, however, could not be left to innumerable state courts, especially as the demonstrations had meanwhile been presented to the public as the spontaneous expression of the people's sentiments. According to the conception of the Oberstes Parteigericht it must, as a matter of principle, be impossible for political offences to be determined and judged by the state court without the Party having the possibility of first obtaining clarification about the happenings, so that, if occasion arises, the Führer could be asked in good time to cancel the proceedings at the state court. This concerns matters, which primarily concern the interests of the Party and which even though this be only from the viewpoint of the perpetrator, are desired by the Party. Due to such considerations, Generalfeldmarschall Party Comrade Göring ... has entrusted the Secret State Police and the Party jurisdiction with the investigation of excesses. The Oberstes Parteigericht has reserved for itself the investigation of killings, severe mistreatment and moral transgressions. On the basis of state police inquiries, the judges of the Oberstes Parteigericht, who were present with their alternates held quick trials of those cases about which facts were ascertained up to 17. January 1939. Gau leaders and Group leaders of the branches served as jurors at the trials and decisions. The decisions, which, for reasons to be discussed later, contain only portions of the statements of the facts, are attached. Party Member Frey, Heinrich, Party Member since 1932, residing in Rheinhausen, Horst Wessel Street 23, was ejected from the Party because of a moral crime and race violation perpetrated upon the thirteen-year old-school girl Ruth Kalter. Frey is in custody and has been handed over to the criminal court (Enclosure 5). Party Member Gerstner, Gustav, Party membership number 3,135,242, SA-Oberscharführer, residing at Niederwern, at present district court prison Würzburg, was expelled from the NSDAP and SA because of theft. Gerstner is in custody and has been handed over to the public court because suspected of race violation. (Enclosure 6).... 4. Party Member Norgall, Franz, Party membership number 342,751, SA-Sturmführer, residing at 58 Neuhoefer street, Heilsberg (East Prussia), was given a warning and sentenced to three years deprivation of the right to hold public office because of disciplinary violation, namely the killing of the Jewish couple Seelig in Heilsberg contrary to orders. (Enclosure 8).... 16. Proceedings against Party Members Aichinger, Hans, SS-Hauptsturmführer, residing at 9 Seilergasse, Innsbruck, and Hofgartner, Walter, SS-Untersturmführer residing at 21 Gavelsberger Street, Innsbruck, for killing the Jews Graubart, Dr. Bauer, and Berger, have already been quashed on the basis of inquiries on the part of the State Police and individual interrogations of the Oberstes Parteigericht (Enclosure 20). With regard to cases 3–16 the Oberstes Parteigericht asks the Führer to quash the proceedings in the State Criminal Courts. The Reich Minister of Justice has been informed of this petition and the decisions on which it was based handed down by the Oberstes Parteigericht. Cases 4–16 are killings committed by order, committed on the basis of a vague or presumed order, committed without orders but motivated by hatred against Jews or in the opinion that vengeance ought to be taken for the death of Party Comrade [Ernst] vom Rath upon the wish of the leaders, or killings motivated by a resolution suddenly formed in the excitement of the situation. The professed object of the entire action was the innermost reason, as well as the thought that reprisals had to be made in some form or other, on behalf of Party Comrade vom Rath. If a clearly defined order is at hand … the request to quash the proceedings against the immediate perpetrator needs no further argument. The order must shift the responsibility from the person who acted to the person who gave the order. Furthermore, the men often had to fight down strongest inner restraints in order to carry out the order. As was repeatedly expressed by the culprits, it is not our SA and SS men's affair to force their way into bedrooms by night, dressed in civilian clothes in order personally to do away with a despised political foe by his wife's side or together with his wife. Investigation into the circumstances under which the orders were given has shown that in all these cases a misunderstanding arose in some link or other of the chain of command, especially due to the fact that it was a matter of course to the National Socialist who was active in the days of the Party struggle that in drives in which the Party does not wish to appear as the organizer, orders are not given with final clarity and with full details. He is therefore used to deducing more from what he reads in such an order than is said literally, just as it had frequently become the practice on the part of the person issuing the order in the interest of the Party to refrain from saying anything to hint what he meant to achieve with the specific order especially when it concerned illegal political demonstrations. Therefore Party Comrade Dr. Goebbels' instruction that the Party was not to organize this demonstration was most likely interpreted by each Party leader present in the town-hall to mean that the Party should not appear as the organizer. Party Comrade Dr. Goebbels probably meant it in that way for politically interested and active circles, who might participate in such demonstrations are members of the Party and its branches. Naturally, they could be mobilised only through offices of the Party and its branches. Thus, a series of subordinate leaders understood some unfortunately phrased orders which reached them orally or by phone to mean that

Jewish blood would now have to flow for the blood of Party Comrade vom Rath, that at any rate the leadership did not attach importance to the life of a Jew, for example, not the Jew Gruenspan but all Jewry was guilty of the death of Party Comrade vom Rath. The German people were therefore taking revenge on all Jewry, the synagogues were burning in the entire Reich, Jewish residences and businesses were to be laid waste, life and property of Aryans had to be protected, foreign Jews were not to be harassed. The drive was being carried out by order of the Führer; the police were withdrawn; pistols were to be brought, and at the least resistance, the weapon was to be used without consideration, as each SA man would certainly know what he had to do etc....

It is another question, whether an intentionally ambiguous order, given with the expectation that the order's recipient would recognise the intention and would act accordingly, is not an example of the discipline of the past. In times of struggle, such an order may, in individual cases, be necessary, in order to achieve political success without giving the government any possibility of discovering the origin of the Party. This viewpoint is now obsolete. The public, down to the last man, realizes that political drives like those of 9. November were organized and directed by the Party, whether this is admitted or not.... (Translation of Document 3063-PS, in *Nazi Conspiracy and Aggression, Vol. V*)

26.08.1942	Wrote the following letter of congratulations to the newly appointed *Reichsjustizminister, SA-Gruppenführer* Dr. Otto Georg Thierack:

Dear Party Comrade Thierack!
I was pleased to read in the V.B. that the "Kaiserless, the terrible time" in the judiciary had finally been ended by the Führer. I am pleased that the Führer chose you and I am especially pleased that he immediately endowed the old Nazi with special powers. Let me offer you my sincerest congratulations on all of this. My wishes go above all in the direction that you may succeed as soon as possible in undoing the outlawry under which the German judge has fallen during the course of the war.

As the son of a lawyer who, after all, made it to the Senatspräsident of an Oberlandesgericht and, according to the Führer's own words, wrote "the first National Socialist book", as well as from 15 years of experience as the highest judge of the NSDAP, I dare to presume a judgement on these things, and even to consider it to be correct.

I do not believe that the mill of Sanssouci has lost its meaning, nor can I agree that the old phrase: "One man's speech is no man's speech, you must hear them both," should no longer be justified. And yet I fear forces at work that want to undermine these foundations. I do not believe that the German people can tolerate a police state, and I refuse to acknowledge that such a state would be worthy of the Führer or his work. Anyone who leads the German Wehrmacht in such a way that it beats the hell out of the enemy wherever it meets him cannot want to fill up the wellspring from which such soldiers grow with police methods.

I am sure you will not find it presumptuous if I wish to talk to you about such questions that have arisen during my 15 years in office and about which I was sometimes allowed to chat with your unforgettable predecessor Gürtner. I would imagine that one day in the not-too-distant future you will visit the Oberste Landesgericht in München. In this case, let me express the hope today that I may then also welcome you to my Oberste Parteigericht. If, on the other hand, my path should first lead me to Berlin, please allow me to contact you then.

It seems to me to be time to call "All hands on deck", so that the Fundamentum Ragnorum does not sink under envious floods of dirt to the detriment of the German people and the Führer's work. Certainly, as one who has suffered in the past, I understand the dislike of the leading men of the movement for the judiciary, but I consider it pernicious to degrade it to the whore of politics. Fettered judiciary must bring ruin, no matter in whose fetters it languishes. Like any other state institution, it can only have one guiding principle: I Serve.

Heil Hitler
Your
Walter Buch
(Bundesarchiv R3001/20055; Translation: Gary Costello)

00.07.1944	Together with several other Party judges, visited *Reichsgau Sudetenland*. During a banquet arranged in his honor by *Gauleiter* Henlein, Buch collapsed from a sudden attack of pleurisy, and was bedridden for some time thereafter.

POSTWAR PROSECUTION:

30.04.1945	Arrested by U.S. Army troops at his estate in Holzhausen am Ammersee.
14.05.1945–12.08.1945	Interned at Central Continental Prisoner of War Enclosure No. 32—known as "Ashcan"—at Mondorf-les Bains, Luxembourg, where he was interrogated numerous times concerning his activities during the Third Reich. He was also interviewed extensively concerning his missing (in later years, confirmed dead) son-in-law, Martin Bormann, who was to be tried in absentia by the Internal Military Tribunal, Nurnberg.
10.08.1945–Autumn 1946	Transferred to Nürnberg, where he was held for a time before being transferred to Dachau.
04.01.1947	Returned to Nürnberg for further interrogation.
03.07.1948	At his first de-Nazification trial, before the *Lagerspruchkammer* in Garmisch-Partenkirchen, classified as a *Hauptschuldiger* (major offender, i.e. placed in de-Nazification *Kategorie I*) and sentenced to five years' hard labor, as well as confiscation of his assets up to 2,000 Marks.
16.02.1949	Appeals hearing before the Weilheim Senate of the *Oberbayern Spruchkammer*. The original sentence of 03.07.1948 was confirmed. He then appealed the sentence and went to the highest court.
29.07.1949	Third de-Nazification hearing, conducted in München. He was again classified as a *Hauptschuldiger* but re-sentenced to three and a half years in a labor camp. Deemed to have served

more than this amount of time in postwar internment, his assets were confiscated, and he was released from custody the same day.

PUBLISHED WORKS:
Nationalsozialismus: Volk und Familie (1932)
Niedergang und Aufstieg der Deutscher Familie (1932)
Fünfzig Jahre antisemitische Bewegung (1937)
Des nationalsozialistischen Menschen Ehre und Ehrenschutz (1939). The following description of this book is excerpted from the report of a 1945 interrogation of Buch: "[Buch wrote it] in order to define the position of the party members, and to establish a code of honor for the party.... Hitler was very satisfied with the book, and ordered Buch to come to some agreement with the army to settle arguments between Army members and members of the party..." (Institut für Zeitgeschichte, München, Akte 4637/71).

DECORATIONS & AWARDS:

00.00.191_	*1914 Eisernes Kreuz I. Klasse*
00.00.191_	*1914 Eisernes Kreuz II. Klasse*
30.01.1942	*Kriegsverdienstkreuz I. Klasse ohne Schwerter*
00.00.1941	*Kriegsverdienstkreuz II. Klasse ohne Schwerter*
04.01.1935	*Ehrenkreuz des Weltkrieges 1914-1918 mit Schwertern*
00.00.1934	*Goldenes Ehrenzeichen der NSDAP*
06.07.1936	*Ehrenzeichen des 9. November 1923 (Blutorden) (Nr. 1.496)*
00.10.1932	*Coburger Ehrenzeichen der NSDAP*
00.00.193_	*Goldenes Hitler-Jugend Ehrenzeichen mit Eichenlaub*
30.01.1942	*Dienstauszeichnung der NSDAP in Gold*
30.01.1940	*Dienstauszeichnung der NSDAP in Silber*
30.01.1940	*Dienstauszeichnung der NSDAP in Bronze*
00.00.1929	*Nürnberger Parteitagsabzeichen 1929*
00.00.1931	*Abzeichen des SA-Treffens Braunschweig 1931*
16.08.1936	*Deutsche Olympia-Ehrenzeichen I. Klasse*
09.11.1935	*Ehrendegen des Reichsführers-SS*
25.12.1934	*Totenkopfring der SS*
00.00.193_	*SS-Zivilabzeichen*
00.02.1934	*Ehrenwinkel für alte Kämpfer*

NOTES:
* Parents:
  - Father: Dr. jur. h. c. *Hermann* Jakob Wilhelm Buch, Senate President of the *Baden Oberlandesgericht* (*28.07.1854, †29.07.1921 in Karlsruhe), son of Hermann Buch (*08.01.1816 in Neustadt, †10.08.1882 in Heidelberg) and his wife Karoline Elisabeth Sofie, *née* Fischer (*15.11.1823 in Heidelberg, †04.12.1895 in Freiburg).
  - Mother: Hedwig Maria Gertrud, *née* Heidlauff. (*02.01.1863 in Lahr)
* Sister: Karola Paula *Hedwig* Buch (*18.04.1886, †00.00.1955 in Loerrach).
* Religion: Protestant.
* Marriages:
  1. 23.09.1908 in Konstanz/Baden to Else Pleusser (*11.05.1887 in Barmen, †29.10.1944 of a heart attack; NSDAP-Nr. 7.732, recipient of the *Goldenes Ehrenzeichen der NSDAP*; NS-Frauenschaft-Nr. 5.721; F.M. [*Fordernder Mitglied*, sponsoring member of the SS]-Nr. 310.542).

2. 00.07.1949 in Inning/Ammersee to Hildegard ("Hilde"), née Sturm (*12.03.1912 in München). Her first husband was *Hauptmann a. D. Dr.* Martin Heinrich *Georg* Gund (*22.12.1889 in Speyer, †25.08.1940). Buch had known Hilde and Georg Gund for many years, and had served with Georg Gund in *Infanterie-Regiment 114* during World War I. After his wartime comrade's death, Buch began to visit Hilde in Inning. After the death of Else Buch, and possibly earlier, they became romantically involved. In 1950, Hilde Buch relocated from Inning/Ammersee to München, emigrating to the United States with her three children in 1962.

* Children of Walter and Else Buch:

Hans-Walter Buch
Kapitänleutnant (Kriegsmarine)
Kapitän zur See (Bundeswehr)

*	11.01.1912 in Biebrich am Rhein (near Wiesbaden).
†	07.08.2001 in Ulm.

Promotions:
Reichsmarine/Kriegsmarine:
26.09.1934	*Seekadett*
01.07.1935	*Fähnrich zur See*
01.01.1937	*Oberfähnrich zur See*
01.04.1937	*Leutnant zur See*
01.04.1939	*Oberleutnant zur See*
01.02.1942	*Kapitänleutnant*

Bundeswehr:
00.00.1956	*Korvettenkapitän*
00.00.1960	*Fregattenkapitän*
00.00.1965	*Kapitän zur See*

Career:
08.04.1934–00.00.193_	Entered *Reichsmarine* service (with Crew 1934, numbering 318 officer candidates), initially undergoing basic training (*Infanterieausbildung*) in Stralsund and shipboard training before participating in a *Fähnrichs-Lehrgang*. *Windjammermatrose* aboard the sailing training vessel *Gorch Fock*.
[00.11.1937]	Junior officer aboard the light cruiser *Köln*.
[00.11.1938]	Assigned as a junior officer to 6. *Zerstörer-Division*.
01.12.1938–13.04.1940	*II. Wachoffizier (II. W.O.)* aboard the destroyer *Z 11 Bernd von Arnim*.
01.04.1940–01.07.1940	*Zugführer* in *Marine-Regiment "Berger,"* a naval infantry unit that participated in the fighting for Narvik (Norway).
01.07.1940–01.03.1941	*Gruppenführer* in *Hafenschutz-Flottile "Molde."*
01.03.1941–01.06.1941	*Kompanieführer* in the *Zerstörer- und Torpedo-Stammabteilung*.
01.06.1941–01.07.1942	*I. Wachoffizier (I. W. O.)* aboard Z 29.
01.07.1942–01.03.1943	*I. Offizier* aboard Z 28.
01.03.1943–01.09.1943	*Kommandant* of the *Torpedoboot Falke*.
01.10.1943–18.08.1944	*Kommandant* of the *Flottentorpedoboot T 30* (commissioned 24.10.1943). On 18.08.1944, T 30 found itself in a mine field and was sunk, 114 men of its 205-man crew losing their lives. Buch survived but was wounded.
00.08.1944–00.10.1944	On convalescent leave due to wounds.

00.08.1944–01.10.1944	*Führer* of *Torpedobootsgruppe Finnenbusen*. Operating in the eastern and central Baltic, *Finnenbusen* played an important role in evacuating some 10,000 German troops and civilian refugees (*Unternehmen Hannibal*) despite the constant threat of enemy aircraft, surface vessels, and submarines.
01.10.1944–08.05.1945	*Kommandant* of the *Flottentorpedoboot T 35* (commissioned 07.10.1944), subordinated to *5. Torpedobootsflotille*.

Postwar Activities:
00.05.1945–00.00.194_	In Allied captivity.
00.00.19__–00.00.1956	*Kapitän* (A6 – Master) of a freighter and *Reederei-Inspektor* (shipping company inspector) of *Reederei Ahlmann-Transport* in Rendsburg/Büdelsdorf/Schelswig-Holstein.
00.00.1956–01.04.1960	Entered service with the *Bundesmarine*, initial assignment(s) unknown.
01.04.1960–01.09.1960	*Kommodore* (m.d.W.d.G.b.) of *3. Zerstörergeschwader* (comprised of the Fletcher Class destroyers *Z 4*, *Z 5*, and *Z 6*). He also commanded *Z 4* during the same period.
01.09.1960–07.08.1962	Assignment(s) unknown.
07.08.1962–31.03.1965	*Kommandeur* of the *Kommando der Troßschiffe* [service vessels command]/*4. Fregattengeschwader/Einsatzflottille 2*.
00.00.1968–00.00.1969	*Chef* of the "DDG Project Management Office" in Washington D.C., including work as *Projektleiter Raketenzerstörer*—project manager for guided missile destroyers, which led to the construction of three Charles F. Adams SCB 155-DDGs for the *Bundeswehr*).
00.00.1972	Retired from the *Bundeswehr*.
00.00.19__–00.00.19__	Member of the *Marine-Offizier-Vereinigung (MOV) e. V.*

Decorations & Awards:
08.08.1944	*Deutsches Kreuz in Gold* as *Kapitänleutnant* and *Kommandant* of *Torpedoboot T 30* in *6. Torpedobootsflottille*.
00.00.1940	*1939 Eisernes Kreuz I. Klasse*
00.00.1939	*1939 Eisernes Kreuz II. Klasse*
00.00.1940	*Zerstörer-Kriegsabzeichen*
00.00.1944	*Verwundetenabzeichen, 1939 in Schwarz*
00.00.1940	*Narvikschild*
c. 1938	*Wehrmachts-Dienstauszeichnung IV. Klasse*

<u>*Bundesrepublik Deutschland*</u>:
00.00.1971	*Verdienstkreuz 1. Klasse (Offizierkreuz) des Verdienstordens der Bundesrepublik Deutschland*
00.07.1992	*Rettungs-Medaille* "Ostsee 1945" for his role, as *Kommandant* of *Flottentorpedoboot T 35*, in the "*größte Rettungswerk der Seegeschichte*" (Greatest Rescue Operation in Naval History). Awarded during the "*7. Ostsee-Treffen*" of the *Kuratorium Erinnerungsstätte Albatros – Rettung über See e. V.* and the "*Ostsee-Archiv Heinz Schön*."

Notes:
* Marriages:
- *c.* 1937 (three children resulting)
- 24.03.1949 to Ursel O. (one child resulting)
- *c.* 1990 to Hildegard ____.

Friedrich *Hermann* Robert Buch
SS-Hauptsturmführer

*	26.02.1920 in Scheuern/Gernsbach.
†	12.11.2012 in a retirement home near Budapest, Hungary. He had resettled to that country with his family on 15.09.2000.
NSDAP-Nr.:	Unknown
SS-Nr.:	357.263 (Joined 01.11.1938)

Promotions:
[Preceding ranks unknown]
00.11.1939	*SS-Junker*
00.00.1939	*SS-Standartenjunker*
00.02.1940	*SS-Standartenoberjunker*
13.06.1940	*SS-Untersturmführer*
30.01.1942	*SS-Obersturmführer*
20.04.1944	*SS-Hauptsturmführer*

Career:
c. 1936–1938	Attended the *NPEA Plön* through graduation.
01.11.1938	Joined the *SS-Verfügungstruppe*.
00.11.1939–00.02.1940	Attended *SS-Junkerschule Bad Tölz*.
00.00.1940–00.00.194_	*Zugführer* in 15. Kompanie/SS-Regiment "Deutschland."
00.11.1941–00.12.1941	*Ordonnanzoffizier* in SS-Kradschützen-Bataillon/SS-Division (mot.) "Reich."
00.12.1941–00.03.1942	*Bataillons-Adjutant* of SS-Kradschützen-Bataillon/SS-Division (mot.) "Reich."
00.03.1942–00.05.1942	*Kompanieführer* of 3. Kompanie/SS-Kradschützen-Bataillon/SS-Division "Das Reich" (mot.).
00.05.1942–00.11.1942	*Bataillons-Adjutant* of SS-Kradschützen-Bataillon/SS-Panzer-Grenadier-Division "Das Reich."
00.11.1942–00.00.194_	*Kompanieführer* of 3. Kompanie/SS-Kradschützen-Bataillon/SS-Panzer-Grenadier-Division "Das Reich."
00.00.194_–00.00.194_	*Kompanieführer* of 15. Kompanie/SS-Panzer-Grenadier-Regiment "Der Führer"/SS-Panzer- Grenadier-Division "Das Reich."
00.00.194_–00.00.194_	Severely wounded, then on convalescent leave.
00.00.194_–00.12.1944	Assigned to *Verwaltungsdienst* (administrative service) at *SS-Junkerschule Bad Tölz*.
00.12.1944–17.01.1945	Temporarily assigned as *Regimentsadjutant* of SS-Panzer-Grenadier-Regiment 4 "Der Führer"/2. SS-Panzer-Division "Das Reich."
17.01.1945–00.05.1945	*Divisions-Adjutant (IIa)* of 2. SS-Panzer-Division "Das Reich". Succeeded Otto Resch. Wounded in action for the seventh and final time, April 1945.

Postwar Activities:
00.00.1945–00.00.194_	In Allied captivity.

00.00.19__–00.00.19__	Editor of *Der Freiwillige* (the *Waffen-SS* veterans' publication), succeeding Helmut Thöle. He was an active member of the *Hilfsgemeinschaft auf Gegenseitigkeit der Angehörigen der ehemaligen Waffen-SS* (HIAG, Mutual Aid Association of Former *Waffen-SS* Members).
22.10.1971	Founded the *"Vereinigung der Freunde der SS-Division 'Das Reich'"* (Association of Friends of the *SS-Division "Das Reich"*) in Rosenheim.

Decorations & Awards:

10.07.1941	*1939 Eisernes Kreuz I. Klasse*
00.00.19__	*1939 Eisernes Kreuz II. Klasse*
00.00.194_	*Infanterie-Sturmabzeichen in Bronze*
00.00.194_	*Verwundetenabzeichen, 1939 in Silber*
00.00.194_	*Verwundetenabzeichen, 1939 in Schwarz*
00.00.1942	*Medaille "Winterschlacht im Osten 1941/42"*
00..00.193_	*Goldenes Hitler-Jugend Ehrenzeichen*
00.00.1938	*Ehrenwinkel für alte Kämpfer*

Daughters:
Gerda Buch-Bormann

*	23.10.1909 in Konstanz am Bodensee.
†	23.03.1946 in the civil hospital of Merano (abdominal or cervical cancer).
NSDAP-Nr.:	120.112 (Joined 00.00.1927)

Notes:

* Married in München-Solln, 02.09.1929, to Martin Bormann (later *Reichsleiter*, head of the *Parteikanzlei der NSDAP*). Ten children resulted from this marriage (an "achievement" for which Gerda Bormann received the *Ehrenkreuz der Deutschen Mutter in Gold*):

  - Adolf ("Krönzi") Martin (*14.04.1930, †11.03.2013), godson of Adolf Hitler.
  - Ilse ("Elke") (*09.07.1931, †00.00.1958), goddaughter of Ilse Hess.
  - Ehrengard Franziska (twin sister of Ilse, *09.07.1931, died soon after birth).
  - Irmgard (*25.07.1933).
  - Rudolf Gerhard ("Helmut") (*31.08.1934), named for Rudolf Hess.
  - Heinrich ("Heiner") Hugo (*13.06.1936), godson of Heinrich Himmler.
  - Eva Ute (*04.08.1938).
  - Gerda (*23.10.1940).
  - Fredrich ("Fred", "Fritz") Hartmut (*04.03.1942)
  - Joseph Volker (*18.09.1943, †00.00.1946)

* Walter Buch grew to detest his son-in-law and fellow *Reichsleiter*. Under interrogation at Nürnberg by Lt. Col. Thomas S. Hinkel, on 31.10.1945, Buch stated:

… I didn't get along with him, and when the *Fuehrer* put Bormann in charge of jurisprudence in the Party [Autumn 1943], my job was practically finished.… The result of it was that the Party Chancellery actually acquired the power to decide on our judgments. In other words, the Party Chancellery would decide that a person should be expelled from the Party, for instance, and then it was up to the Party court to sanction this decision which had been taken beforehand. The procedure, in other words, had been reversed, and, of course, I opposed this change, but could not do anything about it, because the *Fuehrer* had stopped listening to me many years ago. ("Special Report on Walter Buch, *Reichsleiter* and *Oberster Parteirichter*", Special Detention Center "Ashcan"—Detailed Interrogation

Report, in "Interrogation Records Prepared for War Crimes Proceedings at Nuernberg, 1945-1947/ OCCPAC Interrogation Transcripts and Related Records: Buch, Walter Hans"; Publication Number M1270, Record Group RG238)

* During his marriage, Martin Bormann carried on an affair with the young UFA film actress Manja Behrens. This was fully tolerated by his wife.

Lore Buch
*   10.03.1913 in Biebrich am Rhein.
†   01.05.2000 in Gauting bei München.

SOURCES:
Goebbels, Dr. phil. Paul Joseph: *The Goebbels Diaries 1942–1943* (edited by Louis P. Lochner). Doubleday, 1948.
Gordon, Harold J. Jr.: *Hitler and the Beer Hall Putsch*. Princeton University Press, 1972.
Hamilton, Charles: *Leaders and Personalities of the Third Reich, Volume I*. R. James Bender Publishing, 1984.
Höffkes, Karl: *Hitlers politische Generale: Die Gauleiter des Dritten Reiches*. Grabert-Verlag-Tübingen, 1986.
Kienast, *Ministerialdirigent* Ernst (ed): *Der Großdeutsche Reichstag, IV. Wahlperiode, Beginn am 10.04.1938 verlängert bis zum 30. Januar 1947*. Berlin, November 1943.
Krebs, Dr. phil. Albert: *The Infancy of Nazism: The Memoirs of Ex-Gauleiter Albert Krebs, 1923–1933*. New Viewpoints, 1976.
Lang, Jochen von: *The Secretary. Martin Bormann: The Man Who Manipulated Hitler*. Random House, 1979.
Lilla, Joachim; Döring, Martin; & Schulz Andreas: *Statisten in Uniform. Die Mitglieder des Reichstags 1933–1945*. Droste Verlag, 2004.
McKale, Donald M.: *The Nazi Party Courts: Hitler's Management of Conflict in His Movement, 1921–1945*. The University Press of Kansas, 1974.
Mendelsohn, S.: *The Polish Jews behind the Nazi Ghetto Walls*. Yiddish Scientific Institute, 1942.
Miller, Michael D. and Andreas Schulz: *Leaders of the Storm Troops, Volume 1* (1st Edition). Helion & Co., 2015.
National Archives and Records Administration, College Park, Maryland: *SS-Personalakte* of Walter Buch. Microfilm document collection A3343SS
Office of United States Chief Counsel for Prosecution of Axis Criminality: *Nazi Conspiracy and Aggression* (11 volumes). U.S. Government Printing Office, District of Columbia, 1946.
Orlow, Dietrich: *History of the Nazi Party: 1933–1945*. University of Pittsburgh Press, 1973.
Reiche, Erich G.: *The Development of the SA in Nuremberg, 1922–1934*. Cambridge University Press, 2002.
Schirach, Baldur von: *Die Pioniere des Dritten Reiches*. Zentralstelle fur der deutschen Freiheitskampf, 1933.
Tell, Rolf: *Sound and Fuehrer*. Hurst & Blackett Ltd, 1939.
Weinreich, Max: *Hitler's Professors: The Part of Scholarship in Germany's Crimes against the Jewish People*. Yale University Press, 1999.

Right: Buch as a young man. (Source: Walter Buch's personal photo album, in collection of Gary Merlie)

Below: Leutnant Buch, *c.* 1910. Courtesy of Gary Merlie (left image) and (right) from Landesarchiv Baden-Württemberg, Hauptstaatsarchiv Stuttgart, M708/Nr. 411/Bild 1 [1-331965-1].

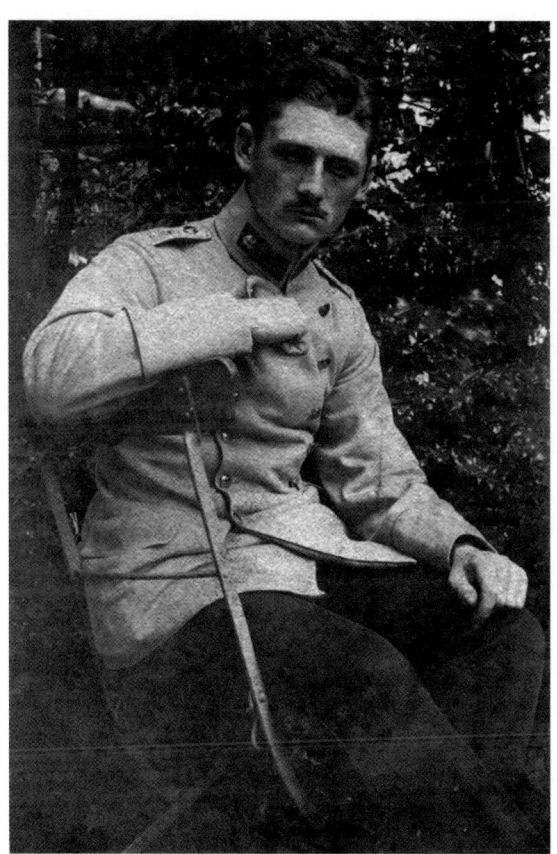

Buch on horseback, c. 1914. (Above, courtesy of Gary Merlie, and below, Landesarchiv Baden-Württemberg, Hauptstaatsarchiv Stuttgart, M708/Nr. 411/Bild 3 [1-331965-3])

Buch with fellow officers, *c.* 1914. (Gary Merlie)

Hauptmann Buch, *c.* 1915. (Landesarchiv Baden-Württemberg, Hauptstaatsarchiv Stuttgart, M708/Nr. 411/Bild 5 [1-331965-5])

Above left: Hauptmann Buch in a trench wearing a steel helmet of the reinforced type designed for snipers, c. 1916. (Gary Merlie)

Above right: Hauptmann Buch and a fellow officer in the trenches on the Western Front. (Gary Merlie)

"*Deutscher Tag der NSDAP*" in Hof, 15.–16.09.1923. Hitler and his entourage tour the area in his open Daimler-Benz. From left to right: Johann Schelshorn (driving), Hitler, Ulrich Graf, Helmuth Klotz, Walter Buch, and Christian Weber. (NARA, Heinrich Hoffmann Collection)

Above left: Walter Buch in civilian attire during the 1920s. (Gary Merlie)

Above right: Walter Buch (left) during the celebration of "*Deutscher Tag*" in Bayreuth, 29.–30.09.1923. Adolf Hitler appears in the background, at extreme left in light-colored overcoat. (Gary Merlie)

24.06.1927: Walter Buch, far left in second row, posing with other Nazis. (Gary Merlie)

02.09.1929: The wedding of Buch's daughter, Gerda, to Martin Bormann.

Above: Left to right: Walter Buch, Gerda Buch, Martin Bormann, and Hitler.

Below: Left to right, behind the bride and groom: Rudolf Hess, August Schneidhuber, Franz Pfeffer von Salomon, Buch, Hitler, and Albert Bormann.

Above left: Walter Buch wearing the short-lived collar tabs for senior officials of the *Reichsleitung der NSDAP* (easily confused with those of an *SA-Gruppenführer*, which were very similar), 1933. (Gary Merlie)

Above right: An informal portrait of Walter Buch wearing the rare *Coburg-Abzeichen*, instituted in October 1932 to recognize participation in the 14.–15.10.1922 "Battle of Coburg." (Gary Merlie)

Right: Walter Buch during an open-air presentation, probably late in 1932. (Gary Merlie)

Above: A gathering of old fighters in München, signed by Prince August Wilhelm ("AuWi"). Left to right: Buch, "AuWi," and Adolf Wagner. (Gary Merlie)

Left: Studio portrait of Walter Buch in brown shirt, 1933. (Gary Merlie)

Walter Buch poses with his family in 1933. (Gary Merlie)

A meeting of the senior Party leadership at the *Preußenhaus* in Berlin, 1933. Left to right: Dr. Hans Frank, Franz Xaver Schwarz, Otto Telschow, Walter Buch, Gottfried Feder, Dr. Joseph Goebbels, Wilhelm Kube, Dr. Otto Hellmuth, and Rudolf Buttmann. (NARA, Heinrich Hoffmann Collection)

Above left: A formal portrait of *Reichsleiter* Buch from an official NSDAP publication.

Above right: *Reichsleiter* Walter Buch, *c*. 1934. (NARA, Heinrich Hoffmann Collection)

Above left: Walter Buch attending the "*6. Reichsparteitag der NSDAP*" in Nürnberg (05.09.1934–16.09.1934). (Still from Leni Riefenstahl's *Triumph des Willens* [1935])

Above right: An informal portrait of *SS-Obergruppenführer* Buch, *c*. 1934. (Max Williams)

Studio portraits of *SS-Obergruppenführer* Buch in 1934. (Gary Merlie)

Walter Buch chats with an NSDAP leader, c. 1935. (Gary Merlie)

Reichsleiter Buch, c. 1935. (Gary Merlie)

Right: *Reichsleiter* Buch visiting a foreign country, possibly Turkey, *c.* 1936. (Gary Merlie)

Below: Walter Buch and Frau Buch (extreme right) dine with SS and *Luftwaffe* officers. Standing, third from left, is *SS-Standartenführer* Felix Steiner, and seated, second from right, is *SS-Standartenführer* Bernhard Voss. (Gary Merlie)

SS-Obergruppenführer and Frau Buch attend a formal gathering, *c.* 1937. In the foreground, back to the camera, is Buch's fellow *Reichsleiter* (and *Oberbürgermeister* of München), Karl Fiehler. (Jeff Clark)

An avid horseman, Buch sits in the saddle in 1937. (Gary Merlie)

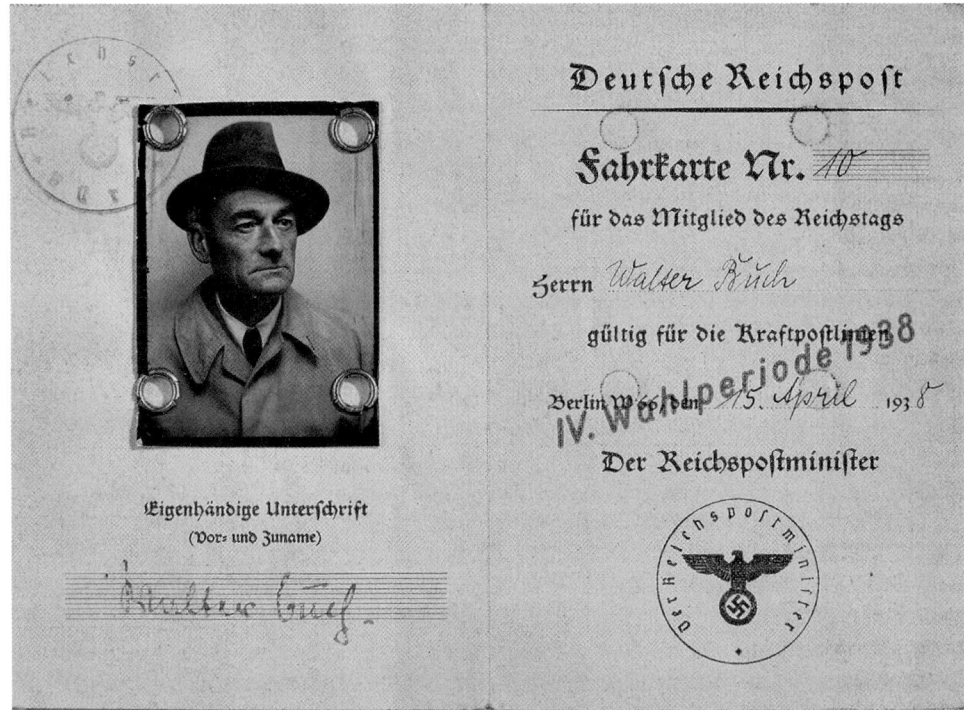

Above: Buch's railway pass as a member of the *Reichstag*. (Hermann-Historica, Auctioneers, München)

Right: Walter Buch and son, 1941. (Gary Merlie)

At a reception for the Japanese Ambassador to Germany, General Hiroshi Ōshima, in München, 1942.

Above: Left to right: Ludwig Siebert, Buch, and General Ōshima. (Gary Merlie)

Below: Left to right: *SS-Obergruppenführer* Werner Lorenz, General Oshima, and Buch. (Gary Merlie)

SS-Obergruppenführer Buch during a visit to *Luftflotte 3* in France, 1942. At his side is the commander of the air fleet, *Generalfeldmarschall* Hugo Sperrle. (Simon James)

09.11.1942: The *Hofbräuhaus* in München during the commemoration of the "*München-Putsch*." Clockwise from left: Christian Weber, Franz Xaver Schwarz, Dr. Robert Ley, Alfred Rosenberg, Max Amann, Dr. Wilhelm Frick, Walter Buch, Philipp Bouhler, and Karl Fiehler.

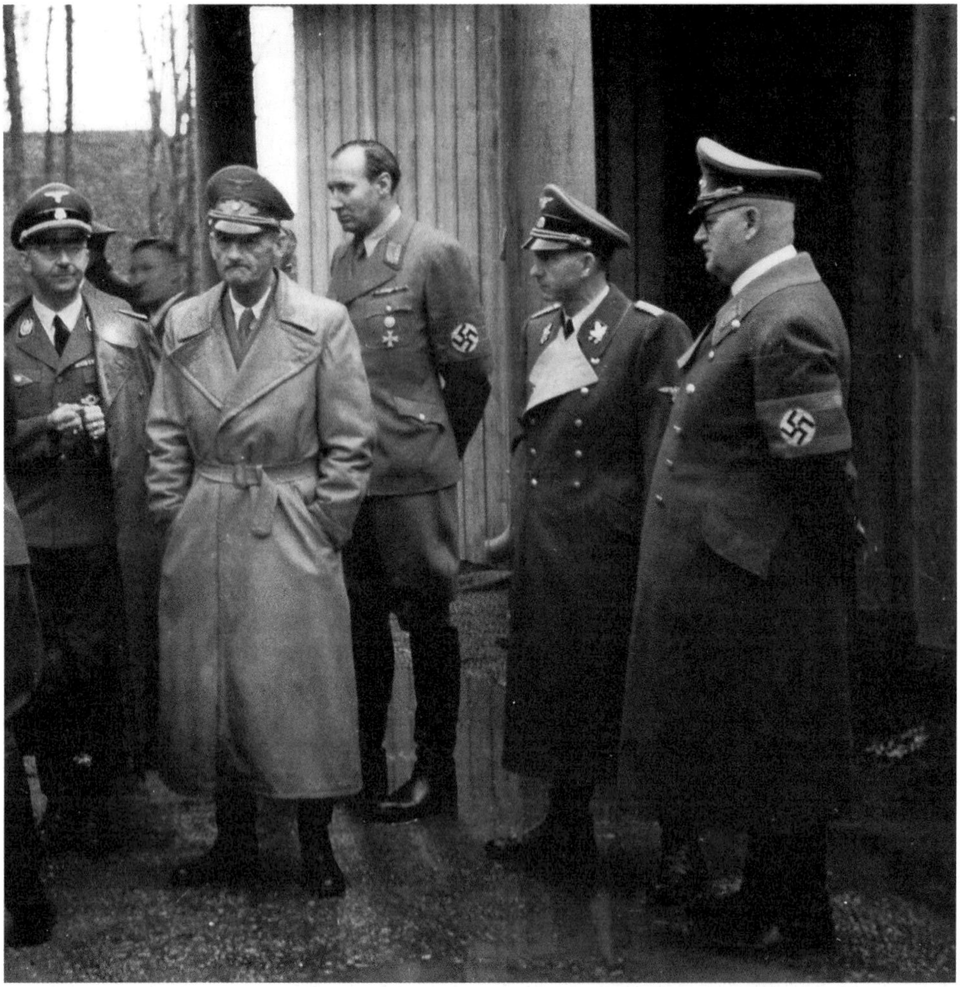

Rastenburg/Ostpreuβen, 07.02.1943: Conference of *Reichs-* and *Gauleiter* at *Führer HQ* "*Wolfsschanze*." Left to right: Heinrich Himmler, Friedrich Hildebrandt, Walter Buch, Emil Stürtz, Dr. Otto Dietrich, and Franx Xaver Schwarz. (NARA, Heinrich Hoffmann Collection)

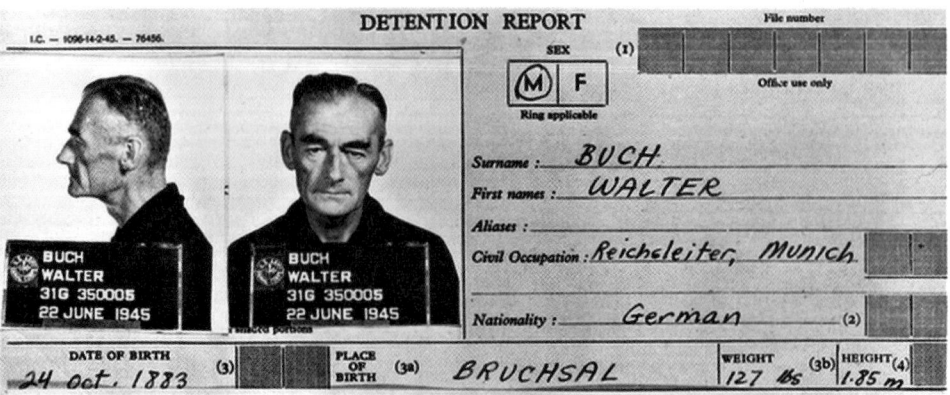

I.C. — 1096-14-2-45. — 76456.

DETENTION REPORT

File number

SEX (1)

M F

Ring applicable

Office use only

BUCH
WALTER
31G 350005
22 JUNE 1945

BUCH
WALTER
31G 350005
22 JUNE 1945

Surname : BUCH

First names : WALTER

Aliases :

Civil Occupation : Reichsleiter, Munich

Nationality : German (2)

DATE OF BIRTH 24 Oct. 1883 (3)

PLACE OF BIRTH (3a) BRUCHSAL

WEIGHT 127 lbs (3b)

HEIGHT (4) 1.85 m

Detention report for Prisoner of War Walter Buch.

Right: Mug shot of a bearded Walter Buch, taken at Nürnberg in 1946. (Ian Sayer)

Below: Walter Buch and family in April 1943. (Gary Merlie)

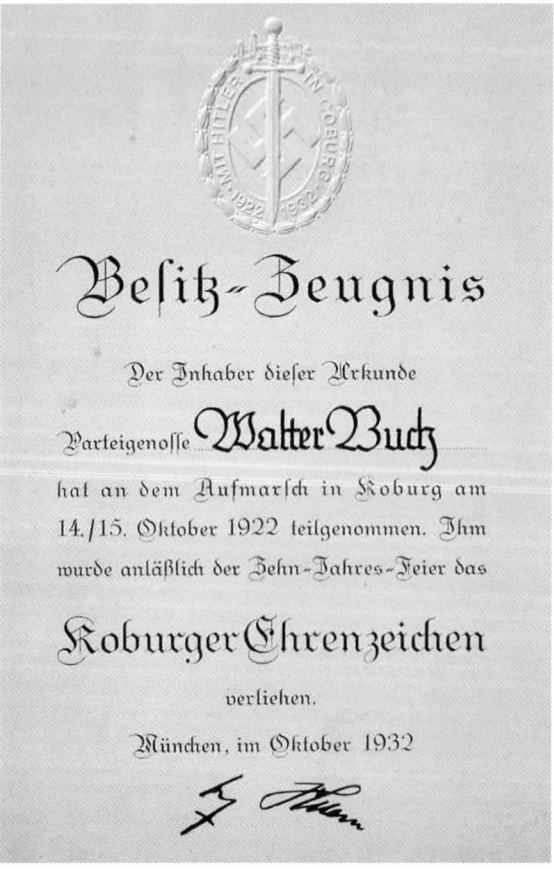

Above: Walter Buch on a boat outing with his daughter, Gerda, *c.* 1935. (Gary Merlie)

Left: The award certificate for Buch's Coburg Badge, marking his participation in the "*3. Deutschen Tag*" in Coburg (14.–15/10.1922).

WALTER BUCH Oberster Parteirichter

Zyb.Nr. 3589/37

München, den 5.April 1937

An die

    Reichsreferentin des BDM,
  Frau Trude B ü r k n e r - Mohr,
              B e r l i n NW. 40,
              Kronprinzenufer 10.

Sehr verehrte Frau Bürkner!

    Erst jetzt nach Rückkehr von einer achtwöchigen Amerikareise komme ich dazu, Ihnen für Ihre beiden Briefe vom 22.1.und 26.2.37., sowie für die Übersendung der beiden entzückenden Alben meinen herzlichen Dank zu sagen. Die Bilder haben mir grosse Freude gemacht. Sowohl bei meiner Frau wie bei meinen Töchtern haben sie helle Begeisterung ausgelöst.

          Heil Hitler!

A letter from Buch, bearing his official letterhead as Senior Party Judge and sent to a senior official of the *Bund Deutscher Mädel*. (Alexander Historical Auctions)

Alfred Max Ludwig Hoffmann
Stellvertretender Kommandeur der SA (16.11.1923-31.01.1924)

*	11.08.1890 in Berlin.
†	18.11.1933 (in Berlin?), of a heart attack shortly after becoming engaged.

NSDAP-Nr.: (Unknown if he held formal membership)

Promotions:

01.04.1909	*Seekadett*
12.04.1910	*Fähnrich zur See*
00.09.1912	*Leutnant zur See*
02.05.1915	*Oberleutnant zur See*
21.01.1920	*Kapitänleutnant*
16.11.1923–31.01.1924	*Stellvertretender Kommandeur der SA*

Career:

c. 1896–c. 1899	*Volksschule* in Wilhelmshaven.
c. 1899–1900	*Vorschule der Oberrealschule* in Kiel.
01.04.1900–00.04.1906	*Städtische Realschule* in Wilhelmshaven (passed his *Einjährigen-Prüfung*).
00.00.1906–00.02.1909	*Städtische Oberrealschule* in Braunschweig (passed his *Abitur*).
01.04.1909–00.00.19__	Entered the *Kaiserliche Marine* as a *Seekadett*, assigned for training to the heavy cruiser SMS *Hertha*.
00.00.191_–00.11.1915	*Adjutant* aboard the battleship SMS *Ostfriesland*.
00.11.1915–00.01.1916	Assigned as *Flaggleutnant* to the *Bereitschafts-Division der Ostsee*.
00.01.1916–00.01.1918	*Wachoffizier* aboard the torpedo boats SM *S 20*, SMS *V 45*, and SMS *V 69*.
00.01.1918–21.06.1919	*Kommandant* of the torpedo boats SMS *V 43* and SMS *V 46*.
22.11.1918–00.00.19__	Interned with the crew of *V 46* at Scapa Flow.
21.06.1919–00.00.1920(?)	After a failed attempt to scuttle the *V 46* at Scapa Flow, interned in England.
13.03.1920–10.09.1920	Service with *II. Marine-Brigade (Brigade Ehrhardt)*.
10.09.1920	Discharged from *Reichsmarine* service.
00.00.1921–00.00.1921	*Leiter* of *Abteilung A (allgemeine Aufgaben)* of "Organisation Consul" (OC).
Spring 1923–09.11.1923	*Chef des Organisationstabes* (IIa) in the *Oberkommando der SA*, tasked with much of the day-to-day business of the organization under the *Oberster SA-Führer*, Hermann Göring. In this capacity, he issued the following guidelines to the members of the SA:

München, 11 July 1923
General guidelines when founding an S.A. [*Allgemeine Richtlinien bei Gründung einer S.A.*]

The S.A. should be the military reflection of the party. The principal task during peacetime is to work together, in close consultation with the party's Ortsgruppenleitung, on all matters concerning the protection of the party's assemblies and events.

Incidentally, the S.A. is a special organization within the National Socialist movement and is to be processed separately from the Ortsgruppen and Parteileitung [Party Leadership]. It is subordinate to a special Befehlsstelle [Command Office], the Oberkommando der S.A. [Headquarters of the S.A.] in München.

The Oberkommando, however, is unable to stay in direct and constant contact with all the individual Gruppen, and eventually after a period of time will issue an order to the effect that, the S.A. will be put under the control of a special national Befehlsstelle.

This Befehlsstelle (S.A. Befehlsstelle) will then take care of everything else on its own and make the decision independently. When it comes to special questions it will then address the O.K. (Oberkommando) which is, naturally, always the höhere Dienststelle of the S.A. Bezirksführers.

As a matter of principle, for the formation of a S.A. the following general rules have been issued:

1) Advertising per word of mouth,

2) scrupulous selection, whoever decides to join, must declare this in a special Verpflichtungsschein.

3) an S.A. man with Unterführer qualification, if possible Feldzugteilnehmer, will take over the leadership und remain the S.A. Führer until further notice is given. After taking office, he should be confirmed by the O.K. or the S.A. Bezirksführer. This confirmation only says that he is S.A. Führer for the time being. If, as the S.A. grows, it becomes apparent that he is not suitable as a Führer, or if he himself declares that he is unable to continue the Führung, then the Bezirksführer will appoint another person as the Führer.

This regulation is necessary as nobody should be held liable for the fact that the Kämpfer for our idea are incorrectly or badly led and are so uselessly sacrificed.

4) Only those who are at least 18 years old, healthy and strong can become members of the S.A.

5) The Führer's immediate main organizational task will consist of forming two Gruppen under his leadership:

   a) those who have served and are trained

   b) those who have not served

The Gruppen should be combined into Züge and later to Hundertschaften.

Strength: Hundertschaften are made up of 9 Gruppen each of 8 men in addition Gruppenführer. 3 Gruppen form a Zug which will be led by a Zugführer, a full Hundertschaft will be made up of:

1 Hundertschaftsführer

3 Zugführer

9 Gruppenführer

72 men (9 x 8 men)

Until allotted an S. A. Bezirksführer, the newly formed S. A. shall be subordinate to the Oberkommando and shall keep it informed of the progress of development.

The newly founded S. A. cannot and must never assume a firm commitment and relationship with any other organizations and associations without the prior approval of the O. K., although it must be emphasized that the S. A. must always and under all circumstances maintain its absolute independence.

F. d. R. [for the record] Das Oberkommando der S.A.
Der Chef des Stabes:
Signed: H o f f m a n n
(Dr. Heinrich Bennecke, *Hitler und die SA*, pp. 236-237; Translation: Gary Costello)

Ernst Röhm writes of Hoffmann: "[Göring's] chief of staff, Kapitänleutnant Hoffmann, was a clear-headed, sober and very industrious officer. I often wished he had had a greater influence on the development of the SA." (Röhm, *Die Geschichte eines Hochverräters*; translated by Eleanor Hancock as *Memoirs of Ernst Röhm*)

The early Nazi publicist and later fugitive, Kurt G. W. Lüdecke, gave a similar assessment of the "calm, composed Kapitänleutnant Hoffmann": "It was Hoffmann, much more than Goering, who had achieved the reorganization of the SA on a military basis, showing himself a very able man and a tireless worker." (Lüdecke, *I Knew Hitler*, p. 173)

08.11.1923–09.11.1923	Participated in the "*München-Putsch*."
15.11.1923	Emigrated to Austria, working in the office of a Salzburg attorney.
16.11.1923–31.01.1924	*Stellvertretender Kommandeur der SA* (Deputy Commander of the SA), operating from exile in Austria.
	He was confirmed in this post by an order issued 16.11.1923 and signed by acting SA adjutant Julius Schreck (but written by Walter Buch, who led the illegal SA in Germany): "The Oberkommando [der SA] is under the command of Kapitänleutnant Hoffmann, whose representatives are Major Buch, Hauptmann Kolb, and Leutnant Weiß."
31.01.1924	Participated in a secret meeting between National Socialist and *völkisch* functionaries in Salzburg regarding future cooperation between the NSDAP and DVFP (*Deutschvölkische Freiheitspartei*). This meeting resulted in his resignation in response to the slanderous remarks of Hermann Esser and Ernst Hanfstaengl.
02.04.1924	Arrested by Bavarian police upon his return from Austria.
27.01.1925–00.00.19__	Employed as a commercial clerk in Offenbach and later Hamburg.
c. 1925	Joined the *Marine-Offizier-Verband*.
00.03.1928	Began employment with *Aug. Scherl G.m.b.H.* in Berlin.
00.12.1930–18.11.1933	*Abteilungsleiter* with *Aug. Scherl G.m.b.H.* in Berlin.

DECORATIONS & AWARDS:

00.00.191_	*1914 Eisernes Kreuz I. Klasse*
00.00.191_	*1914 Eisernes Kreuz II. Klasse*
00.00.191_	*Oldenburgisches Friedrich-August-Kreuz I. Klasse*
00.00.191_	*Oldenburgisches Friedrich-August-Kreuz II. Klasse*

Notes:
* Parents:
  - Father: *Marineoberstabsingenieur* (*Kaiserlichen Marine*) Carl *Ludwig* Hoffmann.
  - Mother: Auguste Emilie Hedwig, *née* Michaëlis.

Sources:
Bennecke, Dr. phil. Heinrich: *Hitler und die SA*. Günter Olzog Verlag, 1962.
Lüdecke, Kurt G. W.: *I Knew Hitler: The Story of a Nazi Who Escaped the Blood Purge*. Charles Scribner's Sons, 1937.

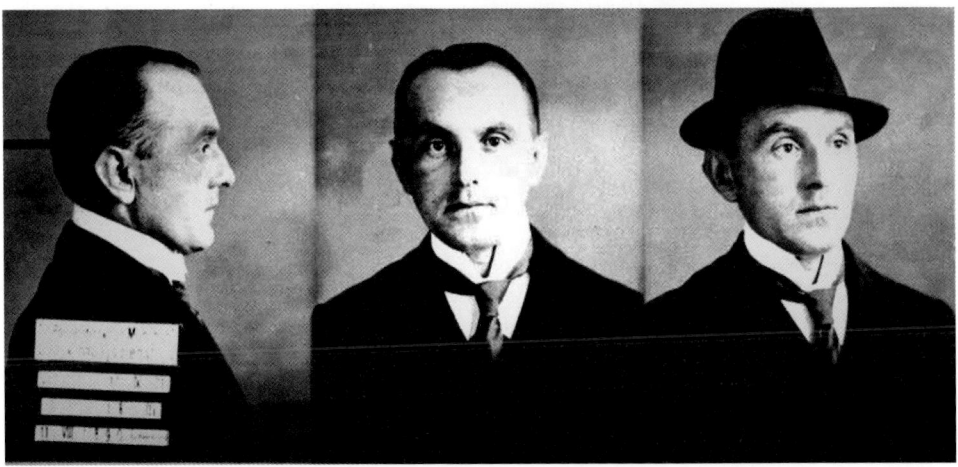

Wilhelm ("Emir") Pleickart Ludwig Adolf Arthur Freiherr Marschall von Bieberstein

"beauftragt mit der Führung der [illegal] *SA"* (00.01.1924-00.05.1924)

*	09.05.1890 in Berlin.
†	31.01.1935 in at air crash at Podejuch near Stettin/Pommern. Following his death, the German airline *Lufthansa* named its Junkers Ju 52/3m, D-ATAK, as *Marschall von Bieberstein* in his honor. The aircraft crashed near Hannover while *en route* from London to Berlin, after a forced landing due to severe icing on 28.11.1936. No injuries were reported.
NSDAP-Nr.:	7.779 (Joined 00.11.1922; Party banned, 09.11.1923–16.02.1925; Reenrolled, 00.00.1925)

Promotions:

00.00.1909	*Fahnenjunker*
00.00.1909	*Unteroffizier*
21.12.1909	*Fähnrich*
22.08.1910	*Leutnant* (*mit Patent vom* 22.08.1908)
25.02.1915	*Oberleutnant*
27.01.1918	*Rittmeister*
00.01.1924–00.05.1924	*beauftragt mit der Führung der (illegalen) SA*

Career:

c. 1896–c. 1903	*Volksschule* (?).
00.00.1903–00.00.1906	*Berthold-Gymnasium* in Freiburg.
00.00.1906–00.00.1909	*Dom-Gymnasium* in Merseburg (passed his *Abitur*, 00.00.1909).
00.00.1909	Entered military service as a *Fahnenjunker*, assigned to *2. Badisches Dragoner-Regiment Nr. 21* (Bruchsal).
c. 1910–00.00.191_	Attended the *Kriegsschule* in Metz.
01.10.1911–00.00.1912(?)	*Offizier-Reitschule* in Paderborn.
00.08.1914–00.07.1915	Assigned successively as *Führer* of *2. Eskadron/Dragoner-Regiment 21* (with which he deployed to the Western Front), then as *Ordonnanzoffizier* of *28. Kavallerie-Brigade*.
00.07.1915–00.01.1916	Assigned to *Flieger-Abteilung 68*, then to *Brieftauben-Abteilung* (carrier pigeon detachment) Ostende.
00.01.1916–00.09.1918	Assigned to *Staffel 3* of *Kampfgeschwader I der OHL* (bomber wing subordinated to the *Obersten Heeresleitung* [Army High Command]).
00.00.1917–00.00.1918	Assigned as a *Staffelführer* and as *stellvertretender Geschwaderführer* to *Kampfgeschwader I der OHL*. He reportedly flew over 300 combat missions during the Great War.
00.00.1919–00.00.19__	Commercial pilot for *Deutsche Luft-Reederei*. In this capacity, he served as *Fahndungsoffizier* (flag officer) in the 19.03.1919 transfer flight to Kristianstad of the first three German commercial aircraft (AEG GV) which had been sold to Sweden.

00.03.1919	Joined the *Freiwilligen Fliegerabteilung* in Mariampol (Lithuania), assigned to *Fliegerabteilung 429* with which he participated in actions against the Red Army.
00.09.1919–00.00.1920	Assigned to the *russischen Detachement Graf Keller*, a component of the *freiwilligen Russischen Westarmee* under Fürsten Awaloff-Bermondt. With the (brevet?) rank of *Oberstleutnant*, he served as *Kommandeur der Luftstreitkräfte der freiwilligen nordwest-russischen Armee* (Commander of the Air Forces of the Voluntary Northwest Russian Army), comprised of the *Truppenfliegerstaffeln 413, 424,* and *426,* as well as *Artilleriefliegerstaffel 427.*
00.00.1920	Returned to Berlin.
26.02.1920	Discharged from military service.
13.03.1920–00.03.1920	Service with the *Sturmabteilung von Pflugk-Hartung* in the "*Kapp-Putsch*."
00.00.192_–00.00.192_	Member of the *Organisation Escherich* ("*Orgesch*").
00.00.192_–00.00.192_	Member of various *Selbstschutzverbänden* (self-defense associations).
00.05.1921–00.05.1921	Brief service early in the month with *Freikorps Roßbach* in Kreuzburg, then with a *Sturmbataillon* in Rosenberg, with *Freikorps "Waterkant"* in Oberschlesien. He was wounded during this period.
21.05.1921–06.06.1921(?)	Assigned to *II. Bataillon* of *Freikorps Oberland* with which he participated in combat in Oberschlesien.
06.06.1921–00.00.1921	Service as a *Zugführer* in *Freikorps von Dömming* (Oberschlesien).
00.11.1922	Joined the NSDAP (*1. Berliner Ortsgruppe*).
00.00.1922–00.00.1923	Assisted in the building of the Turkish Air Force.
00.00.1923–00.00.1923	Actively participated in the "*Ruhrkampf*" against French occupation authorities.
00.00.1923–00.00.1923	Member of the *Stab der Oberkommando der SA* (under Hermann Göring).
09.11.1923	Participated in the "*München-Putsch*," and helped to save the life of *SA-Kommandeur* Göring when the latter was severely wounded by police gunfire during the march to the Feldherrnhalle.
00.11.1923–00.01.1924	*Verbindungsoffizier beim Beauftragten für die Führung der (illegalen) SA.*
00.01.1924–00.05.1924	"*beauftragt mit der Führung der (illegalen) SA*" (charged with leadership of the [illegal] SA), succeeding Walter Buch and Alfred Hoffmann. Succeeded by Ernst Röhm.
00.00.1925–00.00.1925	*Führer* of the *Schlageter-Bund* in Freiburg.
00.00.1925	Reentered the NSDAP.
00.05.1926–00.00.1926	*Führer der SA und SS in Südbaden.*
00.00.1926–00.00.192_	*Kreisleiter der NSDAP* and *Führer der SA* in Freiburg and Breisgau.
Autumn 1926	Began work for the German airline *Lufthansa*.
27.01.1927–02.06.1928	Participated as a *Lufthansa* pilot in the explorer Sven Hedin's Sino-Swedish scientific expedition to Sinkiang Province in northwestern western China. In the introduction, written in Stockholm on 12.12.1942, to his book *History of the Expedition in Asia, 1927–1935*, Hedin remembered his German colleague: "The only foreign member who has died since the expedition came to

an end is Baron WILHELM MARSCHALL VON BIEBERSTEIN, who was killed in a flying accident in Germany in 1935. The thought of his irrepressible good humour and his friendliness will always remain with us as a living and cherished memory."

00.00.1929–00.05.1931	*Führer* of SA-Standarte "Baden."
20.11.1930–14.10.1933	Member of the *Badische Landtag*.
00.03.1933–00.00.1934	*Führer* of the *Untergruppe Berlin der Deutschen Luftsport-Verband* (DLV).
00.00.1933–31.01.1935	*Geschäftsführer* of the *Reichsverband der Deutschen Flughäfen* (Reich Association of German Airports).
00.00.1934–31.01.1935	*Stellvertreter* (deputy) to the *Führer* of *Fliegerlandeskorps X Brandenburg-Grenzmark der DLV* and *Führer* of *DLV-Landesgruppe IV* (Berlin-Brandenburg).
00.08.1934–31.01.1935	*Flugkapitän* and *Leiter* of the *Flugamt* (aviation office) in Königsberg.

DECORATIONS & AWARDS:

18.09.1917	*Ritterkreuz des Hausordens von Hohenzollern mit Schwertern*
00.00.1916	*1914 Eisernes Kreuz I. Klasse*
00.09.1914	*1914 Eisernes Kreuz II. Klasse*
00.00.191_	*Ritterkreuz II. Klasse des Badischer Ordens vom Zähringer Löwen mit Schwertern*
c. 1919	*Baltenkreuz I. Klasse*
00.00.1934	*Ehrenzeichen des 9. November 1923 (Blutorden)* (Nr. 464, mit Wirkung vom 09.11.1933)
00.00.19__	Order of Military Merit __ Class (Bulgaria)
c. 1915	*Harb Madalyasi* (aka "Iron Half Moon" or "Gallipoli Star") (Ottoman Empire)

NOTES:

* Parents:
  -Father: *Adolf* Hermann Freiherr Marschall von Bieberstein (*12.10.1842 in Karlsruhe, †24.09.1912 in Badenweiler).
  -Mother: Marie Luise, *née* Freiin von und zu Gemmingen (*20.02.1862 in Karlsruhe, †28.07.1949 in Schloß Neuerhausen).
  The following is a summary of the career of Adolf Freiherr Marschall von Bieberstein:

00.00.1861–00.00.1865	Studied law at the Universities of Freiburg and Heidelberg.
00.00.1865–00.00.1867	Employed as court trainee.
00.00.1867–00.00.1871	*Referendar* (junior lawyer).
00.00.1871–00.00.1871	*Amtsrichter* (magistrate) in Schwetzingen.
00.00.1871–00.00.1879	*Staatsanwalt* (public prosecutor) in Mosbach.
00.00.1875–00.00.1883	*Abgeordneter* of the *Ersten Badischen Kammer*.
00.07.1878–00.10.1881	Member- as a *deutsch-konservativer* (German Conservative)- of the *Reichstag* (*Wahlkreis Baden 10, Karlsruhe-Bruchsel*).
00.00.1879–00.00.1882	*Landgerichtsrat*.
00.00.1882	Appointed as *Erster Staatsanwalt* in Mannheim.
00.00.1883–00.00.1890	*Badischer Gesandter* (Envoy of the Grand Duchy of Baden) in Berlin.
00.00.1890–00.07.1897	*Staatssekretär [de facto Minister] des Äußeren* (State Secretary and

	de facto Minister for Foreign Affairs) in the cabinet of Bismarck's successor, *Reichskanzler* Leo von Caprivi, until 1894, then under Chlodwig zu Hohenlohe-Schillingsfurst. Dismissed and succeeded by Bernhard von Bülow.
00.07.1897–00.00.1912	*Kaiserlicher Botschafter in Konstantinopel*
15.06.1907–18.10.1907	*Vertreter des Deutschen Reiches* (Representative of the German Reich) to the Second Peace Conference in The Hague.
00.05.1912–24.09.1912	*Kaiserlicher Botschafter in London.*

* Siblings:
  - *Adolf* Otto Wolfram Fritz Freiherr Marschall von Bieberstein (*25.06.1893 in Berlin, †27.09.1946 as a prisoner of war in Moscow)
  - Maria Hilda Marschall von Bieberstein (married name: von Seyfried)
  - Victor Heinrich Marschall von Bieberstein
* Religion: Protestant (baptized 14.06.1890 in the *Garnisonkirche* of Berlin).
* Married on 27.01.1927 to Carola Freiin von Holzing-Berstett (*00.00.1897, †00.00.1960), daughter of Max Freiherr von Holzing-Berstett (*01.01.1867, †09.09.1936) and Elsa Freiin von Holzing-Berstett (*14.02.1875, †11.12.1941). Three children resulted from this marriage, including the later diplomat Dr. jur. Walther Freiherr Marschall von Bieberstein (*29.05.1930, †04.09.2014) who served as ambassador in Bangladesh (1979–1985) and Myanmar (1985–1995).

SOURCES:

Schuster, Peter: *Oberländer: Freikorpskämpfer, Putschisten, NS-Aktivisten, Mitläufer, Geistliche und Widerständler aus dem Freikorps Oberland und dem Bund Oberland. Personalien und Dokumente – Ein Nachschlagewerk.* Nation & Wissen Verlag, 2018.

Above left: Marschall von Bieberstein in civilian attire, c. 1925.

Above right: An official identification photo of Marschall von Bieberstein, c. 1925. (Landesarchiv Baden-Württemberg)

Left: The distinguished German diplomat Adolf Freiherr Marschall von Bieberstein, father of Wilhelm.

Franz Ferdinand Felix von Pfeffer
[Known as Pfeffer von Salomon until 03.07.1941]
Oberster SA-Führer (Reichs-SA-Führer) (01.11.1926–29.08.1930)

*	19.02.1888 in Düsseldorf.
†	12.04.1968 in München/Regierungsbezirk Oberbayern/Bayern. Gravesite: München, Waldfriedhof Solln (Plot 15/Row 3/Grave 71/72).

NSDAP-Nr.: 16.101 (Joined 00.03.1925; Expelled 14.11.1941)

PROMOTIONS:
01.10.1910	*Einjährig-Freiwilliger*
16.02.1911	*Fahnenjunker*
00.00.1911	*Unteroffizier*
23.05.1911	*Fähnrich*
18.08.1911	*Leutnant (mit Patent J6i vom 20.08.1909)*
18.08.1915	*Oberleutnant (L7l)*
20.09.1918	*Hauptmann i. G. (Y)*
00.08.1926–01.11.1926	*"mit der Führung der SA beauftragt"*
01.11.1926–29.08.1930	*Oberster SA-Führer (Reichs-SA-Führer)*
01.04.1930–12.08.1930	*NSAK-Korpsführer*

CAREER:
00.00.1894–c. 1899	*Katholische Mauritzschule* in Münster.
c. 1899–Easter 1907	*Gymnasium* in Münster (graduated and passed his *Abitur*).
17.05.1907	Registered for legal studies at *Rupprecht-Karls-Universität* in Heidelberg.
Winter Semester 1907/08	Studied law at Heidelberg. He exmatriculated after this semester.
Summer Semester 1908	Resumed law studies at the University of Marburg. After this one semester, he returned home.
Winter Semester 1909/10	Resumed law studies at the University of Münster through graduation.
00.00.1910–00.00.1910	After completion of legal studies, worked as a *Referendar* (junior barrister or law clerk) at the *Amtsgericht* (district court) in Dülmen, 35 kilometers southwest of Münster.
00.00.1910	Passed his *Referendarexamen* (legal traineeship examinations) in Hamm.
01.10.1910	Entered service as an *Einjährig-Freiwilliger*, assigned to *9. Kompanie/Infanterie-Regiment "Herwarth von Bittenfeld" (1. Westfälische) Nr. 13* (Münster).
[06.05.1912]	Assigned to *6. Kompanie/Infanterie-Regiment "Herwarth von Bittenfeld" (1. Westfälische) Nr. 13* (Münster).
[06.10.1913]–[06.05.1914]	Again assigned [as a *Kompanieoffizier* or *Zugführer*?] to *9. Kompanie/Infanterie-Regiment "Herwarth von Bittenfeld" (1. Westfälische) Nr. 13*.
00.08.1914–00.08.1915	War service with *Infanterie-Regiment 13*. His precise assignment is unknown to this author, and is not mentioned in the only full-length biography, by Mark Fraschka, of von Pfeffer. Fraschka indicates that he was a *Batterieführer*, likely meaning that he commanded a battery

of 4 to 8 light artillery pieces assigned to this infantry unit. Fraschka writes of von Pfeffer's first months of combat duty:

> His regiment deployed to the Western Front as part of the 13. [Infanterie-] Division in August 1914, being further subordinated to 2. Armee under Generaloberst Karl von Bülow, initially involved in the conquest of Lüttich [Liège], and later in the taking of the Belgian Fort Fléron on 13 August and Fort Chaudfontaine on 14 August. Reims fell on 4 September. Due to their position at Le Petit Morin south of Château-Thierry between 6 and 9 September, the 13. Division was now one of the German units that were trying to provisionally close the gap between Kluck's 1. Armee and Bülow's 2. Armee. The defeat on the Marne then heralded the retreat and the freezing of the fronts.
>
> The regimental records are full of praise for the "ausgezeichneten Führer" ["excellent leader"] von Pfeffer. In the attack on Voormezele in West Flanders, about 30 km north of Lille, Pfeffer had repeatedly distinguished himself as Batterieführer. Here already, through his actions, were emerging the patterns of improvisation and flexibility that would become relevant in his later role as a Freikorps leader. Likewise, the Regimentschronik [Regimental Chronicle] reported on an unbridled violence under Pfeffer's leadership. During the capture of the little town of Voormezele, the battery had "beaten down the bravely defending enemy garrison to one prisoner". A little later, it continues: "The fight was conducted with a particular bitterness, no prisoners were taken." The family lore also reported that Pfeffer's unit was ambushed at Namur. When civilian fire was suspected, Pfeffer gave the order to burn down the village. (Fraschka, *Franz Pfeffer von Salomon: Hitlers vergessener Oberster SA-Führer*, pp. 67-68; Translation courtesy of Gary Costello)

00.08.1915–11.04.1916	*Regimentsadjutant* of *Infanterie-Regiment 193* (formed at Laon, in part from elements of *Infanterie-Regiment 13*). In this assignment, he participated in the autumn battle in the Champagne, during which the regiment was subordinated to *XII. Reserve-Korps* (in the *3. Armee* area of operations).
11.04.1916–Winter 1917	Returned to service with *Infanterie-Regiment 13*. He was twice wounded during this period, and participated in combat operations in the following areas, among others:

31.05.1917–02.08.1917	Chemin des Dames near Verdun
09.08.1917–21.09.1917	*Siegfriedstellung* (defensive positions in northern France
22.09.1917–10.10.1917	In reserve with the *7. Armee*
11.10.1917–25.10.1917	Chemin des Dames near Laffaux-Ecke
16.10.1917–18.12.1917	Rest and training near Sédan and Rémonville

00.01.1918–00.04.1918	Detached from his regiment and assigned to a brief period of *Generalstabsausbildung* (General Staff training) and duty.
00.04.1918–00.11.1918(?)	Returned to the Western Front, assigned as *Kommandeur* of *I. Bataillon/Infanterie-Reserve-Regiment 13* in Flanders.

00.11.1918–00.03.1920	*Führer* of the *Westfälische Freikorps von Pfeffer* (on the Baltic and in Lithuania, Poland, and Oberschlesien). He also participated in the *"Kapp-Putsch"* of March 1920. In a proclamation dated 02.01.1919, von Pfeffer stated:

> Westphalians who do not want to venture into uncertain circumstances alone, and who also want to be among compatriots in foreign countries, join together to form the Westfälische Freikorps "Münster", which will not move out until it is fully equipped and ready for action. A ready-for-action, tightly knit battalion can get through anywhere! Martial discipline and order will prevail in the battalion. Only experienced and long-serving front-line officers. Older NCOs and front-line soldiers from the Western Front preferred. Only those born in 1897 and older. Proper military papers required.… Full field rations, mobile salaries and wages, allowances of 5.-Mark daily. If later used in the East, further increase in monetary pay. Woolen blankets and clothing brought along will be accepted against payment.… Assembly in Münster [at the] Aegidiischule—officers and sergeants 6.1.1919 … non-commissioned officers 9.1.1919 …; enlisted men 14.1.1919.… Hauptmann von Pfeffer R.I.R. 13. (Mark Fraschka, *Franz Pfeffer von Salomon: Hitlers vergessener Oberster SA-Führer*, pp. 89-90, citing Eduard Schulte, ed., *Münstersche Chronik zu Spartakismus und Separatismus Anfang 1919*, p. 8f)

In April 1919, the *Freikorps Pfeffer*, numbering some 3,000 men, proceeded by way of Kaunas in Lithuania to Libau (Liepāja), seat of Latvian nationalist government of Karlis Ulmanis, to reinforce the *VI. Reservekorps* under General Rüdiger von der Goltz. It then participated in driving the Red Army out of Latvia.

00.03.1920–00.00.192_	Worked as a *Zivilangestellter* (civilian employee) with the *Wehrkreiskommando* in Münster.
00.00.1920–00.00.1921	Arrested and detained for his involvement in the *"Kapp-Putsch."* Released on the grounds of an amnesty and the decision of a *Sondergericht* (special court) that he be acquitted.
00.00.1922–00.00.1924	Member of the *Rheinisch-Westfälische Treuebund*.
00.00.1923–00.00.1923	Member of an anti-French sabotage troop in the Ruhrgebiet.
00.00.1924–00.00.1925	Member of the *Völkisch-Sozialer Block* (VSB).
00.05.1924–27.03.1925	*Vorsitzender* of the *VSB Landesverband* in Westfalen.
00.03.1925	Joined the NSDAP.
27.03.1925–07.03.1926	*Gauleiter* of *Gau Westfalen der NSDAP.*
10.09.1925–00.00.1926	Member of the *Arbeitsgemeinschaft der Nord- und Nordwestdeutschen Gaue der NSDAP* (Working Organization of the North and West German Districts of the Nazi Party).
Christmas 1925	Submitted an internal Party memorandum entitled *"Zucht. Eine Forderung zum Programm"* (Breeding: A demand in relation to the Party Program):

> First of all I share with Strasser and all revolutionaries the view that property in Germany is wrongly distributed: property, power, culture are in the wrong hands, misery and ruin are suffered by the wrong people,

and this situation is growing and consolidating itself to such an extent that only the most drastic, ruthless intervention can force German life and Volkstum back into the right paths. Immediately after this common assumption, however, the thinking diverges.

There are those who take as their starting point the equality of human beings, or rather the equality of Germans. This premise leads naturally to the logical conclusion that there can be no reason why among equals a different distribution of property, state power, culture should prevail. If someone who is equal is forced to live in circumstances significantly lower than the mean, then this is naturally "unjust", or a "scandal" with respect to other equals. If someone who is equal is treated markedly better than the average then this is likewise "unjust", for it can only happen "at the expense" of the share the other equals enjoy of property, power, and culture.... In the last analysis I accuse Strasser's program of being rooted in this basic mentality (and I fear I must accuse him of coming out with far too many arguments which in our camp are called "socialist"). It is the Jewish-liberal-democratic-Marxist-humanitarian mentality. As long as there is even a single minute tendril which connects our program with this root then it is doomed to be poisoned and hence 'to wither away to a miserable death.... All Germans are unequal. That is the starting point.... The first logical conclusion to be drawn from inequality is the inequality of value. Some Germans are more valuable than others ("value" is a relative concept, which I use here naturally to refer to value measured in terms of the German, Nordic worldview, and within this measured in terms of what serves the interests of collective German well-being).

A logical consequence of this inequality must be the principle of unequal treatment, that is, unequal share of state power, property, culture. All these must be distributed to people on the basis of how valuable they are....

A further logical consequence of inequality in what people are worth, and the continuous changes brought about by the development of the Volk, is the duty of the state to take charge of this development, which means influencing it in every way possible. Excellence must be increased and enhanced further. Inferiority must be reduced. In plain terms this is a question of breeding. Improving the stock of the race. Breeding human beings....

From the above considerations I can draw up the following programmatic demands of our future state, the "Third Reich":

To determine the degree of higher or lower value of all inhabitants of Germany. The value will be assessed as the function of four criteria:
(1) actual performance in their professions
(2) physical attributes, according to health and racial characteristics
(3) spiritual, moral and cultural traits
(4) hereditary traits evaluated by considering parents and grandparents...

No pity is to be shown to those who occupy the lower categories of the inferior groups: cripples, epileptics, the blind, the insane, deaf and dumb, children born in sanatoria for alcoholics or in care, orphans (= children born out of wedlock), criminals, whores, the sexually disturbed, etc. [*Krüppel, Epileptikern, Blinden, Irren, Taubstummen, Trinkerheilanstalten-* [sic], *Fürsorgezöglingen, Waisen, Verbrechern, Dirnen, Sexualgestörten* u.s.w.] Everything done for them not only means taking resources away from more deserving causes but counteracts the breeding selection process. Nor should we mourn the dumb, the weak, the spineless, the apathetic, those with hereditary diseases, the pathological, because they go under "innocently".

This bottom category means destruction and death. Weighed and found wanting. Trees which do not bear fruit should be cut down and thrown into the fire. (*NSDAP Hauptarchiv*, Hoover Institution Microfilm Collection, reel 44, folder 896, i-ii.)

07.03.1926–20.06.1926	*Gauleiter* of *Großgau Ruhr der NSDAP* (Seat: Elberfeld), together with Dr. Joseph Goebbels and Karl Kaufmann.
07.03.1926–20.06.1926	*Gau-SA-Führer Ruhr.*
00.08.1926–01.11.1926	*"mit der Führung der SA beauftragt"* (Charged with leadership of the SA).
01.11.1926–29.08.1930	*Oberster SA-Führer (Reichs-SA-Führer)*. In his letter of appointment, dated 01.11.1926, Hitler wrote:

The formation of the SA does not follow a military standpoint but what is expedient to the Party. In so far as its members are trained physically the emphasis should not be on military exercises but sporting activities. Boxing and ju-jitsu have always seemed more important to me than any bad, semi-training in shooting.... What we need are not one or two hundred daring conspirators but a hundred thousand, indeed a hundred thousand fighters for our ideology. The work should be carried on not in secret conventicles but in might mass processions; not through the dagger and poison or the pistol can the way be opened for the movement but through the conquest of the streets. We have to teach Marxism that the future master of the streets is National Socialism just as one day it will be the master of the State. (Schumacher Sammlung/403, Bundesarchiv Koblenz, in Geoffrey Pridham, *Hitler's Rise to Power*, pp. 54-55)

Submitted his resignation, 12.08.1930 (see entry for that date below), and succeeded at the end of the month by Hitler. Prof. Bruce Campbell describes Pfeffer von Salomon's leadership of the SA as follows:

By all accounts he was a genuine leader, a strong-willed personality of great energy and ability, but of equally great arrogance and independence, who did not lack enemies within the NSDAP because of his ambition and lack of tact. Clearly he was a man who believed he was right and therefore did not like to compromise. Yet it was only through just such a combination of will, ability, and leadership that he was able to transform the SA into a national organization. And despite a certain inflexibility and brutal directness of character, von Pfeffer had learned to adapt to changing conditions and political contexts … he could see beyond the world of guns and uniforms. It is this political side of von Pfeffer which enabled him to create a new form for the SA, different from that of the Wehrverbände and better adapted to current conditions. Critical of the "dilettantism" of the Beer Hall Putsch, he was able to draw the lesson from it that if the "national revolution" were to succeed, what was needed was not a better organized putsch, which was the solution proposed by many who continued to think in exclusively military terms, but rather entirely new tactics. As Gauleiter of the Ruhr he gained the experience necessary to adapt the paramilitary form of the Wehrverband to the substance of a political movement. In this he was aided by Viktor Lutze. (Campbell, *The SA Generals and the Rise of Nazism*, p. 50)

The former *Gauleiter* of Hamburg, Dr. Albert Krebs, had occasion to work with Pfeffer, and writes of him with scathing disdain in his memoirs:

Without much exaggeration one could say of Pfeffer that it was the uniform alone that made him a man and gave him self-confidence, stability, a purpose. Without the uniform it became all too apparent that he inclined toward the existence of an adventurer, a careless playboy....

This slim man inherited restless blood and an incessantly critical head. Both qualities inhibited him from orderly activity and from a recognition of any authority. People like Pfeffer always feel something approaching primal hatred and contempt for the world of the "citizen". In a well-regulated situation, therefore, they make excellent professional soldiers. It was particularly fateful for Pfeffer and many of his peers of a similar age and status that they were introduced to a "well-regulated situation" only in the years of their early youth. Beginning with the war, which they entered as fresh cheeked soldiers, there commenced the first relaxation and dissolution of the bonds of order. They could still learn the external forms and requirements of their profession, including how to die courageously, but they could not be taught the spiritual values, and metaphysical content of the life of a soldier and an officer. So they remained arrested in a state of spiritual and intellectual adolescence. They learned the techniques and routines of the soldier's craft, but they never became military leaders, officers in the traditional sense. It was therefore sensible for the *Reichswehr* to refuse admittance to the many Free Corps officers despite their extensive battle experience. How could they have maintained and transmitted the ethos of the soldier through the long peacetime period when they had never absorbed it themselves?...

Pfeffer took only the concept of obedience from the entire complex of values included in the term "soldierly discipline" when he came to train the Stormtroopers. For him it was enough that the SA men follow the orders of their immediate superiors. Apart from that they were free to be, in fact they ought to be, thugs. In this approach Pfeffer reflected the triumph of the civil-war mentality in that segment of the German officer corps which never grasped the true morality of the soldier or else had forgotten it and abandons it in the confusion of the war and the postwar era....

The civil-war mentality had come to control him; he did not choose it for himself consciously. Just like cousins Bruno and Ernst von Salomon, Pfeffer was a revolutionary not out of a desire to build something forward-looking but out of reactionary negativistic sentiments. He hated the Weimar Republic because he thought it had destroyed the better and more beautiful past. Among the qualities of this past was the glory of the soldier.... He lived out his memories, his hatreds, his compulsion to action first in the Free Corps, then in the Nazi party, without giving much thought to the ideological connections or justification of his actions. He enjoyed playing the role of the "eternal lieutenant," always available where there was a need for people of his sort, the man who goes into action without a qualm but who also lets himself be put into action. He went along with things and did his job. He lacked the seriousness to ask whether or not he ought to be going along with things. In case of need he dug a few appropriate sounding reasons out of his memory chest.

Thus Pfeffer also held onto his job with the Nazi party as long and as profitably as possible without ever being, I am convinced, a true National Socialist. For the party's program he had only scorn. He was smart enough to recognize its deficiencies and errors. But helping to remove these deficiencies, contributing to an attempt to develop National Socialism as an intellectual movement, that he would not do. For this he lacked ... the seriousness, perhaps also the ability—not the intellectual ability but the spiritual... (Krebs, *The Infancy of Nazism*, pp. 279-282)

Konrad Heiden writes of the ongoing conflict between Pfeffer and Hitler:

[Pfeffer] at heart was no National Socialist at all.... He used his power like a hired captain in the Renaissance; he had exacted the condition that Hitler should have no right to interfere. Pfeffer knew that he could not, on Sundays and Saturday afternoons, make a serviceable military troop out of these students, white-collar workers, and sons of peasants. But the S.A. could be a preparatory school for the army; as many S.A. men as possible should enter the Reichswehr and flood it with rebellion. Hitler trembled at the slightest thought of illegality; they would deport him at once, of that he was certain. Pfeffer ordered the S.A. to engage in military maneuvers; Hitler issued counterorders. Pfeffer's orders were not valid, he declared, unless countersigned by him, Hitler. Violent scenes ensued; ... Pfeffer listened to Hitler's violent outbreaks. Afterward he said to others, "you can't take orders from this slovenly, terrified Austrian!" It was impossible to make those S.A. captains understand that the purpose of the S.A. was expressly not military....

Pfeffer ... would have liked best to hand over the whole SA. To the Reichswehr, calculating that he himself would then become a general, and Hitler, if necessary, could go to the devil. He led the S.A. back to the drill grounds of the Reichswehr and trained them to bear arms; it was beginning to be a repetition of 1923, which Hitler recalled with horror. That must not happen again. The Reichswehr must not be allowed to take "his" S.A. out of his hands.... He forbade his troop any connection with the Reichswehr, on grounds amounting to high treason: "The National Socialist, and first and foremost the S.A. man, has no call to stir so much as a finger for the present state, which has no understanding of our outlook and can only perpetuate the misfortune of our people..." (Heiden, *Der Fuehrer*, pp. 296-297)

03.11.1926	Issued an order on the "SA and the Public (Propaganda)", which included the following:

> The only form in which the SA appears to the public is that of the closed formation. This is at the same time one of the most powerful forms of propaganda. The sight of a large number of inwardly and outwardly calm, disciplined men, whose total will to fight may be unequivocally seen or sensed, makes the most profound impression on every German and speaks to his heart a more convincing and inspiring language than writing and speech and logic can ever do. Calm composure and matter-of-factness underline the impression of strength—the strength of the marching columns and the strength of the cause for which they are marching. The inner strength of the cause leads the German emotionally to deduce its rightness: "For only the right, the honest, the good can release true strength." Where whole hosts purposefully (not in the welling up of sudden mass suggestion) stake life and limb and existence for a cause, the cause must be great and true!…
>
> The SA man is the sacred freedom fighter. The Pg [*Parteigenosse*—Party Comrade] is the instructor and skilled agitator. Political propaganda seeks to enlighten the adversary, to dispute with him, to understand his viewpoint, to go into his ideas, up to a certain point to agree with him—but when the SA appear on the scene, this stops. They are out for all or nothing. They know only the motto (metaphorically): Strike dead! You or me. (Joachim C. Fest, "Ernst Röhm and the Lost Generation" in *The Face of the Third Reich*, pp. 142-143)

05.12.1926–29.08.1930	*Direkter Vorgesetzter der HJ* (Direct Superior of the Hitler Youth). His appointment to this post resulted from his successful demand that the *Hitler-Jugend* be directly subordinated to the SA.
18.08.1927–21.08.1927	Participated in the "*3. Reichsparteitag der NSDAP*" in Nürnberg.
27.10.1927–11.06.1930	*Vorsitzender der Jugendausschuss* (Chairman of the Youth Committee; redesignated *Jugendamt*, 00.00.1928) in the *Reichsleitung der NSDAP*.
19.08.1927–21.08.1927	*Organisationsleiter* (director of organization) for the "*3. Reichsparteitag der NSDAP*" in Nürnberg.
01.03.1928	Created seven new *SA-Oberführer* commands, placing them under the leadership of retired military officers, as follows:

SA-*Oberführer* Ost (Berlin) ....Hauptmann a. D. Walter Stennes
SA-*Oberführer* Nord (Hannover) ....Major a. D. Karl Dincklage
SA-*Oberführer* West (Kassel) ....Oberstleutnant a. D. Curt von Ulrich
SA-*Oberführer* Mitte (Dresden)............Kapitänleutnant a. D. Manfred Freiherr von Killinger
SA-*Oberführer* Süd (München) .... Major a. D. August Schneidhuber
SA-*Oberführer* Ruhr (Elberfeld) ....Oberleutnant a. D. Viktor Lutze
SA-*Oberführer* Ostmark (Wien) ....Hauptmann a. D. Hermann Reschny

01.08.1929–04.08.1929	Participated in the "*4. Reichsparteitag der NSDAP*" in Nürnberg, of which he was a leading organizer.
Autumn 1928	In letters to an SA subordinate in Köln, wrote:

13.10.1928: We are of the opinion that the SA, as the nucleus of the future German army, must be so trained and organized that even today, slowly but surely, a State is formed within the non-State, so that when the National Socialist Greater Germany is created the internal structure will already exist, determined and strong, invincible in every respect.

28.11.1928: The SA is the militant force of the movement-it is the personification of the will to power of a political organization.... As our SA is the expression of a party machine's politically organized will to power which wishes-not with words, but with actions—to accomplish the national and social liberation of the German people, the concept of comradeship in its ranks takes on an entirely different meaning from that in the so-called military and veteran organizations.... The comradeship in the SA formations must, therefore, become such a solid structure that all police bans or other underhand methods will recoil from its granite wall. (Robert M. W. Kempner, "Blueprint of the Nazi Underground—Past and Future Subversive Activities" in *Research Studies of the State College of Washington, Volume XIII, Number 2*, June 1945)

28.12.1929	In a letter to an SA leader in Köln, wrote: "Before you stands but one individual: *Der Führer*. And you obey him. Faith in him is faith in the German people. He commands and you obey. You ask not why nor wherefore. You know the goal." (Robert M. W. Kempner, "Blueprint of the Nazi Underground—Past and Future Subversive Activities", in *Research Studies of the State College of Washington, Volume XIII, Number 2*, June 1945)
01.04.1930–12.08.1930	*Korpsführer* of the *Nationalsozialistische Automobilkorps* (*NSAK*, forerunner of the later *NSKK*). First holder of this post.
00.00.1930–00.10.1934	*Leiter* of the *Abteilung für den kulturellen Frieden* (Department for Cultural Peace) in the *Reichsleitung der NSDAP*.
12.08.1930	Submitted his resignation from the post of *Oberster SA-Führer* and succeeded at the end of the month by Hitler himself (who retained Dr. Otto Wagener as Chief of Staff). According to Dietrich Orlow, his decision to step down was the culmination of a long history of dissatisfaction with the *Führer*'s leadership. It had become clear to him that Hitler's desire was to place further limitations on the autonomy of the SA. Whereas Pfeffer hoped to gain more *Reichstag* seats for his own subordinates in the *SA*, "Hitler," writes Dietrich Orlow, "either refused to allow SA leaders to become members of the *Reichstag*, or else turned down Pfeffer's demand that he, Pfeffer, should control the votes of the SA deputies [In a letter—marked in handwriting 'not sent'—to Pfeffer dated 13.09.1930, Walter Buch stated the latter was true]. In either case, Pfeffer finally withdrew his request and even lamely attempted to explain why the failure to have SA members in the *Reichstag* was best for the organization." (Orlow, *History of the Nazi Party: 1919-1933*, p. 211) In a letter to SA leaders dated 29.08.1930, von Pfeffer wrote that the SA was justified in demanding "other visible and materially noticeable" confirmation that the SA was to benefit from the electoral successes of the NSDAP. Orlow continues:

[Pfeffer] did not specify what proof he had in mind, but it appears that in addition to wanting more money, he demanded more freedom to disintegrate the *Reichswehr* and to train the *SA* as the core of the new German mass army. Since Hitler was particularly unwilling to embark on a campaign of subversion against the *Reichswehr*, Pfeffer had no choice but to resign his position. (Orlow, *History of the Nazi Party: 1919–1933*, pp. 211-212)

On 29.08.1930, on his departure from the post of *Oberste SA-Führer*, he issued the following message to the men of the SA:

Farewell.

SA Men!

For the fourth time, the day is approaching when I was called to München to build, organize, and lead the SA. The goals and requirements I set myself were high and wide. The SA was to be given the form and content that would at the same time enable it to fight through the struggle for freedom in all its phases victoriously, to be equal to the demands in the days of the takeover of the government and to assume the role assigned to it in the Third Reich. On the whole front, I met with so much understanding and fiery enthusiasm for work that we were able to erect the proud SA building during these years, which today serves the movement as a decoration, as a firm support and as a sharp weapon. The sight of our work is our most beautiful reward and our deepest satisfaction.

With that said, I bid farewell to the SA, for I must now resign from the oberste Führung.

In order to continue with my high aims and demands, I consider the moral and material support of the Party leadership to be necessary to such a sharp extent as the Party leadership does not believe it can grant today. On the other hand, I personally cannot do without goals or pace if I really want to be totally absorbed in my work. The latter, however, is to be demanded in such high positions; therefore, he who cannot or can no longer do this should hand over the position to another who is more suitable under the circumstances.

There is no cause for alarm or rumor when there is a change of personnel in a high position every four years: I ask all SA-Führer to engage with our men in this sense. Furthermore, I will continue to manage the organization until my successor has been trained and will then continue to work elsewhere.

From all of you, my comrades and brothers in arms, I bid you farewell with a strong

Kampf-Heil!

The Oberste SA Führer

[Signed:] v. Pfeffer.
(Bundesarchiv NS-18/890; Translation: Gary Costello)

06.11.1932–01.02.1933	Member of the *Reichstag*.
06.12.1932–01.02.1933	*Stellvertretendes Mitglied* (alternate member) of the *2. Ausschuss (Auswärtige Angelegenheiten) der Reichstag* (Second Committee [Foreign Affairs] of the *Reichstag*).
05.03.1933–14.10.1933	Member of the *Reichstag*.
12.11.1933–27.11.1941	Member of the *Reichstag (Wahlkreis 16, Südhannover-Braunschweig)*.
13.03.1934–00.00.193_	*Beauftragter und Verhandlungsführer in der Kirchenfrage der NSDAP* (Representative and Negotiation Leader for Church Questions of the *NSDAP*).
[00.00.1936]	Honorary member of the *Volksgerichtshof*.
00.09.1939–00.03.1940	Interned for seven months at the headquarters of the *Reichssicherheitshauptamt*, per his own account during an interview conducted on 20.02.1953 by the historians Dr. Fritz Freiherr von Siegler and Dr. Helmut Krausnick. Their report of the interview states:

After the outbreak of war Herr v.P. was imprisoned in September 1939 for 7 months in Prinz-Albrechtstraße…. [A] number of higher SS leaders and also Heydrich himself repeatedly visited the imprisoned Herr v.P. while in uniform and expressed their embarrassment as to how he was being treated… (Report of interview by von Siegler and Krausnick, document ZS-177/1-8, dated 20.02.1953, in the archives of Institut für Zeitgeschichte München)

00.00.1941	Briefly arrested in connection with the unauthorized flight of Rudolf Hess to Scotland.
03.07.1941	In accordance with an order by the *Reichsminister des Innern*, Dr. Wilhelm Frick, removed "von Salomon" from his name and subsequently known only as "von Pfeffer." For many years previous, he had already gone by "von Pfeffer" due to the "Jewish" sound of "Salomon."
24.11.1941	Expelled from the NSDAP, with effect from 24.11.1941. This was revealed in *Rundschreiben* (circular letter) Nr. 4742, dated 01.04.1942, by the *Leiter der Partei-Kanzlei, Reichsleiter* Martin Bormann, which read:

It is reported that the former OSAF, Hauptmann a. D. Franz von Pfeffer, was expelled from the party on 24. November 1941.
F.d.R. [für die Richtigkeit/for the record] Friedrichs
[signed] M. Bormann
(Report of an interview of von Pfeffer, conducted in München on 13.06.1963 by former *SA-Obergruppenführer* Dr. Heinrich Bennecke; Document ZS-177/2-49, dated 13.06.1963, in the archives of Institut für Zeitgeschichte München)

The historian Dr. Bennecke, writes of the reasons behind the expulsion, as presented by von Pfeffer:

Hitler believed that Pfeffer had "been behind" Hess's flight to England in May 1941. Before the *Gauleiter*, Hitler made, behind Pfeffer's back … critical remarks, which he declared [should be kept] secret. Pfeffer then sharply complained in writing to Hitler. Hereupon Hitler demanded that v. Pfeffer give the name of the *Gauleiter* who had conveyed to him Hitler's allegations.... [When Pfeffer refused], Hitler then had him arrested by the SS until he spoke. He was accommodated in the Prinz-Albrecht-Palais, Himmler's headquarters, and could not complain about treatment and accommodation. (Report of an interview of von Pfeffer, conducted in München on 13.06.1963 by former *SA-Obergruppenführer* Dr. Heinrich Bennecke; Document ZS-177/2-49, dated 13.06.1963, in the archives of Institut für Zeitgeschichte München)

Despite several months in *Gestapo* detention, Pfeffer refused to provide further information. While in custody, he wrote an aggressive letter in which he denied Hitler's permission to expel him from the Party. Pfeffer had the letter smuggled out, addressed to Hitler care of Hermann Göring. This caused a considerable fuss, and reportedly led Reinhard Heydrich to consider having him shot. However, it led to Bormann, on Hitler's orders, offering Pfeffer a life-long monthly pension for his earlier service as *Oberster SA-Führer* on the condition that Pfeffer keep quiet about the matter.

27.11.1941	Expelled from his seat in the *Reichstag*.
00.00.1942–21.07.1944	Lived on his estate in Pommern.
21.07.1944	In the immediate aftermath of the 20.07.1944 assassination attempt on Hitler and, according to his own account, traveled to various agricultural states in northern Germany under various assumed names. imprisoned for four months.
15.08.1944	On or around that date, reported in writing to Himmler, and despite the *Reichsführer*'s assurances, arrested soon after his reappearance. According to his own account, he was then imprisoned for four months in the prisons at *Lehrter Straße* and *Berlin-Plötzensee*. (Report of interview by von Siegler and Krausnick, document ZS-177/1-8, dated 20.02.1953, in the archives of Institut für Zeitgeschichte München)
00.01.1945	Fled from Pommern to Bayern.
00.00.1945–00.00.1945	*Kommandeur* of a *Volkssturm* unit.

Postwar Confinement:

00.00.1945–00.00.1946	Arrested by U.S. authorities and interned in Heilbronn, then lived in Wiesbaden.
c. 1946	Tried by a de-Nazification court and classified as a *Mitläufer* (fellow traveler).
00.00.1949–00.00.195_	Active member of the *Landesverband Hessen* in the right-wing conservative *Deutsche Partei*.
00.00.1960	Moved to München.

Decorations & Awards:

09.11.1918	*Ritterkreuz des Kgl. Hausordens von Hohenzollern mit Schwertern*
10.10.1915	*1914 Eisernes Kreuz I. Klasse*
00.00.191_	*1914 Eisernes Kreuz II. Klasse*
21.02.1916	*Ritterkreuz II. Klasse mit Schwertern des Kgl. Sächsischen Albrechts-Ordens*
c. 1919	*Balten Kreuz I. Klasse*

c. 1919   Balten Kreuz II. Klasse
c. 1921   Schlesischer Adler 1. Stufe
c. 1921   Schlesischer Adler 2. Stufe
c. 1918   Verwundetenabzeichen, 1918 in Schwarz
c. 1934   Ehrenkreuz des Weltkrieges 1914–1918 mit Schwertern
c. 1933   Goldenes Ehrenzeichen der NSDAP
c. 1929   Nürnberger Parteitagsabzeichen 1929
00.00.194_   Dienstauszeichnung der NSDAP in Silber
00.00.194_   Dienstauszeichnung der NSDAP in Bronze
00.00.1934   Ehrendolch der SA (mit Wirkung vom 03.02.1934)
00.02.1934   Ehrenwinkel für alte Kämpfer

NOTES:
* Parents (Married 23.04.1887):
  - *Father*: *Kgl. preussischer Geheimen Regierungsrat Max* Carl Friedrich Ferdinand Pfeffer von Salomon (*25.04.1854 in Friedeberg in der Neumarkt, †11.08.1918 in Münster as a *Hauptmann der Landwehr*. He was the son of the Prussian *Oberst* of cavalry *Ferdinand* Hubert August Pfeffer von Salomon [*28.04.1822 in Geldern, †00.00.1901; accepted into the Prussian nobility, 14.07.1862] and his wife *Ida* Henriette Gertrud, *née* Hoffmann-Scholtz [*07.08.1834 in Liegnitz, †00.00.1899]).
  - *Mother*: Anna, *née* von Clavé-Bouhaben (*26.07.1862 in Simmern, †28.01.1919 in Münster), daughter of the Prussian *Appelationsgerichtsrat* [appeals court counselor] Franz von Clavé-Bouhaben, an estate owner in Königswinter, and his wife Marie, *née* Coninx.
* Siblings:
  - *Ferdinand* Pfeffer Hubert August Felix Pfeffer von Salomon (*30.04.1889 in Osnabrück, killed in an accident as *Leutnant zur See*, 00.01.1914)
  - Adelheit Pfeffer von Salomon (*00.00.1891)
  - *Friedrich* ("Fritz") Ludwig Ferdinand Felix Pfeffer von Salomon (*19.05.1892 in Berlin-Charlottenburg, †29.10.1961 in Straelen/Niederrhein), NSDAP-Nr. 77.889 (Joined 01.03.1929). As an *SA-Obergruppenführer*, his biography will appear in Volume 2 of the current series.
  - *Ludwiga* Pfeffer von Salomon (*25.08.1894 in Münster, †00.00.1981); married on 09.10.1926 to *Hauptmann* (later *Generalleutnant*) Gustav von Schneidermesser (*04.02.1891 in Düsseldorf, †07.04.1975 in Wiesbaden)
  - *Reiner* Pfeffer von Salomon (*00.00.1895, killed in an action as a *Leutnant* of *Infanterie-Regiment 13* on the Somme, 20.09.1916)
  - *Felix* Pfeffer von Salomon (*00.00.1896, killed in action as *Leutnant* of *Infanterie-Regiment 13* near Verdun, 25.12.1917)
* Among his cousins were the famous *Freikorps* leader and writer (and co-assassin, on 24.06.1922, of German foreign minister Walther Rathenau) Ernst von Salomon (*25.09.1902 in Kiel, †09.08.1972 in Stoekte bei Winsen) and his brother Bruno von Salomon, a leading figure in the *KPD* (*Kommunistische Partei Deutschlands*).
* Religion: Catholic.
* Married in Bakenhof bei Krefeld on 14.01.1922 to *Marie* Sophie Clara Freiin Raitz von Frentz (*01.04.1895 in Altena/Westfalen, †18.05.1984 in Altena/Westfalen). She was the daughter of Adolf Freiherr Raitz von Frentz (*00.00.1843, †00.00.1907], a Prussian *Premier-Lieutenant*, and his wife Sophie Freiin von Lüninck [*00.00.1850, †00.00.1934]). Former Hamburg *Gauleiter* Dr. Albert Krebs describes Frau Pfeffer as follows: "Insofar as Pfeffer criticized the party, he was undoubtedly supported or even encouraged to do so by

his wife. Her repugnance for many leading Nazis, especially Hitler himself, derived from her unhindered instincts and her still solid appreciation of real values and rules..." (Dr. Krebs, *The Infancy of Nazism*, p. 282)

The following children were born to Franz Pfeffer von Salomon and his wife:

- Irmgard ("Ita") (*00.05.1923), Dr. rer. nat., a biologist, married to Friedemann Freiherr von Wintzingerode (*00.00.1913–†00.00.1964), a farmer in South Africa.
- Kunigunde (*00.00.1927), Dr. rer.nat., also a biologist, married to the geologist Dr. phil. Jobst Hülsemann.
- Ferdinand (*00.00.1929), Dr. jur. and attorney in Lünen.
- Max (*00.00.1932), state attorney in Cape Town, South Africa.

Sources:

Bennecke, Dr. phil. Heinrich: *Hitler und die SA*. Günter Olzog Verlag, 1962.
Campbell, Bruce: *The SA Generals and the Rise of Nazism*. The University Press of Kentucky, 1998.
Fest, Joachim C.: *The Face of the Third Reich: Portraits of the Nazi Leadership*. Weidenfeld and Nicolson, Ltd, 1970.
Fraschka, Dr. Mark A.: *Franz Pfeffer von Salomon: Hitlers vergessener Oberster SA-Führer*. Walstein-Verlag, 2016.
Höffkes, Karl: *Hitlers politische Generale: Die Gauleiter des Dritten Reiches*. Grabert-Verlag-Tübingen, 1986.
Höhne, Heinz: *The Order of the Death's Head*. Martin Secker and Warburg, 1969.
Königlichen Herolds-Amtes: *Handbuch des Preußischen Adels*. Ernst Siegfried Mittler und Söhne, Königliche Hofbuchhandlung, 1892.
Königlichen Preußische Kriegsministerium, Geheime Kriegs-Kanzlei: *Rangliste der Königlich Preußischen Armee und des XIII. (Königlich Württembergischen) Armeekorps für 1914 (Nach dem Stande vom 6. Mai 1914)*. Ernst Siegfried Mittler und Sohn, 1914.
—*Rangliste des aktiven Dienststandes der Königlich Preußischen Armee und des XIII. (Königlich Württembergischen) Armeekorps [für 1913] (Nach dem Stande vom 6. Oktober 1913)*. Ernst Siegfried Mittler und Sohn, 1913.
—*Rangliste des aktiven Dienststandes der Königlich Preußischen Armee und des XIII. (Königlich Württembergischen) Armeekorps für 1912 (Nach dem Stande vom 6. Mai 1912)*. Ernst Siegfried Mittler und Sohn, 1912.
Krebs, Dr. phil. Albert: *The Infancy of Nazism: The Memoirs of Ex-Gauleiter Albert Krebs, 1923–1933*. New Viewpoints, 1976.
Lilla, Joachim; Döring, Martin; & Schulz, Andreas: *Statisten in Uniform. Die Mitglieder des Reichstags 1933–1945*. Droste Verlag, 2004.
Morgan, Konrad: *Der Fuehrer*. Houghton Mifflin, 1944.
Miller, Michael D. and Andreas Schulz: *Leaders of the Storm Troops, Volume 1* (1st Edition). Helion & Co., 2015.
Pridham, Geoffrey: *Hitler's Rise to Power. The Nazi Movement in Bavaria, 1923–33*. Hart-Davis, MacGibbon Ltd, 1973.
Siemens, Daniel: *Stormtroopers: A New History of Hitler's Brownshirts*. Yale University Press, 2017.
Stockhorst, Erich: *5000 Köpfe: Wer war was im 3. Reich* (3rd Edition). Arndt-Verlag, 1998.
Wagener, Dr. Otto: *Hitler: Memoirs of a Confidant* (edited by Henry Ashby Turner, Jr.; translated by Ruth Hein). Yale University Press, 1985.
Weiss, Hermann: *Neue Deutsche Biographie*. Duncker & Humblot, 2001.

Above left: Franz Pfeffer von Salomon in 1924. (Bundesarchiv Bild 119-1587A)

Above right: Franz Pfeffer von Salomon, c. 1926.

"*3. Reichsparteitag der NSDAP*" in Nürnberg (19.08.–21.08.1927).

Right: Pfeffer von Salomon and Hitler salute the crowd, with Hess behind them. At far left is Pfeffer's adjutant, Georg Hallermann.

Overleaf above: Left to right: Julius Streicher, Max Amann, Artur Dinter, Georg Hallermann, Pfeffer von Salomon, Hitler, and Ulrich Graf.

Overleaf middle: Hitler delivers a speech to *Reichsparteitag* attendees. Behind him, from left to right: Hess, Streicher, Graf, Ernst Graf zu Reventlow, Pfeffer von Salomon, and Heinrich Himmler.

Overleaf below: Left to right: Himmler, Hess, unknown, Gregor Strasser, Hitler, and Pfeffer von Salomon.

Pfeffer von Salomon with Hitler reviewing a march-past of SA units during the "*Gauparteitag der NSDAP in Essen*," 24.04.1927.

The *Oberster SA-Führer* inspects an SA unit. Georg Hallermann is second from right.

Above: Pfeffer von Salomon and Walther Stennes oversee an SA training exercise in 1928. (Roger Bender)

Left: München, 13.05.1928: Pfeffer von Salomon speaks with Hitler and Rudolf Hess in the rain during the electoral campaign for *Reichstag* and *Landtag* seats. On the right, in overcoat and hat, is Alfred Rosenberg with Julius Schaub in profile. (NARA, Heinrich Hoffmann Collection)

The *Oberster SA-Führer*, in the *Geschäftsstelle der OSAF* at *Schellingstraße Nr. 50*, München, makes preparations for the "*4. Reichsparteitag der NSDAP*" in Nürnberg, together with the Party Treasurer, Franz Xaver Schwarz and Business Manager, Philip Bouhler.

Pfeffer von Salomon participates in the "*4. Reichsparteitag der NSDAP*."

Right: Pfeffer von Salomon and Goebbels salute from the running board of Hitler's car. Standing on the ground at left is Georg Hallermann.

Left to right: Pfeffer von Salomon, Hitler, Franz Ritter von Epp, and Viktor Lutze. Second from the right is Hermann Göring.

Franz Ritter von Epp delivers a speech during a memorial service for Germany's 1914-18 war dead at the *Gefallenen-Ehrenmal* in the *Luitpoldhain*, Nürnberg. Left to right: Ritter von Epp, Hitler, Pfeffer von Salomon, and Rudolf Hess. (Josef H. Krumbach, *Franz Ritter von Epp. Ein Leben für Deutschland*, 1939)

Right: Hitler and Pfeffer von Salomon.

Below: Right to left: Pfeffer von Salomon, Hitler, Ritter von Epp, and Hess. (Walter Frank, *Franz Ritter von Epp. Der Weg eines deutschen Soldaten*, 1934)

Above: The *Direkter Vorgesetzter der HJ* (Direct Superior of the Hitler Youth) reviews the HJ encampment during the rally. To his immediate left is Kurt Gruber, the first *Reichsführer der Hitler-Jugend* (1926–1931). (Heinrich Hoffmann photo)

Left: In conversation with *Gauleiter* Julius Streicher.

The *Führer* in Dresden with senior leaders of the NSDAP, SA, and SS, 1929. First table, left to right: Pfeffer von Salomon, unknown SA leader, Manfred Freiherr von Killinger, Heinrich Himmler (blurred), Georg von Detten, Martin Mutschmann, Hitler, Rudolf Hess, and Gregor Strasser. At the second table are Dr. Goebbels and Dr. Herbert Albrecht (wearing glasses). (NARA, Heinrich Hoffmann Collection)

The *Zirkus Krone*, München, 25.10.1929: Pfeffer von Salomon, Rudolf Hess, and Hitler listen to a speech by the DNVP leader Alfred Hugenberg at a rally of the *Reichsausschuss für das deutsche Volksbegehren* (Reich Committee for the German Referendum against the Young Plan). (NARA, Heinrich Hoffmann Collection)

Plauen, 1930: Hitler and other Party leaders visit the home of the piano maker and early NSDAP financial supporter Edwin Bechstein and his wife Helene. Seated, left to right: Goebbels, unknown, Hitler, Helene Bechstein, Edwin Bechstein, Hans Schemm, and Pfeffer von Salomon. Standing, left to right: Rudolf Hess, Martin Mutschmann, and Dr. Herbert Albrecht. (NARA, Heinrich Hoffmann Collection)

Above: An informal shot of Franz Pfeffer von Salomon, *c.* 1929.

Opposite far: The *Oberster SA-Führer* in full regalia, *c.* 1929. The original caption of this photo, which appears in Heinrich Hoffmann's book, *Das Braune Heer. 100 Bilddokumente: Leben, Kampf und Sieg der SA und SS* (1932), read: "Cool and superior, but wise and valiant. One of the first National-Socialists from Westphalia. A steadfast fighter against the current system. Once, he helped organize para-military 'Freikorps' volunteers; now the S.A.: HAUPTMANN VON PFEFFER."

Opposite near: An artist's rendering of Pfeffer von Salomon, signed by the OSAF.

The "*6. Reichsparteitag der NSDAP*" in Nürnberg (04.–10.09.1934).

Above: Hitler reviews a parade of SA units. Pfeffer stands nearest the camera. (Michal Sika).

Above: Left to right: Pfeffer, Hess, Göring, and Adolf Hühnlein.

Right: Left to right: Pfeffer, Hess, and Göring.

The "*9. Reichsparteitag der NSDAP*"
(06.–13.09.1937):

Left: Right to left: Pfeffer, Göring, Viktor Lutze, and Hess.

Below: Pfeffer and Hess.

The "*10. Reichsparteitag der NSDAP*" in Nürnberg (05.–12.09.1938).

Right to left: Pfeffer, Göring, Hühnlein, NSKK-Gruppenführer Heinrich Jürgensen, and Hess.

Right to left: Pfeffer, Göring, Hitler, Heinrich Himmler, and Kurt Daluege.

Right to left: Goebbels, Streicher, Göring, Hess, Pfeffer, Amann, and Dr. Hans Frank. (Michal Sika)

Pfeffer and Göring stand before the assembled leaders of the SA. (Michal Sika)

Pfeffer and Göring.

Above: Hitler salutes from his car, with Pfeffer in the foreground with Göring to his immediate right. (Michal Sika)

Left: The official announcement of Pfeffer's expulsion from the NSDAP. (Bundesarchiv NS/6-337-0191, courtesy of Gary Costello)

Dr. phil. h. c.
Otto William (Wilhelm) Heinrich Wagener
Stabschef der SA (01.10.1929–31.12.1930)
Obersten SA-Führer (29.08.1930–31.12.1930)

*	29.04.1888 in Durlach/Baden.
†	08.08.1971 in Chieming-Stöttham/Kreis Traunstein/ Regierungsbezirk Oberbayern/Bayern.
NSDAP-Nr.:	159.203 (Joined 01.10.1929)

Promotions:
09.07.1906	*Fahnenjunker*
22.03.1907	*Fähnrich*
18.11.1907	*Leutnant* (*mit Patent vom 22.05.1906*)
08.11.1914	*Oberleutnant*
18.12.1915	*Hauptmann* (M3m)
01.10.1929–31.12.1930	*Stabschef der SA*
29.08.1930–31.12.1930	*Obersten SA-Führer* (m.d.W.d.G.b.)
18.12.1931	*SA-Gruppenführer* (per *SA-Führerbefehl Nr. 6*, 18.12.1931)
01.04.1940	*Hauptmann z. V.*
15.03.1941	*Major z. V.*
01.06.1942	*Oberstleutnant z. V.*
01.08.1943	*Oberst z. V.*
01.12.1944	*Generalmajor z. V.*

Career:
c. 1894–c. 1898	*Volksschule*
c. 1898–00.00.1906	*Gymnasium* in Karlsruhe.
09.07.1906	Entered service as a *Fahnenjunker*, assigned to *Infanterie-Regiment "Markgraf Ludwig Wilhelm" (3. Badische) Nr. 111* (Rastatt).
00.00.19__–30.09.1913	*Bataillons-Adjutant* of *I. Bataillon/Infanterie-Regiment "Markgraf Ludwig Wilhelm" (3. Badische) Nr. 111.*
01.10.1913–00.00.1914	Attended the *Kriegsakademie* in Berlin.
01.07.1914–31.07.1914	Participated in an *Ausbildungskurs* (training course) as a *Flugzeugbeobachter* (aerial observer) with *Fliegerkommando Döberitz*.
01.08.1914–00.11.1914(?)	Deployed to the Western Front with *Reserve-Infanterie-Regiment 55*.
00.11.1914–05.04.1915(?)	Assigned as a *Brigade-Adjutant* of *55. Reserve-Infanterie-Brigade* (dissolved 05.04.1915) under *28. (badische) Reserve-Division* on the Western Front.
05.04.1915–00.12.1915	Assigned as a *Kompanieführer*.
01.02.1916–10.07.1916	*Bataillonsführer* in *3. Reserve-Infanterie-Regiment Nr. 110*.
11.07.1916–07.12.1916(?)	Attached to the *Generalstab* of *Armeegruppe von Stein*.
07.12.1916–00.00.1918	Assigned to the *Generalstab* of *5. Armee*.
06.05.1918	Following a hearing before a court of honor, dismissed from service.
00.00.1919–00.00.1919	Member of a *Freikorps* on the German-Polish border.
Summer 1919–00.00.1920	*Chef des Generalstabes* of the *Deutsche Legion* (*Freikorps*), also known as the *Baltische Legion*, in the Kurland region of Latvia

	and in Lithuania, where it served as part of Colonel (later Major General) Prince Pavel Mikhailovich Avalov-Bermondt's *Freiwillige Russische Westarmee* (also known as the *Freiwillige Deutsch-Russische Westarmee*). The Legion, which had been formed in Mitau, Latvia, on 25.08.1919 (from *2. Infanterie-Brigade*, elements of *1. Garde-Reserve-Division*, and the *Baltische Landwehr*) was disbanded on 18.12.1919, shortly after its return to Germany.
16.11.1919–18.12.1919	*Führer* of the *Deutsche Legion* in Oberschlesien, in the Ruhr, and in Sachsen. Succeeded *Kapitän zur See* Paul Siewert, who had been killed in action on 16.11.1919.
00.00.1919–00.00.1919	Studied economics.
00.03.1920–00.03.1920	Arrested and briefly detained in connection with the "*Kapp-Putsch*."
31.03.1920	Released from *Freikorps* service.
00.00.1920–00.00.1920	*Direktionsassistent* (assistant director) of the *Frankenthaler Maschinen- & Armatur-Fabrik Klein, Schanzlin & Becker AG*.
00.00.1920–00.00.1921	*Landesleiter* of the *Organisation Escherich* in Baden.
End of 1920–00.00.1924	*Direktor* and *Vorstand* (executive) of his father's sewing machine factory *Nähmaschinenfabrik Karlsruhe AG*. It was previously known as *Haid und Neu*, named for Georg Haid and Carl Wilhelm Neu, who had founded the business on 14.04.1860.
00.00.1922–00.00.1924	Lecturer on economic and social policy matters in business college courses at the *Technischen Hochschule* in Karlsruhe and the University of Würzburg.
00.00.1923	Joined the SA.
00.00.1924	Received his doctorate (Dr. phil. h. c.) from the *Philosophischen Fakultät* (philosophical faculty) of the University of Würzburg.
00.00.1924–00.00.1925	Traveled abroad and lectured on matters of economic policy.
00.00.1925–00.00.1929	Part owner of a plywood and veneer business in Villingen.
00.00.1925–00.08.1925	*Vorsitzender* (chairman) of the *Badische Wahlausschuss* (Baden electoral committee) for the *Rechtsblock* in the Reich presidential elections.
00.07.1929	Established contacts with the NSDAP.
01.08.1929–04.08.1929	Participated in the "*4. Reichsparteitag der NSDAP*" in Nürnberg.
01.10.1929	Joined the NSDAP and the SA.
01.10.1929–13.07.1933	Member of the *Reichsleitung der NSDAP*.
01.10.1929–31.12.1930	*Stabschef der SA*. Succeeded by Ernst Röhm.
28.04.1930	Diary entry of Dr. Goebbels: "Night train with Dr. Wagener. He is very smart and we get along well. He also thinks that the Party has to orientate itself more towards Berlin. Seeking above all socio-political power on the level of the empire." (Ralf Georg Reuth, ed., *Joseph Goebbels. Tagebücher 1924–1945, Band 2: 1930–1934*, p. 483)
29.08.1930–31.12.1930	*Obersten SA-Führer* (m.d.W.d.G.b.). Succeeded by Adolf Hitler.
11.09.1930	Diary entry of Dr. Goebbels: "Talk with Hauptmann Wagener. He comes to Berlin a lot now and works for the Party in business circles." (Ralf Georg Reuth, ed., *Joseph Goebbels. Tagebücher 1924–1945, Band 2: 1930–1934*, p. 539)
01.01.1931–00.06.1932	*Leiter* of the *Wirtschaftspolitische Abteilung* (Economic Policy Department) in the *Reichsorganisationsabteilung II der*

Reichsleitung der NSDAP. Succeeded by Dr. Wilhelm Keppler. William L. Patch writes:

> Wagener formulated an original set of economic policies based on corporatist and leadership principles in confidential talks with Hitler and succeeded in recruiting many middle echelon industrial managers and owners of small factories for the NSDAP.... [A confidential draft by Wagener] embraced the ideal of the corporatist "company union" (Werksgemeinschaft) and described the employer as the "Führer" within his factory. All disputes over wages and working conditions would be settled within the "family" of the individual company in the National Socialist state of the future. Trade unions would be responsible merely for vocational training. (Patch, *The Christian Trade Unions in the Weimar Republic, 1918-1933: The Failure of Corporate Pluralism*, pp. 201-202)

Manfred Berg and Martin H. Geyer write of Wagener's approach to Jewish affairs:

> Wagener was a zealous proponent of economic corporativism, a position that identified him with the self-consciously fascist wing among National Socialist intellectuals.... Probably in late 1931 or early 1932, at a breakfast at the party headquarters in Munich, Wagener advised the Führer that the Jewish problem could be solved quite simply by forbidding any further Jewish immigration into Germany. Given the low birth rate among Jews, Wagener calculated, and without replenishment from abroad, they would be condemned to gradual extinction. Until that happened, he advised Hitler, a Nazi regime would need to do little more than bar Jews from positions in government and watch while the Jewish problem solved itself. No Nazi ever proposed a milder solution to the Jewish problem. Hitler obviously did not consider it adequate. (Berg and Geyer, *Two Cultures of Rights: The Quest for Inclusion and Participation in Modern America and Germany*)

00.00.1931	Founder of the *Wirtschaftspolitische Pressedienst* (WPD, Economic Policy Press Service).
00.00.1931–00.00.193_	Editor of the National-Socialist periodical *Wirtschaftspolitischen Briefe*.
18.12.1931	Granted the rank of *SA-Gruppenführer* with assignment as an *SA-Führer z. V.*
00.06.1932–04.09.1932	*Leiter* of *Hauptabteilung IV* (*Wirtschaftspolitik*, Economic Policy) in the *Reichsorganisationleitung der NSDAP.*
04.09.1932–01.04.1933	Designated as *"z.b.V. im Stabe des Führers"* (at disposal of the Staff of the *Führer*).
01.04.1933–13.07.1933	*Leiter* of the *Wirtschaftspolitisch Hauptamt der NSDAP* (Main Office for Economic Policy of the *NSDAP*) and *Sachbearbeiter für Wirtschaftspolitik im Verbindungsstab der NSDAP* (Specialist for Economic Policy in the Liaison Staff of the NSDAP).
01.04.1933	Led an SA squad in the occupation of the business office of the *Reichsverband der Deutschen Industrie*. Peter Longerich writes:

... Wagener demand[ed] changes to [the RDI's] board.... He insisted that the general manager, Ludwig Kastl, was unacceptable on political grounds, that several Jewish members should leave, and that a number of people should be appointed whom the NSDAP could rely on to "coordinate" the RDI's activities with government policy. All attempts by the industrialists to get access to Hitler to persuade him to withdraw these demands proved unsuccessful. (Longerich, *Hitler: A Life*, p. 304)

15.04.1933–13.07.1933	*Regierungskommissar* in the *Geschäftsführung* (business management) of the *Reichsverband der Deutschen Industrie*.
24.04.1933–30.06.1933	*Reichskommissar für die Wirtschaft* (Reich Commissioner for the Economy).
03.05.1933–00.00.1933	*Kommissar des Reiches für den Reichsverband der deutschen Industrie und für die übrige Wirtschaft mit Ausnahme der Landwirtschaft* (Reich Commissioner for the Reich Association of German Industry and for the remaining economy with the exception of agriculture).
00.06.1933–13.07.1933	*Ehrenvorsitzender* (honorary chairman) of the *Reichsarbeitsgemeinschaft der technisch-wissenschaftlichen Arbeit* (RTA, Reich Working Group for Technical-Industrial Work).
13.07.1933	Dismissed from all offices by Hitler, having fallen into disgrace with the *Führer* the previous month.
12.11.1933–28.03.1938	Member of the *Reichstag (Wahlkreis 21, Koblenz-Trier)*.
30.06.1934	Arrested and briefly detained during the so-called "Röhm-Putsch," narrowly avoiding execution. He fled to the Erzgebirge region, working as a farmer in Hohenwedel über Wiesenbad, thereafter avoiding any contact with the NSDAP leadership.
01.04.1937–00.05.1945	Reentered the SA with the rank of *SA-Gruppenführer* and assigned as an *SA-Führer z. V.* to the *Stab der Obersten SA-Führung*.
01.04.1940–12.05.1940	Assigned as an *Ordonnanzoffizier* to the staff of *Armeeoberkommando 6* (6. Armee headquarters).
12.05.1940–31.08.1940	Attached as *Gehilfe* (assistant) to the *1. Generalstabsoffizier* (Ia) in the *Generalstab des Heeres* (Army General Staff).
01.09.1940–00.01.1943	Assigned as *Ia* to the staff of *332. Infanterie-Division*.
00.01.1943–11.02.1944	*Kommandeur* of *Sicherungs-Regiment 177*.
12.02.1944–06.05.1944	*Führer (m.d.F.b.)* of a *Sicherungs-Division*.
06.05.1944–20.07.1944(?)	In *Führerreserve OKH*.
20.07.1944–08.05.1945	*Kommandant Ost-Ägäis* and *Militärgouverneur der italienischen Inseln der Dodekanes* (Military Governor of the Italian Islands of the Dodecanese—Rhodes, Kos, and Leros). Under his command were 6,000 troops, half of them from the punitive *Bewährungseinheiten 999*. On Rhodes, he had established an *Internierungslager* (internment camp) and the concentration camp "Kallithea," where Italian POWs were held. According to the 14.02.1951 issue of the West German magazine *Der Spiegel*, 1,300 death warrants were executed under Wagener's authority in April–May 1945 alone.
08.05.1945	On the island of Symi, signed the unconditional surrender of Axis forces in the Dodecanese Islands to the British. The following is

excerpted from the diary of Herbert Dobson, personal assistant to Major Peter Acland (deputy chief civil affairs officer and chief administrator in Dodecanese Islands in 1945):

8th May 1945:
Today shortly after 10am General WAGNER [sic, WAGENER] with certain staff officers (among whom I recognised Oberleutnant Meeske, Wag[e]ner's representative at the earlier Prisoner and Red Cross supply talks off Turkey) arrived to sign the terms of Surrender....

The Court Room of the Demarkion (Town Hall) had been set out to receive both sides and about 1015 the General came before Brigadier James Moffat, the British Commander. The Brigadier told the General that he had full powers from the Supreme Commander of the Mediterranean Forces to negotiate a surrender and the General replied that he too had the same powers conferred on him by the German High Command. (Heartfield, John: "German Surrender of the Dodecanese Islands" at www.johnhearfield.com/Bob/Dodecanese/Surrender.htm)

POSTWAR PROSECUTION:
00.00.1945–00.01.1947	Held as a prisoner of war at a British camp in Wales.
07.01.1947	Turned over to Italian authorities.
16.10.1948	Sentenced by an Italian military court to fifteen years' imprisonment for the shooting of Italian POWs on Rhodes.
04.06.1951	Released from prison thanks to the intercession of Bishop Alois Hudal and West German Chancellor Konrad Adenauer.
1950s	*Vorsitzender* (chairman) of the *Seeckt-Gesellschaft* and affiliated with nationalist political circles in Bayern.

PUBLISHED WORKS:
Von der Heimat geächtet (Belser, 1920)
Grundlagen und Ziele der nationalsozialistischen Wirtschaftspolitik (Eher-Verlag, 1932)
Nationalsozialistische Wirtschaftsauffassung und berufsständischer Aufbau (Wirtschaftspolitischer Verlag, 1933)
Hitler aus nächster Nähe. Aufzeichnungen eines Vertrauten 1929-1932 (Written in 1946 but published posthumously; edited by Henry Ashby Turner, 1978)

DECORATIONS & AWARDS:
* 05.05.1945	*Ritterkreuz des Eisernen Kreuzes* as *Generalmajor z. V.*, *Kommandant Ost-Ägäis*, and *Militärgouverneur der italienischen Inseln der Dodekanes*
	* Award technically invalid as it was made by the acting Reich Government of *Großadmiral* Karl Dönitz, who did not have authority to make such awards. On 20.05.1945 at 2035 hours, *Generalmajor* Benthack (*Kdr.* of *Festungs-Division Kreta* and *Kdr.* of *Festung Kreta* transmitted a proposal for award of the Ritterkreuz to five men, including Wagener, to *OKW/WFSt* (*Oberkommando der Wehrmacht/Wehrmachtführungsstab*). On 21.05.1945 at 23.33 hours, Dönitz sent a telegram authorizing award of the *Ritterkeuz* to Wagener and four other soldiers "in

	appreciation of the excellent conduct and spirit of the brave garrison of Crete."
17.04.1944	*Ehrenblatt-Spange des Heeres*
29.06.1943	*1939 Spange zum 1914 Eisernes Kreuz I. Klasse*
29.05.1940	*Spange zum 1914 Eisernes Kreuz II. Klasse*
00.00.191_	*1914 Eisernes Kreuz I. Klasse*
00.00.191_	*1914 Eisernes Kreuz II. Klasse*
20.04.1942	*Kriegsverdienstkreuz II. Klasse mit Schwertern*
20.04.1942(?)	*Kriegsverdienstkreuz II. Klasse mit Schwertern*
00.00.191_	*Ritterkreuz I. Klasse mit Schwertern des Königlich Württembergischer Friedrichs-Orden*
25.05.1916	*Großherzoglich Badischer Militär Karl-Friedrich-Verdienstorden*
00.00.194_	*Infanterie-Sturmabzeichen in Silber*
c. 1919	*Verwundetenabzeichen, 1918 in Silber*
c. 1919	*Baltenkreuz I. Klasse*
c. 1934	*Ehrenkreuz des Weltkrieges 1914–1918 mit Schwertern*
00.00.194_	*Dienstauszeichnung der NSDAP in Silber*
00.00.194_	*Dienstauszeichnung der NSDAP in Bronze*
00.00.1929	*Nürnberger Parteitagsabzeichen 1929*
00.02.1934(?)	*Ehrendolch der SA*
00.00.1934	*Ehrenwinkel für alte Kämpfer*

NOTES:

* Parents:
  - Father: Georg Heinrich Wilhelm Wagener, director of a factory (*Nähmaschinenfabrik Karlsruhe AG vorm. Haid & Neu*).
  - Mother: Emma Wagener, née Hofheinz.
* Religion: Lutheran (baptized 03.06.1888).
* Married on 30.12.1930 to Wendula Schmidt.

SOURCES:

Berg, Manfred & Geyer, Martin H.: *Two Cultures of Rights: The Quest for Inclusion and Participation in Modern America and Germany*. Cambridge University Press, 2002.

Reuth, Ralf Georg (ed): *Joseph Goebbels: Tagebücher 1924–1945, Band 2: 1930–1934*. R. Piper GmbH & Co., 1992.

Lilla, Joachim; Döring, Martin; & Schulz Andreas: *Statisten in Uniform. Die Mitglieder des Reichstags 1933–1945*. Droste Verlag, 2004.

Longerich, Peter: *Hitler: A Life*. Oxford University Press, 2019.

Miller, Michael D., and Andreas Schulz: *Leaders of the Storm Troops, Volume 1* (1st Edition). Helion & Co., 2015.

Orlow, Dietrich: *History of the Nazi Party: 1933–1945*. University of Pittsburgh Press, 1973.

Patch, William L.: *The Christian Trade Unions in the Weimar Republic, 1918–1933: The Failure of Corporate Pluralism*. Yale University Press, 1985.

Wagener, Dr. Otto: *Hitler: Memoirs of a Confidant* (Henry Ashby Turner, Jr., ed.). Yale University Press, 1985 (Translation of *Hitler aus nächster Nähe. Aufzeichnungen eines Vertrauten 1929–1932*. Ullstein, 1978).

Dr. Otto Wagener, c. 1933.

Outside the *Reichsgericht* in Leipzig, 25.09.1930: Hitler surrounded by supporters during the so-called "*Ulmer Reichswehrprozeß*," in which three young officers (Richard Scheringer, Hans Friedrich Wendt, and future *SA-Obergruppenführer* Hans Elard Ludin) were tried for national socialist activities. Dr. Wagener stands behind him. At far right is Ernst ("Putzi") Hanfstaengl.

Above left: Dr. Wagener in *Heer* uniform, c. 1940.

Above right: *Generalmajor* Wagener in Allied captivity, 1945.

On the day of Hitler's "*Machtergreifung*" (Seizure of Power)—30.01.1933—Dr. Wagener poses with Hitler and other senior Party leaders at the *Hotel Kaiserhof,* Berlin:

Opposite above: Right to left: R. Walther Darré, Hermann Göring, Ernst Röhm, Hitler, Dr. Joseph Goebbels, Hanns Kerrl, Wilhelm Kube, Dr. Wagener, and seated, Dr. Wilhelm Frick.

Opposite below: Right to left: Paul Körner, Darré, Röhm, Heinrich Himmler, Göring, Kerrl, Kube, and seated, Wagener and Goebbels. (NARA, Heinrich Hoffmann Collection)

The island of Symi in the Aegean, 08.05.1945: *Generalmajor* Wagener signs the surrender of German forces in the Dodecanese Islands to the British. (Imperial War Museum)

Ernst Julius Günther Röhm
Chef des Stabes der SA (05.01.1931–01.07.1934)
Führer der SA (00.03.1925–01.05.1925)

*	28.11.1887 in München/Regierungsbezirk Oberbayern/Bayern.
†	01.07.1934, shot in the chest in Cell 474 at *Strafgefängnis München-Stadelheim* (see the "Career" section, entry of 01.07.1934, for further details). Initially buried in the *Perlacher Friedhof*, his remains were exhumed and cremated on 21.07.1934. His supposed urn was subsequently interred in the *Westfriedhof* in München.
NSDAP-Nr.:	41 (Joined the DAP with Nr. 623, 00.01.1920, and remained in the Party until it was banned in the wake of the *"München-Putsch"* of 09.11.1923; Reenrolled in the NSDAP with Nr. 41 on 01.11.1930)

Promotions:

15.07.1906	*Zweijährig-Freiwilliger und Fahnenjunker*
15.10.1906	*Unteroffizier*
16.02.1907	*Fähnrich*
09.03.1908	*Leutnant*
30.11.1914	*Oberleutnant*
17.04.1917	*Hauptmann (mit Patent vom 17.01.1917)*
00.00.1928	*Teniente Coronel* (lieutenant-colonel, Bolivian Army)
00.03.1925–01.05.1925	*Führer der SA*
05.01.1931–01.07.1934	*Chef des Stabes der SA*
01.05.1931–30.04.1933	*Korpsführer des NSKK*
13.04.1933–01.12.1933	*Staatssekretär*
00.06.1933–01.07.1934	*Reichsleiter der NSDAP*
02.12.1933–01.07.1934	*Reichsminister ohne Geschäftsbereich*

Career:

Fall 1897–Spring 1906	*Königliches Maximilians-Gymnasium* in München. Of his education, Eleanor Hancock writes:

He studied German and classical literature, Latin, Greek, French, history, geography, nature studies, mathematics and physics, drawing and calligraphy, and gymnastics. Whether at school or privately, he also learned to play the piano very well.

He himself described [in his memoirs] his achievements at school as "rather varied" and admitted that he was never a particularly good student. (Hancock, *Ernst Röhm: Hitler's SA Chief of Staff*, p. 8)

15.07.1906–00.00.1919	Entered service as a *Zweijährig-Freiwilliger* and *Fahnenjunker*, assigned to *Kgl. Bayerisches Feldartillerie-Regiment "Prinz Ludwig"* (later redesignated *"König Ludwig"*) *Nr. 10* (Ingolstadt).
25.01.1907	Passed his examinations for promotion to *Fähnrich*.
01.03.1907–07.02.1908	Attended the *Lehrkurs* (instructional course) at the *Kriegsschule* in München. He passed his examinations toward commissioning as an officer on 07.02.1908 and graduated ninety-eighth in a class

of 124. A performance evaluation from this period describes *Fähnrich* Röhm as follows:

> A not yet completely firm character, who however works on himself with good will. His conception of the profession has become more serious. Intellectually of normal capacity, even if partially distracted. Zeal adequate. Physically strong and sufficiently dexterous. Attitude good: he still lacks assurance and certainty of bearing when facing formations. Off duty conduct and social manners are good. Needs supervision. Financial conditions are settled. (Hancock, *Ernst Röhm: Hitler's SA Chief of Staff*, p. 10)

00.00.1908–01.08.1914	Assigned as a *Rekrutenausbilder* (recruit instructor) to *Bayerisches Kgl. 10. Infanterie-Regiment "König Ludwig."* In an evaluation report written in 1912, his company commander, *Hauptmann* Schleicher, wrote:

> [Röhm is] a vigorous, cheerful, capable officer with a well-developed military spirit. Mentally of normal gifts and physically sufficiently dexterous that he is easily deployable in all aspects of service and forms a reliable support of his company chief. He fervently endeavors to fulfill his duties with diligence and conscientiousness. His military knowledge is appropriate for his time of service: his oral and written orders are good. Possesses in addition a good knowledge of French. He is very employable as a platoon leader, understands quickly and circumspectly, sensible and energetic. He treats his subordinates calmly and benevolently. (*"Qualifikations-Bericht zum 1. Januar 1913 über den Leutnant Ernst Röhm im K. 10. Infanterie-Regiment"* in Hancock, *Ernst Röhm: Hitler's SA Chief of Staff*, p. 13)

Röhm experienced some trouble during this assignment, however, when on 09.03.1911, he was punished with three days' confinement to quarters (punishment later suspended) by a *6. Division* court for mistreating a trainee. Eleanor Hancock writes: "… [Röhm] repeatedly push[ed the recruit] lightly in the side during musketry training and [gave] him a smack on the back of the head." (Hancock, *Ernst Röhm: Hitler's SA Chief of Staff*, p. 10)

In another incident, on 22.04.1912, Röhm demanded that three civilians in Ingolstadt's Hotel Adler relinquish their table to him and his fellow officers. Because of their insulting response, Röhm brought charges against the civilians for "defamation of officers." The two men and one woman accused by Röhm were tried and found guilty of the offense on 30.08.1912. It was later determined by his superiors, however, that Röhm had provoked the civilians, and he was ordered to serve a confinement to quarters for two days.

01.06.1912–28.06.1912	Attended the *Pionierkurs* (combat engineer instructional course) of *1. Kgl. Bayerische Pionier-Bataillon*.
25.09.1912–15.10.1912	Attached to *1. Kgl. Bayerisches Reserve-Infanterie-Regiment* under *III. Kgl. Bayerische Armee-Korps*.
27.04.1914–16.05.1914	Attached for training in *Waffeninstandsetzungsgeschäft* (weapons repair) to the *Gewehrfabrik* (artillery factory) in Amberg.

02.08.1914–24.09.1914	Adjutant of *I. Bataillon/10. Kgl. Bayerisches Feldartillerie-Regiment "König"* on the Western Front. In his memoirs, he writes:

[The] Battalion ... marched to Remilly near Metz to provide border and railway protection. I had my baptism of fire during the fight to capture the French artillery training grounds at Flainval from 25 August. Over the next fortnight, near Gellenoncourt, our regiment suffered terrible losses and by 10 September 1914 had only eight active officers left. (Eleanor Hancock, ed., *The Memoirs of Ernst Röhm*, p. 1)

24.09.1914	Severely wounded in the face near Spada in the Chanot Wood, Lorraine, losing the upper portion of his nose. He was subsequently hospitalized in the following medical facilities:

26.09.1914–15.10.1914	*Festungslazarett* in Metz
15.10.1914–10.01.1915(?)	*Distriktkrankenhaus* in Kaiserslautern
10.01.1915–00.04.1915	*Sanatorium* in Reichenhall

00.04.1915–00.04.1915	Assigned to *Ersatz-Bataillon/10. Kgl. Bayerisches Feldartillerie-Regiment*.
17.04.1915–02.06.1915(?)	Returned to active service with *10. Kgl. Bayerisches Feldartillerie-Regiment*, and again assigned as *Adjutant* of its *I. Bataillon*.
02.06.1915–23.06.1916	*Führer* of *10. Kompanie/10. Kgl. Bayerisches Feldartillerie-Regiment*. On 20.06.1916, the commanding general of *III. Kgl. Bayerische Armee-Korps*, *General der Kavallerie* Ludwig Freiherr von Gebsattel, issued the following *Korps-Tagesbefehl* (corps order of the day):

In the name of his majesty the German Kaiser, I award the Iron Cross First Class to Oberleutnant Röhm, 10. Infanterie-Regiment König, in recognition of the extraordinary drive and courage he has exhibited on all occasions since the beginning of the war.
[signed] Freiherr von Gebsattel. (Eleanor Hancock, ed., *The Memoirs of Ernst Röhm*, p. 1)

He received the award shortly before the regiment's capture of the French fortification of Thiaumont near Verdun and the occupation of most of the village of Fleury. The regiments dead in this battle amounted to 150 men (ten officers and 140 NCOs and enlisted men), with seventeen officers and nearly 1,000 NCOs and enlisted men wounded. On the basis of his involvement in these actions, Röhm applied for award of the highest military distinction of the Bavarian Army, the *Militär-Max-Joseph-Orden* (*MMJO*), for actions above and beyond the call of duty. According to his own account, his former battalion commander suggested he submit his name. His application was strongly endorsed by his superiors, including *Generalmajor* Ludwig Freiherr von Tautphoeus (commander of *11. Kgl. Bayerische Infanterie-Brigade*) who wrote that Röhm was "one of the 10th Infantry Regiment's best officers, whose sang-froid, bravery and constant dash had an exemplary effect on his subordinates." (Eleanor Hancock, *Ernst Röhm: Hitler's SA Chief of Staff*, p. 23) However, as Hancock continues:

> Röhm was not awarded the MMJO. Although the order's chapter voted four to three in favor of the award, War Minister von Hellingrath followed the advice of the Chancellery Office of the order and recommended the King reject the award on the grounds that actions like Röhm's occurred frequently and were therefore not over and above the dictates of duty. The King accepted this advice. (Eleanor Hancock, *Ernst Röhm: Hitler's SA Chief of Staff*, p. 23)

Röhm's claim that reasons of finance influenced Bavarian War Ministry's rejection of the award may have been a cover story to assuage his wounded pride and anger. During the attack on the fortifications at Thiaumont on 23.06.1916, Röhm was again severely wounded. He later wrote in his memoirs:

> On 23 June 1916 at Verdun, my company was amongst the first to storm the French trenches and take the fortified redoubt at Thiaumont. That same evening I took a shot through the chest, which passed close to a lung and exited by my shoulder. While I was making my way with two helpers, a sergeant and a private, to the main dressing station, we were forced to seek shelter during an artillery bombardment. Unknown to me, the ridge we chose was the location of a German heavy battery. At the moment we reached the heights, the battery came under fire and I was peppered with shrapnel, receiving twelve more severe wounds. My two helpers were killed. I managed to reach one of the artillery trenches where I was attended by a medical officer. (Eleanor Hancock, ed., *The Memoirs of Ernst Röhm*, p. 2)

00.06.1916–16.08.1916	Hospitalized at the *Reservelazarett Kriegsschule* München
16.08.1916–00.00.1916	Hospitalized at the *Reservelazarett Hohen-Aschau* and classified as "*Felddienstunfähig*" (unfit for further frontline duty).
30.10.1916–27.05.1917	*Adjutant* of the *Armeeabteilung* in the *Bayerische Kriegsministerium* (Bavarian War Ministry). Of this period of service, he writes:

> Once my wounds had healed to the extent that I could be considered "walking wounded", I made numerous enquiries for a posting and at the War Ministry was accepted into the office of Oberst Koller, a friend and colleague. Soon I was appointed as adjutant to the head of the Army Department, Oberstleutnant Freiherr Gustav Kress von Kressenstein.... His department was the most important at the War Ministry. In this period of my career I gained such insight as is only granted to very few, for nearly all orders to and from the War Ministry passed through my hands, all secret reports from the front, including the reports of the Royal Bavarian military plenipotentiaries at the Kaiser's HQ, and I learned of matters and events of which a mere captain of infantry would normally never become aware. (Eleanor Hancock, ed., *The Memoirs of Ernst Röhm*, p. 2)

29.05.1917–08.05.1918	*Ordonnanzoffizier* and *Nachschuboffizier* with the staff of *12. Kgl. Bayerische Infanterie-Division* (comprised of *Kgl. Bayerische 26., 27.,*

	and *28. Infanterie-Regimenter* and *22. Artillerie-Regiment*) in Romania and France. Röhm continues: "At the end of 1917, the Russian and Romanian armistice negotiators arrived at Focsani [Romania] and our division moved to Mizil to retrain for the Western Front. We left Romania on 17 April 1918. My commander, *Generalleutnant* Freiherr von Nagel, had appointed me to the divisional staff." (Eleanor Hancock, ed., *The Memoirs of Ernst Röhm*, pp. 2-3)
09.05.1918–05.11.1918	*2. Generalstabsoffizier (Ib)* of *12. Kgl. Bayerische Infanterie-Division*.
02.10.1918–mid-10.1918	Transferred to the staff of the *Garde-Korps*. He writes of his assignment there: "I was made Ic [*3. Generalstabsoffizier*], a post which involved the collation and evaluation of all reports from the front. It was up to me to suggest when aerial patrols should be flown, observation balloons put aloft, and where we should send scouting parties, and so forth." (Eleanor Hancock, ed., *The Memoirs of Ernst Röhm*, p. 3)
Mid-10.1918	Returned to the divisional staff of *12. Kgl. Bayerische Infanterie-Division*, assigned as *Ib (2. Generalstabsoffizier)*, after the division was withdrawn from the front in Flanders.
00.10.1918	Contracted influenza (the so-called "Spanish flu"), from which he became very ill. Hospitalized at *Feldlazarett 38* on 21.10.1918, he was later transferred to the military hospital in Halle, and after convalescence, returned to duty.
03.11.1918	Returned to the divisional staff of *12. Kgl. Bayerische Infanterie-Division* at St. Sauveur. He soon fell ill again and requested ten days' sick leave in München. He writes in his memoirs: "On my last leave there, I had spoken to Major von Kieffer, departmental chief of personnel at the War Ministry, and had received his promise that I would be given a battalion with my old regiment on 1 December 1918." (Eleanor Hancock, ed., *The Memoirs of Ernst Röhm*, p. 3)
04.12.1918	Reported to *Generalkommando* (Corps HQ) of *I. Bayerische Reserve-Korps*, then sent to *12. Bayerisches Infanterie-Division* in Elberfeld-Barmen, and finally took a train to Landshut (Niederbayern) for the dissolution of the divisional staff.
02.01.1919–31.03.1919	*Adjutant* of *11. Bayerische Infanterie-Brigade* (Ingolstadt, then München), commanded by *Oberst* Max Sämmer. Informed of his appointment to this post on 01.01.1919. On 21.02.1919, he submitted his resignation from this post, having previously "convinced ... Sämmer to discontinue cooperation with the Red headquarters" (Eleanor Hancock, ed., *The Memoirs of Ernst Röhm*, p. 13), whereupon Sämmer and the commanders of his *10.* and *13. Infanterie-Regiment* resigned. On 01.03.1919, after discussions with Sämmer in Ingolstadt, Röhm resumed his post as adjutant. Sämmer then returned to command of the brigade on 05.03.1919.
00.04.1919–00.05.1919	Assigned as *Stabsoffizier* (*Verpflegung und Ausrüstung* [Provisions and Equipment]) to *Freikorps Epp*.
03.05.1919–00.07.1919	*Chef des Stabes* to the *Stadtkommandant* of München (*Oberstleutnant* Adolf Herrgott) and *Offizier für die Abwehr und für politische Angelegenheiten* (Officer for Defense and Political Affairs) with the *Reichswehr* staff in München.

00.07.1919–31.12.1920	*Ib* (*Bewaffnung und Ausrüstung* [staff officer] for armaments and equipment) with the staff of *Schützenbrigade 21/Bayerische Schützenkorps* (commanded by Franz Ritter von Epp).
00.00.1919	Joined the *Deutschnationale Volkspartei* (DNVP, German Nationalist Peoples Party).
00.07.1919	Cofounder of the *Eisernen Faust* ("Iron Fist") club, an organization of radical nationalist officers.
16.10.1919	Attended the first meeting of the *Deutsche Arbeiterpartei* (DAP) addressed by Adolf Hitler. He was probably introduced to the eventual *Führer* by *Hauptmann* Karl Mayr, and the two soon became close friends; Röhm was one of Hitler's few "*Duz-Freunden*" (people permitted to use the informal pronoun "*Du*").
00.01.1920	Joined the DAP.
01.10.1920–05.12.1922	*Adjutant* and *2. Stabsoffizier* to the *Infanterie-Führer VII* (Ritter von Epp). He was also *Leiter* of the *Feldzeugmeisterei* (Quartermaster's Office) in *Gruppenkommando 4* of the *Reichswehr* during this period. The early Nazi publicist, Kurt G. W. Lüdecke, writes of Röhm's actions during this period:

Since 1920, Roehm had been a most practical ally, diverting considerable *Reichswehr* funds to the Nazis, with the consent of his superior, General von Epp. Germany had begun to re-arm the very day the disarmament pact was signed, and Roehm had access to secret appropriations made by the Government to support the so-called "Black Reichswehr"—the illegally armed troops. Now Roehm, who was already a master in "Waffenschiebungen," or arms-bootlegging, practically became master of ordnance for the Nazis. Their arsenals bulged. (Lüdecke, *I Knew Hitler: The Story of a Nazi Who Escaped the Blood Purge*, pp. 144-145)

Late 1921–00.00.1923	*Leiter* of the *München Ortsgruppe* of the *Bund Reichsflagge*, a *Wehrverband* (paramilitary organization) established in the summer of 1919 by his friend and fellow *Reichswehr Hauptmann*, Adolf Heiß.
05.12.1922–03.05.1923	*Stabsoffizier* with *7. Reichswehr-Division* (München).
31.01.1923–00.04.1923	Member of the *Arbeitsausschuss der Landesleitung* (Working Staff of the State Leadership) of *Reichsflagge* and *bevollmächtigter Vertreter* (deputized representative) of *Reichsflagge's Führer*, *Hauptmann* Heiß, in München.
04.02.1923–00.04.1923	*Führer* (*spiritus rector*) of the *Arbeitsgemeinschaft der Vaterländische Kampfverbände* (Working Community of Patriotic Fighting Organizations); simultaneously assigned as a representative of the *Organisation Niederbayern* in München. Within the *Arbeitsgemeinschaft* were the following: *Reichsflagge*, *NSDAP*, *Vaterländische Bezirksvereinen Münchens* (*VVM*), *Zeitfreiwilligenkorps München, Bund Oberland*, and *Bund Unterland*. Röhm led the *Arbeitsgemeinschaft* together with Dr. Christian Roth (former Bavarian Justice Minister), who handled political affairs, and *Oberstleutnant* Hermann Kriebel, responsible for military matters.

04.05.1923	Called to a meeting by *Generalleutnant* von Lossow, which was also attended by Generals Ritter von Epp, Friedrich Freiherr Kress von Kressenstein, and Jakob Ritter von Danner, as well as *Oberstleutnants* Ferdinand Meier and Otto Freiherr von Berchem. He was removed from his assignment to the *Feldzeugmeisterei*, and reassigned to command of a *Kompanie*, von Lossow's reasons being summarized as follows:

1) The events in the dirigible barracks on the night of 30 April–1 May, which indeed were not instigated by Hauptmann Röhm but also were not prevented by him. Hauptmann Röhm, as section chief of the Feldzeugmeisterei, was responsible in part for the grave derelictions of the Transport Section München, subordinate to him.
2) The misuse of the offices of the Feldzeugmeisterei, in which, not only on the afternoon of 30 April, although I had expressly rejected the plans of the Kampfverbände, but also frequently during the preceding weeks, meetings of a purely political character had been held, by means of which the Wehrkreiskommando was compromised. It is an erroneous assumption that such purely political conferences could have taken place in our offices with my consent in view of the existing relations between the Wehrkreiskommando and the patriotic Verbände.
3) The developments in the Kampfverbände in the weeks before 1 May, where, frequently in a manner contrary to discipline, positions were taken against the Landeskommandant or the government in memoranda with the character of [an] ultimatum. The signatures "Reichsflagge" and "Org. Niederbayern" were in these instances equivalent to those of the Reichswehr officers leading these organizations. The holding of militarily useless large-scale field exercises including Reichswehr officers, although it must have been evident that I opposed such exercises.
4) The decision that arose from the above, to forbid Reichswehr officers to belong to the Kampfverbände in question. His very transfer should make it simpler for Hauptmann Röhm to withdraw from Reichsflagge. (National Archives, T79, 72, pp. 1222-23, in Harold J. Gordon, *Hitler and the Beer Hall Putsch*, p. 203)

03.05.1923–00.09.1923	*Kompaniechef* in Bayreuth.
00.09.1923–09.11.1923	Member of the *Deutsche Kampfbund-Kampfgemeinschaft Bayern*.
26.09.1923	Submitted his request for discharge from the *Reichswehr*.
12.10.1923	Founded the *Reichskriegsflagge* in München.
08./09.11.1923	Participated in the "*München-Putsch*," directing the occupation of the *Bayerische Kriegsministerium* building on *Schönfeldstraße*. Several of his men fired shots at *Reichswehr* troops who surrounded the building, resulting in the death of two *Reichskriegsflagge* men, Martin Faust and Theodor Casella. Soon afterward, he surrendered his forces and was arrested by the München police. Röhm recalled the events of 09.11.1923 in his memoirs:

I had ordered no shots to be fired. Thus the Reichswehr advanced unmolested as we watched. The artillery brought up a field gun to

Schönfeld-Strasse and aimed it at us. Machine guns were installed in a building facing us in Ludwig-Strasse, and the mortar company set up on the other side of the road.

Our own machine guns threatened them silently from our windows. One order, one whistle would have done it. The able Semmelbauer had disciplined the machine-gun detachment well, they would have engaged any target ordered. Occasionally I had a notion to do it but I suppressed it. It must not be....

It was lonely around me. The flag fluttered proudly, my friends were close by, stolid and silent. Blood brothers unto death!...

... at midday, I received a visit from General von Epp accompanied by Oberstleutnant [Franz] von Hörauf and Oberstleutnant [Johann-Georg] Hofmann. Hörauf, to whom I was indebted for much in my military life, had hurried to Epp with the intention of urging him to my support with advice and assistance. I was not on particularly good terms with Epp at that time, but he never hesitated to answer the call and came at once. The character of this strange man impressed me greatly that day. I also had a heartfelt gratitude for the noble-mindedness of my regimental comrade Hörauf.

It was suggested I should surrender. I thanked them for their comradely advice, but I could not accept it. I had been ordered here and was determined not to leave without receiving a new order. After Lossow had deserted us, there was only one man who could give it, General Ludendorff. Even the objection of General von Epp, that from now on I was in a besieged fort and had to negotiate alone did not unsettle me.

Ludendorff had left me that morning in the belief that I would hold the district command. No special indication was needed on my part: I had no contact with him, but he had to be able to rely on me. At that moment, Oberstleutnant Hofmann arrived, as he said, as Lossow's spokesman, and called to me, "What else do you want, you have already got everything you wanted. A new government is at the helm in Berlin, and all is in good order!"

No words of friendship or comradeship were brought. As a result of this information I agreed to a two-hour truce. With General von Epp I went to the Reichswehr commander opposite me, Oberst von Pflügel. This meeting affected me deeply. Eyes glistening, Pflügel offered me his hand.

Epp and Pflügel guaranteed the armistice. Hofmann meanwhile wanted to obtain instructions from Ludendorff. I transferred command of the RKF [*Reichskriegsflagge*] to Lieutenant Osswald.

Hauptmann [Josef] Seydel and Graf du Moulin accompanied me with General von Epp to the opposing commander, General von Danner, in the state police barracks....

The meeting with General von Danner and his chief of staff, Oberstleutnant von Saur, was short and bitter. I had difficulty controlling myself.

Danner was unfriendly and cold; to an insulting remark of his I replied in kind... (Eleanor Hancock, *The Memoirs of Ernst Röhm*)

09.11.1923 — Issuance of Ordinance #264 by the Bavarian *Generalstaatskommissar* Dr. Gustav Ritter von Kahr:

In accordance with the existing emergency laws and effective immediately, I command that

1. The Nationalsozialistische Deutsche Arbeiterpartei, Bund Oberland and Reichskriegsflagge are prohibited and dissolved.

2. Legal tender and securities of all types, weapons, armament items, vehicles, bicycles and other means of transport which served the goals of the dissolved organizations or are earmarked to serve, fall to the state and are to be delivered without delay to the nearest police authorities; in München and in Nürnberg-Fürth, to the Polizeidirektion; in the other immediate provinces, to the Staatskommissar.

3. Those who continue to belong to the dissolved parties, who attempt to build new organizations in place of them, who act on behalf of these new organizations, who join one of these organizations, who support these organizations by word or deed, or who disobey the order in paragraph 2, will be sentenced from 1 to 15 years in prison.

München 9 November 1923

Staatskommissar

Dr. von Kahr

(David Jablonsky, *The Nazi Party in Dissolution: Hitler and the Verbotzeit, 1923–1925*, p. 28)

16.12.1923	The ban on the NSDAP in Bavaria was not lifted until 16.02.1925. Discharged from the *Reichswehr*.
26.02.1924–01.04.1924	Tried in the so-called "*Hitler-Prozeß*." Originally charged with high treason, this was soon reduced to accessory to high treason. He was sentenced to fifteen months' imprisonment (with four months' credit for time served). He was in fact released on probation the same day. Regarding defendant Röhm, the official indictment read:

Röhm was probably present at the decisive conference on 8 November. At the latest, he learned of the planned Putsch on the evening of 7 November and then participated in individual consultations on the course and scope of the action. The Reichskriegsflagge celebration, scheduled for 8 November at the Löwenbräukeller presented him with an opportunity to inconspicuously aid and abet the action in the Bürgerbräukeller and to gather as large a striking force as possible. In any case, Röhm occupied the Wehrkreiskommando in the interest of and on the orders of the new rulers, and he made all the preparations to defend the building with guns against a Reichswehr attack. He continued this conduct, although he certainly knew that he was offering open resistance to the legal governmental authority.

(H. Francis Freniere, Lucie Karcic, & Philip Fandek [translators], *The Hitler Trial Before the People's Court in Munich, Volume I*, pp. 23-24)

In his closing argument, delivered on 21.03.1924, Second Prosecutor Dr. Hans Ehard said of Röhm:

At the end of 1923, Röhm was the leader of the remnants of the Reichskriegsflagge in the Kampfbund. As the leader of the

Reichskriegsflagge, he was subordinate to the Kampfbund's leader. Röhm was familiar with the Kampfbund's aspirations; he also participated in a series of conferences in very close, intimate circles. Hitler needed the consent of the other groups' leaders for important actions. Even today, it is a very obvious assumption that Röhm, as the leader of the Reichskriegsflagge, which belonged to the Kampfbund, had already possessed prior knowledge of such decisive steps…. The persons who took part in passing the resolution concerning the undertaking on 8 November deemed it totally unnecessary to notify Röhm in advance, because they knew that they only needed to say—as Röhm himself said—"On such-and-such a date, the Reichskriegsflagge will take stations here and here," then they would be there. Röhm had infinite faith in Hitler. He obeyed him unquestioningly.

As the leader of the Reichskriegsflagge, Röhm had been invited to a party in the Löwenbräukeller on the evening of 8 November. He received an official invitation. The members of the Reichskriegsflagge had been specifically requested to appear in uniform. In particular, members who were abroad were invited, and even on the afternoon of the 8th, they were being summoned by telegram and telephone….

Around 9:00 [p.m.], the news of the creation of a national government came to them from the Bürgerbräukeller. Röhm was notified, and again he had inquiries made in the Bürgerbräukeller concerning whether the news corresponded to the facts. Then he announced the outcome of his inquiries to the meeting and summoned the groups to gather in front of the Löwenbräukeller in order to march to the Bürgerbräukeller and swear allegiance to the new government. On the way there, Röhm received the order, from a motorist coming from the Bürgerbräukeller, to occupy the Wehrkreiskommando with the Reichskriegsflagge and to receive General Lossow with an honor guard.

Lossow did not arrive. Röhm got the impression that something was wrong, and he received information in the Bürgerbräukeller and in the Stadtkommandantur which intensified his misgivings.

Later, Röhm was in the Wehrkreiskommando together with Hitler, Ludendorff, Pöhner, and other leaders. He could no longer have had any doubt of the fact that Kahr, Lossow, and Seisser were not on the side of the undertaking and that they were prepared to take steps against [it].

Hitler, Ludendorff, Pöhner, and Weber left the Wehrkreiskommando around morning. Röhm received instructions to stay in the Wehrkreiskommando, and interpreted these instructions from Ludendorff as an order to hold the building with force. He could only be moved to surrender when Ludendorff's counterinstructions were conveyed to him.

Around noon, the Reichswehr's advance against the Wehrkreiskommando was reported to Röhm. Röhm had the Wehrkreiskommando put in a state of defense. Only when the building was surrounded on all sides, after repeated negotiations, and after a note from Ludendorff arrived, did Röhm decide to lay down his arms and surrender. Röhm did all this in order to support the new authorities. He was even prepared, when the Reichswehr was in the process of resuming possession of their own building, to openly oppose the constitutional power of the State with armed resistance. In addition, he did this when he was still formally an officer of the Reichswehr. This must especially be taken into consideration as cause for aggravating the punishment. On the other hand, the merits which he, as an officer, has won—namely during the march, when he was wounded—are to be put in his favor. It can be conceded that he did not act out of selfish motives either, and that he believed in the moral justification of the movement's goals.

The facts of the case, and Röhm's conduct, indicate that his offense is that of aiding and abetting the crime of high treason. His conduct has not exceeded aiding and abetting. (H. Francis Freniere, Lucie Karcic, & Philip Fandek [translators], *The Hitler Trial Before the People's Court in Munich, Volume I*, pp. 167-169)

Röhm originally chose for his defense attorney Dr. Karl Schramm, a close friend and member of his *Reichskriegsflagge*. Schramm was arrested soon after the *Putsch* for his own involvement in the action, and his father, Dr. Christoph Schramm—who also represented Ludendorff—took over the defense of Röhm. The following is excerpted from the attorney's final statement to the court (25.03.1924):

My client, Major [*sic*] Röhm, did not personally take part in the action. Thus the Prosecutor has amended his charged from high treason to accessory to high treason. However, the judicial fate of the accessory is closely linked with the fate of the criminal....

In Röhm's case the question is, first of all, whether he knew that the operation was to begin on 8 November.... Hauptmann Röhm had no knowledge of the operation. It was not necessary to inform him, because Hitler and Kriebel said, "We can depend on our Röhm."

Hitler, Kriebel, and Weber have unanimously stated that Röhm was not present at the moment when the operation was discussed and decided upon. As far as I can see, any decision in Röhm's case depends entirely on whether you believe he was acting in good faith or whether you think he knew he was violating the law. Röhm was not at the Bürgerbräukeller. He always thought he was serving a legally formed new government. Several factors clearly prove this. Please remember that Hauptmann Röhm went to the Wehrkreiskommando unarmed; there he combined his people with the Reichswehr. When Röhm went to the Stadtkommandantur during the night to see General von Lossow, he asked the Reichswehr officer, Hauptmann Kirschner, to be his deputy. This fact certainly indicates that all Röhm thought and knew was that the fighting units of the Bund and the Reichswehr had become one force.

Then came the news from the Bürgerbräukeller that a national government had been formed. Under these circumstances, is it still realistic to assume that Röhm or anyone else would ask themselves whether or not that was legal; whether or not Herr Karr had transgressed his authority? Röhm knew that the holders of the state authority were at the head of the operation. Would it not have been a terrible insult for the three men if Hauptmann Röhm had told himself, at this point: "Our highest state officials have committed the horrible crime of high treason before the entire nation." You cannot punish Röhm for not having thought of this. You cannot punish him for not being able to imagine that two high officers did not intend to keep their word. You cannot deny that he acted in good faith.

The Prosecutor has tried to explain that even if Röhm was acting in good faith up until 9 November, this showing of good faith was destroyed on the morning of 9 November. I think, however, that the prosecution lacks the evidence to support this argument. The Prosecutor knows as well as I do how difficult it was to get any information through. It is true, I admit, that in the early morning hours this or that piece of information arrived which might have aroused suspicion, but Hauptmann Röhm has assured us that when he read the morning newspaper he was happy to see that his fears had been unfounded, because he now had it down in black and white....

Apart from that, this argument has no validity for Hauptmann Röhm, for the simple reason that at the critical moment, Hauptmann Röhm was asleep at the Wehrkreiskommando. He knew nothing of the visit of Oberst Leupold and was not told about it later. Therefore, no incriminating conclusions can be drawn from it.

When Hitler, Kriebel, and Ludendorff left the Wehrkreiskommando during the morning hours, Hauptmann Röhm received the brief order to stay there until he received further information.

Röhm is an old Bavarian officer. There was nothing left for him to do but obey this order faithfully—he had received it from the highest authorities—and to wait. It was impossible for him to act differently. Hauptmann Röhm is proud of the fact that he heard from Ludendorff personally: "I would not and could not have acted differently."

Hauptmann Röhm first heard of the change in the situation from General Epp and Oberstleutnant [Hans-Georg] Hoffmann; the latter had come on an official mission from the Türkenkaserne. Negotiations started immediately. Röhm went to the Türkenkaserne, conducted negotiations, and returned with the decision to begin calling off the operation. At this point, he received notice from Ludendorff's residence that his order was rescinded. Even if the Hauptmann had known something was wrong, he couldn't have possibly run away and abandoned his people. An operation with 250 men had to be liquidated in a military fashion. If the men had run through the streets aimlessly, nobody could have prevented a disaster.

I would like to take this opportunity to point to the extremely grave consequences that might arise from a verdict of guilty for Röhm. If justice is to be carried out to its fullest, you would then have to indict for high treason the several thousand people who were at the Bürgerbräukeller. The significant question for all of them is whether they were aware of having violated the law. Two more extreme examples: If an enthusiastic listener had put his car at Hitler's disposal to drive to the Wehrkreiskommando, or if another enthusiastic listener had supplied the troops with hot coffee, the two would have to account for their conduct just as does Hauptmann Röhm. These impossible consequences show that a verdict of guilty against Röhm is impossible....

Not one of the defendants, especially not Hauptmann Röhm, is responsible for the blood that was shed on the Odeonsplatz. At the decisive moment he was not even there; he was in the Türkenkaserne. He had given orders not to fire at the Reichswehr, under any circumstances, not even if the Reichswehr should attack.

Röhm has been ready to give his life to his country in countless battles. He has also been seriously wounded. I suggest that you contemplate what this man has done for the Bavarian State. He helped create the Home Guard [Einwohnerwehr] and other matters which I shall mention in closed session. Röhm has been involved in the crush of the Ruhr rebellion and in the liberation of München. I remind you of Röhm's letter to the prosecution which is part of his documents. In this letter, he states that he would take responsibility for the Reichskriegsflagge and the events in the Wehrkreiskommando; he urges the Prosecutor to set his people free since they could not be held responsible for anything. You have heard from Oberstleutnant Kriebel that he gave the order to occupy the Wehrkreiskommando to Röhm since the latter would guarantee that this would be done in a manner appropriate to the dignity of the moment and of the place. Röhm acted in a most selfless way....

Just like the other defendants, he is filled with ardent patriotism. He wanted to contribute to the liberation of his people from servitude. For him, Hitler's act signified the cry for help of an unbearably tormented people. It is impossible to resurrect Germany, to form a new state, unless this is done with new ideals and a new spirit. It was Röhm's most fervent wish to arouse this new spirit. In this endeavor, he succeeded in establishing an almost paternal relationship with his men who admired him. They have retained their loyalty and love for him while he has been imprisoned.

If you think that this man is a criminal, you may perform your difficult task. I personally will never find any peace throughout the rest of my life if he is convicted, because- not as a lawyer, but as a human being- I am convinced of Röhm's innocence. A conviction of all the defendants would be quite a test for our ailing state authority. Carthage is a dubious precedent for Germany. The merchants denied loyalty to their commander because business meant everything to them. At least try to spare Ludendorff and his friends, including Röhm, the fate which the people of Carthage held in readiness for their own commander. (H. Francis Freniere, Lucie Karcic, & Philip Fandek [translators], *The Hitler Trial Before the People's Court in Munich*, Volume 3, p. 273; pp. 277-279; pp. 282-283)

01.04.1924	Tasked by Hitler with the reconstruction of the SA and the *Wehrverbände*. In the following note to Röhm, the convicted *Führer* wrote: "Hauptmann Röhm is military leader of the Kampfbund. I command, therefore, that his ordinances be obeyed by members and particularly leaders of the NSDAP's SA. Those who can't unconditionally follow the commands of Hauptmann Röhm are to be considered as no longer belonging to the SA." (David Jablonsky, *The Nazi Party in Dissolution: Hitler and the Verbotzeit, 1923-1925*, p. 80)
00.04.1924–01.05.1925	*Kommandeur* of *Frontbann*, a cover organization for the SA and other right-wing extremist *Wehrverbände* banned in the aftermath of the "*München-Putsch*." By September 1924, it numbered some 30,000 men throughout Germany. An important collaborator of Röhm during this period, Kurt Lüdecke, later wrote:

... [N]ext to Hitler, the man most impressive to me at that time was Captain Roehm, whose life reads like a novel. Part of it he wrote himself, in his "Story of a Rebel"—Die Geschichte eines Hochverräters, unobtainable in Nazi Germany today.

"On 23 July 1906 I became a soldier." This day seemed to him to mark the birth of his conscious life; apparently the ate of his physical birth, 28 November 1887 was unimportant. "I consider the world, consciously, from a one-sided viewpoint, that of a soldier," is another of his characteristic utterances....

The folkish [völkisch] and in fact the whole Nationalistic movement after the November revolution of 1918 is inconceivable without Roehm, without his practical and successful activity in organizing and doing things. He was a brilliant leader of men, an excellent officer, fearless and straightforward. His massive, round head, battle-scarred and patched, looked like something hammered from rock. He was the living image of war itself, in contrast to his polished manner and exceptional and instinctive courtesy. That, with his naturalness, diplomatic tact and *savoir faire* distinguished him from leading Nazis then and afterwards, who for the most part were boorish and arrogant, or were bullies. For all his one-sided military mind, he was a passionate politician, having, for a soldier, a rare intelligence and understanding for politics. I liked his keen, open gaze and his firm handclasp.

One of Hitler's first backers, Roehm was of decisive importance to the Party, finding money, arms, and men at the most critical times. Without him, the *Fuehrer* could never have dared the Beer Hall Putsch, could never have reached the Chancellorship....

Still on parole for his part in the putsch, Roehm had received from Hitler full authority to reorganize the scattered remnants of the Kampfbund, an absolute carte blanche to carry out on his own responsibility this most delicate of tasks. Starting over again from the beginning, he recruited new troops from the dispersed ranks, and gradually whipped them into a new, semi-military organization called the "Frontbann." Aside from the political difficulties he encountered, it was uphill work to regain the confidence of men who had our disastrous defeat fresh in mind. Roehm could not be everywhere at once; so he asked me to work for him as I travelled through Germany. My part was to persuade the men and the groups with whom I came in contact that the Nazi fight had not collapsed but was still going on. (Lüdecke, *I Knew Hitler: The Story of a Nazi Who Escaped the Blood Purge*, pp. 226-227)

In August 1924, Röhm issued the following public appeal:

Appeal!
The associations and comrades who adhere to the National Socialist Weltanschauung and who unconditionally support Hitler, Ludendorff, and Graefe have united in the Frontbann.

Together with the Frontbann and its affiliated Frontjugend, the Frontkriegerbund, which unites German front-line fighters in its ranks, forms the Frontring.

Germans of all classes, German soldiers, German youth join the ranks of the Frontring!

Applications to the Frontbann should be addressed to the local or national leadership [*örtlichen oder Landesleitungen*] of the Frontbann. Where these are not known, they can be obtained from the information desk in the "Völkischer Kurier", München, Sendlingerplatz 1/II. Telephone 54190.

Applications for the Frontkriegerbund are to be sent to the Bundesleitung, München, Romanstraße 28/1

Ostpreußen, on the day of the Battle of Tannenberg

On the order of: Hauptmann Röhm (*Völkischer Kurier* Nr. 74, 29.08.1924, in Bundesarchiv R 1507; Translation: Gary Costello)

00.00.1924	Member of the *Deutschvölkische Freiheitspartei* (DVFP, German Nationalist Freedom Party).
04.05.1924–20.10.1924	Member of the *Reichstag* (representing the *NS-Freiheitspartei*).
17.05.1924–00.03.1925	*(geschäftsführender) Stellvertretender Kommandeur der SA* ([acting] deputy commander of the [illegal] SA). Succeeded Wilhelm Freiherr Marschall von Bieberstein.
15.08.1924–17.08.1924	Participated in the "*1. Tagung der NS-Freiheitspartei*," held in Weimar under the patronage of *General a. D.* Erich Ludendorff.
00.03.1925–01.05.1925	*Führer der SA*. He met with Hitler in München, 16.–17.04.1925, and exhibited the rebellious spirit which would eventually lead to his death by presenting the *Führer* with a memorandum reading: "I categorically refuse to allow the SA to become involved in Party matters; equally, I categorically refuse to allow SA commanders to accept instructions from Party political leaders." (Röhm, *Die Geschichte eines Hochverräters*, pp. 313-314) Hitler would have none of it; the SA, as a subordinate part of the NSDAP, would have no independence from the Party. On 18.04.1925, Röhm submitted his letter of resignation to Hitler; the *Führer* disregarded it. On 30.04.1925, attempting to salvage his relationship with Hitler, Röhm wrote another letter which ended with: "I take this opportunity, in memory of the fine and difficult hours we have lived together, to thank you and to beg you not to exclude me from your personal friendship." The following day, he resigned from his post as leader of the SA and the *Frontbann* due to his differences of opinion with Hitler. In a conversation with Kurt Lüdecke soon after, he stated:

No need to tell you what Hitler is like. Believe me, I didn't mince words when I last talked with him. But it's useless; if you try to tell him anything, he knows everything already. Though he often does what we advise, he laughs in our faces at the time, and later does the very thing as if it were all his own idea and creation. He doesn't even seem to be aware how dishonest he is. I've never seen a man so magnificently unaware that he's adorning himself with borrowed plumage. Usually, he solves suddenly, at the very last minute, a situation that has become intolerable and dangerous only because he vacillates and procrastinates.... But nobody is perfect, and he has his great qualities. Apparently there's nobody else who would do better than he. (Lüdecke, *I Knew Hitler: The Story of a Nazi Who Escaped the Blood Purge*, p. 287)

00.00.1925–00.00.1926	Door-to-door book salesman for the *Deutsche Nationalverlag*. This was the beginning of a three-year period during which he had to earn an ordinary living as a civilian to augment his modest military pension of RM 335.25 per month. Eleanor Hancock writes, "He struggled in this job, and often found it humiliating." (Hancock, *Ernst Röhm*, p. 83)
00.00.1926–00.00.1928	Applied to the *Reichswehrministerium* for financial aid, receiving RM 1,000 in five payments during this period.
11.10.1926	Sentenced to ten days' jail as a result of his behavior during a conference in München of the *Reichstagsausschuss* "*Feme-Organisationen und Fememorde*" (*Reichstag* Committee "Feme Organizations and Feme Murders", also known as the "*Femeausschuss*"). This committee, chaired by Pal Levi, convened in München 05.10.1926–14.10.1926, and investigated murders of "traitors" by right-wing extremist "*Feme*" detachments. Among these was the 06.10.1920 killing of nineteen-year-old Maria Sandmayr, a waitress in München. She had threatened to report a hidden *Freikorps* arms cache, held inside a castle belonging to a former employer, to the Reich's *Entwaffnungskommissar* (disarmament commissioner). Sandmayr was strangled by the future *SA-Gruppenführer* Hermann Berchtold, with his friend Johann (Hans) Schweighart as an accomplice. A Great War veteran who had risen to the rank of *Leutnant d. R.*, Schweighart was a member of the *Freikorps Epp* in May 1919 and was, in 1920, an employee of Röhm's *Reichswehr* equipment depot in München.

Eleanor Hancock writes that during the committee's hearings:

Röhm and Epp both admitted to helping [Johann "Hans"] Schweighart [the alleged murderer].... In the course of Röhm's interrogation, he refused to answer Levi's further questions and was fined three hundred marks by the committee for contempt [he refused to pay the fine/MdM]. It is not clear what the questions were that Röhm refused to answer, and whether he refused because Levi's questioning was getting close to something legally incriminating. Röhm's own account in his autobiography was marked by anti-Semitic attacks on Levi, which suggests that his anti-Semitism and consequent resentment of Levi's authority led him to refuse to answer the questions. (Hancock, *Ernst Röhm*, pp. 84-85)

On the same date, the *Vertreter der Reichsregierung* (Representative of the Reich Government) in München, *Staatssekretär z. D./Gesandter* Edgar Haniel von Haimhausen, reported on the matter:

Femeausschuss in München.
The witnesses heard today on the 6th day of the hearing of the Femeausschuss were asked to comment on their relationship to Lieutenant Schweikart [Schweighart], who had been arrested in the Sandmeier [Sandmeyer] murder case. Witness General v. Epp stated upon questioning that he had supported Schweikart [Schweighart] with clothing when he came to him in a ragged state after his release from custody. He also took part in a collection of money organised for Schweikart [Schweighart].

	Witness Hauptmann Röhm confirmed in his testimony that he had brought Schweikart [Schweighart] to General v. Epp. In the course of the further examination of this witness, there was a clash between him and the rapporteur of the Femeausschuss, Dr. Levi, in which the witness refused to answer Dr. Levi's questions. The Committee then suspended the further examination of the witness Röhm and fined him 300M. (Bundesarchiv R 707 86b; Translation: Gary Costello)
Late 1926	Worked for two months for the Robel track-building factory, having been referred to its management by Princess Luise of Sachsen-Altenburg. Hancock continues: "Röhm claimed he did well and was considered for a leading position by the firm's founder. Yet, he did not remain there." (Eleanor Hancock, *Ernst Röhm*, p. 83)
00.00.1927–00.00.1927	Worked as a manual laborer for an unknown employer.
09.02.1927–20.02.1927	Imprisoned at München-Stadelheim. In a letter of 27.02.1927 to the office of the *Reichskanzlei*, the *Vertreter der Reichsregierung, Staatssekretär z. D./Gesandter* Haniel (see entry of 11.10.1926, above), wrote:

Hauptmann Röhm in prison.

Hauptmann Röhm, known from the Hitler Putsch, who was sentenced to a fine of 300M. in the Munich session of the Reichstag Feme Investigation Committee because of his behavior towards Dr. Levi, has refused to pay this sum. A recent seizure was unsuccessful. Therefore, due to its uncollectability, the fine was changed to a prison sentence, which Hauptmann Röhm recently began in Stadelheim.

As I have discovered, it would have been easy to raise the aforementioned sum of 300M. from völkisch circles. Röhm, however, refused any support and preferred to serve the prison sentence, presumably foremost because of the propaganda implications.

Signed
Haniel
(Bundesarchiv, R 43 I/2223; Translation: Gary Costello)

c. 1928–00.06.1934	Member of the *Reichsverband Deutscher Offiziere* (RDO, Reich Association of German Officers).
00.08.1928–00.11.1928	*Vorsitzender* of the reestablished *Reichskriegsflagge*, under the new name *Flaggenklub*. His purpose in resurrecting the RKF was not to resume paramilitary activities, but to bring its members into the NSDAP.
Mid-1928	Received an offer from *Major* Wilhelm ("Guillermo") Kaiser, a former Imperial German Army officer serving as temporary Bolivian military attaché in the Netherlands, to work for the Bolivian Army.
25.07.1928–00.11.1928	*Vorsitzender* of the *Wehrpolitische Vereinigung* (WPV, League for Defense Policy).

00.01.1929–00.10.1930   Service with the Bolivian Army as a military instructor and inspector of two infantry regiments. His contract was to run from 01.01.1929 to 31.12.1930. On 14.12.1928, he had embarked for South America aboard the Hamburg-South America liner SS *Cap Polonio*. With him was a nineteen-year-old München art student, Martin Schätzl, and the chief of the Bolivian General Staff (since 09.02.1921), General Hans Kundt. Per Dr. Hancock, "their [Röhm's and Schätzl's] friendship may have arisen through shared political views," however, Schätzl did not share Röhm's sexual orientation. The *Cap Polonio* weighed anchor in Buenos Aires on 31.01.1929, and the trio then went by train to La Paz, arriving there on 05.01.1929. The Bolivians backdated Röhm's service to 05.12.1928. Of his service in South America, Hancock writes:

When Röhm arrived in La Paz in January 1929 he was initially employed as a professor in the Bolivian military college, apparently to allow him to learn Spanish. By the beginning of April 1929 he described his written Spanish as quite good and claimed that he could make himself understood when speaking. Later that month he accompanied Kundt on his inspection of recruits. From June to September 1929 Kundt sent Röhm to inspect various infantry regiments outside the capital. Röhm claimed that "I directed the entire duty, designed all the large exercises, held war games, field discussions, inspections, in the closest agreement with the regimental commanders. I made high demands that were well and cheerfully fulfilled." (Röhm, *Geschichte eines Hochverräters*, fifth edition, p. 360)

In September 1929 Röhm was appointed [by Orden General No. 238 of 07.09.1929] Chief of Staff of the First Division in Oruro under General Carlos de Gumucio. On 22 October, with Röhm commanding, the Blue Division won the annual Bolivian military war games. He remained at the Oruro divisional headquarters until August 1930.

    Röhm's relations with Kundt had deteriorated since his arrival, even though Röhm made friends easily in the German embassy, the German community and among his fellow officers, who remembered him as intelligent, cultivated and agreeable. One Bolivian officer, Colonel Luis E. Saavedra, claimed that Röhm had aroused Kundt's jealousy and that Kundt sent him to Oruro to remove him from the General Staff: "He was undoubtedly more capable than Kundt and that was the origin of their rivalry." Röhm himself did not acknowledge that Kundt was jealous of his ability, though he recognized that his relations with Kundt had worsened. In February 1929 he wrote to Hitler that he was getting on well with Kundt. By April 1930, however, he advised Crown Prince Rupprecht of Bavaria that Kundt saw him as a Bavarian and therefore as second class.... Later—on 22 August—Röhm claimed to the Crown Prince that Kundt had tried everything to remove Röhm and that the plan only failed "as a result of the determined resistance of my followers in the War Ministry." (Hancock, "Ernst Röhm versus General Hans Kundt in Bolivia, 1929-30. The Curious Incident" in *Journal of Contemporary History*, Vol. 47, No. 4 [October 2012], pp. 697-698)

In June 1930, the cabinet of Bolivian President Dr. Hernando Siles Reyes (with whom Kundt sided, and who resigned on 28.05.1930) was overthrown in a coup, and on the 28th of the month, General Carlos Blanco Galindo and other officers established a junta. On 28.07.1930, Kundt left the country. According to Röhm's fellow German officer in the country, Adolf Röpnack, Röhm sided with the anti-Siles uprising, and claimed, Hancock continues, that "Röhm's consent was required for the rebellion of the First Division in Oruro. Röhm's role, according to [the historian Robert] Brockmann, was therefore pivotal in the success of the coup." (Hancock, "Ernst Röhm versus General Hans Kundt in Bolivia, 1929–30. The Curious Incident" in *Journal of Contemporary History*, Vol. 47, No. 4 [October 2012], p. 700) Of Röhm's assignment in the aftermath of the coup, Hancock writes:

Röhm was a friend of Colonel Filiberto Osorio, the guiding force in the new junta. Shortly after the coup Röhm was recalled to La Paz and in August he was appointed expert adviser in the General Staff. His new responsibilities included drawing up the army budget and making the necessary economies in face of Bolivia's large deficit....

[B]y October Röhm had demanded the position of deputy Chief of Staff, had been refused and as a result was leaving for Germany. (Hancock, "Ernst Röhm versus General Hans Kundt in Bolivia, 1929–30. The Curious Incident" in *Journal of Contemporary History*, Vol. 47, No. 4 [October 2012], pp. 702-703)

Mid-10.1930	Recalled from South America by Hitler, who requested that he assume the post of *Chef des Stabes der SA* (chief of staff of the *Sturmabteilung*).
01.11.1930	Reenrolled in the NSDAP.
12.11.1930	Diary entry of Dr. Joseph Goebbels: "Röhm is coming. From Bolivia, where he worked in the army. He is very nice to me, and I like him too. An open, direct soldier's nature. A character."
05.01.1931–01.07.1934	*Chef des Stabes der SA* (chief of staff of the *Sturmabteilung*). Succeeded Dr. Otto Wagener. Succeeded, following his murder, by Viktor Lutze. The following is Röhm's announcement of his appointment:

Comrades of the SA
Appointed by the trust of Adolf Hitler, I take over as Chief of Staff from 5.1.1931.
  I am aware that I have been called to a crucial place at a crucial time.
  Great things have been achieved and greater things are to be completed. The year 1931 will see the movement in further, unstoppable advance towards the inevitable success that will be Germany's success.
  Moving closer to the day of victory depends in no small part on SA.
  In a united front, unconditional loyalty and devotion, it will go its way.
  I have this trust in you, comrades; to be worthy of your trust and to justify the Führer's trust in us will be the content of this year's work for me.
München, 1 January 1931
Ernst Röhm

Röhm built the SA into a massive fighting organization. At the time of his appointment as *Chef des Stabes*, its membership stood at approximately 77,000; within three months, it exceeded 100,000; by 15.12.1931, it had risen to 260,438, a figure that more than doubled in 1932. By the time of Hitler's appointment as *Reichskanzler* on 30.01.1933, Röhm led a paramilitary army of over 500,000 men.

01.05.1931–30.04.1933   *Korpsführer des NSKK (NS-Kraftfahrkorps)*. Succeeded by Adolf Hühnlein.

00.00.1931   Initiation of proceedings against Röhm for *"wiedernatürlicher Unzucht"* (unnatural sex acts). Florence Tamagne details the charges against him as follows:

> A first suit was brought against him and several of his friends; it opened on June 6, at the court of Munich. The waiter Fritz Reif gave a deposition against Röhm. Before Christmas 1930, he had been led by one of his friends, the hotel employee Peter Kronninger [*sic*, Granninger], to a room in a building on Barerstrasse. There lay a man named Ernst, naked on a bed; a few days later, [Granninger] indicated that it was Ernst Röhm. Ernst, after having stripped him, embraced him and masturbated him. Then he turned to [Granninger], who had also been undressed, and continued. [Granninger] had promised Reif money for his services; days passed without the payment arriving and Reif sent a note, threatening to reveal everything to the police if he did not get 25 RM at once. Via [Granninger], he accepted just 8 RM. [Granninger] and Röhm denied the whole thing. [Granninger] had known Röhm for two years, [and] there had never been anything sexual between them. Röhm, for his part, admitted that, from a sexual point of view, he was abnormally inclined. He admitted to having engaged in some lesser offenses but said he had never committed any infringement of §175. The cases were eventually dropped for lack of evidence. (Tamagne, *A History of Homosexuality: Europe between the Wars*, p. 288)

Hitler tolerated and greatly valued Röhm despite the many rumors regarding his lifestyle. He often asserted that the tales of homosexuality on Röhm's part were unproven, and were, in any case, "an entirely private matter." His personal photographer, Heinrich Hoffmann, observed:

> [Röhm] was ... heavily attacked by the leftish press on account of his unfortunate mode of life; this, however, carried no weight with Hitler.
> "In a man like Röhm," he said to me, "who has lived so long in the tropics, a disease like this—for it is as a disease that I prefer to regard his habits—deserves special consideration. With his Army connections, Röhm is very valuable to the Party, and, as long as he remains discreet about things, his private life is of no interest to me; and I certainly should never think of reproaching him or of taking any action against him." (Hoffmann, *Hitler Was My Friend*)

In *"Erlaß Nr. 1"* of that 03.02.1931, Hitler, in his capacity as *Oberste SA-Führer*, declared:

The Oberster SA-Führung has received a number of reports and charges directed against SA leaders and men, mainly consisting of attacks with regard to the private lives of these personalities.

The examination usually reveals that these are things that are completely outside the scope of SA service. In many cases, attacks by political or personal opponents are simply taken over without further ado.

The supreme and senior SA leaders are expected to make decisions about these matters, which are strictly of a private nature.

I reject this imposition in principle and in the strongest manner.

Apart from the fact that valuable time, which is of greater necessity in the struggle for freedom, is being uselessly wasted, I must state that the SA is an assembly of men for a specific political purpose. It is not a moral institution for the education of upper-class daughters, but an association of rough fighters. The only issue that can be examined here is whether or not the SA leader or man fulfils his official duty within the SA. One's private life can only be the subject of scrutiny if it runs counter to essential principles of the National Socialist outlook. The senior SA leaders who receive such denunciations will in future first have to check whether the denunciant, who brings discord and unrest into the SA, should not be called to account and, if necessary, request be made that they be expelled from the SA or the movement.

Adolf Hitler

(Dr. Heinrich Bennecke, *Hitler und die SA*, p. 253; Translation: Gary Costello)

Despite the inherent dangers of exposure, Röhm did little to keep his behavior private. He used his position as SA Chief of Staff to procure partners, with SA men specially allocated as the procurers. His most active pimp was Peter Granninger, installed by Röhm in the *SA-Nachrichtenabteilung* (intelligence department) and intimately linked to the *Stabschef* since 1928:

The head pimp was a shop assistant named Peter Granninger, who had been one of Röhm's partners since 1928 and was now given cover in the SA Intelligence Section. For a monthly salary of 200 Marks he kept Röhm supplied with new friends, his main hunting ground being Gisela High School [in] Munich; from this school he recruited no fewer than eleven boys, whom he first tried out and then took to Röhm.... The general meeting-point for the Granninger circle and the SA homosexuals was Röhm's reserved table in the Bratwurstglöckl, Munich. The proprietor, Karl Zehnter, was a homosexual himself ... Röhm and his highly organized squad of informers generally succeeded in covering their tracks. (Höhne, *The Order of the Death's Head*, p. 82)

The allegations against Röhm soon found their way to the Social Democratic and Communist presses, however, thus creating a significant public relations problem for Hitler and the NSDAP. Tamagne continues:

[O]n April 14, 1931, the socialist newspaper *Münchner Post* published an anonymous letter from a former Nazi, who accused Röhm of being homosexual. In June, the newspaper published several letters which reiterated the same assertion. The June 22 [issue] bore a spectacular headline: "A Hot Fraternity in the Brown House. The sexual life of the Third Reich." On June 24, 1931, *Völkischer Beobachter*, organ of the Nazi party, denied the charges and accused the newspaper of having fabricated the documents. The affair gained steam in 1932. March 7, 1932, in the midst of an election campaign, *Münchner Post* published letters from 1928 and 1929 addressed by Röhm to a friend, Dr. Heimsoth. Röhm was then in Bolivia and he expressed his regrets at not finding any companions. He missed the young Berliners. The socialist press began to describe Röhm's homosexuality in the horrified and hysterical tones usually reserved for the cheapest newssheets. The June 22, 1931 *Münchner Post* speaks about "fornication of the kind referred to in §175, to make your hair stand on end." The March 10, 1932 *Vorwärts* ran a headline about young SA "in the clutches of M. Röhm." The Communist Party, in *Rote Fahne* of March 11, 1932, joined in: "The Hitlerian party is a nest of informants and spies, of intrigues between the leaders and the most horrible corruption!" Welt am Abend talked of "Intrigues and Sexual Hypocrisy around §175 in Hedemanstrasse," and "Captain Röhm abused unemployed young workmen." The campaign sought to reveal the hypocrisy of a party that was claiming it wanted to restore the virtue of the German people and which railed against homosexuality as a Jewish and Bolshevik plague. Leftist parties particularly hoped to upset parents whose children were involved in Nazi movements. (Tamagne, *A History of Homosexuality: Europe between the Wars*, pp. 288-289)

Hitler's foreign press representative, Ernst ("Putzi") Hanfstaengl, writes of Röhm's "perversion":

Fellow officers who had known Roehm during the war always maintained that he had been completely normal and even described orgies in which he had taken part in the Army brothels. He had certainly acquired a syphilitic infection during this period and this may have had some effect on his subsequent development. The scandal started soon after he had returned in October 1930. Letters from his male companions in Bolivia somehow came into the hands of third parties and the accusations started. General von Epp, who had held a high opinion of Roehm's organizational abilities before the Ludendorff Putsch, even taxed him with the rumours at quite an early stage and received Roehm's completely false word of honour that they were not true. Later, about 1932, the scandal became public, and although it was somehow glossed over, Roehm quite openly admitted his aberration to Toni Drexler [Anton Drexler, a cofounder of the *DAP*], because he passed it on to me. Hitler can have had no illusions at any time and his mock horror when he found it necessary to shoot Roehm in 1934 was, of course, pure invention. (Hanfstaengl, *Hitler: The Missing Years*, p. 155)

Kurt Lüdecke summarized his friend's susceptibility to public attack from the enemies of the NSDAP:

But however tolerant the general public might be toward ordinary citizens of doubtful sexual inclinations, Roehm was an exception. His success as head of the much-hated SA made him the target of a savage attack through the loophole of his personal habits. His notoriety was pitilessly exploited by the enemy. The better he did his work for Hitler, the more he suffered from sneers, ridicule, and condemnation which he was powerless to answer because they were at least based on fact. Hitler had always defended him vigorously. But there was no ending the stories or evading the truth that Roehm's vulnerability was bad advertising for the Party. (Lüdecke, *I Knew Hitler: The Story of a Nazi Who Escaped the Blood Purge*, p. 379)

11.10.1931	Participated in the *Tagung der nationalen Opposition* in Bad Harzburg, during which the so-called *"Harzburger Front"* was established.
17.10.1931–18.10.1931	Participated in the "*SA-Aufmarsch in Braunschweig.*"
13.04.1932–14.06.1932	SA banned by the government of Chancellor Brüning.
00.00.1932	Publication of *Halbmast-Heldenbuch der SA und SA*, a tribute to Brownshirts killed in service to the Nazi movement. The book featured forewords by Röhm and Göring, among others. The *SA-Stabschef* wrote:

More than 350 SA comrades gave their lives in fulfillment of the oath they had taken to the Führer and their Fatherland. They died fighting for the Holy German Reich, the truly German Germany, the Third Reich. They were comrades, united in noble fellowship, inwardly connected without regard to origin or race, confession or position. They proved their loyalty to their Führer by sacrificing the most precious thing they could give, their young lives, for him and for the idea. We owe our heroes indelible thanks-thanks for their loyalty, dedication and courage. We will never forget them, but we do not want to lament them in paralyzing grief. We want to draw strength and resilience from their past lives and early deaths, to break the chains and lead Germany out of the dark abyss back to the light of freedom and honor. Germany must live even if we have to die!
[Signed] Ernst Röhm
(Translation: Gary Costello)

10.03.1933–13.04.1933	*Staatskommissar zur besonderen Verwendung* (state commissioner for special assignment) in Bayern.
00.04.1933–02.08.1933	*Ministerial-Kommissar für die Hilfspolizeibeamten der Sicherheitspolizei* (ministerial commissioner for the Auxiliary Police Officials of the Security Police) in the *Preußische Ministerium des Innern*.
13.04.1933–01.12.1933	*Staatssekretär* to the *Reichsstatthalter* in Bayern (Franz Ritter von Epp).
25.04.1933	Appointed as *Staatskommissar z.b.V. in Bayern* (state commissioner for Special Assignment in Bavaria).
01.05.1933–31.12.1933	*Kommandeur der Sicherheitshilfspolizei* (commander of the Auxiliary Security Police) in Bayern.
29.05.1933	Appointed as *Präsident* of the *Deutschen Akademischen Austauschstelle* (German Academic Exchange Office).

30.05.1933 Issued the following confidential status report to the senior leadership of the SA, SS, and HJ:

I do not view the current situation without concern.
Experience shows, however, that in revolutions a certain stagnation occurs after the first big wave.
It is about the bearer of the revolution, the fighting force, withstanding and overcoming this stagnation.
In a simultaneously issued decree, I ordered the SA and SS to visibly refrain from the urge to permanently celebrate festivities from now on. I hold the leaders of the Gruppen responsible for this and ask them to watch over it and demand spot checks that this order is carried through to the Stürmen and is followed scrupulously.
I ask you to take strong action against non-compliance.
There is no mistaking the danger that the SA and SS are to be cast in the role of a mere propaganda force.
I request that, in the spirit of the aforementioned decree, the soldierly principle be vigorously reasserted.
I also have reason to point out that marches etc. may only take place in front of SA or SS Führers and may only be inspected by them.
I enclose for your information two letters which I felt compelled to address to the Stabsleiter of the political organisation and to the Reichsschatzmeister.
I request that these be made known in extracts to the subordinate departments.
I am of the opinion that the SA and SS will certainly be faced with special tasks this year.
I am responsible for ensuring that the Führer has his guards at his disposal at all times, even in serious situations.
You, my SA Führers, are responsible for ensuring that the Revolutionary Guard [Garde der Revolution] is always in a soldierly condition, so that it can meet all the demands placed on it.
Leaders who do not exclusively serve their duty as SA and SS Führers, who are addicted to personal vanity, who would like to become somebody, are to be ruthlessly removed.
I give you the month of June free for the eradication of weaknesses and errors, if such should have taken hold in the SA or SS.
From the 1st of July onwards, I will convince myself through inspections that the old, fresh, simple and uncompromising SA spirit prevails throughout once again.
I also request that the purely propagandistic marches be stopped on your own initiative. In future, even those of a smaller scale are subject to your approval.
SA Führers! We want nothing and must want nothing for ourselves. Leave posts and positions of honor to others.
When the few of us who have taken on such posts in the interests of the SA or SS in addition to our SA or SS Führer posts see that their SA Führer duties suffer, they will gladly give those posts back and be proud to be leaders in the brown army.

Then this alone has turned Germany's fortunes; it will also win and maintain the victory of pure, unadulterated nationalism and socialism.

Heil to the Obersten SA Führer Adolf Hitler.

The Chef des Stabes

Röhm
(Bundesarchiv NS 26/328; Translation: Gary Costello)

00.06.1933–01.07.1934	*Reichsleiter der NSDAP.*
01.07.1933	Appointed as *Präsident* of the *Landesverband Bayern der Deutschen Bühne e. V.* (Bavarian State Association of the German Stage).
31.07.1933	Secretly issued a so-called *"Verfügung betr. Disziplin"* ("disciplinary decree"; *Verf. des OSAF Ch. Nr. 1415/33 v. 31.7.33*), from which the following is excerpted:

I am trying to preserve and guarantee fully the rights of the SA as soldiers in the vanguard of the National Socialist Revolution.... I assume responsibility for all actions taken by the SA which may not necessarily conform to current legal provisions, but which serve the exclusive interests of the SA. In this context it is proper to remember that the leader of an SA organization has the right to execute up to twelve members of a hostile organization in reprisal for the execution of one SA member.

These executions are officially ordered by the Führer; they must be carried out swiftly, and with military rigor.

However, I have been informed of incidents—rare, it is true—in which certain members of SA organizations—I do not wish to designate these men by the name SA, which they do not deserve—have been guilty of inexcusable excesses.

These excesses include the following: the satisfaction of personal vengeance, inadmissible cruelty, extortion and pillage.... [I am indignant with] these profaners of SA honor and the SA uniform [and order the] immediate, exemplary death [of] any responsible SA leader who, through a misconceived sense of indulgence, fails to intervene. (Max Gallo, *The Night of the Long Knives*, p. 27)

14.09.1933–01.07.1934	*Preußischer Staatsrat.*
22.09.1933	Issued the following decree to the SA:

It is evidently for want of some other productive occupation that certain individuals and associations have taken upon themselves the task of carrying out the "moral" reform of the German people.

These reformers may be left to themselves as long as they merely proclaim their ideal aims privately in pamphlets or in such periodicals as agree with them. But real damage is done as soon as such persons, claiming to act on the authority of the State or the Party, proceed to put this pastime into practice. It cannot be denied that this is the case and that a very orgy of reforming is being indulged in by these prudish hypocrites.

E.g., the most stupid regulations have been made regarding bathing costumes and conduct in public baths.

German women have been forbidden to use face powder, or to smoke in restaurants; in the large cities all places of amusement not in keeping with narrow bourgeois standards are to be banned; a campaign is being waged against so-called prostitution, a campaign as hypocritical in its nature as it is brutal in its execution and fatal in its consequences to public health and hygiene.

All this activity is inspired, it is alleged, by a sentiment of sacred responsibility for the good of the nation; in reality it is nothing else but attempts at satisfying repressed complexes which for centuries have repeatedly been made by hypocrites and prudes.

It is clear from evidence at my disposal that there exists a great gulf between theory and practice in the lives of many who in this respect have come to the fore as moral reformers.

More recently I have received new information that even SS- and SA-leaders and men have publicly set themselves up as moral censors, and on these grounds have subjected women to molestations, insults and even maltreatment, in public baths, restaurants and in the streets.

The growing number of such excesses of prudery and worse, which often, too, are of a ridiculous nature, provides me with a welcome opportunity of stating in unequivocal terms that the German Revolution was won, not by philistines and canting morality preachers, but by revolutionary fighters. These alone will safeguard its rights.

It is not the task off the SA to watch over the costume, facial culture and chastity of other persons, but to rouse Germany by their free and revolutionary fighting spirit.

I, therefore, forbid all leaders and members of the SA to lend any active assistance in this direction to those cracked moral aesthetes. This prohibition finds a special application in the case of those members of the SA and SS who have been placed by me at the disposal of the Government as Commissioners of Police or other State Officials.

The Chief of Staff.

Signed: RÖHM.

(Published in the *Hamburger Fremdenblatt*, Nr. 263, 23.09.1933; Translation in Anonymous, *The Persecution of the Catholic Church in the Third Reich: Facts and Documents*, pp. 16-17)

23.09.1933–24.09.1933	Participated in the "*Stahlhelm-Reichsfuhrertagung*" in Hannover.
03.10.1933–01.07.1934	Member of the *Akademie für Deutsches Recht*, München.
00.11.1933–01.07.1934	Member of the *Führerrat der Akademie für Deutsches Recht* (Leadership Council of the Academy for German Law).
08.11.1933	Participated in the ceremonial presentation, on the *Königsplatz* in München, of the flags of several major *Freikorps* ("*Heydebreck,*" "*Kühme,*" "*Lautenbacher,*" "*Pfeffer,*" "*Rossbach,*" "*Oberland,*" etc., as well as "*Sturmregiment Heinz*") to the *Obersten SA-Führung*. Röhm accepted the flags, which were ultimately transferred to the *Braunes Haus*. The event was described as follows in the *Brockauer Zeitung* Landkreis Breslau), issue of 10.11.1933:

The handing over of the flags by the Freikorps.

The unity of will and action of all those who, after the horrific collapse of the German Reich in the days of November 1918, had united as fighters for the revival of patriotic thought and belief, for the honor and freedom of Germany, found its striking expression in the solemn act of the handing over the of the Freikorps flags to the SA.

On the wide space in front of the Glyptothek on the Königsplatz, the delegations of the Freikorps with their glorious flags, the freedom fighters in their old uniforms had lined up, opposite them the long front of the Standarte 16.

To the sound of the presentation march, Stabschef Röhm, who had appeared with the Reichsstatthalter for Bavaria, Ritter von Epp, walked along the ranks of the SA and then greeted the leaders of the flag delegations with a hearty handshake, Dr. Weber, the leader of the Freikorps Oberland, the old warrior Oberleutnant Roßbach and all the others who had once saved the country from the deepest hardship and disgrace at the head of their troops.

After the salute to the Freikorps fighters, Stabschef Röhm stepped in front of the Freikorps' flags and gave a stirring speech.

Stabschef Röhm stated, among other things: In their helplessness, aimlessness and cowardice, presumptuous leaders of 1918 had to turn to the soldiers of 1919 to save Germany again. These soldiers have returned here with their flags and insignia. They have fulfilled their duty, have succeeded in preventing the Bolshevik surge from sweeping over Germany and have restored peace to the German people. Their work stands firm in history. Their work will be cherished, honored and respected by the soldiers for all time. The men who appointed them at that time, of course, and who then gave them the boot again, did not want Germany to become free and great, but only to support their tottering thrones. Thus, the fate of the fighters was temporarily pushed into the background again until other political soldiers stepped onto the stage of German events, took over the word and also the deed and worked to ensure that the whole of Germany was once again filled with a genuine good soldier spirit. By this we understand what today the political soldier proclaims as a National Socialist, the community of all ranks, of all classes, the togetherness of all who are of the same language, of the same blood, the togetherness in good days and in bad, the comradeship of all the good-minded until death. This true soldier characteristic was then, on the whole, taken over by Adolf Hitler's SA. Today, my comrades from the Freikorps, what you also fought for, and what we old soldiers fought for out in the field, has become reality.

We once again have a Germany in which it is worth living and fighting, a Germany in which it is also worth dying for the fatherland, so that these sacrifices benefit the entire people, the entire fatherland. We will ensure that this spirit is and remains the spirit of Germany. The Führer of Germany can be sure that his political soldiers will never leave the path he is leading us along, for Germany's honor and well-being. Germany, dear Germany, may be at peace, we create and fight.

Then Stabschef Röhm accepted the flags from the hands of their leaders and handed them over to the safe custody of the SA. He greeted the leaders of the Freikorps and the Zeitfreiwilligen with a handshake and the words: "The comradeship, which united us in the field, will keep us together in Germany's good times and in bad times!" the Stabschef delivered a Sieg Heil to the old Freikorps fighters. In a solemn procession, the flags were reverently saluted by the densely packed crowds with raised arms and brought into the Braune Haus, where they will be placed in the Hall of Honor next to the Sturmfahnen of the SA. (Translation courtesy of Gary Costello)

12.11.1933–01.07.1934	Member of the *Reichstag*.
02.12.1933–01.07.1934	*Reichsminister ohne Geschäftsbereich* (Reich Minister without Portfolio, sworn in 04.12.1933) and member of the *Reichsverteidigungsrat* (Reich Defense Council).
07.12.1933	Delivered his speech *"Warum SA?"* (Why SA?) to foreign diplomats in Berlin, from which the following is excerpted:

The Storm Troops cannot be compared with any army, any militia or any other military system in the world.… This is absolutely not the case with the Storm Troops according to Adolf Hitler's expressed will. On the contrary, in all the proclamations which deal with relations between the Reichswehr and the Storm Troops he has clearly and unmistakably indicated the dividing line: the Reichswehr is the sole armed force in the state and the Storm Troops are the representatives of the will and ideas of the National Socialist German Revolution. The Reichswehr is charged with the defense of the frontiers and the protection of the interests of the Reich as against foreign countries. The task set the Storm Troops is to form the new German state in mind and will on the basis of National-Socialist ideas and to educate the individual German as a living member of this National-Socialist state. There is no connection whatever between the Reichswehr and the Storm Troops. Thus the German Army took no part whatever in the National-Socialist Revolution, a fact which is probably unique in the history of revolutions.

In spite of their numerical strength of about 2,500,000 men, the Storm Troops are not concentrated in barracks and rationed in common, as is the case with all formations belonging to any military system in neighboring states. They are not paid and are not provided with service clothing. Today, as in the past, service in the Storm Troops is based on the absolutely volunteer system. The Storm Trooper pursues his civil vocation, and merely devotes his leisure hours, in the evening and at night, to Storm Troop service.

The Storm Troops were created as a protective and fighting force for dealing with the internal political opponents of National Socialism, namely Communism and Marxism. For fourteen years the Storm Troops waged the moral fight to obtain power in the state. Their prime task is now to secure the victory of the National-Socialist Revolution.

The Storm Trooper is the exponent of the National-Socialist conception of human existence and its apostle who conveys the principles of National Socialism to the remotest cottage and to all his fellow-countrymen without exception.

In the course of the years of struggle the Storm Troops, with enormous sacrifices, have given convincing proof of their absolute loyalty to the

Führer and to the movement, and thus showed themselves qualified for their task. It will always be a glorious page in the history of Germany that in times of the greatest need hundreds of thousands of men came forward who were ready, from pure idealism and absolutely voluntarily, to defend their principles to the last....

So far it was simply and solely due to the fact that the Storm Troops in the heart of Europe stood for years with consciously anti-Bolshevist aims as a bulwark protecting peace and order in the world, that Bolshevism was unable to lay hands on the western European countries as well. Hence it is absolutely in the interest of foreign countries to see order and discipline firmly established in the German nation. The world ought to be thankful for that, instead of distorting the facts and representing the Storm Troops as a menace to peace....

Nothing is ... more natural than that the National-Socialist State should make use of the old and well-tried champions of this new political faith to educate the entire population to accept in their hearts and really live in accordance with the principles of National Socialism. It would be a contradiction of the totalitarian claim of the National-Socialist State if the State were not to include the party as representing the idea upon which the State is based. This applies even more to the Storm Troops who, as regards their ideas, organization and fighting qualities, are the strongest expression of the power of National Socialism as such. The Storm Troops have got rid of a form of government in spite of the most embittered resistance on the part of its supporters. They have replaced the vanquished state of the November revolution and the Weimar National Assembly by their own State, the National-Socialist state.

Adolf Hitler has now incorporated the Storm Troops in the State. The Storm Troops have thus become not only the representatives of authority but also the bearers of responsibility in their, the National-Socialist state. (Röhm, *Why SA? German Minister Ernst Röhm, Chief of Staff, Addressing the Diplomatic Corps in Berlin on December 7, 1933*)

00.12.1933–01.07.1934	*Bayerischer Staatsminister.*
00.12.1933–01.07.1934	*Bayerischer Staatsrat.*
31.12.1933	One year into his chancellorship, and just months before ordering the massacre of Röhm and other SA leaders, Hitler wrote the following letter which was published in the *Völkischer Beobachter* on 02.01.1934:

My dear Chief of Staff,
The fight of the National Socialist Movement and the National Socialist Revolution was made possible only by the consistent suppression of the Marxist terror by the SA.

If the Army is to guarantee the protection of the nation abroad, it is the task of the SA to secure the victory of the National Socialist Revolution, the continued existence of the National Socialist State and the community of our *Volk* at home.

When I summoned you, my dear Chief of Staff, to your present position, the SA was going through a serious crisis.

It is primarily thanks to you that, in the space of only a few years, this political instrument was able to develop the force which made it possible for me to finally win the struggle for power by overcoming the Marxist opponent.

At the close of the Year of the National Socialist Revolution, I feel compelled to thank you, my dear Ernst Röhm, for the immortal service which you have done to the National Socialist Movement and the German *Volk* and to assure you how grateful I am to Fate to be able to call such men as you fighting comrades [*Kampfgenossen*].
In true friendship and grateful regard,
Yours, Adolf Hitler
(Dr. Max Domarus, ed., *Hitler. Speeches and Proclamations, 1932–1945: The Years 1932–1934*)

05.04.1934	Appointed as *Ehrenführer* of the veterans' organization *Deutsche Reichskriegerbund "Kyffhäuser."*
28.02.1934	Luncheon held for SA and *Reichswehr* leaders at Röhm's headquarters on the *Standartenstraße*, Berlin. This followed a meeting at the *Reichswehr* Ministry, during which Hitler officiated over a reluctant agreement between *Reichswehrminister* General Werner von Blomberg and Röhm in which the *Reichswehr* was deemed "the sole bearer of arms in the Third Reich," and pre- and post-military training would be the province of the SA alone. During the luncheon, Röhm and von Blomberg sealed the agreement with a handshake. Röhm's real goal was more ambitious: to absorb the entire *Reichswehr*, limited by the Treaty of Versailles to just 100,000 men, into the SA, with himself ruling as *Reichswehrminister*. Toward this end, he exploited the discontent within the ranks of the SA, now numbering some 2,500,000 men, which had not benefited in any appreciable way since the seizure of power. Because these plans were contrary to those of the *Führer*, Hitler—under pressure from Göring and Himmler—ultimately decided to eliminate his old comrade Röhm and a number of other SA leaders (see entry of 30.06.1934, below). Almost immediately following the departure of Hitler and the *Reichswehr* leaders from the luncheon, Röhm launched into a tirade before his SA lieutenants, shouting: "What that ridiculous Corporal [Hitler] says means nothing to us.... I have not the slightest intention of keeping this agreement. Hitler is a traitor and at the very least must go on leave.... If we can't get there with him, we'll get there without him." (Heinz Höhne, *The Order of the Death's Head*, p. 110)
A slightly different account is given by Robert J. O'Neill, who writes:

Röhm ... was extremely annoyed. He said that this agreement which he had been forced to sign was a new "*Versailler Diktat*", and referred to Hitler as the "*ignoranter Gefreiter des Weltkriegs*" (ignorant corporal of the World War)....

These events of the afternoon of 28 February 1934 were related to [Generalmajor Maximilian Reichsfreiherr] von Weichs [commanding 3.

Kavallerie-Division in Weimar] by Lutze. Lutze and Weichs were on good terms with each other, if not actually friends. (O'Neill, citing recollections of von Weichs, in *The German Army and the Nazi Party, 1933–1939*, p. 42 and fn.)

In response to these treasonous utterances, the stunned Lutze, whose primary loyalty was to the *Führer*, sought to expose the mutinous spirit displayed by Röhm. In March 1934, he shared his concerns with Rudolf Hess. Making no headway with the deputy *Führer*, he then presented his case directly to Hitler at Berchtesgaden. The *Führer*, hearing of the dangerous rumblings of discontent throughout the SA and rising as high as its top leadership, responded with, "We must let the matter develop." Knowing of Röhm's bitter rivalry with the *Reichswehr*, Lutze later spoke of the matter to *Generalmajor* Walter von Reichenau during military exercises in Braunfels. Von Reichenau was grateful for the information as, unbeknownst to Lutze, he was already working out the details, together with Reinhard Heydrich, for a joint *Reichswehr-SS* action to solve the problems presented by the troublesome Röhm and his clique. Heydrich eventually persuaded Himmler of the need to decapitate the SA, and throughout the Spring of 1934 the two plotted the eventual "Night of the Long Knives." On 22.06.1934, Hitler met with Lutze and informed him of the impending purge to be carried out on the SA leadership, including the removal of Röhm. He advised Lutze that he was to accept orders only from him, and not from München.

18.04.1934 — Delivered his speech *"Die nationalsozialistische Revolution und die SA"* to the diplomatic corps and the foreign press at the Reich Ministry of Propaganda, Berlin:

Under the sign of the Swastika the new National Socialist Germany has nothing but friends in this world. Much has been said and written on this subject.... Most foreigners have failed to understand either the direction or the nature of the German Revolution. The fact that it was not simply a change of political leadership is usually forgotten....

The National Socialist Revolution signifies a spiritual rupture with the thought of the great French Revolution of 1789.

This thought, which takes into account only measurable and enumerable elements, has been raised against it in National Socialism, a new form of idealism before which democracy senses its own disarray, because, by natural necessity, democracy is incapable of understanding the internal principle of National Socialism.

To replace the values of democracy, National Socialism substitutes answers which cannot be precisely measured or weighed, and which cannot be understood by reason and calculation alone: powers deriving from the soul and the blood.

The moral universe of National Socialism and that of democracy, therefore, are located on different conceptual levels....

I am going to speak to you of the SA. The SA is the heroic incarnation of the will and thought of the German Revolution. One can understand the nature and task of the SA only if one understands the nature and goals of the National Socialist Revolution....

The German Revolution began by destroying the internal forms of the Weimar Republic. In place of the red and black system of November, the Revolution substituted the National Socialist regime, which is the incarnation of the political authority of the State.

But as a conception of the world—and the first and final aim of our struggle all these years has been to impose an entirely new conception of the world—National Socialism is not a constitutional problem, and there is no causal link between it and the external form of the State, whatever that may happen to be....

The SA, let us repeat, is the heroic incarnation of the will and thought of the National Socialist Revolution.

The National Socialist Revolution is a process of moral pedagogy. It has been going on for a long time, and will not be finished until the last German incarnates and manifests National Socialism through his acts and thoughts.

When Hitler began his struggle, he was a soldier: combat, combat and more combat have marked his life. Also, by the very nature of the struggle, he subordinated all other considerations to military ones.

To guarantee the execution of his political line, he founded the Brown Army of the Revolution on the basis of two solid supports: the authority of the Führer and discipline.

Only one decision in the SA is voluntary: to enter the ranks of the assault troops of German renewal. From the moment a man puts on the brown uniform, he submits himself without restriction to the law of the SA.

That law is "Obedience until death to the Obersten Führer der SA, Adolf Hitler. My goods and my blood, my strength and my life, everything that I have belongs to Germany."

From the first, Hitler has not fought for small ends.... From the first day, when seven men without names, allies, publicity or money dreamed of lifting Germany from its ruins, the whole power of the State was at stake.

In this struggle, his weapon has been the SA.

The SA is not a band of intrepid conspirators, but an army of believers and martyrs, agitators and soldiers, necessary in this gigantic struggle in which the soul of the German people is at stake.

As circumstances required, Adolf Hitler created a new type of combatant: the soldier of a political idea. To these political soldiers he gave the red flag with its swastika, the new symbol of the German future, and the Brown Shirt, clothing the SA in combat, honor and death.

By its color, the Brown Shirt distinguishes the SA from the masses. It is this fact which justifies it: it is the distinctive sign of the SA, allowing friends and foes alike to recognize immediately those who profess the National Socialist conception of the world....

The SA is the incarnation of National Socialism. With their fists, the SA have opened to the ideas of National Socialism the road leading to victory. And in their progress the SA have drawn the skeptical and the hesitant into this prodigious mass rising of the nation.

The assault of the brown wave under the sign of the swastika calls to those on the sidelines who are waiting to see what will happen: "Come and join us, comrades!"

Without the SA, hundreds of thousands of workers would not have rediscovered the way of the Fatherland.... It is the SA which lifted them from the street, from hunger and from unemployment. These brown battalions have been the school of National Socialism. For in their ranks there are no privileges due to birth, rank or fortune: only the man counts, and the services he has rendered the movement.

Today, the National Socialist State rests on solid foundations. By the millions, the political soldiers of National Socialism watch over this new State, which is their State....

Unfortunately, in the train of the National Socialist Revolution, reactionary elements attached themselves to us. Of course, they were correctly "aligned," and had even pinned the swastika to their lapels to provide that they had always been Nationalists.

However, we did not make a Nationalist Revolution only, but a National Socialist one, and we stress the word "Socialist." ... With amazing mercy, the new regime, on taking power, did not pitilessly eliminate all the representatives of the former system, or of the one which preceded it.... We will wring their necks without the slightest pang if they dare to put reactionary principles into practice.

Reactionaries, bourgeois conformists, specialists in denigration—all these, by natural disposition, consider the Revolution a monstrosity. In return, we feel like vomiting when we think of them.

But an unshakable bastion of the Revolution, the SA rises up against reaction, denigration and conformism. The SA incarnates all the qualities which make the spirit of the Revolution.

During the years of struggle, the Brown Shirt was a formal uniform. It was also a shroud. After our victory, it became the symbol of National Socialist unity, it became the uniform of Germany, which it will remain.

The order and discipline of the SA were, from the outset, a necessity. The SA forged the unity of the revolutionary forces, which, to begin with, were only a loosely linked aggregate. Later, the SA became an instrument of education and the cement of our national community, which can exist only if the individual suppresses himself in every aspect of his life.

Today, it is the expression of a new style of German life. This new style, with its origins in the SA, will impose itself on every aspect of German life.

The SA is the National Socialist Revolution! (Max Gallo, *The Night of the Long Knives*, pp. 295-298)

20.04.1934 — Made the following announcement on behalf of the SA:

The Supreme Commander of the SA, Adolf Hitler, today celebrates his 45th birthday. For us political soldiers of the National Socialist Revolution, he personifies the following: What Germans have been yearning for since they first walked onto the stage of history and which two millennia of German evolution did not accomplish, he has made reality: A Volk which has outgrown the conflicts of rank, class and confession to become united

in a united Reich! Born of his spirit, under his flags, the SA has marched for a National Socialist Germany. Struggle and want, sacrifice and death have bound us to him in a community which nothing and no one can break or separate. We were, we are, and we always will be proud and honored to be at all times his most loyal followers, upon whom the Führer can depend and build in good times and all the more in bad. On this day when, forty-five years ago, Fate bestowed upon the nation in him its savior, the brown and black battalions of the SA present their compliments to their Supreme Commander and renew their oath: to follow in his footsteps and perform his work in unwavering loyalty and never-faltering obedience—to be at the fore, in spirit and deed, at the reconstruction of the State and the evolution of the Germans as a Volk—to serve National Socialist Germany with body and soul unto death. Heil the Führer of the Germans! Heil the Supreme Commander of the SA, Adolf Hitler!
Berlin, 20 April 1934
The SA-Stabschef
Ernst Röhm
(Dr. Max Domarus, ed., *Hitler. Speeches and Proclamations, 1932-1945: The Years 1932-1934*, p. 449)

16.05.1934   Issued the following confidential *Rundschreiben* (circular letter):

Open and hidden enemies of the SA today often dare to fight and harm the SA.

It is not always possible, nor is it always expedient, to oppose them immediately. A defense that does not promise success at the moment, is worse than no defense at all and silent, apparent denial.

However, it is absolutely necessary to put all these things down in writing.

The time may come when these statements will be needed.

I therefore order that in every office, from the standard upwards, an act of

"Hostilities against the SA" [*Feindseligkeiten gegen die SA*]

be written down and is constantly kept up to date. Of course, only accurately verified, absolutely truthful reports may never be submitted. These must contain

Exactly briefly the facts of the case,

Exact place and time,

Names of the plaintiffs, the witnesses and the defendants, or reference to documents, judgments, files etc. with exact indication of the storage, the file number etc.

The files of the standards and the brigades are to be submitted in copy to the groups and to be kept there especially after examination.
The Stabschef:
[Signed] Röhm.
(Translated from Hans Klering, et al., *Weissbuch über die Erschiessungen am 30. Juni 1934*, pp. 46-47)

07.06.1934	Issued an announcement that on the advice of his physician, he was taking several weeks' leave due to a painful nervous disorder, and that the SA would be going on its customary summer leave (to return to duty on 01.08.1934). He added: "If the enemies of the S.A. hope that the S.A. will not be recalled or will be recalled only in part after its leave, we may permit them to enjoy this brief hope. They will receive their answer at such time and in such form as appears necessary. The S.A. is and remains the destiny of Germany." (Frederick L. Schuman, *Hitler and the Nazi Dictatorship. A Social Pathology and the Politics of Fascism*)
00.06.1934	Expelled from the *Reichsverband Deutscher Offiziere*. Kurt Lüdecke writes: "It was a deadly insult, an irreparable blow to a *Reichsminister* and Hitler's chief of staff, and it could hardly have been dealt him without the consent of Hitler and the *Reichswehr*." (Lüdecke, *I Knew Hitler: The Story of a Nazi Who Escaped the Blood Purge*, p. 680)
30.06.1934	Personally arrested by Adolf Hitler at the *Pension Hanselbauer* in Bad Wiessee am Tegernsee. After arriving by plane at the *Flugplatz Oberwiesenfeld* in München, Hitler first arrested *SA-Obergruppenführer* August Schneidhuber and *SA-Gruppenführer* Wilhelm Schmid. He then set out—driven by one of his chauffeurs, Erich Kempka and a large entourage—to deal with Röhm. They arrived unannounced in five cars between 6:00 and 6:30 a.m. Hitler directed the headwaiter of the hotel to knock on the door of Röhm's room (#31). The *Stabschef*, awakened by the knocking, opened the door to hear his *Führer* shout, "Röhm! You are arrested!" and accuse him of treason. He then ordered him to get dressed. By 7:00 a.m., twelve men—among them *SA-Obergruppenführer* Edmund Heines, *SS-Gruppenführer* Robert Bergmann (Röhm's adjutant), *SA-Standartenführer* Ludwig Uhl, and *SA-Obertruppführer* Martin Schätzl—were arrested and transported to Stadelheim Prison outside München. Röhm was driven to Stadelheim separately and was admitted to Stadelheim at 11:00 a.m., given the prisoner number 4034 and placed in Cell 474. Multiple other arrests of senior SA leaders occurred in and around München and Berlin. In 1952, Kempka was interviewed by the German historian Dr. Georg Franz of the *Institut für Zeitgeschichte* in München. His account of the events was as follows:

Hitler sits down beside me and gives the order: "To Wiessee, as fast as possible!"

It must have been about 4.30 a.m., the sky has cleared up, it is nearly bright daylight ... Hitler sits beside me in silence. From time to time, I hear Goebbels and Lutze talking in the back.

Just before Wiessee, Hitler suddenly breaks his silence: "Kempka," he says, "drive carefully when we come to the Hotel Hanselbauer. You must drive up without making any noise. If you see an SA guard in the front of the hotel, don't wait for them to report to me; drive on and stop at the hotel entrance."

Then, after a moment of deathly silence: "Röhm wants to carry out a *coup*."

An icy shiver runs down my back. I could have believed anything, but not a *coup* by Röhm!

I drive up carefully to the hotel entrance as Hitler had ordered. Hitler jumps out of the car, and after him Goebbels, Lutze and the adjutants. Right behind us another car stops with a squad of detectives which had been raised in München.

As soon as I have turned the car so that it is ready to leave in a moment, I rush into the hotel with my gun at the ready. In the hall I meet Standartenführer Uhl, the leader of Röhm's staff guard. Hitler's chauffeur, [Julius] Schreck, is taking him at gunpoint down to the laundry room which for the next hour serves as the first prison for the arrested SA leaders. In passing, Schreck calls out to me: "Quickly! Run up to the boss! He needs you!"

I run quickly up the stairs to the first floor where Hitler is just coming out of Röhm's bedroom. Two detectives come out of the room opposite. One of them reports to Hitler: "My Führer ... the Polizeipräsident of Breslau is refusing to get dressed!"

Taking no notice of me, Hitler enters the room where Obergruppenführer Heines is remaining. I hear him shout: "Heines, if you are not dressed in five minutes, I'll have you shot on the spot!"

I withdraw a few steps and a police officer whispers to me that Heines had been in bed with an 18-year-old SA-Obertruppführer. At last Heines comes out of the room with an 18-year-old fair-haired boy mincing in front of him.

"Into the laundry room with them!" cries Schreck.

Meanwhile, Röhm comes out his room in a blue suit and with a cigar in the corner of his mouth. Hitler glares at him but says nothing. Two detectives take Röhm to the vestibule of the hotel where he throws himself into an armchair and orders coffee from the waiter.

I stay in the corridor a little to one side and a detective tells me about Röhm's arrest.

Hitler entered Röhm's bedroom alone with a whip in his hand. Behind him were two detectives with pistols at the ready. He spat out the words: "Röhm, you are under arrest." Röhm looked up sleepily from his pillow: "Heil, my Führer." "You are under arrest" bawled Hitler for the second time, turned on his heel and left the room.

Meanwhile, upstairs in the corridor things are getting quite lively. SA leaders are coming out of their rooms and being arrested. Hitler shouts at each one: "Have you had anything to do with Röhm's schemes?" Naturally, they all deny it, but doesn't help them in the least. Hitler usually knows about the individual; occasionally, he asks Goebbels or Lutze a question. And then comes the decision: "Arrested!"...

We follow Hitler into the yard and here he tells his chauffeur, Schreck, to charter a bus as quickly as possible to take the SA leaders who are in the laundry room to München.... More and more SA leaders arrive from outside and are brought into the laundry room. I stand at the hotel entrance and hear Röhm order coffee from the hotel manager for the third time....

Now the bus arrives which had been fetched by Schreck. Quickly, the SA leaders are collected from the laundry room and walk past Röhm under police guard. Röhm looks up from his coffee sadly and waves to them in a melancholy way....

At last Röhm too is led from the hotel. He walks past Hitler with his head bowed, completely apathetic. Now Hitler gives the order to leave... (Transcript of interview [25.03.1952] by Dr. Franz, in Herbert Michaelis, et al., eds, *Ursachen und Folgen: Vom deutschen Zusammenbruch 1918 und 1945 bis zur staatlichen Neuordnung Deutschlands in der Gegenwart*; Translation in Jeremy Noakes and Geoffrey Pridham, eds, *Nazism, Volume 1*, pp. 178-180)

30.06.1934 Expelled from the *Preußische Staatsrat* by order of Hermann Göring.

30.06.1934 At 15:00 hours on that date, Hitler issued a decree to the German press removing Röhm from the SA and NSDAP. The next day, the following article, beginning with Hitler's decree, appeared in a special edition of the *Völkischer Beobachter*:

Röhm excluded from the Party and the SA. The Reich press bureau of the NSDAP reports the following decree issued by the *Führer*:

"As of today I have relieved the Chief of Staff Röhm of his position and have ejected him from the Party and the SA [*"Ich habe mit dem heutigen Tage den Stabschef Röhm seiner Stellung enthoben und aus Partei und SA ausgestossen."*]. I am appointing Obergruppenführer Lutze as chief of staff. SA Leaders and SA men who do not obey his orders or who oppose him will be ejected from the SA and the Party and consequently will be arrested and convicted.
Signed: Adolf Hitler
Oberster Führer der Partei und der SA"

******

The Führer to the new Chief of Staff: München, 30. June 1934
The Führer has sent the following letter to SA-Obergruppenführer Lutze:
"To SA-Obergruppenführer Lutze
My Dear SA-Führer Lutze!
The gravest failures on the part of my former chief of staff have compelled me to relieve him of his position. You, my dear Obergruppenführer Lutze, have for many years in good and bad days been an always reliable and ideal SA-Führer. If I am appointing you today as chief of staff it is done with the conviction that you will succeed through your reliable and obedient work in making of my SA the instrument which the nation needs and which I imagine. It is my wish that the SA be built up as a reliable and strong part of the national socialist movement. Full of obedience and blind discipline, they must help to create and form the new German citizens.
Signed: Adolf Hitler"
(Translation of Document 2407-PS, in *Nazi Conspiracy and Aggression, Volume VIII*)

In a statement of 30.06.1934, the Reich Press Office of the NSDAP declared:

For many months now, individual elements have attempted to drive wedges between the SA and the Party and between the SA and the State and to create conflicts. More and more evidence arose in support of the suspicion that these attempts were attributable to a limited clique with a definite purpose.

Chief of Staff Röhm, in whom the Führer had placed a rare trust, did not combat these manifestations but unquestionably promoted them. His known unfortunate predisposition gradually became such an insupportable burden that the Führer of the Movement and Supreme Commander of the SA was driven into an extremely difficult moral dilemma.

Chief of Staff Röhm made contact with General Schleicher without the knowledge of the Führer. In doing so, he made use of the services of an obscure character from Berlin of whom Adolf Hitler most strongly disapproves as well as those of another SA leader. Due to the fact that these negotiations—likewise, of course, without the Führer's knowledge—ultimately involved a foreign power or, respectively, its representatives, an intervention was no longer avoidable, both from the standpoint of the Party and from the standpoint of the State.

Strategically initiated incidents culminated in the fact that the Führer left Westfalen after he had toured labor camps there, flying from Bonn to München at 2:00 a.m. this morning to order that the most seriously incriminated leaders be removed from office and placed under arrest. The Führer proceeded to Wiessee in person with a small escort in order to nip any attempt at resistance in the bud. The act of arresting the men was accompanied by such morally pitiful scenes that every trace of sympathy was necessarily banned. A number of the SA leaders had taken Lustknaben [lust boys] with them. One of them [Edmund Heines] was surprised in a most revolting situation and arrested.

The Führer issued the order to ruthlessly eradicate this plague spot. In the future he is no longer willing to tolerate that millions of decent people are incriminated and compromised by isolated persons with pathological leanings. The Führer issued the order to the Prussian Minister-President Göring to carry out a similar action in Berlin and particularly crack down on the reactionary accomplices to this political conspiracy.

At 12:00 noon, the Führer made a speech to the higher-ranking SA leaders who had convened in Munich, in which he stressed his unshakable alliance with the SA, but at the same time announced his decision to show no mercy from now on in exterminating and destroying undisciplined and disobedient characters and asocial or diseased elements. He pointed out that service in the SA was an honorary service for which tens of thousands of upright SA men had made the most difficult sacrifices. He expected from the leader of each SA division that he prove himself worthy of these sacrifices and be a living example to his organization. He also pointed out that he had defended Chief of Staff Röhm for years against the heaviest attacks but that the most recent development had forced him to place all personal feeling second to the welfare of the Movement and to that of the State, and that above all he would eradicate and nip in the bud any attempt to propagate a new upheaval by ludicrous circles of pretentious characters. (Dr. Max Domarus, ed., *Hitler. Speeches and Proclamations, 1932–1945: The Years 1932–1934*, pp. 472-473)

01.07.1934 According to the account included by Heinz Höhne in *The Order of the Death's Head*, p. 121, three SS officers arrived at Stadelheim Prison at approximately 17:00 hours on that date and demanded to see Röhm in his cell. They were *SS-Brigadeführer* Theodor Eicke (*Kommandant* of Dachau), his adjutant *SS-Sturmbannführer* Michael Lippert, and *SS-Gruppenführer* Heinrich Schmauser (*Führer* of *SS-Gruppe Süd*). They were escorted to Cell 474 where Eicke reportedly confronted Röhm with the words, "You have forfeited your life. The *Führer* gives you one more chance to draw the consequences." He set a loaded revolver on a table in the cell and advised the SA leader that he had ten minutes to use it. The SS officers left the room and waited for the shot. After fifteen minutes of silence, Eicke and Lippert returned to the cell with pistols drawn. Eicke shouted, "*Stabschef*, get ready." The SS officers each fired a shot into Röhm, who collapsed to the floor, mortally wounded and groaning, "My *Führer*, my *Führer*." The cynical Eicke replied, "You should have thought of that earlier; it's too late now." At 18:00 hours, the *coup de grâce* was fired into Röhm's heart by either Eicke or Lippert. A different account of the events was presented in 1949 by Dr. Robert Koch, the former governor of the prison:

… Nobody was allowed to leave the prison that night either. Next morning (Sunday 1 July 1934) two SS men asked at the reception desk to be taken to Röhm. Zink, who was at the entrance, in view of the strict instructions he had been given, refused.

It was about 9.30 a.m. When the two tried to force their way in, Zink alerted the prison governor and the green police, who at once occupied the corridors and prevented any intrusion. The governor ascertained that neither of the SS men had proper authorization. It therefore took hours of telephoning to check their papers; even the Reich Chancellery was rung up. When at least it became clear that they had an order from Hitler, the two murderers had to be taken to Röhm in the new building.

There they handed over a Browning to Röhm, who once again asked to speak to Hitler. They ordered him to shoot himself. If he did not comply, they would be back in ten minutes and kill him…. When the time was up, the two SS men re-entered the cell, and found Röhm standing with his chest bared. Immediately one of them from the door shot him in the throat, and Röhm collapsed on the floor.

Since he was still alive, he was killed with a shot point-blank through the temple. The bullet not only penetrated his skull, but also the ceiling of the cell below…. (Translation from Hans-Adolf Jacobsen and

Werner Jochmann, eds, *Ausgewählte Dokumente zur Geschichte des Nationalsozialismus 1933–1945, Bd. I*, in Jeremy Noakes and Geoffrey Pridham, eds, *Nazism: A History in Documents and Eyewitness Accounts, 1919–1945*, document 124, p. 180)

Eleanor Hancock writes:

Eicke told the prison officials that medical help for Röhm was forbidden. Eicke and Lippert left, taking four SA prisoners with them to Dachau. Prison records showed 6:00 p.m. on July 1 as the time of Röhm's death. His body was put in a coffin after twilight and buried toward 10:00 p.m. in section 1, plot number 24 at the Perlacher Forst cemetery....

On July 10, [*Gauleiter* Adolf] Wagner instructed the Munich police to exhume and cremate the corpses of the SA leaders buried at Perlacher Forst. The ashes were then released to their families with strict instructions as to how and when they could be buried. Röhm's ashes were buried in the same grave as his father on July 21, 1934. Röhm's grave was watched, and those who visited it came under surveillance.

On July 16, 1934, the Amtsgericht München issued a death certificate for Ernst Röhm, giving his place of death as Stadelheimerstrasse 12 in Munich, and describing him as a "single, retired captain," since he had been stripped of his office as Chief of Staff by Hitler on June 30. Röhm died without leaving a will, with an estate of some 41,600 marks. Initially, his entire estate was confiscated by the political police, and then the Oberste SA-Führung....

On February 1, 1935, in its capacity as an inheritance court, the Amtsgericht ruled that Röhm's mother would inherit half the estate, and his siblings one-quarter each. Before this ruling was handed down, however, Emilie Röhm had died from heart trouble, aged seventy-seven, on January 6, 1935. Only one doctor had been willing to treat her. She had rejected the pension Hitler had offered direct dependents of those killed, saying "I will not take money from the murderer of my son." Robert Röhm and his family fell under suspicion, and were subject to surveillance and harassment until 1945. (Hancock, *Ernst Röhm: Hitler's SA Chief of Staff*, pp. 161-163)

In August 1956, Bavarian police arrested Lippert and the former leader of the *Leibstandarte Adolf Hitler*, Josef ("Sepp") Dietrich (who had overseen the execution of SA leaders at Berlin-Lichterfelde), charging them with manslaughter for the killings of June–July 1934 (Lippert being charged specifically for the murder of Röhm). They were soon released on bail, and their trial finally began on 06.04.1957. Lippert claimed he had waited in the corridor while Eicke (killed on the Eastern Front, 26.02.1943) committed the murder on his own. On 14.05.1957, Lippert and Dietrich were sentenced to eighteen months' imprisonment, the president of the court stating that even twelve years after the war, Lippert was "filled with a dangerous and unrepentant fanaticism".

In addition to Röhm, the following senior SA leaders were murdered during the purge:

SA-Obergruppenführer Edmund Heines	Führer of SA-Obergruppe VIII, Breslau	†30.06.1934
SA-Obergruppenführer Fritz Ritter von Kraußer	Leiter of the Führungsamt der OSAF	†01.07.1934
SA-Obergruppenführer August Schneidhuber	Führer of SA-Obergruppe VII, München	†30.06.1934
SA-Gruppenführer Georg von Detten	Leiter of the Politischen Amt der OSAF	†02.07.1934
SA-Gruppenführer Karl Ernst	Führer of SA-Obergruppe III, Berlin	†30.06.1934
SA-Gruppenführer Hans Hayn	Führer of SA-Gruppe Sachsen	†30.06.1934
SA-Gruppenführer Peter von Heydebreck	Führer of SA-Gruppe Pommern	†30.06.1934
SA-Gruppenführer Wilhelm Schmid	Führer of SA-Gruppe Hochland	†01.07.1934
SA-Gruppenführer Konrad Schragmüller	Führer of SA-Gruppe Mitte	†01.07.1934
SA-Brigadeführer Hans Koch	Führer of SA-Gruppe Westmark	†01.07.1934
SA-Brigadeführer Hans Ramshorn	Führer of Gruppenbefehlstellen Oberschlesien	†30.06.1934
SA-Brigadeführer Karl Freiherr von Wechmar	Führer of Gruppenbefehlstellen Niederschlesien	†30.06.1934
SA-Brigadeführer Willi Klemm	Führer of Gruppenstaffel Schlesien	†01.07.1934

Kurt Lüdecke, Röhm's colleague from the earliest years of the Nazi movement, penned the following epitaph for his murdered friend:

Ernst Röhm had met his end in the very prison where he had been incarcerated eleven years earlier for his valiant efforts in support of Hitler in the "Beer Hall Putsch." He was sentenced to death, imperishably branded as traitor, and traduced in his grave as criminal and beast by the man who only a few months before had appointed him Reichsminister in his cabinet and had praised him for his services, thanking destiny for permitting him to number such men as Röhm among his friends and comrades-in-arms.

It is not my wish to make an entire martyr of Röhm. He was admittedly shaping plans which aimed to influence the trend of the Nazi revolution. But compared to others more fortunate, an honest revolutionary who always ranked the idea above the leader, and Germany highest of all. He was incapable of treason. Someday history will affirm that he deserved a better fate. (Lüdecke, *I Knew Hitler*, p. 683)

In an editorial regarding the significance of Röhm's elimination and the purge as a whole, the Berlin-based Prussian-Lithuanian-born American journalist Otto D. Tolischus wrote:

History offers no parallels, but with many qualifications, certain analogies in the French Revolution still present themselves. The victory of Herr Hitler and General Goering on June 30 may be compared with the victory of the Rightist Girondists against the revolutionary and socialistic Jacobins.

On the other hand, it was Hitler and Goering who adopted and adapted Robespierre's famous revolutionary dictum:

"It is with regret that I pronounce the fatal truth: Louis ought to perish rather than a hundred thousand virtuous citizens. Louis must die that the nation may live."

It may strain the imagination to compare Captain Ernst Roehm with Louis XVI, but the two have this much in common, that both fell under the same revolutionary law, except that Roehm did not even have the

	benefit of a mock trial. ("Mass Phase Ended in Nazi Revolution" in *The New York Times*, 15.07.1934)
02.07.1934	Posthumously expelled from the NSDAP.
03.07.1934	Issuance of the *"Gesetz über Maßnahmen der Staatsnotwehr"* (Law Relating to National Emergency Defense Measures), which read:

The Reich Government has enacted the following law, which is hereby promulgated:

The measures taken on 30 June and 1 and 2 July 1934 to suppress attempts at treason and high treason are legal emergency measures in defense of the state.
Berlin, 3. July 1934
The Reich Chancellor: Adolf Hitler
The Reich Minister of the Interior: Frick
The Reich Minister of Justice: Dr. Gürtner
(*Reichsgesetzblatt*, 1934, I, p. 529)

Prior to issuance of the law, a conference of the various Reich Ministers was convened under the chairmanship of Hitler, who outlined his justifications for the purge. He reiterated them in greater detail during a speech to the *Reichstag* on 13 July. The following are excerpts from the minutes of the meeting:

The Reich Chancellor gave the following detailed account of the events which led to the revolt of 30 June and to the measures necessary for their suppression.

For over a year he had been watching the activities of the former Chief of Staff, Röhm, and had hitherto refrained from taking ruthless action only because of the political situation in which Germany was placed. Under Röhm's leadership there had been formed a select clique of SA leaders, which was held together not by loyalty to the Movement but merely by personal ambition and a peculiar tendency. The former Chief of Staff, Röhm, who had repeatedly given him, the Reich Chancellor, his word of honor and for whom he, the Reich Chancellor, had time and again covered up, had betrayed him most grievously. The unfortunate tendency of the former Chief of Staff explained not only why the posts of SA leaders were filled with inferior personnel but also why he [Röhm] had deliberately waged war on the Wehrmacht. This clique, under Röhm's leadership, had attacked him in a slanderous way, because he had seemed to them to be too lenient. Their attacks upon the composition of the Reich Cabinet were in reality directed against the spirit of National Socialism. It would have been an inconceivable disaster for the German people if these men had come to power.

On 30 January 1933, he had deliberately adopted an attitude by which he intended to stretch out a hand to all his fellow-countrymen who were men of good will. The formation and composition of the Cabinet and its unreserved profession of confidence in the Wehrmacht had also been based on this attitude.

The former Chief of Staff, Röhm, had for a whole year consistently been making preparations for a revolution. He had transformed the SA into an instrument which he, the Reich Chancellor, had rejected. It was Röhm's wish that the SA should be turned into a State within the State. He [Hitler] had even quite recently entreated the former Chief of Staff, in a four-hour conversation, 3 to cease his activities. It had all been in vain. Röhm had indeed promised him all he had asked for, but behind his back he had done the exact opposite. Nor had Röhm adhered to the agreement between the Reichswehr and the SA, which it had taken considerable effort to achieve. After his talk with him, the Chancellor, Röhm had taken the SA leaders aside and had told them that the Reich Chancellor had spoken to them in this way because of the international situation but that he really shared Röhm's views. He was accusing the former Chief of Staff of disingenuousness and disloyalty.

The most diverse groups had in the course of time coalesced, amongst them also circles who themselves had not intended a coup d'état, but who had, nevertheless, been interested in a change in present conditions. He had known for a long time of the relations between Röhm and Schleicher, which had been established by the agency of Herr von Alvensleben. It was from this quarter that contacts with France had been made, with the aim of obtaining assurances that France would not make any difficulties for an alternative Government in Germany. Gregor Strasser had also taken a considerable part in this action. Schleicher himself, however, had rejected the idea of forming a new Government or becoming a member thereof.

The former Chief of Staff's tactics had been to represent his action as being, in itself, not directed against Hitler, and he had thus deliberately betrayed the confidence of decent SA men. He had wanted to confront him, the Chancellor, with the choice of either giving him more independence in his capacity of Chief of Staff or of accepting his resignation. This threat of resignation had been nothing but a piece of impertinent blackmail.

When Röhm saw that he was not achieving his object in this way he had ordered a month's leave for the whole of the SA. His plan was to have acts of terrorism committed by special groups during this period in order to create the conviction amongst the people that no Government was possible without the SA. At the same time, he had issued orders to the SA groups to the effect that the SA should be armed in every possible way. The Reichswehr Minister had submitted a document to him, the Reich Chancellor, from which it emerged that this order for the supply of arms had been given. The former Chief of Staff had done this with the idea of being able someday to put up a solid opposition to the Reichswehr. The fact of high treason had thus been completely established.

Röhm and the SA leaders engaged in this plot with him had surrounded themselves with staff guards who were almost exclusively men who had previously served heavy prison sentences.

According to reports received, the action prepared by Röhm was to have started at 4 p.m. on Saturday 30 June. It was necessary to act at once in order to prevent a catastrophe, especially as Röhm's tactics were to be to win over the SA men to his side by telling them that Hitler was no longer behind them.

He, the Chancellor, had thereupon convened a meeting of all the SA leaders at Wiessee, the place where the former Chief of Staff was staying. He had intended to announce personally at this meeting of the leaders that Röhm was under arrest. In the meantime, however, he had been informed that the mobilization of the SA had already been ordered in Berlin for Saturday afternoon. He had therefore decided to take immediate action, the success and details of which were known to the members of the Reich Cabinet.

If certain quarters were to raise objections on legal grounds to the way in which the revolt had been suppressed, he could only reply that it was a case of military mutiny for which there could be no proceedings in the nature of a trial. If mutiny broke out on board ship, it was not only the Captain's right but his duty to suppress this mutiny at once. If he, the Chancellor, had not taken prompt action, fighting between the SA and the police would have broken out in many places in the Reich. This could not be allowed to happen. To make an example of them as he had done was not only a matter of putting down the revolt but also of making it clear to every single one of the leaders and men of the SA that he risked his neck if he in any way conspired against the present regime.

Although the extent of guilt had not been fully established in all cases and he himself had not ordered all the executions under martial law, he assumed full responsibility for the execution of forty-three traitors, since the Reich and possibly the lives of innumerable other people had thus been saved.

He had appointed a new Chief of Staff of the SA whose main task it would be to train and build up a better SA and to bring about better relations between the SA and the Wehrmacht. There was no question of subsequent trials. The example he had made would serve as a salutary lesson for all time. He had firmly established the authority of the Reich Government forever.

He asked the Reich Cabinet to pass the bill he had submitted on measures for the defence of the State in an emergency [*Massnahmen der Staatsnotwehr*]. This bill was not being enacted in order to cover up an infringement of the law but to legalize an action by which the whole nation had been saved from incalculable harm.

The Reichswehr Minister thanked the Chancellor on behalf of the Reich Cabinet for the resolute and courageous action by which he had saved the German people from a civil war. The Chancellor, as became a statesman and a soldier, had acted in a spirit that had called forth from the members of the Reich Government and from the whole German nation a solemn vow of toil, loyalty and devotion at this grave hour... (*Documents on German Foreign Policy 1918–1945, Series C [1933–1937], The Third Reich: First Phase, Volume III, June 14, 1934–March 31, 1935*, pp. 119-122)

On 04.07.1934, the French Ambassador in Berlin, André François-Poncet, met with German Foreign Minister Konstantin Freiherr von Neurath. The following is excerpted from von Neurath's memorandum of the meeting, dated the following day:

M. Poncet ... spoke about the events of 30 June here and complained that, in journalistic circles and amongst the public here, it was openly being said that the foreign Power mentioned in the official announcement was France and that, in particular, he and members of the Embassy were being accused of having conspired with the plotters against the German Government. M. Poncet asked for an official statement by me that this accusation was erroneous. I replied that, firstly, no official quarter had asserted that France was the foreign Power referred to. I was not responsible for rumors amongst journalists or the public....

M. Poncet then told me in detail about his relations with Herr von Schleicher, which he did not deny in any way. He also admitted to accepting, together with Chief of Staff Röhm, an invitation from Herr [Wilhelm] Regendanz [a banker].... No hints regarding the plans of the conspirators, nor any attempts to persuade him or his Government to adopt a friendly attitude in the event of the conspiracy succeeding, had, he could assure me, been made... (*Documents on German Foreign Policy 1918–1945, Series C [1933–1937], The Third Reich: First Phase, Volume III, June 14, 1934–March 31*, pp. 134-135)

François-Poncet's contacts with Röhm were also the subject of a 27.07.1934 memorandum ("François-Poncet's relations with General von Schleicher and with Röhm") Roland Köster, German Ambassador in Paris, to the German Foreign Ministry. The following is an excerpt:

Ambassador Poncet had maintained the greatest reserve towards Röhm, although he was a Reich Minister, by reason of his being head of a formation the legality of which was doubtful under the Versailles Treaty. Röhm had often made it clear to Ambassador Poncet that he would be pleased to enter into relations with him and would like to issue an invitation to him. François-Poncet had let him know that he would neither accept an invitation from him nor issue an invitation to him. He had no wish to be discourteous to Herr Röhm in his capacity of Reich Minister and had, therefore, at the same time, let him know that he would always be pleased to meet him at the houses of others. They had met for the first time on 21 February 1934, on the occasion of a reception given by the Chief of Protocol at his home. The conversation with Röhm had concerned the significance of the SA and the role which its founder gave it in the National Socialist movement. Three months later Herr Regendanz had let Ambassador Poncet know that Röhm wished to see him again. Regendanz had invited him to a meal in order to bring about a meeting between him and Röhm with a few of his colleagues without their being disturbed by the presence of others....

As Regendanz was not suspect, he saw no reason to reject the meeting with Röhm proposed by him, more particularly as Röhm was at this time one of the most important persons in the Reich and a member of the Government, and as there was no sign of any sort that he was in conflict with the Führer. This dinner took place on 24 May 1934; in Ambassador François-Poncet's view it was in no way secret in character, and he had, therefore, not preserved secrecy about it to others. Present at the dinner were Röhm and his three assistants, Herr von Detten, Count Spreti and Herr von Falkenhausen, as well as the host and the Ambassador. After dinner a conversation took place between Röhm, von Detten and François-Poncet, while Count Spreti and von Falkenhausen had a conversation in an adjoining room with Herr Regendanz's adopted son who is himself an SA officer. The conversation with Röhm was of a general nature and concerned German-French relations since the peace treaty. The Ambassador had tried to explain to his questioners the reasoning and the attitude of France. The others made no remarks of any interest. Röhm had looked absent-minded and ill, and mentioned that he had had to have medical treatment for neuritis. M. Léger also assured me here that François-Poncet had not informed the Foreign Ministry here either orally or in writing, officially or privately. Shortly afterwards Regendanz proposed to the French Ambassador another meeting with Röhm and at Röhm's request added that the latter had the feeling that he had not made a good impression on Ambassador François-Poncet. Poncet declined the invitation on the grounds that he was too busy and intended to leave Berlin shortly. François-Poncet had further reported that he had not known that Röhm had attached such great importance to the conversation, and that the latter had intended to refrain from reporting the conversation to the Führer; in any case Röhm had not said anything of the kind to him. Since March of this year Röhm had obviously been attempting to get a footing in Berlin society and in diplomatic circles. He had given big dinners and receptions at which all the Ambassadors and Heads of Missions, with the exception of the French Ambassador, had been present. François-Poncet had refused to follow the example of his colleagues and especially that of the Italian Ambassador, who was most frequently to be seen at Röhm's. In answer to the question which I put to the Secretary General in view of despatch II Fr. 2459 of July 13–15 of this year, as to whether the French Ambassador had ever met Röhm and Schleicher together anywhere, M. Léger informed me that, according to the Ambassador's report which lay before him , such a meeting had never taken place, and neither Schleicher nor Röhm had ever spoken to him of their relations. In view of the contradictory statements on this point, the Secretary General assured me afresh that there could be no misunderstanding and, after he asked François-Poncet for another report, he assured me that Poncet adhered to the above statement. The Secretary General asked me to inform my Government of François-Poncet's reports, and, in so doing, to point out that French officials had not been in touch, either directly or indirectly, with General von Schleicher or Chief of Staff Röhm, and that in their opinion the French Ambassador could in no way be reproached for having such relations with the persons named as would have been incompatible with his position of Ambassador and contrary to the interests of the German Government. (*Documents on German Foreign Policy 1918–1945, Series C [1933–1937], The Third Reich: First Phase, Volume III, June 14, 1934–March 31*, pp. 262-264)

In his memoirs, François-Poncet wrote of his 24.05.1934 dinner with Röhm:

Röhm came, flanked by six or seven youths striking in their smartness and good looks; the SA chief presented them to me as his aides-de-camp. There was nothing secret about the dinner.... The meal was dismal, the conversation insignificant. I found Röhm sleepy and heavy; he woke up only to complain of his health and the rheumatism he expected to nurse at Wiessee. Returning home, I cursed our host for the evening's boredom. But after June 30 he and I were the sole survivors, and he owed his safety only to the fact that he managed to escape to Britain....

In so far as I was concerned, I declared that I would not allow the insinuations of the press to disturb me. If I was suspected of plotting with Röhm, then let this be frankly stated, let the argument be produced and let the proofs of my alleged complicity be established. Naturally no such proof was ever found, let alone published. (François-Poncet, *The Fateful Years. Memoirs of a French Ambassador in Berlin, 1931–1938*, pp. 140-141)

At 19:00 hours on the evening of Sunday, 01.07.1934, Goebbels, having accompanied Hitler on the Bad Wiessee raid of the previous day, delivered the following radio speech:

Volksgenossen and Volksgenosseninnen!
I can still see the Führer standing on the terrace of the Rheinhotel Dreesen in Godesberg at the midnight hour of Friday evening. Down on the open square, the large band of the West German Labor Service has lined up for the last post. The Führer looks earnestly and thoughtfully into the dark night sky that has settled over the wide landscape blurred in harmony after a cleansing thunderstorm, and with a raised hand he greets the enthusiastic cheers of the Rhenish people. As yet, none of the many people down there knows what is imminent. Only a few of those standing on the terrace above have been informed. The Führer has again, as so often in serious and difficult situations, acted according to his old principle of always saying only what needs to be said, to who needs to know and then when he needs to know. For us, he is admirable in this hour. Not even a twitch on the tense face betrays the slightest inner movement. And yet, we few people who stand with him now, as in all difficult hours, know how deeply wounded his soul is, but also how firm he is in his resolve to act with all ruthlessness and to throw down the reactionary rebels who, under the cue of a second revolution, want to break faith with him and the movement and plunge the country into incalculable turmoil.

While the last notes of the Horst Wessel song fade away and the song of the Saar is heard in the distance across the Rhine, grave news comes from Berlin and München. There is no time to lose now. A consultation of two or three minutes and then the Führer's decision is made not to wait until the morning, but to leave immediately by plane for München to root out the nest of conspirators in person. Half an hour later, the heavy, three-engined Junkers aircraft climbs from Hangelar airfield near Bonn into the misty night sky. It is just 2 o'clock in the morning. The Führer sits silently on the foremost seat of the large cabin and stares immovably into the vast darkness. Only now and then is the monotonous whirring of the propellers interrupted by brief questions, information or interjected advice.

At 4am we are in München. The day has already dawned. At the airfield, the Führer receives a detailed report on the situation, and we then proceed immediately to the Bavarian Ministry of the Interior. Elements of the München SA took to the streets in the evening, deceived through false and mendacious proclamations. Their leaders who broke their word and their loyalty are cited immediately. In two sentences of massless indignation and contempt, Adolf Hitler throws all their shame into their faces, which are pale and disfigured with fear and helplessness. Then he personally tears the badges of honor of an SA Führer from the uniform. They will meet their hard but just fate in the afternoon. Now there is no more time to lose.

The Führer is determined to personally visit the nest of conspirators in Wiessee in order to radically and mercilessly smoke it out. In addition to his regular SS escort, his loyal comrades Brückner, Schaub, and Schreck as well as the Reichspressechef of the NSDAP, Dr. Dietrich, and myself are allowed to travel with him.

We now set off at breakneck speed towards Wiessee. There is not a soul to be seen. The streets of the villages are deserted and empty. Around 7 a.m. we arrive in Wiessee. Finding no resistance, we can enter the house and surprise the conspirators' guild while they are still asleep and arrest them immediately. The Führer personally carries out the arrest with unparalleled courage. I will spare myself the task of describing the repulsive and almost nauseating scenes that present themselves before our eyes. A simple SS man summed up our outraged mood in the right words: "I only wish that now the walls would fall down and the whole German people could be witness to this event, to understand how good the Führer is doing to call those responsible to account very harshly and without mercy and to make them pay for their crime against the nation with their death". Shortly after the arrest, a Röhm Stabswache arrives from München. Upright and masculine, the Führer confronts them and gives them the order in one sentence to start the return journey immediately. With a Heil to him, the command is immediately carried out.

Our return journey to München takes place under dramatic circumstances. Sometimes at intervals of only a few minutes we meet the cars of the SA Führer travelling to the conference in Wiessee. The old and loyal comrades-in-arms among them, who have no idea of anything, are briefly oriented, and the guilty traitors involved in the plot are personally arrested by the Führer and handed over to his SS guard.

The reports from the Reich, which are available in München, are quite satisfactory. The whole operation went very smoothly. In Berlin, our party comrade Göring did not hold back. With a firm hand he seized the nest of conspirators and reactionaries there and, true to the orders of his leader, took measures which, though harsh, were necessary to save the Reich from incalculable misfortune. Then the Führer addresses the assembled SA-Führer and political leaders. His speech is a single judgement on the small guild of criminals who have now been arrested, who, in alliance with the Reaktion, wanted to seize power and did not hesitate, regardless of the overall situation and the grave responsibility borne by the Führer, to establish relations with a foreign power in order to speed up the maturing of their wickedly ambitious plans. They have brought the honor and reputation of our SA into disrepute and discredit through a dissolute lifestyle without equal. They have openly mocked the movement's laws of simplicity and personal cleanliness through ostentation and feasting. They were about to bring the whole leadership of the party under suspicion of a shameful and disgusting sexual abnormality. They have tried to thwart the Führer's plans, which are set for the long term, by narrow-minded and malicious short-sightedness, only for the sake of their personal lust for power. On the whole country lay the nightmare pressure of a doom, of which no one but a few insiders felt and sensed its origins, but everyone felt and sensed its almost inevitable coming.

They had believed that the leniency shown to them by the Führer could be mistaken for weakness. This highly treacherous clique had built its project on such a foundation. The Führer then watched in silence for a long time. Time and again, the responsible men, whom he took into his closest confidence, issued warnings in public.

Their warnings were thrown to the wind or even dismissed with arrogant and cynical smiles.

Where kindness did not work, force had to be used. And just as the Führer is great in goodness, he can also be great in harshness. This was now to be shown by this example. And also the ranks of the Reaktion, which were in league here, should now know that the fun is over and the seriousness begins.

The Führer and his loyal followers cannot and will not allow their work of reconstruction, begun at the unspeakable sacrifice of the entire nation, to be jeopardized by the intrigues of unscrupulous political dilettantes. We have spent two months standing in front of the masses of the Nation, evening after evening, to make them understand the difficult situation in which Germany finds itself. We have responded with unparalleled forbearance to the injustice done to us by the reactionary cliques. The nation, with an admirable rationality, has approved our thought processes and has continued to express its confidence in us. Every day we could call to the ballot box without having to fear that even one of the great front of the 12th of November 1933 would be disloyal to the Führer.

This small clique of professional saboteurs, however, did not want to rest. They did not want to understand our indulgence, and now the Führer has called them to order with the force of his severity.

Excessively embittered and outraged by the unscrupulous actions of the conspirators' guild, the SA Führer and political leaders stand before the man who, even in this critical situation, has proved that he is truly a man and that, when the interest of the nation demands it, he can make decisions without regard for the rank and dignity of those whom the law of his action affects, and actually carries them out. His whole life is dedicated to the German people, who love and revere him because he is great and kind, but can also be merciless when it becomes necessary. The Führer is wont to do everything he does in its entirety. As in this case. If at all, then fully. But the eternal obstructionists may learn from this example what it means to tamper with the security of the German state and the sanctity of the National Socialist regime. We are far from taking too tragically the petty grumblings and niggles that are the nature of many people.

But anyone who consciously and systematically rises up against the Führer and his movement should be convinced that he is playing a frivolous game with his head.

On Saturday afternoon, the situation in the whole Reich is already completely calm and settled. The conspirators' nests have been uprooted and now, in his decrees, the Führer informs the nation about the reasons for his actions. The twelve points of his proclamation to the new Stabschef of the SA, our old comrade Viktor Lutze, expose with unsparing harshness the errors and weaknesses that had crept into public life as a result of the irresponsible activities of the Conspirators' Guild.

Now the slate will be wiped clean and the boil, after it had matured, will be lanced. The cleanliness and decency of the party and all its organizations has been restored through the eradication of these questionable elements before the nation. The millions of our party comrades, SS and SA men welcome this cleansing thunderstorm. As if released from a nightmare, the whole nation breathes a sigh of relief. They have once again seen that the Führer is determined to show no mercy when the principle of decency, simplicity and public cleanliness is touched, and that the higher the person it affects, the harsher the punishment.

We who had the good fortune to be with him in these decisive hours have once again learned to admire him without limits for his bravery, for the speed and penetrating power of his resolutions, for his personal grit, for his will to commit himself to his cause and not to remain at the rear when it is necessary to dare to make this commitment. And the nation instinctively felt what we experienced. From the thousands upon thousands of congratulations and expressions of loyalty, the Führer can see that he has once again acted in accordance with the heart of the people.

Once again, let it be said to all: every hand that reaches out to us shall receive our hand of friendship. Every clenched fist raised against the Führer and his regime shall be broken open, if necessary by force. We want the cooperation of the entire nation, rich and poor, high and low; but whoever tries to disturb the Führer and the nation in their work for Germany's future will be beaten to the ground. And pestilence, hotbeds of corruption, disease-symptoms of moral barbarism that show themselves in public life will be burned out, down to the flesh.

The conspirators peddled the opinion in their covens that a second revolution had to be made. Well this second revolution has come, but not the way they thought it would. They had already called upon the foreign press, which is hostile to us, to help them. They had been blathering about crises in the system for weeks. They may now know where strength and authority are to be found in Germany. Never has a government anywhere stood so firm as ours, and never has it been led by a man of such great personal courage as this one. We often said that we saw the voles, but we wanted to let them come out of their holes and hiding places first. They did not understand us and they came out. And now they have met their deserved fate.

However, the nation can only congratulate itself for the events of the 30th of June. The broad masses of our SA comrades, who had nothing to do with the reprehensible activities of the conspiratorial clique, can be assured that a leader of cleanliness and decency now stands at their helm once again. The SS and its leadership deserve the highest praise and the nation's thanks for their exemplary loyalty and discipline, which they have shown again, as so often in difficult situations.

But let it be said to our own nation and to the whole world: There is peace and order in the whole of Germany. Public safety has been restored. Never was the Führer so in control of the situation as in this hour. Speculation about internal strife in Germany is out of place. The nation is getting back to work. The Führer has acted. The fruits of his actions will benefit the whole nation. May a kind fate grant us the grace to complete our great work with Adolf Hitler. He and his followers promise the nation that they will not spare themselves and are determined to work and fight for Germany's life and greatness.

The Reich stands and above us stands the Führer.

("Dr. Goebbels im Rundfunk" in *Rheinsberger Zeitung*, 03.07.1934; Translation: Gary Costello)

19.07.1934   Memorandum from the *Staatssekretär* in the *Reichskanzlei* (Dr. Hans Heinrich Lammers):

1.) To the Reich Main Treasury [*Reichshauptkasse*]
Following the payment order of the 15th of December of last year—Rk 13. 955/33 Ang. 2.

On the 30th of June of this year, Reich Chancellor Adolf Hitler, as Supreme Party and SA Leader, removed the Chief of Staff of the SA of the National Socialist German Workers Party, Ernst Röhm, from his position and expelled him from the Party and SA. Röhm was shot on the 1st of July 1934.

The Reich Main Treasury is instructed to cease payment of the official allowance due to the former Chief of Staff Röhm as Reich Minister without Portfolio on the basis of the Reich Ministers Act, at the end of the month of July 1934. The payment of the second installment of the official allowance for July 1934 will not be made.

2.) To the Berlin Pension Office [*Versorgungsamt V Berlin*]
Further to my letter of the 27th of May this year-Rk.3753-34.

On the 30th of June of this year, Reich Chancellor Adolf Hitler, as Supreme Party and SA Leader, removed the Chief of Staff of the SA of the National Socialist German Workers Party, Ernst Röhm, from his position and expelled him from the Party and SA. Röhm was shot on the 1st of July 1934.

The payment of survivors' benefits is out of the question.

(Bundesarchiv NS 26/328; Translation: Gary Costello)

Published Works:
Die Geschichte eines Hochverräters (memoirs, 1928)
Die nationalsozialistische Revolution und die SA (Speech before the diplomatic corps and foreign press in Berlin on 18.04.1934)

Decorations & Awards:
20.06.1916	*1914 Eisernes Kreuz I. Klasse*
00.00.191_	*1914 Eisernes Kreuz II. Klasse*
08.02.1920	*Kgl. Bayerischer Militär-Verdienstorden IV. Klasse mit der Krone und mit Schwertern*

29.12.1914	*Kgl. Bayerischer Militär-Verdienstorden IV. Klasse mit Schwertern*
00.00.1921	*Schlesisches Bewährungsabzeichen (Schesischer Adlerorden) 1. (?) Stufe*. Per his own account, in *Die Geschichte eines Hochverräters*, awarded for his role in shipping weapons and other military materials to the men of *Freikorps Oberland* who were engaged in fighting Polish insurgents in Oberschlesien.
00.00.1918	*Verwundetenabzeichen, 1918 in Silber*
00.00.1905(?)	*Prinzregent-Luitpold-Medaille in Silber*
00.00.1933	*Goldenes Ehrenzeichen der NSDAP*
00.00.1934	*Ehrenzeichen des 9. November 1923 (Blutorden) (Nr. 2, mit Wirkung vom 09.11.1933)*
00.00.1932	*Frontbann-Abzeichen*
00.00.1931	*Abzeichen des SA-Treffens Braunschweig 1931*
00.00.1934	*Ehrendolch der SA*
00.02.1934	*Ehrenwinkel für alte Kämpfer*
26.05.1934	*Ehrenbürgerrecht der Stadt Stettin*
00.05.1934	*Ehrenbürgerrecht der Stadt Ingolstadt*
24.08.1933	*Ehrenbürgerrecht der Stadt Bad Reichenhall* (revoked 10.07.1947)
20.04.1933	*Ehrenbürgerrecht des Freistaates Bayern.*
00.00.1933	*Ehrenbürgerrecht der Stadt München* (revoked after 1946)
00.00.193_	*Ehrenbürgerrecht der Stadt Magdeburg* (revoked after 1946)

Notes:
* Parents:
  - Father: Guido *Julius* Josef Röhm (*08.07.1847 in Langenzenn near Nürnberg, †03.03.1926), a *Kgl. Bayerisches Eisenbahnoberinspektor* (Royal Bavarian senior railway inspector) and son of the forester Friedrich Wilhelm Bernhard Röhm (*00.00.1824, †00.00.1897) and his wife Meta Johanna, *née* Weigel (*00.00.1827, †00.00.1900). Eleanor Hancock writes:

Julius Röhm was … the second oldest of eight children of an estate forester. As a middle level railway official, he had status to uphold, but little money on which to do so. His family had been officials in Thuringia, and then Franconia, for centuries. He traveled widely as a young man and made his own way in life. He eventually rose into the senior ranks of the railway service, retiring as a railway chief inspector.… In later life, Röhm indicated that he never felt particularly close to his father or brother. He described his father as strict, but conceded that—once Julius Röhm realized that he achieved better without exhortation—he gave him much freedom and allowed full scope to his interests. (Hancock, *Ernst Röhm: Hitler's SA Chief of Staff*, pp. 7-8)

  - Mother: Sofia Emilie Röhm, *née* Baltheiser (*15.12.1857 in Wunsiedel, †06.01.1935 of a heart ailment). Eleanor Hancock continues: "… Röhm was very close to his mother and his sister. Both in public and in private, for Röhm, his mother was 'the best wife and mother in the world. As her youngest, who loves her above all, I can say no more.'" (Hancock, *Ernst Röhm: Hitler's SA Chief of Staff*, p. 8, citing excerpt from Röhm's memoirs)

* Siblings:
  Robert Heinrich Bernhard Röhm
  Offizier-Aspirant
  * 29.04.1879 in Schweinfurt.
  † 31.05.1974.

Promotions:

01.10.1898	*Einjährig-Freiwilliger*
01.07.1899	*überzähliger Gefreiter*
12.03.1915	*etatmäßiger Unteroffizier*
01.09.1918	*Vizefeldwebel der Landwehr II (2. Aufgebot)*
06.09.1918	*Offizier-Aspirant*

Career:

00.00.____–00.00.____	Served as a *nichttechnischer Eisenbahn-Sekretär* (non-technical railways secretary) in Mühlthal.
01.10.1898–30.09.1899	Entered service as an *Einjährig-Freiwilliger*, assigned to *4. Kompanie/1. Kgl. Bayerisches Infanterie-Regiment*.(München).
30.09.1899	Transferred to the reserives.
24.07.1900–17.09.1900	Participated in a training exercise with *I. Bataillon/1. Kgl. Bayerisches Infanterie-Regiment*.
25.07.1902–18.09.1902	Participated in a training exercise with *2. Kompanie/Kgl. Bayerisches Infanterie-Leibregiment*.
03.08.1914	Called up for service with the *Bayerischen Eisenbahn-Bataillon*.
04.08.1914–16.09.1914	Assigned to *bayerischen Eisenbahn-Betriebs-Kompanie Nr. 3*.
17.08.1914–08.09.1914	On official business in the *Kriegsgebiet* (war zone) of Belgium.
28.08.1914–14.09.1914	Hospitalized in the *Vereinslazarett "Dominikanerkloster"* in Düsseldorf due to cellulitis of the left foot.
08.09.1914–17.09.1914	On official business in the *Kriegsgebiet* of northern France.
17.09.1914	After recovery from illness, transferred to *Ersatz-Abteilung/ Bayerischen Eisenbahn-Bataillon*.
18.09.1914–21.06.1915	Attached to *1. Ersatz-Kompanie/Bayerischen Eisenbahn-Ersatz-Bataillon*.
21.06.1915–02.08.1915	Attached to *2. Ersatz-Kompanie/Bayerischen Eisenbahn-Ersatz-Bataillon*.
03.08.1915	Assigned to the *Rekruten-Depot/bayerischen Eisenbahn-Hilfs-Kompanie 5* (Straßburg/Elsass).
01.12.1915–09.12.1915	Again ill with cellulitis.
08.01.1916–27.01.1916	Attached to *1. Ersatz-Kompanie/Bayerischen Eisenbahn-Ersatz-Bataillon*.
28.01.1916–07.07.1916	Attached to *bayerischen Eisenbahn-Betriebs-Kompanie 8* with which he saw combat during the Battle of Verdun (21.02.1916–08.04.1916).
09.04.1916	Participated in an *Ausbildungskurs* (training course) with the *Bayerischen Eisenbahn-Ersatz-Bataillon*.
08.07.1916–15.04.1917	Assigned to *Bayerischen Eisenbahn-Betriebs-Kompanie 7* in Serbia.
16.04.1917–06.11.1918	Assigned to the *Bayerischen Eisenbahn-Betriebs-Abteilung* in Macedonia.
06.11.1918–17.01.1919	Hospitalized in the following facilities:
06.11.1918–12.11.1918	*Reservelazarett Neudeck* (?)
13.11.1918–10.12.1918	*Reservelazarett Zeithain*
11.12.1918–17.01.1919	*Reservelazarett B München*
20.01.1919–20.02.1919	Attached to *2. Demobilmachungs-Kompanie/Bayerischen Eisenbahn-Abteilung*.
20.02.1919	Transferred to *1. Demobilmachungs-Kompanie/Bayerischen Eisenbahn-Abteilung*.

- Meta Eleonore (Lore) Sofie (*14.05.1880 in Schweinfurt), married to the *Hofrat* and *Forstrat* Adolf Lippert (ironically the same surname as one of the men, Michael Lippert, who murdered her brother).
* Religion: Protestant (baptized by the town curate of the Evangelical Church, Röhmeder, on 11.12.1887). Julius Baltheiser, senior district judge in Herieden and a relative of his mother, was his godfather.
* Foreign language proficiency: French, Latin, and Spanish.

Sources:

Anonymous: *The Persecution of the Catholic Church in the Third Reich: Facts and Documents*. Pelican Press, 2003.

Bayerisches Hauptstaatsarchiv, München, Abteilung IV Kriegsarchiv: Excerpts from various *Kriegsranglisten* containing data on the Royal Bavarian Army service of Ernst Röhm.

Bennecke, Dr. phil. Heinrich: *Hitler und die SA*. Günter Olzog Verlag, 1962.

Bundesarchiv, Berlin-Lichterfelde: *Personalunterlagen von SA-Angehörigen: SA-Personalakte* of Ernst Röhm.

Campbell, Bruce: *The SA Generals and the Rise of Nazism*. The University Press of Kentucky, 1998.

François-Poncet, André: *The Fateful Years. Memoirs of a French Ambassador in Berlin, 1931–1938*. Harcourt, Brace and Company, 1949.

Freniere, H. Francis; Karcic, Lucie; & Fandek, Philip (translators): *The Hitler Trial Before the People's Court in Munich* (3 volumes). University Publications of America, 1976.

Gallo, Max: *The Night of the Long Knives*. Harper & Row, 1972.

Gritschneider, Otto: *Der Führer hat sie zum Tode verurteilt*. C. H. Beck, 1993.

Hancock, Eleanor: *Ernst Röhm: Hitler's SA Chief of Staff*. Macmillan, 2008.

—*The Memoirs of Ernst Röhm* (translation of *Die Geschichte eines Hochverräters*). Frontline, 2012.

Hanfstaengl, Ernst Franz Sedgwick ("Putzi"): *Hitler: The Missing Years*. Arcade Publishing, 1957.

Höhne, Heinz: *The Order of the Death's Head*. Martin Secker and Warburg, 1969.

Hoffmann, Heinrich: *Hitler Was My Friend*. Burke, 1955.

Jablonsky, David: *The Nazi Party in Dissolution: Hitler and the Verbotzeit, 1923–1925*. Psychology Press, 1989.

Klering, Hans, et al.: *Weissbuch über die Erschiessungen am 30. Juni 1934*. Verlagsgenossenschaft Ausländischer Arbeiter in der UdSSR, 1935.

Lang, Jochen von: *The Secretary. Martin Bormann: The Man Who Manipulated Hitler*. Random House, 1979.

Lilla, Joachim; Döring, Martin; & Schulz Andreas: *Statisten in Uniform. Die Mitglieder des Reichstags 1933–1945*. Droste Verlag, 2004.

Lüdecke, Kurt G. W.: *I Knew Hitler: The Story of a Nazi Who Escaped the Blood Purge*. Charles Scribner's Sons, 1937.

Miller, Michael D. and Andreas Schulz: *Leaders of the Storm Troops, Volume 1* (1st Edition). Helion & Co., 2015.

Noakes, Jeremy, & Pridham, Geoffrey (eds): *Nazism, 1919–1945. A History in Documents and Eyewitness Accounts. Volume 1: The Nazi Party, State and Society, 1919–1939*. Schocken Books, 1983.

Office of United States Chief Counsel for Prosecution of Axis Criminality: *Nazi Conspiracy and Aggression* (11 volumes). U.S. Government Printing Office, District of Columbia, 1946.

O'Neill, Robert J.: *The German Army and the Nazi Party, 1933–1939*. Cassell and Company, 1966.

Orlow, Dietrich: *History of the Nazi Party: 1933–1945*. University of Pittsburgh Press, 1973.

Rentsch-Roeder, F. Karl (ed.): *Halbmast-Heldenbuch der SA und SA*. Braune Bücher, 1932.

Röhm, Ernst: *Die Geschichte eines Hochverräters* (memoirs). Franz-Eher-Verlag, 1928.
— *Why SA? German Minister Ernst Röhm, Chief of Staff, Addressing the Diplomatic Corps in Berlin on December 7, 1933.* Reprint by "Sons of Liberty," a Louisiana-based American antisemitic organization, 1975.
Schirach, Baldur von: *Die Pioniere des Dritten Reiches.* Zentralstelle fur der deutschen Freiheitskampf, 1933.
Schuman, Frederick L.: *Hitler and the Nazi Dictatorship. A Social Pathology and the Politics of Fascism.* Robert Hale & Company, 1934.
Siemens, Daniel: *Stormtroopers: A New History of Hitler's Brownshirts.* Yale University Press, 2017.
Tamagne, Florence: *A History of Homosexuality: Europe between the Wars.* Algora, 2003.
Toland, John: *Adolf Hitler.* Doubleday, 1976.
U.S. Department of State: *Documents on German Foreign Policy 1918–1945, Series C [1933–1937], The Third Reich: First Phase, Volume III, June 14, 1934–March 31, 1935.* U.S. Government Printing Office, 1959)

Above left: Fahnenjunker Röhm in 1906. (Röhm, *Die Geschichte eines Hochverräters*, 1928)

Above right: Leutnant Röhm in 1908. (Röhm, *Die Geschichte eines Hochverräters*, 1928)

Above: Kompanieführer Röhm (third from left) at the front, c. 1915. (Röhm, *Die Geschichte eines Hochverräters*, 1928)

Left: Hauptmann Röhm, c. 1918.

Inspection of a *Kraftfahrabteilung*, 1919. Left to right: Röhm, Franz Ritter von Epp, unknown, and Hermann Höfle. (Walter Frank, *Franz Ritter von Epp. Der Weg eines deutschen Soldaten*, 1934)

Dortmund, May 1920: Röhm (third from right, in profile) speaks with Franz Ritter von Epp during the departure of Epp's *Schützenbrigade* from the Ruhrgebiet. (Röhm, *Die Geschichte eines Hochverräters*, 1928)

Röhm with the *Kraftwagenstaffel* of Epp's *Schützenbrigade*, September 1920. (Röhm, *Die Geschichte eines Hochverräters*, 1928)

Röhm in 1921, while assigned to the staff of *Infanterie-Fuhrer VII* (Franz Ritter von Epp) in Munchen. (Röhm, *Die Geschichte eines Hochverräters*, 1928)

München, 09.10.1921: *Hauptmann* Röhm, second from left, stands behind Ritter von Epp during a celebration of "*Trauer- und Opfertag.*" (Röhm, *Die Geschichte eines Hochverräters*, 1928)

The staff of *Infanterie-Fuhrer VII* in Munchen, 1922. *Hauptmann* Röhm is second from right in the middle row, next to Ritter von Epp. (Helmut Weitze Militärische Antiquitäten KG)

München, 09.11.1923: *Hauptmann* Röhm (far right) and members of his *Reichskriegsflagge* position themselves outside the *Kriegsministerium* building during the "*Putsch*." Next to Röhm is future *SS-Gruppenführer* Siegfried Seidel-Dittmarsch and, holding the flag, Röhm's future nemesis as *Reichsführer-SS*, Heinrich Himmler.

Ernst Röhm as a defendant in the "*Hitler-Prozeß*," April 1924. Left to right: Robert Wagner, Heinz Pernet, Wilhelm Brückner, and Röhm. (NARA, Heinrich Hoffmann Collection)

München, 01.04.1924: Group photo of defendants in the "*Hitler-Prozeß*" on trial for their part in the "*München-Putsch*" of 09.11.1923. From left to right: Pernet, Dr. Friedrich Weber, Dr. Wilhelm Frick, Hermann Kriebel, Erich Ludendorff, Hitler, Brückner, Röhm, and Wagner.

"*Deutscher Tag*" in Weimar, 15.–17.08.1924, a meeting of the *NS-Freiheitsbewegung Großdeutschland*, with 12,000 people in attendance. Ernst Röhm and Wilhelm Brückner follow the retired *General der Infanterie* Erich Ludendorff. (Roger Bender)

Above: From NARA, Heinrich Hoffmann Collection.

Opposite below: Röhm with fellow *NS-Freiheitspartei* leaders. Right to left: Röhm, Albrecht von Graefe, and Georg Ahlemann.

Above left: Heinrich Hoffmann's studio portrait of Ernst Röhm, *c.* 1924.

Above right: A portrait of Röhm in formal attire, inscribed to a friend, _____ von Proeck on 12.09.1924. (Roger Bender)

Röhm (third from right) participates as a military umpire during Bolivian Army maneuvers in 1930. (Röhm, *Die Geschichte eines Hochverräters*, 1928)

Ernst Röhm in Bolivian Army uniform, *c.* 1930. (Röhm, *Die Geschichte eines Hochverräters*, 1928)

Above left: Röhm in civilian attire, c. 1930.

Above right: 01.01.1931: Röhm announces his appointment as *SA-Stabschef* (*Völkischer Beobachter*, 02.01.1931). For a translation, see the "Career" section, entry of 05.01.1931.

Above left: Ernst Röhm in January or February 1931, soon after his appointment as *SA-Stabschef*. Behind him, from left to right, are Karl Leon Graf Du Moulin-Eckart, Wolf Heinrich Graf von Helldorff, Curt von Ulrich, and Walter Buch.

Above right: Röhm attends an open-air NSDAP function. At right is his adjutant, Rolf Reiner, and behind him, *SS-Oberführer* Georg Aumeier.

Above: Bad Harzburg in the Freistaat Braunschweig, 11.10.1931: Formation convention for the right-wing, anti-democratic alliance known as the "*Harzburger Front.*" Right to left: Josef ("Sepp") Dietrich, Wilhelm Friedrich Loeper, Göring, Walter Buch, Adolf Hühnlein, Franz Ritter von Hörauf, Curt von Ulrich, Karl Leon Graf Du Moulin-Eckart, Röhm, Himmler, and Gerret Korsemann. (NARA, Heinrich Hoffmann Collection)

Left: A postcard photo of Röhm, giving the German equivalent of his Bolivian Army rank (*Oberstleutnant*, or lieutenant colonel). (Hermann-Historica, Auctioneers, München)

Formal portraits of Röhm as SA Chief of Staff.

Above left: From NARA, Heinrich Hoffmann Collection.

Above right: From Hermann-Historica, Auctioneers, München.

Right: An official portrait used on the cover of Heinrich Hoffmann's book, *Das Braune Heer. 100 Bilddokumente: Leben, Kampf und Sieg der SA und SS* (1932). The original caption read:

"In wartime, the bravest of officers; in peacetime, a fanatic revolutionary; never despairing, never humbled, and never complaining; unshakeable in his hope for Germany's future, unchangeable in his loyalty: SA-STABSCHEF HAUPTMANN RÖHM."

Hitler with the senior leaders of his paramilitary forces in 1931. From left to right: Josef ("Sepp") Dietrich, Röhm, Hitler, and Himmler.

The *Flugplatz Tempelhof*, Berlin, 13.06.1932: Röhm with Hitler and Göring.

Above: The *Rheinhotel Dreesen* in Bonn-Rüngsdorf, 1933. Left to right: Unknown, Fritz Dreesen, Röhm, unknown, Hitler, Franz Ritter von Epp, and unknown. (NARA, Heinrich Hoffmann Collection)

Right: An autographed portrait of the *SA-Stabschef*. (Hermann-Historica, Auctioneers, München)

Röhm and Goebbels with Hitler in January 1933.

Röhm and other senior leaders of the SA pose for a group photo at the *Reichsführerschule der SA* in München early in 1933. First row, left to right: Hans Fuchs, Hermann Reschny, Röhm, and Franz Ritter von Hörauf. Second row, right to left: Fritz Vielstich, Wilhelm Freiherr von Schorlemer, Adolf Kob, and Dr. Heinrich Bennecke. (NARA, Heinrich Hoffmann Collection)

Right: Berlin, 06.04.1933: Röhm and Hitler during the "*SA- und SS-Appell*" at the *Sportpalast*. (NARA, Heinrich Hoffmann Collection)

Below: *Flugplatz München-Oberwiesenfeld*, 10.04.1933: Göring prepares to depart for his official visit to Rome. Left to right: Hermann Esser, unknown, Göring, Röhm, August Schneidhuber, and Adolf Wagner. (NARA, Heinrich Hoffmann Collection)

Dortmund, 09.07.1933: Röhm during the "*Aufmarsch der SA-Gruppe Westfalen*" (*SA-Westfalentreffen*).

Röhm participates in the "*Erster Schutzstaffel-Appel der Gruppe Ost*" (First SS Muster of SS Group East) in Berlin-Döberitz, 11.–12.08.1933.

Above left: Röhm and Himmler. (Michal Sika)

Above right: Röhm with Himmler and Daluege. At right is *SA-Gruppenführer* Wilhelm Schmid. (Bundesarchiv Bild 102-14886)

Below: Röhm and *SA-Obergruppenführer* Edmund Heines on horseback. Behind them are Fritz Ritter von Krauß er and, in SS uniform, Rolf Reiner. (NARA, Heinrich Hoffmann Collection)

The "*5. Reichsparteitag der NSDAP*" in Nürnberg (30.08.1933–03.09.1933).

Left: Röhm in conversation with Hitler. (Bundesarchiv_Bild_146-1982-159-21A)

Below: First row, left to right: Röhm, Ritter von Epp, Hess, Hitler, Willy Liebel, Julius Streicher, Dr. Otto Dietrich, Alfred Rosenberg, and Baldur von Schirach. Second row, left to right: Fritz Sauckel, Hanns-Günter von Obernitz, Walter Buch, Hermann Göring, Dr. Robert Ley, Dr. Hans Frank. Third row, left to right: Wilhelm Grimm, Ludwig Siebert, Franz Xaver Schwarz, and in the background, various *Gauleiter* and other Party officials. (NARA, Heinrich Hoffmann Collection)

Berlin, 17.09.1933: The wedding of *SA-Gruppenführer* Karl Ernst (*Führer* of *SA-Gruppe Berlin-Brandenburg*) and his bride, Minna Wolf. Just over ten months later, Karl and Minna Ernst would be taken into SS custody while attempting to embark on their honeymoon, and the thirty-year-old *SA-Führer* was shot by a firing squad at Berlin-Lichterfelde on 30.06.1934.

Above: The happy couple with *Stabschef* Röhm. (Michal Sika)

Right: Röhm and Göring stand behind the newlyweds. Behind Röhm: Paul Körner and Peter Menthe. Behind Göring: *SA-Sturmbannführer* Gerhard Sudheimer (*Adjutant* of *SA-Gruppe Berlin-Brandenburg*) and *SS-Gruppenführer* Rolf Reiner.

The "*Stahlhelm-Reichsführertagung*" at the *Stadthalle* in Hannover, 23.–24.09.1933, during which Hitler declared to his fellow Great War veterans: "Each of us knows one thing: We have become what we are only because of what we went through out there." Over 55,000 people attended the event.

Above left: Left to right: Röhm, Julius Schaub, an unknown *Stahlhelm* leader, Viktor Lutze, Hitler, Franz Seldte, and Adolf Hühnlein.

Above right: Left to right: Röhm, Himmler, and Lutze. (Greg Pearce)

Below: Right to left: Werner von Blomberg, Franz von Stephani, Schaub, Seldte, Dr. Hans Heinrich Lammers, Himmler, unknown Schutzpolizei officer, Hitler, Lutze, and Röhm. (National Digital Archives of Poland)

Röhm with Crown Prince Wilhelm (in *Stahlhelm* uniform) during an SA rally in Breslau, 08.10.1933. Behind the *Stabschef* are *SA-Obergruppenführer* Friedrich-Wilhelm Krüger and Röhm's personal assistant, *SA-Sturmbannführer* Hans Erwin von Spreti-Weilbach. (NARA, Heinrich Hoffmann Collection)

Röhm at his desk.

Left: From NARA, Heinrich Hoffmann Collection.

Below: December 1933. (Michal Sika)

Above left: A formal portrait of the *SA-Stabschef* in full regalia, including his unique *SA-Führer* dagger bearing the symbols of the SA and SS denoting his leadership of both organizations. (Roger Bender)

Above right: Röhm attending a Party rally in Berlin. (NARA, Heinrich Hoffmann Collection)

Right: The *Reichsführerschule der SA*, München: Röhm chats with the schools commander, *SA-Obergruppenführer* Kurt Kühme and other SA officers in 1933. (NARA, Heinrich Hoffmann Collection)

Ernst Röhm and Rudolf Hess, *c.* December 1933. (Michal Sika)

Röhm with von Spreti-Weilbach.

The *Sportpalast*, Berlin, 30.01.1934: Hitler, Röhm attend a concert presented by SS musicians on the first anniversary of the "*Machtergreifung*." (NARA, Heinrich Hoffmann Collection)

Berlin, 31.01.1934: Röhm delivers a memorial address to *SA-Sturmführer* Hans Maikowski on the anniversary of his death. On 30.01.1933, the day of the Nazi seizure of power, Maikowski, as *Führer* of *SA-Sturm 33*, was mortally wounded by gunfire in a largely leftist area of Berlin-Charlottenburg. He died the following day. The *Stabschef* is flanked by Edmund Heines (left) and Karl Ernst (right). (NARA, Heinrich Hoffmann Collection)

Röhm and other senior leaders visit the *Rheinhotel Dreesen* in Bonn-Rüngsdorf.

Above: Röhm speaks with Fritz Dreesen and his wife. Behind him in profile is Heinrich Himmler and, in the foreground, *SS-Gruppenführer* Siegfried Seidel-Dittmarsch (†20.02.1934).

Below: Left to right: *SS-Brigadeführer* Robert Bergmann (Röhm's wartime comrade and later adjutant), Röhm, and Seidel-Dittmarsch.

Left: SA-Stabschef Röhm, wearing the recently introduced *Ehrenwinkel für alte Kämpfer*, speaks with Party leaders in his office. (NARA, Heinrich Hoffmann Collection)

Below: 08.03.1934: The opening of the "*Internationale Automobil- und Motorrad-Ausstellung*" (International Automobile and Motorcycle Exhibition) (08.03.1934–18.03.1934). From right to left: Wilhelm Brückner, Hitler, Göring, Röhm, Dr. Hans Heinrich Lammers, Paul von Eltz-Rübenach, and Adolf Hühnlein. (Roger Bender)

The *Ausstellungspark* on the *Theresienhöhe*, München, 11.03.1934: *Staatsakt* (act of state) to commemorate the first anniversary of the "*Machtübernahme in Bayern*" (Seizure of Power in Bavaria). Right to left in the first row: Dr. Hans Frank, Adolf Wagner, Röhm, Hitler, Franz Ritter von Epp, Hermann Esser, Hans Schemm, and Heinrich Himmler. (Michal Sika)

The Reich Ministry of Popular Enlightenment and Propaganda, Berlin, 18.04.1934: Röhm delivers his speech "*Die nationalsozialistische Revolution und die SA*" to the diplomatic corps and the foreign press.

Right to left: Louis P. Lochner (head of the Berlin bureau of the Associated Press), *General der Artillerie* Werner Freiherr von Fritsch, Walther Funk, Dr. Joseph Goebbels, Röhm, Eric Phipps (British Ambassador to Germany), and Vittorio Cerruti (Italian Ambassador to Germany).

Vittorio Cerruti (left) and Eric Phipps chat with Röhm. In the background, second from left, is Robert Bergmann.

Ernst Röhm and his mother. (NARA, Heinrich Hoffmann Collection)

The Röhm Family plot in München's *Westfriedhof*. (Photo by David Holt, 2013)

Karl Bauer's charcoal portrait of *SA-Stabschef* Röhm.

The eighth edition of Röhm's memoirs (1934).

Viktor Heinrich Lutze
Stabschef der SA (30.06.1934–02.05.1943)

*
†

28.12.1890 in Bevergern/Kreis Tecklenburg/Westfalen.
02.05.1943 (at 22:30 hours) during an operation at the *Städtischen Krankenhaus*, Potsdam, as a result of injuries sustained in an auto accident near Michendorf. This occurred at 14:30 hours on 01.05.1943 as Lutze, his wife, his seventeen-year-old daughter Inge, oldest son Viktor Jr., and chauffeur were returning on the *Reichsautobahn* from Bevergern to Berlin. Viktor Jr. was reportedly driving and fell asleep at the wheel, the car then careening over an embankment, at in excess of 60 mph. Jill Halcomb, referencing a 03.05.1943 press report issued by Dr. Sommer, describes the accident:

Suddenly, from the grass median several pedestrians stepped into the path of Lutze's speeding car. The driver slammed on the brakes, and apparently hit some of the pedestrians. The sudden braking caused the car to change direction and roll with great velocity down the highway for more than fifty meters. Lutze was thrown against the windshield of the car. At first Lutze was not thought to be seriously injured, but late in the day he grew increasingly worse; a blood clot had formed in his lungs. He was rushed into surgery, but Lutze died soon after. His daughter, who had been riding in the rear seat of the car, died earlier, from her severe injuries. (Halcomb, *The SA: A Historical Perspective*, pp. 81-82)

In an official announcement to the press, *SA-Brigadeführer* Thomas Girgensohn (*Amtschef* in the *Adjutantur des Stabschefs der SA*) wrote:

On 1 May 1943, at about 14.30 hours, the Stabschef's car on the Reichsautobahn, in the curve forming the junction of the railroad from Hannover with that from Leipzig, hit the median, raised and cemented at this point, which separates the two carriageways. The vehicle was thrown out of the lane and crashed down the high embankment. The Stabschef, who as usual was in the front on the right side of the driver, was pressed against the windshield in such an unfortunate way that, in addition to serious injuries to the right shoulder, he suffered bruises, several broken ribs and a concussion. The injuries, the serious nature of which became apparent immediately during the first examination after his admission to the hospital [in Potsdam], did not immediately threaten the life of the Stabschef. In the course of Sunday, the Stabschef's condition worsened due to increasing obstruction of breathing and circulation… (*SA-Personalakte Viktor Lutze*)

In his diary entry of 05.05.1943, Goebbels wrote: "… In fact, the car accident was due to improper speed and senseless driving by Lutze's son. Of course, one cannot say that in public; one would completely destroy the son with that…"

Despite intensive treatment by the renowned surgeon Prof. Dr. Ferdinand Sauerbruch, Dr. Otto Nordmann (the Lutze Family's personal physician), and Dr. Werner Forßmann, clinic director of the *städtischen Krankenhaus* in Potsdam (a recipient, in 1956, of the Nobel Prize in Medicine for his work with cardiac catheterization), Lutze died at 20:30 hours due to a collapsed lung. ("*Stabschef* Lutze *schwer verletzt*" in *Bremer Nachrichten*, 03.05.1943; "*Schwerer Kraftwagenunfall des Stabschefs* Lutze" in *Völkischer Beobachter* [Berlin], 03.05.1943) In his diary entry of the 3rd, Goebbels wrote:

In the evening at about 9 o'clock, the Führer calls me to inform me that Lutze died at ½ 9 o'clock in the Municipal Hospital in Potsdam. The death occurred after an operation had become necessary and he could no longer be helped. The Führer asks me to go immediately to Frau Lutze and convey his condolences to her, but above all to encourage the young Viktor Lutze. He was driving the ill-fated car, and the Führer fears that he might harm himself in his initial despair. I immediately drive out with Magda to Paula Lutze. We find her in a very sad but composed mood. We speak courage to her and have some success with it. The details of the funeral are set. Viktor Lutze has left a will that is downright harrowing. From this will again, one can see that he was a one hundred percent upright Nazi. I make another brief visit to the bedside of young Viktor Lutze. He is very shaken and cries like a child. I encourage him; above all, I take him by the Portepée and tell him, on behalf of the Führer, that he must now behave like a man, that a great family tradition rests on him, and that his duty now is to assume its leadership as the only male survivor of the family. He promises me in his hand to act according to the order of the Führer. The will left by Viktor Lutze contains a number of poignant personal details. What he writes about his funeral and about his burial place is moving to tears. Even if his misfortune could have been avoided with some prudence, one says to oneself at this hour: What does that mean! He was one of our oldest and most loyal comrades. Above all, he was very closely connected with me personally. He is the one among the well-known Nazis whom I have known the longest. I still make a midnight trip to Potsdam to the municipal hospital. There he lies laid out in a small hall next to the entrance. His face is very bloated, giving him a completely different appearance. I can hardly recognize him. The moment when I step in front of his bier is very upsetting for me. In this hour I take leave of one of my most faithful and best friends....

The loss of Viktor Lutze is extraordinarily difficult for the old Party comrades. Of course, his position will be filled again; but we will hardly find an equally idealistic and upright fighter of the Führer again....

On the evening of the 3rd, Lutze's long-time deputy and acting successor, SA-Obergruppenführer Max Jüttner delivered a memorial broadcast in honor of his deceased chief. ("*SA. gedachte* Viktor Lutze-*Rundfunksendung für den Stabschef*" in *Der Angriff (Reichsausgabe)*, 05.05.1943; "*Gedenksendung für den Stabschef der SA*", in *Völkischer Beobachter* (Berlin), 05.05.1943)

Arved Fredborg writes:

A scandal which lately did enormous harm to the Party concerned Viktor Lutze.... On their way back to Berlin, with Lutze's son at the wheel, a pedestrian crossed the road and the son twisted the wheel to avoid hitting him. The car skidded and turned over—at 70 m.p.h.... What annoyed people most was not that the pleasure trip was made in an official car, but that, after the accident, geese, hams, eggs and packages of butter were strewn along the highway. (Fredborg, *Behind the Steel Wall: A Swedish Journalist in Berlin, 1941–43*, p. 232)

On the 7th, beginning at noon, Lutze was honored with a state funeral in the *Mosaiksaal der Neuen Reichskanzlei*, with Hitler and Dr. Goebbels giving memorial addresses (see the "Notes" section, below). In his diary entry of 08.05.1943, Goebbels wrote:

At noon the state funeral for Viktor Lutze was held in the new Reichskanzlei. It developed into a huge demonstration of the solidarity of the Party and especially of the SA. Never since the founding of our Reich have such high honors been accorded to a man at his burial as were accorded Viktor Lutze. The ceremony itself was a very dignified one. My memorial address created a deep impression. The Führer himself then took the floor and in a brief tribute honored Lutze. He concluded by conferring upon him the highest category of the German Order. Thereby an honor was accorded Lutze and the SA that far exceeds the customary. But I am glad Viktor Lutze received it. He was such a decent and fine fellow that this decoration at least had to be awarded to him posthumously. I escorted Paula Lutze and the other members of the family out of the Mosaic Hall. Outside, in the Wilhelmstraße, a very impressive funeral parade was held. (Louis P. Lochner, ed., *The Goebbels Diaries 1942–1943*)

On 07.–08.05.1943, a motorized train of *SA-Standarte "Feldherrnhalle"* and funeral cortege led by *SA-Oberführer* Hermann Rennecker conveyed the late *SA-Stabschef*'s remains from Berlin to his hometown of Bevergern. Along the way, the train stopped in Magdeburg, Helmstedt, Braunschweig, and Hannover; in the last city, at 11:00 hours on 08.05.1943, a memorial hour was held with *Gauleiter* Hartmann Lauterbacher and *SA-Brigadeführer* Karl Körner as speakers. On the 9th, he was buried in Bevergern, with memorial addresses delivered by *SA-Obergruppenführer* Jüttner and *Gauleiter* Dr. Alfred Meyer. In June 1943, the Reich Treasurer of the NSDAP, Franz Xaver Schwarz, added Lutze's name to the "*Totenliste der NSDAP*" (List of the Dead of the NSDAP) "*wegen seiner hervorragenden Verdienste um die Bewegung*" ("because of his outstanding services to the movement").

In August 1943, it was determined that the late *Stabschef* held assets, unreported to the tax authorities, in the amount of 396.000 RM for which he had not paid taxes for years.

In his diary entry of 09.05.1943, Goebbels wrote that according to criticism arising in Party circles, *Frau* Paula Lutze "had not exactly behaved nobly in the accident.... Nevertheless, nothing of this should be made public, if only for the sake of the memory of our deceased chief of staff." When the widow refused to leave Lutze's official villa, despite being offered several large apartments, Goebbels wrote, on 21.08.1943: "In any case, Paula Lutze has forfeited all sympathy with the *Führer* by her behavior." Further critical remarks were made by *SS-Obergruppenführer* Gottlob Berger (*Chef, SS-Hauptamt*), who wrote to *Reichsführer-SS* Himmler on 24.06.1943: "According to consistent reports, both Frau Lutze and the young Lutze in Norway have spoken very sharply and spitefully about the SS in particular. It cannot be assumed that a change in the political attitude of the family has occurred in the meantime." (Eckhard Steinmetz, *"Nordmark voran". Beiträge zur Geschichte der SA* [unpublished manuscript])

NSDAP-Nr.: 84 (Joined 21.02.1922 with a different number; Party banned, 09.11.1923–16.02.1925; Unofficially reenrolled 25.02.1925; Officially reentered the Party, 22.03.1926, and later granted the very low membership number of 84 *"in Anerkennung seiner Verdienste"* [in recognition of his meritorious service])

Promotions:

11.04.1907	*Postgehilfe (Anwärter für die gehobene Postbeamtenlaufbahn)*
28.12.1912	*Postassistant*
01.10.1912	*Einjährig-Freiwilliger*
00.00.191_	*Unteroffizier*
[12.04.1916]	*Vizefeldwebel d. R.*
19.01.1917	*Leutnant d. R.* (*"durch Allerhöchster Kabinettsorder"* – by most high cabinet order)
00.08.1919	*Charakter als Oberleutnant d. R.*
00.00.1919	*Postsekretär*
00.00.1923	*SA-Mann*
00.00.1925–00.00.1925	*Stellvertretender Gauleiter der NSDAP*
00.07.1925–26.09.1925	*Gauleiter der NSDAP*
27.09.1925	*Gau-SA-Führer*
00.06.1926–00.00.1927(?)	*Stellvertretender Gauleiter der NSDAP*
01.03.1928	*SA-Oberführer*
02.04.1931	*SA-Gruppenführer* (*Der Oberste SA-Führer, Führerbefehl Nr. 4, 14.10.1931*). Reinstated at that rank, 01.07.1932, when the government ban on the SA was lifted).
01.01.1933	*SA-Obergruppenführer* (*Der Oberster SA-Führer, Führerbefehl Nr. 10* [*Neujahrs-Befehl*], 15.12.1932). Formally granted this rank by Adolf Hitler, 04.01.1933.
15.02.1933–25.03.1933	*Polizeipräsident*
25.03.1933–29.05.1933	*Stellvertretender Oberpräsident*
29.05.1933–28.03.1941	*Oberpräsident*
30.06.1934–02.05.1943	*Stabschef der SA*

20.07.1934–02.05.1943	*Reichsleiter der NSDAP*
30.01.1938	*DRK-Generalhauptführer*

CAREER:

00.00.1897–c. 1901	*Volksschule* in Bevergern.
c. 1901–00.00.190_	*Rektoratsschule* in Ibbenbüren.
00.00.190_–00.03.1907	*Gymnasium Dionysianum* in Rheine (received *Einjährigen-Zeugnis*, authorizing *einjährig-freiwilligen Militärdienst* [one-year voluntary military service]).
11.04.1907–30.09.1912	Entered the *Postdienst* as a *Postgehilfe* (postal assistant). Initially underwent practical training with the *Reichspost* in Rheine, assigned as a *Wochenendfahrer* (weekend driver). He then underwent training with the *Oberpostdirektion* in Münster as an *Anwärter für die gehobene Beamtenlaufbahn* (civil service candidate).
01.10.1912–30.09.1913	Military service as an *Einjährig-Freiwilliger* with *Infanterie-Regiment "Graf Bülow von Dennewitz" (6. Westfälisches) Nr. 55* (Höxter).
01.10.1913–02.08.1914	Employed as a *Postbeamter* (postal official).
03.08.1914–31.03.1919	War service, assigned as *Zugführer*, then *Kompanieführer* in *6. Kompanie/Infanterie-Regiment 369* and *Reserve-Infanterie-Regiment 15*; final assignment as *Adjutant* of *Ersatz-Bataillon/Reserve-Infanterie-Regiment 15* in Unna. He participated in combat near Mondsee (01.10.1914–25.04.1915) and in trench fighting near Flirey (31.01.1916–12.03.1916). Lightly wounded on 12.04.1916 while serving with *6. Kompanie/Infanterie-Regiment 369*, he was wounded a further three times by war's end (including the loss of his left eye to shrapnel).
00.00.1919–00.00.1921	Moved from Unna to Elberfeld.
30.03.1919	Discharged from military service.
01.04.1919–31.12.1922	*Postsekretär* at the *Hauptpostamt* (main post office) in Elberfeld.
00.00.1921–00.00.1925	Operator of a small metal foundry in Elberfeld (closed due to insolvency, 00.00.1925).
Autumn 1921–00.00.192_	*Stellvertretender Vorsitzender* of the *Ortsgruppe Elberfeld* of the *Jungdeutschen Orden* (*Jungdo*, Young German Order).
21.02.1922	Joined the NSDAP/*Ortsgruppe Elberfeld*. He did so against the wishes of his father. It was here that he made the acquaintance of the later *Gauleiter* Dr. Joseph Goebbels, Karl Kaufmann, and Erich Koch.
00.00.192_–00.00.1922(?)	Member of the *Deutschvölkischen Schutz- und Trutzbund* in Elberfeld (under the chairmanship of future *Gauleiter* Karl Kaufmann).
00.00.1923–00.00.192_	*Geschäftsführer* (business manager) of the firm *Schwelmer Messingwerk Albert Klein GmbH*, then worked as a salesman in Elberfeld and later Hannover.
00.00.1923–00.00.192_	Founder and *Führer* of *Kameradschaft Schill* which engaged in acts of sabotage against the French occupation of the Ruhrgebiet. Among its members were the *"Märtyrer der Bewegung"* (Martyr of the Movement) Albert Leo Schlageter (*12.08.1894 in Schönau im

	Schwarzwald, †26.05.1923 on the Golzheimer Heide/Düsseldorf, shot by a French firing squad) and Karl Kaufmann. In Elberfeld on 27.05.1923, Lutze participated as a pallbearer in Schlageter's funeral. The other pallbearers were Erich Koch, Karl Kaufmann, Hans Hayn, and two SA leaders, Jürgens and Hugenell.
00.00.1923	Joined the SA as an *SA-Mann*.
00.00.1923–00.00.1923	Actively participated in underground resistance and sabotage against to the French occupation of the Ruhrgebiet as a member of the *Gruppe Hauenstein* (led by Heinz Oskar Hauenstein).
25.02.1925	Unofficially reenrolled in the NSDAP/*Ortsgruppe Elberfeld*.
00.03.1925	Appointed as one of ten members of the *Gauvorstand der Gau Rheinland-Nord der NSDAP*.
00.00.1925–00.00.1925	*Stellvertretender Gauleiter* of *Gau Rheinland-Nord der NSDAP* (appointed by *Gauleiter* Axel Ripke).
00.07.1925–26.09.1925	*Gauleiter* of *Gau Rheinland-Nord der NSDAP* (jointly, as *SA-Führer*, with Dr. Joseph Goebbels and Paul Schmitz). In his diary entry of 31.08.1925, Goebbels wrote: "Lutze, our *S.A. Führer*, has become my friend. A splendid fellow."
27.09.1925	Participated in a meeting, held in Düsseldorf, of 200 representatives of NSDAP *Ortsgruppen* in the Ruhrgebiet. During this event, Karl Kaufmann was elected as successor to Axel Ripke as *Gauleiter* of *Gau Rheinland-Nord* and Lutze was appointed as *Gau-SA-Führer Ruhr*.
06.03.1926	Participated in the *"NSDAP-Parteitag"* in Essen, attended by 4,000 people, during which the *Großgau Ruhr der NSDAP* was established and placed under the leadership of Karl Kaufmann.
00.03.1926	Together with Kaufmann and Goebbels, met with Hitler in München.
22.03.1926	Officially reenrolled in the NSDAP/*Ortsgruppe Elberfeld*.
27.09.1925–01.03.1928	*Gau-SA-Führer Ruhr*.
06.06.1926–30.09.1928	*Stellvertretender Gauleiter* of *Großgau Ruhr der NSDAP*. Succeeded by Erich Koch.
03.07.1926–04.07.1926	Participated in the *"2. Reichsparteitag der NSDAP"* in Weimar as part of a delegation from the Ruhr consisting of Dr. Joseph Goebbels, Karl Kaufmann, Erich Koch, and Helmuth Elbrechter.
26.11.1926	Participated in the *"Treffen der NSDAP-Ortsgruppenführer des Ruhrgebiets"* at the *Gasthaus Märker* in Hattingen. Also in attendance were Hitler, Goebbels, and Wilhelm Schepmann.
06.01.1927	Elected by the *Ortsgruppe Elberfeld der NSDAP* as *SA-Führer für Elberfeld*.
00.00.1927	Appointed as *Gausturmführer Ruhr*.
19.08.1927–21.08.1927	Participated in the *"3. Reichsparteitag der NSDAP"* in Nürnberg.
01.03.1928–06.10.1930	*"Selbständiger SA-Oberführer Ruhr"* (Wuppertal-Elberfeld)
01.03.1928–00.10.1930	*SA-Oberführer Ruhr* (Wuppertal-Elberfeld).
00.06.1928	In his internal party power struggle with *Gauleiter* Karl Kaufmann, the Elberfeld *Bezirksleiter* Erich Koch accused Lutze of embezzling Party funds. At the same time, he accused Kaufmann, Lutze and the Essen *Bezirksleiter* Josef Terboven of standing together only because they had each other in the palms of their hands through

	"women and money stories." Lutze and Terboven then applied to the *Reichs-Uschla* of the NSDAP for Koch's expulsion from the Party. Finally, Walter Buch, the chairman of the *Reichs-Uschla*, had to come to Elberfeld to investigate the case on the spot. Since he determined a certain justification of Koch's accusations, he gave Kaufmann leave for the further course of the investigation. Lutze and Terboven, however, continued the fight against Koch, during the course of which they soon descended to the level of personal insults. This brought the political activities of the NSDAP in the *Gau* to an almost complete standstill. Under pressure from Lutze and Terboven, Josef Wagner, who in the meantime had been appointed provisional Gauleiter, expelled Koch on 10.07.1928, however this was not recognized by the *Reichsleitung der NSDAP* in München. The conflict was finally resolved by Koch's reassignment to the post of *Gauleiter* in Gau Ostpreußen on 03.09.1928.
08.02.1929	Appointed to the *Stab der Obersten SA-Führung* during a conference involving Hitler and senior *SA* leaders (all of whom were likewise appointed to the *Stab OSAF*).
01.08.1929–04.08.1929	Participated in the "*4. Reichsparteitag der NSDAP*" in Nürnberg.
27.07.1930	Nominated as an NSDAP candidate for the *Reichstag* elections of 14.09.1930
14.09.1930–04.06.1932	Member of the (5.) *Deutschen Reichstag* (*Wahlkreis 23, Düsseldorf-West*; after 31.07.1932, *Wahlkreis 16, Südhannover-Braunschweig*; after 29.03.1936, *Wahlkreis 7, Breslau*).
07.10.1930	Transferred to Hannover where, despite the loss of his left he, he obtained a pilot's license.
07.10.1930–02.04.1931	*Oberster SA-Führer Nord* (Hannover). Successor to *Major a. D.* Karl Dincklage, who died in Davos on the same day he was appointed, having "had to resign from the SAF [*SA-Führung*] for health reasons" a few days earlier. Until Lutze took up his duties, Dincklage's adjutant, Gerret Korsemann (who also continued to serve Lutze in that capacity), had managed the affairs of the *Osaf-Nord*. (Communication from the *Gauführung des Gaues Rheinland der NSDAP* dated 07.10.1930 in Bundesarchiv R 1501/113123).
20.02.1931	Appointed by *SA-Stabschef* Röhm as the future *Führer* of *SA-Gruppe Nord*, leading all SA units in the *Gaue Schleswig-Holstein, Hamburg, Mecklenburg, Hannover-Ost*, and *Hannover-Süd*. (*Verfügung des Stabschefs der SA v. 20. Februar 1931* "Betr.: Neueinteilung der Gruppen").
02.04.1931–13.04.1932	*Führer* of *SA-Gruppe Nord* (Hannover) (m.d.F.b. until 13.10.1931, then permanent from 14.10.1931). (*Der Oberste SA-Führer, Verfügung v. 31.03.1931* – Ia No. 1321/31; *Der Oberste SA-Führer, Verfügung v. 15.04.1931* – Ia No. 1612//32; *Der Oberste SA-Führer, Führerbefehl Nr. 4, 14.10.1931*)
17.10.1931–18.10.1931	Presided over the "*SA-Aufmarsch in Braunschweig*" as "*Organisator und Aufmarschleiter*" (organizer and marching leader). The event, attended by over 100,000 men, had as its primary purpose the demonstration of loyalty by members of the SA and SS.

07.12.1931–18.12.1931	Participated in the *"7. Lehrgang"* at the *Reichsführerschule der SA* in München. This was the *"mündliche[r] Lehrgang der Reichspropaganda-Abteilung II in den Räumen der Reichsführerschule"* (Public speaking course of the *"Reichspropaganda-Abteilung II* in the rooms of the *Reichsführererschule"*, under the direction of future *SA-Obergruppenführer* and *Staatssekretär in the Reichsfinanzministerium*, Fritz Reinhardt, who headed the *Rednerschule der NSDAP* [School for Orators of the NSDAP] in Herrsching am Ammersee).
01.02.1932–13.04.1932	*Führer* (m.d.F.b.) of the newly established *SA-Gruppe Nordmark-Hamburg*, formed from the *Untergruppen Nordmark* and *Hamburg*. Succeeded by Heinrich Schoene. The new *Gruppe* was established via the following order by *SA-Stabschef* Röhm:

Subject: Division of the S.A. The present Gruppe Nord shall be divided into two Gruppen effective 1 February 1932: Gruppe Nord, consisting of the Untergruppen Hannover-Ost, Hannover-Süd, and Weser-Ems, Gruppe Nordmark-Hamburg, consisting of the Untergruppen Nordmark and Hamburg. Gruppenführer Lutze is appointed Führer of Gruppe Nord and at the same time charged with the leadership of Gruppe Nordmark-Hamburg until further notice.... Oberführer Jahn is appointed Stabsführer of Gruppe Nordmark-Hamburg.... The Chief of Staff: gez. Röhm (*Der Oberste SA-Führer I/IIa No. 212/32, 25 January 1931* [sic, 1932]).

13.04.1932–14.06.1932	Official ban on the SA and SS throughout the Reich.
01.07.1932–14.09.1932	*Inspekteur Nord der Obersten SA-Führung (SA-Gruppen Nordmark, Nordsee, Niedersachsen,* and *Mitte)* in Hannover (*Der Oberste SA-Führer, Führerbefehl Nr. 1,* 01.07.1932, p. 2).
31.07.1932–12.09.1932	Member of the *(6.) Deutschen Reichstag (Wahlkreis 16, Südhannover-Braunschweig)*. Already on 07.07.1932, just four weeks before the *Reichstag* election on the 31st, Lutze had committed himself in writing, "that even in the event of possible departure from the National Socialist German Workers' Party, I will not join any other party as a deputy and also not declare myself factionless, but in such a case my mandate at the request of the Party leadership resign." (*PK-Akte Viktor Lutze*)
15.09.1932–30.06.1933	*Führer* of *SA-Obergruppe II (SA-Gruppen Niedersachsen, Westfalen, Niederrhein,* and *Nordsee)* in Hannover. (*Der Oberste SA-Führer, Führerbefehl Nr. II,* 09.09.1932, p. 4)
08.10.1932–16.02.1933	*Führer* (m.d.F.b.) of *SA-Gruppe Nordsee* (Bremen). (*Der Oberste SA-Führer, Führerbefehl Nr. 10 (Neujahrs-Befehl),* 15.12.1932, p. 2)
06.11.1932–01.02.1933	Member of the *(7.) Deutschen Reichstag (Wahlkreis 16, Südhannover-Braunschweig)*.
15.02.1933	Appointed as *Polizeipräsident* of Hannover.
17.02.1933–25.03.1933	*Polizeipräsident* of Hannover. Officially commenced the duties of the post and assumed the post on 17.02.1933. Succeeded *Oberregierungsrat* Johannes Habben. On 20.02.1933, per decree of the Prussian Ministry of Interior, officially entered into office as *Polizeipräsident* of Hannover with effect from 17.02.1933.

	On 24.02.1933, granted *Besoldungs-Dienstalter* (BDA, salary seniority) effective from 17.02.1933. On 25.03.1933, by decision of the *Preußische Staatsministerium* (*Kommissare des Reiches*), immediately transferred to *einstweiligen Ruhestand* (temporary retirement), with Habben again assuming the post.
01.03.1933	Entered active service with the *Deutsches Rotes Kreuz* (DRK, German Red Cross). (*Dienstaltersliste des Deutschen Roten Kreuzes 1939*, p. 371)
05.03.1933–14.10.1933	Member of the *(8.) Deutschen Reichstag* (*Wahlkreis 16, Südhannover-Braunschweig*).
25.03.1933–28.03.1941	*Oberpräsident* of *Provinz Hannover* ("*vertretungsweise mit der Verwaltung der Stelle der Provinz Hannover in Hannover beauftragt*", temporarily charged with administration of the office until 29.05.1933, then officially assigned to the post). On 01.06.1933, he was permanently assigned with effect from 16.05.1933, succeeding Friedrich Carl Ludwig von Velsen.

After formal assumption of the office, he was additionally assigned to the following posts:

- *Vorsitzender* of the *Spruchkammer für Siedlung und Auseinandersetzung der Provinz Hannover* (Arbitration board for settlement and argument in the Province of Hannover).
- *Leiter* of the *Hannoverschen landwirtschaftlichen Berufsgenossenschaft* (Agricultural Professional Association of Hannover).
- *Vorsitzender* of the *Hannoverschen Provinzial-Beratungsstelle für Kriegerehrungen* (Provincial Advisory Office for War Honors).
- *Chef* of the *Wasserstraßendirektion* (directorate for canals) in Hannover.
- *Leiter* of the *Vermögensverwaltung des Herzogs von Cumberland* (Administration Office for the Assets of the Duke of Cumberland).
- *Vorsitzender des Aufsichtsrates* of *Hannoverschen Siedlungsgesellschaft mbH*, Hannover.
- *Staatlicher Kommissar der Technische Hochschule und der Tierärztlichen Hochschule in Hannover* (Government Commissioner of the Technical University and Veterinary College in Hannover).

	Succeeded by *Gauleiter* Hartmann Lauterbacher. On 01.04.1941, Reich Interior Minister Dr. Frick ceremonially accepted Lutze's resignation in Hannover. ("Acht Jahre Oberpräsident" in *Völkischer Beobachter*, 02.04.1941)
00.00.1933	Appointed as *Ehrenvorsitzender* (honorary chairman) of the *Kunstverein Hannover* (artists' association of Hannover).
12.05.1933	Appointed to the following posts by *SA-Stabschef* Röhm:

- *Sonderkommissar des Obersten SA-Führers beim Oberpräsident der Provinz Hannover*
- *Sonderkommissar des Obersten SA-Führers für den Freistaat Oldenburg.*
- *Sonderkommissar des Obersten SA-Führers für den Freistaat Braunschweig.*

	- *Sonderkommissar des Obersten SA-Führers für die Freie und Hansestadt Bremen.* (*Der Oberste SA-Führer, Verfügung v. 12.5.33 – I Nr. 1173/33*) (BArch NS 23/515)
01.07.1933–30.06.1934	*Führer* of *SA-Obergruppe VI*, comprised of *SA-Gruppen Niedersachsen, Nordsee, Niederrhein,* and *Westfalen*) (HQ: Hannover). The *SA-Gruppen Niederrhein* and *Westfalen* were transferred to *SA-Obergruppe X* in May 1934. (*Der Oberste SA-Führer, Führerbefehl Nr. 15*, 01.07.1933, p. 4)
07.07.1933–09.07.1933	Participated in the *"Gau-Parteitages 1933 des Gaues Westfalen-Süd der NSDAP"* and the *"Westfalen-Treffens der SA"* in Dortmund.
30.08.1933–03.09.1933	Participated in the *"5. Reichsparteitag der NSDAP"* in Nürnberg.
14.09.1933–02.05.1943	*Preußischer Staatsrat.*
15.09.1933	After attending the funeral of eight SA men killed in a traffic accident near Solingen, Lutze's own car was struck broadside by another vehicle and completely smashed. Lutze and his companions survived with only minor injuries. ("Kraftwagenunfall des Oberpräsidenten von Hannover", in *Vossische Zeitung* [evening edition], 15.09.1933)
23.09.1933–24.09.1933	Participated, together with Hitler, Rohm, Himmler, and Franz Seldte, in the *"Stahlhelm-Reichsführertagung"* in Hannover.
00.00.1933–01.04.1941	*Präsident der Provinzialrat* (President of the Provincial Council) for *Provinz Hannover.*
12.11.1933–29.03.1936	Member of the *(9.) Deutschen Reichstag* (*Wahlkreis 16, Südhannover-Braunschweig*).
20.01.1934–23.01.1934	Participated in the *"SA-Führertagung"* in Friedrichsroda and Berlin.
28.02.1934	Following a joint event of high representatives of the *Reichswehr*, SA, and SS at the *Reichswehrministerium*, Berlin on the occasion of the 101st birthday of *Generalfeldmarschall* Alfred von Schlieffen (1833–1913). *SA-Stabschef* Röhm, still dreaming of a "National Revolution," addressed the SA leaders present, including Lutze, and gave free rein to his anger and disappointment over the "betrayal" by his close friend Hitler: "Hitler is disloyal and must at least go on leave," the *Stabschef* said, adding "If not with, then we will do the job without Hitler." (Heinz Höhne, *Mordsache Röhm*, p. 205, fn)
00.03.1934	At the beginning of the month, spoke to Hitler's deputy, Rudolf Hess, informing the deputy *Führer* of Röhm's outrageous speeches against Hitler. Hess was uncertain of what to do with the information, and Lutze then traveled to Berchtesgaden to inform Hitler directly, also reporting on the bad morale then prevailing in the SA.
22.06.1934	Meeting with Hitler in Berlin, during which the *Führer* informed him of the planned removal of Röhm. In his diary, Lutze later wrote:

… At first, the Führer only thought of deposing Röhm. He told me so himself on 22 June 1934. On that day, the Führer called me in Hannover. He pulled me out of a meeting of Regierungspräsidenten, ordered me to come to Berlin immediately, and sent me his own plane for this purpose. When I arrived in Berlin, the Führer received me immediately, went with me to his study, obliged me with a handshake and by oath to remain silent until the whole matter was settled, and then went into the actual matter. To questions as to whether I had taken part in meetings with Röhm or with men around Röhm, I had to dutifully answer "No". To further questions whether I knew or had heard that such meetings had taken place, I also had to answer "No". In answer to my questions as to what had been discussed, the Führer told me that several such meetings had taken place with various Ober- and Gruppenführer and that the following had been explained and discussed: "The Reichswehr is reactionary, does not stand behind the Führer, is trying to smash National Socialism, to falsify it or at least to water it down, to smash and eliminate the bearer of the National Socialist idea, the SA- the other organizations do not recognize the situation or are already in tow. For this purpose, the Führer would possibly have to be brought into the hands of the Reichswehr (captured), in order to then carry out the action with the Führer's name. Then the opponent of the Reichswehr would be finished, and it would then have a completely free hand. That would be the thought processes and the intentions of the Reichswehr. The Führer himself would know this, but could do nothing outwardly himself, and now the SA would have to free the Führer again, so that National Socialism would become free again and could be carried out further. Therefore, the SA was to be fully armed and had to be ready." I could only confirm to the Führer once again that I knew nothing of all this and could not believe it at all. The Führer said that he had known from the beginning that I would not be called in for such things, but it was a fact that he had these and quite other messages from the Gestapo. From now on I was not to obey any more orders from München, but only his own. That in itself was the end of the conversation… (*Frankfurter Rundschau*, May 14, 1957) (Heinz Höhne, in *Mordsache Röhm*, p. 239, incorrectly gives the date of the meeting as 19.06.1934)

28.06.1934 — Accompanied Hitler to Essen for the wedding of the Essen *Gauleiter* Josef Terboven. During the wedding celebration, Hitler was informed by *Reichsführer-SS* Himmler about alleged plans for a *Putsch* by Röhm. Hitler immediately retreated with his closest associates, including Göring and Lutze, to Essen's *Kaiserhof* Hotel, and ordered sharp countermeasures: "I have had enough. I will make an example." (Höhne, *Mordsache Röhm*, p. 256)

30.06.1934 — Shortly after 06:30 hours, accompanied Hitler and his entourage (including Goebbels), as well as a raiding party of selected SS men and police officers, during the storming of the *Pension Hanselbauer* at Bad Wiessee. Numerous senior SA leaders were sleeping there, having been called by Hitler himself to a special meeting. Hitler had Röhm and most of the other SA leaders present arrested. According to recollections recorded by Lutze in his diary, Hitler called the *Stabschef* a traitor and declared "Röhm, you are under arrest!" (*"Röhm, du bist verhaftet!"*). Following the discovery of

SA-Obergruppenführer Heines sharing his bed with an eighteen-year-old *SA-Obertruppführer*, Heines pleaded "Lutze, I haven't done anything, help me!", to which Lutze replied that Heines "shouldn't act like a whiner and [should] be quiet." (Excerpt from Lutze's diary, quoted in *Frankfurter Rundschau*, 14.05.1957, part of a series of articles, "'Hitler: Ich warte nicht bis 11.00 Uhr…' Röhms Nachfolger, der SA-Stabschef Lutze, schildert die Ereignisse des 30. Juni 1934", printed in the *Frankfurter Rundschau*, 14., 15., and 16.05.1957) The arrested SA leaders were then transferred to the Munich-Stadelheim penitentiary, where at around 19:30 hours, Edmund Heines, Hans Hayn, Hans Peter v. Heydebreck, Wilhelm Schmid, August Schneidhuber, and Hans-Joachim Graf von Spreti were shot by an eight-man SS firing squad.

Following the events at the *Pension Hanselbauer*, at around 11:30 a.m., Hitler and his entourage arrived at the München Party headquarters, the "*Braunes Haus.*" Hitler then convened a meeting to discuss the anticipated fate of the arrested SA leaders. Rudolf Hess and Max Amann were bickering over the "privilege" of murdering Röhm. Lutze, despite his important role in bringing about the SA purge, had not expected things to proceed in such a violent way. He expressed his ignorance when Hitler asked which SA leaders were most incriminated in Röhm's alleged conspiracy and could give no answer to the *Führer*'s question of who should be put to death. Also at this time, the *Führer* appointed Lutze as the new *SA-Stabschef* in the presence of several SA leaders, including *SA-Brigadeführer* Max Jüttner and *SA-Gruppenführer* Karl Schreyer. In the afternoon, the Reich Press Office of the NSDAP announced Hitler's decree on the change in SA leadership:

As of today, I have relieved Chief of Staff Röhm of his position and expelled him from the party and SA. I appoint as chief of staff Obergruppenführer Lutze. SA leaders and SA men who do not obey his orders or who act contrary to them will be removed from the SA and the Party or arrested and tried.

Adolf Hitler, Oberster Partei- und SA-Führer (*Das Archiv*, 30.06.1934, p. 325)

At the same time, Hitler addressed a letter directly to Lutze:

To SA-Obergruppenführer Lutze
My Dear SA-Führer Lutze!
Serious misconduct on the part of my previous chief of staff forced me to relieve him of his position [*Schwerste Verfehlungen meines bisherigen Stabschefs zwangen mich, ihn seiner Stellung zu entheben.*]. You, my dear Obergruppenführer Lutze, have for many years, in good and bad times, always been an equally loyal and exemplary SA-Führer. If, as of today, I appoint you Chief of Staff, it is with the firm conviction that your faithful and obedient work will succeed in creating out of my SA the instrument which the nation needs and which I envision. It is my wish that the SA will be formed into a faithful and strong member of the national socialist

movement. Filled with obedience and blind discipline, it must help to form and shape the new man.
Signed: Adolf Hitler. (*Das Archiv*, 30.06.1934, p. 326)

Lutze himself later confided to his diary:

… But one thing is certain for me—and I say this and can say this after I have gained sufficient distance from things and clearly see the connections—Röhm never wanted a Putsch against the Führer on 30 June 1934!!! If he had anything in mind, it was not a Putsch to eliminate the Führer, but to eliminate the reactionary and unsocialist military!…
(*Frankfurter Rundschau*, May 14, 1957)

In his *Reichstag* speech of 13.07.1934, in which he offered his justifications for the purge of the SA, Hitler gave special recognition to those leaders of the SA:

… who made no secret of their inner disgust and reprobation [at the activities of Ernst Röhm and his followers] and were in consequence in part removed from responsible posts, in part thrust aside, and in many respects left out of it. At the head of this group of SA leaders, who because of their fundamental decency had been hardly treated, stood the present Chief of Staff, Lutze, and the leader of the SS, Himmler.

30.06.1934–02.05.1943 *Chef des Stabes der SA*. Succeeded Ernst Röhm. As far back as 05.10.1932, Martin Bormann—in a letter to Hitler's personal secretary Rudolf Hess—had proposed Lutze as a candidate to replace the embarrassing renegade Röhm. He wrote: "… I am convinced that the post of [SA] chief of staff could be filled by any SA leader with an understanding of people and a talent for organization (Lutze)…" (Jochen von Lang, *The Secretary*, p. 388) On 01.07.1934, the following statement appeared in a special edition of the *Völkischer Beobachter*:

Röhm excluded from the Party and the SA. The Reich press bureau of the NSDAP reports the following decree issued by the Führer:
"As of today I have relieved the Chief of Staff Röhm of his position and have ejected him from the Party and the SA. I am appointing Obergruppenführer Lutze as chief of staff. SA Leaders and SA men who don't obey his orders or who oppose him will be ejected from the SA and the Party and consequently will be arrested and convicted.
Signed: Adolf Hitler
Oberster Führer der Partei und der SA"

Immediately after appointing Lutze to the post, Hitler issued the following twelve demands to his new *Stabschef*:

1. From the SA-Führer, just as from the SA man, I demand blind obedience and unconditional discipline.

2. I demand that every SA-Führer, like every political Führer, is aware that his behavior and performance must be exemplary for his unit, indeed for all our followers.

3. I demand that SA-Führer—just like political Führer—who are guilty of misconduct in their public behavior be removed from the party and the SA without delay.

4. I demand, especially from the SA-Führer, that he be a model in simplicity and not in expenditure. I do not wish the SA-Führer to give or attend sumptuous dinners. We were not invited to them in the past, we have no business there now. Millions of our people still lack the basic necessities of life, they are not envious of those whom fortune has blessed more, but it is unworthy of a National Socialist to widen the gap, which is incredibly large between need and fortune, even more. In particular, I forbid the use of Party funds, SA funds, or any public funds at all, for feasts and the like. It is irresponsible to be feasting on funds that come in part from the pennies of our poorest fellow citizens. The luxurious Stabsquartier in Berlin, where, as has now been established, up to 30,000 marks per month were spent on banquets etc., are to be dissolved immediately. I therefore prohibit the hosting of so-called banquets and dinners from any public funds for all party entities. And I forbid all Party and SA-Führer from participating in such. The only exception to this is the fulfillment of obligations required by the state, for which the Reich President and then the Reich Foreign Minister are primarily responsible. In general, I forbid all SA-Führer and all Party Führer to give so-called diplomatic dinners. The SA-Führer has not to exercise representation, rather he has to fulfill his duty.

5. I do not wish SA-Führer to go on official trips in expensive limousines or convertibles or to use official funds to purchase the same.

6. SA-Führer or political Führer who get drunk in public are unworthy of being leaders of their people. The ban on nagging criticism obliges one to adopt an exemplary attitude of one's own. Mistakes can be forgiven at any time, bad performance cannot. SA-Führer who therefore behave in an unworthy manner in the eyes of the public, rampage or even organize excesses, are to be removed from the SA immediately without hesitation. I hold the superior authorities responsible for the enforcement. From the state authorities I expect that in such cases the sentence is higher than for non-National Socialists. The National Socialist Führer and especially the SA-Führer should have an elevated position in the nation. He thereby also has elevated obligations.

7. I expect all SA-Führer to help maintain and solidify the SA as a clean and pure institution. In particular, I want every mother to be able to give her son to the SA, the Party and the Hitlerjugend without fear that he might become morally corrupt there. I therefore wish all SA-Führer to be scrupulously vigilant that misdemeanors under Paragraph 175 are met with the immediate expulsion of the guilty individual from the SA and the Party. I want to see men as SA-Führer and not ridiculous primates.

8. I demand of all SA-Führer that they answer my loyalty with their own and support it with their own. But I particularly demand of them that they seek their strength in the area that is given to them and not

in areas that belong to others. Above all, I demand of every SA-Führer that he conduct himself in unconditional openness, loyalty and fidelity towards the Wehrmacht of the Reich.

9. I demand from the SA-Führer that he does not expect more of his subordinates in terms of courage and sense of sacrifice than he himself is prepared to apply at any time. I therefore demand that he prove himself to be a true leader, friend and comrade in his conduct and in the treatment of the German people entrusted to him by me. I expect him to value virtues over numbers in his unit.

10. I expect you, as Chef des Stabes, not to forget the old loyal Parteigenosse, the long-standing fighter in the SA. I do not wish bloating with a thousand unnecessary but costly staffs, and I want promotions to be based not so much on abstract knowledge as on innate ability to be leaders and many years of proven loyalty and willingness for sacrifice. I have in my SA a tremendous stock of loyal and dutiful followers. It is they who conquered Germany, not the clever latecomers of 1933 and later.

11. I want the SA man to be educated mentally and physically to be the best trained National Socialist. Only in the ideological anchoring in the Party lies the unique strength of this organization.

12. I want obedience, loyalty and comradeship to prevail as principles throughout. And just as every Führer demands of his men, so I demand of the SA-Führer respect for the law and obedience to my command.

("Befehl des obersten SA-Fuhrers" in *Rheinsberger Zeitung*, 03.07.1934; Translation: Gary Costello)

After Lutze's death, his deputy, *SA-Obergruppenführer* Max Jüttner was designated *"mit der Wahrnehmung der Geschäfte des Stabschefs der SA beauftragt,"* holding this post from 03.05.1943 until 17.08.1943 when Wilhelm Schepmann was appointed as Lutze's permanent successor.

In his testimony before the tribunal at Nürnberg on 13.06.1946, Jüttner spoke of Lutze's minimal power in the hierarchy of the Third Reich:

Chief of Staff Lutze was only a Reichsleiter in the Party. In spite of that fact he had no influence on the Party leadership. In the last few years, already before the war, he avoided Gau- and Reichsleiter meetings. Lutze did not become a Reich Minister, therefore he had no influence whatsoever on the conduct of Government affairs. (*Trial of the Major War Criminals Before the International Military Tribunal, Nuremberg, Vol. XXI*)

In the following article, Lutze revealed an obsequious and fanatical loyalty toward his *Führer*:

1920: Adolf Hitler, then an unknown front-line soldier, announces a new idea to a handful of people: National Socialism!

These few believe in this idea and its messenger. It is out of faith that their task arises: To convey the world views of Adolf Hitler to their fellow citizens, to introduce them to the idea, to recruit them for the movement! This task has no time limit and has therefore not ended with the achievement of the first concrete goal—the seizure of power!

The most active promoter of this idea was and still is the SA.
Enlightenment, persuasion and education for National Socialism—this is the movement's route to fulfilling further goals!

As always, the Sturmabteilungen march as trailblazers: the fist, the propagandist arm of the movement. Hand in hand with the National Socialist press, which was already a loyal comrade-in-arms of the Sturmabteilungen during the Kampfzeit and followed wherever the SA man prepared the ground for the Führer's idea.

This created the resonance for the first victory!

The demand to influence and administer the state and its institutions in the National Socialist sense, which was made to the movement with the assumption of power, was important but self-evident!

Beyond this and all other demands of time, the eternal task remains: To lead the German people time and again towards the National Socialist idea!

For us, too, and for the following generations in particular, the poet's words apply: what you have inherited from your fathers, acquire it in order to possess it!

That is the end—we are the means! This is the task of the movement and that of the SA in particular.

Be bearers of faith! This is the ground on which we have to build, on which we must build, if the foundation of the state is to be solid!

Be a faith-bringer! This is the eternal mission of the National Socialist Order among the German people, led by the men of the SA, the activists of the idea!

Keepers of the faith, guardians of fidelity, guarantors of honor and freedom: that is what the Führer wants us to be!

His will is our deed
("Glaubensträger und Glaubensbringer – unsere SA", Der Alemanne, 05.03.1937; Translation: Gary Costello)

20.07.1934–02.05.1943	*Reichsleiter der NSDAP.*
28.07.1934	During the *"Wagner-Festspiele"* in Bayreuth, complained to Hitler that the judiciary was conducting criminal proceedings against some *"alte Kämpfer"* in the SA, including those whom he "wishe[d] to keep in the SA." Hitler then had the chief of the *Reichskanzlei,* Lammers, call the Reich Ministry of Justice from Bayreuth and say that he did not want this continued "because [in light] of incidents that occurred before 15 July 1934, it would be best to refrain from proceedings"). (Lothar Gruchmann, *Justiz im Dritten Reich 1933-1940. Anpassung und Unterwerfung in der Ära Gürtner,* p. 431)
02.08.1934	In cooperation with the *Oberster Parteirichter der NSDAP* (Supreme Party Judge of the NSDAP), Walter Buch, established an *SA-Sondergericht* (special court), under the chairmanship of *SA-Gruppenführer* Arthur Böckenhauer, for the *"inneren*

	Säuberung" (internal cleansing) of the SA leadership. At the same time, Lutze sent a submission to Hitler in which he once again requested immunity from punishment for SA men and their associates in connection with the *"Niederschlagung"* (suppression) of the so-called *"Röhm-Putsch"*; on Hitler's orders, the SA crimes were punished on the basis of the of the *"Gesetzes Gewährung Straffreiheit"* (Law Granting Impunity) of 07.08.1934.
09.08.1934	Ordered a *"Säuberungsaktion innerhalb des SA-Führerkorps vom Sturmführer einschließlich an aufwärts"* (Purge within the SA Leadership Corps of [SA-]*Sturmführer* upwards" and the formation of a *Untersuchungsausschüssen* (investigative committees) in all *SA-Gruppen*. (Michael E. Holzmann, "… *und steht die Legion auf dem ihr zugewies'nen Posten." Die Österreichische Legion als Instrument früher NS-Aggressionspolitik*, p. 264f)
[00.10.1934]	Member of the *Präsidialrat der Deutscher Roten Kreuz*.
26.06.1935–02.05.1943	Member of the *Akademie für Deutsches Recht*, München.
04.09.1934–10.09.1934	Participated in the "*6. Reichsparteitag der NSDAP*" in Nürnberg. On the second night the celebrations, to a crowd of thousands of SA men, Lutze declared:

Comrades! Many of you here knew me when I was an SA-Mann and marched in rank and file with you know me from those early years of our movement when I marched rank and file during the first years of our movement. Just as I was an SA-Mann then, so I am still an SA-Mann now. We SA-Männer know only how to be loyal to our Führer and fight for him. [Goebbels' response in his diary entry of 10.09.1934: "Lutze redet Quatsch…" – "Lutze speaks nonsense."]

Also in attendance was the American journalist William Shirer, who wrote in his diary:

Hitler faced his S.A. storm troopers today for the first time since the bloody purge. In a harangue to fifty thousand of them he "absolved" them from blame for the Röhm "revolt." There was considerable tension in the stadium and I noticed that Hitler's own S.S. bodyguard was drawn up in force in front of him, separating him from the mass of the brown-shirts. We wondered if just one of those fifty thousand brownshirts wouldn't pull a revolver, but not one did. Viktor Lutze, Röhm's successor as chief of the S.A., also spoke. He has a shrill, unpleasant voice, and the S.A. boys received him coolly, I thought. (Shirer, *Berlin Diary*, p. 28)

00.10.1934	Appointed as a member of the *Präsidialrat des Deutschen Roten Kreuzes*.
11.10.1934	Goebbels' diary: "… *Viktor Lutze meckert. Er meckert sehr viel…*" (Viktor Lutze grumbles … he grumbles a lot…).
31.10.1934–01.11.1934	*Leiter* of the "*Besprechung der SA-Gruppenführer im Reichsministerium für Volksaufklärung und Propaganda*" (Conference of *SA-Gruppenführer* in the Reich Ministry for Public Enlightenment and Propaganda), Berlin, during which Hitler announced guidelines for the future organization of the SA.

00.12.1934	Start of a conflict between Lutze and the *Chef des Ausbildungswesens* (*Chef AW*), *SA-Obergruppenführer* Friedrich-Wilhelm Krüger, resulting from the latter's conduct during the so-called "*Röhm-Putsch*." On 11.12.1934, Lutze was informed in a short letter from *SA-Obergruppenführer* Dietrich von Jagow (*Führer* of *SA-Gruppe Berlin-Brandenburg*), about the accusations of Wilhelm Kube (*Gauleiter* of Kurmark) against Krüger. According to the letter, Krüger himself had told Kube that during the "*Röhm-Putsch*" on 30.06.1934, he had arranged for the arrest of the *SA-Obergruppenführer* Manfred Freiherr von Killinger (*Ministerpräsident* of Sachsen and former *Führer* of *SA-Obergruppe IV*), and had expressed regret that Killinger had not been shot. Lutze then asked Krüger, on 20.12.1934, to comment on these accusations. Since the accused Krüger had not commented on this even after five weeks to the now very angry Lutze, the latter informed von Killinger and suggested that he call the *Obersten Parteigericht* "with the aim that Pg. Krüger be expelled from the Party and relieved of his duties in the movement." A similar letter was sent to *Obersten Parteirichter* Walter Buch, to whom Lutze pointed out von Killinger's high rank in the SA. Only a few days later, Buch informed Lutze that he had forwarded the matter to the deputy of the *Führer*, Rudolf Hess, who omitted to respond for several months. When finally questioned about the accusations, Krüger denied everything. Martin Bormann, chief of staff to Hess then wrote to Lutze on 09.05.1935, that there was no interest on the part of the Party leadership in a trial against Krüger; Bormann wrote: "Since in the event of a Party trial the events of 30.06.1934 would have to be reopened, at least in part, we should refrain from initiating the Party trial." (Bert Wawrzinek, *Manfred von Killinger (1886–1944). Ein politischer Soldat zwischen Freikorps und Auswärtigem Amt*, p. 203f)
18.01.1935–20.01.1935	Conducted an inspection of *SA-Gruppe Nordmark*, during which, at an *SA-Führerbesprechung* (leadership conference) in Kiel, he declared: "The SA has not become obsolete, as so many ne'er-do-wells think..." ("*Die SA ist nicht überflüssig geworden, wie so viele Neunmalkluge meinen...*"). (*Das Archiv*, 18.01.1935, p. 1430f)
22.01.1935	Chaired a conference of *SA-Gruppenführer* in the *Reichspropagandaministerium* in Berlin. (*Das Archiv*, 22.01.1935, p. 1433)
27.01.1935	Attended the "*SA und SS-Skiwettkämpfe*" (skiing competition) in Garmisch-Partenkirchen together with *Reichsführer-SS* Himmler and the *Reichssportführer*, *SA-Gruppenführer* Hans von Tschammer und Osten.
00.00.1935–00.00.1937	Had a house, known as the "*Saltenhof*," built for himself and his family on the Saltenwiese in Hörstel near Bevergern (today a hotel).
25.05.1935–26.05.1935	Participated in the "*1. Nordmarktreffen*" (involving members of the SA, SS, and HJ) in Kiel.
26.06.1935–02.05.1943	Member of the *Akademie für Deutsches Recht*.
00.00.1935–02.05.1943	Member of the *Große Rat der Nordische Gesellschaft* (Supreme Council of the Nordic Society).
06.07.1935 and 07.07.1935	Speaker at the "*Gautreffen 1935 der NSDAP des Gaues Westfalen-Nord*" in Münster (05.–07.07.1935).

03.08.1935	Discussion with Goebbels in Essen concerning conflicts of interest between the SA and *Wehrmacht*. In his diary entry of the 5th, Goebbels wrote: "[Lutze] is worried about the R.W. [*Reichswehr—sic*; redesignated *Wehrmacht*, 21.05.1935]. But he also doesn't know how to give the S.A. a new impulse. He only grumbles. He doesn't get anywhere with ranting either."
04.08.1935	Delivered a speech during the *"Gauparteitag des Gaues Essen"* in Essen. His speeches at the *Gauparteitagen* in Münster (06. and 07.07.1935) and Essen were published in 1939 under the title *Reden an die SA. Der politische Katholizismus*, the tenth booklet in the series *Hier spricht das neue Deutschland!* (twenty-four pages).
10.08.1935	Conducted an inspection of the SA in Danzig.
11.08.1935	Visited the leaders and men of *SA-Brigade 1 "Memelwacht"* in Gumbinnen.
17.-18.08.1935	Participated in a *Bierabend* at the *Hotel "Preußenhof"* in Stettin. Also present were Franz Schwede (*Gauleiter* of *Gau Pommern*), *SA-Gruppenführer* Hans Friedrich, *Oberbürgermeister* Dr. Werner Faber, some twenty SA men, and three SS officers (*SS-Standartenführer* Robert Schulz, *Führer* of *SD-Oberabschnitt Nord*; *SS-Hauptsturmführer* Hellmut Willich, Schulz's adjutant; and *SS-Obersturmführer* Theodor Weissig). According to Schulz's official report of the incident, an increasingly inebriated Lutze became unable to hold his tongue with regard to the purge of the SA leadership the previous year, and shortly before 2:00 a.m. loudly proclaimed: "One of these days the unjust and arbitrary action of 30 June [1934] will be avenged. The German is a fair-minded being and this violation of justice will one day rebound upon those responsible and their end will be a bitter one." (Heinz Höhne, *The Order of the Death's Head*, p. 148, citing report of the *SS-Führer* Schulz, Willich, and Weissig, dated 21.08.1935, in *SA-Personalakte Viktor Lutze*)

Schulz retorted: "Unfortunately we did not exterminate them root and branch. We were far too indulgent. Some people who escaped and are still in the SA, knew perfectly well what Rohm was up to." But Lutze went on:

Who was always urging Röhm to live it up? Who was always swearing loyalty to him? Was it some old SA Commander or any SA Commander at all? Shall I tell you who it was? Who has been up to their necks in what Rohm was supposed to have done? Was it the SA? These bestialities were not the SA's work or, at least, not the SA alone; the other side [Himmler and the SS] was much worse. Shall I give you names? I can produce names straightaway! (Heinz Höhne, *The Order of the Death's Head*, p. 148, citing report of the *SS-Führer* Schulz, Willich, and Weissig, dated 21.08.1935, in *SA-Personalakte Viktor Lutze*)

Heinz Höhne writes:

Schulz interjected hurriedly: "Chief of Staff, it's nearly two o'clock. We'd better go to bed." He summoned the waiter and *called* for the bill. The party broke up. Viktor Lutze swayed out but he had the last word and it was loud enough for everyone to hear: "I shall go on saying this, even if I am dismissed tomorrow and sent to a concentration camp." (Heinz Höhne, *The Order of the Death's Head*, p. 148, citing report of the SS-Führer Schulz, Willich, and Weissig, dated 21.08.1935, in SA-Personalakte Viktor Lutze, p. 149)

10.09.1935–16.09.1935	Participated in the "*7. Reichsparteitag der NSDAP*" in Nürnberg.
19.09.1935	With effect from 15.10.1935, Lutze prohibited the affiliation of SA leaders and men with the *Kösener Senioren-Convents-Verband* (*Kösener S.C.*, the powerful organization of German, Austrian, and Swiss student associations), since that organization, according to public notification by the Chief of the *Reichskanzlei* (Dr. Hans Heinrich Lammers), had rejected implementation of the *"Arier-Grundsatz"* (Aryan Principle). (*Verfügung des Obersten SA-Führers vom 19.9.1935* – Ch Nr. 54879)
24.01.1936	Delivered a speech to the diplomatic corps and representatives of the foreign press on the "*Wesen und Aufgaben der SA*" (Nature and Tasks of the SA). He declared that the SA was the guarantor of the inviolability of the National Socialist worldview and an indomitable fortress against communism, providing protection against any enemy of the state. Personally, however, Lutze had come to a different conclusion, as he confided to his diary:

For now—it is the beginning of 1936—it becomes a conviction to me that we will go a difficult, indeed a very dangerous way with Germany. For now, it is certain to me that the Führer does not want to give the SA. the place in the Party, in Germany, that it deserves according to its merit, but above all for the safeguarding of the German future. On the other hand, it became clear that the Führer is ill-advised and that he is thus in the hands of people who—be they stupid, negligent, or deliberately bad—can never want the best for Germany. (Steinmetz, "Nordmark voran". Contributions to the History of the SA, Kiel [undated and unpublished manuscript]).

29.03.1936–09.04.1938	Member of the *(3.) Deutschen Reichstag* (*Wahlkreis 7, Breslau*).
04.04.1936–02.05.1943	Member of the *Reichskultursenat* (with title of *Reichskultursenator*).
15.04.1936–02.05.1943	Member of the *Reichsarbeitskammer* (with membership number 3).
23.05.1936–24.05.1936	Participated in the "*2. Nordmarktreffen*" in Kiel.
06.06.1936–07.06.1936	Attended the "*Tag der SA-Gruppe Nordsee*" in Bremen, during which he reviewed a march of 45,000 SA men in the *Pauliner Marsch*.
18.06.1936	At a meeting with Goebbels, Heinrich Himmler, who had just been appointed chief of the German police, grumbled about Lutze. In his diary on the 19th, Goebbels wrote: "He complained to me a lot about Lutze. Viktor also does many stupid things. He scolds and drinks. Two evil qualities." Despite their longstanding friendship and years of work together, Goebbels wrote negatively of Lutze on numerous occasions. The following are examples from his diary:

07.08.1936 (regarding a meeting with Hitler the previous day): "[The *Führer* speaks] sharply against Lutze and his wife."
29.08.1936 (regarding a meeting with Lutze that date): "…Viktor Lutze complains that the S.A. receives too little attention. That is his fault and his alone. He doesn't do any tasks.… But Viktor prefers to scold rather than to work. He is a good guy, but a bad leader…"
27.01.1937 (Regarding a meeting between Lutze and Hitler the previous day): "… Lutze gets a whipping from Hitler for his irresponsible chatter and is very affected by it. But he deserves it …"
03.03.1937: (Regarding a concert evening with Goebbels in the Leipzig Gewandhaus the previous date): "… Viktor Lutze behaves in an excessively stupid manner, rages against Wagner and also talks nonsense as usual…"
04.03.1937: "The good Viktor is stupid beyond measure." (*Der gute Viktor ist maßlos dumm*).
07.03.1937 (Regarding a report by Goebbels to the Führer about Viktor and Paula Lutze): "He does not hold either of them in high esteem. S.A. has no idea and no drive. Lutze incapable of making anything of it."
17.03.1937 (Re: Meeting with Lutze the previous day): "Lutze declares his and the SA's willingness to cooperate in the anti-Comintern work. He bristles with pomposity and lack of luster."
07.05.1937: "… Himmler has spoken to the police officers. In the future they will come only from the S.S. That is good. Lutze looks to the moon with his S.A. He's bickering and doing nothing else. The S.A. has never had a real leader…"
20.05.1937: "… Himmler is too ambitious. He is too much what Lutze is too little…"
24.05.1937 (Re: Goebbels' complaint the previous day to the *Führer* of *SA-Gruppe Berlin-Brandenburg, SA-Obergruppenführer* Dietrich von Jagow): "… S.A. has no idea and no task anymore. Lutze pushes everyone over the head, brambles and does nothing.… I will now soon lecture the Führer about this. Something must happen, otherwise the S.A. goes once again to the dogs…"
31.07.1937 Goebbels: "… The so-called. 'S.A. Künstler' [SA Artists], an invention of Lutze, are pale dilettantes. They do not deserve artistic promotion. Lutze only makes nonsense…"
10.08.1937 (After Goebbels was unable to prevent the planned transfer from Berlin of *SA-Brigadeführer* Werner Schwarz, who had fallen out of favor with Lutze): "… I will then disassociate myself from the S.A. It should do what it wants. As long as Lutze leads it, it can't be helped…"
16.08.1937 (After a joint visit to an SA sports festival the previous day): "… [Lutze is] A good guy, but totally incompetent…"
25.08.1937: "… Lutze writes an essay about S.A. Stupid and provocative. Without valid arguments. The good Viktor has just little sense. Yet he is otherwise so nice…"
08.09.1938: "Lutze rails mightily against Himmler and the Gestapo. But that is probably more competitive envy."
11.05.1939 [following a conversation with *Gauleiter* Terboven]: "[we agree] that Lutze [has] failed so badly. He only makes nonsense and is completely unpredictable in many ways…"

22.12.1940 [following a conversation with *Gauleiter* Terboven]: "… Terboven, like all of us, has a lot on his plate with Lutze. He's a decent guy, but he bickers too much for my liking."

27.02.1941 [regarding a meeting with Lutze the previous day]: "[Lutze] has a lot to criticize about the Party and about Bormann.… Viktor is a real man and a proper old Nazi [*ein echter Kerl und ein richtiger alter Nazi*]."

15.04.1941: "Lutze pays a visit and brings me a whole lot of complaints. He is an unhappy character. Everywhere he sticks his nose in, everywhere he criticizes and grumbles. The nearest work is not done by him; instead he occupies himself with all kinds of nonsense that have nothing at all to do with the war. Everywhere he smells treachery and betrayal, everywhere he believes that the SA is being set back, and in the process, he also feels personally set back. In the meantime, however, he organized meetings with the deposed Gauleiter [Josef] Wagner, maintained personal contact with Brauchitsch, and so on. I hardly believe that he can still be helped…"

20.04.1941 [regarding his prevention of Lutze's planned speech for the *Führer's* birthday]: "… I succeed in halting a big speech by Lutze. Viktor is a good guy, but not a spiritual light."

15.10.1941: "Viktor Lutze is extraordinarily sanguine; he prefers to see things in black rather than white, and thus gets himself into many mischiefs and annoyances."

22.11.1941 [regarding a visit with Hitler the previous day]: "[I present] the Lutze case to the Führer. The Führer has had enough of the Stabschef. The Stabschef has committed a series of imprudent acts. He grumbles all the time, rails against the SS, plays himself up as a great wise seer. Recently, he has been to the front and has taken a stand there that can almost be considered defeatist. Moreover, he drinks and then, in his drunkenness, provokes events that cannot be approved of at all…"

27.11.1941 [regarding a meeting with Lutze and Goebbels' discussion about him with Hitler]: "Goebbels informs his friend Lutze about the conversation with Hitler about him: 'He is somewhat upset, and I give him the urgent advice to register now as soon as possible for a lecture with the Führer, in order to clear up his affairs there. Above all, he must stop drinking so much. The Führer cannot tolerate that in itself, but least of all now with a leading man in the war. Viktor also understands this…'"

12.12.1941 [regarding a visit from Lutze that evening]: "Lutze appears at Goebbels' in the evening: 'He is very broken-hearted, since he has been told that the Führer has something against him. Now he sees ghosts and white mice and foolishly applies a whole series of passages in the Führer's speech to his person, which is of course childish…'"

18.12.1941: Generalfeldmarschall von Brauchitsch must resign from the leadership of the Army.… He has shown himself to be completely ungrown to his task. It is also typical that he is Lutze's most intimate friend. He resembles him in character and attitude. Both are defeatists, both are under the slippers of their wives, and both have a narrow horizon, both lack clarity of purpose and generosity of action. They differ in only one thing: Viktor Lutze no longer runs to church, while Brauchitsch is a real church runner…

28.06.1936	Participated in the *"Gautreffen 1936 des Gaues Westfalen-Nord der NSDAP"* in Gelsenkirchen.
25.07.1936	Involved in an auto accident near Genthin.
08.09.1936–14.09.1936	Participated in the *"8. Reichsparteitag der NSDAP"* in Nürnberg.
31.10.1936	Participated in a tenth-anniversary ceremony marking the establishment of *SA Berlin-Brandenburg* in Berlin.
22.11.1936–29.11.1936	Participated in the *"4. Reichsbauerntag"* (4th Reich Farmers' Rally) in Goslar.
06.09.1937–13.09.1937	Participated in the *"9. Reichsparteitag der NSDAP"* in Nürnberg. Hamilton T. Burden writes: "[Lutze's] speech contained the Party's first public attack on the church and its followers in Germany. Although his threats were by no means veiled, they were extremely vague. Christians were accused of not serving their country as devotedly as they should. A good Christian was defined by Lutze as a man who served his country well." (Burden, *The Nuremberg Party Rallies*, p. 145; speech reported in the *Völkischer Beobachter* of 12.09.1937) In his diary entry of 12.09.1937, Goebbels wrote: "Lutze gives a speech [on 11.09.] to honor the winners [of the *NS-Kampfspielen*]. A terrible tomato salad. As the Führer rightly says: also an obstacle course. But what can you do! He just can't do it any better…"
21.10.1937–22.10.1937	At the invitation of *Großadmiral* Erich Raeder (*Oberbefehlshaber der Kriegsmarine*), participated in a two-day Baltic Sea trip aboard the *Segelschulschiff* (sail training ship) *Horst Wessel*.
27.10.1937–29.10.1937(?)	In Rome as a member of the German delegation, led by Rudolf Hess, to ceremonies marking the fifteenth anniversary of the fascist "March on Rome." Other delegates included *Reichsleiter* Dr. Hans Frank as well as *Gauleiter* Josef Terboven and Adolf Wagner.
01.01.1938–08.06.1939	*Landesführer* of *Landesstelle XI des DRK* in Hannover. Resigned via the following message sent on his behalf by *SA-Sturmbannführer* Schorm (*Adjutantur des Stabschefs der SA*) to the *Oberpräsidium* in Hannover: "By order of the Führer, the Stabschef resigns his office as Landesführer of the Deutschen Roten Kreuz and at the same time declares his resignation from the Deutschen Roten Kreuz." (Message from the adjutant's office of the chief of staff of the SA, in *SA-Personalakte Viktor Lutze*, BArch R 1501/208810)
23.02.1938	In commemoration of the murder of *SA-Sturmführer* Horst Wessel (23.02.1930), issued the following *Tagesbefehl* (Order of the Day) to the SA:

(Horst Wessel Day)

Comrades!

Today we lower the flags and standards in memory of the one who proudly and bravely laid down his life for the cause that we serve.
   Today, the nation sings Horst Wessel's song,
   But his death is entwined in the victory of faith that fills our hearts, in the loyalty that binds us to the Führer.

> SA marches! That's the way it should remain! That which was mortal about Horst Wessel decayed. His spirit lives on in the marching columns of our brown battalions.
>
> By honoring our dead comrade, we commit ourselves for the future.
> Long live Germany! Long live the Führer!
>
> Der Stabschef
> Lutze.
> (Bundesarchiv R-38/3499; Translation: Gary Costello)

24.02.1938	Attended the celebration marking the anniversary of the establishment of the NSDAP at the *Hofbräuhaus*, München.
11.03.1938	Together with other senior NSDAP leaders, including *Reichsführer-SS* Himmler, visited KL-Dachau.
14.03.1938	Trip to Wien to implement the "*Übernahme der österreichischen SA in den Gesamtverband der SA*" (Takeover of the Austrian SA into the General Association of the SA). ("Stabschef Lutze in Wien" in *NS-Telegraf*, 14.03.1938; "Viktor Lutze Stabschef der SA" in *Tages-Post* [Linz], 30.03.1938; "Männer des Führers – Stabschef der SA. Viktor Lutze" in *Salzburger Zeitung*, 31.03.1938; "Viktor Lutze" in *Salzburger Volksblatt*, 01.04.1938)
02.04.1938	Participated in a "*Heldenehrung*" (Heroes' Tribute) ceremony during the "*Tag der Legion*" at the *Heldendenkmal*, Wien. (*Illustrierte Kronen-Zeitung* [Wien], 03.04.1938)
10.04.1938–02.05.1943	Member of the *Großdeutschen Reichstag* (*Wahlkreis 7, Breslau*).
00.04.1938–00.04.1938	Participated in the "*Führertagung der SA-Gruppe Westfalen*" in Dortmund. During the event, at a rally before 12,000 SA men, Lutze once again took a stand on the events of 30.06.1934 (the so-called "*Röhm Putsch*"). The SA, he declared, was "just as immaculate and pure as it had been in the past." With the sentence, "We want to be bearers of ideas, but not bearers of swords" [*Ideenträger wollen wir sein, aber keine Degenträger*], he also publicly attacked *Reichsführer-SS* Himmler with reference to his practice of awarding the *SS-Führerdegen*. (Jochen von Lang, *Der Adjutant. Karl Wolff: Der Mann zwischen Hitler und Himmler*, p. 37)
26.05.1938	Attended the foundation-stone laying ceremony for the *Volkswagenwerke* in Fallersleben (Wolfsburg). There he approached *General der Artillerie* Wilhelm Ulex, the commanding general of *XI. Armee-Korps*; during their private meeting, Lutze stated that the recent SS-engineered purging of Army chief of staff *Generaloberst* Werner Freiherr von Fritsch, on false charges of homosexuality, should be used as the basis for a *Wehrmacht* revolt against Himmler. According to Ulex's postwar recollections, Lutze proclaimed himself and the SA firmly on the side of the *Wehrmacht*. Ulex advised Lutze that, provided the SA leader obtain proof that the charges against von Fritsch had been manufactured by the SS, he would convey Lutze's plan for a revolt to von Fritsch and *Generaloberst* Walther von Brauchitsch (von Fritsch's successor). One or two weeks later, *SA-Gruppenführer*

Erich Reimann reported to Ulex with news that Lutze could now provide supporting documentation that the statements of von Fritsch's accuser, Otto Schmidt, had been false and the result of coercion by the *Reichsführer-SS*. When Ulex shared this information with von Brauchitsch, however, the senior officer refused to play any part, stating: "If these gentlemen want to do it, they must do it alone." (Höhne, *The Order of the Death's Head*, p. 470) Interestingly in light of Lutze's attempts to forge a conspiracy with von Brauchitsch, the 03.02.1939 issue of *Der SA Mann* contained a photograph of Lutze and von Brauchitsch, reviewing a unit of the SA. It was captioned "We [the SA] will be the bridge between the Party and the *Wehrmacht*."

28.05.1938–29.05.1938	Participated in the "*4. Nordmarkttreffen*" in Kiel.
24.06.1938–02.07.1938	Official visit to Rome at the invitation of *Luogotenente Generale* Luigi Russo, chief of staff of the fascist *Milizia Volontaria per la Sicurezza Nazionale* (M.V.S.N., Volunteer Militia for National Security). On 01.07, Lutze and Russo met personally with Mussolini. ("Stabschef Lutze als Gast der faschistischen Miliz" in *Frankfurter Zeitung*, 25.06.1938; "Abschied Lutze von Mussolini" in *Völkischer Beobachter* [*Münchner Ausgabe*], 04.07.1938; "Braunhemd und Schwarzhemd – Nach der Italienreise des Stabschefs der SA" in *Wiener Zeitung*, 07.07.1938)

Lutze was accompanied by a sizable entourage, which included: *SA-Obergruppenführer* Hanns Elard Ludin (*Führer* of *SA-Gruppe Südwest*), *SA-Brigadeführer* Leonhard Gontermann (*Führer* of *SA-Marinebrigade 4*, Kiel), *SA-Standartenführer* Willi Besserer (*Abteilungschef* in the *Adjutantur des Stabschefs*), *SA-Standartenführer* Albert Wiczonke (*Führer* of *SA-Standarte 404*, Bütow/Pommern), *SA-Obersturmbannführer* Hans Peter Hermel (Lutze's adjutant), *SA-Obersturmbannführer* Willi Körbel (Editor-in-Chief of *Der SA-Mann*), and *SA-Obersturmbannführer* Willi Bültmann (*Führer* of *SA-Standarte 1*, Berlin). ("Lutze fährt nach Italien" in *Der Angriff*, 23.06.1938)

14.07.1938–22.07.1938	Hosted *Luogotenente Generale* Russo during a tour of Germany (Berlin–Schleswig-Holstein–Ostpreußen–Rheingau). On 17.07.1938, they attended the "*Reichswettkämpfen der SA*" on the *Reichssportfeld* in Berlin.
05.09.1938–12.09.1938	Participated in the "*10. Reichsparteitag der NSDAP*" in Nürnberg.
19.09.1938	Appointed as a member of the *Gaubeirat des Gaues Ost-Hannover der NSDAP* for the "*Winterhilfswerk des Deutschen Volkes 1938/39*."
01.10.1938	Telex from the Berlin *Polizeirevier 111* (Police Station 111) to the Reich Interior Ministry:

[At about 04:00 hours, Lutze] got into an argument [with the Swiss diplomat Max Graeßli in the Königin-Bar on the Berlin Kurfürstendamm] because the latter had allegedly overheard his conversation. In the course of the confrontation, Stabschef Lutze took Dr. G.'s diplomatic identity card from him, telling him to fetch it from the Reichskanzlei. At the request of Stabschef Lutze, Dr. G. was taken to the police station [111] and released after his personal details had been established. (Telex from Berlin Police Station 111 dated October 1, 1938 to the RMdI. [*SA-Personalakte Viktor Lutze*])

00.10.1938	During the occupation of the Sudetenland, personally flew one of the 160 Junkers Ju 52 aircraft advancing southward from Breslau into Czechoslovak airspace.
03.11.1938	On the occasion of the visit of the Reich Minister of the Interior, Dr. Frick, to Bremen, Lutze met with *Gauleiter* Otto Telschow (*Gau Osthannover*) and Carl Röver (*Gau Weser-Ems*).
09.–10.11.1938	Attended the annual commemoration of the *"München-Putsch"* at the *Bürgerbräukeller*, following which he hoped to enjoy an evening with Frau Lutze on what was their twentieth wedding anniversary. Dr. Goebbels announced during this meeting of "Old Fighters" that antisemitic outbreaks were occurring in various German cities as a "spontaneous" protest to the murder of German diplomat Ernst vom Rath in Paris. He further stated that the *Führer* had decided such demonstrations should not be discouraged by German authorities but permitted to occur without the appearance of government or Party involvement. While many of those present raced to the telephone to relay orders for the inconspicuous organization and carrying-out of anti-Jewish agitation, Lutze, assisted by the SA administrative chief (*SA-Verwaltungs-Obergruppenführer* Georg Mappes), took aside his SA leaders and "ordered them not to participate in any actions against the Jews." (John Toland, *Adolf Hitler*) In many cases, Lutze's orders were ignored, with SA units playing a leading role in what became known as *"Reichskristallnacht."*

In testimony before the International Military Tribunal, Nürnberg on 14.08.1946, Lutze's former deputy, *SA-Obergruppenführer* Max Jüttner, stated:

The participation of SA members in this action consisted of irresponsible actions by individuals which were in gross contradiction to the directive of Staff Chief Lutze's executives. Staff Chief Lutze was in Munich in the old city hall. There, in connection with the speech made by Dr. Goebbels, he immediately assigned the chief of the administrative office, Obergruppenführer Matthes [sic, Mappes], to go to the Hotel Rheinhof, where a part of the SA leaders present had already retired, in order to give these SA leaders strict orders not to participate in any action against the Jews. About an hour later, when he received the news that the synagogue in Munich had been set on fire, Lutze, in my presence, repeated this order to the SA leaders who were still present in the Munich city hall and said that it was to be passed on to all units immediately. This was actually done, which is confirmed by the fact that in many places no actions were carried out at all, and numerous SA men state under oath that they received this order....

As was ascertained afterwards, certain individuals let themselves be misled by agencies which were undoubtedly under the influence of Dr.

> Goebbels. As an actual fact, compared with the SA, relatively few real members of the SA participated in this action, although public opinion later blamed the SA for this entire action. And here again it so happened that everyone in a brown shirt was considered an SA man. That the SA was in no way the sponsor of this action may also be seen from the fact that, as I have read in the press in the last few months, in certain trials, for example in Bamberg, Stuttgart, and, I believe, in Hof, people were convicted who had destroyed synagogues and yet did not belong to the SA. The fact also that in many places SA men upon instructions from the leadership offered to afford protection to Jewish installations against plundering by shady elements, et cetera, created a popular impression that the SA had committed these misdeeds. In any event, Staff Chief Lutze one or two days later gave voice to his indignation to Dr. Goebbels about the action itself and the unjustified accusation against the SA, and strongly condemned the irresponsible way in which the SA men had been incited to commit these misdeeds. Soon after he issued an order that in the future SA men were not to place themselves at the disposal of other agencies for any tasks or actions unless he himself had given express approval. Staff Chief Lutze punished the guilty ones whom he discovered, and if the case warranted it, they were turned over to the regular courts for judgment. (*Trial of the Major War Criminals Before the International Military Tribunal Nuremberg, Volume XXI*)

It is likely that the manner in which the pogroms were carried out offended the disciplined officer in Lutze. He was certainly no friend to the Jews, declaring in 1937:

> *Der Sturmer* has an essential role in seeing that each German today views the Jewish question as the crucial question of the nation, and the honor of having put racial thought in popular language. (*Der Sturmer, 1937/Nr. 11*)

19.01.1939	Issuance of a *Führererlass* (*Führer* decree) designating the SA as "*Träger der vor- und nachmilitärischen Ausbildung*" (Bearer of Pre- and Post-military Training) for all German men. Shortly after 09.11.1938, Lutze had received an order from Hitler to negotiate the regulations for military education before and after regular military service with the commander-in-chief of the army, von Brauchitsch. In the weeks that followed, Lutze and his *Stabsführer*, *SA-Obergruppenführer* Otto Herzog, had held numerous talks with Brauchitsch, his chief of staff (*General der Artillerie* Franz Halder), the commander-in-chief of the *Luftwaffe* (*Generalfeldmarschall* Hermann Göring), and the commander-in-chief of the *Kriegsmarine* (*Großadmiral* Erich Raeder). The relationship between the SA and the *Wehrmacht*, which had previously been disturbed by the efforts of the former *SA-Stabschef* Röhm, was thus redefined.
27.01.1939	*Leiter* of the "*Arbeitstagung der Führer der SA-Gruppen sowie der Hauptamts- und Amtschefs der Obersten SA-Führung*" (Working Conference of the Leaders of the SA Groups as well as the Main

	Office and Office Chiefs of the Supreme SA Leadership) in Berlin. ("Stabschef Lutze vor den SA-Führern" in *Niedersächsische Tageszeitung*, 29.01.1939)
31.01.1939–00.02.1939	Official visit to Italy and the Italian colony of Libya, accompanied by Frau Lutze and *SA-Obergruppenführer* Karl-Siegmund Litzmann. On 01.02, as guest of honor of Benito Mussolini's and *Luogotenente Generale* Russo, he attended ceremonies marking the sixteenth anniversary of the establishment of the fascist M.V.S.N. on the *Piazza Venezia* in Rome. The following day, he met personally with Mussolini. ("Stabschef Lutze in Rom" in *Dortmunder Zeitung*, 01.02.1939; "Stabschef Lutze in Messina" in *Hamburger Nachrichten*, 08.02.1939)
00.02.1939	After the official SA newspaper (*Der SA-Mann: Kampfblatt der Obersten SA-Führung der NSDAP*) printed what Goebbels characterized in his diary (26.02.1939) as "a stupid article against nude dancing," Hitler had the newspaper banned "forever." Lutze was, per Goebbels, "beside himself with dismay."
17.02.1939	Accompanied Hitler during his visit to the *"Internationale Automobil-Ausstellung"* in Berlin.
21.02.1939	Participated in the *"Tagung des Kulturkreises der SA"* (Conference of the Cultural Circle of the SA) in Berlin.
11.03.1939	Published an article, "Die SA-Wehrmannschaften," in the *Völkischer Beobachter*, in which he praised the transfer of pre- and post-military military education to the SA.
26.03.1939	In the *"Durchführungsbestimmung zur vor- und nachmilitärischen Wehrerziehung"* (implementing regulation for pre- and post-military education), decreed that *Wehr- und Jungwehrmannschaften* (military and young SA military teams) were to be formed and divided according to weapon categories.
21.05.1939	Oversaw the swearing-in of 200,000 Austrian and south Moravian SA men in Wien, then conducted an inspection tour of the *Gaue* of Niederdonau, Oberdonau, and Salzburg. ("Stabschef Lutze vereidigt 200.000 Mann SA auf den Führer" in *Illustrierte Kronen-Zeitung* [Wien], 22.05.1939)
01.06.1939	Formation of the *Wehrstab* of the OSAF (headed by *SA-Brigadeführer* Georg von Neufville) as a liaison between Lutze and the supreme commanders of the three *Wehrmacht* branches.
09.06.1939–10.06.1939	Two-day visit to Danzig, during which he inspected the SA in that city together with *Gauleiter* Albert Forster, *Senatspräsident* Arthur Greiser, and *SA-Obergruppenführer* Heinrich Schoene.
21.07.1939–23.07.1939	Attended the *"Reichswettkämpfe der SA"* in Berlin.
22.09.1939–01.04.1941	Member of the *Verteidigungsausschuss* for *Wehrkreis XI*.
21.10.1939	Discussion with the *Generaloberst* von Brauchitsch, on questions of possible promotion of the numerous SA leaders called up to the Army.
23.10.1939–26.10.1939	Tour of Slovakia, during which he held meetings with German Ambassador Hans Bernard, Slovak President Dr. Jozef Tiso, Foreign Minister Ferdinand Ďurčanský, Interior Minister Dr. Vojtech Tuka, Minister of Defense General Ferdinand Catlos,

and the commander-in-chief of the Hlinka Guard, Alexander ("Šaňo") Mach, as well as the *Volksgruppenführer* of the *Slowakei-Deutschen*, *Staatssekretär* (and *SA-Oberführer*) Franz Karmasin.

27.10.1939 Unsuccessfully requested a frontline assignment.

00.12.1939 Letter from the *Oberbefehlshaber des Heeres, Generalfeldmarschall* Walther von Brauchitsch, to *SA-Stabschef* Lutze:

Dear Stabschef!
I read your report on the deployment and activities of the SA since the beginning of the war with great interest.

From the report and from my own observations, I am pleased to see that our good cooperation in peace and the agreements confirmed by the Führer's decree are now also bearing fruit in war. I am particularly pleased that the majority of all SA men are at the front in the field gray uniform. In this I see the most beautiful expression of the front-born SA spirit.

With comradely regards
and Heil Hitler
Your,
[signed] von Brauchitsch.
(*SA-Obersturmführer* Rudolf von Elmayer-Vestenbrugg, *SA.-Männer im feldgrauen Rock. Taten und Erlebnisse von SA.-Männern in den Kriegsjahren 1939–1940*, pp. 281-282; Translation: Gary Costello)

Around the same time, a similarly complimentary letter was sent by *Generaloberst* Wilhelm Keitel (*Chef, Oberkommando der Wehrmacht*):

With great interest I have taken note of the report of 14 October 1939 on the deployment and activities of the SA since the beginning of the war, for the transmission of which I am most grateful.

In the past weeks of the war, the Wehrmacht has felt particularly grateful that the members of the SA and its Führerkorps, recognizing the requirements of this historic time, have taken account of the given circumstances in an exemplary spirit of community and with disregard for all interests not directly serving the war. The readiness for action instilled in all members of the SA had an exemplary effect in all cases within the Wehrmacht, especially before the enemy and in the great patriotic tasks to secure the vital necessities of the Reich and the people. In particular, the cooperation between the SA and the Wehrmacht in the implementation of mobilization and in the transfer of clothing and equipment to the Wehrmacht also functioned without any problems. The additional education of the conscripts will certainly help us to achieve further successes together.
Heil Hitler
[Signed] Keitel
(*SA-Obersturmführer* Rudolf von Elmayer-Vestenbrugg, *SA. Männer im feldgrauen Rock. Taten und Erlebnisse von SA.-Männern in den Kriegsjahren 1939–1940*, pp. 282-283)

22.02.1940	Canceled his participation in the *"Tagung der Reichs- und Gauleiter der NSDAP"* of that date. His absence from the important conference prompted Goebbels to write in his diary the following day: "… I no longer know how to help the good Viktor. He is digging his own grave.… Everyone agrees with me: Viktor Lutze is difficult to help…"
12.03.1940	*SS-Brigadeführer* Gottlob Berger, *Chef* of the *SS-Führungsamt* and a staunch Himmler supporter, denounced Lutze in a letter to Himmler's chief of staff, *SS-Hauptsturmführer* Dr. Rudolf Brandt:

> Dear Doctor! I beg to submit the following to the Reichsführer: The conduct of Stabschef Lutze is gradually becoming a danger to the SS, if not to the Party. The comradeship evenings [*Kameradschaftsabende*] organized by him, especially those attended by the Wehrmacht, are always used to make propaganda against individual sections of the movement in general and against the SS in particular, and in a form unworthy of any decent man.… It would be necessary, in my opinion, to monitor Stabschef Lutze and to nail him at the next opportunity, and to do so in such a way that the matter can be properly brought to the attention of the Führer… (Heiber, *"Reichsführer!" !... Briefe an und von Himmler*, p. 89f.)

In his prison memoirs, Alfred Rosenberg wrote of Lutze's conflicts with Himmler:

> Lutze, staff chief of the Sturmabteilung, was also watching Heinrich Himmler expand his influence, not so much by means of positive accomplishments as by sly pressure made possible by executive power entrusted to him by the state. It may be that Lutze lacked the gift of finding new tasks for the slighted Sturmabteilung that really would have given it a new lease on life; but, historically speaking, it is also possible that the Sturmabteilung was so exclusively identified with our battle for power that it would have taken a long time before such new tasks could have been found for it. Many Obergruppenführer complained to Lutze. The sports insignia of the Sturmabteilung seemed inadequate, nor did the plans for a large German sports competition to be held during the Party Day at Nürnberg satisfy them. Thus the Sturmabteilung lost a number of its old leaders to the foreign diplomatic service, and others to the SS. Himmler countered Lutze's aversion, which he considered a purely personal prejudice, by stating that it was he who had suggested Lutze as chief of staff to succeed Röhm. The Führer, he claimed, had also offered him the leadership of the Sturmabteilung, but he hadn't wanted to fall heir to the leadership of an organisation that others had led during battle. Now Lutze showed his gratitude by making these unjust accusations. Later on, secure in his personal victory, Himmler declined even to see Lutze. However, this antagonism was by no means personal but, rather, a matter of principle. How justified it was, now becomes apparent at Nürnberg. When we discussed this matter, Lutze told me that every young state needed a harsh police executive which occasionally had to use methods running counter to accepted morality, quite without regard to party affiliations. Thus, it was bad for the National Socialist movement that a

Party organisation should be so intimately tied through a personal union with the Sicherheitsdienst, the Staatspolizei [*Gestapo*], and the rest, and that a man like Himmler should draw these ties even tighter. This was necessarily harmful to the Party's reputation among the people, who began to identify certain necessary steps taken by the state with the party and its political identity. In addition, Lutze said, instances of vile corruption in SS leadership as well as indefensible chicanery on the part of the police had occurred. Just then—and this was already during the war—he couldn't bother the Führer with such things. But later on he would submit all his material to the Führer together with an either-or. But even noble Viktor Lutze couldn't possibly guess at that time what Himmler and Heydrich were really up to. (Rosenberg, *Memoirs of Alfred Rosenberg*)

24.04.1940 — Following internal disputes in the Hannover/Braunschweig area, addressed a request to Hitler for dismissal from his office as *Oberpräsident*:

My Führer!
As a result of the new tasks assigned to me, the work for the national defense [*Arbeiten für die Landesverteidigung*], together with my work as Stabschef, are taking such a toll on me that I can no longer do the work in the Hanover High Presidium as I want to do it and am used to doing it. I therefore ask you, my Führer, to relieve me of the office of Oberpräsident of the Provinz Hannover.
   As an SA man you have placed me in Hanover, as an SA man I am yours in old loyalty!
Heil my Führer!
[Signed] Lutze
(*SA-Personalakte Viktor Lutze*, BArch R 1501/208810)

14.05.1940 — Topping-out ceremony of a new office building in Bevergern. The *Bauherr* (contractor) was Lutze, who officially donated the building to his hometown on 11.04.1941.

26.06.1940 — In a letter to the deputy *Führer*, Rudolf Hess, Lutze complained about disadvantages of SA men in the *Gestapo* and police service, asserting that unless they were willing to join the SS, they were placed under massive pressure. Hess forwarded the letter to the *Reichsführer-SS* on 11.07.1940, and on the 22nd, Himmler demanded concrete examples from Lutze. (*Heinrich Himmlers Taschenkalender 1940*, p. 300f)

19.07.1940 — In his *Reichstag* speech of that date, Hitler gave special recognition to various high-ranking Party leaders (Rudolf Hess, Heinrich Himmler, Konstantin Hierl, *Dr.-Ing.* Fritz Todt, Dr. Joseph Goebbels, and Lutze) "... who, among innumerable others, have won the greatest merit in the struggle to make it possible for the new Germany to celebrate victory." In summarizing Lutze's contributions, Hitler declared: "Lutze, Chief of Staff of the Sturmabteilung, who has organized the millions of Storm Troopers in the spirit of the greatest sacrifice to the State and assured their preliminary training and their subsequent careers..."

20.07.1940	Issued the following *Tagesbefehl*:

Men of the SA!

Yesterday, before the forum of the German nation, the Führer appointed the first SA Führer as Reichsmarschall of Greater Germany and expressed his highest praise for the SA.

This praise from our Obersten SA-Führer goes to all of you who have crossed the seas in U-boats, who, as paratroopers, are living symbols of the courage cultivated in the SA, and who in the ranks of the best infantry in the world and in all other formations of the Wehrmacht have contributed to the great victories.

The Führer's proud recognition also goes to you who, in accordance with orders, had to remain at home and who, in the old idealism and selflessness, performed your SA service alongside your increased professional work.

We are all particularly satisfied by the Führer's statement that it was and is his Sturmabteilungen, the infantry of the movement, which have ensured the pre- and post-military training of millions of German men fit for military service as the organization designated by the Führer for this purpose, and in this way have helped to prepare to the highest degree the victory of German arms, which is no less a victory of German faith.

Men of the SA!
And now as always. In old SA spirit to even greater achievements.
Long live the Führer
[Signed] Viktor Lutze
(*SA-Obersturmführer* Rudolf von Elmayer-Vestenbrugg, *SA.-Männer im feldgrauen Rock. Taten und Erlebnisse von SA.-Männern in den Kriegsjahren 1939–1940*, p. 285; Translation: Gary Costello)

06.10.1940	Attended the *"SA-Geist ist Wehrgeist"* (SA Spirit is Military Spirit) event in Bremen.
21.10.1940–00.10.1940	Conducted an inspection tour of the *Reichsgau Wartheland* lasting several days. ("Der Stabschef der SA Viktor Lutze im Warthegau" in *Ostdeutscher Beobachter* [Posen], 22.10.1940)
00.10.1940–00.10.1940	Visited Marienburg/Westpreußen, where he laid a wreath at the gravesite of *SA-Obergruppenführer* Joachim Meyer-Quade (killed in action during the Polish Campaign on 12.09.1939), then proceeded to Posen where he inspected the newly formed *SA-Standarte "Hans von Manteuffel"* (also known as *SA-Standarte "Posen"*). He then participated in celebrations of the *"Tag der Freiheit"* in Litzmannstadt before proceeding to a ceremony at *Generalgouverneur* Dr. Frank's headquarters at Wawel Castle in Kraków.
10.01.1941	Discussion with Goebbels, who wrote in his diary the following day:

… Extensive discussion with Viktor Lutze. He is most sharply opposed to Himmler and the S.S. Entirely on the side of Brauchitsch, who also has the S.S. on number. He also tells me some things about Himmler that

	are anything but nice. But he is biased and too clumsy. I tell him that too. Otherwise, however, a kind-hearted comrade and a fine Nazi [*ein herzensguter Kamerad und prima Nazi*].
15.05.1941–24.05.1941	Visit to France together with *SA-Obergruppenführer* Jüttner. During this tour, he and *Admiral* Karl Dönitz inspected the crew of *U-94* (*Kapitänleutnant* Herbert Otto Kuppisch) at Lorient on the Atlantic coast.
06.06.1941	Delivered a speech during the swearing-in ceremony for newly established *elsäßischer SA-Einheiten* (Alsatian SA units) in Straßburg.
09.06.1942	Attended the funeral of Reinhard Heydrich in the *Mosaiksaal* of the *Reichskanzlei*, Berlin.
23.07.1942	Received by Hitler, together with *SA-Obergruppenführer* Jüttner, at *Führerhauptquartier "Werwolf"* near Vinnitsa (Ukraine) for a lecture on the activities and deployment of the SA in the war. Lutze then conducted a tour of the Eastern Front. ("Stabschef Lutze beim Führer" in *Deutsche Polarzeitung* [Tromsö], 26.07.1942)
20.08.1942	In his diary entry of that date, Goebbels wrote:

Lutze was summoned to the Führer's headquarters, and there the Fuehrer gave him all the instructions he could. The Führer reproached him with all the things I had already been told so often, and warned him seriously against continuing to use defeatist or negativist language. Lutze was very meek and vowed to improve.... His relationship with Brauchitsch is indicative of his level. Both are stupid...

12.09.1942	Meeting with the chief of the general staff of the fascist M.V.S.N., *Luogotenente Generale* Enzo Galbiati, in Berlin. In his diary entry of the 13th, Goebbels wrote: "... The visit of General Galbiati has been prepared by the SA in a rather imperfect manner. For example, Lutze brings ... an interpreter who is hardly able to translate a sentence correctly. There is not much going on with the SA; one can hardly work with it because everything there is built on unreliability and unsoundness."
03.10.1942	Paid a visit to the deputy *Reichsprotektor*, *SS-Oberst-Gruppenführer und Generaloberst der Polizei* Kurt Daluege, in Prague.
04.10.1942	Flew with Daluege to Mährisch-Ostrau and attended the *SA-Wehrkämpfe* (SA war games).
21.11.1942	Visit to Norway at the invitation of the *Reichskommissar*, *Gauleiter* Josef Terboven, in Oslo. ("Stabschef Lutze in Norwegen" in *Deutsche Zeitung in Norwegen*, 23.11.1942; "Der Stabschef in Norwegen" in *Rostocker Anzeiger*, 25.11. 1942)
05.01.1943	In his diary entry of that date, Goebbels again criticized Lutze's leadership of the SA, stating that the *Stabschef* had let "the SA degenerate quite a bit" and had "completely misunderstood a great task.... If one compares what Himmler made of the SS and what Lutze made of the SA, one can see here an enormous difference in personal performance."

23.01.1943	Together with *Gauleiter* August Eigruber, participated in the swearing-in ceremony for the newly appointed *Führer* of *SA-Gruppe Alpenland*, *SA-Gruppenführer* Wilhelm Dittler, in Linz.
24.01.1943	In the company of *Gauleiter* Dr. Gustav Adolf Scheel, delivered a speech to an assembly of 2,000 SA men (in commemoration of the twentieth anniversary of *Gau Salzburg*, on 30 January).
18.02.1943	Goebbels delivered his infamous "*Sportpalast-Rede*" (on the topic of "Total War"), of which Lutze wrote in his diary:

… The worst thing, however, about which I am horrified, is the speech given by Goebbels in the Sportpalast. I have not listened to it at all—thank God not—but I have read it now. This is the worst kowtowing to the gutter. He will be surprised about the spirits he has called with it. Instead of braking and holding the masses in the hand, he gets out of his Minister's chair and goes into the rioting crowd, no even worse, he makes them do it in the first place, he stirs them up. In my opinion, he has done the very worst thing that has been done so far in these 3 ½ years of war. (Eckhard Steinmetz, "*Nordmark voran*". Beiträge zur Geschichte der SA)

26.02.1943	In a letter of that date, Himmler informed *Reichsleiter* Bormann that Lutze had taken up temporary residence in *Generalgouverneur* Dr. Frank's villa and taken a cure in Bad Kryniza. Himmler wrote: "I regard Lutze's visit to a spa in the *Generalgouvernement* as unfortunate; I consider it would be better if he took his cure in some German spa" (Heinz Höhne, *The Order of the Death's Head*, p. 472), and complained that the *Kurhäuser* (spas) in the *Generalgouvernement* were supposed to "give shelter and rest to soldiers wounded and brought out of Stalingrad." (*Die Organisation des Terrors. Der Dienstkalender Heinrich Himmlers 1943–1945*, p. 162f)
Spring 1943	Acquired a small parcel of land adjacent to his "*Saltenhof*" residence in Bevergern and decreed in his will on 08.04.1943 that he would like to be buried here.

DECORATIONS & AWARDS:

07.05.1943	*Deutscher Orden des Großdeutschen Reiches, I. Klasse, 1. Stufe mit Lorbeerkranz und Schwertern* (fourth recipient; posthumous award)
00.00.191_	*1914 Eisernes Kreuz I. Klasse*
00.00.191_	*1914 Eisernes Kreuz II. Klasse*
31.03.1941	*Kriegsverdienstkreuz I. Klasse mit Schwertern*
00.00.1940(?)	*Kriegsverdienstkreuz II. Klasse mit Schwertern*
19.01.1919	*Fürstlich Lippisches Kriegsehrenkreuz für heldenmütige Tat*
30.05.1919	*Fürstlich Lippisches Offiziersehrenkreuz mit Schwertern*
00.00.1918	*Verwundetenabzeichen, 1918 in Silber*
00.00.1939	*Medaille zur Erinnerung an den 1. Oktober 1938*
00.00.1939	*Medaille zur Erinnerung an den 13. März 1938*
c. 1934	*Ehrenkreuz des Weltkrieges 1914-1918 mit Schwertern*
00.00.1933	*Goldenes Ehrenzeichen der NSDAP*
17.05.1939	*Goldenes Hitler-Jugend Ehrenzeichen mit Eichenlaub*. Presented by *Reichsjugendführer* Baldur von Schirach

30.01.1942	*Dienstauszeichnung der NSDAP in Gold*
30.01.1940	*Dienstauszeichnung der NSDAP in Silber*
30.01.1940	*Dienstauszeichnung der NSDAP in Bronze*
00.09.1933	*Abzeichen "Reichsparteitag Nürnberg 1933"*
00.00.1929	*Nurnberger Parteitagsabzeichen 1929*
00.00.1931	*Abzeichen des SA-Treffens Braunschweig 1931*
26.05.1933	*Schlageter Gedächtnis-Abzeichen (Nr. 7)*
00.00.193_	*Großkreuz des Ehrenzeichens des Deutschen Roten Kreuzes mit Eichenlaub (Halsorden)*
10.06.1939	*Ehrenzeichen des Roten Kreuzes der Freien Stadt Danzig.* Presented by Danzig *Senatspräsident* Arthur Greiser during the "SA-Gruppenwettkämpfen in Danzig." ("Senatspräsident Greiser überreicht Stabschef Lutze das Ehrenzeichen vom Roten Kreuz der Freien Stadt Danzig" in Danziger Neueste Nachrichten, 12.06.1939)
20.10.1940	*Kreuz von Danzig I. Klasse*
24.08.1936	*Deutsches Olympia-Ehrenzeichen I. Klasse*
13.12.1939	*Deutsche Schutzwall-Ehrenzeichen*
26.06.1938	*Silbernes Treudienst-Ehrenzeichen*
00.00.1936	*Ehrenplakette für die Mitglieder des Reichskultursenats*
00.00.193_	*Deutsche Reiterabzeichen in Bronze*
31.03.1941	*Dankschreiben des "Führers."* Letter of Appreciation from Adolf Hitler to honor his service as *Oberpräsident* of Hannover.
28.12.1937	*SA-Ehrendolch für Führer der SA-Standarte "Feldherrnhalle"* with the following inscription on the blade: *Ihrem Stabschef im alten SA-Geist* *zum 28.12.1937* *Das Führerkorps der Standarte Feldherrnhalle*
28.12.1940	*Ehrendolch des Deutschen Heeres* (Honor Dagger of the German Army. Presented on the occasion of his fiftieth birthday by *Generalfeldmarschall* Walther von Brauchitsch. ("Stabschef Lutze 50 Jahre alt", Hamburger Fremdenblatt, 27.12.1940; "Der Stabschef der SA" in Frankfurter Zeitung, 28.12.1940; "Stabschef der SA Lutze 50 Jahre" in Illustrierte Kronen-Zeitung [Wien], 28.12.1940; "Ein Lebenswerk für des Volkes Wehrkraft – Zum 50. Geburtstag des Stabschefs der SA" in Ostdeutscher Beobachter [Posen], 28.12.1940)
03.02.1934	*Ehrendolch der SA*
00.00.1937	Gold-plated *Walther PP* 7.65 mm pistol with ivory grips bearing his initials—"*VL*" and serial number 972851. Engraved "*Ehrengabe der Waffenfabrik Walther-Zella-Mehlis/Th.*" and "*S.A.-Pistolenschiessen 1937*". The weapon was manufactured by *Carl Walther Waffenfabrik Zella-Mehlis/Thüringen*
28.12.1938	*Luftwaffen-Zivilabzeichen.* ("Hermann Göring ehrt seinen Kampfgefährten Lutze" in Das Kleine Volksblatt [Wien], 10.01.1939; "Göring ehrt Lutze" in Pommersche Zeitung, 11.01.1939)
00.02.1934	*Ehrenwinkel für alte Kämpfer*
18.12.1931	*Tyr-Rune*

13.05.1939	*Ehrenbürgerrecht der Stadt Schwelm* (title revoked by the *Rat der Stadt Schwelm*, 25.08.1983)
13.05.1939	*Ehrenbürgerrecht der Stadt Schwelm* (title revoked by decision of the city council, 25.08.1983)
26.06.1937	*Ehrenbürgerrecht der Stadt Göttingen* (title revoked by decision of the *Hauptausschuss der Stadt Göttingen*, 25.08.1952)
23.06.1936	*Ehrenbürgerbrief der Stadt Gelsenkirchen* (presented 28.06.1936 by *Oberbürgermeister* Karl Böhmer)
07.10.1934	*Ehrenbürgerbrief der Stadt Bevergern*. ("Chef des Stabes Viktor Lutze in seiner Heimat-Ueberreichung des Ehrenbürgerbriefes" *Münsterischer Anzeiger*, 08.10.1934; "Die westfälische Heimat umjubelt den Chef des Stabes, Viktor Lutze" in *Völkischer Beobachter*, 09.10.1934)
00.00.193_	*Ehrenbürgerrecht der Stadt Hattingen* (Ruhr)
00.00.193_	*Ehrenbürgerrecht der Stadt Rinteln*
00.00.1937	Order of Saints Maurice and Lazarus, Grand Cross (*Gran Croce dell'Ordine dei Santi Maurizio e Lazzaro*)
01.11.1937	Honor Dagger of the *Milizia Volontaria per la Sicurezza Nazionale* (M.V.S.N., Volunteer Militia for National Security)
01.07.1938	Photograph of *Il Duce* (Benito Mussolini) inscribed to *"Al Camerato Viktor Lutze in Kameradschaft"*). ("Abschied Lutzes von Mussolini" in *Völkischer Beobachter* [Münchner Ausgabe], 04.07.1938)
00.00.193_	*Österreichische Kriegserinnerungsmedaille*
16.07.1918	Commander's Cross of the Royal Bulgarian Military Service Order with War Decoration
30.09.1940	Grand Cross of the Royal Bulgarian Order of Civil Merit

NOTES:

* Parents:
    - Father: *August* Anton Heinrich Lutze (*02.12.1859 in Bervergern, †23.03.1947 in Bevergern), a master shoemaker and smallholder. From 1895 to 1938, he was a *Stadtverordneter* in Bevergern, and in November 1935 was appointed as an *Ehrenbeamter auf Lebenszeit* (honorary lifetime official) and member of the *Kreisausschuss* (district committee) of Tecklenburg (*Frankfurter Zeitung*, 24.11.1935).
    - Mother: Maria *Sophia* Lutze, née Kockmeyer (*27.02.1863 in Püsselbühren/Kreis Tecklenburg, †02.02.1932 in Bevergern).

    The marriage produced three children, of which Viktor was the second (and oldest son).
* Religion: Roman Catholic.
* Married in Hausberge (Porta) on 09.11.1918 to *Paula* Minna Friederike Lehmann (*07.09.1900 in Hausberge an der Porta, †23.06.1954 in Bevergern), daughter of the deceased businessman Oswald Lehmann and his wife Ida, née Kahle. She was herself a member of the NSDAP and recipient of its *Goldenes Ehrenzeichen*. From the marriage of Viktor and Paula Lutze were born the following children:
    - Viktor Lutze, Jr. (*29.02.1924 in Wuppertal-Elberfeld, killed in action as a *Leutnant* with 6. Kompanie/Panzer-Grenadier-Regiment 192/21. Panzer-Division northwest of Hottot in Normandy, 20.06.1944). During a private conversation on the night of 03.–04.01.1942, Hitler made the following remarks concerning Viktor Lutze, Jr.:

Young Lutze has gone off to the front as a volunteer. Let's hope nothing happens to him. He's truly a pattern of what a young man should be—perfect in every way. When he has had a long enough period of training at the front, I'll take him onto my staff. He has plenty of breeding. On one occasion, Inge and he had come to Obersalzberg. They must have been thirteen and fourteen years old. Inge had done something that was not too well-behaved, no doubt. He turned to us and made the observation: "What young people are coming to, nowadays!" (H. R. Trevor-Roper, ed., *Hitler's Table Talk 1941–1944*)

- Adolf-Hermann ("Addi") Lutze (*23.07.1936, killed in a car crash on 17.08.1957).
- *Ingeborg* (Inge) Kriemhilde Lutze (*23.11.1925, killed in the accident that mortally injured her father on 01.05.1943).

* The following is Hitler's summary of Lutze's life and career, delivered during his funeral at the *Reichskanzlei* on 07.05.1943:

In a time when the war demands of our Volk the painful sacrifice of so many men, women, and regrettably even children, it takes a particularly heavy toll of blood from our National Socialist Party. There are members and sympathizers of our movement in all formations of the Heer, Kriegsmarine, Luftwaffe, and Waffen-SS, and they fulfill their duty in an exemplary fashion. From the National Socialist Reichstag to the higher age groups of the Hitler Youth, the numbers of our movement's dead represent a far higher percentage of the total than the average of the rest of the Volk.

Alas, the war not only claims our men and women, it also brings truly saddening misfortune. It is particularly tragic for me to have to witness almost every year how the one or other irreplaceable fighter, coworker, and fellow designer of our new Reich is called to join the flock of those whom the poet of the National Socialist revolutionary song has accompany us in spirit. After the plane crash that took the unforgettable and irreplaceable party comrade Dr. Todt from us, it is a car crash this time that robs the SA of its chief of staff and me personally of a man who was always loyally attached to me.

What can be said about the life story of this old National Socialist fighter has been said by the speaker before me, who was one of his oldest friends. I met the SA Führer Viktor Lutze for the first time in Westfalen in 1925–1926. Since then I have become attached to him and his family not only through the common fight but also in a profound personal friendship. Nevertheless, on this day, I wish to commemorate primarily the man who unconditionally tied his own destiny to mine, who throughout the years was such a loyal and unshakable comrade in arms for me that, in a most bitter and painful hour, I felt I could entrust the leadership of my SA to him, as the most competent man.

As one of my most staunch supporters, he fulfilled his mission and developed the SA into an instrument which was capable of carrying out all the great tasks which I set for it in the course of the year.

My SA chief of staff, Viktor Lutze, was a soldier all his life. Because of this way of thinking, he had the fervent desire to be allowed to go to the front himself, a request which he made to me and which I was unable to grant.

Nevertheless, he has now died in a manner which puts a manly end to his life as a National Socialist.

I want to express my profound gratitude to you, my dear Lutze, before the movement, the SA, and the entire German Volk, for your loyal fight. From the mighty struggle, in the midst of which we find ourselves today and to which you so richly contributed through your life's work, will one day emerge the goal which once led us to each other and for which we fought over many decades in a sacred faith and with the greatest devotion: The Greater German Reich, secured by its own power against its enemies and supported by a true Volksgemeinschaft! In the annals of history, the name of Chief of Staff Viktor Lutze will live on eternally as one of the founders of the new Reich.

My dear Frau Lutze, you have my heartfelt sympathy on the death of your husband and your child. I wish both your sons a speedy recovery.

I believe that I cannot secure a worthier future significance for the highest medal that our party can award than by awarding it to the first pioneers of the new Reich and, thus, to the deceased. Through this, it is ennobled for all those who will one day have the honor of bearing it while alive.

* The memorial address by Lutze's early Party colleague, Dr. Goebbels:

My Führer! Dear Lutze family! My old party members and comrades! Dear mourners!

As I stand before his bier in this farewell hour as one of the oldest friends and companions of our Stabschef, to bid him our last farewell in the name of the Führer, his comrades from the ranks of the Reichsleiter, Gauleiter, Obergruppen- und Gruppenführer der SA., many millions of SA. men and party comrades, yes, I can say in the name of the entire German people, I do so with a feeling of sincere and deep pain.

When the news of the Stabschef's car accident reached us in the early afternoon of last Saturday, myself and all his friends and comrades were still clinging to the hope that he would remain with us after all. For hours we hung between fear and hope and fought in spirit with him the struggle against a relentless death, which he had so often faced fearlessly in his life in the trenches of the World War and in the positions of political struggle. Our hope was in vain. As I stood before the dead Stabschef for the last time, I am not ashamed to admit that I was deeply moved when, in those silent minutes, my thoughts progressed through the past 20 years once again, in which I was allowed to be his friend and comrade.

For those of us who established and built the party in the Gau Ruhr, he was the symbol of an eternally fighting German youth. Only we can understand what it means then to release someone from this company. This is also what moves us, those closest to the Führer, and he himself most deeply in this hour, that Viktor Lutze, in his passing away, takes with him a part of our own stormy youth. What he achieved for the Führer, the Party and the nation, the historiography of our times will not be able to pass over in silence. But today, before his grave, I would like to bear witness to his radiant personality, to the brave masculinity it embodied, to his great friend's heart, to all that he was to us, his old comrades and companions, and all that is irretrievably lost with him. Every day brings new events and new concerns. They will also gradually cause the pain of the loss of our Stabschef to fade away; but it will flare up in us once again when the Führer, at the first Party Congress after our victory on the day of the SA, passes through the ranks of his men on his way to the hero's memorial and he does not walk by his side. Then the thoughts of all the hundreds of thousands who, with bated breath, attend this solemn ceremony will certainly linger with him for a minute.

His old comrades will rush to him in spirit, and he will be with them. They are now gathered with the Führer around his bier, to let his rich fighter life pass before their eyes once again.

As early as 21 February 1922, he joined the NSDAP, with the membership number 84, and thus made his first contact with the Führer, which would later become his whole purpose in life. On joining the SA. he is still the unknown SA-Mann Viktor Lutze, who for the first time becomes a member of the political combat organization, whose Stabschef he is later to become. From level to level, he rises higher and higher and the assumption of power sees him in the middle of the political struggle. The severe crisis of 1934 finds in him a strong and powerful factor of unswerving loyalty. It seems only natural that the Führer should appoint him Stabschef of the SA. on June 30, 1934.

This marks the beginning of an organizational structure that reaches far beyond the scope of the party's immediate history. The Stabschef Viktor Lutze can be considered the creator and spiritual father of the organizational and educational development of the SA. What he achieved in this field in the years from 1934 until the day of his passing belongs not only to the history of the Party, but to the history of the German people. Never before has Viktor Lutze's dedication to his work and his idea been more convincingly justified than during this war.

Just as, during the time of struggle, the SA. man was deployed wherever decisions were made in the struggle for political power, so today he is again fighting on the battlefields where the future of the National Socialist Reich is decided. When, until the very end, Viktor Lutze visited his men on the fronts again and again, then it may have been the greatest satisfaction for him to discover that they remained what they always were, even in their field-gray uniforms: Idealists of the Party and the Führer and old SA men. I have little to add to this sketch of a militant life. It speaks for itself.

In contrast, its abrupt conclusion seems almost senseless to us. On May the 1st, the Stabschef returns from a business trip and picks up his family, who have visited his almost 84-year-old father, on the way. On the Reichsautobahn his car starts to skid in a curve, the vehicle is thrown off course and crashes down the high embankment. The Stabschef, who as always sits to the right of the driver, is pressed against the windshield in such an unfortunate way, that, in addition to serious injuries to his right shoulder, he suffers contusions, several broken ribs and a concussion. The injuries, the serious character of which is immediately apparent at the first examination after admission to hospital, do not at first immediately threaten the life of the Stabschef. In the course of Sunday, his condition worsens due to increasing obstruction of breathing and circulation. The doctors perform a procedure that brings only temporary relief to his struggle with death. On Sunday evening, Viktor Lutze succumbs to his severe injuries.

In interpreting the deep feelings of sympathy that we all have for the Lutze family in the face of this tragic accident, I know that, in particular, I am speaking from the heart of their old circle of friends. In warm participation in their pain, we reach out to the grieving widow, his sons, the old, deeply bowed father, who in Viktor Lutze loses the pride of his old age. The party itself, and especially the SA whose unforgettable Stabschef the deceased was and remains, bows in pain to its dead comrade one last time.

Viktor Lutze, dear friend and loyal comrade, farewell! Our moved hearts call to you as we say goodbye: You can rest in peace now. What you have so faithfully fought for at our side is now reality. The greater Reich is ours, and it will never pass away. (*Völkischer Beobachter* [*Wiener Ausgabe*], 08.05.1943; Translation: Gary Costello)

* In a sworn affidavit submitted at Darmstadt on 18.06.1946, former *SA-Gruppenführer* Prof. Dr. med. Kurt Blome (later acquitted in the "Doctors Trial" before the U.S. Military Tribunal, Nürnberg) stated:

I know the former SA Chief of Staff Victor [*sic*] LUTZE from the SA, to which I belonged since 1931. I was last the medial local leader at the disposal of Supreme SA Command. Although this position had no connection with the duties of the SA I often met Staff Chief LUTZE, so that I had good comradely relations to LUTZE. These meetings were mostly short and casual, but during the war in 1940, on the occasion of an incidental common journey in the sleeper Berlin-Munich, or vice versa, we had the opportunity to indulge in a lengthy intimate discussion. From this meeting I recall chiefly 2 points of conversation:

1) The general situation,
2) The events of 8/9 November 1938.

Re 1.
Chief of Staff LUTZE complained of the general political development, especially of the fact that, from his point of view, a gradual distinction had developed between the true national socialism as it was represented during the fighting period and in the party programme, and the present regime which he called "Nazism". As the essential feature of the latter he mentioned the suppression of every individuality and every honest expression of opinion. From the desired national socialist people's state

has arisen an intolerant Police State. He talked about a general complete "uniformity" not only in outward visible forms but also in the intellectual sphere. The world would have reconciled itself with the old, decent national socialism; Nazism, however, has brought upon us the hate of all. If a basic change is not made here, a gloomy future awaits us. He himself was sorry for most of the men of the SA, who had been deeply disappointed by the course of the development. LUTZE expressed himself to me similarly on the occasion of my visit to him in Berlin Vo[β]strasse, about February 1941.

When in 1942 I congratulated Chief of Staff LUTZE on his 50th [sic, fifty-second] birthday in his apartment in Berlin, he took me aside, lead me into one of the rooms and said to me almost literally the following:

"Last night the Fuehrer was here in order to congratulate me. There (he pointed to a seat) we two sat alone for more than 2 hours. I told the Fuehrer frankly all my worries and misgivings. He promised me he would do all he can to provide for a change."

He, LUTZE, then expressed his joy on the Fuehrer's promise. Now he hoped to be able to inspire the SA, for years treated like a step-child, with new buoyancy in the old traditional sense.

Re 2:
On this point LUTZE talked to me in an outspoken lively manner. He had known nothing of the matter, otherwise he would have prevented it. I believe he mentioned Dr. GOEBBELS to me as the instigator. By this the SA, quite unjustly, was put in an unfavorable light, which, considering its decent basic motives, it did not deserve. If SA men really took part in it, it was due to their thoughtlessness and the imposition of orders which had not been issued by him. Wherever he, LUTZE, turned up, great disappointment was shown about these events.
[Signed] Prof. Dr. Kurt BLOME.
(IMT Nuremberg Archives, H-5126, International Court of Justice, in the Taube Archive of the International Military Tribunal Nuremberg, 1945–46, Stanford University Libraries)

SOURCES:
Bennecke, Dr. phil. Heinrich: *Hitler und die SA*. Günter Olzog Verlag, 1962.
Burden, Hamilton T.: *The Nuremberg Party Rallies*. Frederick A. Praeger, Publishers, 1967.
Campbell, Bruce: *The SA Generals and the Rise of Nazism*. The University Press of Kentucky, 1998.
Elmayer-Vestenbrugg, SA-Obersturmführer Rudolf von: *SA.-Männer im feldgrauen Rock. Taten und Erlebnisse von SA.-Männern in den Kriegsjahren 1939–1940*. Hase & Koehler, 1941.
Fredborg, Arvid: *Behind the Steel Wall: A Swedish Journalist in Berlin 1941–43*. Viking Press, 1944.
Gisevius, Hans Bernd: *To the Bitter End*. Houghton Mifflin Company, 1947.
Goebbels, Joseph: *Die Tagebücher von Joseph Goebbels*. Commissioned by the Institut für Zeitgeschichte and with the support of the State Archive Service of Russia. Published by Elke Fröhlich. Teil I: Aufzeichnungen 1923–1941, Band 2/I: Dezember 1929–Mai 1931. Edited by Anne Munding. K. G. Saur, 2005.
—*Die Tagebücher von Joseph Goebbels*. Commissioned by the Institut für Zeitgeschichte and with the support of the State Archive Service of Russia. Published by Elke Fröhlich. Teil I: Aufzeichnungen 1923–1941, Band 3/I: April 1934–Februar 1936. Edited by Angela Hermann, Hartmut Mehringer, Anne Munding, and Jana Richter. K.G. Saur, 2005.
—*Die Tagebücher von Joseph Goebbels*. Commissioned by the Institut für Zeitgeschichte and with the support of the State Archive Service of Russia. Published by Elke Fröhlich. Teil I: Aufzeichnungen 1923–1941, Band 3/II: März 1936–Februar 1937. Edited by Jana Richter. K.G. Saur, 2001.

—*Die Tagebücher von Joseph Goebbels*. Commissioned by the Institut für Zeitgeschichte and with the support of the State Archive Service of Russia. Published by Elke Fröhlich. Teil I: Aufzeichnungen 1923–1941, Band 4: März–November 1937. Edited by Elke Fröhlich. K.G. Saur, 2000.
—*Die Tagebücher von Joseph Goebbels*. Commissioned by the Institut für Zeitgeschichte and with the support of the State Archive Service of Russia. Published by Elke Fröhlich. Teil I: Aufzeichnungen 1923–1941, Band 5: Dezember 1937–Juli 1938. Edited by Elke Fröhlich. K.G. Saur, 2000.
—*Die Tagebücher von Joseph Goebbels*. Commissioned by the Institut für Zeitgeschichte and with the support of the State Archive Service of Russia. Published by Elke Fröhlich. Teil I: Aufzeichnungen 1923–1941, Band 6: August 1938–Juni 1939. Edited by Jana Richter. K.G. Saur, 1998.
—*Die Tagebücher von Joseph Goebbels*. Commissioned by the Institut für Zeitgeschichte and with the support of the State Archive Service of Russia. Published by Elke Fröhlich. Teil I: Aufzeichnungen 1923–1941, Band 7: Juli 1939–März 1940. Edited by Elke Fröhlich. K.G. Saur, 1998.
—*Die Tagebücher von Joseph Goebbels*. Commissioned by the Institut für Zeitgeschichte and with the support of the State Archive Service of Russia. Published by Elke Fröhlich. Teil I: Aufzeichnungen 1923–1941, Band 9: Dezember 1940–Juli 1941. Edited by Elke Fröhlich. K.G. Saur, 1998.
—*Die Tagebücher von Joseph Goebbels*. Commissioned by the Institut für Zeitgeschichte and with the support of the State Archive Service of Russia. Published by Elke Fröhlich. Teil II: Diktate 1941–1945, Band 2: Oktober–Dezember 1941. Edited by Elke Fröhlich. K.G. Saur, 1996.
—*Die Tagebücher von Joseph Goebbels*. Commissioned by the Institut für Zeitgeschichte and with the support of the State Archive Service of Russia. Published by Elke Fröhlich. Teil II: Diktate 1941–1945, Band 4: April–Juni 1942. Edited by Elke Fröhlich. K.G. Saur, 1995.
—*Die Tagebücher von Joseph Goebbels*. Commissioned by the Institut für Zeitgeschichte and with the support of the State Archive Service of Russia. Published by Elke Fröhlich. Teil II: Diktate 1941–1945, Band 5: Juli–September 1942. Edited by Angela Stüber. K.G. Saur, 1995.
—*Die Tagebücher von Joseph Goebbels*. Commissioned by the Institut für Zeitgeschichte and with the support of the State Archive Service of Russia. Published by Elke Fröhlich. Herausgegeben von Elke Fröhlich. Teil II: Diktate 1941–1945, Band 7: Januar–März 1943. Edited by Elke Fröhlich. K.G. Saur, 1993.
—*Die Tagebücher von Joseph Goebbels*. Commissioned by the Institut für Zeitgeschichte and with the support of the State Archive Service of Russia. Published by Elke Fröhlich. Teil II: Diktate 1941–1945, Band 8: April–Juni 1943. Edited by Hartmut Mehringer. K.G. Saur, 1993.
—*Die Tagebücher von Joseph Goebbels*. Commissioned by the Institut für Zeitgeschichte and with the support of the State Archive Service of Russia. Published by Elke Fröhlich. Teil II: Diktate 1941–1945, Band 9: Juli–September 1943. Edited by Manfred Kittel. K.G. Saur, 1993.
Gruchmann, Lothar: *Justiz im Dritten Reich 1933–1940. Anpassung und Unterwerfung in der Ära Gürtner*. R. Oldenbourg Verlag, 1988.
Halcomb, Jill: *The SA: A Historical Perspective*. Crown/Agincourt Publishers, 1985.
Heiber, Helmut (ed.): *"Reichsfuhrer!"... Briefe an und von Himmler*. Deutsche Verlag, 1968.
Himmler, Heinrich: *Heinrich Himmlers Taschenkalender 1940* (annotated edition), edited by Markus Moors and Moritz Pfeiffer. Ferdinand Schöningh, 2013.
Höffkes, Karl: *Hitlers politische Generale: Die Gauleiter des Dritten Reiches*. Grabert-Verlag-Tübingen, 1986.
Höhne, Heinz: *The Order of the Death's Head*. Martin Secker and Warburg, 1969.

Holzmann, Michael E.: *"... und steht die Legion auf dem ihr zugewies'nen Posten". Die Österreichische Legion als Instrument frührer NS-Aggressionspolitik.* LIT Verlag, 2018.

International Military Tribunal, Nürnberg: *Trial of the Major War Criminals Before the International Military Tribunal Nuremberg, Volume XXI.*

Lang, Jochen von: *The Secretary. Martin Bormann: The Man Who Manipulated Hitler.* Random House, 1979.

—*Der Adjutant. Karl Wolff: Der Mann zwischen Hitler und Himmler.* Verlag Ullstein GmbH, 1989.

Lilla, Joachim; Döring, Martin; & Schulz, Andreas: *Statisten in Uniform. Die Mitglieder des Reichstags 1933–1945.* Droste Verlag, 2004.

Meindl, Ralf: *Ostpreußens Gauleiter. Erich Koch—eine politische Biographie.* Fibre Verlag, 2007.

Miller, Michael D. and Andreas Schulz: *Leaders of the Storm Troops, Volume 1* (1st Edition). Helion & Co., 2015.

—*Gauleiter, The Regional Leaders of the Nazi Party and their Deputies, 1925–1945. Volume 2: Georg Joel to Dr. Bernhard Rust.* R. James Bender Publishing, 2017.

Orlow, Dietrich: *History of the Nazi Party: 1933–1945.* University of Pittsburgh Press, 1973.

Rosenberg, Alfred: *Memoirs of Alfred Rosenberg.* Ziff-Davis, 1949.

Schirach, Baldur von: *Die Pioniere des Dritten Reiches.* Zentralstelle fur der deutschen Freiheitskampf, 1933.

Shirer, William L.: *Berlin Diary. The Journal of a Foreign Correspondent, 1934–1941.* Alfred A. Knopf, 1942.

Siemens, Daniel: *Stormtroopers: A New History of Hitler's Brownshirts.* Yale University Press, 2017.

Steinmetz, Eckhard: *"Nordmark voran". Beiträge zur Geschichte der SA.* Kiel, year unknown [unpublished manuscript]).

Toland, John: *Adolf Hitler.* Doubleday, 1976.

Trevor-Roper, Hugh Redwald: *Hitler's Table Talk 1941–1944.* Translation of Dr. Henry Picker & Gerhard Ritter, *Tischgespräche im Führerhauptquartier 1941–1942* [1951]. Weidenfeld and Nicolson, 1953.

Wawrzinek, Bert: *Manfred von Killinger (1886–1944). Ein politischer Soldat zwischen Freikorps und Auswärtigem Amt.* Deutsche Verlagsgesellschaft (DVG), 2003.

Above left: Viktor Lutze (left) in the trenches on the Somme, December 1916.

Above right: Viktor Lutze in civilian attire, *c.* 1924.

Essen, 1925: Viktor Lutze as *Gau SA-Führer* in the Ruhr. (*SA-Obersturmführer* Karl H. W. Koch, *Das Ehrenbuch der SA*, 1934)

The "*2. Reichsparteitag der NSDAP*" in Weimar, 03.–04.07.1926

From right to left in the first row: Viktor Lutze, Dr. Joseph Goebbels, Gregor Strasser, and Josef Wagner. (NARA, Heinrich Hoffmann Collection)

Lutze (eighth from left) and Goebbels (eleventh from left). (*SA-Obersturmführer* Karl H. W. Koch, *Das Ehrenbuch der SA*, 1934)

Hitler and Lutze inspect SA men during the "*2. Reichsparteitag der NSDAP*" in Weimar, 03.–04.07.1926. At left is Heinrich Unger, *Ortsgruppenleiter* of the NSDAP in Essen

The *Gasthof Märker* in Hattingen, 26.11.1926: Hitler, Goebbels, Karl Kaufmann (3), and Lutze (1) as guests at a meeting of *NSDAP Ortsgruppenführer* in the Ruhr. Also present is future *SA-Stabschef* Wilhelm Schepmann (2). (*SA-Obersturmführer* Karl H. W. Koch, *Das Ehrenbuch der SA*, 1934)

Viktor Lutze as *SA-Oberführer Ruhr*, c. 1929.

Hitler consecrates new *SA-Standarte* banners by touching them to the *"Blutfahne."* Viktor Lutze, third from right, next to the Austrian *SA-Oberführer* Hermann Reschny, looks on. At far left are Rudolf Hess and Manfred Freiherr von Killinger.

Right: The *Braunschweiger Hauptfriedhof* (main cemetery), 18.10.1930: Lutze and Hitler attend the memorial service for Karl Dinklage (deputy to the *Obersten SA-Führer* and *Oberster SA-Führer Nord*). At left are Franz Pfeffer von Salomon and Werner von Fichte. (*SA-Obersturmführer* Karl H. W. Koch, *Das Ehrenbuch der SA*, 1934)

Below: Hitler and Lutze inspect the SA in Oldenburg. From left to right: Otto Herzog, Hitler, Gerret Korsemann, Lutze, and Rudolf Hess. (*SA-Obersturmführer* Karl H. W. Koch, *Das Ehrenbuch der SA*, 1934)

Hitler visits Oldenburg, Autumn 1930:

Above: Left to right: *Gauleiter* Carl Röver, Hitler, Lutze, Rudolf Hess, and Otto Herzog. (Roger Bender)

Below: Left to right: Wilhelm Jahn, unknown, Hitler, and Lutze. (Roger Bender)

Above left: SA-Oberführer Lutze in 1931. (Baldur von Schirach, *Die Pioniere des Dritten Reiches*, 1933)

Above right: SA-Obergruppenführer Lutze in 1933.

The *Reichstag*, Berlin, 13.07.1934: The newly appointed *Stabschef*, still wearing the insignia of an *SA-Obergruppenführer*, listens to Hitler as the *Führer* speaks of the recent SA purge. In the row behind him are, from left to right, Konstantin Hierl, Heinrich Himmler, and Karl Hanke. (NARA, Heinrich Hoffmann Collection)

Viktor Lutze in full regalia, wearing the newly introduced insignia for the rank of *SA-Stabschef* in 1934. (NARA, Heinrich Hoffmann Collection)

SA-Obergruppenführer Lutze and *SA-Gruppenführer* Josef Seydel accompany Hitler during a Party function in 1933. (Roger Bender)

Nürnberg, 20.08.1934: Lutze and Hitler with the film director Leni Riefenstahl during preparations for the "6. *Reichsparteitag der NSDAP.*" (NARA, Heinrich Hoffmann Collection)

Above, opposite and overleaf: 28.07.1935: Lutze boards a Junkers Ju 52 for a flight from Hannover to Berlin. (NARA, Heinrich Hoffmann Collection)

Right: A Heinrich Hoffmann postcard of *SA-Stabschef* Lutze. The collar insignia has been modified in this photo; Lutze was an *SA-Obergruppenführer* when it was originally taken. (NARA, Heinrich Hoffmann Collection)

Below: München, 09.11.1934: Lutze delivers a speech at the commemoration of the "*Putsch*" eleven years earlier. (NARA, Heinrich Hoffmann Collection)

Above left: Lutze delivers a speech during the "*7. Reichsparteitag der NSDAP*" in Nürnberg (10.09.1935–16.09.1935). (NARA, Heinrich Hoffmann Collection)

Above right: Lutze and Göring in 1935. In the background at left are *NSKK-Korpsführer* Adolf Hühnlein and *Generaloberst* Werner von Blomberg. (NARA, Heinrich Hoffmann Collection)

An autographed portrait of *SA-Stabschef* Lutze, dated 11.08.1935. (Hermann-Historica, Auctioneers, München)

Berlin, 31.01.1936: Lutze and Hitler review SA troops.

Reichsführer-SS Himmler, followed by Lutze, leads an inspection tour of workshops at *KL-Dachau* on 08.05.1936.

SA-Stabschef Lutze and *Generalfeldmarschall* Göring lead a procession of high-ranking SA leaders. In the background, from left to right, are Fritz Görnnert, Arthur Böckenhauer, Walther Heitmüller, Siegfried Kasche, Herbert Fust, and Dr. Erich Gritzbach.

Lutze with *Reichsleiter* Dr. Ley, *c.* 1935. (Dave Overcash)

Lutze and *Gauleiter* Dr. Alfred Meyer during the "*Gautreffen des Gaues Westfalen-Nord der NSDAP*" in Gelsenkirchen, 25.–27.06.1937. (Dave Overcash)

4.–15.07.1938: The state visit of Lutze's Italian counterpart, *Luogotenente Generale* Luigi Russo, Chief of Staff of the *Milizia Volontaria per la Sicurezza Nazionale* (*M.V.S.N.*, Volunteer Militia for National Security, or "Black Shirts") from 04.10.1935 to 29.10.1939.

Left: Lutze greets General Russo at the *Hauptbahnhof* in München, 14.07.1938.

Opposite above: Lutze sees General Russo off before his departure from Berlin-Tempelhof, 15.07.1938.

The *Führer* poses with Lutze and Russo at the Berghof on the Obersalzberg, afternoon of 14.07.1938.

Rome, July 1938: *SA-Stabschef* Lutze, General Russo, and German Ambassador Hans Georg von Mackensen (in white SS uniform) salute the *Tomba del Milite Ignoto* (Tomb of the Unknown Soldier) at the *Altare della Patria*, Rome.

Formal portraits of Viktor Lutze. From NARA, Heinrich Hoffmann Collection (above and opposite) and Hermann-Historica, Auctioneers, München.

Above: Lutze congratulates Hitler on the occasion of his fifty-first birthday, 20.04.1940. In the background are *SA-Obergruppenführer* Hanns Kerrl and *Dr.-Ing.* Fritz Todt.

Left: Lutze in conversation with Constantin Freiherr von Neurath, the *Reichsprotektor* of Bohemia and Moravia and former Reich Foreign Minister, in 1941. In the background are *SA-Obergruppenführer* Max Luyken (right) and, in *Luftwaffe* uniform at left, *SA-Obergruppenführer* Dr. Horst Raecke. (Alexander Historical Auctions)

Lutze and Goebbels converse with military officers, including several Knight's Cross holders, in September 1940. The Army officer third from left is Horst von Petersdorff (also an *SA-Brigadeführer*). From left to right in the first row: *Hauptmann d. R.* Otto Zierach, *Hauptmann z. V.* Horst von Petersdorff (also an *SA-Brigadeführer*), Goebbels, Lutze, and *Oberleutnant d. R.* Ludwig Klotz. (National Digital Archives, Poland)

Lutze visits his *Führer* at *Führer HQ "Wehrwolf"* near Vinnitsa, 22.07.1942.

The Volkhov Front, August 1942.

Above: Left to right: *SA-Hauptsturmführer* Hans Hoffritz, *Generalfeldmarschall* Georg von Küchler (*Oberbefehlshaber* of *Heeresgruppe Nord*), Lutze, an unidentified officer, and an unidentified general. (Todd Gylsen)

Left: Lutze inspects and decorates men of *Infanterie-Regiment* "Feldherrnhalle" (*Illustrierter Beobachter*, 13.08.1942)

Right: SA-Stabschef Lutze inspecting *SA-Gruppe Pommern*, 14.08.1942. (Roger Bender)

Below: 10.09.1942: Viktor Lutze and General Enzo Galbiati (head of the M.V.S.N.) visit *Führer HQ "Wehrwolf"* at Vinnitsa in the Ukraine, escorted by *SS-Hauptsturmführer* Richard Schulze. (NARA, Heinrich Hoffmann Collection)

11.09.1942: Lutze hosts General Galbiati during his visit to Berlin. (NARA, Heinrich Hoffmann Collection)

Right: An official portrait of *SA-Stabschef* Lutze by Walter Frentz. (Roger Bender)

Below: Lutze and *Reichsleiter* Dr. Ley at the "*Arbeitstagung der DAF*" at Berlin's *Haus der Flieger*, 00.11.1942. (NARA, Heinrich Hoffmann Colection)

SA-Stabschef Lutze and *SA-Obergruppenführer* Oberlindober during an inspection of *SA-Wehrmannschaften* troops at Zakopane, south of Kraków in the *Generalgouvernement*. (National Digital Archives, Poland)

Above: Right to left: Oberlindober, Lutze, an unknown *Generalgouvernement* official, and *SA-Oberführer* (later *Brigadeführer*) Kurt Peltz (*Stabsführer* of the *Führungsstab der SA* in the *Generalgouvernement*, 01.07.1942–00.05.1944).

VÖLKISCHER BEOBACHTER

Wiener Ausgabe
124. Ausg. 56. Jahrg. Einzelpreise: Wien-Stadt 15 Pf. / Auswärts 20 Pf.

"Freiheit und Brot"

Kampfblatt der nationalsozialistischen Bewegung Großdeutschlands

Wiener Ausgabe
Wien, Dienstag, 4. Mai 1943

Stabschef Viktor Lutze gestorben

dnb. Berlin, 3. Mai

Der Stabschef der SA. Viktor Lutze ist am Sonntagabend im Städtischen Krankenhaus Potsdam seinen bei dem Kraftwagenunfall erlittenen schweren Verletzungen erlegen.

Wir senken die Standarten

Ein Mann und ein Kämpfer

Sowjetluftwaffe verlor im vergangenen Monat 1082 Flugzeuge
Im April 423.000 BRT. versenkt
Kriegsschiffsverluste des Feindes: Ein Flugzeugträger, ein Kreuzer, fünf Zerstörer, sechs U-Boote

dnb. Aus dem Führer-Hauptquartier, 3. Mai

Die Gezeiten des U-Boot-Krieges
vb. Wien, 3. Mai

Neue Ritterkreuzträger

Das Urteil der Wissenschaft über Katyn

The front page of the 04.05.1943 Völkischer Beobachter *is devoted to the death of* SA-Stabschef *Lutze.*

Lutze lying in state in the *Führermesse* in Gütersfelde bei Berlin, guarded by members of *Panzer-Grenadier-Regiment* "*Feldherrnhalle.*" Foreground left: *SA-Standartenführer* Friedrich Christian Prinz zu Schaumburg-Lippe (*Stab, SA-Standarte "Feldherrnhalle"*). Foreground right: *SA-Hauptsturmführer* and *Hauptmann* Bahne (*Kommandeur* of *Grenadier-Ersatz Bataillon "Feldherrnhalle"*). Rear left: *SA-Obersturmbannführer* Bethge (*Führer* of *I. Sturmbann/ SA-Standarte "Feldherrnhalle"*). Rear right: *SA-Hauptsturmführer* and *Oberleutnant* Wieland (*Chef* of the *Genesenden-Kompanie* [convalescent company] in *Grenadier-Ersatz-Bataillon "Feldherrnhalle"*).

Hitler bids farewell to his longest-serving *SA-Stabschef*, 07.05.1943.

Hitler offers his condolences to the widowed Paula Lutze while a somber Goebbels and the mother of the deceased look on.

Lutze with his father.

Left: Viktor and Paula Lutze attend the Summer Olympic Games in Berlin, August 1936. In the foreground is *SS-Brigadeführer* Julius Schaub. Behind Lutze is Dr. Hans Frank.

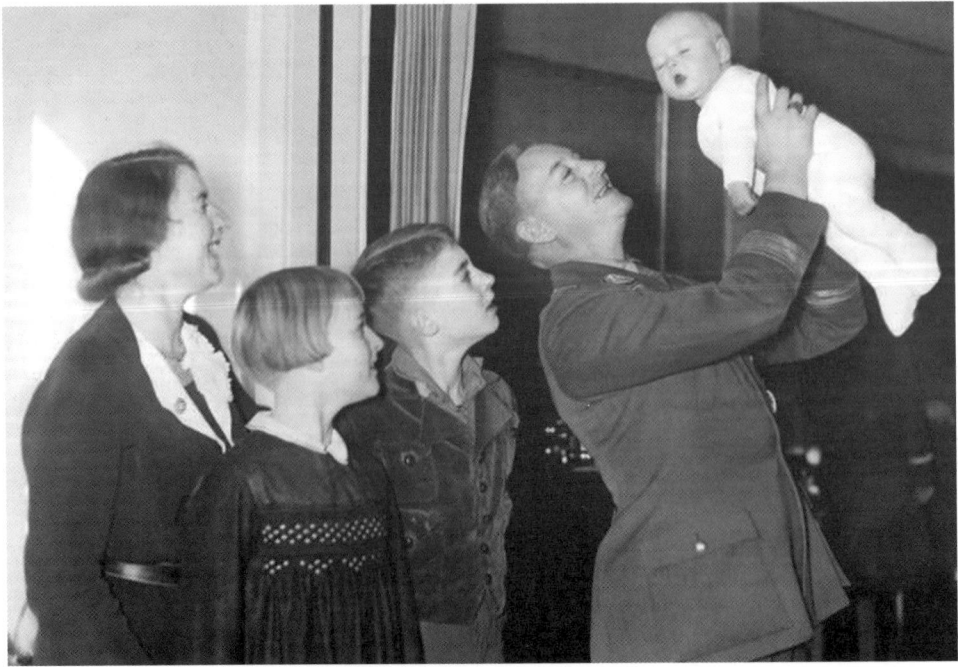

Above left: Hitler and Inge Lutze.

Above right: Paula Lutze and her three children.

Right and opposite below: Viktor Lutze and his family, c. 1935.

Berlin, 27.12.1940: Hitler pays a visit to his *SA-Stabschef* the evening before the latter's fiftieth birthday. Second from left is Paul Lutze, while Viktor Jr. is visible between Hitler and Lutze. (NARA, Heinrich Hoffmann Collection)

The final photo of the Lutze family, taken shortly before the car crash that took the lives of Viktor and his young daughter.

Right: A pencil portrait of Viktor Lutze by Carl Rosemann (Berlin), *c.* 1938, and signed by the *SA-Stabschef*. (Alexander Historical Auctions).

Below: *SA-Stabschef* Lutze is presented with the *SA-Ehrendolch für Führer der SA-Standarte "Feldherrnhalle"* on his birthday, 28.12.1937. At left is his personal adjutant, *SA-Gruppenführer* Erich Reimann. In the background are *SA-Brigadeführer* (later *Gruppenführer*) Walther Heitmüller (*1. Adjutant* to the *SA-Stabschef*) and Lutze's daughter.

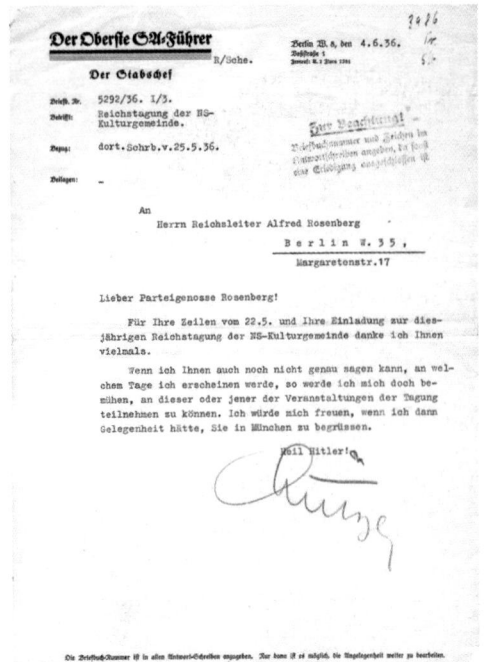
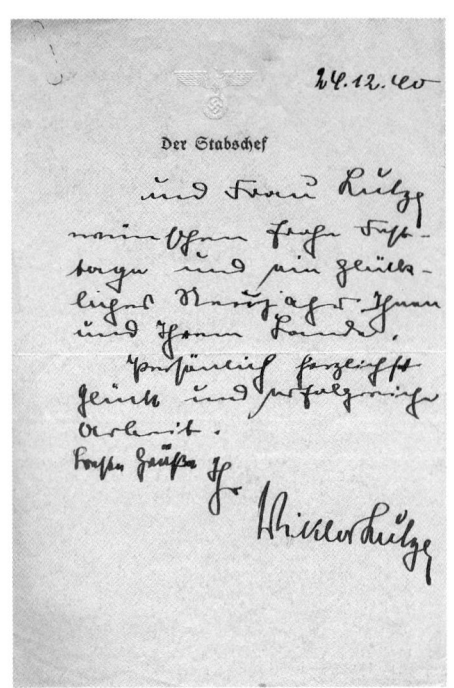

Samples of ephemera signed by *SA-Stabschef* Viktor Lutze.

Above left: A letter to Alfred Rosenberg, thanking his fellow *Reichsleiter* for an invitation to the annual conference of the National Socialist Cultural Community.

Above right: A handwritten note on Lutze's personal stationery.

Below: Signed Christmas and New Year greetings from the *Stabschef der SA*. (Credit for all photos: Alexander Historical Auctions)

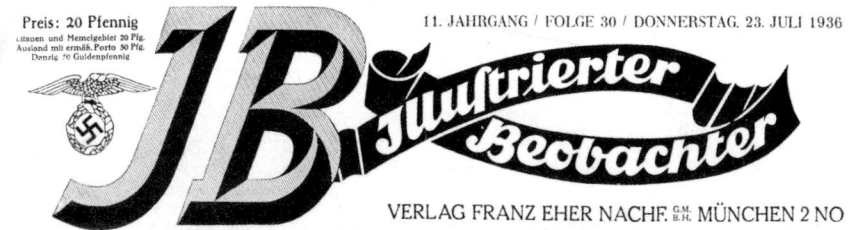

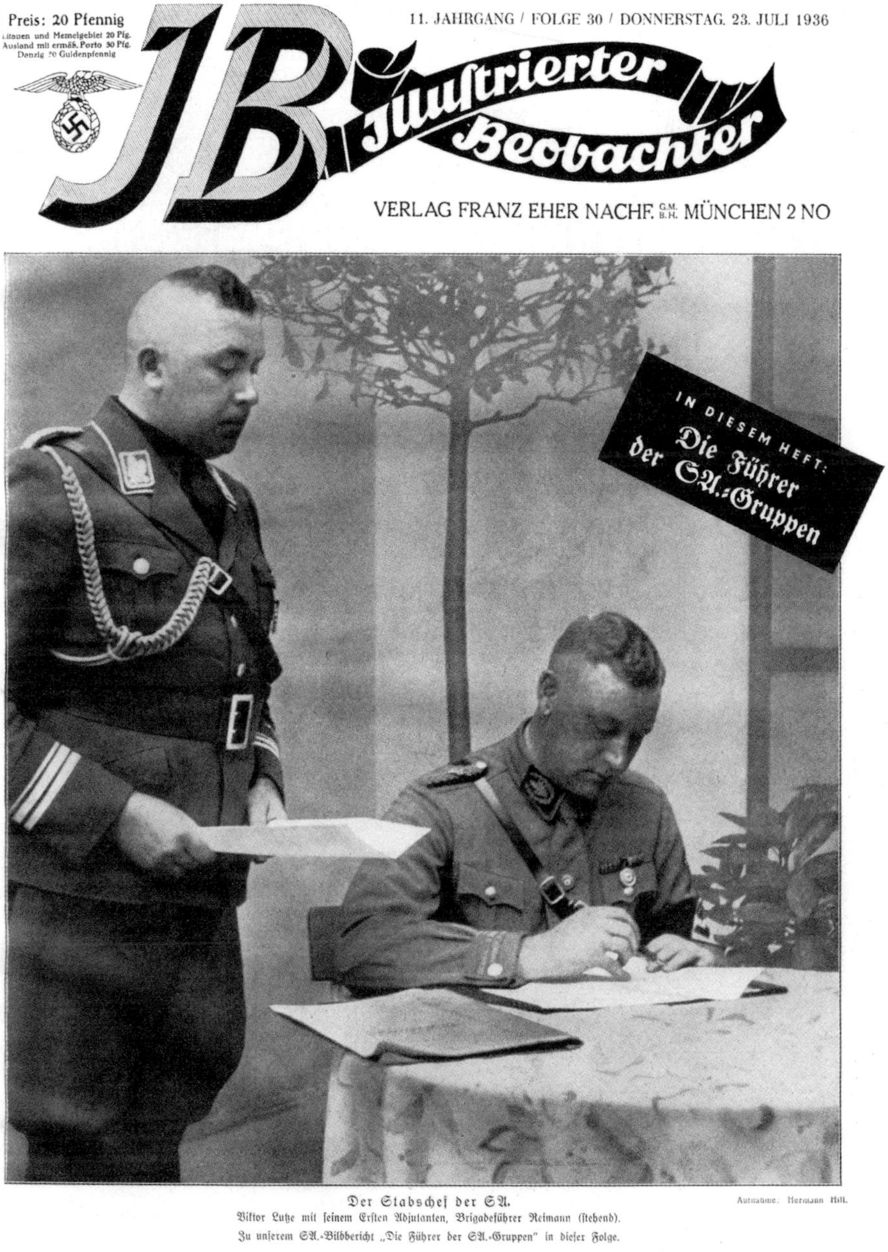
Preis: 20 Pfennig
Litauen und Memelgebiet 20 Pfg.
Ausland mit ermäß. Porto 30 Pfg.
Danzig 20 Guldenpfennig

11. JAHRGANG / FOLGE 30 / DONNERSTAG. 23. JULI 1936

IB Illustrierter Beobachter

VERLAG FRANZ EHER NACHF. G.M.B.H. MÜNCHEN 2 NO

IN DIESEM HEFT: Die Führer der SA.-Gruppen

Der Stabschef der SA.
Viktor Lutze mit seinem Ersten Adjutanten, Brigadeführer Reimann (stehend).
Zu unserem SA.-Bildbericht „Die Führer der SA.-Gruppen" in dieser Folge.

Aufnahme: Hermann Hill.

Lutze and *SA-Brigadeführer* Reimann, appear on the 23.07.1936 issue of the *Illustrierter Beobachter*.

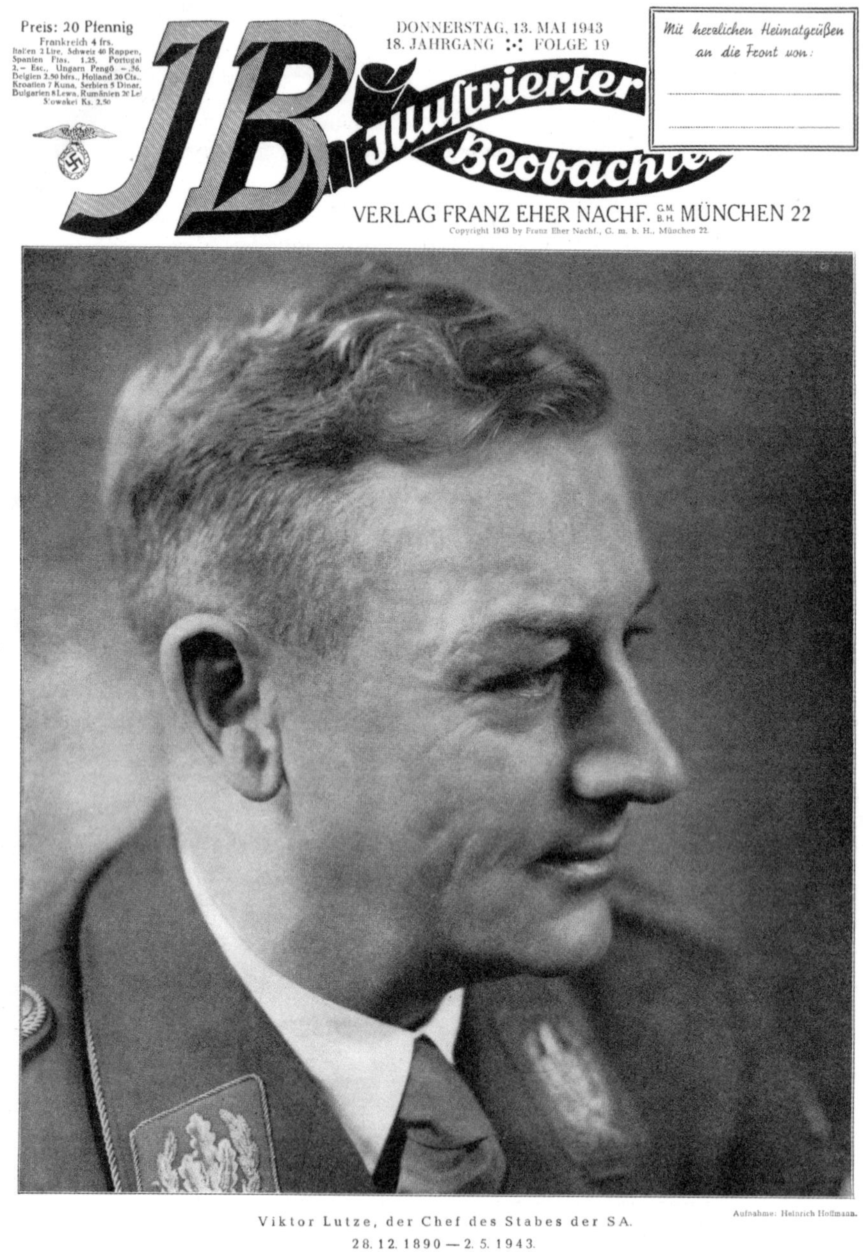
Preis: 20 Pfennig
Frankreich 4 frs.
Italien 2 Lire, Schweiz 40 Rappen, Spanien Ptas. 1.25, Portugal 2,— Esc., Ungarn Pengö —.36, Belgien 2.50 bfrs., Holland 20 Cts., Kroatien 7 Kuna, Serbien 5 Dinar, Bulgarien 8 Lewa, Rumänien 20 Lei Slowakei Ks. 2.50

IB Illustrierter Beobachter

DONNERSTAG, 13. MAI 1943
18. JAHRGANG :·: FOLGE 19

Mit herzlichen Heimatgrüßen an die Front von:

VERLAG FRANZ EHER NACHF. G.M.B.H. MÜNCHEN 22
Copyright 1943 by Franz Eher Nachf., G. m. b. H., München 22

Viktor Lutze, der Chef des Stabes der SA.
28. 12. 1890 — 2. 5. 1943.

Aufnahme: Heinrich Hoffmann.

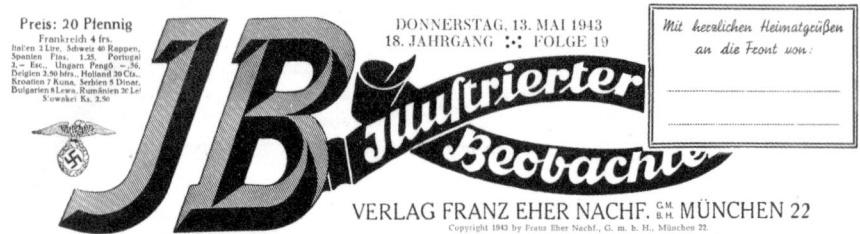

SA-Stabschef Lutze is memorialized on the 13.05.1943 cover of the *Illustrierter Beobachter*.

Max Paul Wilhelm Werner Jüttner
SA-Obergruppenführer/"mit der Wahrnehmung der Geschäfte des Stabschefs der SA beauftragt"
(02.05.1943-08.08.1943)

*	11.01.1888 in Saalfeld/Saale/Thüringen.
†	14.08.1963 in München/Regierungsbezirk Oberbayern/Bayern.

NSDAP-Nr.: 2.039.331 (Joined 28.01.1923 with Nr. 19.500; Party banned, 09.11.1923-16.02.1925; Reenrolled 01.07.1933 with effect from 01.05.1933)

Promotions:
22.03.1906	*Fahnenjunker*
18.08.1907	*Leutnant* (*mit Patent vom* 14.02.1906 A6a)
08.10.1914	*Oberleutnant*
18.12.1915	*Hauptmann*
01.11.1933	*SA-Brigadeführer* (per *SA-Führerbefehl Nr. 20*, 01.12.1933)
20.04.1935	*SA-Gruppenführer*
09.11.1937	*SA-Obergruppenführer*
00.00.19__	*Major z. V.*
02.05.1943–18.08.1943	*"mit der Wahrnehmung der Geschäfte des Stabschefs der SA beauftragt"*

Career:
00.00.1894–00.00.1897	*Vorschule* in Saalfeld.
00.00.1897–00.03.1906	*Reformgymnasium* in Saalfeld (passed his *Abitur*, 00.03.1906).
22.03.1906–00.10.1906	Entered service as a *Fahnenjunker*, assigned to *2. Thüringische Feldartillerie-Regiment Nr. 55* (Naumburg/Saale).
00.10.1906–00.06.1907	*Kriegsschule* in Glogau.
00.06.1907–01.10.1911	*Batterieoffizier*(?) in *2. Thüringische Feldartillerie-Regiment Nr. 55*. The regimental commander assessed him as follows:

Kommando　　　Jüterbog II 25 May 1911
der Feldartillerie Schule
Sekt. 1.Nr. 41Oe/11.

Judgement
on the Leutnant of 2. Thüringische Feldartillerie-Regiment 55, Jüttner, who was ordered to the Second Training Course for Lieutenants 1910/11 (from 5 February to 25 January 1911). His appearance at the front is determined and resolute. In all branches of service he showed appreciative interest. He directs the fire of a battery with certainty even under difficult conditions.
Artillery equipment [knowledge]: very good
Ballistic: very good

Suitable for use in a training regiment.

Signed Kuhn
Oberst und Kommandeur
(Bundesarchiv R 43/890; Translation: Gary Costello)

01.10.1911–24.10.1914(?)	*Adjutant of II. Abteilung/Feldartillerie-Regiment 55.* Deployed to the front from 01.08.1914. In an assessment of 01.12.1913, his regimental commander wrote:

Qualification report of 1 December 1913 on Hauptmann Max Paul Wilhelm Werner Jüttner.

Tall, slim officer, particularly good military appearance. Modest in appearance, tactful, with very good official manners, very sociable. Exceptionally popular comrade. Despite his youth, he has an excellent influence on his younger comrades. Fills his position very well and is suitable for promotion. Mentally and militarily very well-disposed, of a calm, serious nature, yet intellectually active and filled with scientific aspirations, so that he earned the recognition of his higher superiors in a military scientific thesis. As department adjutant, as well as deputy regimental adjutant, he has proven himself to be very diligent, reliable and extremely skillful.

Naumburg a/ d. S. 23.09.1913

von Sandrart
Oberst und Regimentskommandeur
(Bundesarchiv R 43II/890; Translation by Gary Costello)

24.10.1914–10.12.1914	*Adjutant of Feldartillerie-Regiment 55.*
10.12.1914–25.08.1916	*2. Adjutant of 4. Landwehr-Division.*
26.08.1916–06.12.1916	Assigned to the *Generalkommando* (Corps HQ) of the *Landwehr-Korps*. His superior officers assessed his brief service in this assignment as follows:

Qualification report of 1 January 1917 on Hauptmann Max Paul Wilhelm Werner Jüttner.

Tall, particularly good military appearance. He expresses his view clearly and very determinedly while maintaining the best manners. With a maturity beyond his years, he combines youthful freshness that makes every superior's interaction with him enjoyable. He certainly promises to be a particularly good general staff officer. Very socially adept and of impeccable manners. He was extremely popular with his superiors and comrades.

Signed
von Knauer
Major und Chef des Generalstabes des Landwehrkorps

Totally agree with the above assessment. Hauptmann Jüttner promises to be a good general staff officer.

Signed Graf von Kirchbach
General der Infanterie und kommandierender General des Landwehrkorps
(Bundesarchiv R 43II/890; Translation: Gary Costello)

07.12.1916–06.03.1917	Assigned as *2. Generalstabsoffizier* (Ib) to the general staff of *225. Infanterie-Division*. An evaluation by his superior officer, as well as an endorsement by the divisional commander, read:

225 Inf. Division   D. St. Q. 24.02.17
Generalstabsoffizier
I a Nr. 664 Pers.

Report on Hauptmann Jüttner in a general staff post of 225. Inf. Div. with the uniform of Feldartl. Regt. Nr. 55.

Hauptmann Jüttner was transferred to the 225. Inf. Div. by A. K. O. of 7.12.1918 in a General Staff post retaining his previous uniform, and has been 2nd General Staff Officer of this division since 20.12.16. He is 29 years old, a very good, imposing military appearance and has an extraordinarily likeable, fresh character. He has extensive military knowledge, works very independently and presents his views briefly, clearly, firmly and in the best possible form. His official and social appearance and behavior are impeccable; superiors and comrades hold him in equally high esteem as a soldier and as a person.

Signed
Potthoff
Hauptmann im Generalstabe
der 225 Inf. Division

225 Inf. Division

Hauptmann Jüttner was unfortunately only attached to the Division as 2. Generalstabsoffizier for 3 months. During this time and under difficult conditions, he managed the entire supply of the division, the movement of the numerous columns and trains and the extensive work of maintenance and new construction with prudence and the fullest understanding of all the needs of the troops to the best of his ability. A very capable young general staff officer, a kind comrade, whose departure from our group and from the division is sorely regretted by all.

9.III.1917
Signed [Wilhelm] von Woyna, Generalmajor und Div. Kommandeur
(Bundesarchiv R 43II/890; Translation: Gary Costello)

13.07.1917–00.00.1917	Assigned to the *Generalstab der Armee*.
00.06.1917–03.08.1917	Assigned for eight weeks as acting *1. Generalstabsoffizier* (Ia) to the general staff of *Armee Woyrsch*. In the following qualification report, his superior officers evaluated his service during this period:

Generalkommando Landwehrkorps.   K.H.Q. 5.8.1917
Chef des Generalstabes

Transferred to the General Staff, Captain Jüttner has been a member of the Landwehrkorps again since 6.02.17. The above favorable assessment has found further confirmation in every way. Hauptmann Jüttner has substituted for the on leave or detached 1. Generalstabsoffizier (Ia) for 8 weeks to particular satisfaction and in this augmented activity has proved himself to be a skillful and hard-working General Staff Officer.

Signed
v. Knauer
Major und Chef des Generalstabes des Landwehrkorps

I fully support the view expressed above. Captain Jüttner deserves and enjoys full all-round trust, he has a particularly valuable character and a never-failing devotion to duty.

Signed
v. Brietzke
General der Infanterie und Kommandierender General des Landwehrkorps
(Bundesarchiv R 43II/890; Translation: Gary Costello)

A very accomplished general staff officer who deserves special attention.

Signed
Heye
Oberst und Chef des Generalstabes der Heeresgruppe Woyrsch
(Bundesarchiv R 43II/890; Translation: Gary Costello)

04.08.1917–20.11.1917	Attached to the staff of the German *Gouverneur* in Metz.
21.11.1917–08.01.1918	Attached to the *Generalkommando of XIII.* and *XIV. Armee-Korps*.

His superiors assessed his service in these assignments as follows:

Gruppe Caudry   17.11.17
Generalkommando XIII.(K.W.)
Armeekorps
Appraisal of Hauptmann v. d. Armee Max Jüttner, assigned to General Command XIII A.K. for use in the General Staff Service.

Does the appraisee fulfill his position?
Yes
Is he suitable for higher general staff duty and for which?
General staff officer in an Infantry division.
Brief description of the personality of the appraisee.
Clear, determined, hard-working. Good skillful style. Quickly found his bearings in very difficult conditions—the battle of Cambrai—and did an excellent job.

Signed
Müller Loebnitz
Major und Chef des Generalstabes XIII A.K.

Gruppe Busygny   K.H.Q 8 February 1918

Hauptmann Jüttner only belonged to the Gruppe from 22.07–12.01 and during this time was on leave from 27.07–08.01 to recover from frost damage suffered during a training flight. During this short period of service, however, he devoted himself to his field of work with such freshness and energy that he fully fulfilled his task-reorganizing the rear connections as well as the accommodation and road development in the group area. The very favorable impression I had already received of Hauptmann Jüttner during his earlier assignment in the East (with A.A. Woyrsch) has only been confirmed by his short service here. The departure of this very capable general staff officer and very popular comrade is sincerely regretted by the Gen. Kdo.

Signed
Gudewius
Major und Chef des Generalstabs XIV. AK.
(Bundesarchiv R 43II/890; Translation: Gary Costello)

09.01.1918–20.09.1918   Attached to *Armeeoberkommando 6 (AOK 6)*. He was appraised by his superiors as follows:

Oberkommando 6. Armee   A.H.Q. 18.04.1918

Hauptmann Jüttner handled ammunition supplies at the AOK in an exemplary manner during the preparation period and during the conduct of the battle of Armentieres and supervised the execution of the orders given by the AOK to the troops in a tireless, prudent and forward-looking manner. Based on the overall impression of his personality and the practical skills he has shown, I consider him absolutely suitable to be the 1st General Staff Officer of a division.

Lanz
Chef des Generalstabs AOK 6

Very hard-working, usable, capable general staff officer, independent worker, good comrade.

28.09.1918 Herrgott
Adjutant Chef des Generalstabes 6. Armee
(Bundesarchiv R 43II/890; Translation: Gary Costello)

21.09.1918–09.12.1918   *1. Generalstabsoffizier (Ia)* of *2. Infanterie-Brigade*. In Quedlinburg on 12.12.1919, *Major a. D.* von Platen (formerly *Chef des Generalstabes* of LI. [51.] *Armee-Korps*) wrote the following assessment of Jüttner's performance in this assignment:

Hauptmann Jüttner was under my command as general staff officer of the Radfahrbrigade-Armeereserve (cycling brigade army reserve of 2. Armee in the October days of [19]18. During this period, fighting took place on the Sembre Canal near Lanecies and the extensive forests north of the canal between Landrecies and Le Quesnoy.

A time in which one had to hold out against the strongly superior enemy with inferior means and in which the nerves of the leadership played one of the most essential roles. Hauptmann Jüttner has supported his commander excellently in this respect, perseverance, great work performance and a comprehensive, persevering willpower.

Hauptmann Jüttner supported his commander excellently in this respect, perseverance, great work performance and a comprehensive, persevering willpower of this general staff officer contributed in the main to the fact that the excellent Jäger-Brigade always approached the most difficult, loss-ridden tasks with good courage and solved them to the complete satisfaction of the general command. Hauptmann Jüttner supported his commander excellently in this respect, perseverance, great work performance and a comprehensive, persevering willpower of this general staff officer contributed in the main to the fact that the excellent Jäger Brigade always approached the most difficult, loss-ridden tasks with good spirits and solved them to the complete satisfaction of the general command. It was a joy to have such a fresh, fighting force under safe leadership during this bitter time.

[Signed] von Platen
Formerly Major and Chef des Generalstabes of 51. A.K.

Naumburg, 6.7.1920
For the correctness of the copy.
[Official seal and signature of the *Bürgermeister* of Naumburg an der Saale, Karl Roloff]
(Bundesarchiv R 43II/ 890; Translation courtesy of Gary Costello)

09.12.1918–00.01.1919(?)	1. *Generalstabsoffizier (Ia)* of *119. Infanterie-Division.*
00.01.1919–01.08.1919	*Führer* of the *Zeitfreiwilligen-Verband Mitteldeutschland* of the *Landesjägerkorps* in *Regierungsbezirk* Halle-Merseburg. On 07.10.1919, *Generalmajor* Georg Maercker- *Kommandeur* of the *Freiwillige Landesjägerkorps* and later a leading member, with *Oberstleutnant a. D.* Theodor Duesterberg, of the antisemitic faction in the "*Stahlhelm*"-*Bund*- wrote the following *Dienstleistungszeugnis* (certificate of service) concerning *Hauptmann* Jüttner:

Hauptmann Jüttner established the Zeitfreiwilligen units in the Brigade area. He has confirmed the reputation as a hard-working independent worker and capable organizer that preceded him from his military activity as a general staff officer in the field. In a generous way and with amazingly little means, he has created an exemplary organization of Zeitfreiwilligen units and Einwohnerwehren spanning the territory of the Landesjägerkorps. He was helped by his conciliatory nature and his gift for interacting with people. His open, frank, truthful nature has earned him the trust of even radical workers, who have repeatedly called on him to arbitrate in serious wage disputes.

His freshness, energy and organizational skills make him particularly suitable for higher administrative posts.

[Signed] Maercker
Generalmajor, Kommandeur des freiwilligen Landesjägerkorps.

Naumburg, 5.7.1920.
For the correctness of the copy.
[Official seal and signature of the *Bürgermeister* of Naumburg an der Saale, Karl Roloff]
(Bundesarchiv R 43II/ 890-10; Translation courtesy of Gary Costello)

On 03.07.1920, Helmuth von Schele (*Landrat* for Kreis Naumburg/S.) gave the following assessment:

Herr Hauptmann Jüttner has held this position since the establishment of the Kreisräte [district councils]. He initiated the Einwohnerwehr organization in our area. He was extremely skillful in his treatment of the population. He was excellent in the completion of written work.

He combines the most pleasant style with his efficiency in service, as he is an impeccable person in every respect, whom I can recommend to everyone with a clear conscience and whom I wish the best progress on his future path in life.

[Signed] Freiherr von Schele
Landrat.

Naumburg, 6.7.1920.
For the correctness of the copy.
[Official seal and signature of the *Bürgermeister* of Naumburg an der Saale, Karl Roloff]
(Bundesarchiv R 43II/ 890; Translation courtesy of Gary Costello)

01.08.1919	Discharged from military service.
00.00.1919–00.00.1921	Studied law and economics (five semesters) at the universities of Halle and Jena.
01.09.1920–00.00.1921	Coal miner in the lignite mines of Halle.
15.09.1919–31.10.1933	Member of the "Stahlhelm"-Bund der Frontsoldaten/Ortsgruppe Halle/Saale.
00.00.1920–00.01.1923	Member of the *Deutschnationale Volkspartei* (DNVP).
00.00.1921–30.11.1933	Employed- first as a clerk, later as *Abteilungsleiter (Prokurist) für Sozial- und Wirtschaftspolitik*- with the *Deutschen Braunkohlen-Industrie-Verein* in Halle, and ultimately as *Prokurist* of *Anhaltische Kohlenwerke*.
00.05.1921–00.06.1921	*Führer* of the *Studentenbataillon Jena* in Oberschlesien, with which he participated in fighting against Polish insurgents.
00.01.1923	Participated in the "*1. Standartenweihe der NSDAP*" (first ceremonial consecration of Nazi Party flags).
28.01.1923	Joined the NSDAP/*Ortsgruppe München*.

30.01.1923–31.10.1933	*Gauführer* of the *"Stahlhelm"-Bund* in *Gau Halle*. It was in this capacity, on 28.10.1924, that he delivered a speech in Halle/Saale (published in print as a leaflet and appearing in an official *Stahlhelm* pamphlet), praising Hitler in messianic terms:

Dear comrades!
It is now almost a year since the day when one of the best of us front-line soldiers, Adolf Hitler, took action out of the most burning love for the people suffering in boundless hardship, as he could no longer stand by and watch the terrible misery, shame and disgrace, Adolf Hitler, the pioneer of the freedom movement [*Vorkämpfer der Freiheitsbewegung*] and one of our front-line comrades, who fought in the war with the most selfless devotion to his German heritage and Fatherland, is still behind prison walls; the man who, after the collapse, was the first to reawaken in thousands and thousands man's reverence for himself, as belonging to a great whole, to his people. That which is irresistibly powerful about Adolf Hitler, to those who are capable of feeling it at all, is his sheer being. He embodies the longing of the nation. That is why the soul of the people cheers for this man, because it recognizes in him its own innermost being. Adolf Hitler is not and never has been a party man, he stands freely and unbound before my soul, solely as the bearer of an idea which has as its elemental force the love of the brother, which goes as far as death, and the hatred of meanness. And because this is the case, my friends, I believe I am acting in all your interests when I express my indignation at the fact that Adolf Hitler is still being held prisoner and that they want to deny him entry to Austria even at the moment of his release.

The heart bleeds and aches and threatens to burst when one thinks of what is being done to him, whose essence is truth, to him in whom the original German heroic sagas become reality. (Bundesarchiv R 43 II/ 890; Translation courtesy of Gary Costello)

00.00.1926–00.00.1929	Member of the *Provinziallandtag* for *Provinz Sachsen*.
00.00.19__–31.10.1933	*Stellvertreter des 2. Bundesführers des "Stahlhelm"* (deputy to the second *Bundesführer* of the *"Stahlhelm"-Bund*, Theodor Duesterberg).
12.04.1933–31.10.1933	*Landesführer* of the *Landesverband Mitteldeutschland der "Stahlhelm."*
01.07.1933	Reentered the NSDAP/*Ortsgruppe* Halle an der Saale (transferred to the *Ortsgruppe Braunes Haus der NSDAP* on 01.12.1935).
01.11.1933	Joined the SA at the request of Ernst Röhm.
01.11.1933–30.11.1933	*Wehrstahlhelmführer der SA* (m.d.W.d.G.b.).
01.11.1933–30.11.1933	*Beauftragter der Wehrstahlhelm* to SA-*Obergruppe IV* (comprising SA-*Gruppen* Sachsen and *Thüringen*) in Halle an der Saale.
12.11.1933–08.05.1945	Member of the *Reichstag (Wahlkreis 11, Merseburg)*.
01.12.1933–20.09.1934	Appointed as a *hauptamtlicher SA-Führer* and assigned as *Leiter* of the *Abteilung Ausbildung und Organisation* (Department for Training and Organization) in the *Führungsamt im Stab der Obersten SA-Führung* (München). In testimony before the International Military Tribunal at Nürnberg on 13.08.1946, Jüttner stated:

> My appointment into the SA leadership was connected with the incorporation of the Stahlhelm into the SA. The Central German Stahlhelm enjoyed a good reputation even among its political opponents. My especially good relations with the miners and also with the trade unions were well known to Röhm. The Central German Stahlhelm was especially successful in the social field. All this might have contributed to my appointment. I left the mining industry voluntarily and became a professional SA Führer...
> (*Trial of the Major War Criminals Before the International Military Tribunal, Nuremberg, 14 November 1945–1 October 1946, Vol. XXI*)

01.12.1933–20.09.1934	*Verbindungsführer der SA zur Reichswehr* (head of liaison between the *SA* and the *Reich* Armed Forces).
27.07.1934–01.11.1937	*Chef der Führungsamt* (chief of the Leadership Office) in the *Obersten SA-Führung* (m.d.W.d.G.b. until 19.09.1934, then permanent from 20.09.1934). Upgraded to *Hauptamt* status, 01.11.1937. Among his functions in this assignment was the organization of SA marches at the annual *"Reichsparteitäge der NSDAP"* in Nürnberg.
04.09.1934–10.09.1934	Participated in the *"6. Reichsparteitag der NSDAP"* in Nürnberg.
10.09.1935–16.09.1935	Participated in the *"7. Reichsparteitag der NSDAP"* in Nürnberg.
30.04.1936–00.09.1936	Charged with the *Gesamtleitung des Aufmarsches der SA, SS, NSKK und Flieger beim "Reichsparteitag der Ehre 1936"* in Nürnberg.
08.09.1936–14.09.1936	Participated in the *"8. Reichsparteitag der NSDAP"* in Nürnberg.
00.03.1937–00.09.1937(?)	Charged with *Leitung einschließlich der Festsetzung der Stärken der Marschsäulen sowie der Kommandoführung beim Appell der SA, SS, des NSKK und des DLV* (management, including the fixing of the strengths of the marching columns and the command leadership, at the roll call of the SA, SS, NSKK, and DLV) for the *"9. Reichsparteitag der NSDAP"* in Nürnberg.
06.09.1937–13.09.1937	Participated in the *"9. Reichsparteitag der NSDAP"* in Nürnberg.
01.11.1937–08.05.1945	*Chef* of the *Führungshauptamt* in the *Obersten SA-Führung*.
[00.00.1938]	*Abwehrbeauftragter der Obersten SA-Führung*.
05.03.1938–08.05.1945	*Führer* of the *Deutsche Schützenverband* in the *Nationalsozialistischer Reichsbund für Leibesübungen* (NSRL, National Socialist Reich League for Physical Exercise under *SA-Obergruppenführer* Hans von Tschammer und Osten).
05.09.1938–12.09.1938	Participated in the *"10. Reichsparteitag der NSDAP"* in Nürnberg.
01.10.1938–30.10.1938	*Verbindungsführer der SA* to the *Sudetendeutsche Freikorps*. In this role he was tasked with organization of the *Freikorps* and with furnishing it with equipment, clothing, food, and transportation for refugees.
07.02.1939–00.00.1939	Member of the *Deutsche Olympische Ausschuss* (German Olympic Committee) for Germany's participation in the planned 1940 Olympic Games in St. Moritz and Helsinki.
15.06.1939–08.05.1945	*Stabsführer* of the *Obersten SA-Führung* and *ständiger Stellvertreter des Stabschefs der SA* (permanent deputy of the chief of staff of the SA).
07.03.1942	Letter from Jüttner to Helmuth Friedrichs of the *Parteikanzlei*:

> As you know, Reichsleiter Dr. Frank, in his capacity as Generalgouverneur, ordered the formation of so-called Wehrschützenbereitschaften for the

area under his command, in order to first of all gather together in them all the German-blooded people of the Generalgouvernement, to train them there and to make them physically fit, before proceeding to build up the Party's structures.

Recently, in accordance with the order of the Reichsführer-SS of 03.02.1942, it was ordered that an SS-Sturmbann Ost be formed for the Generalgouvernement. A copy of this order is attached. According to this, the aforementioned measure by the Generalgouverneur must be regarded as obsolete and the Oberste SA-Führung consequently considers it advisable to gather the SA men in the Generalgouvernement into SA units, which naturally goes hand in hand with the formation of SA-Wehrmannschaften in the sense of the Führer's decree of 19.01.1939 for the purpose of enhancing military strength and promoting military training.

The Oberste SA-Führung requests that this be noted and that approval of the measure intended by the Oberste SA-Führung be communicated as soon as possible. (Bundesarchiv NS19/2648; Translation: Gary Costello)

02.05.1943–08.08.1943	*Mit der Wahrnehmung der Geschäfte des Stabschefs der SA beauftragt.* Assumed the duties of *SA-Stabschef* following the death of Viktor Lutze, and until the appointment of a permanent *Stabschef* (Wilhelm Schepmann).
00.11.1944–00.05.1945	*Mit Führungsaufgaben beim Aufbau des Volkssturms beauftragt* (charged with managerial responsibilities for the creation of the German People's Army).
00.04.1945–00.04.1945	*Führer* of the *Volkssturm-Kampfgruppe* "Jüttner," numbering approximately 160 men, in München.

POSTWAR CONFINEMENT & ACTIVITIES:

11.05.1945–00.00.194_	Arrested by American troops while commanding his *Volkssturm* unit in the Oberhaushammer Hütte south of Schliersee, then held successively in the camps of Bad Aibling, Neu-Ulm, Heilbronn, Ludwigsburg, Camp 74, Seckenheim and Kornwestheim (Camp 75). He lost 65 lb. while in U.S. custody.
13.08.1946–16.08.1946	Appeared before the International Military Tribunal at Nürnberg as a defense witness on the subject of the SA. The following are excerpts from his testimony:

13.08.1946:

JÜTTNER: I know the Leadership of the SA, its aims, and the SA leaders, especially the higher SA leaders, very well. I do not propose to gloss over anything. A small fraction of SA leaders who had turned out to be mere troopers was eliminated. Even those SA leaders had in the past, during the First World War as brave soldiers, and later as members of the Free Corps under the government of Ebert and Noske, deserved well of their country. Their attitude and their way of life, however, were opposed to the principles of the SA, therefore they had to leave. But the rest, that is the bulk of the SA Leadership Corps, were decent and clean, and irreproachable in their sense of justice and duty.

HERR BÖHM: Tell us about the professional Leadership Corps.

J: As to the active leaders, the Obergruppenführer and the Gruppenführer, I know their history, their way of life and their political and ethical attitude. Apart from the insignificant number who had to leave, these SA leaders were irreproachable. Not one of them had a police record, not one of them was what one might call a failure, all of them had a civil profession before they were taken into the Leadership Corps of the SA. Their way of life was simple and modest. They received, however, in relation to comparable positions of civil servants or businessmen, extremely low salaries. All incomes from other sources were charged against them; there was no one in the SA who was allowed more than one source of income; no one could enrich himself personally owing to his position, and only he could spend money on social activities who had means of his own. Of the Gruppenführer and Obergruppenführer who in 1939 were active in the SA Leadership Corps or with the SA Gruppen, half the number lost their lives in the war. They gave their lives in the belief that they had fought for a just cause. They were patriots, and they committed no wrong or ungodly acts. And even today, I pride myself on having belonged to such an upright leadership corps.

B: Were the SA leaders paid?

J: Up to 1933 there were no paid SA leaders. Only the leaders of the so-called Untergruppen, of which there was one in each Gau, received a remuneration of about 300 marks a month. After 1933 a wage scale was established. In 1940 there was a small increase in pay. The maximum basic salary for an Obergruppenführer was 1,200 marks a month. From Scharführer up to Obersturmbannführer inclusive, all SA leaders, with the exception of the auxiliary personnel, were honorary workers. Of the entire Leadership Corps, including the nominal leaders, roughly two percent were paid.

B: How was the SA Leadership Corps organized?

J: In the SA we differentiated between: SA leaders, SA administrative leaders, SA medical leaders. The SA leaders formed the leadership staffs and led the units. The SA administrative leaders handled the budget, financial matters, and the audit. Together with the administrative leaders of the other branches and of the Party they formed a special leadership body and had to follow the directives of the Reich Treasurer. The medical leaders were physicians and pharmacists; they were charged with the medical care of the SA. The administrative and medical leaders had no influence whatsoever on the running of the SA, and they had no right to that. Besides, the SA had leaders for special purposes, the so-called "z. V." leaders and honorary leaders, some of whom are among the main defendants here.

B: Was not one of the main defendants an honorary leader?

J: Yes, I believe several of them were honorary leaders, such as Göring, Frank, Sauckel, Von Schirach, Streicher, and, to my knowledge, perhaps Hess and Bormann. I might add in this connection that the honorary leaders were never informed about the business affairs of the SA. They had neither the opportunity nor the authority to exert any influence on training, leadership, or use of the SA. They had merely the right to wear the SA uniform and, at meetings and festivities, to take their positions in the ranks of the SA leadership. Even Hermann Göring—who in 1923 headed the SA temporarily when it numbered but a few thousand men—no longer exerted any influence on the SA after that time, nor did he have any time to do so. His nomination as chief of the "Standarte Feldherrnhalle" was only a formal honor, similar to the honors that were extended in the days of the Kaiser to military leaders of merit, or members—even feminine members—of royal families. Herr Frank was appointed leader of the SA for the former Government General by Chief of Staff Lutze. That too was and remained only a formal honor, because the administration itself was carried out by a special administrative staff under Brigadeführer Peltz, and later Kuhnemund. He did not receive any orders concerning the administration of the SA in that region from the Chief of Staff. Such orders went to the administrative staff who, in turn, were responsible to the Supreme SA Leadership. The "z. V." whom I have mentioned could temporarily be called in for duty if they were willing. They were advisory duties, for example on legal and social questions.

B: Of what types of people did the SA in general consist?

J: From the beginning, the SA was made up of former soldiers of the First World War, that is, soldiers and young idealists who loved their country above all. The SA was not, as the witness Gisevius asserted, a mob of criminals or gangsters, but rather, as Sinclair Lewis is said to have written, pure idealists. Many clergymen, many students of theology, belonged to the SA as active members, some until the very end. Each and every SA man will be able to confirm that never at any time were criminal actions demanded of him, and that the SA leadership never pursued criminal aims....

B: What was the opinion and the attitude of the SA on the Jewish question?

J: The SA demanded that the influence of the Jews in national affairs, in the economy, and in cultural life, be reduced in accordance with their position as a minority in Germany. It advocated a numerus clausus.

B: And what was the reason for this demand or this attitude?

J: This demand, which was not only that of the SA, became general in Germany when after the first World War, in 1918 and 1919, great numbers of Jewish people emigrated from Poland to Germany and entered into the economic and other spheres of life, where they gained considerable influence in an undesirable manner. Through certain large judicial proceedings all this profiteering and this disintegrating influence had become known, and it caused much ill-will and resulted in a movement of opposition. Even Jews who had lived in Germany for a long time, and societies of German citizens of the Jewish faith, took position against these influences in a decided manner. So one can readily see that the demand of the SA was well-grounded.

B: Did the SA incite, others to active violence against the Jews?

J: No, in no way. Never did the Chiefs of Staff, Röhm, Lutze, or Schepmann treat the Jewish question in their speeches, or issue any directives in that respect, much less incite others to violence. The concept of a so-called "master race" was never fostered in, the SA; that would have been quite contrary to reason, for the SA received its replacements from all strata. The extermination of a people because of its type was never given any support by the SA, and actions of violence against Jews were not favored by the SA. Quite the contrary, the leadership always objected most strongly to actions of that kind.

14.08.1946:

B: Witness, yesterday we left off in your examination with the manner in which the Jewish question was handled by the SA. Now I should like to ask you how the participation of members of the SA in actions against the Jews in November 1938 can be explained?

J: The participation of SA members in this action consisted of irresponsible actions by individuals which were in gross contradiction to the directive of Staff Chief Lutze's executives. Staff Chief Lutze was in Munich in the old city hall. There, in connection with the speech made by Dr. Goebbels, he immediately assigned the chief of the administrative office, Obergruppenführer Matthes [sic, Mappes], to go to the Hotel Rheinhof, where a part of the SA leaders present had already retired, in order to give these SA leaders strict orders not to participate in any action against the Jews. About an hour later, when he received the news that the synagogue in Munich had been set on fire, Lutze, in my presence, repeated this order to the SA leaders who were still present in the Munich city hall and said that it was to be passed on to all units immediately. This was actually done, which is confirmed by the fact that in many places no actions were carried out at all, and numerous SA men state under oath that they received this order.

B: Then how did it come about that, in spite of that, members of the SA participated in the destruction of Jewish establishments?

J: As was ascertained afterwards, certain individuals let themselves be misled by agencies which were undoubtedly under the influence of Dr. Goebbels. As an actual fact, compared with the SA, relatively few real members of the SA participated in this action, although public opinion later blamed the SA for this entire action. And here again it so happened that everyone in a brown shirt was considered an SA man. That the SA was in no way the sponsor of this action may also be seen from the fact that, as I have read in the press in the last few months, in certain trials, for example in Bamberg, Stuttgart, and, I believe, in Hof, people were convicted who had destroyed synagogues and yet did not belong to the SA. The fact also that in many places SA men upon instructions from the leadership offered to afford protection to Jewish installations against plundering by shady elements, et cetera, created a popular impression that the SA had committed these misdeeds. In any event, Staff Chief Lutze one or two days later gave voice to his indignation to Dr. Goebbels about the action itself and the unjustified accusation against the SA, and strongly condemned the irresponsible way in which the SA men had been incited to commit these misdeeds. Soon after he issued an order that in the future SA men were not to place themselves at the disposal of other agencies for any tasks or actions unless he himself had given express approval. Staff Chief Lutze punished the guilty ones whom he discovered, and if the case warranted it, they were turned over to the regular courts for judgment.

B: Had things been different up to that time when Lutze took this particular line? Was the Political Leadership in a position to use SA members for its own purposes?

J: The Political Leadership only had authority to use the SA for certain tasks, which included the following: participation in Gau and Kreis rallies; demands for the use of the SA in cases of disaster, and also for propaganda purposes; for collection drives for the Winter Relief, for collecting clothing and the Like. These were the usual demands which the Political Leadership made on the SA in the course of the year. So far as I know, at no time did the Political Leadership make any other demands of an illegal nature of the SA. But Lutze issued this order to prevent those offices which were under Dr. Goebbels' influence from leading SA men astray in the future....

B: Did the SA, leadership have any influence on politics?

J: After the death of Röhm none at all. The SA was completely unsuited for exerting any influence on politics, both by its organization and its leadership. Even the misuse of the SA for war-mongering purposes was quite out of the question. Militarism such as the glorification of military activities, uniforms, drilling, jingoism, or the creation of a warlike spirit, was never approved by the SA; Röhm's attitude toward neighboring countries and Lutze's attitude toward war in general, in themselves speak for that....

B: ... Herr Jüttner, now I should like to put: my final question to you. Did the political aims of the SA have a criminal character?

J: The things which the SA did and the aims which its leaders pursued need never fear the light of day. The SA leadership did not pursue any criminal aims and did not even know of any criminal aims of any other agencies. The SA, as an organization, never carried out any actions which could justify its defamation as a criminal organization. The SA, Mr. President, had many followers in the Reich, that is, in the former Reich, and even beyond its boundaries. The SA had opponents as well. Many of these opponents raised their voices, and out of hate or envy created prejudices against the SA. Not the truth-only prejudices of the kind which, as is well known in history, have caused the downfall of many a brave man, could lead to a situation where five or six million men who belonged to the SA in the last two and a half decades would be stamped as criminals.... For these men, for these five or six million men and for the many millions in their families, I can solemnly declare under oath that the SA never had a criminal character. Mr. President, my entire life has been guided by the rule that one should stand by whatever one has done, whatever the risk may be, and fear nothing, not even death itself, save only dishonor.

I consider it to be dishonorable to evade responsibility by putting an end to one's Life, or to become untruthful. In this respect, Mr. President, my consciencel is clear. Therefore, with my declaration on the blamelessness of the SA I can stand in front of the Highest Judge.

15.08.1946:

I shall be very brief, Your Lordship. To conclude the questions put to me I should like to assure you upon my oath that we of the SA did not do anything bad. We did not want a war and we did not prepare for a war. We of the SA, the leadership and the organization itself, did only those things which in other countries are expected of the men of the nation as their moral duty, which Mr. Truman or Marshal Stalin or the statesmen of England and France expect of their men, namely, to do everything to protect the home country and to maintain peace. We of the SA did not commit any crimes against humanity, either. The leadership did not decree them, nor did they tolerate them, nor allow the organization to become guilty of any of them. When individuals committed misdeeds they should be punished and it is our will, too, that they should be brought to just punishment. We therefore do not ask for mercy or sympathy by portraying our domestic distress. We ask only for justice; for nothing else, for our conscience is clear. We acted as patriots. If patriots are to be labelled as criminals, then we were criminals. (*Trial of the Major War Criminals Before the International Military Tribunal Nuremberg, Volume XXI*)

c. 1950	Returned to work in the mining industry.
[00.00.1957]	Working as a trade representative in München-Solln.
00.05.1957	Appeared as a witness in the trial of Josef ("Sepp") Dietrich for overseeing the killing of SA leaders during the "Röhm-Putsch."

DECORATIONS & AWARDS:

18.06.1915	*1914 Eisernes Kreuz I. Klasse*
01.10.1914	*1914 Eisernes Kreuz II. Klasse*
18.05.1918	*Kgl. Bayerisches Militär-Verdienstorden IV. Klasse mit Schwertern*
15.12.1916	*Hamburgisches Hanseatenkreuz*
20.03.1915	*Sachsen-Meiningensches Ehrenkreuz fur Verdienste im Kriege*
09.03.1915	*Österreichisches Militar-Verdienstkreuz III. Klasse mit Kriegsdekoration*
13.06.1918	*Verwundetenabzeichen, 1918 in Schwarz*
22.03.1935	*Ehrenkreuz des Weltkrieges 1914–1918 mit Schwertern*
11.01.1938	*Goldenes Ehrenzeichen der NSDAP*
00.00.1934	*Ehrendolch der SA*

NOTES:
* Parents:
  - August Jüttner (*02.01.1838 in Stendal/Altmark, †26.10.1903), owner of a printing company in Saalfeld.
  - Anna Jüttner, *née* Franke (*16.06.1856 in Saalfeld, †04.01.1931), daughter of the tannery owner Hermann Franke.
* Siblings: two brothers and two sisters.
* Religion: Lutheran.
* Married on 10.02.1913 to Erna Nies (*23.11.1899 in Zobtau). One son (Klaus, *29.10.1915, killed in Stalingrad, 21.01.1943) and two daughters (*24.02.1914 and 01.09.1920) were born to this marriage. Both of his sons-in-law lost their lives in World War II (Walther Rohde, *18.10.1906 in Loitz, killed in action 10.08.1941 as a *Leutnant* 2.5 km. west of Ludwigshöhe near Salla/Karelia, and Georg Wiedemann, *05.06.1908 in Isny, died in Soviet captivity as an *Obergefreiter* in Golubowka [Don Basin], 09.11.1944).

SOURCES:
Bayerisches Hauptstaatsarchiv, München, Abteilung IV Kriegsarchiv: Excerpts from various *Kriegsranglisten* containing data on the Royal Bavarian Army service of Max Jüttner.
Bundesarchiv, Berlin-Lichterfelde: *Personalunterlagen von SA-Angehörigen: SA-Personalakte* of Max Jüttner.

Campbell, Bruce: *The SA Generals and the Rise of Nazism*. The University Press of Kentucky, 1998.

International Military Tribunal, Nürnberg: *Trial of the Major War Criminals Before the International Military Tribunal Nuremberg, Volume XXI*.

Kienast, *Ministerialdirigent* Ernst (ed.): *Der Großdeutsche Reichstag, IV. Wahlperiode, Beginn am 10.04.1938 verlängert bis zum 30. Januar 1947*. Berlin, November 1943.

Lilla, Joachim; Döring, Martin; & Schulz Andreas: *Statisten in Uniform. Die Mitglieder des Reichstags 1933–1945*. Droste Verlag, 2004.

Miller, Michael D. and Andreas Schulz: *Leaders of the Storm Troops, Volume 1* (1st Edition). Helion & Co., 2015.

Leipzig, 19 November 1933: A signed portrait of Hans Jüttner in uniform as a leader of the "*Stahlhelm*"-*Bund der Frontsoldaten*, c. 1925 (note helmet pin above his pocket). (Helmut Weitze Militärische Antiquitäten KG, Hamburg)

Above: November 1933: Newsreel stills of Max Jüttner during the ceremonial transfer of his men from the *"Stahlhelm"-Bund* to the SA. Behind him is *SA-Obergruppenführer* Manfred Freiherr von Killinger.

Right: An artist's rendering of Jüttner from the same timeframe as the opposite photograph.

Max Jüttner in civilian attire.

SA-Brigadeführer Jüttner in 1934. (NARA, Heinrich Hoffmann Collection).

A signed photo of *SA-Brigadeführer* Jüttner in his office. (Helmut Weitze Militärische Antiquitäten KG)

Formal portraits of *SA-Gruppenführer* Jüttner, *c.* 1937.

Jüttner discusses preparations for the "*7. Reichsparteitag der NSDAP*" *(*10.09.1935–16.09.1935) with an unidentified *SA-Standartenführer*. (NARA, Heinrich Hoffmann Collection)

Jüttner at his desk in 1935.

Above left: *SA-Gruppenführer* Jüttner shakes the Führer's hand during the "*9. Reichsparteitag der NSDAP*" in Nürnberg (06.09.1937–13.09.1937).

Above right: *SA-Gruppenführer* Jüttner in 1936. (*Illustrierter Beobachter*, 24.09.1936).

Hans Jüttner in 1938 as head of the *SA-Führungshauptamt* with two of his closest assistants, *SA-Brigadeführers* Rolf Michaelis and Walter Nibbe (heads of the *Amt Körperliche Ertüchtigung* [Office Physical Training] and *Amt Organisation und Einsatz* [Office of Organization and Operations], respectively). Second from right is Jüttner's adjutant, *SA-Sturmbannführer* (later *Standartenführer*) Johannes Berenbrock.

Above left: SA-Obergruppenführer Max Jüttner, *c.* 1938. (Igor Karpov)

Above right: SA-Obergruppenführer Jüttner, *c.* 1939.

Left: Jüttner congratulates Viktor Lutze on his fiftieth birthday, 28.12.1940. (*Der SA-Führer*, January 1941)

Above: SA-*Stabschef* Lutze and *Obergruppenführer* Jüttner visit the elite *Reichsschule der NSDAP Feldafing on the Starnberger See*. At left is the school commander, *Oberdienstleiter* and SA-*Brigadeführer* Julius Görlitz. (Stephen Tyas)

Right: SA-*Stabschef* Lutze and *Obergruppenführer* Jüttner meet with Hitler at *Führer HQ "Wehrwolf"* near Vinnitsa, Ukraine, 23.07.1942. Second from right is Hitler's physican, Dr. Theodor Morell.

Above: Jüttner attends a sporting event in Prague, 1943. To his left are *Staatsminister* and *SS-Obergruppenfüher* Karl-Hermann Frank, *SA-Obergruppenführer* Franz May, and *Generalleutnant* Rudolf Toussaint. (Michal Sika)

Left: Nimes, southern France, 20.06.1943: Acting *SA-Stabschef* Jüttner inspects *60. Panzer-Grenadier-Division* "*Feldherrnhalle.*" Beside him stands the divisional commander, *Generalmajor* Otto Köhlermann.

Right: *SA-Stabschef* Wilhelm Schepmann converses with *Reichsleiter* Dr. Ley during an SA leadership conference, 23.05.1944. At far right is Max Jüttner.

Below: *SA-Stabschef* Schepmann decorates wounded soldiers with the *SA-Wehrabzeichen für Kriegsversehrte* (SA Military Sports Badge for War Wounded) on 15.07.1944. *SA-Obergruppenführer* Jüttner stands at far left. (NARA, Heinrich Hoffmann Collection)

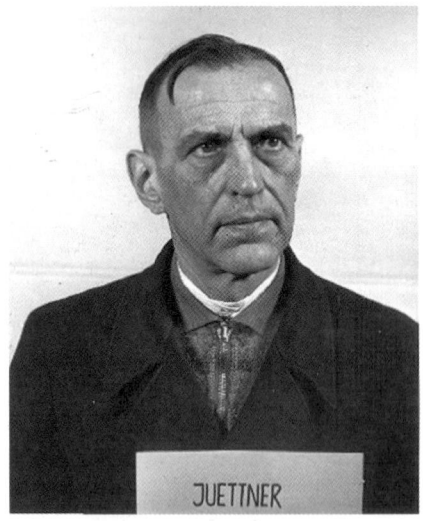

Left: Witness identification photo of Max Jüttner, taken in Nürnberg in 1946. (Ian Sayer)

Below: Nürnberg, August 1946: Jüttner testifies before the International Military Tribunal, Nürnberg.

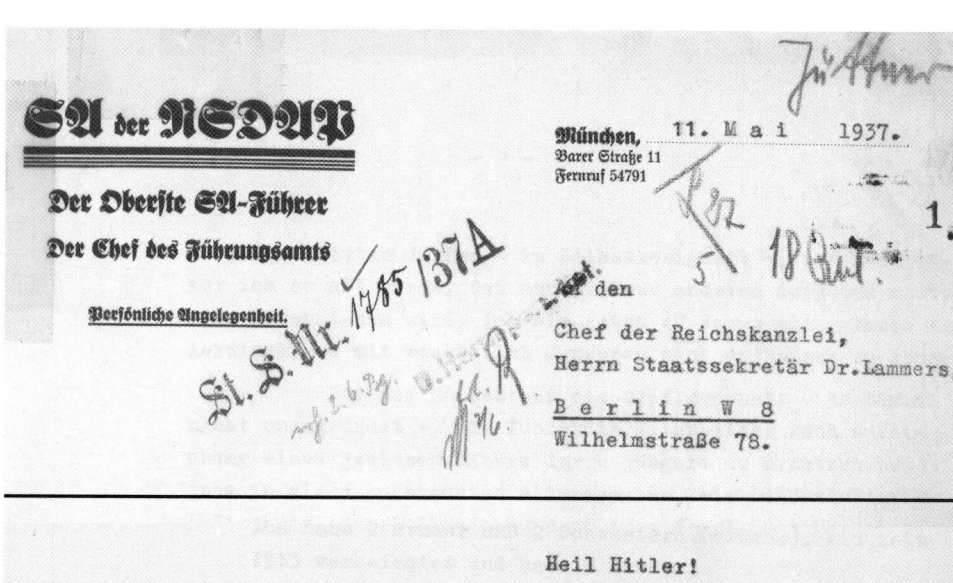

Above: The letterhead and signature of Max Jüttner. (Helmut Weitze Militärische Antiquitäten KG)

Right: A handwritten letter from Jüttner to *SA-Gruppenführer* Edmund Diehl, July 1943. (Helmut Weitze Militärische Antiquitäten KG)

Below: The spartan business card of *SA-Obergruppenführer* Max Jüttner. (Alexander Historical Autographs)

Friedrich *Wilhelm* ("Willi") Schepmann
Stabschef der SA (18.08.1943–08.05.1945)

*	17.06.1894 in Baak/Ruhr (today an Ortsteil- suburb- of Hattingen in Nordrhein-Westfalen).
†	26.07.1970 in Gifhorn/Niedersachsen.

NSDAP-Nr.:	26.762 (Joined 00.00.1922 with unknown number; Party banned, 09.11.1923-16.02.1925; Reenrolled 01.12.1925)

Promotions:

00.11.1914	*kriegsfreiwilliger Rekrut*
00.00.1915	*Offizieraspirant des Beurlaubtenstandes* (officer candidate on leave of absence)
27.01.1916	*Leutnant d. R.*
00.00.1927	*SA-Standartenführer* (as a post, not a rank; the rank did not exist at that time)
00.00.1931	*SA-Oberführer*
01.11.1932	*SA-Gruppenführer* (*Der Oberste SA-Führer, Führerbefehl Nr. 11, 25.01.1933*)
15.02.1933-10.11.1934	*Polizeipräsident*
09.11.1936	*SA-Obergruppenführer* (*Der Oberste SA-Führer, Führerbefehl Nr. 45, 09.11.1936*)
c. 1940	*Hauptmann d. R.*
18.08.1943-09.11.1943	*mit der Führung der Geschäfte des Stabschefs der SA beauftragt* (entrusted with the management of the affairs of the Chief of Staff of the SA)
09.11.1943-08.05.1945	*Stabschef der SA*

Career:

00.00.1900-00.00.1904	*Volksschule* in Baak.
00.00.1904-00.00.1909	*Progymnasium* in Hattingen (Ruhr).
00.00.1909-00.00.1912	*Präparandenanstalt für Lehrer* in Soest.
00.00.1912-00.00.1914	*Lehrerseminar* in Hattingen.
00.11.1914	Entered service as a *Kriegsfreiwilliger* with *Westfälischen Jäger-Bataillon Nr. 7* ("*Bückeburger Jäger*").
00.11.1914-00.11.1918	War service with *Jäger-Bataillon 7, Reserve-Jäger-Bataillon 7,* and *Infanterie-Regiment 56*. Among his assignments were *Bataillonsadjutant* of *Ersatz-Bataillon Jäger 7* (Bückeburg), *Gerichts- und Unterrichtsoffizier* (court and education officer), *Zugführer,* and *Kompanieführer*. He was lightly wounded in September 1917 and later severely wounded on two occasions.
01.07.1919	Passed his *2. Lehrerprüfung* (2nd teaching examination) in Winz bei Hattingen (Ruhr).
00.08.1919-00.12.1930	Entered the *Volksschuldienst* (public school service) and assigned as a *Volksschule* teacher in Winz and Hattingen.
00.00.19__-00.00.19__	Member of the *Kameradschaftskreis der Jäger-Bataillon 7*.
c. 1920-00.00.1922	Member of the *Deutschvölkische Schutz- und Trutzbund*.
00.00.192_	Joined the *Kameradschaftskreis der Jäger-Bataillon 7*.

00.00.1922	Joined the NSDAP/*Ortsgruppe Hattingen*.
00.00.1922-00.00.1923 (?)	*Propagandaleiter* of the *Ortsgruppe Hattingen der NSDAP*.
00.00.1923-04.02.1928	*Führer* of *SA-Sturm Hattingen*.
09.05.1924	Arrested and allegedly mistreated by French occupation troops due to his activities on behalf of the National Socialist movement.
24.10.1925	Participated in the *"Gautagung der NSDAP"* in Dortmund.
01.12.1925	Reenrolled in the NSDAP/*Ortsgruppe Hattingen*.
26.11.1926	Participated in the *"Treffen der NSDAP-Ortsgruppenführer des Ruhrgebiets"* at the *Gasthaus Märker* in Hattingen. Also in attendance were Hitler, Goebbels, and Lutze.
00.00.192_-00.00.19__	*Vorsitzender* of the *Gau-Uschla des Gaues Ruhr der NSDAP*.
00.00.1927-01.02.1929	*Führer* of *SA-Standarte "Ruhr"*, then *Führer* of *SA-Brigade II* (*SA-Bezirksführer der Großbezirk Essen*).
00.00.1928	Appointed as a *Parteiredner der NSDAP*.
20.05.1928	Unsuccessful candidate of the NSDAP for election to the *Preußische Landtag* and *Reichstag*.
18.11.1928-00.00.19__	*Gemeindevertreter der Deutsch-evangelischen Wahlvereinigung für die evangelische Gemeinde des Bezirks der Stadt Hattingen* (Community representative of the German Protestant Electoral Association for the Protestant community of the district of the city of Hattingen).
22.01.1929	At his own request, relieved of his SA position by the *Gausturmführer Ruhr*, Viktor Lutze. Schepmann's resignation led to massive criticism within the Hattingen SA. Schepmann's official statement on the matter related that he was "forced for professional resigns to resign from the SA leadership of the Großbezirk Essen after years of fighting against my authority. This fact was used by W. [Albert Wallwey, *Führer* of *SA-Standarte Hattingen*] to make an attempt to intrigue against me by rather dubious means..." ("Äußerung des Pg. Schepmann, Hattingen zu der Beschwerde Wallwey gegen Schepmann" [Statement by Pg. Schepmann, Hattingen on the Complaint by Wallwey against Schepmann", dated 08.05.1929, in *Obersten Parteigericht-Akte* {OPG-Akte}] Wilhelm Schepmann). The following statement was made in a letter of 24.04.1929 from the *Untersuchungs- und Schlichtungsausschuss* (USCHLA, Investigation and Arbitration Committee of the NSDAP) to the *Ortsgruppe Hattingen der NSDAP* read:

After the resignation of Pg. Schepmann, voices were raised in the S.A. which expressed the opinion that it was not acceptable for a Kopfarbeiter [brainworker] in a leadership position to resign from his leadership post in order to save his character, which might be at stake. From the side of the manual workers, remarks were made such as: "He can also go on the dole, just as well as we have to..." (*OPG-Akte Wilhelm Schepmann*).

01.08.1929-04.08.1929	Participated in the *"4. Reichsparteitag der NSDAP"* in Nürnberg.
10.12.1929-00.00.19__	*1. Schriftführer* (1st secretary) of the *Stadtverordnetenversammlung Hattingen* (Hattingen Municipal Assembly).

10.12.1929-00.00.19__	Member of the *Wahlkommission* (election commission) in the *Stadtverordnetenversammlung Hattingen*.
17.11.1929-00.00.1933	*Stadtverordneter* in Hattingen and member of the *Kreistag* for *Eppene-Ruhr-Kreis*.
00.00.1930-00.00.193_	*Gausturmführer* of *Gausturm Essen* (Bochum).
00.00.1930-00.00.1931	*Gauorganisationsleiter* of *Organisationen I und II* in the *Gauleitung Westfalen-Süd der NSDAP*.
00.00.1930-00.00.1931	*Gaupropagandaleiter* and *Gaufachberater für Kommunalpolitik* of the *Gauleitung Westfalen-Süd der NSDAP*.
00.10.1930-00.00.1933	*Fraktionsführer* (parliamentary group leader) of the *NSDAP-Stadtratfraktion* in Hattingen and the *NSDAP-Fraktion* in the *Kreistag* of *Ennepe-Ruhr-Kreis*. Succeeded Arthur Etterich who had resigned from his position as a *Stadtverordneter*.
29.10.1930-00.00.19__	Member of the *Kontrolausschuss der Stadtverordnetenversammlung Hattingen* (Control Committee of the Hattingen Town Council). Succeeded Arthur Etterich.
08.12.1930	Suspended from the public school service with loss of pension rights due to his NSDAP activities.
00.00.1931	Appointed as a *hauptamtlicher SA-Führer*.
19.03.1931	Following an NSDAP event in Dortmund the prior day, which ended in pandemonium, Schepmann was taken away by the police. The city's *Polizeipräsident*, Karl Zörgiebel, then issued an order against Schepmann and *Gauleiter* Josef Wagner (*Gau Westfalen-Süd*) appearing in public meetings, whether as a speaker or meeting coordinator, in Dortmund. ("Redeverbot für die Nationalsozialisten Wagner, Schepmann und Marschner", in *Hördener Volksblatt*, 20.03.1931)
31.03.1931	In a complaint to *SA-Stabschef* Röhm, *Gauleiter* Dr. Alfred Meyer (*Gau Westfalen-Nord*) objected to the appointment of Werner von Fichte as *OSAF-Stellvertreter West*, as this impeded his desire to see Schepmann appointed as *SA-Führer* for the *Gaue Westfalen-Nord* and *-Süd*.
28.04.1931	In a letter to *Reichsorganisationsleiter* Gregor Strasser, *Gauleiter* Dr. Meyer complained about "the current SA conditions in my Gau". He added that he had "no confidence in Herrn v. Fichte" and asked that "Pg. Schepmann be entrusted with leadership of the SA in Westfalen." (*SA-Disziplinarakte* Werner von Fichte)
29.04.1931	Now writing directly to Hitler, Dr. Meyer pleaded that the *Führer* "arrange for the appointment of Pg. Schepmann as Oberführer over the SA in the whole of Westfalen." (*SA-Disziplinarakte* Werner von Fichte)
00.05.1931	Dismissed from the public school service without entitlement to pension by the *Disziplinargericht* (disciplinary court) of Regierungsbezirk Arnsberg due to his National-Socialist political activities.
00.00.1931	Appointed as a *hauptamtlicher SA-Führer*.
00.00.1931-13.04.1932	*Führer* of *SA-Untergruppe Westfalen-Süd*.
13.09.1932	Participated in the "*Gautag der NSDAP Westfalen-Süd*" in Bochum.

13.04.1932-14.06.1932	SA banned by the government of Chancellor Heinrich Brüning.
24.04.1932-14.10.1933	Member of the *Preußische Landtag* (*Wahlkreis 18, Westfalen-Süd*).
24.06.1932	In a well-received speech to the *Westfälische Landtag*, Schepmann painted a picture of an impending civil war in the Ruhrgebiet. He described the police as an incompetent organization infiltrated by communists. If his SA were given police power for only 48 hours, he claimed, the danger of civil war would be immediately averted. (Daniel Schmidt, *Schützen und Dienen: Polizisten im Ruhrgebiet in Demokratie und Diktatur 1919-1939*, p. 311)
01.07.1932-31.10.1932	*Führer* of *SA-Untergruppe Westfalen-Süd* (resumed command following the lifting of the ban on the SA). (*Der Oberste SA-Führer, Führerbefehl Nr. 1*, 1. Juli 1932, S.
01.11.1932-14.03.1934	*Führer* of *SA-Gruppe Westfalen* (Westfalen-Nord und -Süd, Lippe, Schaumburg-Lippe) (Dortmund; initially m.d.F.b., then permanent). Succeeded Werner von Fichte. (*Der Oberste SA-Führer, Führerbefehl Nr. 11*, 25. Januar 1933)
15.02.1933-10.11.1934	*Polizeipräsident* in Dortmund (assumed the post on 17.02.1933). Resigned at his own request and succeeded by *SA-Gruppenführer* Otto Schramme.

On 27.02.1933, he held a press conference in which he announced that, as *Polizeipräsident*, he would "put the idea of the Führerprinzip [Führer Principle] in the foreground in all my actions." He added that he wished to "clean up the administrative apparatus where it is necessary… so that Dortmund will once again be the stronghold of cleanliness, order, and a sense of honor." [*der Hort der Sauberkeit, der Ordnung und des Ehrgefühls wird*] (*Dortmunder Zeitung*, 28.02.1933).

Immediately after taking office, he initiated a wave of purges within the Dortmund police apparatus. Among other things, the so-called *"Schepmann-Liste"*, which had presumably been drawn up in November 1932 and contained the names and brief assessments of 51 police officers and officer candidates, was sent to the Prussian Ministry of the Interior on 17.03.1933. Five days before his press conference, on 22.02.1933, he had already proposed the first ten police officers for dismissal. On 25.03.1933, he had several police officers suspended and disciplinary proceedings initiated with the aim of dismissing them without pension rights (Müller: "Bei uns sitzt Schepmann, da ist alles in Ordnung.", p. 85; Schmidt, pp. 296, 348). |
00.03.1933	Appointed as *Präsident* of the *Kreistag* in Hattingen.
03.04.1933	Delivered the eulogy at the funeral of *SA-Standartenführer* Hermann Pantföder, *Führer* of *SA-Standarte 174* (*24.11.1896 in Rogätz/Kreis Wolmirstedt [Magdeburg], †31.03.1933 in the area of Milse between Bielefeld and Herford [auto accident]) in the *Rathaus* of Herford. Some 5,000 SA men were in attendance. ("Grabgeleit des Standartenführers Pantföder", in *Westfälische Neueste Nachrichten/Bielefelder General-Anzeiger*, 04.04.1933)
20.04.1933	In response to the *Dortmunder General-Anzeiger* printing an unauthorized portrait of Hitler- drawn by Emil Stumpp and which "maliciously [gave his] facial expression a distorted and

mean-spirited appearance" – Schepmann had the editorial office and printing plant occupied by *SA-Hilfspolizei* that afternoon (incidentally, also the *Führer*'s birthday). A large portion of the circulation was confiscated and the editor-in-chief, Westhoff, taken into *"Schutzhaft"* (protective custody). In his place, the editor-in-chief of the Nazi newspaper *Rote Erde* took over the management and continuation of the newspaper for the time being. The headline of the next day's edition proclaimed that the paper was now *"im Dienst der nationatsoziatistischen Revolution"* (in the service of the National Socialist revolution) ("Polizeiaktion gegen den Dortmunder General-Anzeiger", in *Dortmunder Zeitung*, 21.04.1933)

30.05.1933 Played a role in organizing and carrying out the *"Bücherverbrennung"* (Book Burning) in Dortmund's *Hansaplatz*, described in the following passage by Christina Witte:

In Dortmund, the book burning seemed to have been organized and carried out by the SA, SS, the Hitler Youth and the Bund Deutscher Mädel (BDM), led by the NS-Lehrerbund (NSLB). In the run-up to the cremation ceremony, a library examination committee of the Dortmund NSDAP headed by NSLB member and teacher Dr. Hans Woelbing the book inventory of the local libraries. 4,000 to 5,000 books and volumes of journals were collected, most of which came from the library holdings of the trade union building, which SA men had already occupied on 18 April 1933. Since the city and state library in Dortmund was considered a scientific library, no books were removed from it. The literature classified as 'un-German', in particular scientific Marxist writings, were locked away with one copy each. On the evening of 30 May 1933, at 9 p.m., the above-mentioned NS mass organizations marched on the centrally located Hansaplatz. The great sympathy of the citizens of Dortmund led to an estimated 50,000 people gathering around the fire.

In imitation of the student book burnings, several fire speeches were held on the evening of this non-student action, which resembled those of the students and university teachers or university rectors in their rhetoric and symbolism. In addition to Woelbing and a few other speakers, the Dortmund Polizeipräsident and SA-Gruppenführer Wilhelm Schepmann gave the main speech. Finally, the writings carted onto Hansaplatz by truck were burned. In Dortmund mostly Marxist and socialist leaflets and fewer books were burned. Nevertheless, the names of the authors whose works were to be banned from German literature were read out. The black, red and gold national flag of the Weimar Republic was also impaled on pitchforks by SA men and thrown into the flames. The burning of the flag was given a special theatricality by the accompaniment of a chant. (Witte, "10. Mai 1933 – Die 'Aktion wider den undeutschen Geist' – Nationalsozialistische Bücherverbrennungen", at the Internet-Portal Westfalische Geschichte, https://www.lwl.org/westfaelische-geschichte/portal/Internet/finde/langDatensatz.php)

Schepmann's speech:

German men, German women and German youth! Holy German flame devour un-German spirit! We know no half-measures, and history does not know half-measures. The men of today's government have to make history because they act consistently with their whole personality and are consistent, means to be German. It is not acceptable that licentiousness is freedom. License is bondage and un-German. But we fight with all our might against every un-German spirit…

The renewal of the German spirit is not yet complete. In the spirit of National Socialism, we will carry out the renewal of the people according to the German spirit and make the German spirit and German freedom valid all over the world and thus also reach out to the last man of our people. The symbolic renewal at this sacred fire will shine in families, libraries, and in the last human being who was still a stranger to us today. In this sense, too, the flame should completely destroy everything that is not German. Only he who is related by blood is German. Everything else is un-German and cowardly. Just as the sacrificial death of German men in the World War was heroic and sacred, so the post-war period was cowardly and un-German, and in remembrance of the sacrificial death of our fellow Germans we must carry out the renewal of every German person. Everyone who is related to us by blood, who feels and thinks German is German. If we have heard the names of the authors who were burned here, or at least their writings, we need not say: You shall recognize them by their names. We swept them away in the new Germany because they were not of our blood, but had the blood of cowardice and not the heroic German blood in them.

But the future will not be shaped by cowardice, but by the ability of men who are genuinely German in style and loyalty. Everyone is welcome who wants to go with us from this point of view. If we want to see action and men, let's look only at our government today. It is not the individual who makes history there, but the whole. You have awakened us from the time of deepest shame and a leader has arisen for us, who we stand behind today with all our strength and who will lead Germany on a new path, as heaven has prescribed. If we look at our role models of German men, we know that they will lead us in the right direction with their whole German spirit and with their whole personality and energy. The voice of her blood has bound her to us, and the people are chained to them by the voice of blood to the last man. Battle-hardened and determined, they will lead us to the blessing of our Homeland and Fatherland and will be an example to us for all the battles that they first took on years ago. ("Undeutscher Geist ging in Flammen auf. Eindrucksvolle Kundgebung auf dem Hansaplatz/ Begeisterte Beteiligung der Dortmunder Bevölkerung/Ansprachen der Pgg. Goldmann, Dr. Woelbing, Kaiser, Polizeipräsident Schepmann, Eilers und des Hitlerjugendführers Sürenhagen", in *Dortmunder General-Anzeiger*, 31.05.1933)

07.07.1933-09.07.1933	Participated in the *"Gau-Parteitag 1933 des Gaues Westfalen-Süd der NSDAP"* and the *"Westfalen-Treffens der SA"* in Dortmund
09.07.1933	Leiter of the *"Aufmarsch der SA-Gruppe Westfalen"*. During the event, Schepmann marched at the head of 60,000 SA men, 5,000

	SS men, and 15,000 HJ boys. He also accompanied Hitler and Röhm as they inspected the troops.
00.08.1933	Appointed as a member of the future *Provinzialrat der Provinz Westfalen*.
31.08.1933-03.09.1933	Participated in the "*5. Reichsparteitag der NSDAP*" in Nürnberg.
16.09.1933-17.09.1933	Participated in and spoke at the "*Westfalentag*" in Münster (with 200,000 attendees).
00.11.1933	Issued a proclamation that read:

The Ministerpräsident [Hermann Göring] ordered long ago that the firearm should be used immediately against enemies of the people if the legal requirements are met. Every communist still active today must be ostracized as a traitor to the Fatherland and enemy of the people, persecuted and rendered harmless. (*Dortmunder Generalanzeiger*, 14.11.1933, in Maximilian Scheer, *Das Deutsche Volk klagt an: Hitlers Krieg gegen die Friedenskampfer in Deutschland*)

12.11.1933-08.05.1945	Member of the *Reichstag* (*Wahlkreis 18, Westfalen-Süd*; after 29.03.1936, *Wahlkreis 28, Dresden-Bautzen*).
23.10.1933-10.07.1934	*Sonderbevollmächtigter des Obersten SA-Führers für die Provinz Westfalen* (Special Plenipotentiary of the Supreme SA Leader for the Province of Westfalen). (*Anlage zur Verfügung des Obersten SA-Führers Ch.Nr.1560/33 vom 23. Okt. 1933*; Bundesarchiv NS 23/515); "Polizeipräsident Schepmann Sonderbevollmächtigter des Obersten SA.-Führers für Westfalen", in *Bochumer Anzeiger*, 28./29.10.1933)
27.11.1933-10.07.1934	*Sonderbevollmächtigter des Obersten SA-Führers für den Freistaat Lippe-Detmold.* (*Anlage 2 zur Verfügung des Obersten SA-Führers Ch.Nr.1560/33 II. Ang. v. 27.11.1933*; Bundesarchiv NS 23/515)
27.11.1933-10.07.1934	*Sonderbevollmächtigter des Obersten SA-Führers für den Freistaat Schaumburg-Lippe* (Bückeburg). (*Ibid.*)
20.01.1934-23.01.1934	Participated in an "*SA-Führertagung*" convened by Röhm in Friedrichroda. It concluded in Berlin with Hitler present, and brought together the *Führer* of *SA-Obergruppen* and *-Gruppen*, the high leadership of the *SA-Reserve*, and the *Amtschefe* (office heads) of the individual *Abteilungen* (departments) of the *Obersten SA-Führung*. (*Völkischer Beobachter*, 21./22.01.1934)
25.01.1934-15.02.1934	*Vorsitzender* of an *SA-Ehrenhof* (court of honor) to investigate and clarify allegations of corruption by *SA-Brigadeführer* Willi Veller (*Polizeipräsident* of Wuppertal).
24.02.1934-25.02.1934	Participated in the "*Gauparteitages 1934 des Gaues Westfalen-Nord der NSDAP*" in Münster.
15.03.1934-30.06.1934	*Führer* of *SA-Obergruppe X* (comprising *SA-Gruppen Westfalen* and *Niederrhein*; HQ: Dortmund; m.d.F.b. until 04.04.1934, then permanent). (*Der Oberste SA-Führer, Führerbefehl Nr. 24*, 02.05.1934, p. 8)
10.07.1934-00.08.1943	*Führer* of *SA-Gruppe Sachsen* (Dresden) (m.d.F.b. until 15.09.1935, then permanent). He actually assumed the post on 17.07.1934, succeeding Hans Hayn (who had been murdered in the purge of

	the SA leadership). (*Der Oberste SA-Führer, Führerbefehl Nr. 26*, 31.10.1934, p. 11)
23.07.1934	Ordered the arrest of one of the most senior SA leaders in Sachsen, *SA-Gruppenführer* Arthur Heß (*Führer* of *SA-Brigade 36* in Plauen), probably on orders of Martin Mutschmann (*Gauleiter* and *Reichsstatthalter* of Sachsen), for alleged involvement in the "*Röhm-Revolte*". Heß later told the *Obersten Parteigericht* that Mutschmann had ordered his leave of absence because he had been angry that he, Heß, had become the *Landeshandwerksführer für den Treuhänderbezirk Sachsen* (State Crafts Leader for the Trustee District Sachsen) and not Mutschmann's brother (Andreas Wagner, *"Machtergreifung" in Sachsen*, p. 320). Ultimately, on 25.09.1934, Heß was acquitted by the *SA-Sondergericht* of the *Obersten SA-Führung* of any suspicion of involvement in the "*Röhm-Revolte*" ("No accusations of any kind can be made against *Gruppenführer* Hess that connect him with the intentions of the former Chief of Staff, or that were directed against the P.O. or, for that matter, against the Führer."). Although the *II. Kammer* of the *Obersten Parteigericht*, on 08.02.1935, concluded that Hess was "guilty of a violation of Section 4, Paragraph 2 b of the statutes," but also acquitted him of the accusation that he had obtained the post of *Landeshandwerksführer* by fraud. His career within the SA in Sachsen was finished, however. On 09.01.1935, he was appointed *Reichsinnungsmeister der Reichsinnungsverband des Schuhmacherhandwerks* (Reich Guild Master at the Reich Guild Association of the Shoemaker's Craft). (*SA-Personalakte Arthur Heß*).
30.07.1934	Indicted by the *Obersten Parteigericht der NSDAP* in connection with the so-called "*Röhm-Affäre*", charged with violation of § 4 Abs. 2 b of the *Satzung* [Statute] *der NSDAP*, at the initiative of *Gauleiter* Josef Wagner. Also charged was his subordinate, *SA-Brigadeführer* Paul Giesler (*Führer* of *SA-Gruppe Westfalen*). They were specifically accused of planning an armed SA rebellion on 30.06.1934 and of acting against the authority of *Gauleiter* Wagner and the SS. Wagner accused Schepmann of, among other things, failing to inform Hitler that *Gauleiter* Julius Streicher had engaged in acts endangering the state with Westphalian industrialists in 1932; of defending Röhm's refusal to shoot himself on 01.07.1934; and of agitating within the SA against the NSDAP, the NSBO, and Wagner. (Peter Hüttenberger, *Die Gauleiter: Studie zum Wandel des Machtgefüges in der NSDAP*, p. 87) Proceedings against him were opened before the OPG on 08.08.1934 but vacated on 24.10.1934 (see entry for 10.04.1935, below).
04.09.1934-10.09.1934	Participated in the "*6. Reichsparteitag der NSDAP*" in Nürnberg.
31.10.1934-01.11.1934	Participated in a "*Tagung der Gruppenführer der SA*" (conference of *SA-Gruppenführer*), chaired by *SA-Stabschef* Lutze and with the *Obersten SA-Führer* (Hitler) present, at the Reich Propaganda Ministry, Berlin. During this meeting, the Führer announced guidelines for the future organization and employment of the SA.

06.11.1934	In a 19-page statement, Schepmann rejected accusations made against him by the *Obersten Parteigericht* and asked "for the speedy restoration of my National-Socialist honor in the movement and in public" ("*um die baldige Wiederherstellung meiner national-sozialistischen Ehre in der Bewegung und in der Öffentlichkeit*"). (*SA-Personalakte Wilhelm Schepmann*)
22.01.1935	Participated in a second "*Tagung der Gruppenführer der SA*" in the *Reichspropagandaministerium*, Berlin. (*Das Archiv*, 22.01.1935, p. 1433)
10.04.1935	Together with Paul Giesler and Paul Fischer, fully exonerated and acquitted by the *II. Kammer* of the *Obersten Parteigericht* under the chairmanship of *Reichsleiter* Wilhelm Grimm. The following are the specific offenses of which he had been accused:

Pg. Schepmann is accused of:

1.) Despite knowledge of negotiations between General Schleicher, who had been shot, and Rheinland-Westfalen industrialists, which posed a danger to the state, he did not report these events to the Führer, although he would have been obliged to do so on the basis of his oath of service to the Führer.

2) To have covered up for the traitor Röhm to Pg. Löbbert by saying "If Röhm believes that he is not guilty, then he has no reason to shoot himself; that is one thing."

3.) To have tacitly tolerated at a Führer meeting in Dortmund on 3.7.1934, that SA-Brigadeführer [Paul] Giesler performed a tribute to the high and national traitors who had been shot.

4) To have continued to take an outrageous stand against the political leadership, especially against the Gauleitung Westfalen in the period before 30 June 34, for example, to have threatened with immediate dismissal any SA leader who would allow SA formations to march past the Gauleiter.

5.) To have ordered the SA to be on the alert in the afternoon of 30 June 34 and to have ordered that special attention be paid to the SS and that any intrusion into the office be prevented by force of arms.

6.) To have ordered in the days before June 30, 34, that the SA should line up to be divorced into loyalty to Röhm and Hitler.

7.) To have tolerated that the former Gruppenführer Giesler closed the last big SA leaders' meeting in Dortmund before June 30, 34, in his presence with a Heil to the Chief of Staff Röhm.

8.) To have kept Dr. Jung Johann from Siegen as an instructor in the SA-Führerschule Lippstadt despite of the greatest swine-like behavior.

9.) To have appointed Dr. [Walter] Blume [later *SS-Standartenführer*], whose admission to the Party was rejected in 1933, as head of the Staatspolizeistelle Dortmund.

10) To have ordered the confiscation of weapons from the SS and police authorities by Sturmhauptführer Irmer of the Dortmund Secret State Police and Standartenführer [Richard] Odendahl of Siegen on June 27 and 28, 34, on the grounds that a large parade of armed SA was to take place in Dortmund on June 30, 34.

11.) To have instructed all SA brigades and ranks in the last days before June 30, 1934, to procure large sums of money by all means in order to be able to buy weapons and equipment.

12) To have withheld from the Führer the secret order of the Obersten SA-Führung of 23.5.34 concerning the arming of the SA and the use of closed SA units against the Reichswehr and to have forwarded it to other offices.

13) To have attempted to make SS-Abschnitt-Führer [Fritz] Schlessmann abandon his duty to the Führer by referring to the Chief of Staff.

14) To have tolerated serious excesses on the part of the SA, such as the sadistic maltreatment of the political prisoners of conscience by Standarte 441 in Bochum on 12.11.34 [sic!, correct: 12.11.33], the beatings of Sturmbannführer Lerchner in Scharfenberg and Thülen, the brawls of Oberführer [Hermann] Lohbeck and his men in the pub "Bunte Bühne", Düsseldorf.

15) To have tolerated serious indiscipline on the part of SA leaders, such as the threats made by Brigadeführer Giesler to Detective Linde in the Willsdorf burglary case and to a police officer in the theft case at the Sieghütten ironworks by Brigadeführer [Albert] Schönborn, as well as the abuse and mistreatment of PO and SS men by Sturmbannführer Struck. These interventions were even carried out with reference to his capacity as police chief.

16) To have tolerated the irresponsible stirring up of public opinion against the political leadership by Brigadeführer Giesler, who repeatedly spoke of rolling heads, and by Oberführer Lohbeck in Düsseldorf, who openly spoke of a second revolution against the bigwigs, and thus to have been jointly responsible for the attempt on June 30.

17.) To have tolerated the PO hostility, nepotism and gluttony of Brigadeführer [Heinrich Philipp] Reutlinger in Wiesbaden.

18.) To have tolerated lack of discipline in the SA, as evidenced by the various thefts of SA members and assaults on SS and police people...
(Quoted in the decision of the 2nd Chamber of the OPG of 10.04.1935, in OPG file Wilhelm Schepmann).

00.00.1935-00.00.1935	Member of the *Ehrenausschuss* for the *"2. Sächsische Sängerfest"* in Leipzig (28.-30.06.1935).
10.09.1935-16.09.1935	Participated in the *"7. Reichsparteitag der NSDAP"* in Nürnberg.
30.03.1936-01.01.1939	*Kreishauptmann* of the *Kreishauptmannschaft Dresden-Bautzen* (*"kommissarisch mit der Verwaltung beauftragt"* until 01.06.1936, then permanent).
08.09.1936-14.09.1936	Participated in the *"8. Reichsparteitag der NSDAP"* in Nürnberg.
06.09.1937-13.09.1937	Participated in the *"9. Reichsparteitag der NSDAP"* in Nürnberg. In the course of this event, Schepmann found himself in an argument with *SA-Gruppenführer* Kurt Lasch regarding the bad treatment of old Saxon SA leaders by *Gauleiter* Martin Mutschmann, which culminated in Lasch calling Schepmann a "minion of Röhm" (*"Günstling Röhms"*) and the matter having to be arbitrated by the *Ehrenhof der Obersten SA-Führung* (Court of Honor of the Supreme SA Leadership). (Andreas Wagner, *"Machtergreifung" in Sachsen. NSDAP und staatliche Verwaltung 1930-1935*, p. 321 fn. 95)

21.09.1938	Accompanied the *Führer* of the *Sudetendeutschen Partei* (SdP), Konrad Henlein, on his *"Besichtigungsfahrt durch sächsische Flüchtlingslager"* (sightseeing tour through Saxon refugee camps) of the SdP. ("Konrad Henlein besucht die Flüchtlinge", in *Das Kleine Volksblatt* [Wien], 23.09.1938, p. 6)
01.01.1939-00.08.1943	*Regierungspräsident* in *Dresden-Bautzen* (with effect from 22.03.1936).
11.08.1939-13.08.1939	Participated in the *"Marinebundestag"* of the *NS-Deutscher Marine-Bund* (a component of the *NS.-Reichskriegerbund*) in Dresden.
18.08.1939-20.08.1939	Visit to Trieste to attend the Swimming Championship of the Italian *Milizia Volontaria per la Sicurezza Nazionale* (M.V.S.N., Volunteer Militia for National Security). He had been invited to the event by the Chief of Staff of the M.V.S.N., *Luogotenente Generale* Luigi Russo. (*Vorarlberger Tagblatt*, 19.08.1939, p. 9: *Sportallerlei*)
00.00.1939-00.00.1940	Army service with successive assignment as *Kompanieführer*, *Ordonnanzoffizier*, and *Regimentsadjutant* in an *Infanterie-Regiment*.
26.03.1943	In a conversation with *Reichshauptamtsleiter* Helmuth Friedrichs of the *Parteikanzlei*, regarding a successor to the *Reichssportführer SA-Obergruppenführer* Hans von Tschammer und Osten, who had died the day before, Goebbels suggested Schepmann as a possible candidate. In his diary entry of 27.03.1943, the Propaganda Minister wrote:

... Friedrichs comes to me as Bormann's emissary to discuss the succession of Tschammer-Ostens. I strongly plead against a change in the organizational statute of the Reichssportführer, as demanded by Lutze. One cannot simply subordinate the entire sports movement to the SA. Sport is a people's affair, not a Party affair, or even an affair of an organization of the Party. It must be conceded to the SA that it has a certain right to the post of Reichssportführer. But there are, after all, quite a number of group and Obergruppenführer in the SA who are suitable for this task. I suggest, among others, Jagow, Ludin, Helldorff, and Schepmann. I would prefer Jagow, but I don't know if he can be spared in Budapest. Otherwise, Schepmann would come into question, who has shown great diplomatic skill in his Saxon task; after all, it means something to endure a whole series of years next to [Gauleiter] Mutschmann without coming to blows. Helldorff, of course, has all the prerequisites; only, unfortunately, he is somewhat easygoing. But perhaps this could be changed by some supervision...

The post ultimately went to von Tschammer und Osten's former deputy, *SA-Oberführer* (from 20.04.1944, *Brigadeführer*) Arno Breitmeyer.

16.08.1943-08.05.1945	*Stabschef der SA* (m.d.F.d.G.b. until 09.11.1943, then permanent). Succeeded Max Jüttner, who attended to the duties of *Stabschef* in the months following the death of Viktor Lutze. Dr. Goebbels' assessment of Schepmann's appointment, from his diary entry of 19.08.1943:

... Schepmann has been provisionally entrusted with the management of the affairs of the SA-Stabschef... Lutze's successor... is very well qualified for this task. I am also very pleased that one of our old Ruhr-Garde has been appointed to this post. I will undoubtedly be able to work well with Schepmann [Mit Schepmann werde ich zweifellos gut arbeiten können]...

In a telegram of 18.08.1943, *Reichsführer-SS* Heinrich Himmler wrote:

Dear Parteigenosse Schepmann,

First of all, my warmest congratulations on your appointment as Stabschef of the SA. You are taking on a very difficult position. I will do everything in my power to restore the relationship between the SA and the SS, which has unfortunately been so severely marred by many unfortunate circumstances and through no fault of my own, to one of complete cordiality. You can count on my comradely help and support in this, as well as in your entire task, in any form at any time.

With sincerest comradely greetings.
Heil Hitler
Your H. Himmler
(Bundesarchiv NS 19-3287; Translation: Gary Costello)

Schepmann's answer, dated 19.08.1943:

Dear Parteigenosse Himmler,

I am very grateful for the congratulations and the warmth with which they were expressed. Let me assure you that we will be united by a national socialist comradeship that no one can interfere with. First and foremost, this is the will of the Führer. This will is sacred to me. Then I will cultivate this comradeship even more, on account of the fact that we have known each other personally for years.

In comradely solidarity.
Heil Hitler
As always, your W. Schepmann
(Bundesarchiv NS 19-3287; Translation: Gary Costello)

Daniel Siemens writes of the status of the SA under Schepmann:

By the autumn of 1943 even the notoriously optimistic... Schepmann had to concede that the situation of the organization was critical. In a long speech at a meeting of the Reichsleiter and Gauleiter in Posen on 6 October 1943 [see entry of that date, below], he explained that his organization should be judged not by its immediate results (or lack thereof), but by its long-term impact. The general tone of his speech was defensive. Schepmann repeatedly emphasized that the role of the SA was as an instrument of the party and of Hitler. Consequently, he was eager to improve its relationship with other party organizations, particularly the Hitler Youth and the SS. In direct talks with Himmler, Schepmann seems to have unconditionally accepted the preeminent role of the SS and the Waffen-SS, at least during wartime. He explicitly stated that he would not pursue plans for a Waffen-SA, which would comprise exclusively SA men, even as he claimed that Himmler had previously agreed to establish such a group. Modelled along the lines of the Standarte Feldherrnhalle, but under the command of the Wehrmacht, the projected SA combat unit to complement the Waffen-SS was never established. It is highly unlikely that Himmler ever intended to form such a unit. He most likely made the promise merely to demonstrate goodwill toward the new SA Chief of Staff and ensure his obedience. An agreement between the SA and SS from the year 1944, allowing stormtroopers to volunteer for the 18th SS volunteer Panzergrenadier Division "Horst Wessel", served the same purpose. (Siemens, *Stormtroopers*, p. 272)

20.08.1943	First visit with Hitler following his appointment as *Stabschef*. In his diary, Goebbels wrote: "Schepmann has shown his best side during this discussion."
24.08.1943	First meeting with Himmler in his new function, during which they discovered the settlement of disagreements between the SA and SS. (*Die Organisation des Terrors. Der Dienstkalender Heinrich Himmlers 1943-1945*, p. 418)
25.08.1943	First meeting as newly appointed *SA-Stabschef* with the *SA-Gruppenführer* in Berlin. On the same day, he made his inaugural visit to Goebbels, who wrote in his diary the next day:

... The new Chief of Staff of the SA, Schepmann, pays me an inaugural visit. I talk to him at length about the new tasks of the SA. The program that Schepmann develops is very clear and unambiguous. He wants to give the SA a task again and, above all, bring it closer to the Party. If he succeeds in this, he will undoubtedly earn a great deal of merit for the SA, which, to a large extent, still has the old idealists in its circles. Schepmann makes an extraordinarily sympathetic, calm, and clear impression during the interview... It is now becoming more and more apparent that Viktor Lutze was only partially suited to his position. He had let a lot of things go to waste in the SA. His wife talked too much into the affairs of the SA and politics in general. Schepmann will see his first task in eliminating all this as quickly as possible and giving the SA back its old face...

27.08.1943	Inaugural visit with *Reichsleiter* Franz Xaver Schwarz, Reich Treasurer of the NSDAP. ("Obergruppenführer Schepmann beim Reichsschatzmeister", in *Badener Zeitung*, 28.08.1943, p. 2)
01.09.1943	Delivered his first major public address to the SA, described in the German press as follows:

SA in the Spirit of Defensive Manhood.

On Thursday evening, in the ballroom of the Kunstlerhaus in München, Obergruppenführer Wilhelm Schepmann, entrusted with leadership of the administration of the Stabschef der SA, at the start of an inspection tour through the SA-Gruppen, in a first foundational speech, made a rousing declaration of faith in the unwavering loyalty to the Führer, the unity of the party and the unshakeable confidence in victory in front of the Führer of the SA Standort München, the birthplace and capital of the movement.

[Schepmann] was welcomed by SA-Gruppenführer Ritterkreuzträger Bernhard Hofmann, the newly appointed Führer of SA-Gruppe Hochland. He extended special greetings to General Ritter von Epp and Gauleiter Paul Giesler. In his large-scale address, SA-Obergruppenführer Schepmann highlighted the close ties between the Party's branches, especially the SA, and the political leadership: "The Party is the foundation and the root of this Reich and must be all the more so in wartime. According to the Führer's will, it remains the great and glorious task of the SA to instill the National Socialist spirit into the fortified German manhood."

He further emphasized that the SA only had legitimacy through the Party. Everyone would have to be a National Socialist first if he wanted to be a fully-fledged SA-Mann. The SA-Wehrabzeichen was designated by the Stabschef as a badge of honor for the man who was ready and able for military service. Therefore, even if more than 70 per cent of the SA men were at the front, the SA-Wehrkämpfe were an absolute necessity, especially in wartime.

From the SA-Führer, SA-Obergruppenführer Schepmann demanded open comradeship, authority based on exemplary conduct and joyful submission. The German Volk must always see a role model in the men that wear the uniform. "What we", the Stabschef concluded his gripping speech, "have begun in the time of struggle, we will continue until death." ("*Was wir in der Kampfzeit begonnen haben, wollen wir fortführen bis zum Tode.*") ("SA im Geist wehrhaften Mannestums", in *Hakenkreuzbanner* [Mannheim], 04.09.1943; Translation: Gary Costello)

05.09.1943	Inaugural visit as *SA-Stabschef* to *Reichsmarschall* Göring in the latter's headquarters. ("Stabschef der SA bei Göring", in *Wiener Kronen-Zeitung*, 06.09.1943, p. 3 and "Stabschef Schepmann beim Reichsmarschall", in *Znaimer Tagblatt*, 10.09.1943, p. 2)
06.10.1943	Participant and speaker ("on the ideological task of the SA" – "*über die weltanschauliche Aufgabe der SA*") at the meeting of *Reichsleiter, Gauleiter,* and *Verbandsführer der NSDAP* (under the leadership of *Reichsleiter* Bormann in Posen). In his diary entry of the following day, Goebbels wrote:

The SA has always had great misfortune in its supreme leadership... I do not believe, after all that Schepmann will be up to the task on the whole... The great stature that belonged to turn the wild bunch of the SA into a decent and disciplined fighting organization. is apparently lacking in him...

07.10.1943	Participated in a "*Tagung des Reichs- und Gauleiter*" at Führer HQ "Wolfsschanze" in Rastenburg/ Ostpreußen. ("Das

	Parteiführerkorps im Hauptquartier", in *Wiener Kronen-Zeitung*, 09.10.1943, p. 1 and "Tagung der Parteiführerschaft", in *Znaimer Tagblatt*, 09.10.1943, p. 1)
	That evening, at 1700 hours, he conferred with the *Reichsführer-SS* Himmler in the latter's *Feldkommandostelle Hochwald*. (*Die Organisation des Terrors. Der Dienstkalender Heinrich Himmlers 1943-1945*, p. 489)
15.10.1943	Led an *"Apell des SA-Gruppenführerkorps"* (roll call of *SA-Gruppenführer*) in Hamburg. ("SA im Einsatz gegen Bombenschäden", in *Kleine Volks-Zeitung* [Wien], 16.10.1943, p. 2)
27.10.1943	Diary entry of Dr. Goebbels: "The SA is extremely unlucky. Never in its existence did it possess a leader of stature." (Translation in Daniel Siemens, *Stormtroopers*, p. 426 fn. 185)
31.10.1943	Delivered a speech to the *Führerkorps* of SA-Gruppe Oder in Frankfurt/Oder. ("Stabschef Schepmann in Frankfurt", in *Wiener Kronen-Zeitung*, 01.11.1943, p. 2)
03.11.1943	Delivered a speech to SA men during the *Reichsfeier "Der Toten Tatenruhm"* in the *Stadtsaal* of Speyer:

My comrades!
We have gathered at a site of historical significance for all of us in order to commemorate with pride in these serious times those Germans whose heroic deeds fill our people, whose lives were a single commitment to the German mission and whose death was the heroic culmination of their manly efforts. Here in Speyer Cathedral lie the bones of the German emperors from Salian times. We stand reverently before their coffins and acknowledge their deeds, whose fame fills the world and whose effectiveness we still feel today. Konrad II was a supreme power and leader of his people, whose commitment to the eternal leadership of the Germans in the Germanic region is reflected in the saying:

"When the King has died, the kingdom remains, as the ship remains whose helmsman perishes"

His grandson, Heinrich IV, had to accept defeats and humiliations in his embattled life, but he was not discouraged by any situation and always took up the fight against the opponents of the empire for the unrestricted claim to leadership of the German rulers. Thus his aspirations and his fighting spirit place him in the ranks of the great emperors of our past. He, too, now rests within the walls of this old German imperial city on the Rhein, on the German river that, steeped in legend, is the epitome of German will and desire. In our imagination, neighboring Worms is associated with the shining figure of Siegfried, castles and towns are witnesses to the stormy development of the nation. Heidelberg's ruins remind us of the empire's decline. Blücher's crossing of the Rhein appears to us as a symbol of the storming will for freedom against Napoleonic oppression. And the question "Who wants to be the guardian of the river?" was answered unanimously by the reunited nation in 1870, 1914 and 1939 with the marching of able-bodied men.

We today are the descendants of great generations. It is from the memory of the deeds of our ancestors that we draw the strength for the struggle to which our people are called. We have a thousand years of heritage to defend, which we have to hand over strengthened and invigorated into the hands of future generations. If we do not fully engage in this struggle with all that we are and all that we have, our sons and daughters- accusing us- would perish, a rich inheritance would be lost. Our people know such moments in their history when a failure on the internal course could have destroyed the fruits of centuries of struggle and labor. In times of such danger, providence has repeatedly given us Germans men who, as true leaders, have been able to lift our people out of failure and stagnation and lead them to victory over cowardice and betrayal, over enemy and adversary. The great Friedrich, who was able to develop all the strength of the Prussian nucleus after the decline of the medieval empire, is so close to our hearts because he led his people from an apparently hopeless situation to victory and glory, because we descendants in the Great German Empire live from his deeds. A quarter of a century ago, after the November betrayal, when Germany seemed to be doomed to ruin, Providence gave us, the people of today, the Führer. He brought us the National Socialist idea, that worldview which has its roots in the pagan, which professes its allegiance to the great figures of our history, whose goal is the unity and freedom of our people, for which no sacrifice can be called too great, no commitment too precious.

The despisers of all human greatness, the Jews and the democrats and Marxists who sprang from their thinking, had endeavored, not without success, to alienate the great figures of our history from our people, to eradicate all reverence for the sacrifice of the individual for the whole. Their influence made even the proud confession to our brothers, fathers and sons who died in the First World War fall prey to a ridiculousness that must be scorned by a "enlightened" people. A "drama" was allowed to pass over alleged German stages, which dared to dismiss the fallen German soldier with a "dispose of the dirt". The National Socialist moral doctrine has restored to our German feelings that which belongs inseparably to our nature: reverence for those who gave everything for their people.

This affirmation of the heroic was also the basis for the struggle of National Socialism in the years before the seizure of power. The march to the Feldherrnhalle, the 20th anniversary of which we will be celebrating in a few days, is a declaration of commitment to an idea. Those eighteen who, coming from all strata of our people, fell before the steps of the Bavarian temple of glory, went to their deaths for this idea and in loyalty to the creators of the new world view, out of innermost desire, out of firmly rooted conviction. That is why, year after year, we stand at their bier and acknowledge these dead who live on in us: The Eternal Vigil.

They were followed over the years by hundreds of men who sealed their commitment to the National Socialist worldview with death. One of them, the SA-Sturmführer Horst Wessel, murdered by a cowardly hand, lives on eternally in our national song. The struggle that these men waged was particularly marked by the fact that here Germans were confronting Germans, that the organization of the people, their own state, led by foreigners, was the fiercest opponent. The soldier of 1914, who rushed to the flags in those August days, to which his Supreme Commander had called him, faced the enemy conscious of the power and strength of the Reich. His enthusiasm grew out of this awareness. And although in the development of the ever-widening struggle the State and its leader did nothing, absolutely nothing, to show him the aim of the struggle, to penetrate it ideologically, but on the contrary allowed all the forces to work undisturbed which strove only for the destruction of our national will, the German Army accomplished deeds whose glory over Verdun and Flanders, Tannenberg and Gorlice, Turkey and the Balkans, Africa and the oceans outshone everything that German national power had been able to achieve up to that time. "May thousands of years pass" says the Führer, "one will never be allowed to speak and tell of heroism without remembering the German army of the World War." And the soldierly poet Walter Flex lets the dead heroes speak:

> "We sank down for Germany's splendor.
> Blossom, Germany, as our wreath of death."

When everything that the German soldier had fought for, that had meant power and glory, collapsed, that which had embodied this state also disappeared from his consciousness. Everything was empty and stale, the community form seemed to have lost its meaning, self-interest was the order of the day. Bolshevik trickery, Jewish influences had a paralyzing toxic effect on the German. Then, from the ranks of the unknown soldiers of the war, the savior arose for us: The front-line soldier Adolf Hitler lifted up the best of our people in the all-encompassing National Socialist movement and created in his world view the prerequisite for rebuilding the will to fight back against the blows that fate had dealt our people. In an-historically speaking-unbelievably short time, he reached his goal: In 1933, the German people followed him unanimously on the path prescribed by honor and understanding. Greater Germany comes into being and its people are ready to follow the path whose direction is determined by two basic principles of the National Socialist world view: "Common good takes precedence over self-interest" and "Blood and soil".

No sooner do the first successes of the new endeavors become apparent than the old opponents from the outside appear on the scene. All the attempts that the Führer makes, offering the greatest of völkisch sacrifices, to come to an understanding with the so-called democracies of all shades, fail because of the firm will of the opponents not to give Germany the air it needs to breathe. Thus the Führer calls the German people to a community of arms, the ultimate and highest form of coexistence of a people. "Never forget" he says, "that the most sacred right in this world is the right to soil that you want to cultivate yourself, and the most sacred sacrifice is the blood that you shed for that soil."

When the die is cast in 1939, a united people goes off to fight and its sons perform heroic deeds worthy of those of the fathers of 1914, worthy of Germany's past. Poland and France collapsed under the weight of

German power. German soldiering developed to its highest splendor when the confrontation with the most relentless enemy, Bolshevism, demanded the unleashing of all the people's strength, when terror and the will to exterminate involved women and children at home in the bloody confrontation.

Now the formative power of the National Socialist worldview becomes apparent. Germany's sons have always been the best soldiers in the world. Even ancient Rome was shaken to its foundations when Cimbrians and Teutons established the fame of the Germanic warriors. But no sooner had the Cheruscan Hermann succeeded in crushing the Roman legions attacking his native soil in the Teutoburg Forest than internal strife and party-political discord prevented the exploitation of the military successes. This völkisch discord runs like a red thread through our history. The terrible climax of this inner struggle of all against all was experienced by our generation from 1919 – 1932. When our SA men began the march for the Führer's idea in the streets of the city and the countryside, they were clearly aware that the brute force of the enemy would only be broken by a fight that was determined and prepared to the last resort, but they were animated by a fanatical belief in victory. This faith was so strong that it swept away the hesitant, converted the opponents. Certainly, the French Revolution of 1789 spiritually shaped the nineteenth century and is still present in our environment today in its pernicious materialistic effects. History, however, will one day attribute to the appearance of Adolf Hitler and his National Socialist teachings the significance of having decisively influenced a millennium. The miracle when our whole nation was gradually seized by the idea of the movement, and in this way something came into being for the first time that had never been achieved in the past, probably also because the time was not yet ripe: the German national community. Our opponents around us realized much earlier that a united German nation, growing together into a coherent one, would represent a core in the heart of Europe that could never be overcome and would therefore be decisive, against which all usurpatory desires for power would be shattered. That is why they had always tried everything to prevent the German people from becoming a nation. Richelieu and Mazarin had no other goal than Clemenceau and Churchill. Therefore, the Führer had to reckon with furious resistance from all these forces when he proclaimed the German national community. We know, however, that the very concept of this national community, which no longer needs to be explained to our people, is the root of the strength that enables our people to master the tasks facing them. But because we knew that we had to defend this highest good of the German national community against our opponents all over the world, it was the duty of the movement-and in it especially that of the SA-to ensure that this national community, if you the fight against it was announced, could prove itself as a military community. And this has been achieved!

Today, our nation stands like a steel block at the front as well as at home. Imperturbable, men and women carry out their duty, defying death. New glory transfigures the heroic struggle of our battalions, the daring of our submarines, the audacity of our aviators makes the eyes of our youth light up again. The heroic greatness with which old and young bear the infernal terror of destruction through degenerate warfare, will arouse the admiration of the coming generations again and again. The whole of Germany is prepared to give its all for victory and the greatness of the nation. So today we stand reverently before the sacrifices made by the front and the homeland in the struggle for destiny, and we all pledge, young and old, man and woman, to show ourselves worthy of those who gave their lives in a thousand years of German history and today in the present, so that Germany may endure.

The Edda says:

> "Property dies, clans die,
> You yourself die like them,
> I know one thing that lives forever:
> The glory of the dead."

(Original in the Bundesarchiv; Translation courtesy of Gary Costello)

08.11.1943	Participated in a *"Reichs- und Gauleitertagung"* in München, followed by a meeting of the Party's *"Alten Garde"* (Old Guard) in the *Löwenbräukeller*. ("Der Führer vor der Alten Garde in München", in *Kleine Volks-Zeitung* [Wien], p. 1)
11.11.1943	Accompanied by *Gauleiter* Dr. Gustav Adolf Scheel and *SA-Gruppenführer* Wilhelm Dittler, inspected *SA-Gruppe Alpenland* in Salzburg. During a visit to the *Festung Hohensalzburg*, he was introduced to *Oberbürgermeister SA-Standartenführer* Anton Giger, who greeted him on behalf of the city. In the afternoon, he addressed local SA leaders in the ranks of *Sturmführer* and above during a *Führerappell* in the *Großen Saal des Mozarteums*, and in the evening, he stayed with the SA leaders in the *Mirabellkasino*. (*Salzburger Zeitung*, 11./12.11.1943
13.11.1943	Inspected *SA-Gruppe Donau* in Wien, delivering a speech to 2,500 SA leaders. ("Stabschef Schepmann vor 2500 Führern der SA-Gruppe Donau", in *Das Kleine Volksblatt* [Wien], 14.11.1943, p. 5; "Stabschef Schepmann vor 2500 Führern der SA-Gruppe Donau", in *Wiener Kronen-Zeitung*, 14.11.1943, p 5; "Stabschef der SA Schepmann gab vor den Führern der SA-Gruppe Donau in Wien die Parolen für die Arbeit der SA", in *Znaimer Tagblatt*, 15.11.1943, p. 3)
15.11.1943-16.11.1943	Inspection of *SA-Gruppe Südmark* in Graz. On the 15th he delivered a speech to the officers of the *SA-Gruppe*. The next day, together with *Generaloberst* Eduard Dietl, he spoke at a public assembly of the NSDAP in the *DAF-Sälen* (halls).
21.11.1943	During a roll call of the *Führerkorps* of *SA-Gruppe Pommern* in Krössinsee announced the *Führer*'s institution of the *SA-Wehrabzeichen für Kriegsversehrte* (SA Military Badge for the War-Disabled). ("SA-Wehrabzeichen für Kriegsversehrt. Stabschef

	Schepmann verkündet die Stiftung des Führers", in *Tages-Post* [Linz], 22.11.1943, p. 1; "Stiftung des SA-Wehrabzeichens für Kriegsversehrte. Stabschef Schepmann verkündet den Erlass des Führers", in *Wiener Kronen-Zeitung*, 22.11.1943, p. 3)
01.12.1943	Oversaw an *Arbeitstagung* (working conference) of the entire *SA-Gruppenführerkorps* in Breslau. ("Apell des SA-Gruppenführerkorps in Breslau", in *Znaimer Tagblatt*, 03.12.1943, p. 1)
28.02.1944	Keynote speaker at the *"Abschlusskundgebung der SA-Winterwehrkämpfe"* (Closing Rally of the SA Winter Military Competitions) in the *Großen Stadtsaal*, Innsbruck. ("Der Führer bleibt keinen Schlag schuldig!" -Stabschef Schepmann sprach auf der Abschlusskundgebung der SA-Winterwehrkämpfe", in *Innsbrucker Nachrichten*, 29.02.1944, p. 3)
04.03.1944-06.03.1944	Lecturer on *"Die Reichsidee als politischer Auftrag"* (The Reich Idea as a Political Mission) at the *"2. Arbeitstagung der Dienststelle Berlin der Obersten SA-Führung"* (2nd Working Conference of the Berlin Office of the Supreme SA Leadership) in Posen.
30.03.1944	Delivered a speech to 500 frontline officers in Berlin. ("Stabschef Schepmann vor Offizieren", in *Das Kleine Volksblatt* [Wien], 31.03.1944, p. 4)
00.04.1944	Delivered a speech at a meeting of all *SA Verwaltungsführer* (administrative leaders) in the Reich. ("Der Stabschef der SA in Wien und Niederdonau", in *Neues Wiener Tagblatt*, 16.04.1944, p. 5)
10.05.1944	Accompanied Goebbels during a reception in Berlin for a delegation of soldiers from *Panzer-Grenadier-Division "Feldherrnhalle"* (then deployed to the Eastern Front). ("Dr. Goebbels empfing Abordnung der Panzergrenadierdivision "Feldherrnhalle", in *Znaimer Tagblatt*, 12.05.1944, p. 1)
12.05.1944	Delivered a speech during a *Gruppenführerlehrgang* at the *Reichsschule der Reichsarbeitsdienst*, Berlin. ("Der Stabschef beim RAD", in *Marburger Zeitung*, 13./14.05.1944, p. 2)
17.05.1944-19.05.1944	Participated in a large *Arbeitstagung* of higher-ranking *SA-Führer* in Salzburg.
03.06.1944	Speech to officers of a *Panzertruppenschule*. ("Stabschef Schepmann sprach vor den Offizieren einer Panzertruppenschule", in *Das Klein Blatt* [Wien], 04.06.1944, p. 2)
21.06.1944	Delivered the memorial address at the funeral of the *Regierender Bürgermeister* of Bremen, *SA-Obergruppenführer* Johann Heinrich Böhmcker. ("Trauerfeier für SA-Obergruppenführer Böhmcker", in *Neues Wiener Tagblatt*, 22.06.1944, p. 2)
11.07.1944-13.07.1944	Oversaw an *Arbeitstagung* for the *Führer* of all the *SA-Gruppen* and the *Hauptamtschefs* of the *Obersten SA-Führung*.
12.07.1944	Awarded the *SA-Wehrabzeichen für Kriegsversehrte* to 100 wounded soldiers (*Znaimer Tagblatt*, 14.07.1944, p. 3).
00.09.1944	Charged by the *Chef des Generalstabes des Heeres* with the formation of a *Landsturm*, a reserve militia, in Ostpreußen. This plan was discontinued with the foundation of the *Volkssturm* later in the month.

26.09.1944-00.05.1945	*Inspekteur für die Schießausbildung* (Inspector for Marksmanship Training) of the *Deutschen Volkssturm*. In his diary entry of 12.09.1944, Dr. Goebbels wrote:

Ley, Schepmann and Himmler are arguing about this. I agree with the opinion of the Führer that Himmler is the only one who can build up the Landsturm along generous lines. If it were given to Schepmann, it would soon be eaten up by the lethargy of the SA, and if it were taken over by Ley, it could only become a pure nonsense. |
03.10.1944	Participated in the official memorial service for *Gauleiter* Josef Bürckel (†28.09.1944) in Saarbrücken.
00.10.1944	Delivered a speech to 2,000 *Fahnenjunker* (officer candidates) of the German Army (*Znaimer Tagblatt*, 20.10.1944, p. 2).
18.10.1944	Participated in the state funeral for *Generalfeldmarschall* Erwin Rommel in Ulm.
19.10.1944	In the following *Tagesbefehl* (Order of the Day), declared:

SA-Men! The Führer has called the working homeland to arms. The strength of the whole nation will be provided in the German Volkssturm. It is necessary at this critical moment of the war, to secure victory in our favor.

The Volkssturm will fight at the burning borders of the Reich. It will defend its beloved homeland to the last breath. The SA will employ all the strength and experience of its National Socialist and military education in the Volkssturm. In this grave hour it renews its profession of action and loyalty to the Führer. Wherever the SA man stands in the Volkssturm, he is to fulfill his duty with a passionate heart, National Socialist thoroughness and the ever-practiced selfless devotion. I expect the SA Führer in particular to be a pioneer and an example in terms of performance and commitment to the National Socialist idea. Hail to the Führer!
Wilhelm Schepmann, Stabschef der SA
(*Neues Wiener Tagblatt*, 20.10.1944, p. 1) |
| 13.11.1944 | Delivered a speech during the swearing-in of *Volkssturm* troops in Danzig, during which he declared "Better to go down with honor than to be broken by the inhuman slavery of the enemy." (*Kleine Wiener Kriegszeitung*, 14.11.1944, p. 4 and *Znaimer Tagblatt*, 15.11.1944, p. 1) |
| 06.03.1945 | Visited SA men and *Panzergrenadiere* of the *Kampfgruppe "Feldherrnhalle"* in Marienburg "In recognition of the outstanding part [they] ha[d] played in the defense of [the city]." (*Kleine Wiener Kriegszeitung*, 07.03.1945, p. 3) |
| 16.03.1945 | In Düsseldorf to inspect units of the *Volkssturm*, SA, and SA-Standarte "Feldherrnhalle" in action on the Western Front. In a speech to these men, he declared:

In a few days, you too will fight the enemy who is devastating your homeland and has inflicted untold suffering on so many of our |

countrymen. Go to meet him in this decisive hour with the hatred he has awakened in in us, and with the hardness which your bleeding homeland expects of you...

As men of the SA we have unconditionally bound ourselves to serve in the struggle for freedom of the Reich. Therefore the SA man must fight in the foremost lines. Live and act as SA men according to the old German watchword, "It is better to fight and die honorably than to lose one's freedom and soul." (The National Archives [UK], Ref.: WO 208/4499)

Following the inspection, he met with the *Gauleiter* of Düsseldorf and Essen (Friedrich Karl Florian and Fritz Schlessmann), as well as the leaders of the *SA-Gruppen* in those areas.

Postwar Prosecution and Activities:

00.05.1945-00.08.1947	In the final days of the war, fled by car with his wife to Budweis in Böhmen. It was during this journey that Schepmann learned of Germany's surrender. He responded by burning his SA uniform and all his papers, then had the *Wehrmacht* issue him new papers in the name of "Hauptmann Willy Schuhmacher". After a brief internment under this name, presumably by the U.S. Army, he made his way to Gifhorn where he again registered under the name "Willy Schuhmacher" and found employment as an unskilled worker in an enamel factory near Hannover. He grew a beard, which he later shaved off, and lived in complete seclusion with his wife. He was a member of the SPD during this period. ("Schepmann ist heilfroh", in *Westfälische Nachrichten*, 14.05.1949, p. 4)
00.08.1947-28.04.1949	*Geräteverwalter* (materials administrator) in the *Kreiskrankenhaus Gifhorn*.
28.04.1949	Arrested by British security forces.
02.05.1949	Declared before the *Untersuchungsrichter* (investigating judge) in Lüneburg that "he had never been a Nazi. Although Schepmann admitted that he had been head of the SA since 1943, that, he said, did not mean that he had been a Nazi." (Translated from "Ich war kein Nazi", in *Nordwest-Zeitung* (NWZ) Nr. 51, 03.05.1949, p. 1)
03.05.1949	Handed over by the British police to German authorities. He was subsequently detained in Lüneburg prison. There he was questioned by a Bielefeld public prosecutor after the Bielefeld *Spruchgericht* (Court of Appeal) issued an arrest warrant against Schepmann.
16.05.1949	Sentenced by a Lüneburg court to 2 months' imprisonment for violation of identification regulations.
05.07.1949	Discontinuation by the Bielefeld *Spruchgericht* of proceedings against Schepmann due to a lack of evidence. The local press reported:

It could not be proven that he had belonged, after 1 September 1939, to an organization declared criminal by the verdict of the [International Military Tribunal at] Nürnberg. Schepmann, however, remained in custody because the public prosecutor in Dortmund had initiated

	an investigation against him for crimes against humanity. He was subsequently remanded in custody in the Dortmund remand prison." (NWZ Nr. 80, 09.07.1949, p. 3)
	He was subsequently remanded to custody in the *Dortmunder Untersuchungsgefängnis* (remand prison).
00.00.1949	Joined the *Bund der Heimatvertriebenen und Entrechteten* (BHE, Union of the Homeless and Deprived).
25.01.1950	During an interrogation by the Dortmund *Staatsanwaltschaft* (public prosecutor's office), falsely claimed that "there was never an order in the SA according to which SA-Führer or SA-Männer were allowed to independently arrest people for political dissent." (Translated from Yves Müller, "Bei uns sitzt Schepmann, da ist alles in Ordnung", p. 105)
23.02.1950	Charged by the *Staatsanwaltschaft* (public prosecutor's office) of Dortmund with "*Verbrechen gegen die Menschlichkeit, Freiheitsberaubung, gefährliche Körperverletzung und Nötigung*" (crimes against humanity, deprivation of liberty, grievous bodily harm, and coercion) in at least 48 cases during his time as *Polizeipräsident* of Dortmund and *Führer* of the Westphalian SA ("Schepmann angeklagt", in *General-Anzeiger für Bonn und Umgebung/Westdeutsche Zeitung* Nr. 18360, 22.03.1950, p. 2 and "Anklageschrift gegen Schepmann" in *NWZ* Nr. 69, 22.03.1950, p. 2) The attempt by his lawyer, Prof. Dr. Friedrich Grimm (a member of the *Reichstag* from 1933 to 1945), to have the proceedings overturned prematurely failed on 10.05.1950 due to resistance from the *Staatsanwaltschaft*.
14.06.1950	Beginning of trial before the *Schwurgericht* (assize court) of Dortmund. He was "accused of having known about or tolerated 48 cases of crimes against humanity during his tenure as Polizeipräsident (17.02.1933-10.11.1934). He was also accused of serious coercion in office and of denouncing General [Kurt von] Schleicher..." Schepmann admitted, "I was a convinced National Socialist," but denied any guilt: "I have always been a decent person and have always been a soldier." During the trial, witnesses included the *Oberbürgermeister* of Dortmund Fritz Henßler, *Staatssekretär a. D.* and *SS-Brigadeführer a. D.* Ludwig Grauert, *Regierungspräsident a. D.* Kurt Matthaei, *General der Artillerie a. D.* Edgar Theißen, *General der Panzertruppe* Ludwig Crüwell, and the first head of the Gestapo, former *SS-Oberführer* Rudolf Diels. *Oberbürgermeister* Henßler (*12.04.1886 in Altensteig, †04.12.1953 in Witten) was a former SPD delegate to the Reichstag and manager of the *Westfälische Allgemeine Volkszeitung* (news organ of the SDP in Westfalen). He testified that Schepmann, as *Polizeipräsident*, had threatened him in 1933, saying that all Marxists were criminals and that he would eradicate Marxism. Schepmann denied the accusation. In 1936, Henßler had been arrested by the Gestapo and sent for one year to the Gestapo-administered prison Steinwache in Dortmund. He was then

immediately transferred to *KL-Sachsenhausen*, where he remained from 1937 to 1945.

Former *Staatssekretär* Grauert testified that Schepmann was one of the most upright officials he had ever met, while Kurt Matthaei expresses a similar opinion. ("... als Mensch einer der vorbildlichsten", in General-Anzeiger für Bonn und Umgebung/ Westdeutsche Zeitung Nr. 18433, 22.06.1950, p. 3, and "Der Schepmann-Prozess", in Westfälische Nachrichten, Nr. 141, 22.06.1950, p. 8)

The retired Generals Theißen and Crüwell testified at to their skepticism that Schepmann had been involved in the denunciation of former *Reichskanzler* Schleicher (murdered during the purge of 30.06.1934). Rudolf Diels sought to "exonerate Schepmann, especially in the Schleicher case" ("Zeugen entlasten Schepmann", in *General-Anzeiger für Bonn und Umgebung/Westdeutsche Zeitung* Nr. 18434, 23.06.1950, p. 2 and "Gestapochef sagt für Schepmann aus", in *Westfälische Nachrichten* Nr. 143, 24.06.1950, p. 3)

27.06.1950　Demand by the *Staatsanwaltschaft* of Dortmund for a 39-month prison sentence in the case of Wilhelm Schepmann:

Schepmann is charged with 49 counts of deprivation of liberty and bodily harm, 26 of which were committed while in office, including one count of coercion while in office. Schepmann is also to be held responsible for the sale of the 'Dortmunder General-Anzeiger', a 12 million mark property, for 150,000 marks to the then Nazi mayor of Herne, because he intimidated the owners by occupying the newspaper with SA men. However, the defendant should be acquitted of the denunciation of General von Schleicher. (Translated from "39 Monate Gefängnis für Schepmann beantragt", in Westfälische Nachrichten Nr. 146, 28.06.1950, p. 7)

Schepmann's defense attorneys Grimm and Vogelbruch, on the other hand, requested acquittal for their client. Prof. Grimm's plea, calling for a general pardon for Schepmann ("Pass a courageous verdict, acquit the defendant!"), is met with applause from the audience, and the presiding judge responds with the words: "Your words have touched our minds and hearts." Even the prosecuting attorney Dr. Cohaus, whom Grimm strongly attacked in his closing argument, shook the defense attorney's hand afterwards. ("Der Hauptverteidiger im Schepmann-Prozess beantragt Freispruch", in *General-Anzeiger für Bonn und Umgebung/Westdeutsche Zeitung* Nr. 18438, 28.06.1950, p. 2; "Wahrheit wie ein reinigendes Gewitter", in *General-Anzeiger für Bonn und Umgebung/Westdeutsche Zeitung* Nr. 18440, 30.06.1950, p. 3)

01.07.1950　Sentenced by the Dortmund *Schwurgericht* to 9 months' imprisonment, due to coercion in office (in the case of the liquidation of the newspaper *Dortmunder Generalanzeiger*, when his SA men occupied its offices on 20.04.1933 in retaliation for their publishing a caricature of Hitler), but this sentence was later annulled. He was released from *Zuchthaus Werl* (Werl Prison) the same month.

21.08.1951	In a proceeding before the *Entnazifizierungshauptausschuss* of Regierungsbezirk Lüneburg, placed in *Gruppe III* ("*Minderdbelasteten*", minor offenders).
18.12.1951	Discontinuation, on unspecified grounds, of de-Nazification proceedings. Schepmann was simultaneously reclassified in *Gruppe V* ("unbelastete Personen", unincriminated persons).
09.11.1952	*Kommunalwahlen* (local elections) in Niedersachsen. Schepmann was elected, as candidate of the BHE, to the *Stadtrat* and the *Kreistag* in Gifhorn. The following article appeared in the 17.11.1952 issue of *Time* magazine:

In Lower Saxony, an old friend of Hitler's emerged from a wooden hut where he is living, unemployed, on a dole of $6.90 a week, to win a seat on both the town and county councils of Gifhorn. He was Brownshirt Wilhelm Schepmann, 58, last chief of staff of Hitler's Storm Troopers. Schepmann won easily, without even bothering to campaign. In other local elections in Lower Saxony the neo-Nazis campaigned on the slogan: "Stand fast. Remain German... We shall return." The Refugee Party, which had the Nazis' support, won 17% of the total vote.

13.11.1952	At the request of the Dortmund *Staatsanwaltschaft*, the 4. *Strafsenat der Bundesgerichtshof* (4th Criminal Senate of the Federal Court of Justice) overturned one point of the Dortmund jury court's ruling of 01.07.1950 referred the case back to the *Strafkammer* (criminal chamber) of the *Landgericht* in Dortmund for a new trial. At the same time, Schepmann's appeal against his sentence of 9 months on another charge (coercion in office) was dismissed. ("Schepmann erneut vor Gericht", in Frankfurter Allgemeine Nr. 266, 15.11.1952)
18.11.1952	Waldemar Kraft, *Bundesvorsitzender* (federal chairman) of the *Gesamtdeutscher Block/BHE* (GB/BHE), criticized Schepmann's election to the *Kreistag* and *Stadtrat* of Gifhorn, on the grounds that Schepmann's nomination demonstrated a lack of political tact on the part of both the local *Kreisverband* (district association) of the GB/BHE and the candidate himself. ("Kraft verurteilt Kandidatur und Wahl von Schepmann", in Die Neue Zeitung [Frankfurt/Main] Nr. 274, 20.11.1952)
28.11.1952-09.06.1961	Member of the *Kreistag* of Landkreis Gifhorn (representing the GB/BHE).
28.11.1952-09.06.1951	*Ratsherr* (member of the *Stadtrat*) in Gifhorn (representing the GB/BHE).
28.11.1952-08.11.1956	Became a *Beigeordneter* (delegate) to the *Verwaltungsausschuss* (administrative committee) of Gifhorn.
29.11.1952-30.11.1952	At a meeting of the *Bundesvorstand des "Deutschen Blocks (BHE)"* (Federal Executive Committee of the German Bloc (BHE)" in Hannover, it was decided to summon Schepmann:

Schepmann is to report on his attitude toward democracy in general and BHE policy in particular. After that, a decision will be made as to

	whether the BHE will continue to support Schepmann or distance itself from him. ("BHE-Bundesvorstand tagte", in *Delmenhorster Zeitung* Nr. 278, 01.12.1952, p. 3)
26.05.1954	As a former *Volksschule* teacher, awarded a monthly pension of DM 395.35 by decree of the *Niedersächsischen Kultusministerium* (Lower Saxon Ministry of Education and Cultural Affairs), along with a one-time back payment of DM 3,177. ("Schepmann – SA marschiert", in *Der Spiegel* 21/1961, 17.05.1962, p. 31)
00.00.1954	Appointed to serve as a teacher at a *Volksschule* in Gifhorn, however the *Kultusministerium* of Niedersachsen prohibited him from teaching. On 26.05.1954, the Ministry granted him a one-time payment of 3.177 DM in addition to his monthly retirement benefits of 395.35 DM.
09.11.1956-17.05.1961	*1. Beigeordneter* (i.e., *stellvertretender Bürgermeister* [deputy mayor]) of Gifhorn.
18.04.1961	Reelected as *1. Beigeordneter* of Gifhorn with the votes of the CDU, which "leads to a dispute within the municipal parliament that goes far beyond the municipal sphere". ("Krach um SA-Schepmann", in *Westfälische Nachrichten* Nr. 108, 10.05.1961, p. 1)
17.05.1961	Amid public protests, resigned from office. He had earlier declared: "So that the world can continue to turn in peace, I renounce my office the next month, on 17.05.1961" (*"Damit die Welt sich wieder in Ruhe weiterdrehen kann, verzichte ich auf mein Amt"*). ("Wilhelm Schepmann legt Amt nieder", in *NWZ* Nr. 114, 18.05.1961, p. 1; "Schepmann legt Bürgermeister-Amt nieder", in *Die Welt* Nr. 114, 18.05.1961; "Schepmann zurückgetreten", in *Westfälische Nachrichten* Nr. 114, 18.05.1961, p. 2)
18.05.1961	Announced that he did not intend to resign from his positions as *Ratsherr* and *Kreistagsabgeordneter*. ("Schepmann behält Mandate", in *NWZ* Nr. 115, 19.05.1961, p. 2)
09.06.1961	Resigned from his remaining municipal offices in Gifhorn. ("Der ehemalige SA-Stabschef Schepmann", in *Westfälische Nachrichten* Nr. 133, 12.06.1961, p. 2)
16.08. 1961	Ruling by the *Landesverwaltungsgericht* (state administrative court) in Hannover that Schepmann was not entitled to a pension. ("Keine Pension für Schepmann", in *NWZ* Nr. 191, 17.08.1962, p. 2)
27.08.1961	Removed from the pension rolls by the *Amtsgericht* of Niedersachsen, in Hannover, which ruled that despite the fact that he had committed no crimes against humanity, he had nonetheless "violat[ed] the principles of the legal state".
00.05.1965	Reelected as *Vorsitzender des Kreisverbandes des "Bundes der Vertriebenen"* (Chairman of the District Association of the "Federation of Expellees" [BdV]). (*NWZ* Nr. 112, 14.05.1965, p. 5)

PUBLISHED WORKS:

Aufbau und Aufgaben der SA. Vom Stabschef der SA Schepmann. Vortrag, gealten auf der Befehlshabertagung in Bad Schachen am 11. Oktober 1943.

DECORATIONS & AWARDS:

00.00.1940	*1939 Eisernes Kreuz I. Klasse* (awarded for his part in the breakthrough of the Maginot Line)
00.00.1940	*1939 Spange zum Eisernen Kreuz II. Klasse*
00.07.1916	*1914 Eisernes Kreuz II. Klasse*
00.00.194_	*Kriegsverdienstkreuz I. Klasse ohne Schwerter*
00.00.194_	*Kriegsverdienstkreuz II. Klasse ohne Schwerter*
31.05.1917	*Schaumburg-Lippisches Kreuz für treue Dienste 1914*
00.00.1918	*Verwundetenabzeichen, 1918 in Schwarz*
05.10.1940	*Medaille zur Erinnerung an den 1. Oktober 1938*
05.10.1940	*Medaille zur Erinnerung an den 13. März 1938*
c. 1934	*Ehrenkreuz des Weltkrieges 1914-1918 mit Schwertern*
00.00.1934	*Goldenes Ehrenzeichen der NSDAP*
00.00.194_	*Dienstauszeichnung der NSDAP in Gold*
00.00.194_	*Dienstauszeichnung der NSDAP in Silber*
00.00.194_	*Dienstauszeichnung der NSDAP in Bronze*
00.12.1943 (?)	*Gau-Ehrenzeichen des Gaues Sudetenland der NSDAP*
00.00.1933	*Gauehrenzeichen der Alten Garde von 1923*
00.09.1933	*Abzeichen "Reichsparteitag Nürnberg 1933"*
00.00.1931	*Abzeichen des SA-Treffens Braunschweig 1931*
00.00.1929	*Nürnberger Parteitagsabzeichen 1929*
00.00.19__	*Silbernes Treudienst-Ehrenzeichen*
00.00.193_	*SA-Sportabzeichen in Bronze*
03.02.1934	*Ehrendolch der SA*
00.02.1934	*Ehrenwinkel für alte Kämpfer*
09.11.1934	*Dank- und Anerkennungsschreiben des Preußischen Ministerpräsidenten*
09.11.1934	*Dank- und Anerkennungsschreiben des Reichs- und Preußischen Ministers des Innern*
24.12.1933	*Ehrenbürgerbrief der Stadt Hattingen* (status revoked, 00.00.1945)
08.05.1933	*Ehrenbürgerrecht des Amtes Sprockhövel*
10.02.1944	Entered in the *Goldene Buch der Stadt Bremen*
24.09.1943	Entered in the *Goldenes Buch der Stadt Rawitsch* (Posen)
17.06.1944	RM 100,000 *Dotation* (cash award) from the Führer (for his 50th birthday)
00.00.193_	Commemorative Medal of the War of 1914-1918 with Swords (Hungary)
00.00.193_	Medal for Participation in the European War 1915-1918 (Bulgaria)

NOTES:

* Parents:
  - Father: Richard Schepmann, a miner.
  - Mother: Caroline Wilhelmine Schepmann, née König (†00.08.1914).
  Wilhelm was the youngest of their six sons. Schepmann's brother Hugo, who together with another brother, August, had run the country produce store *Gebr. Schepmann* on *Kleine Weilstraße* in Baak, fell near Ypres on 14.11.1914. August Schepmann
* Religion: Protestant.
* Married in 1920 to the Braunschweig merchant's daughter Gertrud Schümann (*00.00.1898, †00.00.1959), daughter of a merchant in Braunschweig. They had been engaged since May

1918. The couple produced one son, Richard Schepmann. He was to become owner of the neo-Nazi publishing house *Teut-Verlag*, based in Wetter/Ruhr, and described by Nicholas Goodrick-Clarke as "specializ[ing] in reprints from the *Nordland-Verlag* of the *Ahnenerbe* and dossiers on Nazi UFOs" (Goodrick-Clarke, *Black Sun. Aryan Cults, Esoteric Nazism, and the Politics of Identity*, p. 163 and 191). In 1983 he was convicted of inciting racial hatred, receiving a 6-month suspended jail sentence and a considerable fine.

* Schepmann's essay "Task and Role of the SA", published in *Der Politische Soldat*, Nr. 12, October 1944):

As Stabschef responsible to the Führer for the SA, I consider it right that I should once more define explicitly the task and role of the SA within the Party and the Reich, in order to clear up once and for all any obscurity concerning the task of the SA.

During the early years of the movement, it was the SA which, in accordance with the will of the Führer, as part of the Party brought together the activist forces as the sword-arm of the National-Socialist movement. For the National-Socialist who was ready for action, membership in the SA was a matter of course. It was just as much a matter of course that the SA man became a party member and considered himself first and always a National-Socialist. As an SA man, it was his pride and his honor always to be in the forefront of the fight. Where propagandists, collaborators within the inner circle of the Party, dare-devils, helpers for Party members in trouble, everywhere where men ready for action were needed, the SA was there and naturally the SA was called upon. In his calling the SA man was at all times a fanatical representative of the National-Socialist Weltanschauung. The Party was unimaginable without the SA, just as the SA was never an independent power outside the Party, but exclusively a part and an organ of the movement. From this role of the SA as the organization of the activist men of the Party, from its indispensability for the carrying out of National-Socialist activities, and not from the training of the SA or any other branch of their self-education, is derived the justified self-confidence of the SA man. From this role resulted also the esteem of the SA within the whole movement. Tested SA men, capable as political leaders, were continually transferred to the political directorate of the Party, to advance there to leading positions. Almost every one of the old men in authority [Hoheitsträger] in the Party was also an SA man in the years of struggle.

Prerequisite to this success of the SA in the party struggle was its construction according to military principles, was the SA man's unconditional duty to obey, his education in discipline, was above all the constant schooling of the SA man to become a conscious and fanatical political soldier of the Führer. In the narrow sense this is the goal which the work of the SA served. Just as, however, the peace-time training of a soldier does not have significance except as future or at least possible action is in view for the actual defense of the life of the nation, so work within the SA was only a means to an end. The end was the completion of the manifold tasks of the SA in support of the Party's struggle in the field of internal politics, was the victory of the National-Socialist movement.

After Hitler came to power the SA was at first in danger of developing into a defense organization with a military foundation, as a result of a misconception of the order given by the Führer from the beginning that it should educate all German men to have a military, National-Socialist attitude. This led to a loosening of its spiritual ties to the Party and thus necessarily to serious setbacks. Open and veiled alienation between political leaders and SA leaders was the inevitable consequence. The result was unsatisfactory for both sides and disadvantageous to the Party. Many a Party endeavor would have attained easier success if the right use had been made of the largest and strongest formation of the Party, the SA—tightly organized and disciplined down to the last detail, and comprising millions of zealous men from all classes of the people. By and large, however, the SA got stuck in its own field of service. SA work in the narrow sense, the training of units in the evening and on Sundays, became too exclusively the sum and substance of SA activities in general. Above all, this work determined, to too great an extent, the conception of the present task of the SA which was held by the German people, by the Party, and finally even by many SA men.

To be sure, the Führer himself again and again provided fresh impetus, for example, by his order for the military education of German manhood by means of SA training for the Wehrabzeichen and by other assignments. These assignments, however, because they were often not approached in the right way, did not come to fruition. Partly in the Party, partly in the SA Itself, they were regarded too much as independent individual tasks of secondary importance and top little as important constituents of the entire Party's work of educating and leading the whole German people. Thus for a long time the position of the SA and the self-confidence of the SA men remained shaken, they remained so, even though the SA, in this time of outward stagnation and self-imposed limitation achieved results of which they are fully entitled to be proud.

One could not judge as well in peacetime, and even the SA man himself was often never aware, what a great work of education had been done. Especially in the psychologically difficult conditions in which he had to lead his men, the SA leader gained almost unequalled experience in the field of human leadership. In a wide measure, as well; he gained organizational knowledge in the course of the numerous SA internal undertakings. The entire SA, however, became a body of men who had learned how to be strict with themselves and to stand by the Führer and Party in the most difficult circumstances. Now, during the war, it has been shown how valuable this work of the SA was in itself. The SA men in the units on the fighting front have stood the test, like all real National-Socialists, and have proved to be the backbone of the forces. The SA leaders who remained at home, however, put their knowledge and experience at the disposal of the Party and justified, by their achievements, the Führer's order to instill the spirit of National-Socialism in the German men eligible for military service. Thus we have every reason to do away with the old inhibitions. It is the will of the Führer and my task as Stabschef of the SA to clear up these questions conclusively. Every SA man and every Party member, no matter what his position, must come to realize:

As in the period of struggle, it remains the task of the SA to stand to the fore in all matters in which the Party needs an active representation among the people of its will and its measures. The SA man must be the most active propagandist of the Party, the most courageous warrior of the Party in the air war, the most active collaborator with the political leaders in war-time welfare work, the most active National-Socialist in the Wehrmacht, and also, if must be, again the most active fighter against grumblers and defeatists.

The SA is nothing outside the Party's field of duty, and the Party cannot deny itself the use of an army, millions strong, of staunch National-Socialists, comprising the best men of all classes of our people. The National-Socialist leadership of the Wehrmacht knows that the SA men in its units with the other men of the National-Socialist Party represent a nucleus of determined warriors. It cannot refuse to call upon these men— these political soldiers, in the best sense, educated to display unswerving zeal even in difficult situations it cannot fail to call upon them for leadership, education, and spiritual strengthening of the troops.

The SA man himself must know, however, that he is always committed, wherever he may be, as an SA man, as the most active champion of the will of the Party. It makes no difference whether he does SA service in his unit in continuation of his peace-time work, whether he helps with the pre-military training of untrained citizens, whether he conducts military sports contests or military shooting contests, whether in groups or alone, in uniform or mufti, he works in the air war, in the auxiliary police, in the NSV relief work, or in one of the thousand other fields of war service: he is always committed, first of all, as an SA man, as a warrior of the Party, and performs definite tasks in this capacity.

To a special degree all those SA men who have been called up as soldiers today must consider themselves as SA men at work—they more than the rest of the SA. It does not matter whether they are used as generals or staff officers, as leaders of military units or National-Socialist guidance officers, as non-commissioned officers or common soldiers. They all have, along with their military tasks, the political assignment of being examples of the National-Socialist will-to-fight, of sternness and comradeship, the embodiment of the will of the movement. They all have to carry out this assignment as part of their SA service.

Thus every SA man, down to the last one, gains the self-confidence which he absolutely must have to perform his great and wonderful, timeless task. The SA man will, then, always be judged by all other members of the Party and by the whole German nation in the way which the SA and he himself deserve and must claim. The heart of the matter is end remains: T9he work of the SA can only be understood correctly as an integral part of the Party's task of leading the German people and infusing into them the National-Socialist ideology. In this it is not if a number of subordinate auxiliary tasks which is involved, but the I utilization of the units of the Party in all fields of the Party's work. The SA man is everywhere and always on duty as an SA man.

I demand this attitude of every SA man, no matter whether he be a general (SA) or a private, no matter whether active or not, no matter whether honorary or paid. But I also ask all other National-Socialists, from Reichsleiter and Gauleiter down to Blockleiter and even to inactive Party members, from National-Socialist guidance officer to unit leader, to make this attitude the basis of their co-operation with the SA.

This will only be of benefit to the National-Socialist movement.

Nothing of this will change after the war, for what is involved is the lasting task of the SA within the framework of the Party. In our work one task will come to the fore: the SA will be charged with the extra-military National-Socialist education for defense. It will have to bring together the mass of men capable of bearing arms after their discharge from the Wehrmacht, for the preservation and education of their National-Socialist readiness for defense and for the preservation and training of their valiant capacity for action. Naturally special consideration will be given psychologically to the soldiers returning from the front. The service in the reserve corps of ex-service men will be so arranged that it can be performed by everybody. This assignment, too, has to be regarded in the first instance as an essential part of the National-Socialist educational duty of the Party to the German nation. The aim of making every German man into a resolute warrior for the National-Socialist Reich, into a thoroughly convinced and loyal follower of the Führer, is our first and most important aim. The means to this end is training in defense. Detached from the political goal, however, this training would be only a job half-done.

That is how we SA men regard our task, that is how we value it, and that is how we wish, thereby, to serve the Party, our people, and our beloved Führer. In order that cowardice and treachery may never again be able to creep into the German nation and that our children and grandchildren may be able in the future to lay the final stone of the mighty, storm-defying edifice of the National-Socialist Greater German Reich of Adolf Hitler!

Sources:

Beck, Friedrich Alfred: *Kampf und Sieg. Geschichte der Nationalsozialistischen Deutschen Arbeiterpartei im Gau Westfalen-Süd von den Anfängen bis zur Machtübernahme.* Westfalen-Verlag, 1938.

Bundesarchiv, Berlin-Lichterfelde: *Personalunterlagen von SA-Angehörigen: SA-Personalakte* of Wilhelm Schepmann, BArch R 9361-III/569270.

—*Personalakte Wilhelm Schepmann*, BArch VBS 1009 (NS 23) ZA VI 0520 A.01-16.

—*OPG-Akte (Oberstes Parteigericht) Wilhelm Schepmann*, BArch R 9361-I/33784.

Campbell, Bruce: *The SA Generals and the Rise of Nazism.* The University Press of Kentucky, 1998.

Der Spiegel 21/1961, "Schepmann – SA marschiert", 17.05.1961, pp. 30-32.

Goebbels, Joseph: *Die Tagebücher von Joseph Goebbels. Im Auftrag des Instituts für Zeitgeschichte und mit Unterstützung des Staatlichen Archivdienstes Russland. Herausgeben von Elke Fröhlich). Teil I: Aufzeichnungen 1923-1941, Band 2/II: Juli 1931 – September 1932.* Bearbeitet von Angela Hermann. K.G. Saur, 2004.

—*Die Tagebücher von Joseph Goebbels. Im Auftrag des Instituts für Zeitgeschichte und mit Unterstützung des Staatlichen Archivdienstes Russland. Herausgegeben von Elke Fröhlich. Teil II: Diktate 1941-1945, Band 7: Januar-März 1943.* Bearbeitet von Elke Fröhlich. K.G. Saur, 1993.

—*Die Tagebücher von Joseph Goebbels. Im Auftrag des Instituts für Zeitgeschichte und mit Unterstützung des Staatlichen Archivdienstes Russland. Herausgegeben von Elke Fröhlich. Teil II: Diktate 1941-1945, Band 9: Juli-September 1943. Bearbeitet von Manfred Kittel.* K.G. Saur, 1993.

—*Die Tagebücher von Joseph Goebbels. Im Auftrag des Instituts für Zeitgeschichte und mit Unterstützung des Staatlichen Archivdienstes Russland. Herausgegeben von Elke Fröhlich. Teil II: Diktate 1941-1945, Band 10: Oktober-Dezember 1943. Bearbeitet von Volker Dahm.* K.G. Saur, 1993.

—Die Tagebücher von Joseph Goebbels. Im Auftrag des Instituts für Zeitgeschichte und mit Unterstützung des Staatlichen Archivdienstes Russland. Herausgegeben von Elke Fröhlich. Teil II: Diktate 1941-1945, Band 13: Juli-September 1944. Bearbeitet von Jana Richter. K.G. Saur, München-New Providence-London-Paris 1995.

Goodrick-Clarke, Nicholas: *Black Sun. Aryan Cults, Esoteric Nazism, and the Politics of Identity.* NYU Press, 2003.

Hüttenberger, Peter: *Die Gauleiter: Studie zum Wandel des Machtgefüges in der NSDAP.* Deutsche Verlags-Anstalt GmbH, 1969.

Lilla, Joachim; Döring, Martin; & Schulz Andreas: *Statisten in Uniform. Die Mitglieder des Reichstags 1933-1945.* Droste Verlag, 2004.

Lilla, Joachim: *Leitende Verwaltungsbeamte und Funktionsträger in Westfalen und Lippe (1918-1945/46). Biographisches Handbuch.* Veröffentlichung der Historischen Kommission für Westfalen XXII A, Landschaftsverband Westfalen-Lippe, Aschendorff, Münster 2004.

Miller, Michael D. and Andreas Schulz: *Leaders of the Storm Troops, Volume 1* (1st Edition). Helion & Co., 2015.

Müller, Yves: "'Bei uns sitzt Schepmann, da ist alles in Ordnung.' Wilhelm Schepmann-SA-Gruppenführer, Polizeipräsident,

Stabschef", in *Beiträge zur Geschichte Dortmunds und der Grafschaft Mark*; March 2016, pp. 73-106.

—"Wilhelm Schepmann-der letzte SA-Stabschef und die Rolle der SA im Zweiten Weltkrieg, in *Zeitschrift für Geschichtswissenschaft* 63 (2015), 6, pp. 513-532.

Orlow, Dietrich: *History of the Nazi Party: 1933-1945.* University of Pittsburgh Press, 1973.

Priamus, Heinz-Jürgen: *Meyer. Zwischen Kaisertreue und NS-Täterschaft. Biographische Konturen eines deutschen Bürgers.* Klartext, 2011.

Scheer, Maximilian: *Das Deutsche Volk klagt an: Hitlers Krieg gegen die Friedenskampfer in Deutschland.* Laika-Verlag, 2012 (reprint of the original 1936 edition)

Schirach, Baldur von: *Die Pioniere des Dritten Reiches.* Zentralstelle fur der deutschen Freiheitskampf, 1933.

Schmidt, Daniel: *Schützen und Dienen: Polizisten im Ruhrgebiet in Demokratie und Diktatur 1919-1939.* Klartext Verlag, 2008.

Siemens, Daniel: *Stormtroopers: A New History of Hitler's Brownshirts.* Yale University Press, 2017.

Stadtarchiv Hattingen/Ruhr: Geburtsregistereintrag Friedrich Wilhelm Schepmann (Geburtsregister Standesamt Winz Nr. 161/1894)

Uhl, Matthias et al (ed): *Die Organisation des Terrors. Der Dienstkalender Heinrich Himmlers 1943-1945*, published on behalf of the Deutschen Historischen Instituts Moskau. Piper Verlag, 2020.

Wagner, Andreas: *"Machtergreifung in Sachsen. NSDAP und staatliche Verwaltung 1930-1935.* Sonderausgabe für Sächsische Landeszentrale für politische Bildung.

Weidemann, Sabine: "Vom SA-Chef zum SPD-Ratsmitglied" (20.08.2013), online at https://www.waz.de/staedte/hattingen/vom-sa-chef-zum-spd-ratsmitglied-id8335445.html

Right: Wilhelm Schepmann in civilian attire, *c.* 1932. (Baldur von Schirach, *Die Pioniere des Dritten Reiches*, 1933)

Below: Wilhelm Schepmann and Viktor Lutze during the 1928 *"Kundgebung der SA"* in Düsseldorf. (*SA-Obersturmführer* Karl H. W. Koch, *Das Ehrenbuch der SA*, 1934)

Bochum, *c.* 1930: Schepmann in his office as *Gausturmführer Essen*. (NARA, Heinrich Hoffmann Collection)

SA-Oberführer Schepmann and *SS-Gruppenführer* Curt Wittje inspect an *SA* unit in 1932. (*SA-Obersturmführer* Karl H. W. Koch, *Das Ehrenbuch der SA*, 1934)

Dortmund, 13.05.1933: *Polizeipräsident* Schepmann, *Gauleiter* Dr. Alfred Meyer (far left), and *Vizekanzler* Franz von Papen (in dark suit) view a parade of the *"Stahlhelm"-Bund*.

Dortmund, 09.07.1933: *"Aufmarsch der SA-Gruppe Westfalen"* in Dortmund (also known as the *"SA-Westfalentreffen"*).

Left to right: Josef Wagner, Schepmann, unknown, Hitler, Adolf Hühnlein (behind the *Führer*) and Viktor Lutze. (NARA, Heinrich Hoffmann Collection)

Left to right: Heinrich Himmler, Prinz August Wilhelm von Preußen, Viktor Lutze, Schepmann, Wilhelm Jahn, Adolf Hühnlein, Heinrich Knickmann, Siegfried Seidel-Dittmarsch, Ernst Röhm, Josef Wagner, and an unidentified *SA-Führer*. (Michal Sika)

SA-Gruppenführer Schepmann with Hitler in 1933. Also present, from left to right: Wilhelm Brückner, Josef ("Sepp") Dietrich, Julius Schaub, and Hans-Joachim Riecke. (NARA, Heinrich Hoffmann Collection)

SA-Gruppenführer Schepmann's foreword to *SA-Obersturmführer* Karl H. W. Koch's *Das Ehrenbuch der SA* (1934). It reads:
The SA in its nature and organization is unique.

The foundations of the SA are the best traditions, strength, popularity, loyalty, and comradeship.

As long as these foundations form the core of SA, it is steadfast.

It is the duty of every SA Führer and SA man to nurture, shape and maintain these foundations.

This conception of duty secures power for the Führer and thus the German future. (Translation: Gary Costello)

Rudolf Hess receives flowers from girls of the BDM in 1934. At far left is Wilhelm Schepmann. (NARA, Heinrich Hoffmann Collection)

Recklinghausen, August 1933: *SA-Gruppenführer* Schepmann as *Führer* of *SA-Gruppe Westfalen* attends a rally with *SA-Standartenführer* (later *Gruppenführer*) Paul Faßbach, *Führer* of *SA-Standarte 143*. (Robert Bailey)

Reichsminister Dr. Goebbels inspects SA units in Essen in 1935. From left to right: Wolf-Heinrich Graf von Helldorff, *Gauleiter* Josef Terboven, Karl Gutenberger, Schepmann, an unknown *SA-Standartenführer*, and Goebbels. (NARA, Heinrich Hoffmann Collection)

Another view of Dr. Goebbels during a visit to Essen, 1935. Left to right: Graf Helldorff, Josef Terboven, Schepmann, and Goebbels. (NARA, Heinrich Hoffmann Collection)

Above left: An official portrait of *SA-Gruppenführer* Schepmann, *c.* 1936.

Above right: *SA-Obergruppenführer* Schepmann, *c.* 1937. (Igor Karpov)

The *Marktplatz* in *Schluckenau,* 19.10.1938: *SA-Obergruppenführer* Schepmann welcomes the *Oberbefehlshaber* of *Heersgruppenkommando 1, Generaloberst* Fedor von Bock, following the occupation of the Sudetenland.

SA-Obergruppenführer Schepmann just before his appointment as acting *SA-Stabschef*, August 1943.

Schepmann's Order of the Day announcing his appointment as *Stabschef der SA*. It reads:

Men of the SA!
   The Führer has entrusted me with conducting the duties of the Chief of Staff of the SA.
   During the hardest struggle of our Volk for it's external freedom, I am appointed by the trust of the Führer to assume command over you and greet all my comrades at the front and in the homeland.
   It is our duty as National Socialists to serve the Führer in unwavering loyalty and selfless devotion. Our struggle, our commitment and our work are focused on one goal: German victory.
   Hail to the Führer!
   Berlin, the 16th of August 1943
      Wilhelm Schepmann

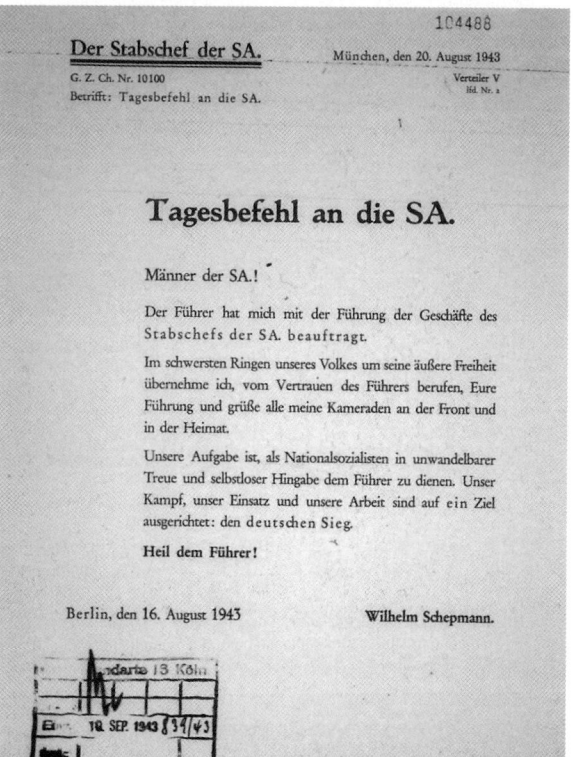

Above left: 27.08.1943: *SA-Obergruppenführer* Schepmann, as acting *Stabschef* of the SA, in conversation with the Reich Treasurer of the NSDAP Franz Xaver Schwarz. (NARA, Heinrich Hoffmann Collection)

Above right: Schepmann meets with *Reichsmarschall* Göring at Carinhall, 06.09.1943.

Schepmann meets with senior officers of *SA-Gruppe Berlin-Brandenburg* at the Kroll Opera House, 12.09.1943. Left to right: Willi Kunemund, Schepmann, Prinz August-Wilhelm, Konrad Mesmer, Johannes Fuhsel, and Walther Mahl. (NARA, Heinrich Hoffmann Collection)

Wilhelm Schepmann wearing the interim insignia introduced specifically for him during the period that he was acting SA-Stabschef. Upon his official appointment, he began wearing the style of insignia worn by his predecessor, Viktor Lutze.

Right: Schepmann meets with senior officers of *SA-Gruppe Berlin-Brandenburg* at the Kroll Opera House,12.09.1943. Left to right: *SA-Brigadeführer* Willi Kunemund, Schepmann, *SA-Obergruppenführer* Prinz August-Wilhelm ("AuWi") von Hohenzollern, *SA-Brigadeführer* Konrad Mesmer, *SA-Oberführer* Johannes Fuhsel, and *SA-Oberführer* Walter Mahl. (NARA, Heinrich Hoffmann Collection)

Above left: Courtesy of Roger Bender.

Above right: Rastenburg/Ostpreußen, 07.10.1943: *SA-Stabschef* Schepmann chats with *Reichsleiter* Alfred Rosenberg during the conference of *Reichs-* and *Gauleiter* at *Führer HQ iWolfsschanze."* (NARA)

Above and below: Formal portraits of *SA-Stabschef* Schepmann, taken by Heinrich Hoffmann.. All are from NARA, Heinrich Hoffmann Collection, except below center and right, which are courtesy of Jerry Luis.

"*Führerappell der SA-Gruppe Pommern,*" 22.11.1943. (NARA, Heinrich Hoffmann Collection)

Above: October 1943: The *SA-Stabschef* in conversation with army generals. Left to right: *General der Infanterie* Viktor von Schwedler, *General der Infanterie* Karl Kriebel (younger brother of the late *SA-Obergruppenführer* Hermann Kriebel), and *General der Infanterie* Werner Kienitz. (NARA, Heinrich Hoffmann Collection)

Left: *SA-Stabschef* Schepmann with, at left, *SA-Hauptsturmführer* Wittfoth. (Roger Bender)

SA-Stabschef Schepmann inspects competitors in the *"Winterwehrkämpfe der SA"* in *Reichsgau Tirol-Vorarlberg*, 03.02.1944. (NARA, Heinrich Hoffmann Collection)

19.04.1944: *SA-Stabschef* Schepmann on a firing range in *Reichsgau Tirol-Vorarlberg*, with *Gauleiter* Franz Hofer observing. (NARA, Heinrich Hoffmann Collection)

Above and below: SA-Stabschef Schepmann oversees rifle firing instruction in his capacity as Inspector for Marksmanship Training of the *Deutschen Volkssturm*, Autumn 1944.

Opposite below: SA-Stabschef Schepmann and *Gauleiter* Albert Forster lead the swearing-in ceremony for the *Volkssturm* in Danzig, 12 November 1944. In the top right frame, at far right, is the distinguished U-Boat commander *Kapitän zur See* Werner Hartmann (holder of the Oak Leaves to the Knight's Cross) who played a key role in organizing the Danzig *Volkssturm*. (Newsreel stills from *Die Deutsche Wochenschau Nr. 741*, 16.11.1944)

Above: Danzig, 12.11.1944: Schepmann delivers a speech during the swearing-in of *Volkssturm* troops. Behind him are, from right to left, *Gauleiter* Albert Forster, an unidentified HJ leader, *SS-Gruppenführer und Generalleutnant der Waffen-SS und Polizei* Fritz Katzmann (*Höherer SS- und Polizeiführer Weichsel*), an unidentfied NSDAP official, an *SA-Sturmbannführer*, *SA-Gruppenführer* Dr. Lorenz Ohrt (acting *Führer* of *SA-Gruppe Weichsel*), and *General der Infanterie* Karl-Wilhelm Specht (*Oberbefehlshaber* of *Wehrkreis XX*). (National Digital Archives, Poland)

19.-22.01.1945: Schepmann speaks with highly decorated officers of *Panzer-Division "Feldherrnhalle,"* including, from left to right, *Oberst d. R.* and *SA-Sanitäts-Standartenführer* Dr. Franz Bäke, *Hauptmann d. R.* and *SA-Oberführer* Ewald Bartel, and *Oberleutnant* Otto Erdmann. (NARA, Heinrich Hoffmann Collection)

A letter to *Reichsleiter* Alfred Rosenberg, signed by Wilhelm Schepmann in his capacity as acting *Stabschef* of the SA. It reads:

Dear Pg. Rosenberg!

Your promotion proposals of 9.11.1943 for the

Obersturmführer Erich Otto
Obersturmführer Dr. Ruprecht
Obertruppführer Dr. [Werner] Rittich

could unfortunately no longer be taken into account, since the order had already been completed and printed. I have given the Personnel Main Office the instruction to examine the promotion proposals and possibly to make a note of them for 20.4.1944.

In the matter of Pg. [*SA-Standartenführer* Dr. Siegwalt] Benatzky, I will send you news as soon as it has been clarified.

Above: 19.-22.01.1945: Schepmann speaks with Knight's Cross holder *Unteroffizier* Josef Fink during a reception for men of *Panzer-Division* "*Feldherrnhalle*." (NARA)

Right: Wilhelm Schepmann in May 1961.

Above: The hunting permit of *SA-Gruppenführer* Wilhelm Schepmann for 1935–36. (Personalakte Wilhelm Schepmann, BArch VBS 1009 [NS 23] ZA VI 0520 A.01-16)

Left: "*Stabschef der SA Wilhelm Schepmann*" by Otto Rost. Exhibited at the "*Große Dresdner Kunstausstellung,*" 1943. Photo from the official catalog of the exhibition.

Appendices

Appendix I: Comparative Table of Ranks

Sturmabteilung	Schutzstaffel	Reichsheer	U.S. Army
Oberster SA-Führer (OSAF) (Adolf Hitler)	Reichsführer-SS	No Equivalent	No Equivalent
SA-Stabschef	SS-Oberst-Gruppenführer	Generalfeldmarschall	General of the Army (5-star)
SA-Obergruppenführer	SS-Obergruppenführer	Generaloberst	General (4-star)
SA-Gruppenführer	SS-Gruppenführer	General der Infanterie, Kavallerie, Artillerie, etc.	Lieutenant-General (3-star)
SA-Brigadeführer	SS-Brigadeführer	Generalleutnant	Major-General (2-star)
SA-Oberführer	SS-Oberführer	Generalmajor	Brigadier-General (1-star)
SA-Standartenführer	SS-Standartenführer	No Equivalent	No Equivalent
SA-Obersturmbannführer	SS-Obersturmbannführer	Oberst	Colonel
SA-Sturmbannführer	SS-Sturmbannführer	Oberstleutnant	Lieutenant-Colonel
SA-Sturmhauptführer	SS-Hauptsturmführer	Major	Major
SA-Obersturmführer	SS-Obersturmführer	Hauptmann or Rittmeister	Captain
SA-Sturmführer	SS-Untersturmführer	Oberleutnant	First-Lieutenant
SA-Haupttruppführer	SS-Sturmscharführer	Leutnant	Second-Lieutenant
SA-Obertruppführer	SS-Hauptscharführer, SS-Standartenoberjunker	Stabsfeldwebel, Stabswachtmeister	Sergeant Major
SA-Truppführer	SS-Oberscharführer	Oberfeldwebel, Oberwachtmeister (Hauptfeldwebel), Oberfähnrich	Master Sergeant
SA-Oberscharführer	SS-Scharführer	Feldwebel, Wachtmeister	Technical Sergeant
SA-Scharführer	SS-Unterscharführer	Unterfeldwebel, Unterwachtmeister	Staff Sergeant
SA-Rottenführer	SS-Rottenführer	Unteroffizier, Oberjäger	Sergeant
SA-Sturmmann (after 1938, SA-Obersturmmann)	SS-Sturmmann	Stabsgefreiter, Obergefreiter	Corporal
SA-Mann (after 1938, SA-Sturmmann)	SS-Mann	Gefreiter	Private

Appendix II: Glossary of German Military and Political Terms

Term	Abbreviation	Definition
Abitur	Abi.	Most prestigious of several certificates issued after completion of secondary schooling in Germany. It typically allowed admission to university in any subject.
Abschnitt	Abs.; Abschn.	Sector; district. In the SS: Regional division of Germany and its headquarters; In the SD: Subordinate Regional HQ and its area.
Abteilung	Abt.; A.	Unit; battalion; department.
Abwehr	Abw.	The intelligence service of the *Wehrmacht*.
Abwehrpolizei	Abw.Pol.	Counter-espionage police. A function of the *Grenzpolizei* under the jurisdiction of the *Gestapo*.
Abzeichen	Abz.	Badge of rank, appointment, or distinction.
Adjutantur		i. Staff department dealing with routing personnel and administrative matters; ii. The earlier title of the *Persönlicher Stab RfSS*.
Agrarpolitischer Apparat	a.A.	The NSDAP's Office for Agricultural Policy.
Ahnenerbe Forschungs- und Lehrgemeinschaft		Society for Research into and Teaching of Ancestral Heritage. Administered by the Pers.Stab RFSS, this office promoted research of family and national hereditary history and dissemination of racial theories.
Akademie für Deutsches Recht		The Academy of German Law, founded by *Reichsleiter* Dr. jur. Hans Frank in 1933 and based in München.
Allgemeines Heeresamt	AHA	General Army Directorate.
Allgemeine-SS	Allg. SS	The general body of the SS, composed of part-time, full-time, and honorary members.
Allgemeines Wehrmachtsamt	AWA	General Armed Forces Office in OKW, concerned with matters of personnel, training, equipment, etc.
Alte Kämpfer		"Old Fighter." Designation applied to members of the NSDAP or its affiliated organizations prior to the Nazi assumption to power on 30.01.1933.
Amt		A main office, branch, or directorate of a ministry, or an independent ministry such as the *Auswärtiges Amt* (Foreign Office).
Amtsgruppe		Office group. A subordinate branch of a *Hauptamt* (Main Office).
Anhaltelager		Temporary detention camp.
Anschluß		The unification of Germany and Austria on 13.03.1938.
Anwärter	Anw.	Cadet or candidate.
Arbeitsgemeinschaft		Labor collective. Associations of former *Freikorps* members formed to facilitate finding employment and maintaining contact as a covert military force.
Armee-Korps	A.K.	Infantry corps.
Armee-Oberkommando	A.O.K.	Headquarters of an *Armee*.
Artillerie-Kommandeur	Arko	Artillery commander of an *Armee* or *Korps*.
Artillerie-Regiment	Art.Rgt.; A.R.	Artillery regiment.

German	Abbr.	Definition
Aufsichtsrat		Supervisory board; board of directors.
Aufklärung	Aufkl.	lit. enlightenment; military reconnaissance.
Aufstellungsstab	Aufst.St.	Formation staff.
Ausbildung	Ausb.	Training.
Ausbildungs- und Ersatz	Ausb.- u.Ers.; A.-u.E.	Training and replacement.
Ausland/Abwehr	Ausl./Abw.	Amt (previously an *Amtsgruppe*) of OKW responsible for espionage, counterespionage, sabotage, and foreign information. Headed by Admiral Wilhelm Canaris until his arrest for anti-Nazi activities in 1944, whereupon it was absorbed by the RSHA.
Auslands-Organisation der NSDAP	AO	The Foreign Organization of the NSDAP, concerned with care and supervision of Germans in foreign countries. Ranked as the 43rd *Gau* of the NSDAP under *Gauleiter* and Foreign Office *Staatssekretär* Ernst Wilhelm Bohle.
Aussendienststelle or Aussenstelle	Aust.	Outstation or outpost of the Sipo or SD.
ausser Dienst	a. D.	Retired; on the inactive list.
Auswärtiges Amt	A.A.	Foreign Office; The Reich Ministry for Foreign Affairs.
Bahnschutzpolizei		Railway protection police. Transferred to SS control in 1942.
Bann		A subdivision of the *Hitler-Jugend Gebiet* (region), approximately comparable to a *Kreis* (district) of the NSDAP.
Bataillon	Btl.	Battalion.
Batterie	Bttr.	Battery (artillery troops).
Bayern		Bavaria. The southernmost *Land* (State) of Germany, comprising the following *Regierungsbezirke* (government districts; capital cities follow in parentheses): Unterfranken (Würzburg); Oberfranken (Bayreuth); Mittelfranken (Ansbach); Oberpfalz (Regensburg); Niederbayern (Landshut); Oberbayern (München); and Schwaben (Augsburg).
Bayerisch	Bayer.	Bavarian.
Bayerische Landtag		Bavarian State Parliament.
Beamter		An official or functionary.
Beauftragt	b.	Authorized; commissioned; in charge.
Beauftragter	Beauftr.	A representative, commissioner, or administrator.
Befehl		An order or command.
Befehlshaber	Bef.	Senior commander.
Befehlshaber des Ersatzheeres	B.d.E.	Commander-in-Chief of the Replacement Army.
Befehlshaber der Ordnungspolizei	BdO	Commander of the Orpo in a *Wehrkreis* or similar territory.
Befehlshaber der Sicherheitspolizei und des Sicherheitsdienstes	BdS	Commander of the Sipo and SD in a *Wehrkreis* or similar territory.
Behörde	Beh.	An authority or administrative body.
bei/beim	b.	On; near.

Bereitschaftspolizei		Mobile barracks police units of the *Landespolizei*, administered by the various *Länder* before the police were centralized in 1935/1936.
Bevollmächtigter	Bev.	Plenipotentiary.
Bezirk	Bez.	A district; sub-region; administrative unit.
Blockleiter		Lowest official of the NSDAP, responsible for the political supervision of forty to sixty households. Subordinate to a *Zellenleiter*.
Bund		League, Federation.
Bund Deutscher Mädel	BDM	League of German Girls. The *Hitler-Jugend* organization for girls aged fourteen to eighteen.
Bund Oberland		A *Wehrverband* (paramilitary formation) of predominantly Bavarian membership formed from the *Freikorps Oberland*. Under the leadership of Dr. med. vet. Friedrich Weber, it was the primary ally of the Nazi Party during the *"München-Putsch"* of 08.–09.11.1923.
Bund Wiking		A *Wehrverband* formed by Hermann Ehrhardt, led by members of his former *Freikorps*.
Bürgermeister		Mayor of a mid-size town or smaller community.
Charakterisiert	Char.	Brevet rank (a temporary promotion, generally render as "*Charakter als* [Oberst, etc.]").
Chef	Ch.	Chief.
Chef des Ausbildungswesens	Chef-AW	A covert military training organization based in part on the SA which instructed young men in military skills, 1933–1935.
Chef der deutschen Polizei	*Ch.d.Dt.P.*; *ChdDtP*; *ChdDtPol.*	Commander-in-Chief of the German Police (Heinrich Himmler).
Chef der Heeresrüstung und Behlehlshaber des Ersatzheeres	Ch.H.Rü.u.B.d.E.	Chief of Army Equipment and Commander of the Replacement Army (*Generaloberst* Friedrich Fromm until July 1944, then Heinrich Himmler).
Chef der Ordnungspolizei	CdO	Chief of the Order Police (1936–1943: Kurt Daluege, then Alfred Wünnenberg (1943–1945).
Chef der Sicherheitspolizei und des SD	CSSD	Chief of the Security Police and SD (Reinhard Heydrich until 04.06.1942, then Himmler until 30.01.1943, and finally Dr. jur. Ernst Kaltenbrunner.
Chef der Zivilverwaltung	CdZ	Head of the Civilian Administration in an occupied territory.
der Reserve	d. R.	of the Reserves.
deutsch	dt.	German.
Deutsche Arbeitsfront	DAF	The German Labor Front. Largest of the NSDAP's affiliated organizations comprising all the corporations, guilds, and professional associations. Led by *Reichsleiter* Dr. Robert Ley.
Deutsche Arbeiterpartei	DAP	German Workers' Party. Founded in München, January 1919. Later redesignated National-Socialist German Workers' Party.
Deutsches Rotes Kreuz	DRK	The German Red Cross.

Deutsch-Völkischer Schutz- und Trutzbund	DVSuTB	German-Folkish Protection and Defense League. Founded in 1919 with support of the Pan-German League. An antisemitic organization specializing in publication of propaganda and rallies among the folkish movement in Germany. Its branch leaders were designated as *Gauleiter*, and this system was duplicated by the NSDAP. This league was officially banned in 1922.
Deutsches Jungvolk	DJV; DJ	German Young People. The *Hitler-Jugend* branch for boys aged ten to fourteen.
Deutschnationaler Handlungsgehilfen Verband	DHV	German National Trade Assistants' Association. A rightist union of white-collar clerks.
Deutschnationale Volkspartei	DNVP	German Nationalist People's Party. The leading German conservative party during the Weimar era.
Deutsch-Sozialistische Partei	DSP	German Socialist Party. An antisemitic political party that merged with the NSDAP in 1923.
Deutsche Volkspartei	DVP	German People's Party. A moderate political party active during the Weimar years.
Deutschvölkische Freiheitspartei	DVFP	German Völkisch Freedom Party. A splinter party of the DNVP with an antisemitic slant operating in northern Germany until *c*. 1929.
Dienststelle		Headquarters, administrative office, station, or depot.
Dr. agr.		Doctor of Agricultural Sciences.
Dr. chem.		Doctor of Chemistry.
Dr. h. c.: doctor honoris causa		Honorary doctor's degree.
Dr.-Ing.		*Doktor-Ingenieur* (Doctor of Engineering).
Dr. jur.		*Doctor juris* (Doctor of Jurisprudence/Law).
Dr. med.		*Doctor medicinae* (Doctor of Medicine; M.D.).
Dr. med. vet.		Doctor of Veterinary Medicine.
Dr. phil.		*Doctor philosophiae* (Doctor of Philosophy; Ph.D.).
Dr. rer. nat.		*doctor rerum naturalium* (Doctor of Natural Science).
Dr. rer. pol.		*doctor rerum politicarum* (Doctor of Political Science).
Dr. theol.		*doctor theologiae* (Doctor of Theology or Divinity).
Durchgangslager	Dulag	POW transit camp.
Ehrenbürger		Honorary citizen of a town, city, or other community.
Ehrenbürgerrecht		Honorary citizenship of town, city, or other community.
Ehrenführer		Honorary leader. Distinction accorded by Himmler to leading NSDAP and State figures nominally attached to his staff.
Ehrenhalber	e.h.	Honorary.
eingetragener Verein	e.V.	A registered society.
Einheit	Einh.	Unit.
Einjähriger Freiwilliger	Einj.Frw.	One-year volunteer. A type of voluntary officer cadet in the Imperial German Army.
Einsatz		Action; operation; employment.
Einsatzgruppe	Egr.	Operational group or task force of the Sipo and SD for special missions (particularly liquidations of Jews, communist officials, etc.) in occupied territory.
Einsatzkommando	Ekdo.	Detachment of the Sipo and SD; subordinate element of an *Einsatzgruppe*.

Einwohnerwehr		Part-time citizens' militia formed by the German Government during the revolutionary period, 1918–19.
Ergänzungs	Erg.	Reserve; supplementary.
Erlaß		Edict, decree, or order.
Ernährung	Ern.	Food; nutrition.
Ersatz	Ers.	Training; depot; reinforcement.
Europäisch		European.
Fachreferat		A specialist subsection or "desk" in an office or headquarters
Fähnrich	Fähnr.	Officer candidate (second stage).
Fahnenjunker	Fhj.	Officer candidate (first stage).
Feldgendarmerie		Military police.
Feldjägerkorps	FJK	A shock formation of the SA, dissolved 1935 and incorporated into the Police.
Feldkommandantur	FK	Administrative headquarters in occupied countries (of regimental status).
Feldlazarett	Feldl.	Field hospital.
Feme		The following is Robert M. W. Kempner's definition of this term: "'Feme' refers to the criminal practice of the German secret para-military organizations, such as the Free Corps, of executing their members for disciplinary reasons, and for informing the State authorities about details of these secret organizations. These executions were made without trial during the period from 1918–33, at which time such procedure became the 'legal' right of the [SS]. Democratic groups in the country and in the *Reichstag* which exposed the *Feme* were stigmatized as 'Feme agitators' by the National Socialists. Furthermore, the Feme organizations murdered outstanding representatives of the new democratic regime, among them the Reich Finance Minister Matthias Erzberger (August 26, 1921) and the Reich Foreign Minister Walther Rathenau (June 24, 1922). The Feme organizations were financially supported by secret funds of the Army and certain industrialists." (Robert M. W. Kempner, "*Blueprint of the Nazi Underground—Past and Future Subversive Activities*" in *Research Studies of the State College of Washington, Volume XIII, Number 2, June 1945*)
Feuerschutzpolizei	FSchp.	Fire Protection Police; a branch of the *Ordnungspolizei*.
Fördernde Mitglied der SS	F.M.	Sponsoring member of the SS paying monthly dues for that status; did not hold actual SS rank. In many cases the wives of SS officers held this title.
Freiherr	Frhr.	Baron (aristocratic title; e.g. Constantin Freiherr von Neurath).
Freikorps	F.K.	Temporary and voluntary paramilitary formations created by the German Army and Navy during the 1918–19 revolutionary period in Germany.
freiwilligen	freiw.	Volunteer.

Freiwilliger Arbeitsdienst	FAD	Voluntary Labor Service. Formed under Government control as a remedy to unemployment during the Great Depression. Forerunner of the obligatory *Reichsarbeitsdienst*.
Gau		Main territorial division of the NSDAP. There were forty-two *Gaue* in the Reich and annexed territories, with a further 43rd *Gau* comprising the *Auslandsorganisation* (AO; Foreign Organization of the Nazi Party).
Gauleiter	GL	Highest ranking NSDAP official in a *Gau*, with responsibility for all matters of politics, economics, labor mobilization, and civil defense.
Gauwohnungskommissar		Regional Housing Commissioner, title held by the majority of the *Gauleiter*. In this capacity, they were subordinated to *Reichsleiter* Dr. Robert Ley, who was appointed as "*Reichskommissar für den sozialen Wohnungsbau*" (Reich Commissioner for Social Housing Construction on 15.11.1940 (redesignated as *Reichswohnungskommissar* [Reich Housing Commissioner] on 23.10.1942).
Gebirgs-Armee		Mountain Army; a formation of the German Army.
Gebirgs-Division	Geb.-Div.	Mountain Division of the *Heer* or *Waffen-SS*.
Gebirgs-Korps		Mountain Corps (a formation of the *Heer* or *Waffen-SS*).
Geheim	geh.	Secret.
Geheime Feldpolizei	GFP	Secret Field Police.
Geheimes Staatspolizei	Gestapo	Secret State Police; *Amt IV* of the *Reichssicherheitshauptamt* from 01.10.1939.
Gemeinde	Gem.	Municipality, community.
Gemeindepolizei	Gem.Pol.	Municipal Police.
genannt	gen.	Called; named; known as.
Gendarmerie	Gend.	Rural police, including motorized traffic control units.
Generalbevollmächtigter	Gen.Bev.	Plenipotentiary General.
Generalgouvernement	Gen.Gouv.; GG	Government General. German-occupied Poland and the administration thereof under Dr. jur. Hans Frank.
Generalkommando	Gen.Kdo.	Headquarters of an Army Corps.
Generalquartiermeister des Heeres		Quartermaster-General of the German Army.
Generalstab des Heeres	Gen.St.d.H.	The German Army General Staff.
Germanizche Leitstelle		Germanic Liaison Office of the *SS-Hauptamt*, responsible for supervision of Germanic SS.
Gesellschaft		Society; association; company.
Gesellschafter		Associate; partner; member of a society or company.
Gottgläubig	Ggl.	Lit.: "God-believing." Essentially a form of agnosticism, this designation was used in place of a religious denomination after one had left the church ("*Kirchenaustritt*"). This action was strongly encouraged and expected of SS members by Himmler, however it was not mandatory.

Graf		Count (aristocratic title; e.g. Georg-Henning Ernst Adolf Graf von Bassewitz-Behr).
Grenadier	Gren.	adj.: Infantry; n.: infantryman.
Grenzpolizei	Grepo; GP	Frontier Police (a branch of the *Gestapo*).
Grenzschutz		Border protection. Military formations tasked with the defense of Germany's, particularly in the east and northeast following the First World War.
Groß	gr.	Great; large.
Großdeutsche Volksgemeinschaft	GDVG	Greater German People's Community. Organization composed of the NSDAP remnants in southern Germany, 1924–1926.
Großer Generalstab	Gr.Gen.St.	Great General Staff. The General Staff of the Imperial German Army.
Gruppe	Gr.	Group; section. From 1927 to 1931, term used to identify a group of three to thirteen men (redesignated as *Schar* in 1931). From 1931 on it was applied to a large regional unit of the SA and SS (*SS-Gruppen* were redesignated as *SS-Oberabschnitte* in late 1933).
Gymnasium	Gymn.	Type of secondary school in German-speaking countries. Its primary purpose was preparation for university study and positions of higher administrative work. The following are names for the different grades in a *Gymnasium*: 5th grade = *Sexta* 6th grade = *Quinta* 7th grade = *Quarta* 8th grade = *Untertertia* 9th grade = *Obertertia* 10th grade = *Untersekunda* 11th grade = *Obersekunda* 12th grade = *Unterprima* 13th grade = *Oberprima* Passing into the *Untersekunda* equals a *Hauptschulabschluß* (basic-level school graduation); successfully finishing the *Untersekunda* is equal to the *Realschulabschluß* (mid-level school graduation); successfully finishing the *Unterprima* means having *Fachholschulreife* (qualification for certain general higher education studies); and successful completion of the *Oberprima* means having *Abitur*, i.e., the *Hochschulreife*, necessary for university studies (e.g., in medicine or law). A *Gymnasium* provides a classical education including subjects such as history, geography, biology, and foreign languages (including Latin).
Handelshochschule	HH	University of Commerce.
Handelsschule		Secondary school emphasizing business skills.
Hauptamt	HA	Main office.
Hauptamtlich	hauptamtl.	full time; fully paid; professional.
Hauptaussenstelle	HAust.	Large branch office of the SD.
Heer		Army.
Heeresgruppe	Hgr.	Army group.

Hilfspolizei	Hipo	Auxiliary Police formed by Hermann Göring in 1933 from SA, SS, and *Stahlhelm* members.
Hitler-Jugend	HJ	Hitler Youth. The Nazi youth organization.
Höhere SS- und Polizeiführer	HSSPF	Higher and Police Leader.
Hundertschaft		Century. Units of around 100 men, approximately equivalent to a company (often found in the Polizei and SA).
in; im	i.	In; in the.
Infanterie	Inf.; I.	Infantry.
Infanterie-Division	Inf.-Div.; I.D.	Infantry division.
Infanterie-Regiment	Inf.-Rgt.; I.R.	Infantry regiment.
Ingenieur	Ing.	Engineer.
Inspektor; Inspekteur	Insp.	Inspector.
Inspekteur der Ordnungspolizei	IdO	Original title for the *BdO* (see *Befehlshaber der Ordnungspolizei*).
Inspekteur der Sicherheitspolizei und des Sicherheitsdienstes	Insp.d.Sipo u.d.SD; IdS	Inspector of the Security Police and Security Service.
Inspektion	Insp.; In.	Inspectorate.
Jäger	Jäg.	Hunter.
Kadettenanstalt		Designation for a military academy of the Imperial German or Austro-Hungarian Army.
kaiserlich und königlich	k.u.k.	Of or pertaining to the Imperial and Royal armed forces of the Austro-Hungarian Empire.
Kampfbund für Deutsche Kultur	K.f.D.K.	Fighting League for German Culture. A Nazi organization established to combat Jewish influences in German cultural life.
Kaserne	Kas.	Barracks.
Kavallerie	Kav.; K.	Cavalry.
Kavallerie-Division	Kav.Div.; K.D.	Cavalry division.
Kavallerie-Regiment	Kav.Rgt.; K.R.	Cavalry regiment.
Königlich	Kgl.	Royal.
Kommandant	Kdt.	Commandant.
Kommandantur	Kdtr.	Administrative headquarters; Garrison headquarters.
Kommandeur	Kdr.	Commander.
Kommandeur der Ordnungspolizei	KdO	Commander of the uniformed police in a general commissariat; subordinate to the BdO.
Kommandeur der Sicherheitspolizei und des Sicherheitsdienstes	Kdr.d.Sipo u.d.SD; KdS	A regional Commander of the Security Police and Security Service.
Kommando	Kdo.	Command; detachment; detail.
Kommissarisch	komm.; k.	Acting; temporarily put in charge.
Kompanie	Komp.	Company (military unit)
Konzentrationslager	KL (official); KZ (unofficial)	Concentration camp.
Kraft durch Freude	KdF	The Nazi "Strength through Joy" movement.
Kreis	Kr.	District (U.S.: County).
Kreisleiter	KL	District Leader. Head of an NSDAP *Kreis*.
Kriegs	K	War-; wartime.

Kriminalpolizei	Kripo	Criminal Police; Amt V of the *Reichssicherheitshauptamt* from 1939.
Kriminalpolizei-Aussendienststelle	KPAuDSt.	Large branch office of the *Kripo*.
Kriminalpolizei-Aussenposten	KPAuP	Small branch office of the *Kripo*.
Kriminalpolizei-Leitstelle	KPLSt.	A regional HQ of the *Kripo*.
Kriminalpolizeistelle	KPSt.	A sub-regional HQ of the *Kripo*.
Kyffhäuserbund		A large German veterans' organization which evolved into the *NS-Reichskriegerbund*, the primary veterans' organization of the Third Reich.
Land		State or Province (Plural: *Länder*). One of the fifteen territorial divisions of Republican Germany, each with its own government. Controlled by the central Reich government through *Reichsstatthalter* from 1933.
[*kasernierte*] *Landespolizei*	Lapo	[Barracks-housed] State Police. Militarized Barrack Police Forces of the *Länder*; taken over by the Reich after 1935 and placed under *Wehrmacht* control.
Landwirtschaft	Landw.	Agriculture.
Landtag		The parliament of a *Land* (State).
Lehrerseminar		Training college for teachers.
Leitabschnitt		Regional HQ of the SD, approximately coinciding with a *Wehrkreis*.
Legationsrat	Leg.Rat	Legation or embassy counselor in the Foreign Office.
leitend(er)		Governing; leading; executive.
Leitender Regierungsdirektor	Ltr.Dir.	Title of an executive assistant in a high government office.
Leiter	Ltr.	Chief; head; director; coordinator.
Leitstelle		Regional HQ: of the *Gestapo* or *Kripo*, established at the HQ of a *Wehrkreis* or capital of a *Land*.
Luftschutzpolizei	LSP	Air raid protection police established in 1942 from personnel of the SHD and TeNo as an element of the *Schutzpolizei*. Recruited primarily from reservists of the *Polizei*.
Marine Küsten Polizei	MKP	Naval Coastal Police.
Mark	Mk.	Region; province; type (e.g., of a weapon).
Maschinengewehr	MG.	Machine gun.
Militär; militärisch	mil.; milit.	Military.
Ministerialdirektor	Min.Dir.	Executive official in a Ministry approximately equivalent to a *Generalmajor*.
Ministerialdirigent	Min.Dirig.	A senior civil service official. Department head in a ministry with the approximate equivalent of *Generalleutnant*.
Ministerialrat	Min.Rat	Senior <u>ministerial</u> counselor in civil service; usually head of a section within a ministry; approximately equivalent to an *Oberst*.
Ministerpräsident	Min.Präs.	Minister-President; Prime Minister of a *Land* government.
Mit	m.	With.
mit der Führung beauftragt	m.d.F.b.	Temporarily charged with leadership or command.

mit der Wahrnehmung der Geschäfte beauftragt	m.d.W.d.G.b.	Temporarily charged with the conduct of affairs.
Mitglied	Mitgl.	Member.
Mitglied des Reichstages	M.d.R.	Member of the *Reichstag*.
mit Patent vom	m.Pat.v.	A term relating to seniority for promotion (later known as *"Rangdienstalter"* [RDA]; see below). An example: If an officer was promoted *Oberstleutnant der Polizei* on 18.12.1934 *mit RDA vom* 01.10.1934, he would actually receive the promotion on 18.12.1934 but the date of calculation for salary, retirement pay, etc. would be 01.10.1934. Term later replaced by *Rangdienstalter*.
mit Wirkung vom	m.W.v.	With effect from; effective date (e.g., of rank). For example, if an officer was promoted to *SS-Obergruppenführer* on 08.04.1944 *mit Wirkung vom* 20.04.1944, he was not entitled to wear the uniform or receive the salary of that rank until 20.04.1944. Between 08.04.1944 and 20.04.1944, the officer in question would remain in the rank of *Gruppenführer*.
Motorisiert	mot.	Motorized.
München		Munich. Capital city of the German state of Bayern (Bavaria) an of the Nazi movement (*"Hauptstadt der Bewegung"*).
Nachrichten	N.; Na.; Nachr.	Signals.
Nationalsozialistische Betriebszellenorganisation	NSBO	National-Socialist Industrial Cell Organization. The Nazi factory workers' organization.
Nationalpolitische Erziehungsanstalten	NPEA; Napola	National Political Educational Institutes. Secondary schools organized along the lines of the *Hitler-Jugend* and under the jurisdiction of the *Dienststelle Heißmeyer*.
Nationalsozialistische Deutsche Arbeiter Partei	NSDAP	National-Socialist German Workers' Party (commonly known as the Nazi Party).
Nationalsozialistische Deutscher Ärzten-Bund	NSDÄB	National-Socialist German Association of Physicians.
Nationalsozialistische Deutscher Juristen-Bund	NSDJB	National-Socialist German Association of Jurists.
Nationalsozialistische Freiheitsbewegung	NSFB	National-Socialist Freedom Movement. Formed as a continuation of the völkisch movement during the ban on the NSDAP and other such organizations following the *"München-Putsch"*.
Nationalsozialistische-Fliegerkorps	NSFK	National-Socialist Flying Corps. The NSDAP flying enthusiasts' organization.
Nationalsozialistische-Kraftfahrkorps	NSKK	National-Socialist Motor Corps. Played an important role in the military and paramilitary training. Initially known as the *Nationalsozialistische Automobilkorps* (NSAK).
Nationalsozialistische Volkswohlfahrt	NSV	National-Socialist People's Welfare Organization. Primarily responsible for the care of mothers and juveniles and headed by *SS-Gruppenführer* Erich Hilgenfeldt.
Nord	N	North.

Nordost	NO	Northeast.
Nordwest	NW	Northwest.
Nummer	Nr.	Number.
Ober	O.	Higher; senior.
Oberbefehlshaber des Heeres	OB d. H.	Commander-in-Chief of the Army.
Oberbürgermeister		Lord Mayor of a large city.
Oberkommando		Headquarters staff.
Oberkommando des Heeres	OKH	High Command of the Army.
Oberkommando der Luftwaffe	OKL	High Command of the Air Force.
Oberkommando der Marine	OKM	High Command of the Navy.
Oberkommando der Wehrmacht	OKW	High Command of the Armed Forces (Hitler was supreme commander, while *Generalfeldmarschall* Wilhelm Keitel headed OKW).
Oberpräsident	OPräs.; OPrs.	Chief administrator and government executive of a Prussian Province.
Oberrealschule		Higher modern school (modern languages, mathematics, science; nine-year course).
Oberregierungsrat	ORR	Senior government counselor of the civil service; approximately equivalent to a lieutenant-colonel.
Oberschlesien	O.S.; OS.	Prussian Province of Upper Silesia.
Oberste SA-Führer	OSAF	Supreme SA Leader (title held by Adolf Hitler from 1930).
Oberstes Parteigericht	OPG	The Supreme NSDAP Court under *Reichsleiter* Walter Buch.
Offizier	Offz.; Off.	Officer.
Offiziers-Aspirant		Probationary or aspirant officer.
Panzer	Pz.	Armor; tank.
Parteigenosse	Pg.	"Party Comrade," a term of solidarity and respect used among members of the NSDAP.
Parteikanzlei	PK	Hitler's chancellery as leader of the NSDAP. Headed by *Reichsleiter* Martin Bormann.
Personalhauptamt	SS-PHA	Main personnel office of the SS, responsible for records of all SS officers.
Politische Bereitschaft		Political alarm squad. Forerunner units of the *SS-Verfügungstruppe*.
Politische Organisation		The NSDAP's political organization (as separate from its paramilitary branches, such as the SS and SA).
Polizeidirektor	Pol.Dir.	Police Director. Head of the regular police in a small city.
Polizeipräsident	Pol.Präs.	Police President. Head of the regular police in a large city.
Polizeiverwaltung	PV	Police administration.
Polizeiverwaltungsgesetz	PVG	Police Administration Law.
Präparandenschule		Training college for elementary school teachers.
Preußen/preußisch		Prussia/Prussian.
Preußische Landtag		Prussian State Parliament.
Rangdienstalter	RDA	A term relating to seniority for promotion (previously known as "Patent" [see "*mit Patent vom*" above for definition]).
Rasse- und Siedlungshauptamt	RuSHA	SS Race & Settlement Main Office. Responsible for racial purity of the SS and settlement of SS colonists in occupied territories.

Realschule		A non-classical secondary school (six-year course), less prestigious than the Gymnasium, with the purpose of preparing students for employment in practical or technical fields.
Redner		Speaker/orator.
Referat		A sub-section or "desk" within an *Amtsgruppe*.
Referent		Official in charge of a *Referat*.
Regierungsbezirk	Reg.Bez.	Sub-division of a Prussian province. Also, an administrative district of Bavaria.
Regierungsdirektor	Reg.Dir.	Rank of administrative official in a regional government, approximately equal with that of Colonel.
Regierungspräsident	Reg.Präs.	Senior government official in a *Regierungsbezirk*
Regierungsrat	Reg.Rat; RR	Government counselor. Lowest rank in the higher civil service; approximately equivalent to the rank of Major.
Reichsarbeitsdienst	RAD	Reich Labor Service. A national compulsory labor service, organized along paramilitary lines (superseded the earlier *Freiwilligen-Arbeitsdienst* [FAD]).
Reichsarbeitsministerium	RAM	Reich Labor Ministry.
Reichsbevollmächtigter		Reich Plenipotentiary controlling the civil affairs of an occupied country (e.g., SS-*Obergruppenführer* Dr. jur. Karl Werner Best in Denmark)
Reichsfinanzministerium	RFM	Reich Ministry of Finance.
Reichsführer-SS	RFSS	Reich Leader of the SS. The following men held this title: Joseph Berchtold: 1926–1927 Erhard Heiden: 1927–1929 Heinrich Himmler: 1929–28.04.1945 Karl Hanke: 30.04.1945–08.05.1945
Reichsführer-SS und Chef der Deutschen Polizei	RF SS u.Chef d.Dtsch.Pol.	Reich SS Leader and Chief of the German Police. Heinrich Himmler's title from 17.06.1936 to 28.04.1945. He was succeeded by Karl Hanke,
Reichsführung-SS		Supreme command of the SS, comprising the *Persönlicher Stab RFSS* and the *Hauptämter*,
Reichsgau		One of eleven regions formed from territories annexed from Austria, Czechoslovakia, and Poland in 1938 and 1939.
Reichsgesetzblatt	RGB	Official legal gazette issued in two parts by the *Reichsministerium des Innern*. Part 1 concerned current legislation; Part 2 dealt with international treaties, etc.
Reichsjustizministerium	RJM	Reich Ministry of Justice.
Reichskommissar für die Festigung Deutschen Volkstum	RKFDV	Reich Commissioner for the Strengthening of Germanism. Title given to Heinrich Himmler in October 1939 when Hitler entrusted him with the repatriation of *Volksdeutsche* ("racial Germans") and the settlement of German colonies in the East. A *Stabshauptamt RKFDV* was established under Ulrich Greifelt to put Himmler's plans for Germanic mastery into effect.

Reichskommissariat	RK	Title for the German civil administration in various occupied territories, headed by a *Reichskommissar*. The occupied Eastern Territories were divided into *Reichskommissariat* Ostland (comprising the Baltic States [Latvia, Estonia, Lithuania] and White Russia), under *Reichskommissar* Hinrich Lohse while *Reichskommissariat* Ukraine, under *Reichskommissar* Erich Koch, controlled the Ukraine and portions of the Crimea and Caucasus. These *Reichskommissariate* were broken down into *Generalbezirke* [general districts] under the control of *Generalkommissare*. Subordinate to the *Generalbezirke* were *Kreisgebiete* [district regions] headed by *Gebietskommissare*).
Reichskriminalpolizeiamt	RKPA	The headquarters of the *Kriminalpolizei* (*Amt V* of the RSHA).
Reichsleiter	RL	The highest rank in the NSDAP hierarchy.
Reichsluftschutzbund	RLB	Reich Air-Raid Protection League.
Reichsministerium für die besetzten Ostgebiete	RMBO; Ostministerium; Ostmin.	Reich Ministry for the Occupied Eastern Territories, run by *Reichsminister* Alfred Rosenberg and his deputy, *Gauleiter* Dr. Alfred Meyer from 1941 to 1945.
Reichsministerium des Innern	RmdI.	Reich Ministry of the Interior (Dr. Wilhelm Frick, 1933–1943; Heinrich Himmler, 1943–1945).
Reichsnährstand	RNS	Reich Food Estate. Established in 1933 by Richard Walter Darré to control agricultural production.
Reichsführer-SS und Chef der Deutschen Polizei	RFSS u. Chef d. Dtch.Pol.	Reich SS Leader and Chief of the German Police. Heinrich Himmler's title from 17.06.1936 to 28.04.1945. He was succeeded by Karl Hanke.

Reichsparteitag der NSDAP	RPT		Reich Party Day of the *NSDAP*. The annual Nazi Party Congress. On 30.08.1933, Hitler designated the city of Nürnberg as the *"Stadt der Reichsparteitage."* A total of ten *RPTs* were held as follows (the eleventh, very ironically named the *"Reichsparteitag des Friedens"* (Reich Party Day of Peace), was cancelled due to the outbreak of war on 01.09.1939). Dates: City: Title: 27.–29.01.1923 München -- 03.–04.07.1926 Weimar -- 19.–21.08.1927 Nürnberg -- 01.–04.08.1929 Nürnberg -- 30.08–03.09.1933 Nürnberg *"Reichsparteitag des Sieges* [Victory]" 04.–10.09.1934 Nürnber *"Reichsparteitag der Einheit und Stärke* [Unity and Strength]" 10.–16.09.1935 Nürnberg *"Reichsparteitag der Freiheit* [Freedom]" 08.–14.09.1936 Nürnberg *"Reichsparteitag der Ehre* [Honor]" 06.–13.09.1937 Nürnberg *"Reichsparteitag der Arbeit* [Labor]" 05.–12.09.1938 Nürnberg *"Reichsparteitag Großdeutschland* [Greater Germany]" [To start 02.09.1939] Nürnberg*"Reichsparteitag des Friedens* [Peace]"
Reichsrat			One of two legislative organs under the Weimar Republic in Germany. The *Reichsrat* was the representative body for the various German *Länder* (states), superseding the former *Bundesrat* in 1919, while the *Reichstag* dealt with the nation as a whole.
Reichssicherheitshauptamt	RSHA		Reich Security Main Office.
Reichsstrafgesetzbuch	RStGB		Reich Penal Code.
Reichstag			The German National Parliament. Largely a figurehead body after its legislative powers were taken away and granted to the Reich Government by way of Hitler's "Enabling Act" of 24.03.1933.
Reichsstatthalter	Rsth.		Reich Governor; Hitler's representative in a German *Land* or *Reichsgau*.
Reichsverteidigungskommissar	RVK		Reich Defense Commissioner. Official in charge of a *Reichsverteidigungsbezirk* (Reich Defense Region). These regions originally corresponded to the Wehrkreise, but following a decree of 16.11.1942, they were made identical to the forty-two NSDAP *Gaue* in Germany. From that date onward, each *Gauleiter* also held the post of *Reichsverteidigungskommissar*.

Reichswehr	RW	Reich Defense. The armed forces of Germany from 06.03.1919 until the enactment of the *Wehrgesetz* (Defense Law) of 21.05.1935; on that date, its title was changed to *Wehrmacht*.
Reichswirtschaftsministerium	RWM	Reich Ministry of Economics.
Reifeprüfung		School-leaving examination (also known as *Abitur*).
SA-Aufmarsch in Braunschweig ("*SA-Treffens Braunschweig 1931*")		A rally of over 100,000 SA and SS members held in Braunschweig on 17.–18.10.1931. It was hosted by *SA-Gruppe Nord* (under then-*SA-Gruppenführer* Viktor Lutze). John R. Angolia writes of the rally in *For Führer and Fatherland, Volume II*: "It was at this assembly, which followed closely on the heels of the Stennes putsch, that Hitler gained the assurance of the *SA* rank and file and at which Lutze gained a reputation as a totally loyal Party member.… It was at this meeting also that Hitler authorized the creation of 24 new Standarten, thus expanding the *SA*, and recognized the *Motor-SA* and NSKK. All Party members who had officially attended the rally were authorized to wear the [*Abzeichen des SA-Treffens Braunschweig 1931* {see Awards Glossary}] on their left breast."
Sachbearbeiter		Officer or official responsible for a specific matter.
Sanitätsdienst		Medical service.
Schar		An SS or SA unit consisting of three to thirteen men.
Schutzmannschaften	Schuma	Auxiliary police units composed of foreign elements and *Volksdeutsche*; the first *Schuma* unit was set up in the Ukraine in August 1941.
Schutzpolizei	Schupo; Schp.	Protection Police. The regular uniformed municipal and country police forces, comprising most of the membership of the *Ordnungspolizei*.
Schutzstaffel	SS	lit. Protection or Guard Detachment. Officially established in 1925, the SS became, under Heinrich Himmler, the most powerful organization in the Third Reich.
Selbstschutz		i. A German nationalist self-protection organization formed in Silesia in 1920; ii. A self-protection militia recruited from the *Volksdeutsche* in Poland by the SS; iii. Self-Protection Service, an element of the *Luftschutzdienst* composed of air raid wardens and other nonmilitary air raid protection personnel.
Sicherheitsdienst des RFSS	SD	The *SS* Security Service established by Reinhard Heydrich in 1931 as the intelligence organization of the Nazi Party.
Sicherheitspolizei	Sipo	Security Police, composed of the *Gestapo* and *Kripo*.
Sicherheits- und Hilfsdienst	SHD	Security and Assistance Service. An auxiliary police unit responsible for air raid-related tasks. Superseded by the *Luftschutzpolizei*, 1942
Sigrunen		The runic double "S" insignia (ᛋᛋ) of the *Schutzstaffel*.

Sonderkommando	Skdo.	Special commando of the Sipo or SD.
SS- und Polizeiführer	SS- u.Pol.F.; SSPF	SS and Police Commander in the occupied territories, subordinate to an HSSPF
Staat		State; country.
Staatssekretär	St.Sek.	State Secretary in a Reich or Land Government Ministry.
Stab	St.	Staff.
Stabschef:		Chief of Staff of the SA.
Stabsführer	Stabs.	Chief of Staff (e.g., to the *Führer* of an *SS-Oberabschnitt*).
Stadthauptmann		Senior administrative official in a *Stadthauptmannschaft*, a subdivision of a district in the *Generalgouvernement* (occupied Poland).
Stadtrat		Town-council; town-councilor; alderman.
Stadtverordneter		Town councilor.
"Stahlhelm"-Bund		"Steel Helmet League," also known as the *Bund der Frontkämpfer* (League of Front Soldiers). The most prominent German veterans' organization, established by the later *Reichsarbeitsminister* and SA-Obergruppenführer Franz Seldte on 25.12.1918.
Standortführer		Garrison commander.
Stellvertreter	Stellv.	Deputy.
Sturmabteilungen	SA	Storm Troops. The original defense formations of the NSDAP, founded in 1921. Purged in June–July 1934 when it became too radical and unwieldly for Hitler's tastes, prompting him to wipe out numerous members of its leadership, including SA-Stabschef Ernst Röhm. The purge of the SA was carried out by Himmler's SS, initially a subunit of the SA, and in its wake the SS gained considerable power.
Sturm		A company-sized unit of the SS, SA, or NSKK, consisting of several *Truppen*.
Sturmbann		A battalion-sized unit of the SS, SA, or NSKK consisting of several *Stürme*.
Technische Nothilfe	TeNo; TN	Technical Emergency Corps, established in 1919. Auxiliary force of the *Ordnungspolizei* consisting of engineers, technicians, and specialists involved with construction work, communications, salvage, public utilities, etc.
Teilkommando		A sub-unit; Smallest element of an *Einsatzgruppe* of the Sipo and SD.
Totenkopfverbände	SS-TV	Death's Head units, employed in the concentration camps as guards. Formed the nucleus of the *SS-Totenkopf-Division* when it was formed in October 1939.
Trupp	Tr.	Squad or detail. An SA (and in its early years, SS) unit equivalent to a platoon, composed of several Scharen.
Truppenübungsplatz	Tr.Üb.Pl.	Troop training area.
Unterführer		Non-commissioned officer of the SS, SA, or NSKK.
Unternehmen		Operation; undertaking; enterprise.

Verband	Verb.	A formation or unit.
Verbindungsoffizier or *Verbindungsführer*	Verb.Offz. or Verb.Fhr.	Liaison officer.
Verwaltung	Verw.	Administration.
Verwaltungspolizei		Administrative branch of the *Ordnungspolizei* and *Sicherheitspolizei*.
Völkisch		"An adjective denoting an ultranationalist, antidemocratic populism that claimed to represent a kind of integral Germanness. Xenophobic in general, the *völkisch* movement was particularly identified with a virulent antisemitism. It was strongly influenced by Social Darwinism." (definition from Prof. Bruce Campbell's *The SA Generals and the Rise of Nazism*)
Verein [later redesignated *Volksbund*] *für das Deutschtum im Ausland*	VDA	The League for Germans Abroad. Pre-Nazi organization concerned with activities of the *Volksdeutsche* (ethnic Germans). Taken over by the NSDAP, 1930 and eventually absorbed by the Volksdeutsche Mittelstelle under *SS-Obergruppenführer* Werner Lorenz.
Volksdeutsche		Ethnic German.
Volksdeutsche Mittelstelle	VoMi	Ethnic German Assistance Office. Established as the *Büro von Kursell*, 1936 and renamed in 1937. Led by *SS-Obergruppenführer* Werner Lorenz, it obtained the status of a Hauptamt of the SS in 1941.
Volksgruppe		Ethnic group.
Volkstum		Nationality.
Vorsitzender		Chairman.
Vorsitzender des Aufsichtsrates		The Chairman of a Supervisory Board (in business and industry).
Waffen-SS	W-SS	The fully militarized combat formations of the SS.
Wehrkreis	Wkr.	Military district.
Wehrmacht		The armed forces of the Third Reich, consisting of the German Army (*Heer*), Navy (*Kriegsmarine*), and Air Force (*Luftwaffe*).
Wehrmachtbefelshaber		Senior Armed Forces commander in an occupied territory.
Wehrmachtführungsstab		Armed Forces Operations Staff, headed by *Generaloberst* Alfred Jodl.
Wehrwirtschaft		Military or war economy.
Wehrwirtschaftsamt		War Economics Directorate of OKW.
Wien		Vienna. The capital city of Austria.
zur besonderer Verwendung	z.b.V.	For special utilization.
Zellenleiter		Cell leader. An NSDAP official responsible for four to five blocks of households; subordinate to an *Ortsgruppenleiter*.
Zollgrenzschutz	ZGS	Border Customs Protection Service. Controlled by the *Sicherheitspolizei*, with personnel from the Customs Service.
Zug		Platoon.
Zugführer	Zugfhr.	Platoon leader.

Appendix III: Glossary of German Military, Political, and Civil Decorations and Awards

Term	Abbreviation	Description
Abzeichen des SA-Treffens Braunschweig 1931		Badge of the SA Meeting at Braunschweig 1931. Instituted 1931 and officially recognized as a Party honor award on 06.11.1936. Issued to commemorate the rally of 100,000+ members of the SA and SS at Braunschweig on 17.–18.10.1931.
Ärmelband "Afrika"		"Afrika" cuff title. Instituted by order of Army General Staff, 15.01.1943. Equivalent of a campaign medal.
Allgemeines-Sturmabzeichen	Allg.St.Abz.	General Assault Badge. Instituted by order of the *Oberbefehlshaber des Heeres, Generaloberst* Walther von Brauchitsch, 01.06.1940.
Bandenkampfabzeichen	BKA	Anti-Partisan War Badge. Instituted by *Reichsführer-SS* Heinrich Himmler on 30.01.1944. Issued in three classes (bronze, silver, and gold).
Coburger Ehrenzeichen der NSDAP		Coburg Badge. Instituted by Hitler on 14.10.1932 to commemorate participation in the patriotic rally—known as the "3. *Deutscher Tag in Coburg*"—of 14.–15.10.1922 (to which Hitler and other Nazis, including 700 or 800 SA men, had been invited); the rally was occasioned by many street skirmishes between Nazis and communists, Hitler's followers emerging victorious (436 men were registered as recipients of this extremely rare award, which was declared an official NSDAP and Reich decoration by *Führer* decree on 06.11.1936).
Danzig Kreuz (aka *Kreuz von Danzig*)		Danzig Cross. Instituted 31.08.1939 to recognize meritorious service to the NSDAP in Danzig. Awarded in two classes.
Deutsche Olympia-Ehrenzeichen		German Olympic Games Decoration. Instituted by Hitler on 04.02.1936 in two classes (*I. & II. Klasse*) to recognize contributions toward the preparation and execution of the XIth Summer and IVth Winter Olympic Games (in Berlin and Garmisch-Partenkirchen, respectively).
Deutscher Orden		German Order. Instituted by Hitler on 11.02.1942 as the highest decoration of the Nazi Party. The first award was presented posthumously to *Reichsminister/SA-Obergruppenführer Dr.-Ing.* Fritz Todt after his death in an air crash on 06.02.1942.
Deutsches Kreuz	DK	Shortened form of *Kriegsorden des Deutschen Kreuzes* (War Order of the German Cross). Instituted by Adolf Hitler on 28.09.1941. Issued in Gold (DKiG; for combat bravery or leadership) and Silver (DKiS) for meritorious service in furtherance of the war effort.

Deutsches Reichssportabzeichen		German National Sport Badge. Instituted in 1913 by the *Deutsche Reichsbund für Leibesübungen* (German National Physical Training Union). Initially available only in Bronze and Gold, a silver edition was introduced in 1920. Award was based on various tests of physical skill, endurance, and completion time of athletic events.
Deutsches Reitersportabzeichen		German Horseman's Sports Badge. Instituted by the German National Federation for the Breeding and Testing of Thoroughbreds, 09.04.1930. Awarded in three classes: 3rd class (bronze) for achievement in horse racing; 2nd class (silver) for achievement in equestrian shows and tournaments; 3rd class (gold) for outstanding accomplishments in equestrian sports.
Deutsches Schutzwall-Ehrenzeichen		German Defense Wall Honor Award. Instituted 02.08.1939 to recognize planning and labor (between 15.06.1938 and 31.03.1939) which led to completion of the "Siegfried Line" defenses.
Dienstauszeichnung der NSDAP	D.A. d. NSDAP	Long Service Awards of the NSDAP. Instituted by Hitler on 2.04.1939 in three classes: Bronze (for ten years' service in the NSDAP); Silver (for fifteen years); and Gold (for twenty-five years). The *Kampfzeit* ("Time of Struggle") years 1925 to 1933 counted as double toward service time accumulation).
Ehrenblatt-Spange des Heeres	EBSdH	Honor Roll Clasp of the Army. Instituted by order of Adolf Hitler on 30.01.1944. Awarded to those who already held the Iron Cross 1st Class and again distinguished themselves in action.
Ehrendegen des Reichsführers-SS:		Sword of Honor of the *Reichsführer-SS*
Ehrendolch der SS		Honor Dagger of the SS
Ehrenkreuz des Weltkrieges 1914-1918		Honor Cross of the World War 1914–1918. Instituted by *Reich* President *Generalfeldmarschall* Paul von Hindenburg on 13.07.1934. Issued in three forms: 1) *für Frontkämpfer* (for Combatants); with Swords 2) *für andere Kriegsteilnehmer* (for non-combatants) 3) *für Witwen und Eltern* (for widows and parents)
Ehrenplakette für die Mitglieder des Reichs-Kultur-Senats		Honor Badge for Members of the National Senate of Culture. First awarded on 28.11.1936 (to all 125 members of the *Reichskultursenat*).
Ehrenwinkel für alte Kämpfer:		Honor Chevron for Old Fighters. Issued for wear by all persons who had entered the NSDAP, the SS, SA, NSKK, or any other Party affiliated organizations prior to Hitler's assumption of power on 30.01.1933. Another version, the *Ehrenwinkel mit Stern* (Honor Chevron with Star), was instituted on 25.07.1935 to recognize SS members who had formerly served in the *Wehrmacht* and *Polizei*.

Ehrenzeichen des 9. November 1923 (Blutorden)		Honor Decoration of 09.11.1923 (also known as the Blood Order). Instituted 15.03.1934 by Hitler to honor participants in the *"München-Putsch"* of 09.11.1923. The conditions were expanded on 30.05.1938, with the inclusion of non-*Putsch* participants who had rendered outstanding service to the Party during the "Time of Struggle." These included: 1. Receipt of a death sentence (later commuted to life imprisonment); 2. Imprisonment for one or more years for Nazi political activities; 3. Suffering severe wounds in the service of the NSDAP.
Ehrenzeichen des Deutschen Roten Kreuzes		German Red Cross Decoration. Originally instituted in 1922. Redesigned with Third Reich motifs in 1934. Issued in a number of classes. Superseded by *Führer* order of 01.05.1939 with the introduction of the *Ehrenzeichen für Deutsche Volkspflege* (German Social Welfare Decoration), as Hitler believed awards should cover all facets of social welfare, rather than the limited area of the Red Cross).
Ehrenzeichen für Deutsche Volkspflege		German Social Welfare Decoration. Instituted 01.05.1939 to supersede the *Ehrenzeichen des Deutschen Roten Kreuzes* (see above).
Ehrenzeichen "Pionier der Arbeit"		Pioneer of Labor Decoration. Instituted by Hitler, 07.08.1940 to recognize exceptional achievement in industry and society.
Eisernen Kreuzes	EK	Iron Cross. The basic German award for bravery. Originally instituted in 1813, reinstituted again in 1870, 1914, and finally on 01.09.1939 by Adolf Hitler. Awarded in two classes (*Eisernes Kreuz II. Klasse/EK II* and *Eisernes Kreuz I. Klasse/EK I*) for bravery in combat. Open to all members of the *Wehrmacht*, *Waffen-SS*, personnel in organizations providing direct support to the German military, and personnel of Germany's Axis allies and foreign volunteer units. In cases where an individual had received one or both classes of the Iron Cross in the First World War, he would receive the *1939 Spange zum 1914 Eisernes Kreuz I. or II. Klasse* (1939 Clasp to the 1914 Iron Cross).
Flugzeugführerabzeichen		*Luftwaffe* Pilot's Badge. Instituted by Hermann Göring on 12.08.1935. Awarded to all active military personnel who had qualified for a military pilot's license.
Frontbannabzeichen		*Frontbann* Badge. Instituted 1932 by *SA-Gruppe Berlin-Brandenburg* (under Kurt Daluege). Officially recognized as an honor badge of the NSDAP in 1933. Authorization for wear of this badge was discontinued in 1934.

Frontflug-Spange		Operational Flight Clasp (*Luftwaffe*). Instituted by Hermann Göring on 30.01.1941, initially in three design patterns (for Fighters, Bombers, and Reconnaissance), later expanded and broadened to include *Tagjäger* (Day Fighters), *Kampf- und Sturzkampfflieger* (Heavy, Medium, and Dive Bombers), and a number of other categories of air units. Issued in Bronze for twenty operational missions, silver for sixty, and gold for 110.
Gau-Ehrenzeichen des Gaues Sudetenland der NSDAP		Commemorative Badge. Instituted by *Gauleiter* Konrad Henlein on 25.12.1943.
Gau-Traditionsabzeichen Berlin		*Gau Berlin* Commemorative Badge. Instituted by *Gauleiter* Dr. Goebbels on 29.10.1936, awarded in silver and gold classes.
Gau-Traditionsabzeichen des Gaues Danzig-Westpreußen		*Gau Danzig-West Prussia* Commemorative Badge. Instituted *c.* 05.1939 by *Gauleiter* Albert Forster.
Gau Wartheland-Traditionsabzeichen		*Gau Wartheland* Commemorative Badge. Instituted by *Gauleiter* Arthur Greiser, probably early in 1940, to commemorate the establishment of the Warthegau on 26.10.1939.
Gau-Traditionsabzeichen Essen		*Gau Essen* Commemorative Badge. Instituted by *Gauleiter* Josef Terboven, 1935 in commemoration of the tenth anniversary of the establishment of *NSDAP Gau Essen*.
Goldenes Ehrenzeichen der NSDAP (aka *Goldenes Parteiabzeichen*)		Golden Badge of Honor of the NSDAP. A *Führer* decree of 13.10.1933 stated that all NSDAP members with uninterrupted service since 27.02.1925, and with NSDAP-Nr. 1 to 100,000, were to receive the badge on 09.11.1933. In later years, the award was presented to certain individuals who, though not meeting the original criteria as to NSDAP membership number or entrance date, had made significant contributions to Party and State. Such honorary awards were bestowed upon *Gauleiter/SS-Obergruppenführer* Konrad Henlein (NSDAP-Nr. 6.600.001), *Generalfeldmarschall* Werner von Blomberg (honored for his contributions to Germany's military rebirth), and numerous others. 1,795 women received the award.
Goldenes Hitler-Jugend Ehrenzeichen		Golden Hitler Youth Honor Badge. Instituted by *Reichsjugendführer* Baldur von Schirach on 23.06.1934.
Goldenes Hitler-Jugend Ehrenzeichen mit Eichenlaub		Golden Hitler Youth Honor Badge with Oakleaves. Instituted by *Reichsjugendführer* Baldur von Schirach in 1935. Awarded to members of the Hitler Youth, as well as various non-members (such as *Reichsführer-SS* Heinrich Himmler) who had contributed to the growth and advancement of the Nazi youth movement.

Infanterie-Sturmabzeichen	Inf.St.Abz.	Infantry Assault Badge. Instituted on 20.12.1939. Initially awarded only in silver (for infantry and mountain infantry), a bronze edition was made available on 01.06.1940 to recognize troops of the motorized infantry.
Julleuchter der SS		Yule candleholder of the SS. Earthenware candleholders used to adorn the Yuletide tables of SS families, manufactured by the Allach Porcelain company at Dachau.
Kriegsorden des Deutschen Kreuzes		Official title of the *Deutsches Kreuz* (see above)
Kriegsverdienstkreuz	KVK	War Merit Cross. Instituted by *Führer* order on 18.10.1939 to recognize meritorious service in furtherance of the war effort of a non-combatant nature. Awarded "*mit Schwertern*" (with swords) for bravery and "*ohne Schwerter*" (without swords) for service. Issued in the following classes: *Ritterkreuz des Kriegsverdienstkreuzes* (Knight's Cross of the War Merit Cross [*mit Schwertern* or *ohne Schwerter*]) (118 awarded with swords and 137 without swords); Two awards in gold (both without swords) were presented on 20.04.1945.
Luftschutz-Ehrenzeichen		Air Raid Protection Honor Badge (1. & 2. *Stufe*). Instituted 30.01.1938 for honorable service in the *Reichsluftschutzbund* (*RLB*, Reich Air Raid Protection League), the *Werkschutz*, the *Ordnungspolizei*, the *Feuerschutzpolizei*, and the *Technische Nothilfe*; issued in two classes (*I. & II. Stufe*).
Medaille zur Erinnerung an den 13. März 1938		Commemorative Medal of 13.03.1938. Instituted by Hitler on 01.05.1938 to recognize all military, political, and civil service personnel involved in the annexation of Austria.
Medaille zur Erinnerung an den 1. Oktober 1938		Commemorative Medal of 01.10.1938. Instituted by Hitler, 18.10.1938 to recognize persons who had participated in the occupation of the Sudetenland region of Czechoslovakia (criteria for award expanded to include those involved with the creation of the Reich Protectorate of Bohemia & Moravia, 01.05.1939. For those involved in the occupation of the remainder of Czechoslovakia, Hitler instituted the Spange "Prager Burg" (Prague Castle Bar), a small metal device affixed to the ribbon of the medal.
Medaille zur Erinnerung an die Heimkehr des Memellandes		Commemorative Medal of the Return of the Memel District. Instituted 01.05.1939 by Hitler to recognize participation of military, political, and civil service personnel in the annexation of the Memel (Klaipeda) region of Lithuania.

Medaille "Winterschlacht im Osten 1941/42" (aka *Ostmedaille*)		Medal for the Winter Campaign in Russia 1941–1942. Instituted by Hitler, 26.05.1942 to recognize members of the *Wehrmacht*, *Waffen-SS*, and *Polizei* who had endured the first winter campaign against the Soviet Union.
Nahkampfspange	NKS	Close Combat Clasp. Instituted by Hitler on 25.11.1942 to recognize participation in hand-to-hand combat unsupported by armor. Issued in three grades- *I. Stufe* (bronze); *II. Stufe* (silber); and *III. Stufe* (gold).
Nürnberger Parteitagsabzeichen 1929		Nürnberg Party Day Badge of 1929. Instituted 15.08.1929 to commemorate the 4th Party Rally which convened at Nürnberg from 01.08.1929-04.08.1929. Officially classified a Party honor badge by *Führer* decree of 06.11.1936.
Panzerkampfabzeichen	Pz.K.Abz.	Tank Battle Badge. Instituted on 20.12.1939 for award to all members of German Army tank crews. Initially awarded only in silver, but from 01.06.1940 a bronze edition was available for *Panzer-Grenadiers*, armored car crewmen, and crewmembers of self-propelled assault guns.
Polizei-Dienstauszeichnungen		Police Long Service Awards. Instituted by *Führer* order of 30.01.1938, initially in three classes (*3. Stufe*: eight years' loyal service; *2. Stufe*: eighteen years'; *1. Stufe*: twenty-five years' service). A higher class was authorized on 12.08.1944 to recognize forty years' loyal service; this was indicated by a gold metal device with the number 40 in an oakleaf pattern affixed to the first-class awards ribbon.
[Orden] Pour le Mérite	PlM	Order for Merit (popularly known as the "Blue Max"). Highest military award of Imperial Germany before and during the First World War.
Ritterkreuz des Eisernes Kreuzes	RK d. EK	Knight's Cross of the Iron Cross. Instituted 01.09.1939 by Adolf Hitler for bravery or leadership in combat (approximately 7,300 awards of the RK d. E.K. were rendered between 1939 and 1945). A further award, the *Ritterkreuz des Eisernes Kreuzes mit Eichenlaub*, was instituted on 03.06.1940. The *Ritterkreuz des Eisernes Kreuzes mit Eichenlaub und Schwertern* (Oakleaves & Swords) was instituted on 21.06.1941. To recognize those who performed further outstanding acts of heroism or decisive leadership, the *Ritterkreuz des Eisernes Kreuz mit Eichenlaub, Schwertern und Brillanten* (Oakleaves, Swords, & Diamonds) was instituted on 15.07.1941. Finally, a special award was created specifically for *Luftwaffe* Stuka ace *Oberst* Hans Ulrich Rudel—this was the *Ritterkreuz des Eisernes Kreuz mit Goldenem Eichenlaub mit Schwertern und Brillanten* (Golden Oakleaves, Swords, and Diamonds).

Ritterkreuz des Kriegsverdienstkreuzes	RK d. KVK	Knight's Cross of the War Merit Cross (see "*Kriegsverdienstkreuz*" above for details).
SA-Sportabzeichen	SA-Sp.Abz.	SA Sports Badge. Instituted by *SA-Stabschef* Ernst Röhm on 28.11.1933. Initially issued only in bronze; *Führer* decree of 15.02.1935 introduced a silver and a gold version of the award.
SS-Dienstauszeichnungen	SS-D.A.	SS Long Service Awards. Instituted 30.01.1938 in four classes (4. *Stufe*: four years' loyal service; 3. *Stufe*: eight years' loyal service; 2. *Stufe*: twelve years' loyal service; 1. *Stufe*: twenty-five years' loyal service (the *Kampfzeit* ["time of struggle"] years 1925 to 1933 counted as double toward service time accumulation).
SA or SS-Zivilabzeichen	(SA/SS-Z.A.)	SS or SA Civil Badge. A small circular badge bearing the SS runes or runic-style SA insignia, worn on civilian clothes by members of those organizations.
Totenkopfring der SS		Death's Head Ring of the SS. Instituted by Heinrich Himmler on 10.04.1934 to recognize members of the SS who had exhibited noteworthy achievement, devotion to duty, and loyalty to the SS and Third Reich. Approximately 14,000 had been awarded by 17.10.1944, when Himmler halted further production and presentation of the rings.
Traditions-Gauabzeichen für Thüringen (aka *Gauehrenzeichen "Silberner Adler" des Gaues Thüringen der NSDAP*)		*Gau Thüringen* Commemorative Badge. Instituted by *Gauleiter* Fritz Sauckel, 00.06.1933.
Traditions-Gau-Abzeichen		*Gau* Commemorative Badges. Instituted 1933 for loyalty and meritorious service during the "*Kampfzeit*" (Time of Struggle of the Nazi movement).
Treudienst Ehrenzeichen		Faithful Service Decorations. Instituted by Hitler on 30.01.1938 to recognize loyal civilian service (issued in three classes: 2. *Stufe* in Silver (for twenty-five years' service); 1. *Stufe* in Gold for forty years' service; and a *Sonderstufe* (special grade) for fifty years' service.
Verwundetenabzeichen	Verw.Abz.	Wound Badge. First instituted on 03.03.1918 by Kaiser Wilhelm II; reintroduced by Adolf Hitler on 01.09.1939; issued in three classes: *Schwarz* (black): one to two wounds; *Silber* (silver): three to four wounds; *Gold*: five or more wounds. In the event of loss of eyesight or limb, the silver grade was awarded automatically. The gold award was granted in cases of death or total physical disability.
Wehrmacht-Dienstauszeichnungen	WH-D.A.	Armed Forces Long Service Awards. Instituted by Adolf Hitler on 16.03.1936 in four classes (for four, twelve, eighteen, and twenty-five years of service. A forty-year award was introduced on 10.03.1939).

About the Authors

Michael Miller was born in Torrance, California, on 28 May 1971. He served in the U.S. Navy from 1989 to 1993, achieving the rank of yeoman petty officer third class with assignments to USS *Orion* (AS-18), the Port Services Department of Commander, Submarine Squadron 22 in La Maddalena, Sardinia, and Fleet Air Reconnaissance Squadron Two (VQ-2) in Rota, Spain. His interest in World War II dates back to 1978. Founder of the website *Axis Biographical Research* in 1999, he is the author or coauthor of the following:

Leaders of the SS & German Police, Volume 1: Reichsführer-SS-SS-Gruppenführer (Georg Ahrens to Karl Gutenberger). R. James Bender Publishing, 2006.
Knight's Cross Holders of the SS & German Police, 1940–1945. Self-published, 2009.
Knight's Cross Holders of the SS & German Police, 1940–1945, Volume 1 (Miervaldis Adamsons to Georg Hurdelbrink). Helion & Co., 2016.

With Andreas Schulz:
The SS-Brigadeführer, 1933–1945. Self-published, 2004.
Gauleiter: The Regional Leaders of the Nazi Party and Their Deputies, Volume 1 (Herbert Albrecht–H. Wilhelm Hüttmann. R. James Bender Publishing, 2012.
Leaders of the SS & German Police, Volume 2: Reichsführer-SS-SS-Gruppenführer (Hans Haltermann–Walter Krüger). R. James Bender Publishing, 2015.
Gauleiter: The Regional Leaders of the Nazi Party and Their Deputies, Volume 2 (Georg Joel – Dr. Bernhard Rust). R. James Bender Publishing, 2017.
Gauleiter: The Regional Leaders of the Nazi Party and Their Deputies, Volume 3 (Fritz Sauckel – Hans Zimmermann). Fonthill Media, 2021.

Andreas Schulz was born in Stendal (Altmark) on 12 April 1965. After completing his studies in Magdeburg, he worked as a hydraulic engineer. For over a decade, he has served in the *Bundespresseamt* (Federal Press Office) of the German Government. A diligent and passionate research historian, he is the coauthor of the following works:

With Joachim Lilla and Martin Döring:
Statisten in Uniform. Die Mitglieder des Reichstags 1933–1945. Droste Verlag, 2004.

With Dr. med. Dieter Zinke:
Die Generale der Waffen-SS und der Polizei 1933–1945, Band 1 (Abraham-Gutenberger). Biblio-Verlag, 2003.

Die Generale der Waffen-SS und der Polizei 1933–1945, Band 2 (Hachtel-Kutschera). Biblio-Verlag, 2005.
Die Generale der Waffen-SS und der Polizei 1933–1945, Band 3 (Lammerding-Plesch). Biblio-Verlag, 2008.
Die Generale der Waffen-SS und der Polizei 1933–1945, Band 4 (Podzun-Schimana). Biblio-Verlag, 2009.
Die Generale der Waffen-SS und der Polizei 1933–1945, Band 5 (Schlake-Turner). Biblio-Verlag, 2011.
Die Generale der Waffen-SS und der Polizei 1933–1945, Band 6 (Ullmann-Zottmann). Biblio-Verlag, 2012.

With Michael D. Miller:
The SS-Brigadeführer, 1933–1945. Self-published CD-Rom, 2004.
Gauleiter: The Regional Leaders of the Nazi Party and Their Deputies, Volume 1 (Herbert Albrecht – H. Wilhelm Hüttmann). R. James Bender Publishing, 2012.
Gauleiter: The Regional Leaders of the Nazi Party and Their Deputies, Volume 2 (Georg Joel – Dr. Bernhard Rust). R. James Bender Publishing, 2017.
Leaders of the SS & German Police, Volume 2: Reichsführer-SS-SS-Gruppenführer (Hans Haltermann – Walter Krüger). R. James Bender Publishing, 2015.
Gauleiter: The Regional Leaders of the Nazi Party and Their Deputies, Volume 3 (Fritz Sauckel – Hans Zimmermann). Fonthill Media, 2021.